Handbook of
Transnational
Crime & Justice

Advisory Board

Handbook of
Transnational
Crime & Justice

Editor
Philip Reichel

SAGE Publications
Thousand Oaks ▪ London ▪ New Delhi

For information:

 Sage Publications, Inc.
2455 Teller Road
Thousand Oaks, California 91320
E-mail: order@sagepub.com

Sage Publications Ltd.
1 Oliver's Yard
55 City Road
London EC1Y 1SP
United Kingdom

Sage Publications India Pvt. Ltd.
B-42, Panchsheel Enclave
Post Box 4109
New Delhi 110 017 India

Printed in the United States of America

Library of Congress Cataloging-in-Publication Data

Handbook of transnational crime and justice / edited by Philip Reichel.
    p. cm.
Includes bibliographical references and index.
ISBN 0-7619-2622-4 (cloth)
    1. Transnational crime. 2. Criminal justice, Administration of—International cooperation.
3. Organized crime. I. Reichel, Philip L.
HV6252.H36 2004
364.1′35—dc22   2004009278

04   05   06   07   10   9   8   7   6   5   4   3   2   1

Acquiring Editor:	Jerry Westby
Editorial Assistant:	Vonessa Vondera
Production Editor:	Diana E. Axelsen
Copy Editor:	Linda Gray
Typesetter/Designer:	C&M Ditigals (P) Ltd.
Indexer:	Teri Greenberg
Cover Designer:	Edgar Abarca

Contents

Foreword

MICHAEL LEVI

Cardiff University, Wales, U.K.

Many students of criminology, as well as criminal justice practitioners and policy advisers, are not much interested in events beyond their immediate environments. Typically, we are interested in understanding—and sometimes combating—crimes that occur in our neighborhoods or that affect people we care about there or elsewhere. In addition—stimulated by movies and the gory distortions of crime patterns displayed by news media and by documentaries—we may be intrigued by gangsters and by the psychopathologies of serial killers. How else can we explain the presence of so many "true crime" homicide and gangland books in bookstores?

Although most crimes are experienced—and directly caused—at the local level, it takes only the mildest leap of imagination to understand that some of the etiological factors producing these local crime events arise elsewhere. This link with the wider world lies not just in the sphere of the economy but also in how criminal markets operate. It is to bring readers—both academic and practitioner—to appreciate the wider context, and to understand how theories and crime control policies interact with it, that this *Handbook of Transnational Crime and Justice* has been commissioned and presented here. Among the topics it examines are the development of the way in which we now see the crime problem as having a transnational component; the impact of transnational crime control policies (including those having to do with money laundering and terrorism); our knowledge in different parts of the world of behavior often oversimplistically labeled "organized crime"; and specific themes such as international views about the death penalty, international courts, and juvenile justice. These themes are diverse, but collectively, they aim to stimulate our thinking about the broader challenges brought about by crimes beyond borders. Going beyond conventional transnational crimes and including antiquities, environmental, and war crimes, this important *Handbook*—written by acknowledged international experts in their subject areas—gives students, academics, and practitioners an essential reference guide to the key ideas, data, and evaluative approaches needed to make sense of emerging and ever-mutating phenomena at the cutting edge of criminological understandings and of legal and criminal justice practices in the cyberworld and in the material world.

The image of the receiver of stolen goods—popularized in Dickens's *Oliver Twist*, although criminalized much earlier, in medieval times—may have been the first example of a "criminal market" model, but this was a local or, at most, a national market. Money laundering may have enabled the drift of criminal elites into social respectability in earlier periods, but it was not an explicit part of the crime control model until the mid-1980s. Transnational crime was explicit in piracy, in some commercial frauds, and in 16th century prohibitions against bankrupts fleeing the country to evade their creditors (Levi, 1981), although laws devised for intrastate actions found it hard to cope with jurisdictional complexities. However, it was only with the advent of prohibition—the smuggling of prohibited commodities (drugs, people, some weapons and components) and the evasion of excise taxes on (normally) licit commodities (alcohol and tobacco)—that transnational crime and transnational measures to control crime came into their own. Traditionally, most terrorism has taken place within the nation-state, but the trend toward attacking property and citizens of the "target population" in third-party countries—of which September 11, 2001, is the paradigmatic dramatic example—has reinforced the desire to intervene in other countries' crime control spheres, as has been happening in a more limited way since the 19th-century Opium Wars.

Many countries have experienced a bifurcation of policing, with strong cultural and political pressures to focus at the neighborhood level and, simultaneously, burgeoning national units to tackle transnational and hi-tech crimes, along with endless international meetings to negotiate mutual legal assistance agreements (see Joutsen, Chapter 13, this volume). "Law and order" has become such a major political issue—affecting social welfare and economic development in first and third world alike—in so many countries that central and city governments fear being blamed for failing to control "crime" sufficiently and thus become impatient with developments—whether local or in other formally sovereign countries— that are not reducing the sorts of crimes that interest the media and their electorates.

Money laundering has been the arena where global "responsibilisation" has taken the most advanced form, with peer-pressurized and imposed norms being developed since 1989 to get all nation-states to accept that they have a responsibility not to assist those who commit crimes in other jurisdictions by taking in their money, even though the launderers may not do the banking country's citizens any direct harm (Joyce, Chapter 5, this volume; Levi, 2002; Levi & Gilmore, 2002). Such international harmonization pressures are also manifest in U.S. enforcement around the world (Nadelmann, 1993) and in the growth first of the human rights and criminal policy aspects of the Council of Europe (currently 45 member states) and then of the Justice and Home Affairs component of the European Union (now 25 member states, all of them also members of the Council of Europe), as well as in G8 interest in policing, for example, high-tech crimes. The accumulating U.N. Conventions on Narcotic Drugs (Vienna, 1988), Suppression of the Financing of Terrorism (New York, 1999), Transnational Organized Crime (Palermo, 2000), and Corruption (Mexico City, 2003) illustrate the growth of the political importance of attempts to carve out crime control exceptions to the centripetal tendencies of deregulated economic globalization (although the Suppression of the Financing of Terrorism Convention attracted very few signatures before 9/11). One unintended and possibly undesirable consequence of the political interest in transnational crime is competition between international bodies for influence over control mechanisms: Thus, we have overlapping money laundering (and some anticorruption) programs from the Council of Europe, the European Union, the Financial Action Task Force (under G7), the International Monetary Fund, the Organization for Economic Co-operation and Development (in relation to transnational bribery), the United Nations, and the World Bank, as well as countries and regional bodies around the world. This can lead to evaluation fatigue and to a focus on the more easily measurable phenomena (mostly legal and institutional) at the expense of more fundamental questions such as what we are expecting these actions to achieve and how we will know whether they are working optimally or not. Where there are no direct victims, these questions are particularly difficult to answer, but there has been little interest to date in addressing them seriously (Chawla & Pietschmann, Chapter 9, this volume; Levi, 2002; Naylor, 2002).

Other important aspects of transnational crime and justice are covered in this *Handbook*. We may discover some fresh ideas and evidence to "sell" them with by looking at how other countries have dealt with contentious issues such as juveniles and crime, policing, and the death penalty. The notion of borrowing from other systems, especially those that share our language, has become more common and is not restricted to transnational crimes—for example, drug courts, zero-tolerance policing, and closed-circuit television surveillance. At its worst, such cross-national borrowing can be little more than a voluntary or imposed transfer (by way of overseas aid technical assistance) to facilitate one's own international cases or because "our system is the best," (a) without research rigorously examining whether there has been an impact and, if so, whether the measures caused it, and (b) without properly thinking through whether the conditions that produced the effect could be replicated in the policy-borrowing country or area. Nations, local groups, and moral (and, increasingly via consultancies, financial) entrepreneurs of criminal justice innovations are understandably proud of their achievements: Stimulated by media coverage and electronic news gathering, pressures can build up to adopt policies acclaimed as "successes"

elsewhere, with insufficient respect for local conditions that may make them less effective when transplanted.

It is good to begin with greater modesty in our claims of knowledge about phenomena that require a flexible set of analytical tools, fusing knowledge that we only intermittently reliably collect about crimes, criminals, and how they organize themselves in relation to prevention and law enforcement challenges. Recognizing our present limitations, dealing with organized crimes of different types in many parts of the world, not just in the countries of the North, and with how justice is achieved (or not) in different countries and in those crimes that are inherently transjurisdictional, the *Handbook* seeks to give us the evidential basis we need for making more intelligent decisions about the world we live in. We may need better evidence, and more refined policy-making tools and environment, but this *Handbook* gives us a sound start.

REFERENCES

Levi, M. (1981). *The phantom capitalists: The organisation and control of long-firm fraud.* London: Heinemann.

Levi, M. (2002). Money laundering and its regulation. *Annals of the American Academy of Political and Social Science, 582,* 181–194.

Levi, M., & Gilmore, B. (2002). Terrorist finance, money laundering and the rise and rise of mutual evaluation: A new paradigm for crime control? *European Journal of Law Reform, 4*(2), 337–364.

Nadelmann, E. A. (1993). *Cops across borders: The internationalization of U.S. criminal law enforcement.* University Park: Pennsylvania State University Press.

Naylor, R. T. (2002). *Wages of crime: Black markets, illegal finance, and the underworld economy.* Ithaca, NY: Cornell University Press.

Introduction

PHILIP REICHEL

When I began my academic studies in criminology and criminal justice more than 30 years ago, I recall being intrigued by a comment from one of my professors who boldly told our class: "Crime is everywhere." This was his introduction to that day's lecture on rural crime in the United States and his way of emphasizing that crime occurs in rural communities as well as in urban areas. More recently, while flipping through the *Global Report on Crime and Justice* (Newman, 1999), I was again reminded that "crime is everywhere," but the point now was that no country is without crime—in either its rural or urban areas. This *Handbook* is also about crime being everywhere. But the reference has broadened again, and the point here is that particular criminal acts are occurring everywhere in the world. Furthermore, it is necessary and possible to combat such crime. Those two concepts provide the base for this book's general organization and specific chapters. This Introduction to the *Handbook of Transnational Crime and Justice* explains the book's thesis, importance, and structure, and then provides suggestions for using the *Handbook*.

THE *HANDBOOK'S* GOAL

The *Handbook* is designed to provide libraries, students, scholars, government agencies, and practitioners around the world with essays on the increasingly transnational nature of crime and the cooperative international responses to that crime. All chapters are original works by recognized and respected authors writing in their area of expertise. Authors were recruited by the editor upon recommendation by members of the *Handbook's* advisory board. The "About the Contributors" section in this *Handbook* provides information that you will find interesting about each author.

One of the goals for the *Handbook* was to provide perspectives on transnational crime and justice from scholars around the world. The authors are writing from ten different countries, but they represent even more. Several of the authors with the United Nations are professionals and academics in their home country but are currently working at the U.N. International Centre in Vienna. We believe the international representation provided by our authors provides appropriate balance and perspective to the *Handbook*.

In addition to providing the reader with scholarly material on these important topics, an effort was made to have authors include practical and applied information. As a result, even the more theoretical and historical chapters include material that practitioners should find helpful.

EXPLAINING KEY TERMS USED IN THE HANDBOOK

A difficult decision for the editor and the advisory board members was agreeing on the most appropriate term to describe crimes that occur across national borders. Choices included "global crime," "international crime," and "transnational crime." We eventually chose *transnational crime* because it seems more appropriately descriptive and it is becoming the commonly accepted term among comparative scholars.

Global crime was dismissed rather early in the discussion because it is typically used to explain crime's distribution rather than its typology. Years from now, the crimes discussed here may be so much a part of the world community that it makes no sense to discuss them in terms of regions where the behavior originates, countries through which the criminals operate, and specific places where the crime is completed. Today, however, these crimes are not global in that sense of universality. Deciding between the terms *international crime* and *transnational crime* was more difficult. In the end, we made the distinction based on the understanding that international crime includes acts that threaten world order and security (e.g., crimes against humanity, war crimes, genocide), whereas transnational crime affects the interest of more than one state (Partin, 2003). Following that distinction, a few of the *Handbook's* chapters (Chapters 11 and 16, for example) are more correctly considered as covering international crime, but the *Handbook's* primary focus is clearly on crimes that affect more than one state—but not necessarily the world order.

After deciding on transnational crime as the descriptor for the criminal activity being discussed, a decision had to be made on the terminology used to describe how that crime is fought. Again, several options presented themselves. Sometimes countries, especially bordering countries, enter into bilateral and multilateral agreements to combat crime that occurs across their borders. Increasingly, however, even countries not sharing a common border are joining forces to investigate, arrest, adjudicate, and punish criminals engaged in transnational crime. The term *cross-national*

seems a more appropriate descriptor for those arrangements because it implies action and cooperation among many countries. In addition—and unlike the situation presented by the criminal acts—some efforts to combat transnational crime are identified correctly as international in nature. For example, agreements under the authority of supranational agencies such as the United Nations are clearly international in nature (see Chapter 13). Because both *cross-national* and *international* are appropriate terms when referring to efforts at combating transnational crime, both are used in Part III of the *Handbook*.

STRUCTURE AND SCOPE OF THE HANDBOOK

The *Handbook of Transnational Crime and Justice* contains 24 chapters distributed over four sections. Chapters in Part I introduce the topic of transnational crime and place the *Handbook* in the context of comparative criminology and comparative justice. Part II provides specific examples of transnational crime (e.g., terrorism, drug trafficking, money laundering), and chapters in Part III introduce the topic of cross-national and international efforts to combat transnational crime. Coverage here includes cooperative arrangements in the areas of policing, investigation, adjudication, and sanctioning. Finally, chapters making up Part IV address emerging issues for transnational crime and justice and provide regional coverage of transnational organized crime. There are separate introductions to each part of the *Handbook*, and extensive comments about the chapters in Parts II, III, and IV are found in those introductions.

SUGGESTIONS FOR USING THE HANDBOOK

The *Handbook's* primary purpose is as a reference book. We anticipate the primary users to be scholars and students seeking general and specific information on the broad topics of transnational crime and responses to that crime. In addition, practitioners and policymakers in countries around the world will find the chapter material to be an excellent source of information and ideas. As Dammer, Reichel, and He explain in Chapter 2, a primary reason for comparative studies is to benefit from the experiences of others. When countries understand better the extent, process, and impact of transnational crime, they can combat it more effectively.

Because this *Handbook* was designed primarily as a reference tool, it does not have to be read from start to finish. The chapter titles are descriptive enough that readers will be able to go directly to chapters appropriate for their project. However, the necessary overlap among some topics (e.g., Chapter 5 on money laundering and Chapter 7 on computer crime contain important information on each topic) means that researchers may miss key information by limiting their reading to a single chapter.

To assist in the process of identifying all the *Handbook's* relevant information, an index provides users with quick access to key terms and names.

The editor, advisory board members, and authors thank you for including this *Handbook* among your sources for information about transnational crime and ways to combat it. We trust that you will find that the information provides a current and accurate overview of world knowledge about transnational crime and cross-national justice in the early 21st century.

REFERENCES

Newman, G. (Ed.). (1999). *Global report on crime and justice*. New York: Oxford University Press.

Partin, G. (2003, October 4). *International criminal law*. American Society of International Law. Retrieved December 6, 2003, from www.asil.org/resource/crim1.htm

Acknowledgments

This book is truly the result of exceptionally hard work by many people from around the world. The friendship, vision, and support of Sage acquisitions editor Jerry Westby were instrumental in the book's conceptual origin and its final form. Editorial assistant Vonessa Vondera provided considerable assistance in accomplishing a wide variety of administrative tasks and production editor Diana Axelsen effectively guided (and drove) the project through its various stages. Special kudos go to copy editors Linda Gray and Judy Selhorst, who were somehow able to take material from nearly 40 authors found in at least 10 different countries and make the 24 chapters consistent in style and format. Linda Gray had the additional task of providing consistency in the way citations and references were presented by authors writing under a social science style and others who prepared materials following a legal referencing format. Because of the copy editors' skill, you will find this handbook an excellent reference source that allows the reader to identify easily the remarkably wide range of sources used by the authors.

Obviously, the book would not have come to fruition without the efforts of the authors who willingly and enthusiastically accepted the offer to provide these chapters. The cooperative nature of colleagues around the world who are willing to share their knowledge and expertise about transnational crime and justice issues is one of the reasons I find this field of study so enjoyable. Finally, my appreciation goes to the members of the advisory board who provided content guidance and author suggestions. I thank them all for their active participation and advice.

—Philip Reichel
University of Northern Colorado

PART I

Introduction

The first two chapters, making up Part I of the *Handbook,* set the stage for the remaining chapters. In Chapter 1, Felsen and Kalaitzidis trace the evolution of the concept of transnational crime and offer some historical examples of that crime. Those examples (including slavery and piracy) are good reminders that most contemporary phenomena have historical antecedents that should be taken into consideration in order to have the most complete understanding of an issue.

Dammer, Reichel, and He provide, in Chapter 2, an overview of comparative studies in both criminology and criminal justice. After distinguishing those two subject areas, the authors explain why comparative studies are important. They then provide examples of how comparison is used by criminologists (e.g., comparing crime patterns in two or more countries) and by criminal justice scholars (e.g., identifying similarities and differences in how countries respond to crime). In the chapter's final section on future issues, the authors anticipate changes in how transnational crime is defined and addressed by the world community. In doing so, they provide an excellent introduction to the *Handbook's* remaining parts.

1

A Historical Overview
of Transnational Crime

DAVID FELSEN

AKIS KALAITZIDIS

The interest of scholars and practitioners in transnational crime took off in earnest during the 1990s, amid significant political and economic developments in the international system. The end of the Cold War, the demise of the Soviet Union shortly afterward, and the emergence of new states in Eastern Europe in this period marked the beginning of a new era. By the mid-1990s, the relatively orderly Cold War system had given way to a world of greater uncertainty and an ever-growing number of perceived threats to nation-states. These new developments, coupled with immense technological changes in recent years, have heightened our concern over nation-states' vulnerability to cross-border criminal activity.

This chapter first explores early attention to *transnational actors* in the social sciences.

Next, the chapter traces the evolution of the term *transnational crime*. Third, the chapter briefly looks at historical instances of transnational crime. Then the chapter examines the growing interest in transnational crime in the 1990s at both the theoretical and practical levels. Finally, the chapter concludes with a brief look at the scope of transnational crime today.

THE CONCEPT OF TRANSNATIONALISM IN THE SOCIAL SCIENCES

There have been a number of references to *transnationalism, transnational actors,* and *transnational organizations* in the literature of various disciplines over the past three decades. In the 1970s, international relations introduced the concept of the transnational actor.

The focus on nonstate transnational actors grew out of pluralist theories of the state and its decision-making process. In domestic politics, pluralist theorists have always argued that political outputs resulted from competition among different interest groups.

Similarly, at the international level, scholars began to focus their attention on the role of nonstate entities in the international system, challenging conventional realist assumptions about the nation-state as the principal actor in the international system (Viotti & Kauppi, 1987). In their edited work, *Transnational Relations and World Politics,* Keohane and Nye (1972) asserted that a variety of transnational actors played significant roles in international relations. Transnational actors engaged in a whole host of cross-border activities and processes, involving the movement of money, information, and people across frontiers (Keohane & Nye, 1972; Morse, 1972). The actors might be government bureaucrats or their agencies, who often establish ties with their counterparts in other countries, or they could be private actors pursuing their interests in different countries. It was argued that the communications and actions of transnational actors greatly affected international political outcomes. At times, transnational actors could take actions running counter to their own country's interests.

In the same period, Huntington (1973) dissected the features of transnational organizations. Huntington defined these organizations as having operations and activities located in two or more countries. Transnational organizations, according to Huntington, seek to mobilize their resources and optimize their strategies to efficiently penetrate the territories in which they operate. Rosenau (1980) concisely defined transnational *processes* as "processes whereby international relations conducted by governments have been supplemented by relations among private individuals, groups, and societies that can and do have important consequences for the course of events" (p. 1).

Transnational organizations also became important to political and economic theories of dependency and underdevelopment in the 1970s. These scholars turned their attention toward the growing phenomenon of *multinational corporations,* also termed *transnational corporations,* examining the impact on the economies of less-developed countries of transnational corporations headquartered in advanced industrialized societies. Many argued that the exploitation by transnational corporations of poor countries established a dependency relationship, resulting in underdevelopment of dependent economies and rampant political corruption among the elite of dependent countries. Moreover, profits, rather than being reinvested in the country where the corporation operates, were merely transferred back to the firm's home country, ensuring that benefits to poor countries were minimal (Jenkins, 1987).

Scholars such as Braithwaite (1979) studied specific linkages between transnational corporations and political corruption. The U.N. Center on Transnational Corporations explored the long-term effects resulting from the ongoing relationship between transnational corporations and less-developed countries. These studies proliferated in the late 1970s and 1980s (Jenkins, 1987). It was at this time that the concept of transnational crime entered the criminology lexicon.

EVOLUTION OF THE CONCEPT OF TRANSNATIONAL CRIME

Although practical interest in transnational crime by policymakers and law enforcement officials emerged more concretely in the 1990s, transnational crime entered the discourse of criminology in the 1970s at roughly the same time that *transnationalism* entered the vocabulary of other social sciences. However, early references to transnational *crime* did not delineate a precise criminological phenomenon. Rather, *transnational* was interchanged with *international* or *global* developments. For instance, Clifford's 1975 article "New Dimensions in Criminality: National and Transnational," although distinguishing between domestic and international crime, still employed *transnational* and *international* interchangeably (Clifford, 1975, pp. 74–76; 1976). Transnational references could also be found in discussions of international terrorism—a case in point being Mickolus's (1980) *Transnational Terrorism: A Chronology of Events* (see Mickolus, 1978, 1980; Oots, 1986; Stohl, 1979).

The Fifth United Nations Congress on Crime Prevention in 1975 is where many consider the term to have been actually coined (Mueller, 2001, p. 13; Reuter & Petrie, 1999, p. 7). Yet it is unclear whether the term at that time referred to a distinct criminological phenomenon or whether it referred simply to *economic crimes by transnational corporations* in the sense understood by dependency theorists. For instance, one of the agenda items at the 1975 Congress was a report titled "Changes in Forms and Dimensions of Criminality: Transnational and National," which discussed establishing "more effective control over the abuse of economic power by national and transnational enterprises" (United Nations, 1976, item 5).

During the 1980s, however, transnational crime came to describe a much broader array of criminal activities (MacNamara & Stead, 1982; Smith, 1989). This coincided with an increase in attention to narcotics trafficking, which had become a priority of U.S. law enforcement ever since the war on drugs had been declared by the Nixon administration, and efforts were redoubled during the Reagan years. Other criminal activities addressed by the MacNamara and Stead (1982) edited volume included the smuggling of illegal aliens, arms smuggling, currency offenses, fraud, and terrorism.

It was also in this period that a precise and parsimonious definition of transnational crime was offered by Bossard (1990) in *Transnational Crime and Criminal Law*. According to Bossard, transnational crime is an activity that is considered a criminal offense by at least two countries (p. 5). Bossard's conclusions noted that transnational crime is *as much a political as a legal problem,* that the phenomenon "is largely influenced by the development of world problems" (p. 143) and that it "takes advantage of all forms of progress, especially in international transport, . . . telecommunication and computers" (p. 141). These observations were confirmed by developments in the 1990s.

By the final decade of the 20th century, there emerged a stronger discussion of transnational crime, both at the theoretical and practical levels. Cross-border crime had become a key security issue for policymakers and law enforcement agencies in Europe and the United States (Williams, 2001, p. 58). Their efforts increasingly shifted from domestic organized crime to the international arena and transnational crime. The events surrounding this growing attention to transnational crime in the 1990s will be discussed later; first, however, the next section looks at our different understandings of transnational crime.

CURRENT UNDERSTANDING OF TRANSNATIONAL CRIME

The term *transnational crime* now belongs to the everyday lexicon not only of criminologists but also of policymakers, law enforcement officials, and the public. Although the concept of transnational crime could seldom be found in any legal text or law enforcement handbook before the last decade (Mitsilegas, 2003, p. 82), today the term is commonly employed by specialists and nonspecialists alike. Yet, transnational crime is not a legal concept; it lacks a precise juridical meaning. It remains a concept within criminology that describes social phenomena (Mueller, 2001, p. 13). The term is both sociological, because we are concerned with understanding criminal groups or networks, and political, because transnational criminal actors operate within an international environment structured by nation-states and by politics (Serrano, 2002, p. 16).

However, there remains little consensus over the terminology of this social scientific phenomenon. For example, many scholars highlight the organized nature of transnational organized crime or TOC (Berdal & Serrano, 2002). Others reject TOC's organized nature, arguing that viewing it as organized distorts our understanding of cross-border crime rather than helping to explain it. As one critic notes, "TOC discourse precludes a more subtle understanding of the phenomenon it purports to describe and thereby diminishes the effectiveness of the response to it" (Sheptycki, 2003, p. 142).

Indeed, the use of the term *organized crime* has drawn widespread criticism. The term was introduced by anticorruption reformers in the United States during the nineteenth century. Back then, organized crime referred to the local political corruption extant in large U.S. cities, where politicians and the police protected gambling and prostitution operations. It was only in the postwar era that the term evolved into one that referred to organized associations of gangsters (Woodiwiss, 2003, pp. 4–13). Today, while many see organized crime as having features such as hierarchical structure, division of labor, organizational codes or taboos, continuity in operations, the practice of corruption, and a capability to inflict violence (Lee, 1999, pp. 1–2), numerous experts have shown that criminal activities are often not at all organized but instead are quite disorganized (Reuter, 1985; Van Duyne, 1996).

It is clear that the degree of organization of criminal activity can vary dramatically, with some groups possessing hierarchical structures and other criminals operating within loosely structured, flexible networks. This is so because illegal markets operate like other markets, with many groups supplying goods and services and forming linkages in myriad ways. Consequently, critics argue that the term *organized crime* merely simplifies and mystifies the complexities of criminal activities and functions (Reuter, 1985; Reuter & Petrie, 1999).

This criticism also extends to *transnational* organized crime (Passas, 1999, p. xiii). The notion of transnational organized crime produces an image of numerous tightly knit international criminal groups when, in fact, criminal structures are less stable and networks are more diffuse. At the same time, however, scholars tend to see crime as having a necessary degree of organization (Beare, 2003; Berdal & Serrano, 2002). "Precisely because it involves criminal activities that cross national boundaries, some degree of organization is usually required, generally a considerable amount" (Reuter & Petrie, 1999, p. 8). Nevertheless, although a growing number of scholars and practitioners make use of the more controversial term TOC, this volume views transnational crime as being generally less strictly organized.

Another concern is that transnational crime is frequently confused with other terms that describe the same phenomena—notably international or global crime (Ruggiero, 2000; Serrano, 2002; Viano, 1999). The distinction between transnational and international crime is particularly blurred. Those who distinguish between the two argue that international crimes are crimes prohibited by international laws, norms, treaties, and customs, whereas transnational crimes are specifically concerned with acts criminalized by the laws of more than one country (Bassiouni, 1983; Bossard, 1990). Yet others view the internationalization of criminal law and prohibitions as the main feature characterizing transnational crime (Nadelmann, 1990; Serrano, 2002).

Apart from these terminological issues, there is also little agreement over the formal definition of transnational crime. Bossard (1990) asserts, as discussed earlier, that transnational crime simply refers to acts that violate the laws of more than one country (p. 5). The United Nations has adopted a similar approach, defining transnational crime as "offences whose inception, prevention and/or direct or indirect effects involved more than one country" (quoted in Mueller, 2001, p. 14).

Other scholars prefer broader sociological definitions of transnational crime. For example, Passas (1998) defines transnational crime as "avoidable and unnecessary harm to society, which is serious enough to warrant state intervention and similar to other kinds of acts criminalized in the countries concerned or by international law" and where "offenders or victims find themselves in—or operated through—different jurisdictions" (Passas 1998, p. 3). This definition aims at a wider understanding of crime, much in the tradition of sociologist Edwin Sutherland (Passas, 1998).

In short, although the term *transnational crime* is more widely used today than ever before, it remains a much-debated concept. Differences between transnational and international crime are also less clear in practice. Owing to the many ongoing conceptual controversies such as those discussed above, scholars concede that "academic efforts to reduce the notion of transnational crime and organized crime to a precise and uncontested analytical definition have generally proved fruitless" (Serrano, 2002, p. 14).

Nevertheless, the introduction and widespread use of the term *transnational crime* among law enforcement officials and policymakers has helped focus debate about security priorities in the 1990s. It gives cross-border criminal activities a more concrete label and has prompted better categorization and understanding of these activities. The growing attention to transnational crime itself reflects the way in which law enforcement officials and government policymakers have changed their perception of security and law enforcement priorities. As argued later, these changes with respect to crime resulted from international developments and changes in domestic attitudes and priorities. Before turning to the developments of recent years, this chapter will briefly look at some historical examples of how changing international circumstances and domestic politics refocused policy with respect to transnational criminal activities. The next

section covers the historical cases of slavery, piracy, and smuggling.

HISTORICAL CASES OF TRANSNATIONAL CRIME

Over the past century, we have witnessed the internationalization of criminal law by way of international treaties and domestic legislation (Nadelmann, 1993). For example, money laundering, trafficking in endangered species, even drug trafficking, which were of limited juridical importance 100 years ago, now are key concerns at the dawn of the 21st century (Andreas, 2002, p. 39). Changes are due in large measure to advances in technology, international developments, and changes in moral attitudes in Europe and the United States and have led to the development of new criminal legislation under conditions wherein "a highly interventionist state is promoted to police the illegal sectors" (Andreas, 2002, p. 39).

Furthermore, these shifts in policy priorities often resulted from changed international conditions and changes in moral attitudes and domestic interests. This section focuses on three examples where enforcement against transnational crime developed as a result of changed political, economic, and moral circumstances within states. The cases examined here are slavery, piracy, and smuggling.

Slavery as a Transnational Crime

The crime of slavery has existed since antiquity. Slaves helped build the Parthenon in Athens and the Coliseum in Rome. Large slave markets existed in the cities of Chios, Rhodes, Delos, and Ephesus (Thomas, 1997). Although there was some opposition to the institution, many, including such well-known figures as Aristotle, defended it. Aristotle wrote in *Politics* that "humanity is divided into two: the masters and the slaves; or, if one prefers it, the Greeks and the Barbarians, those who have the right to command and those who are born to obey" (quoted in Thomas, 1997, p. 28).

Slavery largely disappeared for almost a millennium from the European continent but once again reemerged after 1500. The conquest of the Americas in the 16th century prompted the demand for slaves in the New World. The first European power to give permission to transfer slaves was Spain under King Ferdinand (Thomas, 1997, p. 792). The Portuguese, Dutch, French, and British soon followed with their own legislation. In 1672, the King of England granted a charter to the Royal African Company permitting the company to deal in slaves (Thomas, 1997, p. 196). By the end of the 17th century, the slave trade was "considered not only a lawful but desirable branch of commerce, a participation in which was made the object of wars, negotiations, and treaties between different European states" (Wheaton quoted in Bassiouni, 1991, pp. 450–451).

However, the growing commercial and military might of the United Kingdom in the 18th and 19th centuries, coupled with its embrace of new economic ideas and its reduced commercial need for slaves, resulted in the change in course of the Atlantic slave trade. This process began inside British civil society, which enjoyed relatively greater press freedom than elsewhere, and by political and judicial decisions of the period. In London, books and pamphlets appeared condemning the practice of trade in African slaves, leading to changes in attitudes among the political and economic elite, and among the population in general. A pivotal moment was the Quakers' transformation from participants in the slave trade to strong opponents. Groups such as the Anti-Slavery Society became driving forces in Britain of the day (Nadelmann, 1990; Thomas, 1997).

In 1807, the British Parliament made the slave trade illegal at home. However, Britain formally banned slavery in its colonies only later on—in British West Indies in 1838 and

British India in 1843 (Bassiouni, 1991). Once having criminalized the institution in its own empire, the British used its diplomatic and military resources to ban slavery elsewhere, employing its warships in the 1840s as an international police force to suppress the slave trade globally and signing bilateral agreements with numerous states to search vessels for slaves at sea (the United States remained an exception). Brazil, one state that resisted British demands in the first half of the 19th century, had its ships seized and burned in its harbors (Nadelmann, 1990).

Britain also used its clout to bring about recognition of slavery as an international crime as part of various 19th-century treaties. At the Congress of Vienna of 1815, a declaration was signed that condemned slavery, although the declaration did not include practical enforcement mechanisms to bring about the abolition of the slave trade. The Congress of Verona of 1822 also included a multilateral condemnation of slavery, as did other treaties signed in 1841 and 1862. However, the international treaties alone did not result in slavery's abolition (Bassiouni, 1991; Nadelmann, 1990).

Other countries lagged behind Britain in this regard. Most of the states of the United States had passed laws against the institution before the onset of the Civil War, but these were not enforced with any rigor. Moreover, the Act to Prohibit the Importation of Slaves Into Any Port or Place Within the Jurisdiction of the United States was signed into law by President Thomas Jefferson in March 1807 and went into force in 1808. Yet the *Times* of London reported in 1846 that New York City was the greatest slave-trading market in the world (Nadelmann, 1993, p. 32). In short, governments either continued to be directly involved in the slave trade or else tacitly encouraged or approved of the trade. As Bassiouni (1991) notes, "It was difficult for many European countries who had already abolished slavery in their own constitutions and legislation to condemn the slave trade outright, as it was not economically feasible to do so" (p. 451).

The end of support for slavery by European governments and by the United States in the late 1800s and early 1900s had less to do with international treaties and domestic norms in place than with changes in domestic political and economic interests and changes in moral attitudes, which saw a growing chorus of opposition to the institution in Britain. Following this shift on the part first of Britain and then of other European powers and the United States, the 20th century witnessed a slew of new international laws adopted to underpin the moral shift against slavery. These included the Geneva Convention and the 1984 Convention against Torture and Other Cruel, Inhuman or Degrading Treatment or Punishment by the U.N. Commission on Human Rights (Bassiouni, 1991, pp. 491–492).

Piracy as a Transnational Crime

Like slavery, piracy was employed by both nation-states and private actors for economic gain and has also been criminalized under international and domestic laws. Also like slavery, piracy is a phenomenon that has existed since antiquity. It was the subject of Homeric poems, which labeled it as a significant criminal activity (De Souza, 1999, pp. 16–17). The creation of the Delian League in 478 B.C. was motivated by a collective concern over piracy. Moreover, under the leadership of its most famous general, Pericles, Athens and other Greek city-states issued a decree aimed at combating piracy and ensuring the safety of the seas. Pericles got approval from other Hellenic states for naval operations against pirates. Sparta, on the other hand, used piracy as an instrument of state policy to weaken its nemesis Athens, supporting raids on the coast of Attica (see De Souza, 1999, pp. 26–30).

Piracy remained an enforcement challenge as well as a tool of state policy for continental European powers of the Middle Ages. On one hand, European countries had to contend with raids by the Mediterranean Corsairs on their islands and of their shipping. On the other hand, they also turned pirates to their advantage. Since the 1200s, the British Crown supported privateering, employing private sea vessels to assist in its attacks on France. In 1243, Henry III issued privateer commissions, whereby the king would receive half the proceeds from these adventurers (Thomson, 1994, p. 22).

After 1500, with Spain in the ascendancy in Europe, the British overtly encouraged individual pirates such as Francis Drake and others. The naval competition that existed between Spain and Britain at the time, and Britain's concern over Spain's accumulation of treasures and territory in the Americas, led to a rise in acts of piracy (Chambliss, 1989). Although piracy was deemed a criminal act by most European countries at that time, the British policy of encouraging piracy saved the country military resources and allowed the British to avoid direct confrontation with the powerful Spanish Empire (Chambliss, 1989).

In general, most countries cooperated with pirates at various times in exchange for portions of their treasure. For example, the French government told its colonial governors on its islands not to interfere with pirates and to offer their ships safe harbor in exchange for a percentage of their goods. The British admiralty instructed Britain's colonial governors and British naval ships to do the same, offering assistance under the Crown (Chambliss, 1989). The United States in the 1800s also offered sanctuary for pirates in exchange for their treasures. Charleston, South Carolina, for instance, offered safe passage in exchange for goods (Johnson, 1999). Furthermore, the French and English Crowns, and many of the nobility, invested in many pirate ventures, with Francis Drake, England's most famous, receiving a knighthood for his services by Queen Elizabeth I (Naylor 2001, pp. 7–9).

Changing moral attitudes and political circumstances in the late 19th century made piracy and privateering a less attractive tool of state policy and, consequently, made it easier to enforce domestic legislation and international agreements against acts of piracy. In particular, the ascendancy of the British on the high seas was accompanied by more widespread criminalization. In the 19th century, the British introduced norms in both the domestic and international spheres (Williams, 1961). Moreover, there were several naval attacks against pirates by the British, Americans, and Dutch, which had the effect of helping to reduce piracy globally over the course of the 1800s (Nadelmann, 1990, pp. 488–489).

As in the case of slavery, however, the criminalization of piracy spread gradually, as the benefits of piracy as a tool of state policy diminished and as commercial interests saw piracy as more of a hindrance than a help; hence, an end to government-sanctioned piracy was seen as a policy to better secure commercial interests. Moreover, the 19th century witnessed the acceptance of new norms of civilized behavior during peacetime, which entailed a moral obligation not to engage in acts of piracy (Nadelmann, 1990, p. 490).

Nevertheless, piracy continues to flourish today in certain parts of the world. In particular, the problem is acute in the Far East where small city-states often offer safe harbor to pirates in exchange for goods. The situation has worsened in the past two decades because "so many countries, instead of being positive about the difficulties, tend to be recessive and put forward copious arguments claiming either there is not a problem or explaining why they cannot do anything about it" (Abhyankar, 2001, p. 183). One recent report by the International Maritime Bureau, which monitors these incidents, said that piracy has been rising steadily since 2000 ("Piracy Rife," 2003). Piracy poses a strong challenge to the international order and may become one of the faster-growing transnational crimes of the future.

Opium Smuggling as a Historical Transnational Crime

Like slavery and piracy, smuggling has existed throughout history and has been employed both as state policy and by nonstate groups. Smuggling arises because of different laws and regulations that govern markets across borders. Whenever the flow of a commodity is controlled or prohibited by one state, it creates an environment that favors profits through smuggling. State-sponsored smuggling and state sanctioning of illegal trade have been policies of particular importance for European interests. For instance, illegal trade between Britain and Spain's colonies was a deliberate British policy in the first half of the 18th century that helped bring about the collapse of Spain's hegemony in the New World and Spain's entire commercial framework. Owing to the policies of the government and large private British interests such as the South Seas Company, Spanish commerce to the New World was cut from 15,000 tons a year to 4,000 or less by 1737. This caused a decline in profits to Spanish merchants and in revenues to the king of Spain (Nelson, 1945, p. 65).

One particularly salient example of state-sponsored smuggling is the illegal trade in opium by the British, which gave rise to the Opium Wars of the 19th century. Beginning in the 15th century, the Portuguese, Spanish, and British sought to bring opium to China to pay for imports of tea, spices, and pottery. The British were most successful at this. Through their government-sanctioned cartel, the British East India Company, and by way of military force, they were able to establish and maintain lucrative opium markets in China. This policy also resulted in two wars over opium in the 19th century (Abadinsky, 2003).

By the 19th century, just as the British public turned against the slave trade, the British government was establishing an opium market on mainland China in order to improve its trade balance with the country. Britain's East India Company had imported large quantities of tea and spices to Britain since the 17th and 18th centuries, but China bought little in return, creating a huge trade imbalance over the years. The British introduced an opium market, with opium brought in from India in an attempt to remedy this trade imbalance. This policy persisted in spite of opium restrictions in Britain itself.

Opium was soon after declared illegal by the emperor, and the trade went underground, supported by the British and coordinated by Chinese triad gangs (Abadinsky, 2003, p. 280). In 1839, the Chinese military lay siege to Canton and confiscated British merchant ships. In response, in 1840 a British expeditionary force attacked China, seizing Hong Kong and making the emperor pay compensation to the merchants. At the conclusion of the First Opium War in the mid-1840s, there was again an upsurge in opium imported into China.

When the Chinese government once again resisted British opium trade terms in 1856, a second opium war broke out. This time Britain was helped by the French, Russians, and Americans to exploit the militarily weak China (Abadinsky, 2003). Despite the military victory, however, British control over the opium trade from India to China became less commercially lucrative, because an alternative opium source for China, Persia, emerged in the 1870s.

Britain's loss of their opium revenues and their loss of control over the Chinese opium market made it easier for the gradual shift toward criminalizing narcotics at the end of the 1800s and in the early 1900s. This process was led by the United States, principally over the course of the 20th century (Abadinsky, 2003; Nadelmann, 1993). Yet within Britain itself, there grew up a strong anti-opium movement, which paralleled in many ways the antislavery movement. Groups such as the Anglo-Oriental Society for the Suppression of the Opium Trade lobbied the government against Britain's opium exports from India to China, backed by other anti-opium societies and Liberal Party members (Nadelmann, 1990, pp. 503–504). When the British Liberal Party won the elections of 1906, the opium trade was ended. It was considered a "triumph of moral (religious and humanitarian) impulses over political and economic interests" (Nadelmann, 1990, p. 504).

In short, international developments—namely, changes to the opium market, coupled with changes to commercial interests and moral attitudes toward opium trade—resulted in the gradual end to Britain's participation in illegal opium exports to China. It also led to Britain's support over the course of the 20th century of American-led antidrug efforts.

In conclusion, what is common to all three historical cases is that changes in policies toward all three activities were the result of international developments, as well as the result of changes in domestic political and economic interests in addition to moral attitudes. The implementation of new legislation at the domestic level and new norms and treaties at the international level did not suffice in bringing about international recognition of slavery, piracy, and drug smuggling as transnational (international) crimes. Although the 1990s did not deal with the criminalization of actions hitherto engaged in by European countries and the United States, the period did see changes in international circumstances and domestic political and security interests. In addition, there were changes to moral attitudes concerning what constitutes key security threats—as policymakers and law enforcement officials, particularly in the United States, shifted their focus from the battle against Communism toward the battle against transnational crime. These factors all contributed to placing transnational crime at the forefront of the security agenda.

CHANGING INTERNATIONAL CONDITIONS AND PRIORITIES IN THE 1990S

As highlighted above, international developments, changes in domestic political and security interests, and changes in moral attitudes helped bring about changes in security priorities to Europe and the United States during the 1990s. Indeed, as discussed below, the very language to describe transnational crime was borrowed from the lexicon of the Cold War (Woodiwiss, 2003). Some of the key events of these years include the emergence of new states with unstable economic and political structures in Eastern Europe, the development of a common market among European Union (EU) states, and the redefinition of U.S. policy following the demise of the Soviet Union. All these events pointed toward the need to develop a new economic, political, and security framework. At the same time, dramatic advances in technology, notably in the Internet and communications technologies, heightened cross-border linkages and made national frontiers seem more permeable than ever (Passas, 2001, p. 28). For policymakers and law enforcement officials, the rapidly unfolding events led them to replace their commitment to containing Communism with a commitment to containing the growing threat of transnational crime.

The collapse of the economies of the post-Communist East resulted in increased migration by Eastern Europeans across Western Europe's borders. Relatively weak law enforcement and border controls in the post-Communist states also meant an increase in corruption and illegal activities, including drug trafficking; alcohol and tobacco smuggling; trafficking in dangerous materials, firearms, and illegal immigrants; money laundering; and corruption (Joutsen, 2001). The Balkans wars of the 1990s also proved to be the first international political crisis in the post–Cold War order, as well as a law enforcement concern.

Apart from unleashing Europe's first war in almost half a century, the Balkans unleashed a new network of criminal activity. The outbreak of conflict in the region, the breakdown in institutions, and the mass emigration of people from the former Yugoslavia created opportunities for criminals and criminal networks. Organized crime was closely linked to the conflicts there (Koppel & Szekely, 2002).

The instability of post-Communist states greatly affected the policies of Western Europe and the EU. The completion of Europe's single market in 1992 removed barriers to the movement of goods, services, and peoples across borders, thereby highlighting the need for tighter coordination in the sphere of criminal justice. Hence, from the late 1980s onward, the Western European states of the EU attempted to strengthen their own internal institutions to offset the growing challenges that emerged in Europe at the end of the Cold War (Nugent, 1994; Swann, 1995).

Economic and monetary union remained the most visible priority of the EU during discussions of the Maastricht Treaty on European Union in 1991–1992 (Dinan, 1994). However, policymakers grew increasingly concerned about the lack of coordination among national law enforcement agencies to deal with the emerging illegal opportunities that stemmed from the creation of the customs union and the free movement of goods and people across borders. Illegal migration and trafficking, as well as money laundering, were particularly salient issues. With the increasing numbers of illegal non-EU citizens, particularly from Eastern and Southern Europe, coming into Western Europe, there was significant debate in the 1990s concerning the strengthening of "fortress Europe" (Geddes, 2001; Ruggiero, South, & Taylor, 1998). Yet measures to stem the illegal movement of non-EU migrants merely encouraged opportunistic criminals who increased their trafficking in persons into the EU (Taylor, 2002, pp. 125–126).

Similarly, finance officials from EU governments argued that money-laundering activities were expected to proliferate considerably as closer economic integration ensued, in preparation for the launch of the single currency in 1999 (Joyce, 1999). Without legislative and enforcement changes to accommodate integration, it would become harder for the EU and national governments to track financial transactions (Adamoli, 2001).

In response to these institutional weaknesses, the EU took steps to strengthen its Justice and Home Affairs institutions, the so-called third pillar of the European Union structure, which deals with internal issues in the community. The EU adopted new measures as part of Title VI of the Maastricht Treaty of 1992 (Dinan, 1994). Title VI discussed increasing cooperation between European states in the area of international drug trafficking, among other areas. At the same time, the European Council pushed through a proposal to create Europol, the European Police Office, although ratification of the Europol convention had to wait until 1998 (den Boer, 2002, p. 104). Nevertheless, from the early 1990s, European countries gradually increased their cooperation in policing and began harmonizing enforcement policies, above all in the areas of money laundering and counterfeiting (Joyce, 1999).

Although Europe's chief political response to the end of the Cold War was the strengthening of its internal institutions, the only remaining superpower needed to outline its new priorities in the post–Cold War "new world order" at home and abroad. The United States needed to reprioritize how it allocated its resources over the medium term. At this point, new threats and challenges quickly emerged, or were rediscovered, in the 1990s. Prominent among these were drug smuggling, terrorism, and the growing penetration of international organized crime groups into the United States economy and society.

This shift in focus of the United States, away from its Cold War security interests and moral obligations to contain Communism and toward threats posed by a multiplicity of different groups and countries ensured that transnational crime emerged from being a conceptual consideration and became a central security policy issue (Shelley, 1995; Williams, 2001). Whereas before the fall of the Berlin Wall, U.S. law enforcement officials principally focused on domestic criminal organizations operating within or close to its borders, developments in the international system resulted in changed attitudes and priorities of policymakers and law enforcement officials, leading to a renewed focus on transnational crime.

There is much evidence of this change in U.S. policy direction in the early 1990s. One example is U.S. efforts in drug trafficking. Attempts to combat the international drug trade by declaring "war on drugs" started in the early 1970s and expanded under the Reagan administration in the 1980s (Nadelmann, 1993). There occurred a growing number of extradition requests in this period, requests rising from 50 per year in the 1970s to 500 for the year 1990 (Nadelmann, 1993, p. 4). Also, the United States began to focus more attention on producer markets in Latin America. Whereas, in Colombia, between 1920 and 1960, the smuggling of marijuana, heroin, and cocaine was not considered the jurisdiction of law enforcement (Serrano & Toro, 2002, p. 157), by the 1990s, the country was under increasing U.S. pressure to help stem the flow of drugs to the United States. U.S. dissatisfaction with certain Latin American countries' efforts in this regard led to an unprecedented "conditional" certification of Colombia, Bolivia, and Peru in 1995— which threatened antidrug assistance to these countries if these governments did not do their share to stop the production and flow of drugs. Subsequently, the United States fully decertified Colombia in 1996 (Granada, 2002).

Another example of this shift in its security focus can be gleaned from law enforcement's use of terminology in this period. With the Cold War over, law enforcement officials began borrowing Cold War terminology to describe the emerging transnational criminal threats in the 1990s. At a September 1994 conference gathering in Washington, D.C., of high-level U.S. law enforcement and intelligence officials, organizers chose the title "Global Organized Crime: The New Empire of Evil," while the executive summary of the conference stated, "The dimensions of global organized crime present a greater international security challenge than anything Western democracies had to cope with during the cold war" (quoted in Woodiwiss, 2003, p. 26).

In sum, in the early post–Cold War era, Europe and the United States rapidly moved to prioritize transnational crime as a key security issue, both as a consequence of the economic and political instability in post-Communist Europe and as an alternative security strategy following the end of the Cold War. Since the beginning of the 1990s, a growing number of government resources have been allocated to transnational crime, more academic research has been devoted to the subject, and the term has gradually entered the vocabulary and been used with greater regularity. In short, the 1990s signaled a shift toward the internationalization of the concept of transnational crime.

THE INTERNATIONALIZATION OF TRANSNATIONAL CRIME: THE ROLE OF THE UNITED NATIONS

The growing attention paid to transnational crime by the United States and Europe was mirrored by efforts of the United Nations. The United Nations as an institution was facing myriad challenges by the 1990s, as the collapse of the U.S.S.R. and the emergence of new states increased its membership significantly and altered its priorities. The United Nations sought a more pronounced role in the new world order that was emerging. In the post–Cold War era the United Nations sighted an opportunity to

strengthen its lead role in obtaining global cooperation and collaboration toward alleviating poverty and hunger, promoting development, addressing human rights issues, and organizing other quality-of-life initiatives. For the United Nations, the growth of transnational crime represented a threat to its objectives, as well as an opportunity for the international body to take a lead in this area.

The institutional mechanisms of the United Nations in the area of criminal justice were enhanced throughout the 1990s. As early as December 1990, the General Assembly adopted treaties on extradition, mutual assistance on criminal matters, and the transfer of criminal proceeds (Vlassis, 2002, p. 83). In 1991, the U.N. Secretary-General convened a ministerial meeting in Versailles, France, to create a new U.N. criminal justice and crime prevention initiative. The new program was adopted by the General Assembly in December of that year, to be governed by the Commission on Crime Prevention and Criminal Justice (CCPCJ) (Vlassis 2002, p. 84).

The CCPCJ aimed to foster more direct coordination among high-level government officials of different countries to address growing transnational criminality. At the CCPCJ's first session in 1992, it was determined that transnational crime would be a key theme of the Commission's work. The involvement, and subsequent death of Italian magistrate Giovanni Falcone at the hand of organized crime in Italy further galvanized the efforts of the CCPCJ (Gilbert, 1995; McCarthy, 1997).

A key initiative of this agency's activity was the World Ministerial Conference on Transnational Organized Crime, held in Naples in 1994 (Mueller, 2001; Williams & Savona, 1996). The conference was attended by more than 2,000 high-level government officials from 142 countries. The aim was to discuss the challenges posed by transnational crime, as well as how to cooperate to meet those challenges. At the conference's conclusion, the "Naples Political Declaration and Global Action Plan Against Transnational Organized Crime" was adopted. The declaration was subsequently adopted formally by the General Assembly one month later (Sheptycki, 2003; Williams & Savona, 1996).

Following the Naples declaration, transnational crime received an ever-increasing amount of interest on the part of governments around the globe. At the United Nation's 50th anniversary ceremony of June 1995, U.S. President Clinton urged the United Nations to promote cooperation in fighting transnational crime and called for a joint declaration on international crime (Lupsha, 1996; Mitsilegas, 2003). The Clinton administration reaffirmed its commitment to combating transnational crime again in 1996, defining it as a national security priority (Serrano, 2002, p. 27).

By the second half of the decade, a U.N. draft convention on transnational crime was in the works. In 1997, the U.N. General Assembly established an intergovernmental group to begin writing the document. By November 2000, within 3 years, the U.N. General Assembly had adopted the U.N. Convention Against Transnational Organized Crime. The convention aims to address four key areas: criminalization, international cooperation, technical cooperation, and implementation (Vlassis, 2002). In sum, in well within a single decade, transnational crime had ceased to be an infrequently discussed academic concept and had become a practical security priority that engaged the world's most important international body.

THE SCOPE OF TRANSNATIONAL CRIME TODAY

Despite the disagreements that exist over the definition of transnational crime, organized or otherwise, what is clear is that the phenomenon encompasses a wide array of criminal activities. In an attempt to delineate better the nature of transnational crime, in 1994, the United Nations established 18 categories of

transnational crime—a list topped by money laundering and terrorism (Mueller, 2001, p. 14).[1] More recently, Reuter and Petrie (1999) have succinctly categorized the principal transnational criminal activities as follows:

1. Smuggling—commodities, drugs, protected species

2. Contraband (goods subject to tariffs or quotas)—stolen cars, tobacco products

3. Services—immigrants, prostitution, indentured servitude, money laundering and fraud (pp. 11–12)

Although there is a wide array of transnational activities, certain categories have received more interest than others. The activities that seem to have garnered the most attention are smuggling activities—drug smuggling, arms trafficking, smuggling of nuclear material and other weapons of mass destruction (WMDs), trafficking in persons, and money-laundering services.

Before the 1990s, drug trafficking was practically one of the only transnational crime activities that received considerable attention from both law enforcement officials and the public. The war on drugs had been declared before the fall of the Berlin Wall. However, changes in the international system have made drug smuggling an ever-greater threat for nation-states, and a more profitable enterprise for criminal organizations. The zones of production have become more numerous, and distribution has become more sophisticated. There have been growing signs of links between drug trafficking and other forms of crime, notably arms smuggling (Williams & Savona, 1996, p. 22).

The trafficking of arms is another key area of transnational crime. The end of the Cold War has resulted in many groups within post-Communist states, and elsewhere, engaging in the illegal sale of arms. The Yugoslav wars in the 1990s provided a lucrative market for arms smugglers (Koppel & Szekely, 2002). Arms traffickers exploit the breakdown in political institutions both in the country of origin and in the country where the arms are destined. Attempts by groups to circumvent arms embargos imposed on rogue states have also been a problematic issue in recent years.

Another area of rising concern today is the smuggling of nuclear materials and WMDs, which is linked to rising concern over terrorism. The smuggling of nuclear materials, either sponsored by rogue states or orchestrated by terrorist groups, has become a central concern for law enforcement. There has been an increase in discoveries of nuclear smuggling activities by law enforcement officials in Germany, Hungary, and other states that border the former U.S.S.R., as it has been discovered that nuclear materials are often purchased from Russian government-controlled institutions, highlighting the inadequate control by authorities over these institutions (Williams & Savona, 1996). The problem is addressed by the chapter on terrorism in this volume (Chapter 4).

Another area of particular concern is the trafficking in persons. The widening of the gap between rich and poor countries in recent years, advances in transportation technology, and the greater permeability of borders, particularly in Europe, have made illegal trafficking in humans a key transnational crime issue. Trafficking has increased, particularly of women and children from poorer countries, many of whom hope for a better life abroad but are duped and sold into slavery or forced into prostitution. Trafficking in people has risen in the 1990s especially among migrants from Southern and Eastern Europe and from the Far East.

A key criminal service underpinning the above activities is money laundering. Money laundering has grown considerably, owing to the better information and communication technologies that have emerged within the world's financial systems. Moreover, the freer movement of people and goods across borders, the lack of coordination among law enforcement agencies in different countries, banking secrecy, and the discrepancies among nation-states in terms of financial regulation and legislation regarding money laundering have also contributed to the proliferation of tax havens and money laundering (Arlacchi, 2001, pp. 10–11).

Furthermore, although there has been a great deal of discussion of the destabilizing effects of money laundering, it is a phenomenon that is still poorly grasped and an area for which there is little *certain* empirical evidence or statistical data—all this in addition to poor training for staff carrying out research (Van Duyne, 2001, p. 10). This important transnational crime is also discussed in this volume (Chapter 5).

In sum, the challenges posed by transnational crime are many, not least because numerous forms of transnational crime have bourgeoned in recent years. The response of policymakers and law enforcement agencies to the growing threat of transnational crime has enjoyed some successes, although as the chapters in this volume attest, much more can be done.

CONCLUSION

Transnational crime as a concept offers a lens through which we can better discuss and analyze cross-border criminal activity. Although the phenomenon was rarely discussed in the 1980s, the emergence of transnational crime in the 1990s as a security issue resulted from both changes to the international system and changes to domestic attitudes toward security and crime in both Europe and the United States. The result has been the growing acceptance among countries that transnational crime poses significant security challenges to nation-states. The Naples declaration and, more recently, the U.N. convention that addressed transnational crime have further institutionalized transnational crime as a security issue of paramount importance.

NOTE

1. The 18 categories are money laundering, terrorism, theft of art and cultural objects, theft of intellectual property, illicit arms traffic, airplane hijacking, sea piracy, hijacking by land, insurance fraud, computer crime, environmental crime, trafficking in persons, trade in human body parts, illicit drug trafficking, fraudulent bankruptcy, infiltration of legal business, corruption and bribery of public officials/party officials/elected representatives, other offenses by criminal groups (e.g., auto theft) (see Mueller, 2001, p. 14).

REFERENCES

Abadinsky, H. (2003). *Organized crime* (7th ed.). Belmont, CA: Wadsworth.

Abhyankar, J. (2001). Maritime fraud and piracy. In P. Williams & D. Vlassis (Eds.), *Combating transnational crime: Concepts, activities and responses* (pp. 155–194). London: Frank Cass.

Adamoli, S. (2001). Organized crime and money laundering trends and countermeasures: A comparison between Western and Eastern Europe. In P. C. Van Duyne, V. Ruggiero, M. Scheinost, & W. Valkenburg (Eds.), *Cross-border crime in a changing Europe* (pp. 187–202). Huntington, NY: Nova Science.

Andreas, P. (2002). Transnational crime and economic globalization. In M. Berdal & M. Serrano (Eds.), *Transnational organized crime and international security: Business as usual?* (pp. 37–52). Boulder, CO: Lynne Rienner.

Arlacchi, P. (2001). The dynamics of illegal markets. In P. Williams & D. Vlassis (Eds.), *Combating transnational crime: Concepts, activities and responses* (pp. 5–12). London: Frank Cass.

Bassiouni, M. C. (1983). The penal characteristics of conventional international criminal law. *Case Western Reserve Journal of International Law, 15*, 27–37.

Bassiouni, M. C. (1991). Enslavement as an international crime. *International Law and Politics, 23*, 445–517.

Beare, M. (2003). Introduction. In M. Beare (Ed.), *Critical reflections on transnational organized crime, money laundering, and corruption.* Toronto: University of Toronto Press.

Berdal, M., & Serrano, M. (Eds.). (2002). *Transnational organized crime and international security: Business as usual?* Boulder, CO: Lynne Rienner.

Bossard, A. (1990). *Transnational crime and criminal law.* Chicago: University of Chicago, Office of International Criminal Justice.

Braithwaite, J. (1979). Transnational corporations and corruption: Towards some international solutions. *International Journal of the Sociology of Law, 7*(2), 125–142.

Chambliss, W. J. (1989). State-organized crime. *Criminology, 27*(2), 183–208.

Clifford, W. (1975). New dimensions in criminality: National and transnational. *Australian and New Zealand Journal of Criminology, 8*(2), 67–85.

Clifford, W. (1976). New and special problems of crime: National and transnational. *International Review of Criminal Policy, 32*, 3–7.

De Souza, P. (1999). *Piracy in the Greco-Roman world.* Cambridge, UK: Cambridge University Press.

Den Boer, M. (2002). Law enforcement cooperation and transnational organized crime in Europe. In M. Berdal & M. Serrano (Eds.), *Transnational organized crime and international security: Business as usual?* (pp. 103–118). Boulder, CO: Lynne Rienner.

Dinan, D. (1994). *Ever closer union? An introduction to the European community.* London: Macmillan.

Geddes, A. (2001). International migration and state sovereignty in an integrated Europe. *International Migration, 39*(6), 21–41.

Gilbert, M. (1995). *The Italian revolution: The end of politics, Italy style?* Boulder, CO: Westview Press.

Granada, C. (2002). The OAS and transnational organized crime in the Americas. In M. Berdal & M. Serrano (Eds.), *Transnational organized crime and international security* (pp. 95–102). Boulder, CO: Lynne Rienner.

Huntington, S. (1973). Transnational organizations in world politics. *World Politics, 25*(3), 333–368.

Jenkins, R. (1987). *Transnational corporations and uneven development: The internationalization of capital and the third world.* New York: Routledge.

Johnson, P. (1999). *A history of the American people*. New York: HarperCollins.

Joutsen, M. (2001). Cross-border crime patterns between Eastern Europe and the European Union. In P. C. Van Duyne, V. Ruggiero, M. Scheinost, & W. Valkenburg (Eds.), *Cross-border crime in a changing Europe* (pp. 15–32). Huntington, NY: Nova Science.

Joyce, E. (1999). Transnational criminal enterprise: The European perspective. In T. Farer (Ed.), *Transnational crime in the Americas* (pp. 99–116). New York: Routledge.

Keohane, R. O., & Nye, J. S. (Eds.). (1972). *Transnational relations in world politics*. Cambridge, MA: Harvard University Press.

Koppel, T., & Szekely, A. (2002). Transnational organized crime and conflict in the Balkans. In M. Berdal & M. Serrano (Eds.), *Transnational organized crime and international security: Business as usual?* (pp. 129–140). Boulder, CO: Lynne Rienner.

Lee, R. W., III. (1999). Transnational organized crime: An overview. In T. Farer (Ed.), *Transnational crime in the Americas* (pp. 1–38). New York: Routledge.

Lupsha, P. A. (1996). Transnational organized crime versus the nation-state. *Transnational Organized Crime, 2*(1), 21–48.

MacNamara, D. E. J., & Stead, P. J. (1982). Introduction. In D. E. J. MacNamara & P. J. Stead (Eds.), *New dimensions in transnational crime*. New York: John Jay.

McCarthy, P. (1997). *The crisis of the Italian state*. New York: St. Martin's.

Mickolus, E. F. (1978). Chronology of transnational terrorist attacks upon American business people, 1968–1976. *Terrorism, 1*(2), 217–235.

Mickolus, E. F. (1980). *Transnational terrorism: A chronology of events, 1968–1979*. Westport, CT: Greenwood.

Mitsilegas, V. (2003). From national to global, from empirical to legal: The ambivalent concept of transnational organized crime. In M. Beare (Ed.), *Critical reflections on transnational organized crime, money laundering, and corruption* (pp. 55–87). Toronto: University of Toronto Press.

Morse, E. L. (1972). Transnational economic processes. In R. O. Keohane & J. S. Nye, Jr. (Eds.), *Transnational relations and world politics* (pp. 23–47). Cambridge, MA: Harvard University Press.

Mueller, G. O. (2001). Transnational crime: Definitions and concepts. In P. Williams & D. Vlassis (Eds.), *Combating transnational crime: Concepts, activities and responses* (pp. 13–21). London: Frank Cass.

Nadelmann, E. A. (1990). Global prohibition regimes: The evolution of norms in international society. *International Organization, 44*, 479–526.

Nadelmann, E. A. (1993). *Cops across borders: The internationalization of U.S. criminal law enforcement*. University Park: Pennsylvania State University Press.

Naylor, R. T. (2001). *Economic warfare: Sanctions, embargo busting, and their human cost*. Boston: Northeastern University Press.

Nelson, G. H. (1945). Contraband trade under the Asiento. *American Historical Review, 51*(1), 55–67.

Nugent, N. (1994). *The government and politics of the European Union* (3rd ed.). London: Macmillan.

Oots, K. L. (1986). *A political approach to transnational terrorism*. Westport, CT: Greenwood Press.

Passas, N. (1998, June). *Transnational crime: The interface between legal and illegal actors*. Paper presented to workshop on Transnational Organized Crime to Committee on Law and Justice, National Research Council, Washington, DC.

Passas, N. (1999). Introduction. In N. Passas (Ed.), *Transnational crime*. Aldershot, UK: Ashgate.

Passas, N. (2001). Globalization and transnational crime: Effects of criminogenic asymmetries. In P. Williams & D. Vlassis (Eds.), *Combating transnational crime: Concepts, activities and responses* (pp. 22–56). London: Frank Cass.

Piracy Rife in Indonesia Archipelago. (2003, July 24). *The Guardian*. Retrieved April 2, 2004, from www.guardian.co.uk/indonesia/Story/0,2763,1004631,00.html

Reuter, P. (1985). *The organization of markets: An economic analysis*. Washington, DC: National Institute of Justice.

Reuter, P., & Petrie, C. (Eds.). (1999). *Transnational organized crime: Summary of a workshop*. Washington, DC: National Research Council, Committee on Law and Justice.

Rosenau, J. (1980). *The study of global interdependence: Essays on the transnationalisation of world affairs.* New York: Nichols.

Ruggiero, V. (2000). Transnational crime: Official and alternative fears. *International Journal of the Sociology of Law, 28,* 187–199.

Ruggiero, V., South, N., & Taylor, I. (1998). *The New European criminology: Crime and social order in Europe.* London: Routledge.

Serrano, M. (2002). Transnational organized crime and international security: Business as usual? In M. Berdal & M. Serrano (Eds.), *Transnational organized crime and international security: Business as usual?* (pp. 13–36). Boulder, CO: Lynne Rienner.

Serrano, M., & Toro, M. C. (2002). From drug trafficking to transnational organized crime in Latin America. In M. Berdal & M. Serrano (Eds.), *Transnational organized crime and international security: Business as usual?* (pp. 155–182). Boulder, CO: Lynne Rienner.

Shelley, L. I. (1995). Transnational organized crime: An imminent threat to the nation-state? *Journal of International Affairs, 48*(2), 463–489.

Sheptycki, J. (2003). Against transnational organized crime. In M. Beare (Ed.), *Critical reflections on transnational organized crime, money laundering and corruption* (pp. 120–144). Toronto: University of Toronto Press.

Smith, H. (Ed.). (1989). *Transnational crime: Investigative responses.* Chicago: Office of International Criminal Justice, University of Illinois at Chicago, 1989.

Stohl, M. (Ed.). (1979). *The politics of terrorism.* New York: Marcel Dekker.

Swann, D. (1995). *The economics of the common market: Integration and the European Union* (8th ed.). London: Penguin.

Taylor, I. (2002). Liberal markets and the Republic of Europe: Contextualizing the growth of transnational crime. In M. Berdal & M. Serrano (Eds.), *Transnational organized crime and international security: Business as usual?* (pp. 119–128). Boulder, CO: Lynne Rienner.

Thomas, H. (1997). *The slave trade: The story of the Atlantic slave trade, 1440–1870.* New York: Simon & Schuster.

Thomson, J. (1994). *Mercenaries, pirates and sovereigns: State-building and extraterritorial violence in early modern Europe.* Princeton, NJ: Princeton University Press.

United Nations. (1976). *Changes in forms and dimensions of criminality: Transnational and national.* Fifth United Nations Congress on the Prevention of Crime and the Treatment of Offenders, Geneva, 1975. New York: Author.

Van Duyne, P. (1996). The phantom and threat of organized crime. *Crime, Law and Social Change, 24*(4), 341–377.

Van Duyne, P. C. (2001). Cross-border crime: A relative concept and broad phenomenon. In P. C. Van Duyne, V. Ruggiero, M. Scheinost, & W. Valkenburg (Ed.), *Cross-border crime in a changing Europe* (pp. 1–14). Huntington, NY: Nova Science.

Viano, E. C. (Ed.). (1999). *Global organized crime and international security.* Aldershot, UK: Ashgate.

Viotti, P. R., & Kauppi, M. V. (1987). *International relations theory: Realism, pluralism, globalism.* New York: Macmillan.

Vlassis, D. (2002). The UN Convention Against Transnational Organized Crime. In M. Berdal & M. Serrano (Eds.), *Transnational organized crime and international security: Business as usual?* (pp. 83–94). Boulder, CO: Lynne Rienner.

Williams, N. (1961). *Captains outrageous: Seven centuries of piracy.* London: Barrie & Rockliff.

Williams, P. (2001). Organizing transnational crime: Networks, markets and hierarchies. In P. Williams & D. Vlassis (Eds.), *Combating transnational crime: Concepts, activities and responses* (pp. 57–87). London: Frank Cass.

Williams, P., & Savona. E. (Eds.). (1996). *The United Nations and transnational organized crime.* London: Frank Cass.

Woodiwiss, M. (2003). Transnational organized crime: The strange career of an American concept. In M. E. Beare (Ed.), *Critical reflections on transnational organized crime, money laundering, and corruption* (pp. 3–34). Toronto: University of Toronto Press.

2

Comparing Crime and Justice

HARRY R. DAMMER

PHILIP REICHEL

NI HE

During the past two decades, crime has moved from being primarily a domestic social problem to one that is more global in nature. The globalization of economy, opening of previously restricted borders, the exponential growth in information technology, and widespread transcontinental mobility all helped crime to transcend national boundaries.

Two academic disciplines with particular interest in these issues are criminology and criminal justice. These fields of study have much in common but are clearly distinguished. Criminologists are interested in crime as a social phenomenon (e.g., the spread and distribution of crime) and as social behavior (e.g., why people engage in criminal acts). Criminal justice scholars are interested in the people and procedures established by a government in its attempt to maintain social order and accomplish justice in society. In this chapter, we explain why comparing issues of crime and justice cross-nationally is important, describe how comparative criminologists and comparative criminal justice scholars go about their work, and identify some issues we believe will confront both disciplines in the future. We begin with a review of the growth and importance of comparative studies in criminology and criminal justice.

THE GROWTH AND IMPORTANCE OF COMPARATIVE CRIME AND JUSTICE STUDY

In response to the growing problem of transnational crime, those in the academic community have developed an intense and sustained interest in the study of comparative criminology and criminal justice. Although the growth of transnational crime—and surely the September 11, 2001, terrorism events in the United States—have piqued the interest in international crime issues, we can trace the beginnings of the subject area back to at least 1872 and the International Congress on the Prevention and Repression of Crime, held in London. Later, the First International Police Congress was held in Monaco in 1914. Two world wars put interest in the field on hold until the late 1960s when the United Nations developed the first Crime Prevention and Criminal Justice Branch under the direction of G. O. W. Mueller. Over the last 30 years, interest in comparative crime and justice has slowly gained momentum and is now prominent in the academic and professional arenas.

Recently, prominent American scholars have vociferously called for the "globalizing" of criminal justice curriculum (Adler, 1996) and for "internationalizing" criminology and criminal justice study (Friday, 1996). Academic, professional, and governmental organizations have responded to these calls. Since the 1990s, at least three major North American conferences chose the related theme. In November of 1995 and November 1999, the American Society of Criminology titled its annual conferences "Crime and Justice: National and International" and "Explaining and Preventing Crime: The Globalization of Knowledge," respectively. In March 2003, the Academy of Criminal Justice Sciences held its annual conference under the theme of "The Globalization of Crime and Justice." Similarly, international conferences have been held throughout the world, the largest being the International Congress on Criminology, which held its 12th Congress in Seoul, Korea in 1998, and its 13th Congress in Brazil in August 2003.

Comparative criminology and criminal justice courses, and various forms of written and electronic materials on the subject, have also flourished in recent years. Based on several surveys conducted among U.S. researchers, between one third (Cordner, Dammer, & Horvath, 2000; Hippchen, 1977; Terrill, 1983) and one half (Esbensen & Blankenship, 1989; Peak, 1991) of the criminal justice programs offer some comparative or international courses. During one 5-year period, between 1986 and 1991, the number of courses offered in comparative criminal justice more than doubled (Wright & Friedrichs, 1991). In 2002, John Jay College of Criminal Justice developed the first full-fledged bachelor's degree in International Criminal Justice (Natarajan, 2002).

Increased awareness and coverage of cross-national crimes and criminal justice practices can be found in many criminology and criminal justice textbooks published in the United States. It is common for authors in criminology and criminal justice to include paragraphs, inserts, or boxes featuring cross-national crimes, foreign justice practices, or both. Many introductory texts now devote an entire chapter to issues related to comparative criminology, criminal justice, or both (Adler, Mueller, & Laufer, 1995; Albanese, 2002; Schmalleger, 2001). An impressive number of edited books and anthologies with a cross-national focus have been published in the last decade. More important, there are now textbooks devoted entirely to the study of comparative criminal justice systems (Fairchild & Dammer, 2001; Reichel, 2002; Terrill, 2002). Comparative study as a legitimate vehicle for academic publications can also be evidenced by the increasing number of periodicals addressing comparative criminology and criminal justice (Mueller, 1996), and there are thousands more published cross-national studies compared with a mere decade ago (Adler, 1995). Yet some remain skeptical about whether the comparative criminology-criminal justice field has indeed grown out of its "infancy" (Howard, Newman, & Pridemore, 2000) and whether comparative study is still regarded as an "exotic frill" or as "an excuse for international travel" (Bayley, 1996, p. 241). However, this view is sure to change if the field continues to gain academic legitimacy and notoriety.

With the spread of crime throughout the world, many governmental agencies, national and international, have come to see the value in the study and dissemination of information on the subject. Various forms of statistical data are obtained through agencies such as the International Police Organization (Interpol) and the World Health Organization and through organizations such as the Ministry of Justice in the Netherlands that conducts the International Crime Victim Surveys (ICVS). The United Nations has created a large group of criminal justice information providers, including the Dag Hammarskjold Library in New York City and the ever-growing U.N. Crime and Justice Information Network (UNCJIN). UNCJIN has expanded to include the Centre for International Crime Prevention in Vienna and numerous institutes for crime prevention in Japan, Rome, Australia, Italy, Cost Rica, Finland, Uganda, and Canada, and in the United States under the auspices of the National Institute of Justice (NIJ).

The NIJ is the research, development, and evaluation agency within the U.S. Department of Justice. In 1999, the NIJ, recognizing the need to better identify and describe crime and to support those who fight crime, decided to develop the NIJ International Center. The International Center's mission is to stimulate and facilitate research and evaluation on transnational crime and justice issues and to disseminate the knowledge gained throughout the national and international criminal justice communities (Finckenauer, 2000). Since its inception, the International Center

has worked with the United Nations and its various institutes to mount a variety of studies on topics such as transnational organized crime, corruption, and human trafficking.

Criminal justice libraries worldwide have also joined in the search for international criminal justice knowledge. The World Criminal Justice Library Network has been developed to link nearly 100 criminal justice libraries. Active participants include university libraries in the United States (e.g., Eastern Kentucky University, Rutgers University, Sam Houston State University), Canada (e.g., the University of Montreal, and the University of Toronto), Europe (e.g., the Max Planck Institute in Freiburg, Germany), and university and government entities in Australia (e.g., the Australian Institute of Criminology) and Asia (e.g., the Korean Institute of Criminology). Having briefly expressed the reasons for and vehicles contributing to the growth of the field of comparative criminal justice, we now turn to the larger question of why people around the globe should concern themselves with the identification and comparison of issues related to crime and justice.

WHY SHOULD WE COMPARE ISSUES OF CRIME AND JUSTICE?[1]

There are many reasons to study and compare issues of crime and justice. We will concentrate on three: (1) to benefit from the experience of others, (2) to broaden our understanding of different cultures and approaches to problems, and (3) to help deal with the many transnational crime problems that plague the world today.

To benefit from others' experience. "The reason for comparing is to learn from the experience of others, and, conversely, that he who knows only one country knows none" (Sartori, 1996, p. 20). This profound statement by

George Sartori illustrates the importance of international and comparative study. Comparative work in criminal justice is an excellent vehicle for learning more about how others practice criminal justice. With this information, we can begin to solve the many problems related to crime and justice.

In all areas of the criminal justice system—police, courts, and corrections—there are many examples of how nations have adapted others' methods of implementing criminal justice. For example, people wonder why Japan has a much lower crime rate than the United States or, indeed, most Western nations. The Japanese themselves give some credit for their low crime rates to their police methods—most notably, community policing. Many countries have become interested in adapting the Japanese police practices, including the use of Kobans (small local police stations). Some U.S. cities, including Detroit and Houston, have modified the Japanese methods and use them in their local police operations (Bayley, 1991).

Many countries have also adopted rules of criminal procedure that others pioneered. In fact, some criminal procedure rules, such as the right to counsel at an early stage of the criminal process, are becoming universal in Western systems of justice. Many countries have even adopted entire legal codes from the codes of others. The Napoleonic Code of Civil Law, developed in France in the early 19th century, was one such export, as was the French penal code, also developed under Napoleon. Another export in the late 19th century was the German Civil Code. These codes have had an enormous influence on the development of legal systems and criminal justice systems throughout the world (Merryman, 1985).

Corrections strategies also tend to spill over borders. For example, the idea of day fines, which was first developed in Scandinavian countries, has been adopted by Germany and, more recently, by Great Britain and the United States. And New Zealand, Australia, Canada, and the United States have started different kinds of restorative justice programs. Restorative justice is an idea that many victims' rights advocates in the United States cultivated, but it has its roots in the justice practices of many indigenous cultures.

There are many other examples of countries borrowing or adapting criminal justice practices from the United States. In the 19th century, many European countries, especially France, copied American methods of incarceration—specifically, the Auburn system and the Pennsylvania system. More recently, former Communist countries in Eastern Europe have called on the FBI to help train them in the fight against organized crime. Many countries have also improved their ability to collect and disseminate crime statistics using the U.S. models of the Uniform Crime Reports (UCR) and National Crime Victimization Survey (NCVS).

To broaden our understanding of the world. A second reason for studying the administration of justice in other countries is to broaden our understanding of other countries and cultures. This is imperative because the multicultural world we now live in has entered the stage of globalization, whereby the world has become interdependent in terms of the events and the actions of people and governments around the world. In short, globalization is the idea that the world is "getting smaller." Reflecting on the globalization of crime is a recent trend in criminal justice, and many countries, concerned with transnational crime, are developing a serious interest in globalization issues.

Globalization has occurred because of many events in the 20th century. Two of the most prominent are the end of the Cold War and the growth in technology. The end of the Cold War—more specifically, the demise of the former Soviet Union—has led to the opening of many previously regulated borders and, in turn, to an increase in international trade and travel. Over the past 30 years, the number of international passenger flights has increased twentyfold, and the number of global imports has increased tenfold. Along with these increases has been a concomitant increase in crime.

Ease of travel by air has enabled criminals to do their work in other countries or easily escape to a safe haven. As air and sea trade has increased, so has the smuggling of illegal goods such as drugs and guns. Strong evidence suggests that some individuals have even engaged in the illegal smuggling of human body parts to wealthy persons in other countries who need medical assistance. In countries that are in economic or political turmoil, many persons attempt to flee, causing problems such as international criminal activity, refugee flows, the spread of contagious disease, and nuclear weapons and drug trafficking (Cusimano, 2000). When refugees enter a country, either legally or illegally, they experience difficulties adjusting to a new language and cultural norms, and many find themselves in some kind of legal trouble.

Technological growth has also contributed directly to the vast increase in the kind and volume of transnational crime, with computers and telecommunications playing a key role. Cybercrime, crime committed with the use of computers, now ranges from relatively minor acts of consumer fraud to more serious crimes in which drug traffickers move billions of dollars of illegal drug money, to major crimes that can paralyze entire financial networks and national security systems. In sum, "the very networks that legitimate businesses use to move goods so cheaply are the same networks that criminals use to move illicit goods so easily" (Winer, 1997, p. 41).

Broadening our understanding of other countries is also important because, as globalization occurs, we are more likely to fall prey to the problem of ethnocentrism—the belief that one's own country or culture does things "right" and all other ways are "wrong" or "foreign." Ethnocentrism is a common phenomenon; people often think their country, culture, or religion is better than all others. In terms of crime and criminal justice, ethnocentrism is a problem because it can lead to crime within and across borders. LePaulle noted that there is a tendency to view the law of one's own country "as natural, as necessary, as given by God" (quoted in Cole, Frankowski, & Gertz, 1987). This ethnocentric view actually makes the system seem uninteresting and not worthy of scrutiny. After all, why should we need to examine and appreciate what amounts to the only game in town? But, LePaulle continues, the law of any country is more accurately the result of "historical accident or temporary social situations" (p. 19). The way that a nation administers justice often reflects deep-seated cultural, religious, economic, political, and historical realities. Learning about the reasons for these different practices can give us insight into the values, traditions, and cultures of other systems. Such broadening of perspective helps us see our own system in more objective terms.

To deal with transnational crime problems. Finally, a third good reason to study criminal justice from a comparative perspective is the increasing need to address transnational and international crime problems. Crime is universal—there is no country without crime (Newman, 1999, p. 64). And as we begin the 21st century, rapid travel and communication are making us painfully aware that crime is no longer confined by the geographical boundaries of individual countries. It appears that garden variety thefts, robberies, and assaults may become less troublesome to society than offenses such as the internationalization of organized crime, nuclear trafficking, international terrorism, money laundering, and the transnational trafficking of humans and human organs (see, e.g., Collin, 1997; Lee, 1996; McDonald, 1997; Williams, 1999). Criminality in this new century seems less apt to prey on private citizens and more likely to victimize communities, governments, and even entire nations.

Transnational crimes such as terrorism, air and sea hijacking, and drug smuggling are serious concerns that beg for a cooperative international response. Multinational collaboration is occurring, but the needed action requires a level of teamwork that countries of the world are only beginning to consider. Understandably, cooperation often starts with neighboring countries. Their common border not only presents the problem of intercountry crime but also provides both reason and opportunity to do something about it. Besides examples of neighbor cooperation, there are several examples of multinational collaboration as groupings of countries realize the need to develop formal agreements in their quest to control and combat crime.

Benefiting from others' experience, broadening our understanding of the world, and combating transnational crime are clearly three excellent reasons for studying comparative crime and justice. Those reasons express clear goals that appeal to the practitioner, policymaker, and to academics with an applied bent. There is another good reason for comparing issues of crime and justice, but this reason is often neglected because its application is less obvious. Specifically, comparative studies can help build, modify, and advance theoretical analysis of crime and criminal behavior. Obviously, theory informs practice, so it is unfair to suggest that strengthening theoretical analyses cannot be lumped with practical reasons for comparative studies. But a consistent predicament of theoreticians is to have their applied credentials questioned. A brief review of the efforts of comparative criminology will show how comparative studies benefit the growth of theory. We will then turn our attention to comparative justice studies in order to appreciate how that field of study works to achieve some of the other benefits of comparative study.

COMPARATIVE CRIMINOLOGY

Comparative studies have a lengthy history in the social sciences, and despite its seemingly recent appearance, comparative criminology is no exception. Jeremy Bentham, Émile Durkheim, Adolph Quetelet, Gabriel Tarde, and Alexis de Tocqueville would be on many lists of scholars interested in cross-national studies of crime. But just what do comparative criminology scholars study and what have they found? These are important questions when trying to understand the current interest in comparative criminology and when considering the future of this field of study. We briefly consider each question in hopes of whetting the appetite of persons interested in a more rigorous inquiry into comparative criminology.

What is the subject matter of comparative criminology?

As noted at this chapter's start, criminologists are interested in crime as a social phenomenon and as social behavior. Most simply, comparative criminologists are interested in the same things but on a broader scale. Johnson and Barak-Glantz (1983) suggest that comparative criminologists seek to locate commonalities and differences in crime patterns among divergent cultures. Newman and Howard (2001) list issues such as testing at the international level our traditional theories about crime, identifying the distribution and patterning of crime in different countries, and describing how cultures might differ in their relation to crime as topics of interest to comparative criminologists. Helpful as those denotations are, we are drawn to Beirne and Nelken's (1997) succinct definition of comparative criminology as referring to "the systematic and theoretically-informed comparison of crime in two or more cultures" (p. xiii).

Appealing aspects of Beirne and Nelken's (1997) definition are the focus on crime and the requirement that two or more cultures are compared. By restricting comparative criminology to the study of crime, we avoid confusion with comparative criminal justice, which focuses on the policies and procedures established by a culture to achieve social order. As we do at this chapter's beginning, Beirne and Nelken recognize the artificial nature of any line drawn between crime and criminal justice. But doing so helps distinguish fields of study that might otherwise be confused. Similarly, requiring a research effort to involve two or more cultures before being designated an example of comparative criminology seems very reasonable. Research describing homicide in a particular country other than one's own can be very informative, can clearly advance scientific knowledge, and could be a necessary step in developing or refining theories about homicide's occurrence. To be a comparative study, however, homicide in at least two countries should be studied.

Another feature of comparative criminology must be noted. To date, comparative criminology has mostly compared domestic crime events in two or more countries. The growth of criminal acts that cross national borders should also be of interest to comparative criminologists. Other chapters in this book provide examples of transnational crimes such as money laundering and trafficking in illicit drugs. An understanding of these criminal events requires knowledge of their spread and distribution across time and place—a type of inquiry appropriate to comparative criminology. In addition, transnational crime involves the cooperative behavior of people in several countries as they coordinate efforts to accomplish the crime. Explaining such behavior by criminals in different countries is also an appropriate investigation for comparative criminologists. To more accurately reflect contemporary research topics, we propose an expansion of Beirne and Nelken's (1997) definition of comparative criminology to be a systematic and theoretically informed comparison of crime in two or more cultures *or across two or more countries.*

What variables are used in comparative criminology?

Criminologists seeking to understand better the spread and distribution of crime in a particular country have considered the possible influence of social, economic, political, psychological, and biological variables. Comparative criminologists have used these same variables in their attempt to compare crime's occurrence cross-nationally. Especially popular have been variables associated with economic conditions and urbanization.

Economic development and industrialization are among the most popular variables included in comparative research on crime—with homicide and theft often being the crimes of research choice. Most studies have found that neither economic development nor industrialization is significantly related to homicide rate (e.g., He, 1999; LaFree, 1997). However, the majority of research comparing theft rates among countries finds a significant positive effect of economic development and industrialization (e.g., Hartnagel, 1982; He, 1999; Stack, 1984).

Other economic variables of interest to researchers have included unemployment rates and the amount of money the government spends on social service programs. Fiala and LaFree (1988) found no significant effect of unemployment on homicide. Neapolitan (1995) found no evidence to suggest that unemployment has any significant effect on theft in less-developed nations. Using both cross-sectional and pooled data, He (1999) found a significant positive effect of unemployment on homicide, but the effect of unemployment on theft is less consistent.

Several researchers have offered government expenditures on social service programs as a potential correlate to crime (see DeFronzo, 1997). Fiala and LaFree (1988) found a significant negative effect of welfare spending on child homicide victimization among 18 industrialized nations. Similarly, using advanced industrialized nations as samples, Gartner (1990, 1991) and Briggs and Cutright (1994) both found a significant negative effect of "social assistance" on child homicide. Pampel and Gartner (1995) also found that the level of welfare assistance had a significant negative effect on homicide offending among young men in 18 industrialized nations. A significant negative effect of welfare assistance on property crime has been found in single-nation studies (e.g., DeFronzo, 1996).

He (1999) measured the theoretical concept of human investment as the total percentage of the government expenditures in social security, social welfare, health care, and education in his study. Contrary to expectations, He's cross-sectional analysis results indicated no significant effect of government expenditure on social welfare on either homicide or theft.

In addition to economic conditions, researchers have also considered the role urbanization might play in explaining differences in cross-national crime rates. The results here are also mixed. Using population growth rate as measurement of urbanization, two studies found a positive effect of urbanization on homicide (Krahn, Hartnagel, & Gartrel, 1986; McDonald, 1976), but two others did not (Krohn & Wellford, 1977; Messner, 1982). Both Krohn and Wellford (1977) and McDonald (1976) found a significant positive effect of urbanization on theft.

When urbanization is operationalized as the percentage of the population living in urban areas, researchers have not found a significant positive effect of urbanization on either homicide (e.g., Kick & LaFree, 1985; Messner, 1980; Ortega, Corzine, Burnett, & Poyer, 1992) or theft (e.g., Hartnagel, 1982; He, 1999; Kick & LaFree, 1985). In fact, some studies suggest a significant negative effect of urbanization on homicide (e.g., Conklin & Simpson, 1985; Ortega et al., 1992). Obviously, urbanization remains a variable worthy of additional research.

In addition to economic conditions and urbanization, comparative criminologists have considered the potential role played by factors such as political strictures and moral individualism. Lynch, Newman, McDowall, and Groves (1988) tested a hypothesis proposing that the rates of violent and property crime will differ according to world system location. They suggested that core nations would have higher rates of property crime because of the democratic and egalitarian ideologies. Periphery countries will have higher rates of violent crime because of political repression, frustration-aggression reactions, and alienation. Controlling for income inequality and the level of economic development, Lynch et al.'s study supported their hypotheses regarding crimes in the core and the periphery nations. In an attempt to identify patterns for semiperiphery nations, He (1999), using pooled data analysis, found a significant positive effect of both semiperiphery and periphery on homicide. He also found a significant negative effect of both semiperiphery and periphery on theft.

Only a handful of comparative studies have looked into the effect of moral individualism on homicide. Messner (1982) used Protestant religiosity and school enrollment as measurements of moral individualism but did not find a relationship between these two measures and homicide. Huang (1995), upon finding a significant negative effect of individualism (measured by scores on political and civil rights) on homicide, suggested that a society's common sentiment of respect for individuals' political and civil rights might inhibit citizens from killing each other. Neapolitan (1995) tested the effect of political rights on theft in a sample including only the less-developed nations. He found that political rights had a significant positive effect on theft in less-developed nations.

Attempting to make sense of these positive, negative, null, and mixed effects requires researchers to draw on the rich tradition of theory that has developed in criminology. A key question is whether theoretical explanations for crime's occurrence in a particular country have any explanatory power in another country. Continuing our brief overview of comparative criminology, we consider some of the explanations that have been offered to explain crime cross-nationally.

What explanations have comparative criminologists offered?

An entire section of this book is devoted to the research of comparative criminologists as they seek to understand transnational crime (see Part II). Here, we provide a brief account of the more traditional research endeavors that compare domestic crime in two or more countries. This review of classic and contemporary examples of comparative criminology shows the diversity of crimes considered, variables addressed, and theories proposed by scholars interested in comparing crime across cultures.

A popular technique among comparative criminologists has been an attempt to identify commonality among cases of crime to determine a general theory of criminal behavior. Shelley's (1981) *Crime and Modernization* is an early example of this methodology. As the title indicates, Shelley uses empirical evidence to show that modernization provides the best theoretical explanation for crime's evolution in recent history. Specifically, she suggests that social processes accompanying industrial development have resulted in conditions conducive to increased criminality, such as loosened family ties, instability of family, and lack of supervision of younger family members. More recent versions of this approach are grouped as examples of Durkheimian-modernization theory (see Neuman & Berger, 1988). This perspective uses the nation-state or society as the unit of analysis, and it posits that all nations develop through similar stages. Variables such as industrialization, population growth, urbanization, the division of labor, social disorganization, anomie, modern values, and

cultural heterogeneity are used to explain variation in crime rates.

Recent theorizing in the Durkheimian-modernization vein uses the triad of modernization, civilization, and power to explain different criminological developments in diverse societies (Heiland & Shelley, 1992, p. 18). This synthesized modernization-civilization theory is seen by some as strengthening the explanatory power of the Durkheimian-modernization perspective by adding civilization and power variables. The civilization concept, drawn from Elias's (1982) civilization theory, provides the link between the long-term structural changes and the alteration of personality structures. At the individual level, Elias suggests that historically there has been an ever-increasing refinement of customs and manners, an obvious pacification of the conditions of daily life and an intensification of instinctive and affected inhibitions. At the institutional level, Elias found three key societal factors in the development of greater individual control: (1) the monopolization of the instruments of power, (2) the centralization of state power, and (3) the creation of power monopolies.

According to Elias (1982), the limitations on individual behavior can find equilibrium only when they are part of a relatively stable and easily comprehensible arrangement of actions by the broader society. And such a situation occurs when there is a monopoly of social institutions. If Elias's hypothesis holds true, that interpersonal relations vary with the civilization of society, then so should the nature of interpersonal violence and crime (Heiland & Shelley, 1992). And it would not be unreasonable to hypothesize that a more civilized society would have lower volumes of violent crimes but higher volumes of self-inflicted harmful behaviors such as drug use or suicide.

In their assessment of the Durkheimian-modernization perspective, Neuman and Berger (1988) found weak support for the perspective's ability to explain variation in crime rates across countries. Believing other perspectives could work as well, Neuman and

Berger consider a Marxian world-system perspective and an ecological-opportunity perspective. The Marxian world-system perspective defines crime as a sociopolitical concept that reflects production and power relations, which are intrinsically linked to a society's relation to other societies (see, e.g., Humphries & Greenberg, 1981; Lopez-Rey, 1970; Neuman & Berger, 1988). This perspective treats industrialization and urbanization as the outcomes of capitalist expansion. Unlike the Durkheimian-modernization perspective, which sets modernization as a key predictor of crime rates, the Marxian-world system perspective uses modernization only as an intervening variable. In this way, it argues that the effect of industrialization and modernization depends on how modes of production articulate with one another.

Durkheimian-modernization, synthesized modernization-civilization, and Marxian world-system perspectives all provide a macro-level analysis of variation in cross-national crime data. The ecological-opportunity perspective takes a microlevel approach by concentrating on the criminal act itself. This theory argues that crime occurs where environmental conditions are favorable. For example, LaFree and Birkbeck (1991) studied victimization data in Venezuela and in the United States and found that in both countries, robbery typically involves public domains, lone victims, strangers, and incidents taking place outside buildings. Neuman and Berger (1988) see this ability to identify the specific situations that immediately precede in space and time the actual execution of a crime as a strength of the ecological-opportunity perspective. Should comparative criminologists continue to find that crimes occur in similar situations, regardless of country, we will have valuable information about criminal acts—although our knowledge about motivation to commit those acts will not necessarily be advanced.

It is apparent from this review of comparative criminology that it is a field of study in which scholars are drawing on traditional criminological theory and methodology while simultaneously expanding the discipline's enquiry beyond events in a single country. In a similar manner, scholars interested in comparative criminal justice are borrowing from the knowledge base in disciplines such as sociology, political science, and criminal justice as they seek to understand how nations have sought to maintain a system of formal social control. We now turn our attention to this other area of importance—the broad field of comparative studies.

COMPARATIVE CRIMINAL JUSTICE[2]

While comparative criminologists are busily comparing crime patterns cross-nationally, comparative justice scholars are considering the similarities and differences in how countries attempt to maintain social order and accomplish justice. Research has identified the different ways police organizations are structured (e.g., Bayley, 1985), described variation in criminal procedure around the world (e.g., Bradley, 1999), noted how jury systems differ among those countries using juries (e.g., Vidmar, 2000), reported on differences in sentencing policies and practices (e.g., Tonry & Frase, 2001), and offered explanations for variation in the use of imprisonment in different countries (e.g., Neapolitan, 2001). And those are just a very few topics and authors who are building the knowledge base of comparative criminal justice.

As an example of the type of information resulting from comparative justice studies, we offer a descriptive account of how the courts are structured in four different countries. To introduce another comparative technique, the countries are chosen to reflect each of four legal traditions. This concept of legal traditions—also called legal families—refers to a culture's attitudes, values, and norms regarding the nature, role, and operation of law. Following the prevailing contemporary strategy (e.g., Fairchild & Dammer, 2001;

Reichel, 2002), we use the four legal families of civil, common, socialist, and Islamic.

Civil Law Family and German Courts

The oldest contemporary legal family is the civil legal tradition. Persons familiar with the American legal system often find this term confusing because *civil law* in United States jurisdictions refers to private wrongs (such as contract disputes) rather than to the *criminal law,* which handles social wrongs (such as thefts and assaults). Some authors attempt to avoid this confusion between civil law as private wrongs and civil law as a legal tradition by referring to the Romano-Germanic law family. That designation is appropriate because the origins of the civil law tradition are in the *Corpus Juris Civilis* (450 B.C.) and the laws of the Germanic tribes, such as the Franks and the Bavarians, that bordered the Roman Empire in central Europe and eventually conquered most of Europe. Although use of the term *Romano-Germanic* avoids the problems of confusion, especially by Americans, between the civil law family and civil law as private wrongs, most comparative scholars prefer to refer to the civil law tradition. We honor that preference and use the term *civil law* as referring to one of the world's major legal traditions.

A number of different codifications of civil law followed the *Corpus Juris Civilis,* including the famous *Code Napoléon* (1804), which codified the civil law of France. During the first part of the 19th century, the idea of codification spread from France to other parts of Europe and to Latin America. Germany was among the countries finding favor with the idea of codification, but the Germans did not agree with basic principles used in developing the *Code Napoléon.* With significant deliberation and historical research, Germany finally succeeded in creating its version of a civil code (the German Civil Code of 1896), which became effective in 1900.

The German national legislature determines, for the entire country, what behavior is criminal and what will be the accompanying punishment. However, each German state is responsible for administering both the law and the punishment.

Germany's penal code places criminal offenses into one of two categories: felonies, which are punishable by imprisonment for at least one year, and misdemeanors, which are punishable by a shorter term or a fine (Kurian, 1989). The distinction is similar to that used in the United States, but German misdemeanors contain a broader range of offenses and include crimes such as larceny, fraud, or negligent homicide that would be considered felonies in many American jurisdictions.

A distinguishing feature of the civil legal tradition is a reliance on the inquisitorial rather than adversarial process for adjudication. The adversarial process, found especially in the common law tradition, assumes truth will arise from an open competition over who has the correct facts. The prosecution and defense propose their version of the "truth," and the judge or jury determines which side has the most accurate portrayal. Rather than a competition between opposing sides, the inquisitorial process is more like a continuing investigation. All parties in the case are expected to provide all relevant evidence to the court. The judge, not the attorneys for defense or prosecution, then calls and questions witnesses. As a result of this process, the civil legal tradition has a procedurally active judge and rather passive lawyers. This is nearly opposite the adversarial process, which has a procedurally passive judge and rather active advocates.

The German states (Länder) are responsible for administering federal law, so all trials are conducted at the state level. Federal courts exist only to handle appeals from the state courts. Fairchild and Dammer (2001) describe three tiers of criminal courts in the German states. At the bottom are the *Amtsgerichte* courts that hear minor criminal cases. Above them are the *Ländgericht* where major criminal cases are tried. As the uppermost state court, the *Oberländesgerichte* court hears appeals from the lower state courts and will also try some exceptional cases (e.g., treason). Appeals from the state courts may eventually reach the *Bundesgerichtshof,* or the Federal Supreme Court. Five of these supreme courts operate as the court of last resort for appeals in criminal cases coming through the state courts. When the appeal is on a constitutional question, the Federal Constitutional Court decides the issue and returns the case to the lower court for final disposition.

Legal systems following the inquisitorial process seldom use a jury as Americans know the term. Instead, participation from the public is in the form of lay judges. Persons are selected as lay judges from nominees provided by a community council. The lay judges are assigned to trials over a 4-year period, but they serve an average of only 1 day per month. During the trial, the lay judges serve alongside a professional judge. Trials for the less serious crimes are heard by a panel of one professional judge and two lay judges. When the trial is for a more serious offense it will be heard by three professional judges and two lay judges. The verdict is by majority vote, so it is possible that the lay judges have a significant say in the outcome. However, since the professional judge or judges typically dominate the questioning and the deliberation, lay judges have to be especially assertive to have significant influence (Fairchild & Dammer, 2001; Weigend, 1983).

Common Law Family and Canadian Courts

You will recall that the primary source of law in the civil legal tradition is the written code. For the common legal tradition, the primary source of law is custom. The distinction between codification and custom is confusing because it is possible—in fact, likely—that common law is also expressed in written form. However, it is neither necessary nor sufficient that common law be written down for it to have legal authority. A brief review of the origin of common law will make this point more clearly.

In an attempt to return order to an increasingly disrupted kingdom, Henry II (1154–1189) issued the Constitutions of Clarendon (1164), which listed customs said to be the practice in England when the 12th century had begun. The idea was that traditional, consistent, and reasonable ways of deciding disputes provided the appropriate source of law. Determining whether something was "customary" fell to members of the community, who sat as a jury of peers. Judges were expected to follow legal custom by abiding by prior decisions in similar cases. In this manner, custom could be identified by reliance on the people and through reference to several cases. Importantly, however, the case was not referred to as the source of law; it merely provided proof that a legal principle (a custom) was once applied.

Eventually the practice of citing prior cases was done less to show custom and more as a way to reference authority. In this way, common law developed a reliance on precedent or *stare decisis,* wherein courts are expected to abide by previously decided cases. Those cases were in written form, but they cannot be considered written law in the way the civil legal tradition views "written." The prior cases reflected custom, albeit custom in writing, rather than reflecting specific decisions by rulers or legislators. The criminal statutes found in common law countries today must be considered in the same way. When common law legislatures prepare written penal statutes or codes, they are not so much *making* written law (as do civil law legislatures) as they are *proposing* law. That is because final determination regarding the validity of a statute lies with the courts, who will evaluate the legislature's work. In other words, civil law legislation stands on it own because the legislature is the source of law. But common law legislation is not authoritatively established until it passes examination of the courts because custom is the source of law.

Because common law developed in England and influenced the application of law in the British colonies, this legal tradition is the one most familiar to citizens of the United States.

Today, the United States, Canada, Australia, New Zealand, India, and former British colonies in Africa have legal systems counted among those of the common law tradition. Exceptions include parts of those countries where France had great influence in the province's or state's history. So Canada's province of Quebec and the state of Louisiana each have a strong civil law tradition despite being part of a common law country.

The way Canada has classified an offense determines how the case flows through the system. Therefore, it is necessary to understand the classification before being able to follow a case through the courts. Also, it is important to note that the French influence in Quebec gives that province some unique aspects in its court structure and trial process. For that reason, the following description applies generally to the other nine provinces and the two federal territories.

Canada's Criminal Code places crimes into one of three categories. *Summary conviction offenses* are the least serious and result in only slight punishment. They include, for example, committing an indecent act, creating a public disturbance, soliciting prostitution, and driving a motor vehicle without the owner's consent. *Indictable offenses* are the most serious crimes and bring the harshest penalty. Typical indictable offenses are murder, possession of stolen goods, dangerous driving, and sexual assault. Falling between summary and indictable offenses are *hybrid offenses* such as theft of an item valued at less than $1,000 (Canadian), impaired driving, and some types of assault (Griffiths & Verdun-Jones, 1994; Pease & Hukkila, 1990).

Canada's provinces and territories generally have a three-tiered court system going from provincial and territorial courts at the lowest level through superior courts (with name variation by province) to the courts of appeal at the highest level (Griffiths & Verdun-Jones, 1994). The provincial courts carry the greatest workload of any court level because all cases

enter at this level. The majority will also be tried and finally disposed of in the provincial courts, but others (the most serious indictable offenses) will be sent to the superior court for trial.

Provincial courts may have separate divisions to handle family matters, cases of juvenile delinquency, traffic cases, and criminal cases. Most of the criminal cases are those that have been charged as summary conviction offenses. In general, such offenses may be tried only before a provincial court judge sitting without a jury. Accused persons may appear in person at the trial or may send their lawyer to represent them—unless the judge has issued a warrant requiring their attendance. The term *summary conviction* implies that casual and concise justice is dispensed.

Indictable offenses, and hybrid offenses charged as indictable, can be heard at either the superior or provincial court level. Griffiths and Verdun-Jones (1994) explain that the particular form and place of trial in superior court are determined by the category of indictable offense being charged. The most serious indictable offenses (e.g., murder, treason, piracy) may be tried only by a judge of the superior court sitting with a jury, unless the judge and the attorney general consent to forgo the jury. The least serious indictable offenses (e.g., theft, fraud, possession of stolen goods) may be tried by only a provincial court judge. If the charge is on an indictable offense not falling into either of those categories, the accused can choose the mode of trial. Robbery, dangerous driving, assault, and breaking and entering are examples of these "electable" offenses. The choices available to the accused are to have a trial by a provincial court judge, a superior court judge and jury, or a superior court judge. Failure to make a choice sends the case to a judge and jury. At the federal court level, and standing as the country's court of last resort, is the Supreme Court of Canada. The Supreme Court justices are appointed by the federal government from lists prepared by the provinces.

Socialist Law Family and Chinese Courts

The designation of socialist law as a separate legal tradition is the most controversial of the four legal families. In fact, some comparative legal theorists do not see the socialist legal tradition as a separate family. However, valid arguments recognize the similarities between socialist and civil law while maintaining that cultural and philosophical differences between the two allow separate classification. For example, both civil and socialist traditions view law as stemming from written codes, but the civil codes (according to the socialists) are the work of special interest groups, whereas the socialist codes represent the ideals of the people's revolution. In addition to its particular philosophical view of law's role, we consider socialist law as a separate tradition because we can learn much about the nature of law in systems emphasizing communal values at the expense of individualism.

The legal system of the Union of Soviet Socialist Republics (U.S.S.R.) provided the philosophical and technical base for a socialist legal tradition. The "fall" of the U.S.S.R. did not result in the collapse of the socialist legal tradition any more than the fall of the Roman Empire destroyed the civil legal tradition. Countries currently reflecting major aspects of the socialist legal tradition are Cuba, North Korea, Vietnam, and China.

One characteristic setting the socialist legal tradition apart from others is its view of law as artificial. The Romans and Western Continentals viewed law as binding because they appropriately authorized and recorded it. The English viewed law as binding because it recognized immemorial custom. The Russian people, even before the arrival of the U.S.S.R., never came to see law as binding at all. For the Russians, law was an arbitrary work of an autocratic sovereign and a privilege of the bourgeoisie. Russian princes and czars not only created the law, they were above it. This point is important to understanding the role

of law as perceived by Karl Marx and as implemented by Vladimir Lenin.

After the Bolshevik revolution (1917), Lenin, as the head of the new Soviet state, drew on the traditional Russian view of law as artificial. A basic tenet of Marxism-Leninism was that under communism, the need for law would wither away. Because law was artificial, that philosophy was neither surprising nor unreasonable to the Russian people. Nevertheless, until it had faded, law could play an important role in achieving a communist state. Law would, in other words, be used to achieve other ends. Rather than being an absolute value that dictated how people and their government must behave, law would be a tool for accomplishing communist goals. For the Russian people, the idea that law was subordinate to policy was not much different from its being subordinate to the will of princes and czars. Law was, after all, artificial.

Another characteristic setting the socialist legal tradition apart from others is its view of law as subordinate to policy. Law, under this tradition, is used to achieve a desirable end rather than being an absolute value limiting both the leaders' and the people's behavior. The policy to which law is subordinate places the rights of the collectivized economy and the socialist state above any rights the individual might have. Socialists see the subordination of law to policy as an improvement over the civil and common traditions, because subordinated law can be used as a tool to achieve socialist economic and educational goals.

David and Brierley (1978) addressed the economic role played by socialist law when they contrasted it with civil and common law's role in capitalist economies. Law in a capitalist economy tells the citizens that a just and moral society, achieved through law as an absolute value, results in economic order. Under the socialist legal tradition, economic order, achieved through law as a tool, results in a just and moral society. The reversal of attitudes toward law's role in the economy gives the socialist legal tradition different ideas about law than those found in civil and common traditions.

Law's educational role was an important feature for Lenin and remains a key feature in today's socialist law countries. In the former U.S.S.R., the People's Republic of China, and other countries following a socialist legal tradition, law operates to educate people about the principles of socialism and to guide them toward the communist ideal. Socialist judges do not simply apply the law, as they do in civil law countries, nor do they make or validate the law, as they do in common law countries. Judges in the socialist legal tradition must help ensure the success of government policy by educating the people.

Political and economic changes beginning in 1989 had an important affect on the legal systems in the former countries of the U.S.S.R. and in other Central and Eastern European countries. Because an important aspect of that change was a growing appreciation for the rule of law, it seems appropriate to identify those countries as more closely affiliated today with the civil, rather than the socialist, legal tradition. But similar changes have not occurred in all socialist countries. Cuba, Vietnam, North Korea, and the People's Republic of China were less affected by challenges to traditional socialism and provide contemporary examples of the socialist legal tradition. China provides our specific example.

China's formal court system has four tiers. Going from the bottom up, they are the Basic People's Court, the Intermediate People's Court, the Higher People's Court, and finally the Supreme People's Court. The Basic People's Courts, which are found in each county and municipal area, handle the majority of the ordinary criminal trials. The Intermediate People's Courts hear more serious criminal cases and appeals from the Basic People's Courts. Major criminal cases and appeals are heard by the Higher People's Courts, which operate at the province level and in some major cities. The Supreme People's Court serves primarily in an appellate capacity but will also hear major criminal cases that have an impact on the entire country (Situ & Liu, 1996).

The courts are essentially agencies of the central government (i.e., the Communist Party) and as a result do not have judicial independence in the way Westerners think of the term. Court activities at each level are reviewed by a judicial committee. Members of the judicial committees are appointed by the People's Congress at each level, and it is through the People's Congress that the central government has its input and influence.

At the trial, those accused have the right to offer a defense, to argue the case, to explain their innocence, or to request leniency in punishment. Although the defendant can provide self-defense, it is also possible to hire a lawyer or ask a close relative to defend one's case. When cases are at trial with a public prosecutor, the court can appoint a lawyer to speak for the accused (Situ & Liu, 1996).

Like the situation in most civil law countries, China does not use a jury but instead has citizen input through representation of lay judges or *people's assessors*. Minor criminal cases are heard before a single judge, but more serious cases come before a panel of one to three professional judges and two to four people's assessors. The people's assessors are laypersons who have reached age 23 and are eligible to vote.

In addition to its formal justice system, China is recognized as having an especially well-developed system of informal justice. In fact, the informal system is so integral that it sometimes operates alongside the formal system. The Public Security Committees operate in this capacity at the policing level and the People's Mediation Committees (PMC) perform the informal role at the court level. China's constitution requires each urban neighborhood and each rural village to have a PMC. In addition, PMCs can be established at workplaces, schools, and other institutions.

Although the PMCs serve the socialist ideology very well, they have historical ties to Confucianism and the belief that moral education through mediation is the best way for communities to resolve conflict. The PMCs operate under the guidance of local governments and local people's courts. PMC members are elected by the people living or working in the PMC's jurisdiction. When a conflict arises, the parties can ask that a mediator get involved. But the PMC does not need to wait for an invitation. Because the mediators live in the community, they usually hear about problems early on and can respond quickly.

Islamic Law Family and Saudi Arabian Courts

The Islamic legal tradition is unique among legal families in several respects. The first is its perception of law's source as sacred rather than secular. The other legal traditions, especially civil and common, have religious links, but they remain distinct and separate from religion. The Islamic legal tradition, on the other hand, is completely reliant on religion.

Muslims, like Christians and Jews, believe in one God, whom Muslims call Allah. Of Allah's messengers to the world, Muhammad (circa 570–632) is considered the most recent prophet by Muslims. The religion prescribed by Muhammad is Islam (Arabic for *submission*), and its followers are "those who submit to Allah" (Muslims).

Islamic law is called the *Shari'a*, "the path to follow." Its primary ingredients are the *Qur'an* (Islam's holy book) and the *Sunna* (the statements and deeds of Muhammad). These two elements identify both crimes and punishments, but they provide very little information regarding the legal process by which offenders are brought to justice.

Three categories of crime are distinguished in the *Shari'a: hudud, quesas,* and *ta'azir. Hudud,* which are offenses against God,

require mandatory prosecution and must be punished in the manner prescribed in the *Qur'an* or the *Sunna.* The seven *hudud* crimes are adultery or fornication, defamation, drinking alcohol, theft, highway robbery, apostasy (the rejection of Islam by one professing Islamic faith), and rebellion or corruption of Islam. The punishment for *hudud* crimes include death by stoning for a married person committing adultery, hand amputation for theft, and whipping for persons using alcohol (Sanad, 1991).

Quesas crimes are less serious than *hudud* crimes and more serious than *ta'azir* crimes. They are similar to what other criminal codes call crimes against persons and include acts such as voluntary and involuntary homicide, assault, and battery. Punishments for these crimes can be acts of retaliation by the victim or his family (e.g., the eye for the eye, the nose for the nose) or financial compensation by the offender to the victim or his family.

The least serious of *Shari'a* crimes are the *ta'azir.* Included in this category are all offenses not identified as either *hudud* or *quesas* crimes. Examples of *ta'azir* crimes are petty theft, homosexuality, eating pork, neglect of prayers, and acts damaging to the public interest. A *ta'azir* penalty can be execution but is more likely to be whipping, imprisonment, or a fine (Sanad, 1991).

In the *Shari'a,* God identified the crimes and stipulated the penalty, but the law's application fell to humans. Not surprisingly, humans disagreed about how to apply God's law. Some Muslims took a strict interpretation and believed that every rule of law must be derived from the *Qur'an* or the *Sunna.* Others believed human reason and personal opinion could be used to elaborate the law. The latter camp suggested that as the centuries progressed from Muhammad's time, there were new behaviors or situations that had not been directly addressed in the early 7th century. Human reason, these Muslims believed, could be used to fill the gaps.

Because human reason could become human legislation, which is inappropriate because law comes from Allah and not from humans, it was important that the reasoning be subordinate to divine revelation. The result was a process known as *qiyas*, or reasoning by analogy. For example, Lippman, McConville, and Yerushalmi (1988) note that some judges have sentenced committers of sodomy (a behavior not mentioned in the *Qur'an* or *Sunna*) to the same penalty the *Qur'an* provides for adultery by reasoning that sodomy and adultery are similar offenses. The presence of *ta'azir* crimes also allows the *Shari'a* to keep pace with modern society by making criminal any act that might cause damage to the public interest or the public order. In this way, acts not specifically mentioned 14 centuries ago (such as traffic violations, embezzlement, or forgery) are still considered illegal by divine revelation rather than human legislation.

Traditional Islamic societies such as Saudi Arabia mold their court system to ensure that Islamic law is the basis for court proceedings and decisions. There is a dual court system in Saudi Arabia, with *Shari'a* courts handling criminal cases, family law, and some civil law. A separate system of administrative tribunals has jurisdiction over specific issues such as traffic offenses and laws related to business and commerce. Our concern is with the *Shari'a* courts, which follow a four-tiered structure moving from the lower or general courts at the bottom, to the High Courts, then to the Courts of Appeal, and finally to the Supreme Judicial Council.

The general courts are presided over by a single Islamic judge (*qadi*). These courts are found in most every town and deal with minor domestic matters, misdemeanors, small claims, some *ta'azir* crimes, and *hudud* offenses of intoxication and defamation. *Hudud* and *quesas* offenses are heard in the High Courts, which also hear cases on appeal from the lower courts. A single judge hears the case unless a sentence of death, stoning, or amputation is required. A three-judge panel hears those cases (Moore,

1996). Final appeal is before the Supreme Judicial Council, which is also the agency making regulations and policies for administering the country's court system as a whole. The Council, composed of 11 members, cannot alter a verdict but instead refers the case back to the court of appeals for reconsideration.

Although the structure of Saudi courts is not especially unique, some of the procedural law governing the trial process is. Sanad (1991) highlights the rules of evidence as a particularly important distinguishing feature of Islamic law in general. Most Muslim scholars maintain that evidence in criminal cases must be restricted to confession and testimony. Regarding confession, it is not sufficient for the accused to simply admit to the charges. For a confession to be valid, the confessor must be a mature, mentally sound person who gives, with free will, a confession that is neither doubtful nor vague. Coerced confessions presumably are not acceptable or admissible, but Moore (1987) says flogging and long detention of suspects who refuse to confess occur in Saudi Arabia.

For the second type of evidence, testimony, at least two witnesses should provide consistent testimony before a conviction on *hudud* and *quesas* crimes can be given. But just any witness is not acceptable. To be condoned, the witness must be an adult male (one school accepts two females as equivalent to one male), known to have good memory, sound mind, and good character.

In addition to requirements about who can testify, there are rules regarding how many witnesses are required and how the testimony is given. For a conviction on *hudud* and *quesas* offenses, at least two witnesses should provide consistent testimony about the accused's actions. In the case of adultery, four witnesses are required. Because there are seldom times when two devout male Muslims observe a burglary in process or four such witnesses watch adultery taking place, the "evidence" in many criminal trials is incomplete. At this point, the rules regarding how testimony is given come into play in the form of *oaths*.

According to Rosen (1989), witnesses under Islamic law are not sworn in before testifying. In fact, there is even some understanding that less than truthful statements may be made in court as witnesses are speaking freely. However, if testimony reaches a point where neither side has adequately supported its claim, one party may challenge the other to take an oath. If the person challenged does so, he wins the case. Or the person challenged can refer the oath back to the challenger who can secure victory by swearing to his own truthfulness. This process of challenging is not a haphazard one. The *qadi* plays a very important role because he decides which party will first challenge the other to take an oath. That decision is important because the first to swear wins the case. Rosen suggests that the *qadi,* after observing the comments from witnesses and from the parties themselves, looks for the person most likely to know what is true about the case. That person is designated as the one first to be challenged to take the oath. Because false swearers will suffer the consequences of judgment day, devout Muslims take oaths very seriously and, presumably, truthfully.

By categorizing the world's legal systems as falling into one of four legal traditions, comparative justice scholars are encouraging us to benefit from others' experiences, broaden our understanding of the world, and combat transnational crime. They are, in other words, helping us realize the benefits of comparative study as described at this chapter's start.

FUTURE ISSUES FOR THE COMPARATIVE CRIME AND JUSTICE COMMUNITY

Predicting future issues in any area is always risky. But we do not speculate too much when suggesting that the coming decades will see continued increase in transnational crime and more transnational cooperation to combat that crime. These points form the crux of this book, and they are fully developed in the remaining chapters. However, we conclude this chapter with a brief overview of these issues as we set the stage for the more topic-specific chapters.

Predicting an increase in transnational crime is less difficult than defining exactly what acts constitute transnational crime. Typically, when we think of crime, we are considering those events that originate, are carried out, and affect a local area—even if that local area is the nation. The burglar, assailant, or auto thief usually conceives the crime in the same general locale where it is committed. Furthermore, the impact of the crime is mostly on that locale. Transnational crime, on the other hand, has its origin, execution, and impact in two or more nations. Dobriansky (2001) makes the point with the drug ecstasy, which is manufactured primarily in the Netherlands and is trafficked in the United States by, among others, Israeli organized crime groups. That crime's impact is likely felt in all three countries.

Even after accepting a definition of transnational crime that requires the crime's origin, execution, and impact to involve more than one country, there is no agreed-on list of crimes fitting that definition. Most people would agree that cybercrime, drug trafficking, and money laundering are examples of what we mean by transnational crime. There might be less agreement about environmental crime (e.g., pollution from one country causing environmental harm in another country). This lack of specificity regarding the activities constituting transnational crime cannot continue. Our first prediction regarding the future of comparative crime and justice is that we will see greater clarity regarding what activities are examples of transnational crime. Whether a result of action by practitioners, researchers, or policymakers, there will have to be greater agreement regarding the subject matter of transnational crime.

In addition to clarification of what constitutes transnational crime, we also believe there will be increased understanding and appreciation of this phenomenon by citizens of each country. Virtually all corners of the world are affected by at least some type of transnational crime. But there is considerable variation in the attention the crimes receive from a nation's justice agencies, politicians, media, and citizens. American citizens, for example, are very much aware of the transnational aspect of drug trafficking but are often not so familiar with environmental crimes and crimes against a cultural heritage. Citizens in European countries may fully appreciate the transnational aspects of organized crime but may not have much understanding of how cybercrime and money laundering can affect their daily lives. Increased awareness is already occurring, but we believe it will become an even greater aspect of daily life—not necessarily because more individual citizens will be directly affected by a specific transnational crime (although that too will certainly happen) but more because government resources will be directed toward combating transnational crime, so politicians and the media will encourage citizens to become informed.

Finally, we anticipate expanding cooperation among nations in the areas of enforcement and adjudication. At present, Interpol is the premier example of international cooperation in law enforcement. Interpol is not an operational police force; instead, it assists local and national police agencies in conducting crime investigations, collecting and compiling statistics, and delivering arrest warrants ordered by courts. Because of Interpol, police have learned that through collaboration and communication much can be accomplished in the fight against crime. With Interpol firmly in command of international coordination among law enforcement agencies, there is no reason to anticipate anything other than continued sophistication and cooperation at that level. However, changes may occur at regional levels as geographically linked nations collaborate to combat transnational crimes that particularly impact their region. The activities of the European Police Organization (Europol) provide a prime example of such regional cooperation, and we anticipate that nations in other regions will follow the European Union's model and develop specific agencies to coordinate law enforcement efforts in their region.

As more transnational criminals are caught, there will be greater effort to express global outrage toward the offense and the offender. Appropriate and understandable issues of national sovereignty means the majority of transnational offenders will be tried and punished according to the laws of a particular country. However, we also anticipate an increase in the use of international tribunals and supranational courts for a greater variety of transnational offenders.

Current examples of adjudication at a supranational level (see Chapter 16 for extended discussion on these courts) are mostly in cases where a legal solution is required between two countries or when justice must be meted out to offenders responsible for acts that violate international standards or treaties. The judicial mechanisms established for such cases are developing and gaining legitimacy at a rapid pace. For example, the International Court of Justice (ICJ) is the principal judicial organ of the United Nations (ICJ, n.d.). The Court has a dual role of settling, in accordance with international law, any legal disputes submitted to it by the 185 United Nations member states and neutral parties (Nauru and Switzerland) and to give advisory opinions on legal questions referred to it by international organizations.

Another supranational court is the European Court of Human Rights (ECHR). The ECHR allows for individuals to bring cases directly to a judicial body after they have been denied relief in their national courts (Council of Europe, n.d.). Generally, the mission of the ECHR is to interpret and uphold the European Convention on Human Rights and Fundamental Freedoms, a treaty prepared by the Council of Europe in 1950.

The most recently formed transnational court, ratified by United Nations member states in 2002, is the International Criminal Court (ICC). The ICC is the first ever permanent, treaty-based, international criminal court established to promote the rule of law and ensure that the gravest international crimes do not go unpunished (ICC, n.d.). It differs from the ICJ, which does not have criminal jurisdiction to prosecute individuals. When implemented (a number of statutory measures and practical steps still have to be taken before the Court becomes operational), the ICC will have jurisdiction with respect to the crimes of genocide, crimes against humanity, and war crimes. The Court will also have jurisdiction over aggression, but countries have not yet agreed on the definition of aggression. The ICC will not exercise jurisdiction over aggression until the crime has been further defined and conditions under which the Court will exercise its jurisdiction have been agreed on.

As of May 2004, 94 countries had become state parties to the ICC. The United States is not among those countries, but it seems clear that even without U.S. participation, the ICC will be playing a key role in the future of transnational crime and justice. For example, even though the ICC does not have direct jurisdiction over acts of terrorism, it may be able to prosecute terrorist acts when they amount to crimes against humanity—which is under ICC jurisdiction. Also, depending on how the crime of aggression is eventually defined, other transnational crimes may come under ICC jurisdiction.

These developments in transnational crime and justice will also affect the disciplines of comparative criminology and comparative criminal justice. We anticipate that academic programs will continue to create and expand course offerings in comparative criminology and criminal justice and that practitioners will find ever-increasing reasons and opportunities to engage in joint ventures with colleagues in other countries. The other chapters in this book will provide another resource to the increasingly solid foundation being built by scholars and practitioners around the world as we work together to understand the possibilities for a safer and more secure world.

NOTES

1. Material in this section draws heavily from Fairchild and Dammer (2001) and Reichel (2002).

2. Material in this section draws heavily from Fairchild and Dammer (2001), Mukherjee and Reichel (1999), and Reichel (2002).

REFERENCES

Adler, F. (1995). Our American sociology of criminology, the world, and the state of the art: The American Society of Criminology Presidential address. *Criminology, 34,* 1–9.

Adler, F. (1996). A note in teaching "international." *Journal of Criminal Justice Education, 7*(2), 223–225.

Adler, F., Mueller, G. O. W., & Laufer, W. S. (1995). *Criminology* (2nd ed.). New York: McGraw-Hill.

Albanese, J. S. (2002). *Criminal justice* (2nd ed.). Boston: Allyn & Bacon.

Bayley, D. H. (1985). *Patterns of policing: A comparative international analysis.* New Brunswick, NJ: Rutgers University Press.

Bayley, D. H. (1991). *Forces of order: Policing modern Japan.* Berkeley: University of California Press.

Bayley, D. H. (1996). Policing: The world stage. *Journal of Criminal Justice Education, 7,* 241–251.

Beirne, P., & Nelken, D. (Eds.). (1997). *Issues in comparative criminology.* Aldershot, UK, & Brookfield, VT: Ashgate/Dartmouth.

Bradley, C. M. (1999). *Criminal procedure: A worldwide study.* Durham, NC: Carolina Academic Press.

Briggs, C. M., & Cutright, P. (1994). Structural and cultural determinants of child homicide: A cross-national analysis. *Violence and Victims, 9*(1), 3–16.

Cole, G. F., Frankowski, S. J., & Gertz, M. G. (1987). *Major criminal justice systems: A comparative study.* Newbury Park, CA: Sage.

Collin, B. (1997). The future of cyberterrorism. *Crime & Justice International, 13*(2), 14–18.

Conklin, G. H., & Simpson, M. E. (1985). A demographic approach to the cross-national study of homicide. *Comparative Social Research, 8,* 171–185.

Cordner, A., Dammer, H., & Horvath, F. (2000). A national survey of comparative criminal justice courses in universities in the United States. *Journal of Criminal Justice Education, 11*(2), 211–223.

Council of Europe. (n.d.). *General information.* Retrieved May 20, 2003, from www.echr.coe. int/Eng/General.htm

Cusimano, M. K. (Ed.). (2000). *Beyond sovereignty: Issues for a global agenda.* New York: St. Martin's Press.

David, R., & Brierley, J. E. C. (1978). *Major legal systems in the world today: An introduction to the comparative study of law* (2nd ed.). New York: Free Press.

DeFronzo, J. (1996). Welfare and burglary. *Crime & Delinquency, 42*(2), 223–230.

DeFronzo, J. (1997). Welfare and homicide. *Journal of Research in Crime and Delinquency, 34*(3), 395–406.

Dobriansky, P. (2001). The explosive growth of globalized crime. *Global Issues: Arresting Transnational Crime, 6*(2). Retrieved May 19, 2003, from http://usinfo.state.gov/journals/ itgic/0801/ijge/gj01.htm

Elias, N. (1982). *The civilizing process: The history of manners and state formation and civilization* (E. Jephcott, Trans.). Oxford, UK: Blackwell.

Esbensen, F., & Blankenship, M. (1989). Comparative courses in undergraduate CJ curricula. *ACJS Today, 8*(2), 1, 19.

Fairchild, E., & Dammer, H. R. (2001). *Comparative criminal justice systems* (2nd ed.). Belmont, CA: Wadsworth/Thomson Learning.

Fiala, R., & LaFree, G. (1988). Cross-national determinants of child homicide. *American Sociological Review, 53,* 432–435.

Finckenauer, J. O. (2000, July). Meeting the challenge of transnational crime. *National Institute of Justice Journal,* pp. 1–7.

Friday, P. (1996). The need to integrate comparative and international criminal justice into a traditional curriculum. *Journal of Criminal Justice Education, 7*(2), 227–240.

Gartner, R. (1990). The victims of homicide: A temporal and cross-national comparison. *American Sociological Review, 55*(1), 92–106.

Gartner, R. (1991). Family structure, welfare spending and child homicide in developed democracies. *Journal of Marriage and the Family, 53,* 231–240.

Griffiths, C. T., & Verdun-Jones, S. N. (1994). *Canadian criminal justice* (2nd ed.). Toronto: Harcourt Brace.

Hartnagel, T. F. (1982). Modernization, female social roles, and female crime: A cross-national investigation. *Sociological Quarterly, 23*(4), 477–490.

He, N. (1999). *Marx, Durkheim, and comparative criminology.* Lanham, MD: Austin & Winfield.

Heiland, H.-G., & Shelley, L. I. (1992). Civilization, modernization and the development of crime and control. In H.-G. Heiland, L. I. Shelley, & H. Katoh (Eds.), *Crime and control in comparative perspectives* (pp. 1–19). Berlin & New York: Walter de Gruyter.

Hippchen, L. (1977). The teaching of comparative and international criminal justice in graduate schools of sociology and criminal justice. *International Journal of Comparative and Applied Criminal Justice, 1*(1), 57–71.

Howard, G. J., Newman, G., & Pridemore, W. A. (2000). Theory, method, and data in comparative criminology. *Criminal Justice 2000* (Measurement and Analysis of Crime and Justice, Vol. 4, pp. 139–211). Washington, DC: National Institute of Justice.

Huang, W. S. W. (1995). A cross-national analysis on the effect of moral individualism on murder rates. *International Journal of Offender Therapy and Comparative Criminology, 39*(1), 63–75.

Humphries, D., & Greenberg, D. F. (1981). The dialectics of crime control. In D. F. Greenberg (Ed.), *Crime and capitalism: Readings in Marxist criminology* (pp. 209–254). Palo Alto, CA: Mayfield.

International Court of Justice. (n.d.). *General information.* Retrieved May 20, 2003, from http:// 212.153.43.18/icjwww/igeneralinformation. htm

International Criminal Court. (n.d.). *ICC at a glance.* Retrieved May 20, 2003, from www.icc-cpi.int/php/show.php?id=ataglance

Johnson, E. H., & Barak-Glantz, I. L. (1983). Introduction. In I. L. Barak-Glantz & E. H. Johnson (Eds.), *Comparative criminology* (pp. 7–17). Beverly Hills, CA: Sage.

Kick, E. L., & LaFree, G. D. (1985). Development and the social context of murder and theft. *Comparative Social Research, 8,* 37–57.

Krahn, H. T., Hartnagel, T. F., & Gartrel, J. (1986). Income inequality and homicide rates: Cross-national data and criminological theories. *Criminology, 24,* 269–295.

Krohn, M., & Wellford, C. (1977). A static and dynamic analysis of crime and the primary dimensions of nations. *International Journal of Criminology and Penology, 5*(1), 1–16.

Kurian, G. T. (1989). *World encyclopedia of police forces and penal systems.* New York: Facts on File.

LaFree, G. (1997). Comparative cross-national studies of homicide. In M. D. Smith & M. A. Zahn (Eds.), *Homicide studies: A sourcebook of social research.* Thousand Oaks, CA: Sage.

LaFree, G., & Birkbeck, C. (1991). The neglected situation: A cross-national study of the situational characteristics of crime. *Criminology, 29,* 73–98.

Lee, R. W., III. (1996). Nuclear trafficking in former communist states. *Trends in Organized Crime, 2*(1), 62–69.

Lippman, M. R., McConville, S., & Yerushalmi, M. (1988). *Islamic criminal law and procedure: An introduction.* New York: Praeger.

Lopez-Rey, M. (1970). *Crime: An analytical appraisal.* New York: Praeger.

Lynch, M. J., Newman, D., McDowall, D., & Groves, W. B. (1988, November). *Crime in the world system: An introduction to world system theory and its implications for comparative criminology.* Paper presented at the Annual Meeting of the American Society of Criminology, Chicago, IL.

McDonald, L. (1976). *The sociology of law and order.* Boulder, CO: Westview Press.

McDonald, W. F. (1997). Illegal immigration: Crime, ramifications, and control (the American experience). In W. F. McDonald (Ed.), *Crime and law enforcement in the global village* (pp. 65–86). Cincinnati, OH: Anderson.

Merryman, J. H. (1985). *The civil law tradition.* Stanford, CA: Stanford University Press.

Messner, S. (1980). Income inequality and murder rates: Some cross-national findings. *Comparative Social Research, 3,* 185–198.

Messner, S. (1982). Societal development, social equality, and homicide: A cross-national test of a Durkheimian model. *Social Forces, 61,* 225–240.

Moore, R. H., Jr. (1987). Courts, law, justice, and criminal trials in Saudi Arabia. *International Journal of Comparative and Applied Criminal Justice, 11*(1), 61–67.

Moore, R. H., Jr. (1996). Islamic legal systems: Traditional (Saudi Arabia), contemporary (Bahrain), and evolving (Pakistan). In C. B. Fields & R. H. Moore, Jr. (Eds.), *Comparative criminal justice: Traditional and nontraditional systems of law and control* (pp. 390–410). Prospect Heights, IL: Waveland Press.

Mueller, G. O. W. (1996). International criminal justice: Harnessing the information explosion—coasting down the electronic superhighway. *Journal of Criminal Justice Education, 7*(2), 253–261.

Mukherjee, S., & Reichel, P. L. (1999). Bringing to justice. In G. R. Newman (Ed.), *Global report on crime and justice* (pp. 65–88). New York: Oxford University Press.

Natarajan, M. (2002). International criminal justice education: A note on curricular resources. *Journal of Criminal Justice Education, 13*(2), 479–498.

Neapolitan, J. L. (1995). Differing theoretical perspectives and cross-national variation in thefts in less-developed nations. *International Criminal Justice Review, 5,* 17–31.

Neapolitan, J. L. (2001). An examination of cross-national variation in punitiveness. *International Journal of Offender Therapy, 45*(6), 691–710.

Neuman, W. L., & Berger, R. J. (1988). Competing perspectives on cross-national crime: An evaluation of theory and evidence. *Sociological Quarterly, 29*(2), 281–313.

Newman, G. R. (Ed.). (1999). *Global report on crime and justice.* New York: Oxford University Press.

Newman, G. R., & Howard, G. J. (2001). Introduction: Varieties of comparative criminology. In G. J. Howard & G. R. Newman (Eds.), *Varieties of comparative criminology* (pp. 1–8). Leiden, Netherlands: Brill.

Ortega, S. T., Corzine, J., Burnett, C., & Poyer, T. (1992). Modernization, age structure, and regional context: A cross-national study of crime. *Sociological Spectrum, 12*(3), 257–277.

Pampel, F. C., & Gartner, R. (1995). Age structure, socio-political institutions, and national homicide rates. *European Sociological Review, 11*(3), 243–260.

Peak, K. (1991). The comparative systems course in criminal justice: Findings from a national survey. *Journal of Criminal Justice Education, 2*(2), 267–272.

Pease, K., & Hukkila, K. (1990). *Criminal justice systems in Europe and North America.* Helsinki, Finland: Helsinki Institute for Crime Prevention and Control.

Reichel, P. L. (2002). *Comparative criminal justice systems: A topical approach* (3rd ed.). Upper Saddle River, NJ: Prentice Hall.

Rosen, L. (1989). *The anthropology of justice: Law as culture in Islamic society.* Cambridge, UK: Cambridge University Press.

Sanad, N. (1991). *The theory of crime and criminal responsibility in Islamic law: Shari'a.* Chicago: Office of International Criminal Justice.

Sartori, G. (1996). Comparing and miscomparing. In B. E. Brown & R. C. Macridis (Eds.), *Comparative politics: Notes and readings* (8th ed., pp. 20–30). Belmont, CA: Wadsworth.

Schmalleger, F. (2001). *Criminal justice today: An introductory text for the twenty-first century* (6th ed.). Upper Saddle River, NJ: Prentice Hall.

Shelley, L. I. (1981). *Crime and modernization: The impact of industrialization and urbanization on crime.* Carbondale: Southern Illinois University Press.

Situ, Y., & Liu, W. (1996). An overview of the Chinese criminal justice system. In O. N. I. Ebbe (Ed.), *Comparative and international criminal justice systems: Policing, judiciary and corrections* (pp. 125–137). Boston: Butterworth-Heinemann.

Stack, S. (1984). Income inequality and property crime. *Criminology, 22,* 229–258.

Terrill, R. J. (1983). A status report on undergraduate courses in comparative criminal justice offered at colleges and universities in the United States. *International Journal of Comparative and Applied Criminal Justice, 7*(1), 129–135.

Terrill, R. J. (2002). *World criminal justice systems: A survey* (5th ed.). Cincinnati, OH: Anderson.

Tonry, M. H., & Frase, R. S. (2001). *Sentencing and sanctions in Western countries.* Oxford, UK, & New York: Oxford University Press.

Vidmar, N. (2000). *World jury systems.* Oxford, UK & New York: Oxford University Press.

Weigend, T. (1983). Sentencing in West Germany. *Maryland Law Review, 42*(1), 37–89.

Williams, P. (1999). Emerging issues: Transnational crime and its control. In G. Newman (Ed.), *Global report on crime and justice* (pp. 221–241). New York: Oxford University Press.

Winer, J. M. (1997). International crime in the new geopolitics: A core threat to democracy. In W. F. McDonald (Ed.), *Crime and law enforcement in the global village* (pp. 41–61). Cincinnati, OH: Anderson.

Wright, R. A., & Friedrichs, D. O. (1991). White-collar crime in the criminal justice curriculum. *Journal of Criminal Justice Education, 2*(1), 95–121.

PART II

Transnational Crime in the 21st Century

Just as many aspects of our lives have become part of a global village . . . so, too, has crime taken on a global dimension.

—James Finckenauer (former Director of the International Center at the National Institute of Justice)

Citizens of most nations take a rather parochial view of crime. The primary concern, understandably, is how safe they feel in their own neighborhoods. But as the quotation from Finckenauer (2000, p. 3) suggests, it is increasingly difficult to ignore crime's progressively more global nature. When she was U.S. Under Secretary of State for Global Affairs, Paula Dobriansky (2001) used the following examples to make this point:

- The drug ecstasy, manufactured primarily in the Netherlands, is trafficked to the United States by, among others, Israeli organized crime groups.
- A computer virus designed and sent from the Philippines caused computers at many U.S. government agencies to be shut down, some for as long as a week.
- A major U.S. bank discovered it was being used by Russian organized crime to launder money.

These examples emphasize how transnational crime affects American citizens, but similar examples are found for citizens in any country.

The chapters in Part II provide examples of transnational crimes that have already had a significant impact on the world community. Cindy Hill (Chapter 3) begins the section with a review of the problems associated with counting transnational crime. As noted in the *Global Report on Crime and Justice* (Newman, 1999), transnational crimes, because they are composed of many smaller crimes, are very complex and extremely difficult to count. Hill uses robbery and homicide rates to explain some of the problems in recording, reporting, and analyzing crime cross-nationally. By explaining the current problems encountered when measuring traditional domestic crime, she anticipates the likely problems we will encounter when trying to measure transnational crime. Her chapter concludes with suggestions for how those measurement problems might be overcome.

Jonathan White (Chapter 4) begins coverage of specific transnational crimes with his chapter on terrorism. Prior to September 11, 2001, much of North America had been comparatively untouched by international terrorism (see, e.g., U.S. Department of State, 2002). But with the terrorist acts on that day, American citizens came to have a new appreciation for the devastation and trepidation wrought by terrorists. White provides all readers with information and analysis that helps us understand the historical and contemporary context of this terrifying transnational crime. After distinguishing between domestic and international terrorism, he reviews terrorism's transitory stages since 1945 and explains how religion has modified terrorism to be a more clearly transnational affair.

In her coverage of money laundering (Chapter 5), Elizabeth Joyce notes that the fight against global terrorism, along with other international criminal matters and international policy developments, has expanded the concept of money laundering to include several criminal events. In addition to the typical link to drug trafficking, today's anti-money-laundering efforts must also consider how terrorism and corruption are financed. Joyce effectively reviews the intricacies of this complex crime by noting the difficulties of estimating money laundering's magnitude, explaining the process by which the crime is accomplished, and identifying the need for international standards to help combat money laundering.

In Chapter 6, Christine Alder and Kenneth Polk provide information on a crime about which many readers are likely unfamiliar. Crimes against the cultural heritage involve the unlawful procurement or acquisition of archaeological and artistic objects that are part of a country's legacy. In addition to reviewing the historical and contemporary forms of the problem, Alder and Polk explain the crime's impact and discuss some of the cooperative efforts used to combat this form of illicit trafficking.

As Chris Marshall, Hank Robinson, and Dae-Hoon Kwak explain in Chapter 7, the extent of transnational computer crime is difficult to gauge. Part of the problem is determining what activities are examples of this crime. They identify two general categories (crimes where the computer is used as a tool and crimes where the computer is a target) and provide specific examples of each (e.g., money laundering for the former and breaking down network service for the latter). Their chapter also includes a review of criminal law in cyberspace, some examples of international efforts to combat transnational computer crime, and some intriguing questions about the future.

Has a crime occurred when the use of chemical herbicides and the careless disposal of poisonous industrial waste move from their country of origin into neighboring countries? Raymond Michalowski and Kevin Bitten tackle this important issue in Chapter 8 as they discuss transnational environmental crime. They explain that toxins freely travel from country to country on the wind, in surface and ground water, and through the movements of humans and animals. When that ease of transfer is combined with the difficulty of subjecting those environmental harms to legal control, it is apparent that this is an issue presenting many challenges. Michalowski and Bitten address those challenges by identifying the mechanisms affecting the transnational flow of environmental harm, then suggesting how non-governmental organizations are important in bringing these issues to the attention of the public and lawmakers. Examples of international agreements designed to protect the global environment conclude this thought-provoking chapter.

One of the first crimes recognized by the lay public as having a transnational aspect is the trafficking in illicit drugs. In Chapter 9, Sandeep Chawla and Thomas Pietschmann use the trafficking of opiates, cocaine, amphetamine-type stimulants (ATS), and cannabis to explain the extent and trends of drug trafficking. After providing a historical context, Chawla and Pietschmann explain the trafficking patterns associated with each of those four drugs and show how action against trafficking has changed from being primarily national in character to today's more international effort.

Trafficking of humans and smuggling of migrants are activities that today affect almost all nations. Andrea Di Nicola (Chapter 10) explains what behaviors constitute each of these offenses and describes how each is accomplished. His chapter emphasizes the organized nature of these transnational crimes, estimates the extent of the problem, and reviews some of the international and national efforts designed to combat this version of smuggling.

Drawing on his experience as senior trial attorney for the U.N. International Criminal Tribunal for the former Yugoslavia, Grant Niemann (Chapter 11) provides an intriguing analysis of war crimes, crimes against humanity, and genocide. Whereas other crimes covered in Part II are commonly offered as examples of transnational crime, these offenses are more often considered international crimes because they so clearly affect all humans regardless of nationality. For all three crimes, Niemann provides the historical background, then places them in a contemporary context. His discussion is especially appropriate as the last chapter in Part II because he explains how international law is used to combat these crimes—and those cross-national and international efforts are the themes of the chapters in Part III.

REFERENCES

Dobriansky, P. (2001, August). The explosive growth of globalized crime. *Global Issues: Arresting Transnational Crime, 6*(2). Retrieved March 29, 2004, from http://usinfo. state.gov/journals/itgic/0801/ijge/gj01.htm

Finckenauer, J. O. (2000, July). Meeting the challenge of transnational crime. *National Institute of Justice Journal*, p. 3.

Newman, G. (Ed.). (1999). *Global report on crime and justice.* New York: Oxford University Press.

U.S. Department of State. (2002). *Patterns of global terrorism, 2001.* Washington, DC: Author.

3

Measuring Transnational Crime

CINDY HILL

Criminal groups have traditionally been identified with specific countries and areas; the Sicilian Mafia with Palermo, the Chinese Triads and Japanese Yakuza, and the American Mafia families in New York, Chicago, and Las Vegas, to name a few. However, researchers and practitioners began to notice that criminal groups were no longer sharing a regional character; rather, they have evolved into an international or transnational character complete with regional and global alliances. Causes for this change have been attributed to dramatic shifts in social, political, and economic systems around the world in the late 20th century, as well as extraordinary advances in communication technology and transportation. Specifically, a number of landmark events, including the creation of free-trade blocs such as the European Union and the North American Free Trade Agreement (NAFTA), the advent of the Internet, the collapse of the Soviet Union, and the commercialization of China have opened new targets for international or transnational organized criminal activity and new methods of operation (Richards, 1999).

Whatever the geographic scope of the criminal operations, it is clear that organized criminal activity is no longer simply a local or domestic activity. The range of activities pursued by criminal organizations has broadened significantly. As the activities and interests of these organizations became more global, they began to partner with other criminal groups to gain admittance into new markets and to benefit from their allies' unique criminal abilities to outsource certain specialties, such as drug routes into the United States, using contacts for surplus military arms or nuclear materials, or connecting organ "donors" with organ recipients from around the world. As such, transnational crime has emerged as a leading issue in the 21st century. A common grouping of crimes considered to be transnational includes, among others, the illicit trafficking in arms, drugs, women and children, immigrants, body organs, cultural artifacts, and nuclear material; terrorist activities; environmental crime; and money laundering (Mueller, 1999).

Often, the term *organized crime* is used synonymously with *transnational crime*. However, much of the research written on organized crime highlights the characteristics of the crime groups and not the dynamics of the transnational markets that have allowed the activities of these organizations to thrive (Morrison, 2003). Corresponding to the view that organized crime poses a greater threat than other more "ordinary" crimes is the view that transnational organized crime must be more dangerous and ubiquitous (Morrison, 2003). Although many transnational crimes are perpetrated by organized criminal groups, all transnational crimes are not necessarily the work of an organized criminal group. For example, recent worldwide events have caused an increased interest in terrorist organizations. The major sources of income for terrorist groups are organized crime and the trafficking of weapons and drugs. The financing of terrorism takes many forms and represents an economic structure that has many of the same characteristics of international organized crime. Despite the passage of new laws regarding money laundering in several countries, the ability to investigate such transactions is difficult at best.

Providing empirical confirmation of the major trends in transnational criminal activity remains elusive. In developing a protocol for measuring transnational crime, it is first important to focus on the more traditional crimes, to find a consistent methodology, an accurate data set, and a method to compare diverse countries with one another. With such a vast array of crimes classified as transnational, government entities and researchers alike have been perplexed with how to count, measure, or make true approximations on worldwide criminal statistics.

A number of issues relating to transnational crime need to be examined. Like any social phenomenon, crime continues to evolve in response to a constantly shifting legal, economic, and political environment. To inform policy on transnational crime in the hopes of greater cooperative enforcement, an agenda of research is required to address the conceptual dilemmas of current knowledge on the subject. For example, in terms of international cooperation, bilateral or multilateral arrangements with other countries have increased over the years; however, they have failed to synchronize national laws to any great extent. Therefore, to accurately assess the transnational crime problem with the purpose of developing viable solutions, some method of definition and measurement needs to be employed. That method is appropriately chosen from the techniques used by criminologists to define and measure traditional crime.

This chapter briefly introduces some of the problems in recording, reporting, and analyzing crime cross-nationally. Robbery and homicide rates (both generally perceived as violent crimes) are used to illustrate these problems inherent in developing comparative crime statistics. Goals of this chapter are to illustrate how current knowledge regarding problems associated with measuring crime in various countries can help one to understand and anticipate problems associated with measuring transnational crime. This is accomplished by (a) explaining measurement problems for traditional crimes such as homicide and robbery, (b) noting the difficulty in comparing crime cross-nationally, (c) explaining measurement problems for transnational crime as being both similar to and different from those for traditional crimes, and (d) using a typology of several transnational crimes to suggest ways to overcome the measurement problems.

PROBLEMS ENCOUNTERED WHEN MEASURING DOMESTIC CRIME

Reporting, Recording, and Classification Problems

Crimes come to the attention of police not only through reports by victims but also through direct detection by the police. Thus, the proportion of crimes committed that become known to police will also depend on the efficiency and discretionary practices of the police (Riedel, 1990). These, in turn, will depend on the number of police officers, the quality of their training, and the cultural and political pressures to which they are subjected (Reichel, 2002). If these factors vary systematically across nations—that is, by level of development, cultural, or legal system—official police data will also be systematically biased (Wolf, 1971). Results of two studies of the relationship between crime rates and the number of police officers per population suggest that the number of police officers significantly affects crime rates and that crime rates significantly affect the number of police assigned to a particular location (Levitt, 1997; Marvell & Moody, 1996). There is also research indicating that the resources a country devotes to policing and the relative number of police officers in a country have little association to crime rates, indicating that biases introduced by differences in access to police and the efficiency of police are not great (Bennett & Wiegand, 1994). However, police presence is often an overlooked explanatory variable in cross-national crime studies (Neapolitan, 1997). In the 48 cross-national studies surveyed, only one (McDonald, 1976) used size of police force as an exploratory variable.

Not all crimes reported to or detected by police become part of the official records reported to the United Nations or to Interpol (the two most used compilers of cross-national crime data). There are likely to be both unintentional and intentional errors in the collection, recording, and classification of crimes (Hagan, 2003; Vito & Blankenship, 2002). Many police departments do a poor job of completely and uniformly gathering crime data from all sections of the country; this is likely to be more true of developing nations than of more industrialized nations (Groves, McCleary, & Newman, 1985). Thus, there is some evidence that police work in developing nations is less efficient and more biased

toward the powerful than in industrial nations (Arthur, 1991).

All researchers agree there are differences among nations in the proportion of crimes reported to or detected by the police (Neapolitan, 1997). Some researchers argue that there is sufficient evidence that these differences are essentially random and thus do not systematically bias research (Archer & Gartner, 1984; Barclay & Tavares, 2002; Bennett & Wiegand, 1994; van Kesteren, Mayhew, & Nieuwbeerta, 2001). Other researchers have addressed the issue of reporting differences between developing and industrial nations and have concluded that they are not significant (Barclay & Tavares, 2002; Krohn, 1976, 1978; Krohn & Wellford, 1977; van Kesteren et al., 2001; Wellford, 1974).

Police may underreport or overreport certain crimes because of political pressures or cultural values. Political instability and regime changes might influence legal definitions and the recording and classifying of some offenses, as well as the tendency of people to report offenses, all of which adversely affect trend analysis (Hagan, 2003; Vito & Blankenship, 2002). Two examples of countries facing transformations included the African nations of Rwanda and the Congo, both plagued with political volatility and police corruption. Furthermore, some crimes may be tolerated or even de facto decriminalized and thus not handled in an official manner (Arthur, 1991). However, there is little hard evidence regarding any of the above, because such things are difficult to research.

Definitional Problems

Many conventional crimes, such as murder and theft, have ancient origins and thus are quite similarly defined across nations (Kick & LaFree, 1985). The apparent existence of legal universals and consistent cross-national perspectives suggest that some crimes may be cross-nationally comparable. In addition to problems common to most cross-national comparative research, several problems are more specific to cross-national studies of homicide and other crimes (Kick & LaFree, 1985). Perhaps the most basic of these is the problem of classifying crimes in a consistent manner across countries. Even homicide, which is the most easily defined and often the most researched crime cross-nationally, suffers from definitional differences among countries. Classification of casualties as homicides is particularly problematic in nations experiencing war, rebellion, or severe political and civil conflicts (Gartner, 1990; Howard, Newman, & Pridemore, 2000; Huang & Wellford, 1989; Lynch, 1995). Crime statistics from countries such as Cyprus and Colombia, for example, must be critically analyzed to ensure that data represent the homicide definition provided by the researching organization.

Official police data reflect the legal codes and practices of a country, and these might vary considerably among nations (Neapolitan, 1996). The United Nations tries to adjust for this by having nations place crimes in broad categories that include many of the definitional differences among nations. Each country is allowed some latitude in interpretation of the categories provided, and in some cases, legal codes are too different for the categories to be used in a similar manner (see questionnaire's definition of terms in United Nations, 2001). Thus, many nations cannot or do not place the same crimes in the same categories. For example, in contrast to all other Western nations, the Netherlands has no crime category for robbery (Marshall, 1989); therefore, if they report data for robbery categories, it is important to understand what definitions were used. Such classifications may not represent the total crime numbers for a country. Similarly, Japan classifies assaults resulting in death in the assault category and not in the homicide category (Kalish, 1988). Also, when crimes are forced into broad categories, important variations within the category may be concealed. Two countries may report the same number of thefts, but in one country 90% may involve forcible entry, whereas in another country only 20% involve forcible entry (Lynch, 1995). Attempting to measure the phenomenon is often the single most important way of focusing attention on the definitional issues because it requires conceptual clarity (Reuter & Petrie, 1999). Often, the nuances between robbery, burglary, and theft are the most difficult for countries to define in their criminal codes with regard to United Nations or Interpol surveys.

Statistics on crime tell as much about the bureaucracy of the justice system in a given country and about how it is viewed by the general public as they do about the true extent of crime in that country or about how such crime is being dealt with. The problems involved in cross-national analysis have been detailed in many studies (e.g., Krohn, 1976; MacKenzie, Baunach, & Roberg, 1990; Martin, Romano, & Haran, 1988; McDonald, 1976; Messner, 1992; Messner & Rosenfeld, 1997; Neapolitan, 1996; Smith & Zahn, 1999). Most researchers have included as many countries as possible in their research; however, until recently, data have not been available for a sufficient number and diversity of countries to test hypotheses properly and to make generalizations regarding international crime trends (Lynch, 1995; Messner, 1989; Neuman & Berger, 1988; Newman & Howard, 1999; Reichel, 2002).

In addition, data collected must be reliable and accurate. The majority of cross-national crime research uses secondary data. Therefore, it is important to understand the definitions used by the primary researchers and recognize variations in reporting and recording practices.

Selection Criteria for Sample Countries

Of particular importance to any cross-national sample is the distribution of countries included in a sample according to the geopolitical and regional placements of the country.

Perry and Robertson (2002) suggest that a sample population should be divided into four distinct geographical regions (Asia, Sub-Saharan Africa, Latin America, and Arab/Middle East-North Africa) and three distinct geopolitical regions (Arab nations, Commonwealth of Independent States and Eastern European [CIS-EE] nations, and Western industrial and other West European established democracies). These regions reflect conventional geopolitical and regional demarcations for countries across the world (Perry & Robertson, 2002). Furthermore, another transcontinental category should also be created in cross-national comparisons for those countries that are industrial democracies of the West as well as Western Europe, designated as *advanced*. This category includes countries such as Australia, Japan, and the United States.

Often, when crime statistics are compared cross-nationally, they are given in terms of total raw numbers, or ratios. However, this does not take into consideration the individual characteristics of the countries. In accordance with existing research and theorizing on the structural sources of crime across nations, several important structural features of individual nations are taken into consideration to minimize the possibility of observing spurious results (Lee, 2001). One prerequisite referenced throughout the literature for making comprehensive comparisons between individual countries is an understanding of the social, economic, and administrative situations within each country. Crime, thus, is a function of many different factors. It is important, for example, to compare area, population, and population density of the sample population to more accurately compare crime rates between countries. For instance, according to the United Nations Fifth Crime and Justice Survey (United Nations, 1995), the Bahamas and the Russian Federation have similar homicide rates, yet they are vastly different types of countries; they vary in land area, population,

gross domestic product, and police personnel to population ratio, to name a few. Likewise, Canada, Denmark, Russia, and Hong Kong may have similar robbery rates, yet each is very much different when examining them together on characteristics besides crime. Other variables must at least be noted when attempting to assess and compare crime rates cross-nationally.

Problems Encountered When Comparing Domestic Crime Cross-Nationally

Crime analysis allows a researcher to determine who is doing what to whom by its focus on crime against persons and property. It also involves trend correlations to assist in management and in the solving and the prevention of crime (Gottlieb, Arenberg, & Singh, 1994). In the administration of justice, it is important to assess an emerging crime problem, whether at the local, state, or national level. Therefore, many nations have attempted to assess their crime problems by compiling and analyzing reported crimes to the police or by crime victimization surveys. Presently, these types of analyses focus on traditional crimes, such as homicide, robbery, and burglary, particularly when applied to a cross-national setting.

What makes comparisons possible is that crime is ubiquitous. Although many countries have quite different legal systems, based on their individual histories and traditions, one common feature of all countries is crime. However, what is defined as crime and how countries respond to it vary significantly from country to country (Kalish, 1988). The types of crime data collected may also differ considerably from country to country (Newman, 1999; Nowak, 1989; Shichor, 1990). The types of analyses performed may also differ. For instance, in countries with a decentralized police system, identifying which category of offense has occurred is very difficult. In addition, political control of crime recording is a reality that must be recognized when one attempts to interpret crime statistics (Reichel, 2002). For example, human rights organizations dispute the number of executions committed in China each year. Although the Chinese government does not report the number of executions, it is believed that China far surpasses any other country in the number of executions carried out and, furthermore, that the Chinese government attempts to distort the number of political prisoners it currently has incarcerated. Also, some countries may focus their attention and interest on certain types of crimes, such as the "war on drugs" in the United States in the 1980s. As such, there was a significant increase in the rate of these types of reported crimes.

Although cross-national research on crime increased in the 1980s and 1990s, relative to other crime research, it remains quite small (Neapolitan, 1997). Reporting problems in the collection of crime statistics has been very well documented (LaFree, 1999; Neapolitan, 1997; Newman, 1999) and remains a key cause for the low number of cross-national crime studies. Because each country has similar difficulties in recording and reporting crime figures, crime rate comparisons among countries is problematic. Differing definitions, criminal justice and governmental structures, economic developments, and a variety of other factors unique to each country make it difficult to properly compare even the most well-documented crime rates cross-nationally. Although researchers and scholars frequently note that homicide statistics are the most accurately recorded and most universally defined crime category across nations, even homicide can suffer from different recording practices.

Differences in a nation's social environment will also affect crime comparisons. For example, developed countries with telephones may have more crime reported to the police than countries without a contemporary communications infrastructure. In addition, technologically advanced police forces may report and record a higher proportion of crimes than police forces without computer capabilities.

LIMITATIONS OF CROSS-NATIONAL STUDIES

Any cross-national study faces a difficult set of methodological problems in conducting rigorous analyses. The following details some of the problems common to most comparative research and those specific to the study of cross-national crime data collection.

Samples and Data Availability

Most of the general difficulties facing comparative research using countries as the unit of analysis are related to problems of directly transferring common statistical analysis techniques to an analysis environment in which the available sample is severely limited (Newman & Howard, 1999). For example, most common statistical analysis techniques are based on the assumption that the cases being analyzed are randomly sampled from a larger population (Hagan, 2003). However, comparative cross-national studies of crime generally have been based not on random samples but instead on simple data availability. This has several important implications. First, samples are intrinsically biased in that not all countries of the world are equally likely to be studied. In general, comparative cross-national studies more commonly have included developed, Western-styled democracies and less commonly have included developing nations, communist nations, and nations of the former Soviet Union (Perry & Robertson, 2002; van Kesteren et al., 2001). In addition, as stated previously, the relative proportion of industrial countries in a sample may well have a great influence on research results, especially because the level of development is often a key variable in many cross-national crime studies (He, 1999). The industrial or more developed countries of the world constitute about 40%

of the countries represented in Interpol, World Health Organization, and U.N. samples (LaFree, 1999). However, these same countries represent less than 15% of the total number of nations of the world. Thus, most previous research has in all probability been biased by the large proportion of developed Western nations in samples because it would appear that these nations have distinctly different crime patterns and historical and situational contexts from those of developing nations (He, 1999; Howard et al., 2000; LaFree, 1999).

Another sample problem is what to do with the former communist countries currently in transition of Eastern-Central Europe. The political, economic, and social situations of these nations have always made their inclusion in analysis with other nations questionable. The recent changes in these countries, including the creation of more nations, make it even more likely that, in analysis, they might unduly influence research, confounding and confusing results, particularly in longitudinal studies where the time period is before, during, and after the transition (Newman, 1999).

Finally, because the total number of countries with available data is relatively small, sample sizes analyzed are also small. Small sample sizes suggest that results may be highly dependent on only a few cases. In the analysis of cross-national crime rates, a single outlier can sometimes change conclusions. Therefore, it is important to examine the countries sampled multivariately and determine how outliers are affecting the results.

Because of sample size limitations, analyses based on common statistical techniques are severely limited. For example, problems of multicolinearity cannot be solved by increasing the size of the sample. Moreover, statistical techniques generally are limited to relatively simple bivariate direct effects models (Hair, Anderson, Tatham, & Black, 1998). For instance, in exploring 48 cross-national homicide studies from 1965 to 2001, sample sizes range from a low of 14 observations (Landau,

1984) to a high of 1,075 (Bennett, 1991), using pooled time-series techniques. Earlier homicide studies more often relied on simple classifications or measures of central tendency (see, e.g., Quinney, 1965; Wolf, 1971). Of the 10 earliest studies examined, ranging from 1965 to 1980, 7 did not report significance tests for individual variables.

Homicide Rates

As previous research has shown, reported crime changes considerably over time. Crime rates change at different rates for different offenses and for different countries. In a 15-year time period (1980–1994), the average homicide rate in 25 countries increased by roughly 6.5% (Moors, 2003). The pattern of homicide rates when compared with the development status of countries is a bit more difficult to assess. Cross-national crime data indicate that less-developed countries have higher average rates of homicide than do industrialized countries (Krohn, 1976; Lee, 2001; Moors, 2003; Wellford, 1974; Wolf, 1971). Homicide rates in developing countries have been increasing over time. Industrial countries have had a general decrease in crime over the 15-year time period, particularly in the 1990s. This observation has also been made by other researchers (see also Newman, 1999). However, the caveat must be made that the samples countries may play a role in this observation.

Robbery Rates

Over the same time period (1980–1994), the average robbery rate increased more frequently in the 1980s. There was a 25% increase from the early 1980s (1980–1984) to the late 1980s (1985–1989). As previously discussed, this increase may be due to the amount of missing robbery data in the early 1980s or because of bias resulting from the countries sampled. Because cross-national crime data indicate that less-developed countries have higher average rates of homicide than do industrialized countries (Lee, 2001), one could extend that to other violent crimes, such as assault or robbery; however, it was found that industrialized countries had significantly higher average robbery rates than the developing countries sampled (Moors, 2003).

In the past, the lack of quality data has not allowed for reliable cross-national crime research. Therefore, when attempting to make cross-national crime comparisons, the types of countries in the sample population should also be critically examined (e.g., when comparing industrial countries to developing countries; Islamic law countries to common, civil, or socialist law countries; or similar countries by some predetermined characteristic to each other, such as regional location).

Through time, cross-national crime studies have employed increasingly sophisticated multivariate regression analysis, pooled time-series analysis, and LISREL analysis (LaFree, 1999). Furthermore, the numbers of variables used as controls have increased substantially in more recent studies (Howard et al., 2000).

MEASURING TRANSNATIONAL CRIME

Problems Likely to Be Encountered When Tracking Transnational Crimes

The globalization of crime demands a coordinated or transnational criminal justice response (Howard et al., 2000). The difference between traditional crimes and certain types of transnational crimes is that, generally, traditional crimes can be counted as crime analysis. Transnational crimes, on the other hand, involve not only crime analysis but intelligence analysis as well. Intelligence analysis, which focuses on the relationship between persons and organizations involved in illegal—and usually conspiratorial—activities, aids in determining who is doing what with whom (Gottlieb et al., 1994). As such, intelligence analysis is

often difficult for local law enforcement officials to recognize and investigate. The two major sources of cross-national data, the United Nations and Interpol, collect data solely on traditional crimes, which does not accurately reflect a nation's entire crime problem (Neapolitan, 1997).

Martin and Romano (1992) and Newman (1999) agree that the apparent increase in transnational crime has contributed to a greater interest among countries to take notice of the crime situations occurring in other countries. Recent worldwide events have placed greater emphasis on international cooperation and have resulted in changing views regarding the traditional obligations and expectations of one country in relation to its citizens and to other countries (Bloomfield, 2002; Nadelmann, 1993; Richman, 2000). However, the nature of transnational crime takes advantage of the ease of movement between countries, making it even more difficult to establish a unified strategy for hindering such crime problems.

Although it is important that methods for collecting and analyzing cross-national data on nontraditional crimes be developed, previous efforts have not been very successful. The very nature of these types of transnational crime makes it difficult to quantitatively assess. Transnational crimes are often very complex crimes, composed of a number of smaller crimes, which thus makes them extremely difficult to accurately count. No systematic method of accounting for these types of crimes currently exists at the international level, although attempts have been made to compile data on individual crimes, such as arms trafficking, drug trafficking, or illegal immigration.

Traditional crimes are most often collected on a national level. These crimes are relatively discrete events. Therefore, although definitions across countries may differ, most countries have been able to adjust their definitions of crime to those of a survey for international comparison, such as the United Nations Crime and Justice Survey. It is much more difficult to have a common definition for nontraditional crimes. Often, the very definition of what a transnational crime consists of is at the center of the controversy. Different authors have used slightly different definitions over the years (see, e.g., Alder, Mueller, & Laufer, 1994; Martin & Romano, 1992).

The figures currently cited in the literature are based on those crimes that come to the attention of law enforcement entities. However, the ratio between failures and successes is unknown. Therefore, estimates can vary greatly. New ways to measure them must be found that are organizationally sophisticated (Howard et al., 2000). Therefore, providing empirical support in major trends of transnational crime currently is a very problematic undertaking that is still in its initial stages of development.

Providing quantitative indicators for traditional crime is difficult, but finding hard data on illicit enterprises of transnational scope is close to impossible (Williams, 1999). As part of the Fifth United Nations Survey of Crime Trends and Operations of Criminal Justice Systems (1995) efforts were made to assess the prevalence and extent of transnational crime. Transnational crime was defined as "offences whose inception, proportion and/or direct or indirect effects involved more than one country" (para. 9). However, from this initial attempt, it was discovered that few countries record these crimes separately in their official statistics. The penal codes of nations and countries do not categorize "transnational crime," and consequently, no official statistics are available to submit data on such events.

Therefore, there is an urgent need for the development of reliable and uniform data collection at the international level. To have a coordinated law enforcement response to transnational crime, an understanding of the characteristics of these crimes is required. In addition, the operational strengths and weaknesses of crime control systems in other countries, which is an important goal of comparative studies, must be recognized (Howard et al., 2000).

Suggestions for Measuring Transnational Crime

In many countries, there are no serious efforts to collect data about transnational crime, partly because of a lack of resources and expertise. Moreover, little is done to coordinate collection efforts and to combine national statistics about organized criminal activity. The aim of criminal justice systems around the world is policing within national borders. Nevertheless, there has been increased attention devoted to this variety of crime. For the moment, much of the information is anecdotal and depends to a large extent on media accounts of transnational crime, so these data sources bring with them considerable difficulties in terms of validity, as noted by a number of researchers (Howard et al., 2000; Passas, 1995; Williams, 1999).

In general, because of the lack of reliable quantitative data, an accurate assessment of the scale of transnational crime cannot be made. That is not to say that transnational crime cannot be measured; however, very little is currently available to suggest how the measurement task should be approached. For most transnational organized crime activities, there are simply no systematic estimates of size. For example, although the Immigration and Naturalization Service (INS) has recently made attempts to estimate the number of illegal immigrants inside the United States (Stana, 2002), it has not attempted to estimate either the number entering as the result of organized smuggling activities or the revenues generated by such smuggling. Issues such as this must first be recognized in order to see a clearer picture of the problem at hand. As is often the case, agencies may compile and aggregate data, but statistical techniques are often underused. Data may be simply presented in summary expressions.

Official records such as court and regulatory proceedings are currently one of the best sources of useful data on transnational crime. Caveats exist in using such data, however. Court records report only a small and unrepresentative set of activities, usually the most serious ones. Even in the population of actual prosecutions, itself unrepresentative of all criminal activities of these enterprises, most cases do not go to trial but are settled through plea bargaining in the United States. Most indictments identify a set of specific criminal acts that provide only modest illumination of the underlying organization.

Passas (1998) suggests that "criminogenic asymmetries," the differences among nations in law or regulations or in the effectiveness of enforcement, facilitates the development of transnational crime. Thus, one country may provide a safe haven, or at least a safer haven, for conducting criminal activities in the other. Certainly, this applies to the international drug market. For example, Colombia, Peru, and Bolivia are the leading producers of cocaine for the world market because of their low risks of sanctions, along with cheap land labor in these countries (U.S. Department of State, 2002).

Other current possible data sources include investigative records, ethnographic studies and surveys, and informants. Although there are numerous potential data sources for the study of transnational crime, each has substantial weaknesses. Most have an opportunistic element, because they are from operational sources. Much of the data currently available are from one organization that attempts to collect data on one type of crime. For example, the United Nations Office for Drug Control and Crime Prevention has established a modest research program in drugs, people trafficking, and corruption.

The use of liaisons or legal attachés between countries may be another possible link to investigate transnational problems between countries. Also, the use of educational programs such as the International Law Enforcement Academy (ILEA), which brings together law enforcement personnel from around the world, can be a means to collect preliminary information regarding transnational crimes among countries. These types of gatherings can be used as focus groups to discuss the emerging problems and what some possible responses may be.

CLARITY THROUGH TRANSNATIONAL TYPOLOGIES

Although it is difficult to compile one database with all the types of crimes categorized within a transnational definition, the following is a brief overview of some of the offenses that transnational criminal groups are involved in and some possible means to gather data on each crime.

Firearms Trafficking

The arms trafficking industry involves domestic as well as foreign-made weapons. In addition to firearms bought and sold in the United States, many American-made weapons are purchased abroad and then illegally smuggled back into the country. This can make it very difficult to keep accurate counts of this type of transnational crime. Often, end-user certificates, registry of shipments, and fraudulent manufacturer's stamps are used to smuggle weapons. The Organization of American States (OAS) Treaty Against Illicit Trafficking in Firearms (an initiative of the U.S. government's 1998 international crime control strategy), called for a "hemispheric convention to combat the illicit manufacturing of and trafficking in firearms, ammunition and explosives" (White House, 1998). An agreement negotiated at the OAS convention mandates that all member parties establish a single point of contact to coordinate international firearms trafficking issues. Although legal arms sales to developing nations are tumbling, the illicit sale is increasing globally (Shanker, 2002).

The Bureau of Alcohol, Tobacco, Firearms and Explosives (BATF) in the United States is responsible for investigating the illegal movement of firearms, explosives, and ammunition in international traffic and preventing such arms from being used throughout the world to commit acts of terrorism, to subvert restrictions posed by other nations on their residents, and to be used as commodities in organized crime and narcotics-related activities. The BATF has an extensive program designed to curtail the influx of foreign-made weapons, and those American-made weapons being smuggled back into the country. BATF's National Tracing Center (NTC) is the world's only facility with the capability to trace the history of firearms, maintaining transaction records on more than 100 million firearms. In 2000, the NTC processed approximately 210,000 crime gun traces (Department of the Treasury, 2001).

In conjunction with the U.S. Customs Service, BATF also participates in foreign-country firearm trafficking assessments and training programs funded by the U.S. Department of State, Bureau of International Narcotics and Law Enforcement Affairs. Access to such information may be one possible means to initially identify arms trafficking numbers. Although more intelligence and analysis are needed, the relatively small numbers of firearms seized at the site of importation into a country suggest that it is unlikely that criminal demand is being met to any significant degree by the smuggling of firearms (National Criminal Intelligence Service [NCIS], 2003).

Drug Trafficking

The commercial exchange of illegal drugs, including the equipment and substances involved in producing, manufacturing, and using drugs, is known as drug trafficking. The consequences of drug trafficking have created a major challenge for countries worldwide. Of all the transnational illegal markets, the best explored is that for drugs (Reuter & Petrie, 1999). In terms of scale, drug trafficking also represents the greatest organized crime threat, although the high priority attached to it by law enforcement over a number of years may inadvertently have diverted attention from other areas, whose relative importance is currently less well understood as a result (NCIS, 2003). The most recent estimates, those for 2001, give a total of about $65 billion in retail sales in the United States alone, the largest component being cocaine ($36 billion) (Office of National Drug Control Policy [ONDPC], 2003). Worldwide, it is estimated that drug trafficking is a $400 billion trade market (Drug Policy Alliance, 2002).

International drug-trafficking organizations have extensive networks of suppliers and front companies and businesses to facilitate narcotics smuggling and money laundering of illicit proceeds (Reuter & Petrie, 1999). The evolution of the international drug trade has included more worldwide trafficking of synthetic drugs and a growing group of actors (ONDPC, 2003). Increasingly, traffickers from many countries are avoiding traditional practices of partnering with a single ethnic group and have been working together with many in the purchase, transportation, and distribution of illegal drugs.

In addition, nontraditional trafficking groups, such as rebel armies and extremist groups, have also turned to the drug trade as a means of increasing proceeds for their causes. There is evidence that various terrorist groups, such as the Shining Path in Peru and the Revolutionary Armed Forces of Colombia (FARC) tax illicit drug production as a means of financing their activities and operations. Drug-trafficking groups in Central and South Asia and Latin America, where the majority of illicit drugs are produced and trafficked, have expanded their networks to include cross-border cooperation and associations with other drug-trafficking groups. Adapting quickly, international drug-trafficking organizations have found new methods for smuggling drugs, new transshipment routes, and new ways to launder money that make it difficult for law enforcement entities to track. All these are possible with more open borders and modern telecommunications technology.

Some nations have shifted their policy focus toward harm reduction based on the notion that reducing the consumption of drugs will help to contain the flow and production of controlled substances. Despite their best efforts, it is estimated by the Drug Policy Alliance (2002) that only 10% to 15% of heroin and 30% of cocaine is intercepted worldwide. Because drug traffickers earn a gross profit of around 300%, it is estimated that at least 70% of international drug shipments need to be intercepted to substantially reduce the illegal trafficking industry.

The Drug Enforcement Administration (DEA) in the United States manages a number of information-sharing programs that give law enforcement agencies access to database information, such as in intelligence centers like the El Paso (Texas) Intelligence Center. In addition, Organized Crime Drug Enforcement Task Forces (OCDETF), in which DEA participates at the federal level, combine resources of many agencies under one roof to provide a comprehensive approach against criminal organizations. Participating state and local agencies receive information from Federal agencies involved in the individual OCDETF investigations.

On a more international level, the Special Operations Division (SOD) of the DEA is a comprehensive enforcement operation designed specifically to coordinate multiagency, multijurisdictional, and multinational Title III investigations against the command-and-control elements of major drug-trafficking organizations operating domestically and abroad. The investigative resources of SOD support a variety of multijurisdictional drug enforcement investigations associated with the Southwest Border, Latin America, the Caribbean, Europe, and Asia. DEA programs may be an invaluable resource for statistical data on illegal drug trafficking; however, these data are limited to the countries in which the DEA operates. A worldwide drug-trafficking database has yet to be designed.

Illegal Migration

An activity where an effective distribution system is necessary for the crime to be completed is illegal immigration. Illegal immigration comprises people smuggling, where the migrants are essentially willing participants, and where organized criminals profit mainly from facilitating their migration across borders, and human trafficking, where the intention behind the facilitation is to exploit the migrants when they reach their destination. The vast majority of illegal immigrants appear to be willing participants rather than victims of human trafficking. However, the nature of human trafficking is such that it is harder to identify numbers and therefore quantify if persons fall into the trafficking or smuggling category.

Most human-trafficking victims come from Asia, with over 375,000 victims each year. The former Soviet Union is believed to be the largest new source of trafficking for prostitution and the sex industry, with over 100,000 women and children trafficked each year from that region. The U.S. Department of State has estimated that at any given moment, there are hundreds of thousands of people in the trafficking pipeline, being warehoused by traffickers, waiting for new routes to open up or fraudulent documents to become available (Richards, 1999).

The worldwide smuggling of migrants has increased rapidly since the early 1990s. Estimates have as many as 500,000 people from countries such as China and India being smuggled into Western Europe at fees from as low as $250 to highs of $25,000 per person

(Schmid & Savona, 1995). Migrants from South and Central America have "coyotes" (smugglers) take them over the Mexican border into the United States (Nieves, 2002). Chinese immigrants pay smugglers up to $45,000 per person for successful entry into the United States (Chin, 1998). Also, although it is impossible to quantify the effects, the need for organized illegal assistance will have grown in the wake of increased security and border controls around the world following the events of September 11, 2001. Schmid and Savona (1995) note that the criminals involved in smuggling people are often concurrently engaged in arms and drug smuggling.

Identity theft has been a prevalent crime for which aliens can obtain fraudulent documents to enter the United States or other countries illegally or to obtain employment and other benefits. In the fiscal year 2000, the INS reported almost 124,000 fraudulent documents intercepted by INS inspectors (Stana, 2002). INS believes organized crime groups will increasingly use smugglers to facilitate illegal entry of individuals into the United States to engage in criminal activities, such as narcotics trafficking and terrorism. With heightened border security, alien smugglers are expected to increasingly use fraudulent documents to introduce aliens into the United States (Stana, 2002). Illegal migration is often an event-driven statistic. After the September 11th attacks, many of the suspected terrorists arrested were for INS charges. The focus on illegal immigration caused a change in law and a more critical look at the immigration problem as a whole.

The Bureau of Justice Statistics notes that the majority of persons entering the United States illegally are returned to their country of origin without being referred to the criminal justice system (Ward, 2000). The number of noncitizens processed in the federal criminal justice system increased an average of 13% annually from 1984 to 2000. In 1984, 3,462 non-U.S. citizens were prosecuted in federal

district courts, and by 2000, the number had risen to 20,751 (U.S. Department of Justice, 2000). During the same period the number of non-U.S. citizen inmates increased from 4,088 to 20,655. About 55% of those inmates were in the United States legally (U.S. Sentencing Commission, 2001).

The combination of increased freedom of movement, pursuit of better opportunities, diminished legitimate migration possibilities, and demand for foreign labor has resulted in a profound increase in the level of illegal migration. Many immigrants will travel under appalling conditions in the hopes of a better life ("Immigration," 2003). There are numerous cases in which the traffickers have taken the money and left the would-be migrants stranded. Immigration, both in numbers and characteristics, may depend on the strength and stability of the government in the sending country, especially the firmness of the rule of law and the specificity of legislation targeting criminal activities. The opaqueness of many immigrant communities to policing allows organized crime networks to flourish in a relatively safe setting. In addition, the extent to which the receiving country is open to immigrants—providing opportunities for learning the language, culture, and new skills and a niche in the legal economy—may influence the extent to which organized crime can gain a foothold in immigrant neighborhoods.

The United Nations has a Global Programme Against the Trafficking in Human Beings that addresses human trafficking, particularly that of women and children. In a selection of countries, field projects are being carried out to test promising strategies, such as new structures for collaboration between police, immigration, victims' support, and the judiciary, both within countries and internationally (linking countries of origin to destination countries). The Transnational Crime and Corruption Center of American University has performed numerous studies on human trafficking and alien smuggling. Aside from training law enforcement personnel, part of its focus is on quantifying the political, social, and economic costs of trafficking. Such programs are needed to assess the people-smuggling and human-trafficking problems worldwide.

Trafficking in Human Organs

One of the most controversial areas of transnational crime is human organ trafficking. With the advent of organ transplantation more than three decades ago, the human body has quickly become a commodity for replacement parts. Some maintain that organized crime and other criminal elements are exploiting this area (Chang, 1995; Orszag-Land, 1997). In countries such as India, South Africa, and Brazil, persistent reports have suggested a thriving black market in human organs. China has been accused of removing organs from executed prisoners to supply them to recipients from other countries. Although there is little quantitative evidence, supported by sensational personal accounts, that organized transnational trafficking of organs exists, there are good grounds for concluding that a black market in human organs does exist and that because of differential levels of wealth among nations organ trafficking has a transnational dimension. Often, the organ "donors" are from one country, the recipient from another, and the operation is performed in a third country.

Organ trafficking can be understood at one level in simple supply-and-demand terms. The global demand for organs has surpassed organ donation in most cases, thus creating a market economy. A remarkably high demand for body parts has produced predatory competition among tissue and transplant banks. Although illegal immigration and other related crime produces an enormous profit, a single dead body has the potential to yield tens of thousands of dollars to tissue banks and research facilities (Katches, Heisel, &

Campbell, 2000). And with the scarcity of consensual organ donors worldwide, a network of illicit traders, often called body brokers or intermediaries, has emerged. Black marketers understand that trafficking laws are either obscure or limited in their use of penalties (Tass, 1998). The result is a flourishing black market in human body parts, nourished through kidnapping, mutilation, and murder. The expansion of the illegal body part trade must be heavily dependent on collaboration between localized and international gangs (Orszag-Land, 1997).

Britain's National Criminal Intelligence Service believes an illegal black market in cloned body parts will be yet another future market for organized crime rings ("Is Illicit Cloning," 1999). Presently, there are severe organ shortages, and instances of organ trafficking and trading have been reported globally. Activities range from corruption in waiting list distribution, body part theft from morgues, compensated gift giving, outright organ sales, the use of organs from executed prisoners, and even granted release time to prisoners for organ donation.

Although this is a vastly understudied area, Organs Watch was founded in 1999 out of the University of California at Berkeley to investigate reports and rumors of human rights abuses surrounding organ trafficking, identify hot spots where abuse may be occurring, and begin to define the line between ethical transplant surgery and practices that are exploitative or corrupt. Initial data may be available through these reports; however, it is still on the case study level of analysis.

CONCLUSION

The criminal community is enlarging; although traditional crimes are ever present, the international criminal justice community must also deal with emerging nontraditional crimes. Governments are responding to transnational criminal activities, but they are doing too little too late. Arms trafficking, drug trafficking, illegal immigration, and trafficking of human organs are just a few transnational crimes that appear to be growing in numbers. To address the sources and motivations of these crimes, they first must be legally defined as such in an international forum.

One conclusion that might be weakly inferred from the attempts to estimate the scale of drug importing is that consumption-based estimates are likely to be stronger than supply-based estimates (Reuter & Petrie, 1999). However, the large population surveys that exist for drug use do not exist for other illicit commodities and services. Moreover, measuring other markets that have little in common (e.g., illegal immigrant smuggling, organ trafficking, and arms trafficking) with any specificity may prove challenging because of low base rates of consumption compared with rates for drugs, for example. It seems clear that the measurement task will require very different data collection and analytic methods than have thus far been available.

There is a need for nations to continue to develop and communicate a comprehensive strategy on transnational organized crime. Specifically, the nature and scope, as well as current and future risks and threats, need to be assessed and researched. Efforts need to be expanded, especially in the area of reliable and uniform data collection. More sophisticated methodologies need to be devised and greater use made of the information available in the private sector (Williams, 1999).

As a matter of urgency, a central clearinghouse needs to be established with a focus on illicit market activities of all kinds and a recognition of the cross-linkages and synergies being developed. An increased emphasis on coordinated efforts should also be pursued. Coordination and cooperation are key to conducting research that address the problems inherent in transnational crime.

REFERENCES

Alder, F., Mueller, G. O., & Laufer, W. S. (1994). *Criminal justice.* New York: McGraw-Hill.

Archer, D., & Gartner, R. (1984). *Violence and crime in cross-national perspective.* New Haven, CT: Yale University Press.

Arthur, J. (1991). Development and crime in Africa: A test of modernization theory. *Journal of Criminal Justice, 19,* 499–513.

Barclay, G., & Tavares, C. (2002). *International comparisons of criminal justice statistics 2000* (Statistical Issue 05/02). London: Home Office.

Bennett, R. R. (1991). Routine activities: A cross-national assessment of a criminological perspective. *Social Forces, 70,* 147–163.

Bennett, R. R., & Wiegand, R. (1994). Observations on crime reporting in a developing nation. *Criminology, 32*(1), 135–148.

Bloomfield, L. P. (Ed.). (2002). *Global markets and national interests.* Washington, DC: Center for Strategic and International Studies.

Chang, D. H. (1995). A new form of international crime: The human organ trade. *International Journal of Comparative and Applied Criminal Justice, 19*(1), 1–13.

Chin, K. (1998, September). *Transnational organized crime activities.* Paper presented at the International Scientific and Professional Advisory Council conference in Courmayer, Italy. (Available from the School of Criminal Justice, Rutgers University)

Department of the Treasury, Bureau of Alcohol, Tobacco and Firearms. (2001). *FY 2000 accountability report.* Washington, DC: Government Printing Office.

Drug Policy Alliance. (2002). *Drug treatment vs. supply side measures* (fact sheet). Retrieved April 19, 2004, from www.drugpolicy.org/library/factsheets/drugtreatmen/index.cfm

Gartner, R. (1990). The victims of homicide: A temporal and cross-national comparison. *American Sociological Review, 55,* 92–106.

Gottlieb, S., Arenberg, S., & Singh, R. (1994). *Crime analysis: From first report to final arrest.* Montclair, CA: Alpha.

Groves, W. B., McCleary, R., & Newman, G. R. (1985). Religion, modernization, and world crime. *Comparative Social Research, 8,* 59–78.

Hagan, F. E. (2003). *Research methods in criminal justice and criminology* (6th ed.). Boston: Allyn & Bacon.

Hair, J. F., Anderson, R. E., Tatham, R. L., & Black, W. C. (1998). *Multivariate data analysis* (5th ed.). Upper Saddle River, NJ: Prentice Hall.

He, N. (1999). *Reinventing the wheel: Marx, Durkheim and comparative criminology*. Lanham, MD: Austin & Winfield.

Howard, G. J., Newman, G., & Pridemore, W. A. (2000). Theory, method, and data in comparative criminology. In D. Duffee (Ed.). *Measurement and analysis of crime and justice* (Vol. 4, pp. 139–211). Washington, DC: National Institute of Justice.

Huang, W. S. W., & Wellford, C. F. (1989). Assessing indicators of crime among international crime data series. *Criminal Justice Policy Review, 3*(1), 28–47.

Immigration: Our kinda ciudad. (2003, January 11). *The Economist*, p. 23.

Is illicit cloning of body parts a burgeoning business in organized crime? (1999, April 13). *Source Global Briefings*, p. 42.

Kalish, C. B. (1988). *International crime rates* (special report). Washington, DC: Bureau of Justice Statistics.

Katches, M., Heisel, W., & Campbell, R. (2000, April 16). Donors don't realize they are fueling a lucrative business. *The Orange County Register*, p. H1.

Kick, E. L., & LaFree, G. (1985). Development and the social context of murder and theft. *Comparative Social Research, 8*, 37–57.

Krohn, M. D. (1976). Inequality, unemployment and crime: A cross-national analysis. *Sociological Quarterly, 17*, 303–313.

Krohn, M. D. (1978). A Durkheimian analysis of international crime rates. *Social Forces, 57*(2), 654–670.

Krohn, M. D., & Wellford, C. F. (1977). A static and dynamic analysis of crime and the primary dimensions of nations. *International Journal of Criminology and Penology, 5*, 1–16.

LaFree, G. (1999). A summary and review of cross-national comparative studies of homicide. In M. D. Smith (Ed.), *Homicide: A sourcebook of social research* (pp. 125–145). Thousand Oaks, CA: Sage.

Landau, S. F. (1984). Trends in violence and aggression: A cross-cultural analysis. *International Journal of Comparative Sociology, 25*, 133–236.

Lee, M. R. (2001). Population growth, economic inequality, and homicide. *Deviant Behavior: An Interdisciplinary Journal, 22*, 491–516.

Levitt, S. (1997). Using electoral cycles in police hiring to estimate the effects of police on crime. *American Economic Review, 87*, 270–291.

Lynch, J. (1995). Building data systems for cross-national comparisons of crime and criminal justice policy: A retrospective. *ICPSR Bulletin, 15*(3), 1–6.

MacKenzie, D. L., Baunach, P. J., & Roberg, R. R. (Eds.). (1990). *Measuring crime: Large-scale, long-range efforts*. Albany: State University of New York Press.

Marshall, I. H. (1989). Trends in crime rates, certainty of punishment and severity of punishment in the Netherlands. *Criminal Justice Policy Review, 1*(1), 21–52.

Martin, J. M., & Romano, A. T. (1992). *Multinational crime: Terrorism, espionage, drug and arms trafficking* (Vol. 9). Newbury Park, CA: Sage.

Martin, J., Romano, A., & Haran, J. (1988). *International crime patterns: Challenges to traditional criminological theory and research.* (Monograph, Vol. 4, No. 2). Huntsville, TX: Sam Houston State University.

Marvell, T. B., & Moody, C. E. (1996). Specification problems, police levels, and crime rates. *Criminology, 34*, 609–646.

McDonald, L. (1976). *The sociology of law and order*. Boulder, CO: Westview.

Messner, S. F. (1989). Economic discrimination and societal homicide rates: Further evidence on the cost of inequality. *American Sociological Review, 54*, 597–611.

Messner, S. F. (1992). Exploring the consequences of erratic data reporting for cross-national research on homicide. *Journal of Quantitative Criminology, 8*(2), 155–173.

Messner, S. F., & Rosenfeld, R. (1997). Political restraint of the market and levels of criminal homicide: A cross-national application of institutional-anomie theory. *Social Forces, 75*, 1393–1416.

Moors, C. S. (2003). *Crime trends: A cross national comparison of homicide and robbery rates in 25 countries.* Unpublished doctoral dissertation, Sam Houston State University.

Morrison, S. (2003). Approaching organized crime: Where are we now and where are we going? *Crime and Justice International, 19*(72), 4–10.

Mueller, G. O. W. (1999). Transnational crime: An experience in uncertainties. In S. Einstein & M. Amir (Eds.), *Organized crime: Uncertainties and dilemmas* (pp. 3–19). Chicago: Office of International Criminal Justice Press.

Nadelmann, E. A. (1993). *Cops across borders: The internationalization of U.S. criminal law enforcement.* University Park: Pennsylvania State University Press.

National Criminal Intelligence Service. (2003). *UK threat assessment 2002.* London: Author.

Neapolitan, J. L. (1996). Cross-national crime data: Some unaddressed problems. *Journal of Criminal Justice, 19*(1), 95–112.

Neapolitan, J. L. (1997). *Cross-national crime: A research review and sourcebook.* Westport, CT: Greenwood.

Neuman, W. L., & Berger, R. J. (1988). Competing perspectives on cross-national crime: An evaluation of theory and evidence. *Sociological Quarterly, 29,* 281–313.

Newman, G. (Ed.). (1999). *Global report on crime and justice.* New York: Oxford University Press.

Newman, G., & Howard, G. J. (1999). Introduction: Data sources and their use. In G. Newman (Ed.), *Global report on crime and justice* (pp. 1–23). New York: Oxford University Press.

Nieves, E. (2002, August 6). Illegal immigrant death rate rises sharply in barren areas. *New York Times,* pp. A1, A12.

Nowak, S. (1989). Comparative studies and social theory. In M. L. Kohn (Ed.), *Cross-national research in sociology* (pp. 34–56). Newbury Park, CA: Sage.

Office of National Drug Control Policy. (2003). *Drug policy information clearinghouse fact sheet* (NCJ Publication No. 191351). Washington, DC: Government Printing Office.

Orszag-Land, T. (1997). Body traders: Organised crime is moving into a grisly new trade. *International Police Review, 13,* 13.

Passas, N. (1995). The mirror of global evils: A review essay on the BCCI affair. *Justice Quarterly, 12,* 801–829.

Passas, N. (1998, June). *Transnational crime: The interface between legal and illegal actors.* Paper presented at the Workshop on Transnational Organized Crime, Committee on Law and Justice, National Research Council, Washington, DC. (Available from Temple University, Department of Criminal Justice)

Perry, R. L., & Robertson, J. D. (2002). *Comparative analysis of nations: Quantitative approaches.* Cambridge, MA: Westview Press.

Quinney, R. (1965). Suicide, homicide, and economic development. *Social Forces, 43,* 401–406.

Reichel, P. L. (2002). *Comparative criminal justice systems: A topical approach* (3rd ed.). Upper Saddle River, NJ: Prentice Hall.

Reuter, P., & Petrie, C. (Eds.). (1999). *Transnational organized crime: Summary of a workshop.* Retrieved March 9, 2003, from www.nap.edu/openbook/0309065755/html

Richards, J. R. (1999). *Transnational criminal organizations, cybercrime, and money laundering: A handbook for law enforcement officers, auditors, and financial investigators.* Boca Raton, FL: CRC Press.

Richman, D. C. (2000). The changing boundaries between federal and local law enforcement. In C. Friel (Ed.), *Boundary changes in criminal justice organizations* (Vol. 2, pp. 81–111). Washington, DC: Department of Justice, Office of Justice Programs.

Riedel, M. (1990). Nationwide homicide data sets: An evaluation of the uniform crime reports and National Center for Health Statistics data. In D. L. MacKenzie, P. J. Baunach, & R. R. Roberg (Eds.), *Measuring crime: Large-scale, long-range efforts* (pp. 175–205). Albany: State University of New York Press.

Schmid, A. P., & Savona, E. U. (1995). Migration and crime: A framework for discussion. *Trends in Organized Crime, 1*(3), 77–81.

Shanker, T. (2002, August 8). Global arms sales to developing nations are tumbling, study finds. *New York Times,* p. A8.

Shichor, D. (1990). Crime patterns and socioeconomic development: A cross-national analysis. *Criminal Justice Review, 15,* 64–77.

Smith, M. D., & Zahn, M. A. (Eds.). (1999). *Homicide: A sourcebook of social research.* Thousand Oaks, CA: Sage.

Stana, R. M. (2002, June 25). *Identity fraud: Prevalence and links to alien illegal activities.* Statement before the Subcommittee on Crime, Terrorism and Homeland Security and the Subcommittee on Immigration, Border Security, and Claims, Committee on the Judiciary, House of Representatives. (GAO-02–830T). Washington, DC: Government Printing Office.

Tass, T. A. (1998, March-May). The migrant mafia. *Cross Border Control International,* pp. 8–11.

United Nations, Crime Prevention and Criminal Justice Branch. (1995). *The fifth United Nations survey of crime trends and operations of criminal justice systems (1990–1994).* Retrieved March 29, 2004, from www. uncjin.org/ Statistics/WCTS/WCTS5/wcts5.html

United Nations. (2001). *Questionnaire for the seventh United Nations survey of crime trends and operations of criminal justice systems, covering the period 1998–2000.* Retrieved April 18, 2004, from www.unodc.org/pdf/crime/ seventh_survey/InstrumentE.pdf

U.S. Department of Justice, Bureau of Justice Statistics. (2000). *Sourcebook of criminal justice statistics.* Washington, DC: Government Printing Office.

U.S. Department of State, Bureau for International Narcotics and Law Enforcement Affairs. (2002, March). *International narcotics control strategy report.* Washington, DC: Government Printing Office.

U.S. Sentencing Commission. (2001). *2001 Sourcebook for federal sentencing statistics.* Washington, DC: Government Printing Office.

van Kesteren, J., Mayhew, P., & Nieuwbeerta, P. (2001). *Criminal victimisation in 17 industrialised countries: Key findings from the 2000 International Crime Victims Survey.* The Hague, Netherlands: ICVS.

Vito, G. F., & Blankenship, M. B. (2002). *Statistical analysis in criminal justice and criminology: A user's guide.* Upper Saddle River, NJ: Prentice Hall.

Ward, R. (2000). The internationalization of criminal justice. In C. Friel (Ed.), *Boundary changes in criminal justice organizations* (Vol. 2, pp. 267–21). Washington, DC: U.S. Department of Justice, Office of Justice Programs.

Wellford, C. F. (1974). Crime and the dimensions of nations. *International Journal of Criminology and Penology, 2,* 1–10.

White House. (1998). *International crime control strategy: June 1998.* Washington, DC: Government Printing Office. Retrieved March 29, 2004, from www.fas.org/irp/offdocs/iccs/iccstoc.html

Williams, P. (1999). Emerging issues: Transnational crime and control. In G. Newman (Ed.), *Global report on crime and justice* (pp. 221–241). New York: Oxford University Press.

Wolf, P. (1971). Crime and development: An international comparison of crime rates. *Scandinavian Studies in Criminology, 3,* 107–120.

4

Terrorism in Transition

JONATHAN R. WHITE

On October 12, 2000, two members of al Qaeda directed a small bomb-laden watercraft toward the USS *Cole* in Yemen's Aden harbor for the purpose of attacking the mightiest navy in the world. Despite the ambitious nature of the project, neither a rogue nation nor a terrorist state sponsored the bombers. The attack was the result of a transnational effort by a shadowy group of terrorists. It was a suicide mission, and the two *shahidin,* or martyrs, felt they were servants in a holy undertaking. Their goal was to strike the epitome of evil, the United States of America. Steering the boat so that their shaped charge warhead faced the warship, they went through a short ritual and detonated the deadly bomb. Seventeen American sailors were killed along with the two suicide bombers. It took a year to repair the damage to the *Cole,* but the damage to 17 families will never be healed (Gunaratna, 2002, p. 50).

The attack on the USS *Cole* symbolizes many aspects of modern terrorism. It illustrates the increased willingness of some terrorists to die for a cause, and it demonstrates the ability of a small group to attack a superpower. Yet there is something deeper about the attack on the U.S. Navy destroyer. This issue surfaced in a recruiting tape al Qaeda made after the murderous attack (Benjamin & Simon, 2002, pp. 154–155). Opening with a scene of the damaged destroyer, a caption reads, "Destroying the *Cole.*" After glorifying the attack, the film shifts to a panoramic view of the Arabic world, scenes of travail from many countries in the Middle East. It concludes with a segment demonizing the West and Muslims who seek political compromise with the United States, Europe, and Israel. Closing with an appeal from the late Abdullah Azzam, one of Osama bin Ladin's spiritual mentors, the film calls on Muslims to transcend the illusion of nationalism and join a never-ending holy war. The recruiting video uses the attack as a religious call to transnational terrorism.

This chapter focuses on the interplay between religion and transnational terrorism. It begins by describing the slippery nature of definitions, and it separates international and transnational concepts. The three phases of modern post–World War II terrorism are summarized, and an older ideological model of terrorism is recast in terms of religion. The chapter also focuses on the process of religious terrorism, and it contains a brief discussion of asymmetrical warfare. The argument here is that terrorism has gone through three transitory phases since 1945. The first phase was dominated by nationalism, and the second emphasized ethnic and ideological violence. The current phase is dominated by religiously motivated groups. During the first two phases of the postwar experience, terrorism tended to be either a localized or an international affair. Religion has changed the equation, and it provides the base for a transnational terrorism.

DEFINITIONAL PROBLEMS AND TRANSNATIONAL TERRORISM

It is difficult to conceive of terrorism as a manifestation of transnational crime because the definition of the subject changes in time and political space. This is not to suggest that one person's terrorist is another's freedom fighter, but it does suggest that the term *terrorism* means different things at different times. Alex Schmid (1983, pp. 70–111) claims the slippery nature of terrorism is due to its intangible nature. Terrorism is not a physical entity to be measured and defined; it is an ever-changing affair. Despite the elusive nature of the subject, terrorism becomes more concrete when defined in criminal codes. The problem with such codes, however, is that they are not applicable across cultures. Whether approaching terrorism through social or legal meanings, the concept is problematic within the framework of transnational crime.

Terrorism is political activity involving crime, and its characteristics change with historical circumstances and the political environment. As Louise Richardson (1998/ 2003) argues, the term *terrorism* is so pejorative that it has become virtually meaningless. She concludes that many violent political activities are inappropriately labeled terrorism and that terrorists continually seek to avoid being labeled. This irony did not escape the early analysts in the field. H. H. A. Cooper (1978) noted myriad definitional dilemmas nearly four decades ago. Walter Laqueur (1999, pp. 8–10) states that volumes will be written about the definition of terrorism and they will not add one iota to our understanding. Schmid (1983, pp. 70–111) provides the most thorough definition by correlating dozens of different definitions, but even his Herculean efforts fail to bring the problem into focus. The complexity of the definitional dilemma is exacerbated when discussing transnational crime.

On one hand, nothing could be more applicable in a reader on transnational crime than a chapter on terrorism. Name an international criminal activity and chances are terrorists have engaged in it. Physical violence such as hijacking, kidnapping, and murder are on the high end of the scale, with drug trafficking, money laundering, and immigration crimes falling in other areas. Terrorists engage in cybercrimes, and they use information networks for clandestine communication. They establish illegal multinational criminal organizations. They extort money, commit credit card fraud, and counterfeit currency. Terrorists forge documents and rob banks. They commit mass murder and engage in activities that would be deemed war crimes in other circumstances (Dyson, 2001). Terrorism frequently involves local and international criminal activity.

On the other hand, many distinguished analysts have refused to classify terrorism as criminal activity. Two of the illustrious deans in the field, Paul Wilkinson (1974, pp. 37–55) and Cooper (1978), took pains to emphasize the importance of the political nature of terrorism in contradistinction to its criminal characteristics. Wilkinson's classic *Political Terrorism* (1974) identifies three forms of terrorism: criminal, political, and state sponsored. Wilkinson argues that scholars, government leaders, and journalists usually mean "political terrorism" when they discuss the problem of terrorism. Political terrorism can be examined as state repression, ideological revolutionary activities, or nationalistic revolutions. State repression refers to a government's using terror to keep citizens in line, whereas ideological revolutionary terrorism focuses on violence to change a political system. Nationalistic terrorism emphasizes the ethnic structure of government over its ideological underpinnings, and both nationalistic and revolutionary terrorism can be sponsored by states. Wilkinson's focus on political terrorism guided many terrorism analysts away from the study of crime.

As editors of an early presidential commission report on terrorism, Cooper and his colleagues (1976) explain why analysts emphasized the political nature of terrorism. To be sure, Cooper says, terrorists engage in all types of crimes, but their purpose is not criminal. The ultimate objective of terrorism is to change political behavior. Criminal activity enters the equation, Cooper says, because terrorists commit crimes as they conduct political operations. Cooper and his colleagues make a distinction between normative crimes and crimes associated with terrorism. When the purpose of a crime is to achieve economic gain or psychological gratification, criminal activity does not fall into the realm of political terrorism, but violent criminal actions in support of political goals may be terrorism. Not all political criminal activity is terrorism, but violent political crimes that victimize innocent individuals may fall into the category. Agreeing with Wilkinson, Cooper's approach suggests that

terrorism is a subject for political analysis, not criminology.

Continuing in the path established by Wilkinson and Cooper, Walter Laqueur (1999, pp. 79–104) further explains the political nature of terrorism. Criminologists may develop profiles and models of criminal activity, Laqueur writes, because they deal with constant traits of human behavior. It is possible to plot behavior over a period of time, profile certain behavioral types, and predict behavior in various social settings. This works in criminology because conditions and behavior are relatively constant, but nothing could be further from consistency than terrorism. No one can develop a criminological model of terrorism, Laqueur argues, because terrorist behavior does not remain constant. Terrorism is not a psychological phenomenon; it represents violent political behavior. Terrorists do not act from psychological inadequacies but from political circumstances. It is possible to determine general characteristics of political movements, but not to engage in a psychological analysis of terrorist criminality. Such definitional specificity, Laqueur concludes, does not exist.

Brian Jenkins (1998) offers a practical solution to the problem: terrorism is situationally defined. Rather than seeking a complex social definition of the problems of terrorism, Jenkins and his fellow researchers at RAND look at the practical aspects surrounding terrorist events. Although terrorism frequently involves criminal activity, terrorists are not typical criminals. They commit crimes for political purposes. When captured by security forces, they are not usually prosecuted as terrorists but charged with the crimes they commit. Terrorists strike targets for political purposes in a given situation, using crime as an incidental tactic. When terrorists cross national boundaries, they become international terrorists. Furthermore, terrorists are not exceptionally creative; they use a limited array of weapons and tactics. Whether regional or international, terrorists use crime in varying situations for political purposes.

An analysis by Jeffery Ian Ross (1999) differs from earlier research suggesting that both political and social factors can lead to a criminology of terrorism, and he takes the argument further. Terrorism involves violence but criminal behavior is a result of political and social circumstances; that is, terrorism involves variables that can be measured on a criminological scale. The measurable by-product can be examined through psychological factors that vacillate with political circumstances. Ross's conclusions lead to two practical considerations. First, terrorists use both criminal activities and criminal organizations to accomplish political objectives. When using international violence, criminal organizations may pose a problem for national security. Second, as a result of criminal activities, terrorists frequently encounter criminal justice systems even though their primary purpose is not to commit crimes. This presents a policy problem. Terrorism is political activity that can threaten national security on an international scale, yet the criminal aspects of terrorist operations and organizations bring them into contact with justice systems. Should terrorism be handled by the criminal justice system, or should it be considered within the framework of national security? Many countries, including the United States, have yet to answer this question.

There are further complications with the definition when discussing various types of terrorism, and this becomes apparent when examining transnational crime. International terrorism involves groups operating across nation-state boundaries, but transnational terror seeks something greater than nationalistic goals. Richardson (1998/2003) writes that terrorism is politically motivated violence directed at noncombatants or symbols, designed to change behavior through communication. She believes the United States sees terrorism more as an international problem than a transnational one. In other words, American policymakers view terrorist organizations in terms of their links to nation-states, even basing policy on state-sponsored terrorism. Transnational terrorism, political violence transcending the nation state, is not at the forefront of counterterrorist policies. Richardson believes the U.S. government as well as American counterterrorist analysts tend to use the terms *international* and *transnational* interchangeably; however, she separates the definitions. International terrorism crosses national boundaries while acknowledging the legitimacy and function of the nation-state. Transnational terrorism points toward an ideological globalism ignoring a world divided by national frontiers.

If Richardson's (1998/2003) dichotomy is correct, it has two important conceptual ramifications. First, by acknowledging the nature of transnational terrorism, policymakers may come to realize that the structure of terrorism has changed. At least two major international terrorist groups embrace a transcendent ideology—al Qaeda and Hezbollah—and both groups are motivated by religion. In addition, several smaller groups want to follow in their path. Second, at first glance, because many of these groups are Islamic, it would seem to suggest the beginning of religious conflicts beyond nationalistic wars. Indeed, this is part of the thesis of Samuel Huntington's (1996) clash of civilizations. However, when examining Western terrorism, the same transcendent trend seems to be emerging when ideology is used as a surrogate religion. Transcendent ideology dominates modern anarchism, ecological extremism, animal rights activism, anti-genetic-engineering movements, and racial supremacy extremism. Transnational terrorism transcends the nation-state by using religion and surrogate religious values.

ANTICOLONIAL, IDEOLOGICAL, AND RELIGIOUS TERRORISM

Modern terrorism has undergone three fairly distinct phases since World War II with differing ideas dominating each phase: anticolonial terrorism, ideological terrorism, and religious terrorism.

Anticolonial Terrorism

Many revolutionaries in European colonies used terrorism as a tactic after 1945, targeting colonial administrators, foreign nationals, and natives sympathetic to the colonial power. Terrorists formulated their own theories of anticolonial revolution and based much of their activity on earlier revolutionaries such as the Irish Republican Army and the Russian Peoples' Will. Anticolonial rebels used terrorism to make foreign occupation too costly for colonial powers (see Debray, 1967; Fanon, 1982; Guevara, 1968). In modern bureaucratic language, this process is known as asymmetrical warfare.

Few scholars have summarized asymmetrical war better than Bruce Hoffman, one of the foremost terrorism experts of our day. Hoffman (1998, pp. 45–65) points to the changing nature of war in the past 50 years. According to Hoffman, the fall of European colonial possessions to the Japanese in World War II established a revolutionary idea throughout the colonial world. When Japan defeated colonial powers, it demonstrated to native populations in Africa, Asia, and Latin America that European systems were not inherently superior to non-European governments. As a result, colonies clamored for freedom. Their cries intensified when the Western powers signed a declaration asserting the right of nations to control their political destinies. When Europe's colonial powers refused to abandon their empires, even after declaring the right to self-determination, colonies took up the mantle of political revolt.

As violence spread across European colonies, revolutionary leaders quickly realized they could not fight Europeans in a conventional manner. European armies were simply too strong. As a result, revolutionaries found their strategy guided by other principles. The purpose, they reasoned, was not to win a military confrontation against a superior power; their goal was to win a political battle in the court of public opinion. Opinion could be influenced when relatively weak forces attacked stronger forces at their weakest link. Revolutionaries embraced the idea of asymmetry.

Warfare is continually changing, and asymmetry is not a new concept in international conflict. In conventional warfare, the purpose of battle is to bring more resources, troops, and power to a point where the enemy is weak. Successful military leaders create asymmetrical situations. Terrorists essentially follow this logic, with one major exception. Because they are too weak to attack military forces directly, they attack them when they are at rest, or they bypass military targets for civilians. It makes little sense for terrorists to fight in the open against a superior force.

Hoffman (1998, pp. 45–65) examines three anticolonial revolts in Palestine, Cyprus, and Algeria to demonstrate the effectiveness of asymmetry. The process began in Palestine before World War II. Two Jewish terrorist groups, the Irgun Zvai Leumi and the Stern Gang, found they could attack occupying British forces even though the British outnumbered them. The keys to terrorist successes were threefold: (1) Terrorists looked and acted as normal citizens when not engaged in combat; (2) terrorists operated in an urban environment, allowing them to emerge from a crowd and to merge back into it; and (3) symbolic targets created an aura around each attack, making it appear to be more significant than it really was. Terrorists demonstrated that superior numbers of British soldiers could not keep the country safe, and the process continued after the war.

Long before the 24-hour news coverage of CNN, Hoffman (1998) argues, Zionist terrorists were able to focus world attention on a relatively obscure cause. When the terrorists murdered Palestinian Arabs or British soldiers, they did so for the sake of gaining notoriety. They hoped to wear down the security forces psychologically, to create a political climate in Britain that would deem the costs of occupying Palestine to be too high, and to keep the conflict before the eyes of the world. When the British left in 1948, it was partially as a result of a successful terrorist campaign. Other revolutionaries took note: Asymmetrical war worked.

Hoffman's analysis of Cyprus and Algeria reveals similar results. Cypriot terrorists had no desire to kill British soldiers for the purpose of gaining a military victory. They wanted to demonstrate the ability of a weaker force to strike a stronger force at will. Again, the message was asymmetry. The same lesson came into play in Algeria. One Algerian revolutionary leader stated that it was better to kill one enemy soldier in front of the world's media than it was to kill ten of them in a forsaken desert. The purpose of killing was to gain attention. In addition, terrorism in Palestine, Cyprus, and Algeria legitimized civilian targets. Murdering civilians had the same impact as killing soldiers.

Ideological Terrorism

The second phase of modern terrorism evolved from the legacy of anticolonialism. By 1960, ideological and nationalistic terrorists used anticolonial rhetoric to challenge Western society. This led to the growth of left-wing and ethnic violence in the 1960s and 1970s (Pluchinsky, 1982, 1993). As left-wing and nationalistic violence swept the Middle East, Asia, Latin America, and the West, an international ethos of revolutionary terrorism seemed to pit itself against the Western world.

The ideological terrorists of the left, and later the right, used the rhetoric of anticolonialism, but their targets were the economic and social symbols of Western democracies. Some indigenous revolutionary radicals gravitated to these movements, and many more sympathized with them. The political climate spawned by the Vietnam War fueled violent ideological terrorism in Europe and the United States. Third world revolutionaries claimed these new ideologues as their own, and nationalistic terrorist groups in Spain, Ireland, and the Middle East moved from the rhetoric of nationalism to call for international revolution. The revolutionaries claimed to transcend nationalism, whereas their more conservative adversaries traced their support back to nation-states supporting terrorism. In the end, the ideological movements failed even before the collapse of the former Soviet Union. Nationalistic groups in Ireland and Spain lost much of their support, and groups in the Middle and Far East searched for new meanings.

Why had ideological terrorism failed? Why did militants in Palestine, Iran, and Sri Lanka look for another cause? Corrado and Evans (1988) speculate that the impact of democracy was ultimately to blame. Left-wing intellectuals had no moral ground in the Western political frame. Violence de-legitimated terrorism, and left-wing ideas became part of the political dialogue. Dennis Pluchinsky (1993) points out that the extremist groups also ran out of steam. Their unwillingness to compromise and disgusting fascination with violence turned public opinion against them. Pluchinsky also shows that Western political systems were sympathetic to both class and ethnic injustices. When mainstream politicians stole the terrorist agenda, the terrorists had no reason to fight. The same logic did not apply to Asia and Africa. When Western democracies trumped the ideological terrorists, violent groups searched for another supporting structure. They found it in religion.

The Advent of Religious Terrorism

Religious terrorism differed from previous experiences because it introduced a cosmic dimension to violent political struggles. Mark Juergensmeyer's (2000) groundbreaking work, *Terror in the Mind of God*, examines the uncompromising attitude of such philosophy. The mere existence of a demonized enemy is evil, and any deviation from the orthodox path potentially represents the work of the devil. Therefore, tolerance of differences is inconceivable. Violence is mandated, according to Juergensmeyer, as a result of the cosmic necessity to purify creation by purging evil. The call to violence, Juergensmeyer argues, is a call to purify the world from nonbelievers and those who interpret religious tradition incorrectly. If the holy warrior fails, God fails, so the struggle calls for martyrs willing to accept the holy duty of sacrifice. Holy war comes through a tradition that allows only one way of thinking. If the holy warrior falls in a losing cause, the warrior becomes a martyr for hope. On the other hand, successful warriors represent a victory for God. Such holy wars represent uncompromising principles of struggle and sacrifice.

Juergensmeyer examines holy warriors in several differing faith traditions and finds commonalities. It is interesting to apply his logic by comparing one of the al Qaeda manuals, *Declaration of Jihad Against the Country's Tyrants* (n.d-b), with the *Defense Manual* of the American extremist right-wing group known as the Covenant, the Sword, and the Arm of the Lord (1982). Both books begin with theological passages claiming that their interpretations of God are correct. They both quote U.S. Army manuals (al Qaeda does a better job), interspersing tactical directions with lengthy scriptural passages accompanied by violent exegesis. If the manuals are indicative of the mind of the holy warrior, the language of religious terrorism remains constant across cultures. Yet violent domestic religious groups and international groups were never able to grow past regional issues. Al Qaeda differed, becoming a truly transnational terrorist group. A brief examination of recent history explains why.

Lebanon, Sri Lanka, and Afghanistan: Suicide, Religion, and Asymmetry

Holy terror began growing in the Middle East in the wake of the Iranian revolution (1978–1979). Iranian revolutionaries established a theocratic government based on the laws of Shia Islam. When Israel invaded Lebanon in 1982, their tanks rolled through the Shiite villages of Southern Lebanon. Militant Iranians flocked to Lebanon in response, and they spawned a new type of terrorist group with a new tactic, the suicide bomber. Old forms of terrorism gave way to the religious fervor of Hezbollah, the Party of God, as religious terrorists struck the Israeli invaders with human bombs.

The Israeli Institute for Counter-Terrorism (ICT, 2001) developed a thorough description of the process Hezbollah developed to conduct suicide operations. The ICT argues that preparation for a suicide bombing comes from two separate units. The first is a standard military group that focuses on reconnaissance, logistics, and planning. The second unit has a psychological function. It recruits and isolates a suicide bomber, preferably a young man or woman, brainwashing the victim until martyrdom seems to be the only logical course of action. When the victim is ready, the psychological unit turns the martyr *(shahid)* over to the military unit. The military unit straps the suicide bomb on the victim and directs the *shahid* to the target. This two-step process became the Hezbollah model for suicide bombings from 1983 until the mid-1990s.

Other Middle Eastern groups found themselves copying the Hezbollah religious-based model. Violent Palestinian groups broke away from the ethnonationalist Palestine Liberation

Organization and formed religion-based groups such as Hamas. A splinter religious group from the Egyptian Muslim Brotherhood, Palestinian Islamic Jihad, openly praised Hezbollah and followed its example in suicide bombing. Religious terrorist groups sprang up in Egypt and other parts of North Africa. Suicide became a volatile tactic, and other groups found new ways to employ suicide bombers.

New methods of suicide bombing developed in Sri Lanka and Kurdistan. The Liberation Tigers of Tamil Elaam (LTTE or Tamil Tigers) of Sri Lanka waged a campaign of terror based primarily on ethnicity, but they capitalized on religious differences between Buddhists and Hindus. Embracing suicide bombings, the LTTE modified the formula posited by Hezbollah and other Middle Eastern groups. They recruited, conscripted, and kidnapped children, isolating them in training camps and socializing them for years in a cult of martyrdom. As the children matured, they turned into willing candidates for suicide operations. Socialization became a new method to prepare suicide bombers. The Kurdish Workers' Party (PKK) avoided religion altogether, selecting suicide bombers and telling victims that both they and their families would be murdered unless they carried out the attack. The PKK was especially successful at disguising young women, packing explosives around their stomachs to make them appear pregnant. The suicide terror spawned by the LTTE and PKK was deadly and devastating.

Learning from previous experiences with suicide bombings, another variation of religious terrorism developed in Central Asia. In December 1979, the former Soviet Union invaded Afghanistan to bolster a fading Communist regime. The conflict became a surrogate superpower struggle, with Soviet forces engaged against Afghan guerrillas who, in turn, were supported by the United States. In the eyes of the world, the Soviet Afghan War (1979–1989) represented the last battle of the Cold War. In the eyes of the Afghan guerrillas, however, resistance against the Soviets was a holy war, a battle between God's holy warriors—the *mujihadeen*—and the godless Marxists of the former Soviet Union. When the Soviets retreated and the U.S.S.R. collapsed, the *mujihadeen* believed God had defeated the Communists. Some of them prepared to take their battle to other enemies (see Rashid, 2002).

Afghanistan also reinforced the modern allure of asymmetrical warfare. The *mujihadeen* could rarely match the Soviet army in the field, but they could lure it into situations where they had temporary superiority. In addition, they fought on terrain conducive to their hit-and-run tactics. The battles between the Soviets and the *mujihadeen* became classical examples of asymmetry, representing a weak force pitted against a stronger power with the weaker force carrying the day (White, 2003a, pp. 47–63).

There were several religious guerilla groups in the Afghan War, and they believed God stood behind their victory. Martyrdom and suicide operations became a standard course of action (Shay, 2002, pp. 105–146). No leaders seemed to understand this more than the chiefs of al Qaeda—Osama bin Laden and Ayman al Zawahiri. Building on the experiences of previous suicide operations in the Middle East, Kurdistan, and Sri Lanka, they enhanced the effectiveness of their martyrs. Rather than brainwashing young people into committing suicide or forcing unwilling victims, al Qaeda leaders allowed experienced warriors to volunteer for "martyrdom operations." When the *shahid* joined a terrorist cell, he found himself in the presence of a charismatic leader and other warriors who had volunteered for death. Continually emphasizing martyrdom, a theme reinforced in both Christian and Islamic traditions, charismatic leaders were able to maintain a cult of martyrdom where suicide became the highest form of organizational and religious sacrifice

(Gunaratna, 2002, pp. 7–8, 90–97). This allowed al Qaeda to place sleeper suicide agents in deep cover, sometimes lasting for years.

Religion and the Logic of Transnational Terror

Religion also influenced the structure of terrorism. Neither suicide nor asymmetry brought a transnational dimension to terrorism, but religion did. Shay (2002, pp. 52–66) points to a variety of *mujihadeen* groups that grew from the Soviet Afghan War. When the Soviets withdrew, the new Afghan leader, Najibullah, vowed to keep centralized Communist power in Kabul. The *mujihadeen* continued to resist, even though the United States ended its support, turning attention to Saddam Hussein. According to Gunaratna (2002, pp. 4–23), Abdullah Azzam, the cleric who founded al Qaeda, believed that an ideological holy war should continue after the Afghan struggle. This would involve evangelical activities and assisting Muslim guerrillas in the event of war. Osama bin Laden disagreed. Influenced by two Egyptian organizations, bin Laden argued that al Qaeda should embrace the tactics of terror. Azzam was murdered, and the bin Laden/al Zawahiri philosophy took control of al Qaeda. They decentralized command structures and created a loose-knit conglomeration of groups around the globe. They also dispersed decentralized cells, sending al Qaeda fighters throughout the world. This diverse group of terrorists avoided structure, bureaucracy, and hierarchical organization. Al Qaeda, bound together by religious fanaticism, became a transnational terrorist group (see Table 4.1).

The United States refocused on the Middle East when Saddam Hussein invaded Kuwait in 1990. A massive international coalition, headed by American forces, responded and dismantled the Iraqis in a quick campaign. The presence of U.S. forces in Saudi Arabia angered many Muslims, including the reconstituted al Qaeda. The United States soon found that it was the prime target of a transnational terrorist operation.

In the anticolonial and ideological phases of modern terrorism, most terrorist organizations did not seek to transcend the nation-state. For example, Hezbollah reinvented itself as an international terrorist group in the course of the Iranian revolution, leaving Iran to fight the Israelis and eventually the Americans in Lebanon. But Hezbollah's political orientation and logistic links remained firmly attached to Iran, with secondary links to Syria and supporters from Lebanon until the mid-1990s. In the early days, Hezbollah internationalized the Shiite agenda but made no attempt to transcend the state. Al Qaeda took another path. Religion provided the basis for transcending the state, and the process was not limited to Islamic extremists. Seeing the success of al Qaeda, Hezbollah changed its direction. Although still maintaining ties to Iran and Syria, it has branched into a transnational group.

THE THEOLOGY OF TRANSNATIONAL TERRORISM

Religious terrorism in the modern world evolved from earlier forms of terrorism, and holy terror ultimately became a theological process. That is, the transcendent nature of religious violence took place because groups began thinking in religious terms. Symbols, myth, and sacred meanings became the basis for action and for transcending the nation-state.

Suicide bombers represent the epitome of this logic. The media is replete with stories of bombers seeking a reward in heaven for their suicidal exploits, but theology suggests a deeper rationale for suicide bombing. In any religion, humans perform various activities to approach a deity, and one of the most fundamental elements for atonement is sacrifice

Table 4.1   Al Qaeda's Campaign of Terror

Date	Place	Event
12-29-92	Aden, Yemen	Hotel bombing
2-26-93	New York City	First World Trade Center bombing
10-3-93	Mogadishu, Somalia	Firefight, U.S. Army Rangers
Late 1994	Manila, Philippines	Operation Bojinka
11-13-95	Riyadh, Saudi Arabia	Car bomb, U.S. military personnel*
12-26-95	Addo Abada, Ethiopia	Attempted assassination of Hosni Mubarak
6-25-96	Dharan, Saudi Arabia	Truck bomb, U.S. Air Force base*
8-7-98	Dar es Salaam, Tanzania	U.S. embassy bombing
8-7-98	Nairobi, Kenya	U.S. embassy bombing
12-4-99	Port Angeles, Washington	Foiled bombing plot
December 1999	Amman, Jordan	Foiled bombing plot
10-12-00	Aden, Yemen	Boat bomb, *U.S.S. Cole*
12-25-00	Strasbourg, France	Foiled bombing plot
9-11-01	New York City	World Trade Center attacks
9-11-01	Washington, DC	Pentagon attack
9-11-01	Pennsylvania	Attack foiled by hijack victims
9-13-01	Paris, France	Foiled bombing plot
9-13-01	Brussels, Belgium	Foiled bombing plot
9-19-01	Detroit, Michigan	Sleeper cell closed
10-8-01	Sarajevo, Bosnia	Foiled attack
October 2001	Madrid, Spain	Sleeper cell closed
Early 2002	Singapore	Three sleeper cells closed
4-11-02	Djerba, Tunisia	Truck bombing of a synagogue
Summer 2002	Gibraltar	Foiled naval attack
Summer 2002	West Coast, US	Alleged sleeper cell closed
Fall 2002	Buffalo, New York	Alleged sleeper cell closed
10-6-02	Aden, Yemen	Boat bomb, French merchant ship
10-9-02	Kuwait	Marines attacked by two gunmen
10-12-02	Bali, Indonesia	Bombing of a nightclub
11-12-02	Unknown	Tape claiming to be bin Laden praises recent violence

SOURCE: White (2003b, p. 295). Copyright 2003. Reprinted with permission of Wadsworth, a division of Thomson Learning: www.thomsonrights.com.

*The FBI has not established links between al Qaeda and this attack. These attacks may be linked to Hezbollah or a similar group.

(Tillich, 1957). Sacrifice is the conduit for entering holy ground. Campbell (1949) argues that myth has the same power, vicariously placing the community in a hero's shoes as the deity is approached. Seen from this frame, suicide bombing becomes far more than simply an action to gain a reward in the afterlife. It is the supreme act of sacrifice in approaching a deity. Indeed, some people willingly sacrifice themselves for familial and political causes, but religion has a ready-made prescription to justify such sacrifice.

Chip Berlet (1998) complements the portrait of ritual sacrifice by explaining how enemies become unholy. Soldiers, politicians, and others routinely degrade their enemies, but religious terrorists take the matter further. They demonize their enemies, rendering them fit not for holy sacrifice but for destruction. Berlet believes the process begins when a particular group is blamed for a social problem. He calls this process scapegoating. When scapegoats are demonized, they become the representatives of the antideity in a divine struggle. Their destruction is mandated in the sacrifice.

An al Qaeda bombing illustrates the point. In 1998, suicide terrorists destroyed two American embassies in Africa. Ironically, the majority of people killed were Muslims, not Americans or even Christians. According to one of the al Qaeda manuals (Al Qaeda, n.d-a), such killing is permissible because good Muslims will go to heaven. If the victims were not good Muslims, they were part of the enemy's forces and deserved death. In the sacrificial world where the enemy is demonized, there is no middle ground. People are either part of God or part of the devil, and God will reward the innocent people who stand on holy ground. The demonized others are of no consequence.

This concept is not new nor is it limited to major religious traditions. Researchers from the RAND Corporation (Jenkins, 1984) conducted in-depth interviews with a surviving terrorist from the Japanese Red Army after the murder of more than 70 people in Israel's Lod Airport in 1972. The terrorist was temporarily saddened to discover that his group had accidentally murdered Puerto Rican Christian pilgrims instead of Israelis. When confronted with the mistake, he was eventually able to dismiss the problem, claiming that divine justice would make celestial beings of the Puerto Ricans. Innocent victims present no problem for a group that has dichotomized the world between the righteous and the demons.

Religious terrorists also frequently believe they have had some type of sacred enlightenment. A fictional example serves to illustrate the point. In *The Turner Diaries*, a white supremacy novel written by the late William Pierce under the pseudonym Andrew MacDonald (1989), the novel's protagonist goes through a profound religious experience while being initiated into a terrorist group known as the Order. The hero makes the transition from small-time criminal into theological terrorist after the experience. Such life-altering moments are hardly limited to violent escapades, but they are part of religious terrorism. Unfortunately, they also lend legitimacy, in the terrorist's mind, to sacred conflict.

A practical example can be used to emphasize this process. The Aum Shinrikyo was a religious cult based in Japan in the early 1990s. In 1995, it carried out the largest known act of chemical terrorism in the history of the world. Fortunately, the cult's inability to disperse sarin gas prevented massive casualties. Brackett (1996) provides the best in-depth analysis of the cult. Formed by Shoko Asahara, Aum drew professionals into an eschatological grouping that combined apocalyptic Buddhism and Christianity. Operating in Africa, Asia, Australia, North America, and Europe, Aum gradually gathered the ingredients necessary to make weapons of mass destruction. Benjamin and

Simon (2002, pp. 129, 228–229, 433–438) point to both the transnational character of the group and its apocalyptic tendencies. After receiving a religious revelation, Asahara decided to bring about Armageddon by launching a chemical attack on the Tokyo subway system. Several Aum members used sharpened umbrellas to puncture plastic bags filled with a liquid solution that would produce a poison gas when exposed to the air. The attack failed because the agents were not strong enough to bring about massive casualties.

The difficult point for the Tokyo subway attack is not the failed technology but the willingness to induce mass casualties. Technological weaknesses can be overcome. Asahara demonstrated the willingness to induce megadeath through religion. According to Brian Jenkins (1987), the political terrorists of the 1970s and 1980s were unwilling to cross the line from localized destruction to using weapons that would result in massive death. The reason is fairly straightforward. Political terrorists want to influence political opinion and gain power. By introducing massive death, they delegitimize the cause. Religious terrorists, playing to a deity, have no such inhibition. Furthermore, after receiving a mandate to perform such a deed, sacred enlightenment, murderous religious zealots have no logical incentive to hinder mass destruction.

Religious terrorism begins when potential terrorists believe the existing order is a threat to divine structure. Religious terrorists are not in a battle with human forces; they battle evil. Juergensmeyer (2000, pp. 153–195) points out that this leads to a cosmic confrontation. Terrorists operate on a battlefield where their deity's creation is threatened with disorder. Myth, symbols, and sacred ideology are invoked in the holy war, and the struggle assumes much more than historical dimensions. All history hangs in the balance of the confrontation.

Theology has criminological importance. Religious terrorists are able to transcend the state because they behave differently from political terrorists. The process can be illustrated by differentiating criminals from political terrorists. Bodrero (2002) argues that the behavior of ordinary criminals is self-focused, is driven by immediate gratification, is oriented toward escape, and exhibits no particular loyalty to a cause. Terrorists, on the other hand, are focused on the group, willing to defer gratification for a greater good, oriented toward attack, and ultimately loyal to a cause. Hoffman (1995) points out that religious terrorists exhibit characteristics similar to political terrorists except in their attitude toward death. Although political terrorists view death as a necessity, religious terrorists actively seek to maximize death. They do not care about the political ramifications of megadeath, to say nothing of its tragic human toll, because existence is either good or evil, and all evil must be destroyed. This cosmic view transcends nationalized terrorism.

CONCLUSION

Transnational terrorism is changing the function of terrorism in the modern world. The United States has traditionally approached transnational terror as an international problem, but the flattened structures of groups such as Hezbollah and al Qaeda posit true transnational challenges to the West. Terrorists do not tend to be either original or highly innovative, and terrorist organizations change slowly, mimicking the experiences of the past. Trends indicate that terrorism will increasingly decentralize as groups transcend national boundaries. Groups will remain religious or use surrogate causes such as animal rights, the environment, or genetic engineering. The trend toward religious violence not only brings transnational links, it provides the logic for mass destruction. Future counterterrorist policy should take these trends into account. Terrorism has transmogrified into a transnational experience.

REFERENCES

Al Qaeda. (n.d-a). *Al Qaeda manual*. Retrieved March 31, 2004, from www.disastercenter.com/terror

Al Qaeda. (n.d-b). *Declaration of Jihad against the country's tyrants*. (n.p.).

Benjamin, D., & Simon, S. (2002). *The age of sacred terror*. New York: Random House.

Berlet, C. (1998). *Dances with devils*. Somerville, MA: Political Research Associates. Retrieved March 31, 2004, from www.publiceye.org/apocalyptic/Dances_with_Devils_1.html

Bodrero, D. D. (2002, February). Law enforcement's new challenge to investigate, interdict, and prevent terrorism. *The Police Chief*, pp. 41–48.

Brackett, D. W. (1996). *Holy terror: Armageddon in Tokyo*. New York: Weatherhill.

Campbell, J. (1949). *The hero with a thousand faces*. New York: MJF Books.

Cooper, H. H. A. (1978). Terrorism: The problem of the problem definition. *Chitty's Law Journal, 26*, 105–108.

Cooper, H. H. A., and the National Advisory Committee on Criminal Justice Standards and Goals. (Eds.). (1976). *Report of the Task Force on Disorders and Terrorism* (NCJ Publication No. 39469). Washington, DC: Government Printing Office.

Corrado, R., & Evans, R. (1988). Ethnic and ideological terrorism in Western Europe. In M. Stohl (Ed.), *The politics of terrorism* (pp. 379–410). New York: Dekker.

Covenant, the Sword, and the Arm of the Lord. (1982). *Defense manual*. Zaraprath-Horeb (self-defined area between Bull Shoals and Springfield), MO: Author.

Debray, R. (1967). *Revolution in the revolution?* Westport, CT: Greenwood.

Dyson, W. E. (2001). *An overview of terrorism*. Tallahassee, FL: Institute for Intergovernmental Research.

Fanon, F. (1982). *The wretched of the earth*. New York: Grove.

Guevara, E. (Che). (1968). *Reminiscences of the Cuban Revolutionary War*. New York: Monthly Review Press.

Gunaratna, R. (2002). *Inside Al Qaeda: Global network of terror*. New York: Columbia University Press.

Hoffman, B. (1995). Holy terror: The implications of terrorism motivated by a religious imperative. *Studies in Conflict and Terrorism, 18*, 271–284.

Hoffman, B. (1998). *Inside terrorism*. New York: Columbia University Press.

Huntington, S. P. (1996). *The clash of civilizations: Remarking world order*. New York: Simon & Schuster.

Institute for Counter-Terrorism. (2001). *Countering suicide terrorism: An international conference*. Herzliya, Israel: ICT.

Jenkins, B. M. (1984, November). *The who, when, what, where, and how of terrorism*. Paper presented at the Detroit Police Department Conference, Urban Terrorism: Planning or Chaos?

Jenkins, B. M. (1987). Will terrorists go nuclear? In W. Laqueur & Y. Alexander (Eds.), *The terrorism reader* (pp. 350–357). New York: Meridian.

Jenkins, B. M. (1998). "Introduction." In I. O. Lesser, B. Hoffman, J. Arquilla, D. F. Ronfeldt, M. Zanini, & B. M. Jenkins. (Eds.), *Countering the new terrorism*. Santa Monica, CA: RAND.

Juergensmeyer, M. (2000). *Terror in the mind of God: The global rise of religious violence*. Berkley: University of California Press.

Laqueur, W. (1999). *The new terrorism: Fanaticism and the arms of mass destruction*. New York: Oxford University Press.

MacDonald, A. (William Pierce). (1989). *The Turner diaries*. Hillsboro, WV: National Alliance.

Pluchinsky, D. (1982). Political terrorism in Western Europe: Some themes and variations. In Y. Alexander & K. A. Myers (Eds.), *Terrorism in Europe* (pp. 40–78). New York: St. Martin's.

Pluchinsky, D. (1993). Germany's Red Army faction: An obituary. *Studies in Conflict and Terrorism, 16*, 135–157.

Rashid, A. (2002). *Jihad: The rise of militant Islam in Central Asia*. New Haven, CT: Yale University Press.

Richardson, L. (2003). Global rebels: Terrorist organizations as trans-national actors. In R. D. Howard & R. L. Sawyer (Eds.), *Terrorism and counterterrorism: Understanding the new security environment* (pp. 67–73). Guilford, CT: McGraw-Hill. (Reprinted from *Harvard International Review,* 1998, Vol. 20, No. 4)

Ross, J. I. (1999). Beyond the conceptualization of terrorism: A psychological structural model of the causes of this activity. In C. Summers & E. Markusen (Eds.), *Collective violence: Harmful behavior in groups and governments.* New York: Rowman & Littlefield.

Schmid, A. (1983). *Political terrorism: A research guide to concepts, theories, data bases, and literature.* New Brunswick, CT: Transaction.

Shay, S. (2002). *The endless jihad: The Mujahidin, the Taliban, and Bin Ladin.* Herzliya, Israel: Institute for Counter-Terrorism.

Tillich, P. (1957). *The dynamics of faith.* New York: Harper Torch.

White, J. R. (2003a). *Defending the homeland: Domestic intelligence, law enforcement, and security.* Belmont, CA: Wadsworth.

White, J. R. (2003b). *Terrorism: An introduction* (4th ed.). Belmont, CA: Wadsworth.

Wilkinson, P. (1974). *Political terrorism.* New York: Wiley.

5

Expanding the International Regime on Money Laundering in Response to Transnational Organized Crime, Terrorism, and Corruption

ELIZABETH JOYCE

Recent years have seen the most rapid and profound period of international policy development on international criminal matters prompted largely, but not entirely, by the fight against global terrorism. Many of the measures that countries are now attempting to implement, although not new in themselves, have been incorporated for the first time into legally binding international conventions. Some measures, previously thought unfeasible, are now being implemented for the first time.

In the field of anti–money laundering (AML), the international regime of norms and standards was strengthened after September 11, 2001 (9/11), to address the financing of terrorism.

It was strengthened further with the U.N. Convention Against Corruption, which was opened for signature in Mérida, Mexico, on December 9 to 11, 2003. Money laundering is instrumental to corruption and the abuse of public office for private gain. In recent years, several cases of large-scale corruption have come to light in which millions of dollars of state assets have been stolen by senior state officials and deposited in bank accounts in other countries. The battle to freeze and repatriate such assets has to date been only minimally successful.

The need to incorporate within the international regime responses that could address the

AUTHORS' NOTE: Elizabeth Joyce works in the United Nations Office on Drugs and Crime. The opinions expressed in this chapter are those of the author and not those of the United nations.

ways in which money-laundering mechanisms are used for crimes such as the financing of terrorism and corruption has expanded the concept of money laundering beyond its earlier definition that referred in some jurisdictions only to a specific list of crimes or predicate offenses, and in some jurisdictions, until very recently, only to drug trafficking. The linkages between money laundering and the financing of terrorism, and between money laundering and corruption, are now explicit in international law. The political will created by the international response to 9/11 expanded and strengthened the international regime. With the possibilities presented by a strengthened AML regime in terms of international cooperation on criminal matters, other applications for its provisions became more feasible. States have expanded their acceptance of what can occur at the international level, including the incorporation into international law of measures related to the recovery of assets. Thus, addressing the financing of terrorism created a strengthened international AML regime and, indirectly, a political context in which a strengthened regime could be applied to other sensitive international issues involving the seizing and freezing of criminal assets, such as asset recovery in corruption cases.

States have expanded the AML regime to cover new types of crime, some only recently criminalized. They have increased the number of actions that national institutions must take to achieve compliance with international norms and standards. They have also expanded the range of professions and businesses that are now obliged to take responsibility for reporting suspicious financial transactions to the authorities.

The development of an international AML regime is not simply an attempt to codify at the global level existing national or regional norms and standards. Rather, it represents a major change in the way governments address transnational crime.

AML has been a fast-moving, dynamic policy area for more than a decade, as governments have gradually realized the full extent of the challenge of addressing transnational crime and as practitioners' experience has increased. Governments are still developing new ways to address money laundering, rejecting legal and institutional instruments that once seemed promising, and developing new ones. Many of the key approaches that states now apply were initiated only recently when, after 9/11, wider duties and powers of investigation were made available in many countries in relation to suppressing the financing of terrorism. Arguably, the United States passed the most wide-ranging national legislation to address terrorism in the aftermath of 9/11 with the acronym-friendly Uniting and Strengthening America by Providing Appropriate Tools Required to Intercept and Obstruct Terrorism Act (USA PATRIOT Act) of 2001. This legislation creates new crimes, new penalties, and new procedures to counter terrorism, including the financing of terrorism.[1] All other states have also found it necessary to pass new legislation to become compliant with international norms and standards on countering the financing of terrorism (CFT). Because most states are still in the process of incorporating these standards into national law, and all are still struggling to implement them, the full effects of these policies will not be understood for some time.

The expansion of AML has raised concerns. Civil liberties organizations have questioned the increased scrutiny of individuals' financial affairs that some governments have awarded themselves. The private sector has been apprehensive about the financial costs associated with a high level of transaction reporting. However, the rapid development of this international regime has also increased opportunities for greater security resulting from better international cooperation on criminal matters. Governments and international organizations have also acknowledged that money laundering is considered in the broadest sense as the technical means by which money is concealed for illicit purposes, not necessarily just to disguise its criminal origins but also its criminal destination.

QUANTIFYING THE UNQUANTIFIABLE: THE MAGNITUDE OF MONEY LAUNDERING

Attempts to quantify the global value of money laundering, and its effects on countries' economies, were popular in international organizations in the late 1990s, but results were inconclusive. For some governments, the value of quantifying money laundering was more than academic; it was seen as a crucial element of raising public and official awareness that could prompt other governments and other actors to comply with the emerging international AML norms and standards.

It has proved extraordinarily difficult. In 1998, the then-managing director of the International Monetary Fund (IMF), Michel Camdessus, remarked in a speech to the plenary of the Financial Action Task Force (FATF) that money laundering might be equivalent to 2% to 5% of global gross domestic product (GDP). Relying for its credibility on its source, this estimate is frequently cited as authoritative, although the IMF has never formally published it.

An FATF working group to estimate the magnitude of money laundering, which brought together several distinguished statisticians and criminologists, was disbanded in 2000 after its members failed to agree on a methodology for their calculations. An early IMF report, which noted that most of these empirical efforts focused on indirect macroeconomic-based estimates, provides a useful review of the literature, but is itself inconclusive, suggesting merely that the pervasiveness of money laundering may be sufficiently widespread in some countries to exert an independent impact on the macroeconomy.[2]

The problem lies in the lack of empirical data covering all crimes. Money that is laundered is essentially (although no longer exclusively) the proceeds of crime. As a U.N. report commented, "To date knowledge about the nature, structure and operation of illegal markets remains . . . rudimentary."[3]

Some countries do collect useful crime statistics and give a reasonable overview of domestic illegal markets. More is known about some large criminal markets than others. The United Nations, for example, publishes annual estimates of the value of illicit drug production from figures provided by its member states.[4] For some countries where the drug trade is economically important, these might provide a basis for estimates of money laundering at the national or regional level. The attorney general of Thailand, for example, estimated that more than 95% of money-laundering cases filed in 2003 involved drug trafficking.[5] Nevertheless, and notwithstanding the economic importance of the illicit drug market to the global "underground economy," this alone is obviously an inadequate basis for global estimates of money laundering.

It might be argued that estimates of money laundering resulting from large-scale corruption are likely to be more credible, because the investigations might deal with the transactions of only one or a few individuals through the formal financial system and thus be easier to track. The former Shah of Iran was alleged to have misappropriated some $35 million during the 25 years of his reign, largely disguised by foundations and charities. Papa Doc Duvalier and his son, Jean-Claude Duvalier, as presidents of Haiti from 1957 to 1986, were alleged to have extracted between $500 million and $2 billion from the state, an estimated 87% of government expenditure being paid directly or indirectly to Duvalier and his associates between 1960 and 1967. The case against family members of former president of the Philippines, Ferdinand Marcos, is still ongoing more than 15 years after he left office, amid allegations that he misappropriated at least $5 billion of state assets.[6]

More recently, a Pakistani court convicted the husband of former Pakistani Prime Minister Benazir Bhutto, Asif Ali Zardari, of accepting $9 million in kickbacks, and he is known to have channeled funds in excess of $40 million through Citibank private bank accounts between 1995 and 1997. In Nigeria, the late Sani Abacha and his associates are estimated to have removed funds from Nigeria of up to $5.5 billion, mainly from the oil sector. In Peru, a congressional investigation estimated that Vladimiro Montesinos, Peru's former head of intelligence and a close associate of former President Alberto Fujimori, might have acquired as much as $800 million from activities that included kickbacks from military procurement. To date, around $227 million, transferred abroad from Peru under the government of President Fujimori, has been frozen in five foreign countries, and $68 million has been recovered.[7] Former Ukrainian Prime Minister Pavlo Lazarenko is believed to have embezzled around $1 billion from the state while he was in office between 1994 and 1997. Now under arrest in the United States on charges of laundering some $114 million, Lazarenko has admitted to having laundered $5 million through Switzerland, which has repatriated almost $6 million to Ukraine.

Some of these figures are fairly specific, and those referring to amounts seized are verifiable, yet they leave us little closer to a global understanding of the magnitude of this particular set of crimes, let alone the global magnitude of money laundering. Consider an estimate of the Nyanga Declaration on the Recovery and Repatriation of Africa's Wealth: "An estimated $20–40 billion has over the decades been illegally and corruptly appropriated from some of the world's poorest countries, most of them in Africa, by politicians, soldiers, businesspersons and other leaders."[8] It is worth noting the lack of specificity in this statement with regard to the time frame, the countries where this action is alleged to have taken place, and the estimate itself.

The true global extent of money laundering and its economic effects remain virtually unknown. In the longer term, ever more powerful data analysis tools will improve some

states' capacity to undertake strategic analysis as part of their AML law enforcement effort that will advance understanding of illicit markets, which will then provide assistance for determining strategic approaches to transnational law enforcement efforts. Suffice it to say, enough is known now to acknowledge the importance of introducing measures to control money laundering.

THE MECHANISMS OF MONEY LAUNDERING

Money laundering has often been characterized as a three-stage process that requires (1) moving the funds from direct association with the crime, (2) disguising the trail to foil pursuit, and (3) making them available to the criminal once again with their occupational and geographic origins hidden from view.[9] Criminal money is frequently removed from the country in which the crime occurred to be cycled through the international payments system to obscure any audit trail. At the point of integration, criminal proceeds are fully integrated into the financial system and can be used for any purpose.[10] The proceeds of crime at the preliminary placement stage can be filtered initially through a variety of channels, particularly the cash-based retail service sector and businesses that deal in goods of high value, cash, or both, such as gold, gems, and works of art.

A cash-based retail service business—including car washes, laundries, game arcades, video rental stores, tanning salons, bars, and restaurants—remains one of the best covers for placing deposits inside a domestic financial system. Illegal money is mixed with legal, and the total is reported as the earning of a legitimate business.[11] Wire transfer services are used extensively in the money-laundering process, although many governments have recently adopted international standards requiring that the beneficial owner of funds be identified at all stages in the transfer process.

Currency exchange houses are somewhat more difficult to regulate. Remittance houses or financial services companies are used to cash bearer checks. Launderers can also use insurance companies by buying a life insurance policy with a large cash surrender benefit, paying the premium in cash, and later cashing the premium in for payment. Travel agencies and casinos are also used for this type of laundering. Corporate vehicles—including trusts and bearer shares—are misused for money laundering and other illicit activities, particularly those that provide anonymity to beneficial owners. These instruments are often put in place by professionals—lawyers and accountants—who act as financial intermediaries or provide expert advice to launderers.

At the second stage, money that has been moved overseas to disguise its origins in the formal financial system may spend at least part of its time in an offshore trust. In the Caribbean, the Pacific, and Europe, so-called offshore havens sell offshore corporations licensed to conduct business only outside the country of incorporation, free of tax or regulation and protected by secrecy laws. Money launderers have traditionally used offshore trusts in common law jurisdictions to hide and protect dirty money. One of the advantages of a trust is that the owner of the assets conveys ownership irrevocably to the trust, thus preventing the assets from seizure by creditors. Offshore trusts can have an additional level of protection from a "flee clause," which triggers the trustee to shift the domicile of the trust if it is threatened by, for example, war, civil unrest, or law enforcement. The asset protection trust was often offered in many former U.K. dependencies, before recent changes in banking laws. Use of such a trust might involve conveying assets to an offshore company, after which control of the company would be transferred to the offshore asset protection trust. The person transferring the assets would be appointed manager of the company, and the trust deed might stipulate that the

transferor of the assets has the right to buy them back again for a nominal sum, thereby respecting the letter of trusts law but undermining its spirit.[12]

Other forms of layering to disguise the trail of laundered money include capitalizing a company in bearer shares so that the owner of the physical shares is the owner of the company, and no other record of ownership exists. Efficient money laundering can involve layers of interlocking companies and multiple bank transfers, preferably from country to country.

The third stage of money laundering, integration, or making clean money available for use, can also be done in many ways. These include repatriating funds through a debit or credit card issued by offshore banks; casino "winnings," payable-through accounts in correspondent banks (now subject to much greater regulation than before); bogus capital gains on options trading; real estate scams; and so on.[13]

In the past 5 years, the international AML regime has acquired greater leverage to force countries to change their laws on banking secrecy and AML, which has changed the way that most countries regulate their financial systems. Some of the smaller jurisdictions that formerly offered recondite banking services have in effect, under international pressure, closed down their offshore facilities. The cavalier days of labyrinthine trust arrangements, numbered bank accounts, and accountants in shirtsleeves arriving at palm tree–sheltered banks in exotic jurisdictions with suitcases of cash are essentially over.

Generally speaking, the international AML regime that has produced far more regulated offshore sectors has been focused largely on formal financial transactions, with an emphasis on transaction reporting and due diligence. Newer international norms and standards have more recently tried to address the more intractable problems associated with money laundering that does not take place through banks and formal financial institutions. These include the use of nonprofit organizations (NPOs), charities, and casinos, as well as the actions of professional intermediaries, such as lawyers and accountants, to facilitate money laundering or the financing of terrorism. They have also signaled a renewed preoccupation with movements of cash.

Recent concern about the financing of terrorism has also prompted governments to turn their attention once more to the problems associated with cash-based forms of money laundering that evade the formal banking and financial institutions. They realized that individual terrorist operations can be relatively inexpensive and that it was relatively straightforward for a single individual to transport enough money in cash to fund a devastating attack. U.S. government officials estimated that the total cost of all the September 11 attacks was only $300,000 to $500,000.[14] Some countries have overwhelmingly cash-based economies and only a small financial sector; money laundering through banks is not perceived to be a serious problem. Some of the major predicate crimes to money laundering—illicit drug trafficking being the most obvious—still require the processing of large amounts of cash in the first stages of the money-laundering process. Associated with the challenges of tracing and seizing illicit cash is the use of jewels and gold as surrogate forms of cash. Being of high value, low weight, untraceable, and odorless, diamonds, where available, are a useful cash alternative. "According to the Congressional Research Service, a pound of diamonds in 2002 was worth around $225,000, compared with a pound of cash at $45,000, and a pound of gold at $4,800."[15]

The international community is also paying more attention to the problems associated with alternative remittance systems that, in many parts of the world, provide a crucial financial service. The alternative remittance systems or informal funds transfer systems (IFTSs), sometimes known as *hawala*, that are currently causing concern among policymakers and law enforcement, originated in Asia and predate formal banking systems. According to the U.S. Federal Bureau of Investigations (FBI), some of the funding available to the September 11 hijackers was transferred in and out of the United States using a *hawala*-type system.[16] Internationally, law enforcement has known and been concerned about *hawala* systems for years, but international measures to control such systems were put in place only after 9/11.

The FATF defines an alternative remittance system as

> a financial service that accepts cash, cheques or other monetary instruments or other stores of value in a location and pays a corresponding sum in cash or other form to a beneficiary in another location by means of a communication, message, transfer or through a clearing network to which the MVT (money or value transfer) service belongs.[17]

An Interpol report notes that the word *hawala* comes from the Arabic root for "transfer," but in Hindi and Urdu, it has come to mean "exchange of money" or even "trust" because of the great deal of trust required for the system to operate. A *hawala* broker has a network of international connections that he or she uses to arrange the delivery of money or value. No money crosses a border physically and no money enters the conventional banking system. The transaction rests on a single communication between *hawala* dealers and is often not recorded or guaranteed by written contract. The trust between the two bankers secures the debt and allows it to stand with no legal means of reclamation. The debt between the two bankers is eventually cleared, either by remittances requested in the reciprocal direction or through a variety of money movement methods.[18]

Alternative remittance systems are not necessarily an instrument for the transfer of the proceeds of crime or for the purposes of crime. Developed to facilitate trade, in many parts of the world, they are simply a faster, cheaper, and more convenient method of money transfer. Traditionally, a trader traveling abroad would take a letter of credit from a local banker, which in turn would be honored by a counterpart abroad. A small commission would be charged, and the two bankers would balance their books by trade. Underground bankers operated through legitimate businesses, shops, remittance houses, and money changers. For some in the Asian diaspora, this system of banking is the only viable method of remitting cash to relatives in remote rural areas, where formal banking systems are unavailable.

The alternative remittance system, however, also lends itself to other purposes, including all types of capital flight, tax avoidance, the circumvention of exchange controls, the avoidance of customs duties by over- and underinvoicing, smuggling, trafficking in human beings, and the financing of terrorism. A recent joint study by the International Monetary Fund and the World Bank recognized the *hawala* system's traditional role and the attractiveness of its operational characteristics—namely, speed, lower transaction costs, cultural convenience, versatility, and potential anonymity.[19] It found that IFTSs, as the international financial institutions prefer to call them, have important implications for implementing monetary fiscal and financial sector regulatory and supervisory policies—specifically that IFTS transactions could affect the composition of broad money with indirect effects on monetary policy and that they could influence exchange rate operations. The study recommended that efforts should be made to bring such systems closer to the formal financial sector without altering their specific nature even while, where possible, ensuring that *hawala* dealers are registered and keep adequate records.[20] The second approach with regard to regulation was to address the weaknesses in the formal financial sector that led customers to resort to IFTSs.

In international trade, settling accounts by means of a compensating balance works on the same principle as *hawala* and has been in use for as long as international trade has existed. Thus, a business may settle a debt with an overseas company by settling with a local company to which the overseas company owes money. The avoidance of international transactions, wire transfers, and so on, makes such a system useful for those with illicit purposes, yet, like *hawala*, it may also be used because it is cheaper and more convenient. International trade has long used ways to avoid taxes, tariffs, and customs duties, but there is some concern that money launderers will turn to trade to launder money as financial transactions become easier to trace and proceeds of crime become more vulnerable to seizure. Other forms of trade-based money laundering include over- and underinvoicing of imports and exports (a classic means to avoid value added tax, or VAT, but also useful in laundering proceeds of crime) and many other types of invoice fraud.

In the Western Hemisphere, the U.S. government identified the black market peso exchange (BMPE) as a key method of laundering drug money through trade. The Colombian cartels sell drug-tainted U.S. dollars to BMPE houses in Colombia in return for pesos. Once this currency exchange has occurred, the cartel has clean pesos and is out of the process. The peso broker in Colombia, meanwhile, begins the process of laundering the dollars by spending them on products such as cigarettes and electronics and returning the assets to Colombia in the form of imports.

In the medium term, governments might reasonably foresee the need to develop new policies and place a greater emphasis on policing cash-based money laundering, currency smuggling, money laundering by trade, and the many ways in which criminal money is transferred and laundered outside the financial system.

DEVELOPING INTERNATIONAL STANDARDS ON MONEY LAUNDERING

The international community began work on establishing an international AML regime in the late 1980s, starting with efforts to implement the proceeds of crime provisions in the U.N. Convention Against the Illicit Traffic in Narcotic Drugs and Psychotropic Substances in 1988 (the Vienna Convention). The first international treaty to address money laundering, the Vienna Convention covered only the proceeds of offenses related to illicit drug trafficking.

The purpose of addressing proceeds of crime in the Vienna Convention was as a means, to quote the convention's preamble, "to deprive persons engaged in illicit traffic of the proceeds of their criminal activities and thereby eliminate their main incentive for so doing."[21] The convention does not use the term "money laundering"—some U.N. member states were reluctant at the time to accept use of what was then a colloquial term in an international convention—nor does its scope go beyond drug-related offenses. Nevertheless, its legal framework was the basis for all subsequent policy. Almost all the countries of the world are parties to the Vienna Convention—168 as of April 2004—which entered into force in 1990.

As the convention was being opened for signature, the Basel Committee on Banking Supervision had turned its attention to the responsibilities of banks in the prevention of money laundering. In 1988, it issued the statement on Prevention of Criminal Use of the Banking System for the Purpose of Money-Laundering.[22] The statement recognized the risks of misuse of financial institutions for criminal purposes and issued guidance to banks in three main areas: the importance of proper customer identification, the need to comply with money-laundering laws, and the need to cooperate with law enforcement authorities. The details of best practice for customer identification are at the heart of AML and remain among the most heatedly debated technical issues in the prevention of money laundering.

The European Community adopted a money-laundering directive on June 10, 1991. Council Directive 91/308/EEC on prevention of the use of the financial system for the purpose of money laundering was aligned to the relevant provisions of the Vienna Convention on drug trafficking but gives member states the discretion to extend the directive's provisions to "any other criminal activity designated as such for the purposes of this Directive by each Member State" (Article 1).[23] The directive was later amended to compel member states to have in place legislation that covers all serious crimes.

The comprehensive technical framework of the international regime, however, is the 40 Recommendations of the FATF, first published in 1990 and revised in 1996 and 2003. The FATF, established by the G-7 group of countries, has become the key standards-setting body in the fight against money laundering. An intergovernmental body, it has 33 members—each of the European Union member states, Argentina, Australia, Brazil, Canada, Hong Kong, Iceland, Japan, Mexico, New Zealand, Norway, Russia, Singapore, South Africa, Switzerland, Turkey, and the United States, and two regional organizations, the European Commission and the Gulf Cooperation Council. It examines money-laundering techniques and trends and recommends ways of addressing them, reviews countries' legislative efforts and rate of implementation through a process of mutual evaluations, and recommends to countries measures that still need to be taken.

Meetings of the FATF focus on the technical issues associated with the drafting and implementation of standards. Finance ministry personnel with substantive knowledge, rather than diplomats, tend to lead delegations and, perhaps for this reason, the meetings are characterized by a technically skilled, informal, consensus-based approach that produces rapid and effective results. Nonmembers have criticized the FATF member states for having taken it on themselves to set international standards, to evaluate other countries' efforts, and to threaten nonmembers with sanctions for noncompliance, sometimes in circumstances where FATF members have themselves not been fully in compliance with the standards. The FATF response is that AML standards implemented by only a few countries or regions are ineffective and that critical weaknesses in national AML systems serve as obstacles to international cooperation. This idea is crucial for understanding the impetus for action on international criminal matters.

The FATF's Non-Cooperative Countries and Territories (NCCT) process was particularly controversial because it targeted non-FATF members that the FATF judged to be uncooperative in implementing international standards. The original list, released in June 2000, contained 15 countries and territories ranging from Russia to Nauru. By 2003, most had been removed following positive FATF evaluations. The NCCT process polarized some regional AML bodies that concluded that some of their members had been singled out unfairly. These bodies, set up in the FATF's image and known as FATF-style regional bodies, have tended to emphasize their independence of the FATF and, with regard to the NCCT process, they have often acted as a forum for dissent from the pace and form of international policy development, if not its content.[24] Notwithstanding the opposition, the NCCT process triggered a concern with the implementation of new laws and not just with their drafting and was highly effective in improving international AML compliance.

Gradually, standards such as those produced by the FATF and the Basel Committee on Banking Supervision have been given the weight of law in various U.N. conventions. In December 2000, the U.N. Convention Against Transnational Organized Crime (also known as the Palermo Convention) was opened for signature. It entered into force on September 29, 2003. The convention requires governments to put in place a full range of AML countermeasures, based on international standards and best practice, including financial system measures such as customer identification, record keeping, and reporting of suspicious transactions. Most important, it covers all serious crime, not just those crimes associated with drug trafficking.

During this period, there was increasing concern about abuse of the financial system in corruption cases, particularly large-scale corruption. Some countries wanted to introduce at the international level measures that would (a) prevent high-ranking government figures and their associates from transferring state assets to foreign bank accounts, (b) make it easier for governments to be granted freezing orders on those assets in foreign jurisdictions, and ultimately, (c) facilitate the return of money that had been already been stolen. There are now several international instruments linking the criminalization of such acts and money laundering. The Palermo Convention contained general provisions on the criminalization of corruption involving public officials and money laundering. The amended EU directive on money laundering also identifies corruption as a serious crime and thus a predicate offense to money laundering.[25] Others include the Convention on Laundering, Search, Seizure and Confiscation of the Proceeds from Crime and the Criminal Law Convention on Corruption of the Council of Europe, the Inter-American Convention Against Corruption of the Organization of American States, and the Convention on Combating Bribery of Foreign Public Officials in International Business Transactions of the Organization for Economic Co-operation and Development.

By September 2001, the pace of policy development on AML had slowed somewhat. The NCCT process had very effectively raised awareness. Many countries were drafting and redrafting AML and proceeds-of-crime laws. Technical assistance providers, such as the U.N. Office on Drugs and Crime (UNODC), were beginning to turn their attention to delivering technical assistance and training in implementation to states that were finding compliance with the international standards something of a challenge.

COMBATING THE FINANCING OF TERRORISM

After September 11, 2001, the focus shifted. Within weeks, the FATF, which had already established itself as the main international standard setter on AML, released eight special recommendations on terrorist financing.[26] This followed a suggestion from the European Union (EU) finance and economics ministers and the G7 finance ministers that such an initiative be pursued in the framework of measures already taken by the international community to combat money laundering. The FATF Special Recommendation 2 advises jurisdictions to include the financing of terrorism as a predicate offense to money laundering. Thus, CFT measures were linked to the existing AML regime.

Meanwhile, the United Nations condemned the terrorist attacks in the United States (Resolution 1368 [2001]) and, on September 28, 2001, the U.N. Security Council passed Security Council Resolution 1373—not the first, nor the last, Security Council Resolution to address the financing of terrorism but, arguably, the most important, because it characterized terrorism as a threat to international peace and security. This designation triggered the Security Council's option to invoke Chapter VII of the U.N. Charter, making the resolution immediately binding on all member states. Resolution 1373 also established the Counter-Terrorism Committee (CTC) to monitor implementation of the resolution as a whole, thus establishing a mechanism whereby states' CFT efforts could be assessed.

On April 10, 2002, the U.N. International Convention for the Suppression of the Financing of Terrorism entered into force. The speed with which countries ratified this convention illustrates the heightened commitment of the international community to combat terrorism. The convention had first been opened for signature in 1999, but 22 of the 26 ratifications needed for it to enter into force took place after the terrorist attacks on the United States.

The convention establishes three main obligations for states parties. First, it establishes the offense of financing of terrorism in criminal legislation. Second, it obliges states to engage in a wide range of cooperation with other states parties and provide them with legal assistance in matters relating to the convention. Third, it enacts requirements concerning the role of financial institutions in the detection and reporting of evidence in financing of terrorism acts. The convention also contains detailed provisions on mutual legal assistance and extradition that go much further than the nine previous antiterrorism conventions. Arguably, one of the convention's most significant contributions to the construction of an international regime on CFT is the establishment of a detailed framework for international cooperation in this area.

As with the AML regime, effective CFT implementation remains a challenge. The FATF, together with a G7 mandated body, the Counter-Terrorism Action Group (CTAG), has some responsibility for monitoring countries' compliance with new CFT standards. Under this system, which at the start of 2004 was still in a pilot phase, the FATF has been handed the task of coordinating the assessment of countries' technical assistance needs, reports of which will then be submitted to the CTAG.

It was understood that these reports would identify weaknesses in the international CFT regime and would then be used as a basis for the delivery of technical cooperation by G7 countries and international organizations to less compliant countries.

MONEY LAUNDERING AND CORRUPTION

The most recent expansion of the AML regime has occurred in relation to corruption and, in particular, to large-scale public corruption. This type of corruption, sometimes known as grand corruption, usually involves the embezzlement of state assets, including the direct transfer of funds from the public treasury to personal accounts, the physical theft of the state's gold stocks, the misappropriation of revenue and loans from international financial institutions, and in at least one case, the wholesale looting of furniture from the presidential palace.

The most successful individuals manage to organize a comprehensive range of illicit business activities involving the full range of illicit services on a grand scale: the awarding of contracts and concessions to foreign and domestic companies, the granting of economic monopolies to close associates, the soliciting of bribes in exchange for government employment, cash-for-favors, protection money from criminals, extortion, bank loans to political allies, electoral campaign contribution brokerage, and commodity smuggling.

These cases are distinguished from other forms of corruption in terms of their scale and the fact that those involved were public figures, their relatives, or their close associates. Where the individual's net worth increases during a period in public office to a far greater degree than can be explained by official earnings and income from prior assets, there is often a presumption that such funds were dishonestly obtained. The ability to distinguish between legal and illegal funds need not present insurmountable problems to freezing, forfeiture, and repatriation. Records are almost always incomplete, and it is usually impossible to attribute individual assets to specific offenses. However, cases have gone ahead with court rulings that the amount of legal funds formed only a minor portion of the total assets seized.

The theft of state assets by senior public figures has repeatedly occurred over many decades and, in some cases, can almost be regarded as traditional. Citizens might be bitter or cynical but are seldom surprised when new cases came to light. Popular protests are common but usually short-lived. Such cases, especially when the looting is spectacular, serve to reinforce low expectations about political leaders. To some degree, popular acceptance that the theft of state assets is inevitable, that leaders are incorrigible, or that they even have a certain entitlement, often grants this type of theft some legitimacy. Voters can often quite readily be persuaded to overlook the alleged corruption of former presidents when they decide to run again for election. Even in wealthy, developed countries, there can be apathy toward high-level corruption based on low expectations of integrity and probity.[27]

This poverty of expectation on the part of a country's voters explains why anticorruption work carried out by international organizations, including the United Nations, often focuses on broader issues related to governance and the rule of law, with the aim of improving state institutions as a whole and raising expectations about the political leadership. Similarly, much of the work of the nongovernmental organization Transparency International has to do with raising popular awareness and reducing public tolerance of all levels of corruption. These efforts may serve over time to improve institutions and culture. However, the successful repatriation of stolen assets can demonstrate in the most graphic manner that public officials cannot act with impunity, that electorates need not tolerate theft of their property by their own public representatives, and that the international community provides no safe havens for corrupt public figures.

THE ROLE OF THE BANKS

Banking regulation has traditionally existed primarily to ensure the stability of the financial system. Tests of due diligence and compliance with general regulations are not in themselves intended to be an aid to law enforcement in other matters but, rather, to guarantee the integrity of the banking system itself. Consequently, the decision to require financial institutions to establish and maintain reporting standards on suspicion of crimes has amounted, in effect, to a recruitment of the banking system in the service of law enforcement. Thus, the change in perspective required of financial institutions, created by the development of an international AML regime, should not be underestimated.

A major incentive for the banks to ensure that their institutions are compliant with international standards is reputational risk. Their capacity to attract and retain customers depends largely on their maintaining credibility and a reputation for financial probity. In addition to reputational risk, financial institutions without effective due diligence on AML are also exposed to the risk of possible restitution claims from national governments and private individuals and even to criminal changes of money laundering against employees or the financial institution itself. In November 2002, U.S. bank Broadway National Bank pleaded guilty to three felony charges for failing to file suspicious activity reports on $123 million in cash deposits and for failing to establish an AML program, and was fined $4 million.[28]

A decade ago, the notion of serious reputational damage for major banks as a consequence of a failure to identify and control the large-scale illegal transfer of funds by corrupt public officials was largely hypothetical. The attitudes of the banks have changed since then. Citicorp CEO John Reed wrote a letter to the Board of Directors in November 1997 after the U.S. Department of Justice had interviewed him about the Salinas (see below) case, in which he commented:

> I am more than ever convinced that we have to rethink and reposition the Private Banking business. . . . Much of our practice that used to make good sense is now a liability. We live in a world where we have to worry about "how someone made his/her money" which did not used to be an issue. Much that we had done to keep Private Banking private becomes "wrong" in the current environment.[29]

The allegations of massive corruption attributed to the family of former Nigerian President Sani Abacha highlighted once more the role of commercial banks as facilitators of large-scale illegal transfers of funds involving public officials, their families and associates. The banking system's increasing vulnerability is a consequence of the vastly increased volume of business and the improved technology that facilitates it. Increased international commitment to AML measures, as well as a number of high-profile corruption cases, has exposed the banks as never before to external scrutiny.

In the Abacha case, the Swiss Federal Banking Commission took the unusual step of naming the banks it determined had failed to practice due diligence and of identifying the ways in which they had failed.[30] The Abacha case differed from earlier large-scale corruption cases in the degree to which blame was apportioned to the failures of the international banking system. In March 2001, the U.K. Financial Services Authority (FSA) calculated that $1.3 billion of transactions linked to Abacha were conducted through 23 banks, including London branches of foreign banks.

At 15 of the banks, the FSA found significant weaknesses in AML controls, although it declined to name them.

Much of the recent scrutiny has focused, in particular, on the use by corrupt public figures of private banking operations, the range of bespoke (custom-made) banking services that banks and financial institutions offer to wealthy individuals. Private banking operations offer financial services to high-net worth individuals who would usually have around $1 million or more as a minimum deposit. Traditionally, Switzerland has had the largest private banking operations in the world, but major banks are all attracted to the business as a highly profitable concern, offering returns twice as high as many other banking areas. Worldwide total assets currently under management by private banks have been estimated at $15.5 billion. Nevertheless, a private bank account is only one potential destination for looted state assets and the one that has received most recent scrutiny and regulation. Securities brokers and dealers, for example, are also engaged in private bank-type activities but are not subject to the same regulations. The banking system as a whole offers a wealth of services for such purposes. The regulatory practices of Citigroup's private banking business have come under U.S. congressional scrutiny in three other cases, besides that of Abacha: Raúl Salinas, brother of former Mexican President Carlos Salinas; President Omar Bongo of Gabon; and Asif Ali Zardari, husband of former Pakistani Prime Minister Benazir Bhutto.[31] The study found several factors that facilitated the use of private banking by corrupt public figures wishing to deposit large sums of money. They were (a) that private bankers acted as client advocates; (b) that the clients were often extremely powerful; (c) that there was a culture of secrecy, secrecy jurisdictions, and secrecy restrictions on U.S. bank regulators; and (d) that there was a culture of lax AML controls. Citigroup and others have since changed their policies on customer due diligence.

Money laundering via correspondent banking has also attracted official concern.[32] Correspondent banking involves the provision of banking services by one bank (the correspondent bank) to another bank (the respondent bank), thus allowing banks to undertake international financial transactions in jurisdictions where they have no physical presence. Correspondent banking is a key feature of the international payment system, but those characteristics that make it highly effective—speed and geographic availability—also make it a potentially useful means of money laundering. In the past, financial transactions could be rendered invisible through the use of a payable-through account. Instead of securing a license to operate in one country, a foreign bank could open a correspondent master account with a bank in the host country and allow its clients to draw checks on the bank's master account. The account remains legally in the name of the foreign bank.[33] A large bank might have hundreds or even thousands of correspondent relationships. The Senate report found that "high-risk foreign banks" had been able to open correspondent accounts at any U.S. bank and conduct their operations through their U.S. accounts, and argued that this was because U.S. banks had failed to adequately screen and monitor the foreign banks as clients. The United Nations has noted that correspondent accounts "can provide the owners and clients of a poorly regulated, and even corrupt, bank with the ability to move money freely around the world."[34]

International standards have also been introduced to take account of so-called higher-risk customers or politically exposed persons, in particular the *Guidance on Customer Due Diligence for Banks* from the Basel Committee on Banking Supervision, which recommends enhanced know-your-customer (KYC) regulations to establish the identity of customers and monitor their financial activity.

Recommendation VII of the revised FATF 40 recommendations, adopted in June 2003, recommends that banks carry out additional due diligence before entering into a relationship with a correspondent bank, which would include the nature of its business, its reputation, and the quality of its supervision. With regard to payable-through accounts, the bank should be satisfied that the respondent bank has verified the identity and is performing ongoing due diligence on the client.

KYC principles are at the core of AML regulation in the financial sector. These standards confer responsibility on financial institutions to establish the identity of all beneficiaries of an account and to monitor account activity. Institutions are required to file suspicious transaction reports to the competent authorities when they encounter unusual or suspicious activity.

Criteria that establish that KYC requirements are satisfied have evolved over time as a result of experience, developing technology, and public pressure. Yet global implementation is uneven. According to the Bank for International Settlements (BIS), owned by the world's leading central banks, "KYC policies in some countries have significant gaps and in others they are non-existent."[35]

Changes to guidelines and regulations have sometimes met with resistance from some international financial centers and banks, on the basis that the changes threaten the confidentiality of their client relationships. The banking sector has preferred to introduce voluntary codes of conduct. The BIS claims that its KYC rules are wider than the FATF guidelines. In particular, in response to the poor publicity that the U.S. congressional hearings on private banking generated, a group of 12 major banks, which together accounted for around one third of the world's private banking funds, met at Wolfsberg, Switzerland, in October 2000, and agreed on a set of voluntary principles specifically for their private banking operations[36]—the Global Anti-Money Laundering Guidelines for Private Banking (known as the Wolfsberg Principles). Again,

the guidelines emphasized the importance of KYC.

In November 2002, the Wolfsberg Group of financial institutions established a second set of guidelines, this time for AML controls for correspondent banking relationships. The Wolfsberg Group guidelines also bar its members from doing business with shell banks. Keen to avoid a situation in which a bank might have to take responsibility for the integrity of each individual client of its correspondent banking client, the guidelines take a risk-based approach. This involves assessing the depth of due diligence required on a corresponding banking client by examining its domicile, ownership and management structures, business portfolio, and client base.

At the national level, some governments have demanded more due diligence for political leaders. In Switzerland, for example, banks have been obliged since May 1, 1992, to issue internal directives on money laundering, provide staff training, and establish an AML unit. However, Switzerland also has specific measures to deal with the problems of holding accounts for foreign public officials: Swiss banks have had in place policies aimed at avoiding money linked to corruption since the scandals surrounding President Marcos of the Philippines. Since 1987, the Swiss Federal Banking Commission (SFBC) has stipulated that when banks carry out important public functions for a foreign state, they must have internal directives that set out the business policy in connection with such persons. In Switzerland, since May 1, 2000, the intentional acceptance of funds that belong to foreign holders of office and that stem from corruption also renders the bank liable to prosecution.

The U.S. government released advice to banks on January 16, 2001, specifically to deal with the problem of possibly illegal transfers of funds made by corrupt foreign officials and their families and associates. The *Guidance on Enhanced Security on Transactions That May*

Involve the Proceeds of Foreign Official Corruption offers advice on how to build on existing due diligence and AML programs by outlining procedures that banks can use to get information on accounts held by foreign officials. After 9/11, the USA PATRIOT Act criminalized laundering in the United States of the proceeds of foreign political corruption.[37]

PROBLEMS ASSOCIATED WITH THE REPATRIATION OF ASSETS

International investigations to recover funds derived from corruption require authorities to institute legal proceedings to win legal title to assets. Recovery actions can take many forms, including (a) criminal proceedings in the state of origin (the requesting state), with enforcement of the sentence in the state where the funds are located (the requested state); (b) civil proceedings in the requesting state followed by international enforcement of the judgment; (c) criminal or civil proceedings initiated by the requested state leading to forfeiture of the property either to the requesting state directly or to the requested state (which may then share the assets); (d) civil proceedings initiated by the requesting state in the courts of the requested state; or (e) a combination of the above.[38]

In addition, there may be political considerations in large-scale asset recovery cases that help determine their outcome. In the past, many observers claimed that geopolitical concerns sometimes affected the outcome of such cases. Banks tried to justify holding the accounts of overtly corrupt leaders because of the apparent tolerance of those leaders by other governments. It was sometimes claimed that requested countries holding assets were reluctant to assist in recovery efforts because they regarded the new government as hostile.

In effect, serious political considerations will always condition how far a country will modify its legislative framework and its policies to facilitate asset recovery. One rule of thumb is that where a destination country has demonstrated the political will to establish an effective AML regime, it will generally be in a position to undertake a role in asset recovery.

Nevertheless, the pressing of criminal charges against a former head of government will, of necessity, involve complex political considerations for the international community. An urgent instance is that of Slobodan Milosevic who, with his close associates, has been accused of generating illegal funds of at least $1 billion during his 1989 to 2000 period in power in Yugoslavia.

Key problems include the diversity of legal systems, the inability of some requesting states to devote scarce resources to fund a complex and lengthy international case, and the lack of responsiveness of requested states. The central legal problems often involve matters of jurisdiction and territoriality. Where legal systems are incompatible, particularly when cases involve cooperation between civil and common law systems, cooperation is difficult. Mutual legal assistance treaties have proved cumbersome and ineffective when the object is to trace assets as quickly as possible. Overcoming jurisdictional problems slows down investigations, often fatally. By the time investigators get access to documents in another jurisdiction, the funds have moved elsewhere.

The propriety of civil forfeiture is a central legal difficulty in asset recovery cases. Recovery actions, involving the freezing and confiscation of illicitly transferred assets, straddle the boundary between criminal and civil proceedings.[39] Criminal proceedings are generally more effective in terms of the remedy available, but they involve a far higher burden of proof than do civil proceedings. By contrast, civil forfeiture, with a lower burden of proof and fewer legal safeguards, is far more efficient in terms of process—and is essential to the success of many complex cases—but is not recognized by many national legal systems.

Bank secrecy in some jurisdictions still inhibits investigation. Jurisdictions will, in all likelihood, have been chosen precisely because they offer some sort of legal shield against investigation. Legal obstacles to investigation and the operation of one country's law enforcement in another's jurisdiction also complicate an already complicated operation.

There can be legal problems related to due process and evidentiary requirements. Requested countries can vary somewhat in their degree of responsiveness, determined by their own legislative framework. Courts in requested countries often set preconditions about convictions before agreeing to freeze assets or transfer frozen assets to the requesting country. They might demand that the requesting country file a criminal charge or bring a forfeiture proceeding against the individual in question in order to keep the assets frozen, that a final decision be made on criminal prosecution or forfeiture to permit repatriation, and that these proceedings comply with the requested state's own procedural requirements of due process. The courts might also want to establish that proceedings in the requesting countries satisfy human rights principles. Many requesting countries have found some or all of these requirements difficult to fulfill.

In the Abacha case, some efforts to freeze funds in foreign jurisdictions have been prevented by Nigeria's failure to meet requested countries' criteria. The United Kingdom has said that, although willing in principle, it cannot freeze up to $1 billion in accounts belonging to the Abacha family thought to be held in British bank accounts until it receives sufficient information to clarify the nature of criminal proceedings in Nigeria against Mohammed Abacha, son of the late dictator. Abacha family funds have been frozen in Switzerland, Liechtenstein, Luxembourg, and Jersey.

Swiss policy and legislation on responding to requests for the freezing of assets has changed markedly over the years since 1986, partly as a result of the Marcos case. In the late 1980s, the SFBC sought actively to uphold the principle of bank secrecy in relation to the Marcos case, but by 2000 was publicly naming banks that had failed in regulating the accounts of the Abacha family. Key changes to Swiss law, including changes to Article 74 of its mutual assistance law, which allows "anticipatory restitution" in exceptional circumstances, has made Switzerland more responsive to requests than most other jurisdictions.

The complexity of such cases is inevitable. Large amounts of money have usually been acquired by many different means, hidden in multiple accounts in multiple locations, often under multiple identities. A variety of different financial instruments will have been used, some of which will be highly sophisticated. Funds will have been transferred directly from the central bank to public officials' private accounts in some countries. However, arrangements are usually far more intricate. Companies owned by a political leader or his family sometimes control, often at several removes, key aspects of the economy, such as oil revenue. When Sani Abacha was in power, he was estimated to have personally controlled Nigeria's oil sector, which produces more than 90% of the country's foreign earnings.

The state, for obvious reasons, will give an incomplete record of the theft. The corrupt individuals are likely, as in the Marcos case, to have taken steps to destroy evidence of their financial dealings. A rare exception to this rule is the recent case of Vladimiro Montesinos who, as head of Peru's intelligence service, secretly recorded more than 2,000 videotapes of his business dealings, thus leaving a permanent record of his own allegedly corrupt activities and those of many key members of the Peruvian political elite.

Financial institutions through which the money moved will not easily be able to furnish a record of all relevant transactions. Each case is likely to have involved many banks. According to the SFBC, Abacha funds flowed from Swiss banks alone to 524 banks in

Liechtenstein, the United States, the United Kingdom, and Luxembourg. Moreover, recent cases have shown that even where banks have acted with all due diligence to regulate the accounts of suspect public officials, they do not have the capacity to aggregate all financial information about the individual, particularly when the individual is deliberately subverting the banks' own systems.

One of the most important obstacles to seeking out illegal funds and securing their repatriation is lack of capacity in the requesting (and sometimes the requested) country. Short-comings in judicial, administrative, or investigative capacity seriously impede the degree to which a country can undertake such a case successfully, although such cases are almost always of a complexity that would challenge even the most well-functioning state institutions.

Many of the capacity problems lie in the requesting country. Basic record keeping is a problem in some legal systems. Nigeria has said that much of the documentary evidence about the Abacha era is proving extremely difficult to uncover, if it exists at all. In Peru last year, Special Prosecutor José Ugaz, investigating allegations against Vladimiro Montesinos, said he could not carry out an investigation until Congress passed a law barring suspects from leaving the country. The United Nations also received reports that at one stage Ugaz's office did not even have sufficient funds to pay for translations of the letters to the Swiss authorities seeking official information about suspect accounts.

The demands on investigative resources are huge and raise serious problems of international case management. Investigators involved in such cases point out that the usual procedures for tracking assets are simply not strong enough or proactive enough for the demands of these massive international cases and that new procedures need to be put in place.

Much of what can be done in relation to the repatriation of assets depends on the resources available to fund the case. Cases will almost certainly last for several years, and parties to the action are likely to be determined by their ability to fund litigation. It has never been entirely clear how the Marcos family has been able to fund teams of lawyers acting on its behalf against the Philippines government for 15 years, given that their assets in the Philippines, the United States, and Switzerland were frozen in 1986.

The success rates of such cases, when viewed overall, is not encouraging. Most take years to conclude, and all are extremely expensive. It is rare that more than a small proportion of the illegal funds is repatriated to the country from which it was stolen, and the degree of success in repatriating some assets hardly seems commensurate with the years of work and the expense incurred. Legal actions related to the collapse of Bank of Credit and Commerce International (BCCI) took place in 50 to 60 countries, but fewer than 40% were successful. In the Marcos case, after 15 years, only $600 million (much of that interest on the original sum) of more than $5 billion lies in escrow in the Philippines National Bank, and the case shows no signs of being concluded.

Operations that seek to recover state assets are complex, expensive, and time-consuming. Solutions to specific problems are reached on an ad hoc basis, depending on the countries involved and the nature of the case. There are few practitioners in either public or private practice with experience of this type of work, and in many jurisdictions, there is no one at all. Countries impoverished by corruption may lack the financial resources to undertake the costly financial investigations necessary. Many who work in this field perceive a need for innovative legal and administrative procedures and mechanisms that could assist in this type of case. In light of this, the U.N. Convention Against Corruption provides interesting and remarkably detailed mechanisms for addressing some of the existing problems. The challenge for states, as with the AML/CFT regime, lies in the implementation.

NOTES

1. The act expands the government's authority to regulate the activities of U.S. financial institutions, particularly their relations with foreign individuals and entities. It also introduces a number of new crimes, including laundering in the United States of any of the proceeds from foreign crimes of violence or political corruption, and the laundering of proceeds from cybercrime. Charles Doyle, *The USA PATRIOT Act: A Sketch* (Congressional Research Service, Library of Congress, 2002), www.fas.org/irp/crs/RS21203. pdf (accessed April 2, 2004).

2. Peter J. Quirk, "Macroeconomic Implications of Money Laundering" (IMF Working Paper 96/66, International Monetary Fund, Washington D.C., April 1996).

3. Jack A. Blum, Michael Levi, R. Thomas Naylor, and Phil Williams, *Financial Havens, Banking Secrecy and Money-Laundering* (New York: United Nations, 1998), p. 8. Full text available online in English, French, and Spanish at www.imolin.org/research.htm. This report from United Nations Office for Drug Control and Crime Prevention (UNODCCP—now the United Nations Office on Drugs and Crime [UNODC]) still offers some of the best analysis available of the various ways in which the international financial system can be subverted for the purposes of money laundering.

4. United Nations Office on Drugs and Crime (UNODC), *Global Illicit Drug Trends 2003* (Vienna: UNODC), p. 27. Available online at www.unodc.org/pdf/report_2003-06-26_1_executive_summary.pdf.

5. *The Nation*, January, 5, 2004.

6. A 1989 Racketeer Influenced and Corrupt Organization (RICO) Act claim brought in California estimated that the assets amounted to $5 billion. However, a Manila newspaper reported that in February 2001, Marcos's daughter attempted to move $13.2 billion from an account with the United Bank of Switzerland to Deutsche Bank in Dusseldorf, Germany.

7. U.N. General Assembly, Ad Hoc Committee for the Negotiation of a Convention against Corruption, "Global Study on the Transfer of Funds of Illicit Origin, Especially Funds Derived From Acts of Corruption" (Vienna: United Nations, November 28, 2002), p. 3. Available online at www.unodc.org/pdf/crime/convention_corruption/session_4/12e.pdf.

8. Signed on March 4, 2001, by representatives of Transparency International, a nongovernmental organization, in Botswana, Cameroon, Ethiopia, Ghana, Kenya, Malawi, Nigeria, South Africa, Uganda, Zambia, and Zimbabwe.

9. Blum et al. (1998), p. 4.

10. The Vienna Convention refers to the conversion (of cash to another asset) or transfer of property, and concealment or disguise of the true nature, source, location, disposition, movement, rights with respect to, or ownership of property, knowing that such property was derived from an offense and creation of a perception of legitimacy. The Financial Action Task Force refers to the three-stage descriptive model of placement (of cash into the legal economy or out of the country), layering (creation of complex structures to conceal origins of the cash), and integration (returning laundered funds to the licit economy). Blum et al. (1998), p. 4. The academic literature has produced several other analytical models, including division of the phenomenon into three sets of techniques: those designed to circumvent or corrupt legal AML control mechanisms, those designed to disguise the illicit origin of the property, and those designed to hide the true identity of the owner of the assets. Oliver Stolpe, Strategien gegen das Organisierte Verbrechen (Köln, Berlin, München: Carl Heymanns Verlag KG, 2004), pp. 67–70.

11. Blum et al. (1998), p. 8.

12. Blum et al. (1998), p. 9.

13. Blum et al. (1998), p. 10–11.

14. U.S. General Accounting Office (GAO), *Terrorist Financing: U.S. Agencies Should Systematically Assess Terrorists' Use of Alternative Financing Mechanisms* (Washington, DC: U.S. GAO, 2003), p. 6. Available online at www.gao.gov/new.items/d04163.pdf.

15. U.S. GAO (2003), p. 20, note 35.

16. U.S. GAO (2003), p. 19.

17. Financial Action Task Force (FATF), "Combatting the Abuse of Alternative Remittance Systems: International Best Practices," Special Recommendation VI (SR VI) (Paris, France: FATF/GAFI, 2003). Available online at www1.oecd.org/fatf/pdf/SR6-BPP_en.pdf. The FATF issued an interpretative note to SR VI in February 2003.

Available online at www1.oecd.org/fatf/pdf/INSR6_en.pdf.

18. Lisa C. Carroll, "Alternative Remittance Systems Distinguishing Sub-Systems of Ethnic Money Laundering in Interpol Member Countries in the Asian Continent" (Lyon, France: Interpol). Available online at www.interpol.int/Public/FinancialCrime/MoneyLaundering/EthnicMoney/default.asp.

19. Mohammed El Qorchi, Samuel Munzele Maimbo, and John F. Wilson, *Informal Funds Transfer Systems: An Analysis of the Informal Hawala System* (IMF Occasional Paper No. 222, International Monetary Fund, Washington D.C., 2003).

20. The interpretative note to SR VI (see note 17) recommends that jurisdictions license or register *hawala* dealers, ensure that their services are subject to the relevant FATF recommendations, and ensure that they can impose sanctions on such services for failure to comply with them.

21. United Nations Convention Against the Illicit Traffic in Narcotic Drugs and Psychotropic Substances (Vienna: United Nations, 1988), p. 1. Available online at www.unodc.org/pdf/convention_1988_en.pdf.

22. See www.bis.org/publ/bcbsc137.pdf for this document.

23. Published in the *Official Journal of the European Communities* (OJEC) L 166/77 (June 28, 1991): 0077–0082.

24. Regional bodies in the fight against money laundering include the Asia-Pacific Group on Money Laundering (APGML), the Caribbean Financial Action Task Force (CFATF), the Grupo de Acción Financiera de Sudamérica (GAFISUD), Moneyval of the Council of Europe, and the Eastern and Southern Africa Anti-Money Laundering Group (ESAAMLG).

25. On December 4, 2001, the European Union adopted Directive 2001/97/EC of the European Parliament and of the council, amending Council Directive 91/308/EEC dealing with money laundering.

26. For the text of the eight special recommendations, see www.fatf-gafi.org/SRecsTF_en.htm.

27. Tim King, "French Favours," *Prospect* (2004, January), pp. 24–31.

28. Robert F. Worth, "Bank Failed to Question Huge Deposits." *New York Times,* November 28, 2002, p. 1.

29. Quoted in U.S. Senate, Committee on Governmental Affairs, Permanent Subcommittee on Investigations, *Private Banking and Money Laundering: A Case Study of Opportunities and Vulnerabilities,* 106th Congress, 1st session, November 9 and 10, 1999, 888.

30. Swiss Federal Banking Commission (SFBC), *Abacha Funds at Swiss Banks: Report of the Swiss Federal Banking Commission* (Bern: SFBC, September 4, 2000). Available online at www.ebk.admin.ch/e/archiv/2000/neu14a-00.pdf.

31. See Worth, "Bank Failed to Question, 2002."

32. U.S. Senate, *Minority Staff of the U.S. Senate Permanent Committee on Investigations Report on Correspondent Banking: A Gateway to Money Laundering,* February 5, 2001. Available online at www.senate.gov/~gov_affairs/psi_finalreport.pdf.

33. Blum et al. (1998), p. 10.

34. U.N. General Assembly (2002), p. 6.

35. Bank for International Settlements, *Customer Due Diligence for Banks* (Basel Committee Publications No. 85, Basel, Switzerland, October 2001), para. 2. Available online at www.bis.org/publ/bcbs85.pdf.

36. The signatory banks are ABN AMRO Bank N.V.; Banca Commerciale Italiana; Banca del Gottardo; Banco Santander Central Hispano, S.A.; Barclays Bank; The Chase Manhattan Private Bank; Citibank, N.A.; Credit Suisse Group; Deutsche Bank AG; HSBC; J. P. Morgan Société Générale; and UBS AG.

37. Doyle (2003), p. 4.

38. U.N. General Assembly (2002), p. 7.

39. U.N. General Assembly (2002), p. 9.

6

The Illicit Traffic in Plundered Antiquities

CHRISTINE ALDER

KENNETH POLK

For centuries, the antiquities of some countries have been illegally removed and transported transnationally to fill the collections of private purchasers and museums. This chapter examines this international traffic in antique cultural material that has been illegally removed from its cultural setting. Of fundamental concern is the illicit removal from a country of material that is defined as being important to the cultural heritage of that nation or to humankind more generally. Although there is some variation cross-nationally in the definition of *antique*, here the common legal definition of antique as referring to material more than 100 years old will be used. Most objects of concern in this chapter are in fact chapter are much older.

Cultural material is a considerably more complicated term. Much of the material being referred to is considered in developed countries as "art," and the items are likely to be found in art museums. The material covers such a wide range of objects that it is difficult to include them all within one definition (see Conklin, 1994). A recent example is the illegal removal from Italy of 18th- and 19th-century paintings, which were subsequently destined for international auction houses (Watson, 1997). Also covered by the use of the term *cultural material* are archaeological objects from ancient cultures. The material might consist of any items extracted from a site that were part of the life of a past civilization. For example, plundered items from ancient sites have included pottery

AUTHORS' NOTE: The authors would like to acknowledge the support of Professor Elmar Weitekamp and the Department of Criminal Law and Criminology of the Faculty of Law of the University of Leuven (KUL), Belgium, while we were preparing this chapter.

and weapons from Native American sites in the United States, woven materials and gold objects from pre-Columbian sites in Latin America, stone and ceramic material from tombs in China, and stone sculptures from the Khmer sites in Cambodia.

The contemporary traffic in these objects is definitively an international problem (although some of the traffic in such objects may be within one nation, as in the case of Native American objects in the United States or the trade in Roman objects found and traded in England). The fundamental cause of the plunder is the demand for cultural material exerted by the rich market states. This demand exerts an inexorable pull on the cultural resources of the often poor nations that are the source of much of the highly valued cultural goods. Huge sums of money are exchanged in market centers such as New York, London, and Paris for objects illegally extracted from poorer nations around the globe. The consequence is the destruction of the cultural heritage of the source nation and of the cultural heritage of humankind more generally. It is the present argument that as long as that demand is allowed to continue, it will be virtually impossible to develop an effective campaign to stop the plunder. A major purpose of the present discussion, therefore, is to provide an exploration of the dynamics of this traffic as an international market problem.

A BRIEF HISTORICAL OVERVIEW

As the major developed nations expanded their colonial dominions, it was a commonly accepted practice to bring back to the colonial centers objects obtained from the empire. Often, these objects found their way into the major public collections in these countries and can today be appreciated in the major museums of the world, such as the Metropolitan Museum in New York, the British Museum in London, or the Louvre in Paris.

Individuals, too, often considered "tasteful collecting" as one of the major pastimes of

travel in the newly conquered nations or recently established colonies. In fact, this practice has an even longer history. For example, an appreciation of cultural heritage was highly refined in ancient China, where collections of antique relics were often placed in tombs as part of the most valued items of the deceased. The appreciation of such material is recorded, for example, in a Chinese painting from the late 15th century with the title translated into English as "Enjoying Antiquities" (Hearn, 1997, p. 98). Young English gentlemen enjoying their grand tour of Europe in the 18th and 19th centuries often returned carrying cultural objects and items that provided a demonstration of both their wealth and taste.

Collecting and enjoying the artistic features of material from other cultures, in short, has been an important part of our intellectual heritage This appreciation continues to flourish today as demonstrated by the huge crowds attracted to the major museum collections in New York, London, or Paris. In fact, the long tradition of collecting has created a climate of legitimacy around the gathering of these goods that lingers and results in considerable confusion and debate when steps are designed to restrict or prohibit the removal of cultural material from source locations. Furthermore, as measures have evolved in recent years to stop contemporary plunder, major questions have been raised about the appropriateness of earlier practices of removal by the colonial powers, as can be seen in the notable international debate regarding the demands by Greece for the return by England of the Parthenon marbles (Conklin, 1994, pp. 133–134).

CONTEMPORARY FORMS OF THE PROBLEM

The illicit traffic in antiquities operates as an international market where demand from the developed economies results in the transfer of material from source environments. One point to start the analysis, then, is to examine the process whereby the material is initially removed from its context at the source. Virtually all nations that are the source of plundered antiquities today define the unauthorized removal of cultural material as a crime, either by terming the extraction of the objects as a form of theft or by prohibiting the export of the material from the country of origin (or both).

The actual nature of the removal of cultural heritage varies considerably according to the strength of law enforcement, the probability of detection, the nature of the contexts, and the goods being plundered. In some locations where there is more vigorous enforcement, the plunderers may be forced to work at night with a high degree of caution and secrecy, as is the case with the *tombaroli* (tomb robbers) in Italy and some of the tomb robbers in Peru. In remote impoverished sites in countries such as Cambodia, Thailand, or countries in Africa where enforcement is less vigorous, an affluent antiquities dealer may hire a large number of local farmers to plunder a site, often digging up a vast quantity of material in a relatively short (and destructive) time. One antiquities shop in the Southeast Asia region has a picture of such an operation pasted over the display case of the objects being sold, as if to provide some verification that the material has actually been dug from the ground and thereby providing provenance of the goods. In some instances, as when a whole tomb is plundered, there may be a great number of objects taken, whereas in other situations only one object may be involved, as in the robbery of paintings from churches in Italy. Although worldwide the potential penalties faced by plunderers generally are slight, in some cases the stakes are much higher, as in China where tomb robbers, nearly always peasants, may face capital punishment if they are caught.

As is the case with any international illicit market, obtaining the raw material is but a first step. In the case of antiquities, most systematic trade activity is handled in the country of origin by agents, commonly closely linked to antiquities dealers in either source or market countries. These agents in general must have the resources necessary to purchase the goods from those who have done the plundering, and they must have contacts with the marketplace. In addition, they must be knowledgeable about the market, including (a) how the market works and the selling prices of various kinds of objects, (b) some knowledge of the goods themselves so that they are able to rank goods in terms of their quality, and (c) knowledge about the procedures required to remove the objects from their country of origin—that is, contacts with smugglers.

Movement of illicit goods across national boundaries requires two elements. First, there will be networks of smugglers who are able to move goods illicitly from one country to another. In the case of antiquities, there are some known instances where the smugglers involved move not only cultural heritage material but other illicit goods, such as drugs, as well. A recent television program on stolen art showed a customs checkpoint coming out of Turkey where the border officials were removing both illicit drugs and plundered antiquities from a smuggler's van. In most circumstances, especially in terms of the movement of material from Asia and Southeast Asia, it would appear that the smugglers are specialists in moving antiquities, with relatively narrowly defined routes for movement of goods from one country to another. In the case of China, for example, the smuggling routes run primarily from China through Macau or Hong Kong. In Cambodia, much of the material first crosses into Thailand, where it is then passed through centers such as Bangkok or Chiang Mai and then on to the market centers.

The second requirement of such traffic, to ensure consistent success, is that there will most often be some level of corruption of law enforcement and customs officials. In some countries, the large amount of resources involved in the trade in cultural heritage material suggests high-level political involvement in such corruption. In Asia, according to some sources, this can involve top-ranking military officers who often have unique access to the kinds of machines (including trucks, cranes, containers, container vehicles, and even aircraft) that ease the movement of such goods across borders and from source to destination.

The trade in antiquities, like drugs, tends to be differentiated. Just as there are different market patterns for drugs such as cocaine, heroin, and marijuana, so, too, are there different sources, distribution routes, patterns of smuggling, and ultimate market activities for antiquities. Historically, for example, there was a mainstream of traffic of pre-Columbian material that went from Latin America, through to North America, and then outward to a wider international market. In recent years, there has been a vigorous market in material from Africa that moves through markets located in France and Belgium.

Up to this point, the traffic in antiquities looks like many other illicit markets such as the traffic in drugs or human beings, in that there are illegal source activities, smuggling, and corruption. However, there is one fundamental difference. In contrast to other illegal markets, in the case of the trade in cultural material, the trade at the market or demand end is open and quite legal. The goods that may result in the shooting of a peasant looter in China are sold openly, often in very elite establishments, in demand centers such as London, New York, or Paris. This is not a trade, like drugs, where the ultimate market activity is as illicit and hidden as the production and transport processes of the material being sold. In some cases, the prices asked are extraordinary, and as a consequence, the purchasers represent the social and economic elite of the community.

In some respects, the involvement of elites in the purchasing of cultural heritage material represents the continuation of a long tradition of the demonstration of taste and wealth, a kind of social vestige of privilege that extends through the centuries. Some of these elites are well connected with political decision makers in many of the demand countries and have been involved in heated debates regarding whether the nation should participate in international agreements regarding the protection of cultural heritage. Of course, once a nation becomes party to such agreements, this potentially jeopardizes the access and supply of material to potential purchasers. Many leading demand countries (e.g., Belgium and The Netherlands) have yet to sign on to the major treaties.

Those engaged in the traffic of antiquities into the lucrative demand centers therefore face a problem. If goods have been illegally obtained in one country, but they are to be sold legally in another, a transformation must occur so that the objects have legitimate export documentation to enable their legal importation into the destination countries. This transformation of illegal to legal goods occurs in the major transit ports. Most transit locations have a history of being "free ports" with relatively few restrictions on importation and exportation of goods. Once material has arrived at these ports (e.g., Switzerland, Hong Kong, and Macau), export documentation is accessible that then allows the materials to be transferred on to markets as legitimate goods.

In the recent case of material plundered from Iraq, for example, claims were made that the material was flowing outward from Iraq to Jordan, and from there it was shipped to Switzerland (Gottlieb & Meier, 2003; Riding, 2003). Historically, at least two benefits have been derived from moving the material through Switzerland. First, the laws of that country are tilted strongly in favor of "good faith purchasers" so that an individual who has bought an object through most common commercial channels obtains secure title that is exceptionally difficult to dislodge through any legal challenge. Second, once that secure title has been obtained in Switzerland, the object is relatively free to flow onto the market in other centers because legal export papers will be easy to obtain. The material can then appear in venues such as the major auction houses with the all-too-common provenance of "from the collection of a Swiss gentleman."

A critical factor that supports the continued trade of plundered cultural material in the demand centers is the general and widespread acceptance of a shared understanding among sellers and buyers that issues of provenance will not be raised when articles are purchased. Consistently, reviews of auction house and private-dealer catalogues demonstrate that when objects are sold, little or no information is provided regarding the history of the object. Provenance in the art world generally refers to the ownership history of the object. For cultural heritage material, the archaeologists are much more demanding, asking that the ownership history, at least in the ideal case, refer not only to who has owned the object in recent years but include exact information regarding where the material was found, when and by whom the dig was conducted, any information that has been published about the material, and how from that point it has entered the commercial market. It is striking that the common practice in the trade of antiquities is to provide no clues regarding either of these approaches to provenance. The fact that dealers historically have not been forthcoming about the history of the material being traded has meant that awkward questions about illegal digging and export practices could be avoided.

At the same time, this practice poses a dilemma for the dealers. Wherever there is a lucrative trade in cultural objects, there will develop a parallel trade in faked material. Dealers may then be placed in a position where they have to assure potential customers that their material is "authentic" (and therefore "genuinely" looted) while at the same time finessing possible questions of the legality of title. The legal export documents obtained through the transit ports are an essential part of this process. The potential customer can be assured that the material has come from some known (i.e., plundered) site but that its importation has been legal and the purchaser can obtain secure title. Where possible with expensive objects, dealers may be able to obtain technologically elaborate tests of the age of the object (particularly with ceramic material), which are an important feature of the often elaborate "certificates of authenticity" provided to the customer.

WHERE CRIME HAS ITS GREATEST IMPACT

The victimology of antiquities crime is somewhat unique; the ultimate victims of such plunder are those whose collective understanding of a shared cultural heritage is threatened by the loss of antiquities. Once the sites have been plundered, the loss is irrevocable, because what is at issue for archaeologists is the total context of the site, not simply the individual objects that are carried away. Therefore, although the many attempts to return objects to the country from which they have been stolen are laudable, the objects themselves are not the major focus of concern. Future attempts at control must be premised in the objective of the protection of cultural heritage sites from the initial plunder.

The primary impact of the demand for antiquities is found in the destruction that occurs to major sites of cultural heritage, especially when the plunder activities are large scale, rough, and devastating. Whole temples in Cambodia and Guatemala have been destroyed to retrieve a few of the stone statues, and in nations such as Peru, whole areas have been transformed into moonscapes by looters.

A secondary impact occurs when the attempts to restrict trade at the source nation level create widespread corruption. In the poorer nations in particular, the wealth of the antiquities trade can result in the flow of money into the pockets of corrupt customs, police, and military officials.

COOPERATIVE EFFORTS UNDERTAKEN TO REDUCE THIS TRAFFIC

The first attempts at the control of the illicit plunder of cultural heritage material occurred when source nations attempted to restrict the flow of material outside their boundaries. Although some of these laws go back hundreds of years (Blake, 1997; Greenfield, 1996), most of these have been enacted over the past 100 years or so. These laws tend to take two forms: (1) a weak form that involves a restriction on the export of material and (2) a strong form that defines cultural material as property of the state, and its unlawful removal as theft (Kaye, 1996, 1998). The problem with simple export restrictions is that the courts in many of the major market states, including the United Kingdom and the United States, take the position that they will not enforce such regulations, leaving the control to the individual source nations within their own borders. Police and courts in most countries have accepted, however, that they have a responsibility for prosecution in matters of theft. There have been major successful prosecutions in both England and the United States of persons involved in the traffic of antiquities where it could be proved that the material in their possession had been stolen from the country of origin.

One recent and dramatic example of such a prosecution resulted in the conviction of Fred Schultz, one of the leading antiquities dealers in New York, on a charge involving the handling of material that the U.S. government alleged had been stolen from Egypt (Gerstenblith, 2002). Schultz is a former president of the National Association of Ancient, Oriental and Primitive Art, and the charges arose as a result of his sale, for $1.2 million, of a stone head of Amenhotep III and his attempt to sell other material that had been passed on to him by a British citizen who had smuggled the material out of Egypt. The pair had attempted to cover their tracks by inventing a false provenance for the material around a fabricated collection that they claimed had been established in the 1920s ("The Thomas Alcock Collection"). The U.S. government in this case applied U.S. law, specifically the National Stolen Property Act, despite the fact that the actual theft had taken place in Egypt. Schultz was sentenced to a term of imprisonment as a result of the conviction (his accomplice had already served time in English prisons as a result of his earlier conviction in that country).

One lesson available from criminological analysis of international illicit markets is that where demand remains at high levels in economically rich nations, much can be gained by prohibitive legislation in source countries, especially countries whose citizens are locked in poverty. Recent writing in the drugs area, with the exception of official government documents, provides a strident chorus regarding the failure of attempts, especially by the United States, to reduce the flow of illicit drugs by means of policies or interventions that focus on source nations. With regard to drug policies aimed at the supplying countries, Stevenson (1994) has observed,

> For 70 years, the international community, spurred by the USA, has used diplomacy and financial and military assistance to persuade producer countries to control drug production. Despite this effort, supply-side policies have made no discernible impact on the global availability of drugs. (p. 33)

After reviewing the status of drug control efforts of nine countries, including producing nations such as Peru, Colombia, Thailand, and Burma, Tullis (1995) listed some of the unintended consequences observed in many of these countries, including a delegitimizing of the state and aggravated and endemic violence, among others (p. 208). Johns (1992) similarly notes that "criminalization and enforcement have brought about additional social costs (corruption, deflection of police resources, increased illegal profits, criminal justice system overloads, secondary crime, etc.)" (pp. 1–2).

These widely discussed consequences for drug interventions focused on relatively poor source countries are not unfamiliar to observers of the antiquities market. Murphy (1995) has commented, for example that "the art world knows that embargo legislation in developing source nations does not prevent export; it only ensures that the traffic goes underground" (p. 155).

Almost 20 years ago, another analyst argued, "I start with the pessimistic premise that, so long as there is a world market for beautiful objects, a substantial amount of looting will persist no matter what regulatory system is installed, because total prevention would entail unacceptable costs" (Bator, 1982, p. 49)

The lengthy and detailed history of prohibition aimed at source nations, when demand continues in the developed nations, suggests, as Bator concluded, that few positive results will come from attempts to approach the problem of the illicit traffic in antiquities by punitive laws, no matter how draconian, aimed primarily at eradicating supply. This is not to argue that these countries should not press forward with laws and regulations aimed at preserving their cultural heritage (because the content of these laws often sets the parameters of what can be accomplished in the major market states). Rather, the intent here is to establish firmly the principle that such laws in source nations are unable to reach market forces that drive the trade, forces located firmly within the pulls exerted by demand. In fact, as long as the trade in antiquities may be conducted openly in auction houses and dealer's galleries in the market centers, not

only will the flow of material out of the poorer source nations continue, additional social costs will likely result from the creation of organized criminal activity to carry out the organization of the supply of material and its smuggling across borders, including the disastrous effects of corruption of the political process in the source environments.

Over the past three decades, there has been a growing recognition that any reduction in the level of destruction taking place in source nations will require international cooperation to address the problem of the demand exerted by wealthy nations for these cultural heritage goods. After many years of protest and outcry by source nations, one of the first and most important steps was the establishment of the 1970 UNESCO (U.N. Educational, Scientific and Cultural Organization) Convention on the Means of Prohibiting and Preventing the Illicit Import, Export and Transfer of Ownership of Cultural Property. This convention requires that cooperating states attempt to prevent the purchase and import of illegally excavated objects and return certain categories of unlawfully removed cultural material to the country of origin. Equally important, the convention places considerable emphasis on maintaining cultural resources in situ. In calling attention to the issue of context, the convention provides that "cultural property constitutes one of the basic elements of civilization and national culture. . . . Its true value can be appreciated only in relation to the fullest possible information regarding its origin, history and traditional setting" (UNESCO, 1970, p. 2). This treaty, to be effective, requires bilateral agreements between source and market nations. When these agreements are in place, they can serve as a powerful weapon for the return of cultural material to a source nation. The presence of treaties between the United States and Italy, Cambodia, and Guatemala (among others) has proven to be a powerful weapon on one hand, restricting material flowing into the United States from these nations and, on the other, assisting the return of material when its illegal entry into the United States is discovered.

Unfortunately, despite the clear intent of the 1970 UNESCO Convention, it has faced a number of problems in achieving significant outcomes. For one, it becomes fully effective only when a given country agrees to participate, and it also requires numerous bilateral agreements if material is to be returned. More critically, the legal systems of many European nations strongly favor "good faith purchasers." Once goods have been obtained through most common commercial outlets in these nations—for example, at auction—and if the buyer can demonstrate good faith in the purchase, then it becomes close to impossible for the original owners of the property to regain ownership of the material.

To address such problems, the 1995 Unidroit (U.N. International Institute for the Unification of Private Law) Convention on the International Return of Stolen or Illegally Exported Cultural Objects was developed. The main aims of this convention were to (a) deter art theft, (b) provide the means by which the art-rich nations can make claims for the return of stolen or illegally exported goods through the courts of the art importing nations, and thereby (c) reduce the level of looting of cultural property that comes up for sale on the international art market. Specifically, this convention addresses the problem of "due diligence," by attempting to balance protections extended to good faith purchasers against the risks that might arise if buyers are not careful in carrying out a proper search regarding the provenance of objects being bought. These aspects of the convention are aimed directly at a common problem of the secrecy and lack of openness that has been a central feature of the international art and antiquities trade. Unfortunately, this important instrument to date has had limited impact because relatively few of the market states have agreed to sign on, in no small part

because of the strong opposition within the art trading community to these provisions.

Another international agreement relevant to this discussion is the UNESCO 2001 Convention on the Protection of the Underwater Cultural Heritage. This convention contains a number of important elements, three of which are central to present concerns. The first is concerned with the preservation of context: "The preservation *in situ* of underwater cultural heritage shall be considered as the first option before allowing or engaging in any activities directed at this heritage" (UNESCO, 2001, Article 2, Section 5).

The importance of this provision is that the convention from the outset explicitly provides that a first priority is the protection of the archaeological setting. This issue of context must be understood as the issue of paramount importance.

A further section provides a clear prohibition regarding an economic market of maritime cultural heritage goods: "Underwater cultural heritage shall not be commercially exploited" (UNESCO, 2001, Article 2, Section 7). This provision recognizes that the fundamental force motivating the plunder of cultural sites derives from the economic market that exerts a demand for cultural heritage material. Furthermore, the "Annex" to the convention provides "Rules Concerning Activities Directed at Underwater Cultural Heritage"; the second of these specifies concerns about the market:

> The commercial exploitation of underwater cultural heritage for trade or speculation or its irretrievable dispersal is fundamentally incompatible with the protection and proper management of underwater cultural heritage. Underwater cultural heritage shall not be traded, sold, bought or bartered as commercial goods. (UNESCO, 2001, Annex, Rule 2)

This 2001 convention is unique in that it explicitly states that it is the market itself that has to be addressed. It goes on to provide a mechanism by which states will achieve the objectives of this provision: "Each State Party shall take measures providing for the seizure of underwater cultural heritage in its territory that has been recovered in a manner not in conformity with this Convention" (UNESCO, 2001, Article 18, Section 1). This element of the convention, when (and if) it becomes fully implemented, will provide the mechanism by which the provision against an economic market can be enforced. It is anticipated that market actors will be deterred from buying or selling illicitly extracted material by a concern for possible seizure of goods.

These three international approaches to controlling the illicit market in antiquities share a common concern for addressing the forces that fuel this traffic—that is, the demand exerted by purchasers in the developed nations. The focus has thus shifted from earlier attempts to control the market by restricting the flow of goods out of source nations (which would seem to be doomed to failure as long as demand remains strong) to a focus on mechanisms and procedures to restrict or channel demand. Furthermore, that these three measures all developed out of a U.N. framework indicates that international pressure is gradually building (not yet international consensus, to be sure) to reduce the illicit traffic in cultural heritage material.

FUTURE DIRECTIONS: DETERRENCE AS PROBLEMATIC

One of the unique problems that must be confronted in attempts to control the illegal market in antiquities is that some buying and selling of antiquities will be legal. For centuries, there has been a legitimate trade in cultural objects (whatever ethical position one may wish to take today about such a trade). Consequently, there is an enormous amount of material in collections and in the hands of collectors that will continue to flow on and off the market legally regardless of the steps taken to prevent the movement of newly excavated material. Furthermore, there are a number of aesthetic and scholarly reasons for a flow of cultural material, as was recognized in a recent report in Great Britain:

> We further accept that there is a substantial public benefit in a vigorous and honorable market in cultural objects. Aside from its general contribution to the economy, the market is a touchstone of much of our law and practice on cultural property. Many public committees require knowledge of the state of the market in cultural objects in order to operate. Their terms of reference assume both the existence and the desirability of a market. (Department for Culture, Media and Sport, 2000, p. 10)

There may be dangers in attempting to close off areas of legitimate trade; an important consequence might be the creation of an even more problematic underground market (Murphy, 1995; O'Keefe, 1997). The continued existence of this legitimate trade clouds the ethical terrain around the antiquities issues; it creates a climate of demand and acceptance of the legitimacy of at least a partial market for heritage material that may not necessarily be easy to constrain neatly into categories of legal and illegal activity.

As we look to the future of policy regarding the control of the illicit component of the antiquities trade, it is our view that there needs to be a much wider view of the policy options than those currently in place. Most of the present policies, both at the source nation level and at the international cooperation level, rely fundamentally on simple deterrence mechanisms. That is, the suggested policies, including the various treaties and conventions, propose relatively simplistic prohibition approaches to control of the illicit traffic. The rules and regulations that have been put in place are premised on the idea that the task is to identify wrongdoers engaged in the illicit trade and then to implement various civil penalties or criminal penalties to discourage others from considering engaging in the trade. Certainly, when a golden object stolen from Italy that costs several hundred thousand dollars is seized and returned to its country of origin (without compensation to the individual from whom it has been seized), or when a prominent art dealer is convicted to a lengthy prison term, a message is sent to the community of potential sellers and buyers of cultural heritage material.

Such regulatory approaches are consistent with the conventional wisdom of deterrence theory, especially when it is recognized that there is a better than usual correspondence between the traffic in plundered cultural material and the elements of rational choice found in deterrence theories. The buying of antiquities is a considered a transaction where it can be argued that the typical purchaser will balance a number of factors that probably include the perceived appropriateness of the cost and that might include consideration of risk of seizure or prosecution if such risks were attached to the purchase. When objects costing millions of dollars are seized in a blaze of media publicity from purchasers who then see their investment vanish (as happened in the Golden Phiale case where a golden platter bought in the United States for $1.2 million was seized by U.S. Customs and ultimately returned to Italy; Slayman, 1998) or when a dealer is sent to jail as the result of a very public trial (as in the Schultz case), it is only reasonable to anticipate that the market will take notice as the principles of deterrence begin to operate.

Initially, then, it might appear that when it comes to public policy aimed at reducing the plunder of illicit cultural material, legal sanctions might be a key element. It should be noted here that in its routine formulation, deterrence theory refers to the threat of criminal sanctions. In the case of the control of the market for antiquities, it is likely that the most

common legal actions are civil suits that have the result of removing the material from the possession of a purchaser. Some of the most notable of these seizures have occurred in the United States where these purchasers are not compensated for their loss. Given the large amounts of money involved, these civil sanctions obviously constitute a form of legal penalty that can be considered a component of deterrence.

We remain skeptical, however, regarding the success of attempts to control the illicit traffic in cultural material built mainly on the threats of seizure or punishment. This skepticism is based on two different sets of questions. The first set is concerned with the rather dismal record of attempts to control illegal markets through prohibition. The second focuses on arguments regarding the potential contribution of regulations aimed at the task of persuasion and their ability to create a "climate of compliance" wherein individuals will not participate in the illicit market for antiquities.

Illegal markets are driven essentially by demand, and when demand is great enough, as for goods such as drugs and antiquities, they become international in scope. When the demand is high and exerted over an extended time, complex organizational structures emerge to provide the necessary hidden services required for illicit activity, including smuggling and the negotiations with corrupt public officials required if consistent access to travel routes is to be secured. As reviewed above, the record of prohibition to date with respect to both the drug and antiquities markets is not one that would lead to any great optimism that by itself such deterrence-based approaches will bring the illicit traffic under control.

In the United States, Prohibition in the 1920s obviously did not result in the disappearance of alcohol use, and for most objective observers (at least those outside of the U.S. government) the ongoing struggle to control drugs through punitive legislation has similarly failed to stem the flow of drugs into that country. We are not the only observers who question such approaches when they are applied to the antiquities markets. Recall, for example, Bator's (1982) lament that "looting will persist" as long as demand for antiquities remains high.

It is not being argued here that there is no role for punitive legislation aimed at restricting the flow of illicit antiquities. Furthermore, recent actions, such as the 2001 UNESCO Convention, are much more sophisticated in their recognition that the problem arises because of the economic exploitation of (i.e., the market for) cultural material. Although the 2001 UNESCO convention provides for steps such as seizure that could occur in both demand and source countries (as well as transit venues), the fundamental mechanism provided in this convention is still one based in the inherent threat represented by seizure.

Where market demand remains high, and individuals are willing to run the risks of such seizure, or when it is known that there are locations where there is no risk of seizure, it follows that the plunder will continue. Our own work has been focused primarily on the traffic of material from China and Southeast Asia, and it certainly appears that for most goods from these regions, there is still a vigorous market for objects and that this market is supplied by the continued plunder of cultural heritage sites. Thus, on the day that a large object from China was seized by U.S. Customs in New York and ultimately returned (Barnes, 2000), hundreds if not thousands of smaller objects from the same country were openly being sold in the antiquities shops of that city. These objects—for example, ceramic figures from the Han and Tang periods—were offered with little in the way of provenance and in all probability had been recently plundered.

Unfortunately, the current regulations, as provided in the 1970 UNESCO Convention,

are applicable only where rather rigorous conditions are met. They apply only when both source and market nations have signed onto the convention (and the sanctions available are shaped by the specific provisions of the convention that have been adopted). As it has been commonly pursued, the provisions of the convention commonly (but not exclusively) seem most relevant to a few large objects that have been inventoried prior to their removal from their country of origin. The mesh of the net of regulation, in short, is apparently not fine enough to snare the smaller objects being traded in an apparently vigorous market, at least when the focus is on material from Asia.

Even when there are wins, they may be illusory. For example, over the months we have been observing the traffic of Khmer materials out of Cambodia, we have noticed a discernable slowing of the flow in such items through venues such as the River City complex in Bangkok. Our informants suggest this is because of agreements struck between Thai and Cambodian governments designed to reduce the trade in Thailand of material from Cambodia. The antiquities shops in Thailand, however, are still crammed with merchandise. It appears that there is now considerable traffic in wooden objects from Burma and Laos and wooden chests from Tibet (or, more properly, allegedly from Tibet). Because of the apparent continued demand for antique material, there is a kind of "displacement" effect occurring, where as supply is restricted from one source, alternative material is substituted from another. The plunder continues, but its location shifts, at least in terms of the materials publicly displayed in antiquities retail outlets.

In the case of a recently proposed convention (UNESCO, 2001) regarding maritime material, there, too, intent of the convention may also founder on the hard rock of commercial realities. Certainly, one stream of destructive activity in maritime objects is made up of treasure seekers searching for highly valuable items such as gold, silver, and precious jewels. Under current international laws and regulations, at times treasure seekers engage in complex negotiations involving salvors, archaeologists, and national governments whereby as the material is extracted, an attempt is made to carry out a full archaeological survey of the site, and a proper classification of the material produced. One salvage firm, for example, has just announced that such a deal was struck with the British government regarding recovery of a large shipment of gold that was lost in the 17th-century shipwreck of the *Sussex*.

The attempt to establish preservation in situ as the major option for underwater cultural objects and the prohibition against commercial exploitation found in the 2001 convention are unlikely to be respected by those tempted by the search for precious materials. If an attempt was made to have a rigid enforcement of these provisions, the treasure seekers would see little alternative but to abandon any kind of collaborative arrangement as in the *Sussex* wreck. The search for gold and other valuable commodities, unfortunately, will continue as it has for centuries. If treasure trovers have to do their work secretly, they will have scarce regard for the preservation or study of the wreck as part of our cultural heritage. Instead, the techniques will involve snatch and grab, with major destruction of the maritime site a likely result.

In sum, although there have been undeniable gains since the 1970 UNESCO Convention, there continues to be a thriving market for plundered antiquities in the international market centers. Criminal and civil sanctions, despite at times being severe, have not been successful in controlling the plunder. It is the present argument that the current strategies based in deterrence need to be supplemented by additional methods based in persuasion, negotiation, education, and training.

THE ROLE OF PERSUASION: CREATING A "CULTURE OF COMPLIANCE"

The argument for alternatives to deterrence is based partly in psychological theory regarding the effects, and limits, of pain, punishment, and the threats thereof as a tool for shaping behavior. It is well established that punishment (or its threat) can under specific conditions inhibit a pattern of behavior. Unfortunately, it is also well established that this response to conditioning does not extinguish the drive behind that behavior, so the pattern will reemerge when the threat of punishment is removed. Furthermore, although the original pattern may be deterred, alternative behavior may emerge aimed at a similar end where there is no threat of punishment. The logic of conditioning argues that an alternative approach is to support other and desired forms of behavior that compete with the undesirable pattern with positive reinforcement. As these alternative behaviors take hold, are rewarded, and thrive, the original pattern is extinguished.

A slightly different argument focused on the issue of the regulation of white-collar crime can be found in the work of John Braithwaite (1985, 1989, 1993, 2002). Part of his view, as expressed in the title of one of his early works, is that when we deal with white-collar crime we have to make some difficult decisions whether we should "punish or persuade" (Braithwaite, 1985). When it comes to regulation, Braithwaite ultimately urges that we take a bet both ways—that is, that we recognize that both persuasion and punishment need to be part of the regulatory mix but that most of what we do within a regulatory policy should be focused on persuasion. He proposes a "pyramid" metaphor (Braithwaite, 1993), where the bulk of regulatory activity within the policy is at the base of the pyramid and is about education, training, negotiation, arbitration, and other strategies of persuasion. Braithwaite sees a place for appropriate severe punishments when the crimes are particularly serious; he also believes that a symbolic response by the criminal justice system indicated is especially appropriate. But such punitive responses (as indicated by his placement of such actions at the top of the "pyramid") should occur relatively rarely within a healthy regulatory environment.

The central idea of this view of regulation is that the desired outcome is what we might for our purposes term a "culture of compliance." One persuades, educates, trains, and negotiates to create a climate within a market where those involved comply with regulations because they see these regulations as proper and appropriate. The intent, as in behavioral psychology, is to create situations where individuals comply with regulations because they think the regulations are right, not simply because they fear that they will be punished if they violate the rules.

In the antiquities trade, it is our view that the task, similarly, is to create a climate of compliance where dealers will not sell, and consumers will not buy, unprovenanced antiquities, not because they fear that they may be punished but because they understand the consequence of their market behavior. The goal is to eliminate the demand for unprovenanced cultural heritage material, thus removing the basic force that drives the illicit market in antiquities and thereby stopping the plunder.

How might this be accomplished? What we propose is that market centers accept the proposition that only cultural heritage material that has documented and acceptable provenance be offered for sale and that consumers be educated and trained to demand proper documentation before they buy such objects. The form of such documentation would have to be developed, and this might involve collaboration of dealers, art historians, curators of major public collections, archaeologists, and cultural heritage public servants, among others.

It is striking that such documentation is still not an expectation in the sale of material either through antiquities dealers or in auction houses. In an ongoing study of such catalogues involving Chinese and Southeast Asian objects, we have found that almost never do the major dealers and auction houses provide provenance information for material being offered for sale. Where provenance information exists, it most often takes the form of such well-known and ambiguous phrases as "from the private collection of a Swiss gentleman." Rarely is specific information given about whose hands the object has passed through in recent years, and almost never is there any statement about the archaeological origins of the material.

We envision a standard provenance form, perhaps one prepared with the joint sanction of a dealers' association and an archaeological body. Although the exact details would have to be negotiated, it can be assumed that the form would identify (a) the source country; (b) the cultural period from which the object came; (c) the rough date that the material was created originally; (d) the date that the material was removed from the heritage site; (e) perhaps some details of the removal, such as the sponsorship of the dig and the archaeologist who supervised the removal of the material; and (f) some history of the object since it has been placed on the market. For material that has been on the market since before a sunset clause date (often a date in the early 1970s is offered as appropriate to such provenance to conform to the establishment of the original UNESCO convention), it would be acceptable to provide information regarding whose hands the material has passed through since the off date.

Within this argument, the fundamental objective is to stop the plunder of cultural heritage sites. It is assumed that this will be accomplished best by having a market of provenanced cultural heritage material that in essence drives unprovenanced material out of that market. Others, of course, have proposed this argument. O'Keefe (1997), after observing that the levels of destruction and theft of cultural material suggest that current legal strategies "cannot be operating satisfactorily" concludes, "Perhaps the time has come to look at changing the market for antiquities" (p. 61). He then surveys different approaches and proposes that although rendering all collecting antisocial is not an achievable or desirable option, it may be possible to address *some* antisocial collecting:

> Instead of attempting to render all collecting anti-social . . . it would be more productive to bring about change in public attitudes that would render the collecting of certain antiquities unacceptable; antiquities which are undocumented, unprovenanced, looted or stolen. A campaign to this end might be more effective if the flow of antiquities from legitimate sources were maintained or increased. (p. 63)

In making a similar proposal, Murphy (1995) offered one approach whereby

> the developing art-rich nations should treat cultural property as an exploitable national resource, not to be hoarded absolutely, but to be "mined" as a source of income. . . . The income from the sale of excess relics can be made available to finance preservation of the most culturally significant pieces, training of curators, and scientific exploration efforts. Once international demand is satisfied by the creation of a sizeable licit market, the profit is cut out of illicit traffic and the concomitant anti-social behaviour is reduced. In a perfect model, money would be channeled toward preservation and study rather than to bribes. (p. 235)

Two decades ago, the argument was put in its simplest form: "The best way to keep art is to let a lot of it go" (Bator, 1982, p. 322). Such an argument presumes, as did the recent Palmer Panel (Department for Culture, Media and Sport, 2000) in the United Kingdom, that there will continue to be a vigorous market in antiquities.

More critically, and controversially, this proposal allows for the flow of new material onto the market. Although, in fact, many of the traditional source nations for cultural heritage objects now forbid such traffic, there are interesting examples drawn from maritime sites, where in recent years material has been located, studied, excavated, and placed onto the antiquities market. One of these is the large amount of early ceramic material extracted from the *Hoi An* wreck. In that case, an arrangement was made between the Vietnam government, a salvage firm, and a team of marine archaeologists. The site was subjected first to an archaeological survey; then the material was extracted. A proportion of the thousands of ceramic objects was retained by the Vietnam government and distributed to various state museum collections, with the rest placed in an auction conducted by Butterworth's. Whatever one thinks of the consequences of this particular venture, when material from this site circulates in the market, it will carry with it the full provenance documents provided in the course of the auction.

It is possible that further innovations might develop in the processing of material by both archaeologists and source nations, including the possibility, suggested to us by participants at a recent conference, that material is placed on the market on a lease arrangement, where title is retained by the source nation and material is carefully catalogued and identified by archaeologists or cultural heritage staff so that it can be recalled if research purposes dictate the need to reexamine the objects. Such an arrangement meets the requirements of many source nations that they retain ownership of their cultural heritage but also creates a mechanism so that individuals can have personal access to material.

It can be pointed out that it is to be regretted that personal access to cultural heritage material is treated as unethical and problematic. Individual appreciation of these objects has an ancient lineage and resonates today in the widespread appreciation of finely crafted ancient material. It is not the individual possession of one or another object that is the problem. It is the purchase of unprovenanced items, from an illicit market, that should be the focus of our attention. Furthermore, if it were decided that there would be henceforth no commercial traffic in cultural heritage material, alternative mechanisms would have to evolve if the large public collections (including those maintained by universities) are to continue to have access to new material for purposes of research, education, and cultural appreciation.

One of the major problems in implementing a strategy of persuasion is that at present it is not clear how a responsible regulatory unit would be organized, where it would be located, and what powers it might have. The scheme proposed by Braithwaite (1993, 2002) is concerned primarily with the oversight of corporate activity by government bodies such as those dealing with occupational health and safety, coal mine safety, the monitoring of homes for the elderly, and financial organizations such as banks and insurance companies, among others. Typically, these regulatory bodies are governmental units created by the legislative framework that provides the statutes enforced by the unit.

In most market nations, such governmental bodies, dedicated to the control of the antiquities market, do not exist. Instead, there is a complex of interest groups with competing perspectives regarding how the trade might be organized. O'Keefe (1997) for example, identifies a widely dispersed set of groups that have a stake in such activity, including archaeologists, impoverished local populations, indigenous peoples, dealers, auctions houses, art historians, collectors, and the general public. Additional interested parties are public museums, political figures with an interest or stake in public policy relating to antiquities, and public servants (both nationally and internationally) concerned with cultural heritage policy.

In the short term, given both the urgency of the problem and the growing awareness of the need for action by various of these stakeholders, a variety of initial steps can be taken. Those with expertise in the issue of archaeological provenance might come together and make specific proposals for standard provenance protocols that might have the sanction of the associations of academics, dealers, and museums. O'Keefe (1997) speaks of the importance of a "sustained campaign in all media" that would highlight the costs of the destruction involved with the looting of cultural heritage sites, and these, too, might be organized through conferences and seminars by the major stakeholders and professional associations. Organizations such as the International Council of Museums (ICOM) have already played a major role by adopting a set of binding guidelines that require that member museums commit themselves to the principle that they will not acquire unprovenanced cultural heritage material. It is highly likely, however, that for sustained effort organized around the level of "persuasion" that is required, governmental regulatory units within the market countries will have to be established.

To summarize, it is presumed that there is a role for criminal sanctions within a total approach to the control of the market in illicit activities that gives emphasis to *both* punishment *and* persuasion. This formulation assumes that major effort in the future needs to be given to innovative work to shape the education and training required for the persuasion component of this statement. The plunder of cultural heritage sites will stop only when dealers and buyers in market countries come to realize the tragic consequences of the continued trade in unprovenanced material. By itself, the threat of punishment alone is too inexact and blunt an instrument to achieve this end.

REFERENCES

Barnes, J. E. (2000, March 30). Alleging theft, U.S. demands rare sculpture go back to China. *New York Times*, p. 1.

Bator, P. M. (1982). *The international trade in art.* Chicago: University of Chicago Press.

Blake, J. (1997). Export embargoes and the international antiquities market. *Art, Antiquity and the Law, 2,* 233–250.

Braithwaite, J. (1985). *To punish or persuade: Enforcement of coal mine safety.* Albany: State University of New York Press.

Braithwaite, J. (1989). *Crime, shame and reintegration.* New York: Cambridge University Press.

Braithwaite, J. (1993). *Business regulation and Australia's future.* Canberra: Australian Institute of Criminology.

Braithwaite, J. (2002). *Restorative justice and responsive regulation.* New York: Oxford University Press.

Conklin, J. E. (1994). *Art crime.* Westport, CT: Praeger.

Department for Culture, Media and Sport. (2000). *Ministerial Advisory Panel on Illicit Trade report* (Chairman: Professor Norman Palmer). London: Author.

Gerstenblith, P. (2002, Spring). The United States vs. Schultz. *Culture Without Context*, pp. 5–6.

Gottlieb, M., & Meier, B. (2003, May 2). Little has been found of plunder from '91. *International Herald Tribune*, p. 4.

Greenfield, J. (1996). *The return of cultural treasures.* Cambridge, UK: Cambridge University Press.

Hearn, M. K. (1997). *Splendors of imperial China: Treasures from the National Palace Museum, Taipei.* New York: Metropolitan Museum of Art.

Johns, C. J. (1992). *Power, ideology and the war on drugs: Nothing succeeds like failure.* New York: Praeger.

Kaye, L. M. (1996). The future of the past: Recovering cultural property. *Cardozo Journal of International and Comparative Law, 4*(1), 23–41.

Kaye, L. M. (1998). Art wars: The repatriation battle. *New York University Journal of International Law and Politics, 31,* 79–94.

Murphy, J. D. (1995). *Plunder and preservation: Cultural property law and practice in the People's Republic of China.* Oxford, UK: Oxford University Press.

O'Keefe, P. J. (1997). *Trade in antiquities: Reducing destruction and theft.* Paris: U.N. Educational, Scientific and Cultural Organization.

Riding, A. (2003, May 2). Iraq's looted art: The list shortens. *International Herald Tribune,* pp. 1, 4.

Slayman, A. L. (1998, May/June). The looting of Italy: The case of the Golden Phiale. *Archaeology*, pp. 36–49.

Stevenson, R. (1994). *Winning the war on drugs: To legalise or not?* London: Institute of Economic Affairs.

Tullis, L. (1995). *Unintended consequences: Illegal drugs and drug policies in nine countries.* Boulder, CO: Lynne Riener.

U.N. Educational, Scientific and Cultural Organization. (1970). *Convention and means of prohibiting and preventing illicit import, export and transfer of ownership of cultural property.* Paris: Author. Retrieved April 7, 2004, from www.unesco.org/culture/laws/ 1970/html_eng/page1.shtml

U.N. Educational, Scientific and Cultural Organization. (2001). *Convention on the protection of the underwater cultural heritage.* Paris: Author. Retrieved April 7, 2004, from www.unesco.org/culture/laws/underwater/htm l_eng/convention.shtml

U.N. International Institute for the Unification of Private Law. (1995). *Convention on the international return of stolen or illegally exported cultural objects.* Rome: Author. Retrieved April 7, 2004, from www.unidroit.org/ english/conventions/c-cult.htm

Watson, P. (1997). *Sotheby's: The inside story.* London: Bloomsbury.

7

Computer Crime in a Brave New World

CHRIS E. MARSHALL

T. HANK ROBINSON

DAE-HOON KWAK

In this chapter,[1] we will examine a kind of crime that will, in all likelihood, occupy the attention and research of future criminologists and criminal justice experts to at least the extent that "street crime" does today. Computer crime—its variants, its control, its motivations—is new to us, both practitioners and researchers alike. We grope our way into the 21st century.

We have only recently moved to legally define computer crime as distinct from traditional crimes such as fraud and theft. Furthermore, early attempts to control computer crime find sophisticated computer users able to wear the equivalent of electronic gloves to hide their "virtual fingerprints" and identity. Jurisdictional issues related to most Internet-facilitated crime pose procedural roadblocks to obtaining critical evidence (President's Working Group, 2000, p. 22). These obstacles strain criminal justice agencies already spread thin by the duties and efforts required to fight "regular crime." The U.S. Department of Justice's Office of Justice Programs Annual Report to Congress for Fiscal Year 1999 acknowledges that electronic crime presents new obstacles to effective law enforcement effort at all levels (U.S. Department of Justice, 2000b, p. 62).

The need to control computer crime is fairly obvious, even though cybercrime and information warfare have not yet become major security issues in most countries (Speer, 2000, p. 271). Ominous scenarios involving attacks on national power and communication grids; air, vehicle, and train traffic control systems; weather forecasting networks; stock, security, and commodity markets; inventory distribution systems for food, fuel, and medicine; and the banking systems are not difficult to conceive; any one of these kinds of attack could cripple an otherwise vital nation. Although loss of air traffic control is often cited as an example of why the infrastructure must be protected, consider also the disastrous consequences of an attack that breaks down the power grid in the northeastern United States at 10:00 p.m. during a February blizzard marked by subzero temperatures and high wind. Or consider a similar attack executed in Phoenix, Arizona, during mid-August, allowing the temperatures of buildings to rise to a level that even operable computers would have to be shut down to avoid overheating and malfunction. In either instance, the derivative effects on hospitals, law enforcement, and emergency dispatch would be immediate and catastrophic.

That computer crime must be controlled is not in doubt. The question is *how?* Moreover, that computer crime is often committed ignoring national boundaries makes this kind of offense even more difficult to control. Computer crime and its transnational implications are the focus of this chapter.

THE NEW TECHNOLOGY

A computer is "an electronic machine, operating under the control of instructions stored in its own memory, that can accept data (input), manipulate the data according to specified rules (process), produce results (output), and store the results for future use" (Shelly, Cashman, Vermaat, & Walker, 1999, p. 1.3).[2]

The computer is one of the most fantastic tools ever invented by human beings; it very possibly rivals the wheel in its far-reaching effects on the well-being of humankind. The computer began its tool life[3] with important military uses such as (a) helping to break secret German military code in World War II, (b) weapons targeting, and (c) computing complex problems of nuclear fission necessary for the invention of the atomic bomb. Its

later, peacetime uses expanded to include complicated numeric integrations for statistical problems for scientific research; searchable, flexible databases, including criminal databases; playing the world's chess champion; and, of course, the Internet.

New uses of the computer materialize daily. Such promising uses as "robotic insects" that report soil and weather conditions in all parts of large grain fields and nanorobots working inside the human body to repair damaged or diseased cells represent only a small part of the incredible potential of this new tool (Powell, 2000). We can only stand back and look on in awe at the breadth of the computer's utility (for a timeline highlighting the development of the computer, see Shelly et al., 1999, pp. 1.48–1.57). Unfortunately, as with other tools, such as guns and knives and telephones and nuclear energy, all of which have important roles in peaceful human existence, some people choose to deploy the computer to hurt and steal from others. Moreover, the character of the computer enables its use even across national boundaries and large—even interplanetary—distances and with incredible speed. This new tool has a long reach, certainly much longer than any mere handgun.

In its brief history, the Internet has taken a central place in our lives; there are several good accounts of the Internet's history (see, e.g., Lipson, 2002, p. 5; Shelly et al., 1999, pp. 1.48–1.57). The Internet's life began in 1969 as a research network sponsored by the Advance Research Project Agency (ARPA) for the U.S. Department of Defense; the original name of the network was ARPANET. Early justification for the ARPANET project was to maintain the flow of defense-related information in the event of a catastrophic nuclear attack; the idea was that, if a nuclear explosion destroyed one or more sites/nodes in the network (a university or city, for instance), the information packets bearing vital military information would simply be rerouted through other paths and other nodes of the

Table 7.1   Top 15 Internet Users, 2002

Ranking	Country	Internet Users (in 1,000s)	Share %
1	United States	160,000	24.13
2	Japan	64,800	9.73
3	China	54,500	6.71
4	Germany	30,350	8.18
5	United Kingdom	27,150	4.08
6	South Korea	26,900	4.04
7	Italy	20,850	3.13
8	Canada	17,830	2.68
9	France	16,650	2.50
10	India	16,580	2.49
11	Brazil	15,840	2.38
12	Russia	13,500	2.03
13	Australia	10,450	1.57
14	Spain	10,390	1.56
15	Taiwan	9,510	1.43
Top 15 Total		**496,000**	**74.48**
Worldwide Total		**665,910**	**100.00**

SOURCE: Computer Industry Almanac Inc. (2002).

network (Wall, 1997, p. 209). By 1969, ARPANET connected four nodes; specifically, four major research facilities—University of Southern California (USC), Stanford Research Institute (SRI), University of California at Santa Barbara (UCSB), and the University of Utah. By 1973, an international connection with University College of London (England) was established via NORSAR (Norway) (Lipson, 2002, p. 5). By 1982, a means of supporting network-to-network linkages appeared in the form of a standard network protocol.[4] Specifically, this protocol was to become the "glue" that held together the many, many component networks making up the Internet.

Currently, there are about 233 million hosts throughout the world.[5] The number of Internet users around the world is approximately 665,910,000; government and independent market researchers expect that the number of Internet users could reach 1 billion by the year 2005 (Torr, 2003b, p. 13). In the United States, there are approximately 160,700,000 Internet users making up about 24% of the worldwide total (see Table 7.1 along with a visual representation in Figure 7.1. Note that only 15 developed countries represent nearly 75% of the worldwide total of Internet users. This latter fact demonstrates a wide gulf between rich/developed nations and the rest of the world in terms of involvement in the Information Age. But computers are misused by people and organizations in both the developed and less-developed world.

WHAT IS TRANSNATIONAL COMPUTER CRIME?

Transnational is a relatively new term developed by the U.N. Crime and Criminal Justice Branch in 1974. Its main purpose was to help guide U.N. conference discussions of crime[6] (Reuter & Petrie, 2000, p. 7), but the term has gained a more widespread use in discussions of general crime, especially organized crime activities. *Transnational crime* typically implies that the criminal activity involves at least two different countries; sometimes, the term *cross-border crime* is used equivalently. Transnational crime has immediate and

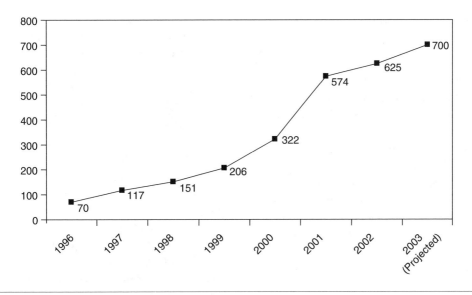

Figure 7.1   Total Web Users Online (in millions), 1996 to 2003
SOURCE: InterGOV International's Office of Public Information (www.intergov.org).

obvious utility for computer crime, given the lack of regard that this kind of crime has for national or continental boundaries.

A wide and diverse range of social theorists argue that today's world is undergoing fundamental and monumental structural changes: This change has often been defined as *globalization*. Globalization is often defined using Harvey's (1989, pp. 284–285) notion of time-space compression; interlinked computers are by their very nature an essential component of the globalizing world. Although there are many uses for the idea of globalization, one involves a world capitalist economic system playing a forceful role in eliminating the primacy, effectiveness, and even the necessity of that most cherished modern form of geopolitical organization—the nation-state.[7] In this perspective, transnational corporations and organizations are eroding and dismantling local structures, traditions, and cultures (Kellner, 2002, p. 285). It follows in this line of reasoning that the death knell for nation-states has been sounded and, lacking any utility, the nation-state

is destined to become an artifact of history. The evolution of a European Union—along with all of the many complications of that experiment (see discussion of European unification in Castells, 1998, pp. 330–354)— might be considered an ongoing object lesson of this kind of trend toward the death of the nation-state.

Needless to say, the computer plays a pivotal role in the internationalization and globalization of the world. The computer is constrained by neither time nor place.

General Types of Computer Crime

Computer crime may be organized into two broad categories: (1) those crimes where the computer is used as a *tool*, as when reproducing copyrighted materials or stalking someone and (2) those crimes where the computer is a *target* as in those acts intended to steal passwords or those meant to break down network service (denial of service) (see Mukhtar, 2001, p. 1).

Cybercrimes I: Computer as Tool

Financial crimes. At one level, money laundering is simple: One's ill-gotten money is converted to a less-suspicious, less-traceable form of asset. However, the process by which this is accomplished can be incredibly complicated. In a sense, the more complicated and convoluted the laundering process, the more layers of safety lie between the original culprit and the dirty money—and, therefore, the better for the criminal. With the advent of computer involvement in money-laundering schemes, even more layers of "safety" can be created. It is estimated that the "total amount of money laundered in the world average between 2 and 5 per cent of the world's GDP [gross domestic product]" (Tan, 2002, p. 277); this is between $600 billion and $1.5 trillion. These amounts place money laundering as the third largest business in the world behind foreign exchange and oil (Tan, 2002, p. 277).

The Financial Action Task Force (FATF), one of the most important intergovernmental organizations dealing with money laundering at this time, was established at the G-7 summit in Paris in July of 1989 (Zombori, 2001, p. 20). The FATF report, *The Forty Recommendations* (1999), is one of the most respected documents on money laundering. The recommendations represent the complexities of modern money-laundering schemes and the need for international cooperation in their control. With respect to the computer and money laundering, Recommendation 13 of that report states, "Countries should pay special attention to money laundering threats inherent in the new or developing technologies that might favour anonymity, and take measures, if needed, to prevent their use in money laundering schemes" (FATF, 1999, p. 4).

Financial frauds constitute another type of computer-aided financial crime. These crimes usually follow a common pattern. Those engaged in fraud typically prey on people who are looking to make a better than average return on their investments (or, to put it a little less charitably, those looking to get something for nothing) or on those in desperate need of a loan (van Fossen, 2002, p. 357). This applies to traditional local forms of fraud as well as to new forms of cross-border fraud.

The advent of the Internet has allowed chat rooms, e-mail, or Web sites to be used as vehicles for conducting fraud. According to National Fraud Information Center (2004), the most frequent Internet fraud in 2003 were online auctions (89%), followed by general merchandise (5%), Nigerian money offers (42%), and information/adult services (1%); the average loss per incident was $527 compared with $468 in 2002. These schemes induce the victims to send money for promised items but then deliver nothing or only an item far less valuable that what was promised (U.S. Department of Justice, 2000a). Other popular forms of Internet fraud include identify theft, credit card fraud, investment fraud, and trademark, copyright, or patent counterfeiting (U.S. Department of Justice, 2000a). All of these have occurred ignoring national borders.

Nigerian scams, mentioned in the foregoing paragraph, bilked innocent victims of $5 billion by 1996 since they were first detected in the early 1980s, and they continue to the present time (The 419 Coalition, 2003, p. 1). A watchdog group, The 419[8] Coalition based in Harrisonburg, Virginia, describes the Nigerian scams,

> The Scam operates as follows: the target receives an unsolicited fax, email, or letter often concerning Nigeria or another African nation containing either a money laundering or other illegal proposal OR you may receive a Legal and legitimate business proposal by normal means. . . . At some point, the victim is asked to pay up front an Advance Fee of some sort, be it an "Advance Fee," "Transfer Tax," "Performance Bond," or to extend credit, grant COD privileges. . . . If the victim pays the Fee, there are many "Complications" which require still more advance payments. (The 419 Coalition, 2003, p. 1)

Yet another, somewhat odd case of fraud—actually many acts of fraud—began in June of 1990 when Mark Logan Pedley founded the Dominion of Melchizedek, a fictional jurisdiction having 300 equally fictional banks, most of which have been used in numerous fraud schemes (van Fossen, 2002, p. 364). The following briefly describes Melchizedek:

> Since 1990 fraudsters have formed a network centering on the Dominion of Melchizedek. . . . a pseudo-state claiming jurisdiction or influence over an increasing number of Pacific Islands but existing primarily in cyberspace . . . Melchizedek registers insurance companies, banks and other entities for clients who would have great difficulty obtaining them . . . Melchizedek serves as a kind of "underground government" which organizes independent entrepreneurial criminals—bringing them together and providing them with connection, pseudo-state corporate entities, diplomatic passports, government positions, and "laws." (van Fossen, 2002, pp. 358–359)

To protect and investigate the increasing Internet financial frauds, the National Fraud Information Center (NFIC) was established in 1992. In 1996, the Internet Fraud Watch was created, enabling the NFIC to offer consumers advice on protecting themselves from fraud schemes. The Internet Fraud Initiative was created in 1999, and recently, the Federal Bureau of Investigation and the National White Collar Crime Center established a joint project, the Internet Fraud Complaint Center established to receive online complaints, analyze the complaints to identify the character of the particular schemes, and refer potential Internet fraud schemes to law enforcement (U.S. Department of Justice, 2000a).

Offensive content. There exists an abundance of what to some are objectionable materials on the Internet, from sexually explicit materials and racist propaganda to instructions for fabricating bombs (Grabosky, 2001, pp. 42–43),

as well as tools and software for finding and hacking into vulnerable computer systems. Examples of offensive material aimed at hurting individuals are many; for instance,

> A rejected suitor posted invitations on the Internet under the name of a 28-year-old woman, the would-be object of his affections, that said that she had fantasies of rape and gang rape. He then communicated via e-mail with men who replied to the solicitations and gave out personal information about the woman, including her address, phone number, details of her physical appearance and how to bypass her home security system. Strange men turned up at her home on six different occasions and she received many obscene phone calls. While the woman was not physically assaulted, she would not answer the phone, was afraid to leave her home, and lost her job. (recounted in Grabosky, 2001, p. 42)

A major concern, especially among the public and political leaders, is the presence of and relatively easy access to pornographic materials on the Internet. The concern centers on children and those who would be adversely influenced by such visual, audio, and textual offensive materials. To some, the problem is easily remedied: Eliminate access to offensive material. However, this solution has many, many ramifications, not the least of which involves defining what is "obscene." And this is a very old problem.

> In 1954, the British philosopher Bertrand Russell told *Look* that obscenity "is whatever happens to shock some elderly and ignorant magistrate." Ten years later, Justice Potter Stewart, an elderly but hardly ignorant U.S. Supreme Court Justice, implicitly endorsed Russell's observation when he wrote that he could not intelligibly define obscenity, but "I knew it when I saw it." (Lane, 2000, p. 124)

As the Internet grows, confrontations between those who would control the content (not only sexual explicit material but hate speech as well) on the Internet to protect citizens thought vulnerable and those concerned that this control infringes on the fundamental value of democracies—freedom of speech—will likely continue and become even more contentious (for fuller discussions and debates regarding free speech and control of Internet content, see Spinello, 2000, pp. 45–69; Torr, 2003a, pp. 92–135). A complicating factor for the transnational perspective is that there exist variations among different countries as to what is considered "offensive content" (child pornography, for instance).

Underlying all arguments of morality and ethics of Internet content is the fact that pornography on the Internet is part of a huge pornography industry, a full-blown sector of the economy in the United States. Even conservative estimates place pornography at about $10 billion per year in gross revenue, which places it at what Americans pay for sporting events and live music performances combined. Of this amount, between 5% and 10% came from adult Web sites in 1998 (Lane, 2000, pp. xiv–xv).

Cybercrimes II: Computer as Target

The sophistication of system attack tools is continually improving; consequently, current antivirus software and intrusion detection systems are severely strained. Also, more and more system vulnerabilities are being discovered and at a faster rate than system administrators can provide and invoke patches to "fill" those vulnerabilities (Householder, Kevin, & Dougherty, 2003, p. 2).

Computer network attacks can be divided into two types: passive attacks and active attacks. Passive attacks generally focus on intercepting data such as passwords, user names, e-mail messages, and even secret data using "sniffing" software.[9] Active attacks, on the other hand, typically attempt to cause harm to computer systems by exploiting system faults and vulnerabilities (Chappell, 2001–2002, pp. 1–2). Most active attacks attempt to overload the victim's computer or system of computers to the point that it either slows to an unusable crawl, hangs, or completely crashes. There are many popular attack tools available to anyone with Internet access to the World Wide Web and requiring little computer sophistication to use.

One type of active attack, the denial of service attack, uses multiple systems to attack one or more victim systems with the intent of denying service to legitimate users of the victim systems (Householder et al., 2003, pp. 2–3). Another type of attack, even more dangerous than denial of service, is the distributed denial of service attack, which can use an entire army of computers to attack the victim system. For example, during a week in February 2000, hundreds of computers overloaded several selected victims, including Yahoo.com, ETrade.com, and CNN.com (Chappell, 2001–2002, pp. 6–7). The third type of active attack, unlike a virus, requires that a user *do something* to continue toward the virus's end goal, such as destroying a hard drive or deleting a set of files. Alternatively, a worm can propagate by itself with no user involvement whatsoever. Worms also can spread through networks and the Internet with no assistance. For example,

> In 1988, Robert Tappan Morris, Jr., a 23-year-old graduate student in computer science at Cornell and the son of a National Security Agency (NSA) computer security expert, wrote an experimental, self-replicating, self-propagating program called a *worm* (99 lines of code, not including object files) and injected it into the Internet. He chose to release it from MIT, to disguise the fact that the worm came from Cornell. (Power, 2000, p. 60)

The Morris worm shut down 60,000 computers across the United States, and although it caused no physical damage, the U.S. General

Accounting Office estimated that between $100,000 and $10 million was lost due to lost access to the Internet. Morris was eventually convicted under the Computer Fraud and Abuse Act (Title 18) and sentenced to 3 years of probation and 400 hours of community service; he was also fined $10,500, plus supervision costs. His appeal in December of 1991 was rejected (Power, 2000, pp. 63–64). This case involved primarily U.S. computers and computer systems, but it can easily be seen how similar attacks may disable computer systems worldwide.

HOW MUCH TRANSNATIONAL COMPUTER CRIME EXISTS?

There is an unhappy fact regarding the level of transnational crime, including computer crime. That fact is that "highly reliable national statistics are rare" (Williams, 1999, p. 221), and we would add that this is even more true with regard to international statistics. In August 1999, President Clinton ordered the establishment of an interagency Working Group on Unlawful Conduct on the Internet. The working group's report expressed considerable concern about the glaring lack of data on Internet crime. Forced to rely primarily on anecdotal materials and press reports, the working group (2000, p. 10) was simply unable to specify the degree of impact of Internet crime in the United States. Furthermore, in addition to not being able to accurately gauge how much Internet crime exists, we also face a vacuum of credible data as to *who* is committing Internet crime.

InterGOV's International Web Police is making a strong effort at the international level to gather reliable information on Web crime. The aim of this international organization is to serve and protect the citizens of the Internet community. InterGOV International acts as a central clearinghouse for reported computer crimes, scams, and terrorist activities and is the regular posting site for the crime

and terrorist activity on the Web. In 1993, there were 640 complaints filed with InterGOV, a rate of about 1.7 complaints per day; by the year 2002, InterGOV received 1,351,897 complaints, a rate of about 3,704 complaints per day.[10] However, only about 31% of the complaints received were considered valid—that is, Web related. The top three types of valid complaint were (1) fraud (scams) complaints, 26%; (2) child pornography complaints, 17%; and (3) stalking complaints, 11% (see Table 7.2). InterGOV evaluates the crime rate increase from 2002 to 2003 at about 61%.

Table 7.2   Type of Reports to INTERGov, 2002

Type of Report/Complaint	Percentage
Fraud (scams)	26
Child pornography	17
Stalking	11
E-mail abuse	9
Harassment/threats	9
Hacking/viruses	9
Children related	6
Copyright violations	4
Terrorism	3
Chat room abuse	2
Other	4
Total	**100**

SOURCE: InterGOV International's Office of Public Information (www.intergov.org).

In the United States, early data collection dealing with attacks on computers was begun in December of 1988. The agency organized to, among other things, collect this type of data was Computer Emergency Response Team (CERT)[11] located at Carnegie Mellon Software Engineering Institute in Pittsburgh, Pennsylvania. According to CERT (see www.cert.org/stats/cert_stats.html), the number of computer security incidents reported to CERT in its beginning year, 1988, was 6; in 2001, it was 52,658; and by September, 2003, it was over 137,529 incidents (p. 5) (see Figure 7.3).

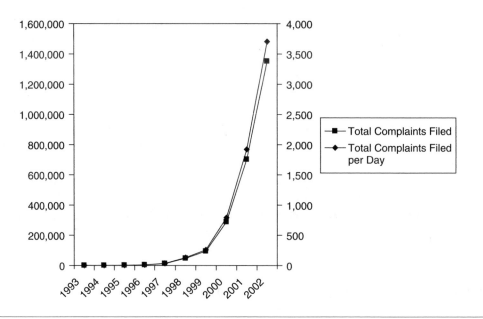

Figure 7.2   Criminal and Civil Web Complaints, 1993 to 2002

SOURCE: InterGOV International's Office of Public Information (www.intergov.org).

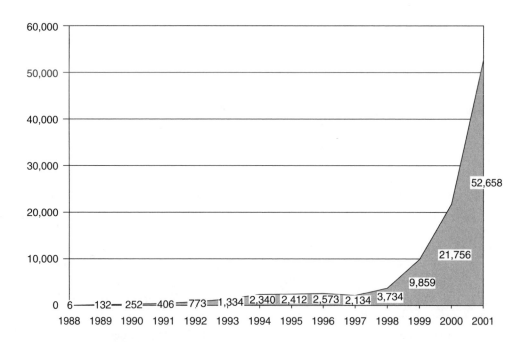

Figure 7.3   Internet Computer Attacks Reported to CERT Coordination Center, 1988 to 2001

SOURCE: Householder, Kevin, and Dougherty (2003). Copyright 2002, Institute of Electrical and Electronic Engineers, Inc. All rights reserved.

In sum, (a) it is very hard to estimate the exact amount of national and international computer crime, and (b) it appears that there is a steady increase in reported computer crime.

TRANSNATIONAL CYBERCRIME CRIMINAL JUSTICE ISSUES

We know of many, many variants of computer crime already, with more waiting to be invented; included among the current wave are computer hacking,[12] stalking, swindle and extortion schemes, computer piracy, theft of money from banking and financial and other industries, terrorism of many kinds, launching computer viruses and worms, denial of service schemes, identity theft, unauthorized use of information systems, sabotage of individual as well as corporate computers and computer networks, espionage, privacy infringement, copyright and intellectual property violations, consumer fraud, the transmission of harmful or illegal information or both related to drug dealing and other "traditional street crime," illegal arms trade, child pornography and obscenity, hate speech, defamation, and other new types no doubt evolving as we write. These different types call for different law enforcement responses. In the following section, a few recent developments in this area are discussed.

Law and Criminal Justice in Cyberspace

In any discussion about the fundamentals of criminal law and cyberspace, it is worthwhile to remember the reasons why criminal and civil laws have traditionally been wielded. Norms are often viewed as society's approximation of proper behavior but are most effectively enforced by small, cohesive groups in which the violators are obvious, deviations can be quickly punished, and the offender tends to be sensitive to group disapproval or sanction. As groups grow larger, more anonymous, and more complex, individuals become less sensitive to informal controls. At this point, the formal methods of social control, civil and criminal law, emerge (Reid, 2000).

Civil law is designed to protect a variety of interests such as preserving the family (divorce law), protecting business relationships (contract law, uniform commercial code), preserving property rights (probate law), and generally motivating reasonably responsible behavior (negligence and product liability actions) (Reid, 2000). In civil law actions, the litigation is structured so that a plaintiff (the injured party) pursues a personal or institutional remedy for damages against the defendant. The harm for which the defendant may be liable can arise from acts that are either negligent or intentional and can include acts such as libel, slander, false imprisonment, assault and battery, causing physical or emotional injury, wrongful death, or product liability. The two primary purposes of civil suits are to compensate an injured party for miscellaneous losses (through financial awards) or to force a party to "do" something through injunctive relief.

In contrast, the parties to a criminal action are the state (representing "society") versus the defendant. Unlike traditional civil actions that tended to rely on causes of action and remedies shaped by the common law (the law created by judicial decisions), criminal actions involve a wrongful act specifically prohibited by law. Within the tradition of American jurisprudence, the main constitutive elements of a criminal law include the following:

a. *Actus reus* or wrongful act: Actor commits a specific act or omission

b. *Mens rea* or guilty mind:
   i. Actor's intention to commit the prohibited act
   ii. May be varying degrees from deliberate to intentional to accidental

c. Concurrence of act and intent: It is not a crime to think bad thoughts or to commit an unavoidable act

d. Harm: Personal/societal interest must somehow be diminished

e. Causation: Harm must result from the act (Nemeth, 2004; Reid, 2000)

The prosecutor must prove the existence of all five elements to win conviction. In contrast to most civil cases in which the plaintiff must prove his or her cause of action by a preponderance of the evidence, the state's prosecutor must present sufficient evidence to convince the judge or jury that the defendant is guilty beyond a reasonable doubt.

To understand how law influences social behavior, it is also important to appreciate the distinction between the substantive criminal law and criminal procedure. The substantive law defines the actual crimes and addresses the specific behavior that the state proscribes—for example, murder, robbery, or speeding (Nemeth, 2004; Reid, 2000). Criminal procedure, on the other hand, sets the rules by which the prosecution may proceed. It has often been said that the state uses the substantive criminal law to keep the citizenry under control, whereas due process provides the leverage by which citizens can keep the state under control.

From a policy-making perspective, the critical hallmarks of a successful response to computer and security concerns include striking the appropriate balance between (a) crime control and due process, (b) accountability and privacy, (c) system integrity and system access, (d) constraints on vulnerability and facilitating entrepreneurial/academic/artistic creativity, and (e) protecting society's general liberty interests and protecting an individual's specific liberty interests.

President Clinton's Working Group on Unlawful Conduct on the Internet (2000) noted, "The rapid growth of the Internet and e-commerce has made such unlawful conduct a critical priority *for legislators, policymakers, industry, and law enforcement agencies*" [italics added] (p. 10). Given the emergence of undesirable behaviors within a society,

these groups face two choices: Develop enforcement and prosecution strategies that rely on existing laws to deter the deviance, or create new criminal statutes that specifically target that behavior.

The reality of political survival provides strong incentives for legislators and policymakers to create new rules and laws.[13] The Uniting and Strengthening America by Providing Appropriate Tools Required to Intercept and Obstruct Terrorist Act of 2001 (USA PATRIOT Act of 2001, P.L. 107–56, 115 Stat.272 (2001)) was actually a set of amendments to the National Information Infrastructure Protection Act of 1996 (18 U.S.C. § 1030) in which several computer crime acts were already prohibited. In general terms, the respective subsections prohibit (a) unauthorized access to computer files (1030(a)(1)); (b) obtaining information from financial institutions, the U.S. government, or private sector computers used in interstate commerce (1030(a)(2)); (c) intentionally accessing government computers without authorization (1030(a)(3)); (d) accessing a protected computer with the intent to defraud and obtain something of value (1030(a)(4)); (e) hacker-related activities that intentionally, recklessly, or negligently impair the "integrity or availability of data, a program, a system, or information" (1030(a)(5)); (f) the trafficking of passwords (1030(a)(6)); and (g) threats to damage a protected computer with the intent to extort something of value (1030(a)(7)); 18 U.S.C. § 1030 (2000) (as amended by 115 Stat. 272) (see Jacobson & Green, 2002, p. 280). Although a perceived need to keep pace with the evolution of new variations in computer crime undoubtedly drove these amendments of the substantive criminal law, the obvious effort that went into assembling a bill title that reduced to the acronym, "USA PATRIOT Act" illustrates Congress's desire to prominently remind constituents of legislators' aggressive disapproval of computer-related misbehavior.

Such legislative action frequently facilitates police and prosecutors' enforcement efforts. New laws convey a strong sense of legitimacy to investigations, arrests, and prosecutions. Challenges to the constitutionality or substantive validity of such laws require time and resources that many defendants cannot muster. As a practical result, police and prosecutors are able to bring the significant weight of state authority to bear against offenders even while society debates the extent to which a behavior should be condemned.

There is an emerging set of international legal regulations focusing on computer crime (see discussions in Cronin, 2002; Gabrys, 2002; Grove, Goodman, & Lukasik, 2000). As in many other areas of international matters—treaties, U.N. decrees, covenants, conventions, and so on—gaining true international cooperation is often problematic. Therefore, international law develops slowly. However, as the risks of cyberattacks against important national information structures increase, it behooves nations to begin to discuss the legal problems of information warfare more openly and candidly (Grove et al., 2000, p. 100). One approach suggested by Grove is to broaden the definition of "armed attack" involving "use of force" current in the U.N. Charter to include destructive and invasive information attacks against U.N. member nations. He argues that certain information technology attacks could cause destruction at least equal to conventional armed forces (Grove et al., 2000, pp. 93–94). The road to progress on international cooperation in dealing with transnational computer crime will be a long one.

PROCESSING TRANSNATIONAL COMPUTER CRIME

International Law Enforcement

When speaking of transnational crime, most current criminological scholars focus on the international aspects of organized crime or economic crime, not computer crime. However, the main problems facing those in law enforcement for those kinds of crime will, no doubt, be in place for transnational computer crime as well: (a) Law enforcement is not sufficiently trained or adept at responding to technological or organizationally complex crime, and (b) law enforcement is faced with significant "regulatory conflicts" arising from international and interorganizational relationships underlying transnational computer crime (Schlegel, 2000, p. 366). And with these difficulties, a compounding problem for law enforcement aiming at transnational crime is that research is very limited; in Schlegel's less-than-optimistic view, "We know precious little about the policing of organized crime and even less about the policing of white-collar crime" (p. 371). This state of affairs does not portend well for understanding organized and white-collar crime, much less with the added complication of high technology.

Countries are taking many varying law enforcement steps to contain this "new crime." For instance, Singapore, China, and Vietnam seek to control citizen use of the Internet by requiring users to register with authorities as well as by directly controlling Internet traffic coming into the country (Wall, 1997, p. 219). The U.S. fight against computer crime involves state-funded non-public-police organizations such as the U.S. Postal Service and the U.S. Securities and Exchange Commission as well as legal measures and technological devices (encryption devices) (Wall, 1997, pp. 219–220). However, the United Kingdom leans toward an approach encouraging Internet service providers to "police" their own services (Wall, 1997, p. 220).

A key problem with law enforcement of transnational computer crime—at least that dealing with the Internet—is that the Internet was not designed to track or trace the behavior of its users or to resist or limit access of "untrustworthy users" (Lipson,

2002, pp. 13–14). Rather, the Internet was originally designed as a free means to connect cooperative and collaborative communities of academic and military researchers. Funds were not made available for security for the early Internet; instead, functionality and performance of the Internet were the funding priorities (Lipson, 2002, p. 13). Lipson comments on the state of affairs of security on the Internet:

> The Internet's original design goals never included the support of today's mission-critical and high-stakes applications in business, energy, transportation, communications, banking and finance, and national defense. These high-stakes Internet applications pose enormously tempting targets of opportunity for criminals, terrorists, and hostile nations, and they overly stress the technology designed for more innocent times. The migration of critical applications from expensive, closed, arcane, and proprietary technology to less costly, open, highly-distributed Internet applications, based on widely available COTS (commercial off the shelf) or public domain software, makes these applications much more accessible and more easily attacked by malicious adversaries. (pp. 15–16)

It is well-known that the current state of law enforcement will have to undergo major changes to deal with the threat of cybercrime. Many scholars and practitioners are attempting to forge new inroads in dealing with crime having a transnational scope. Choudhury (2001) suggests that the biggest challenge to international law enforcement of transnational computer crime is to "think globally and act locally" (p. 77). Although in the long run, the following institutions and agencies may well become extinct, they currently represent the frontline for international law enforcement effort in controlling transnational crime: (a) Interpol, (b) International Association of Chiefs of Police, and (c) the United Nations

and multinational institutions such as the World Bank (involved because of fraud and money laundering concerns among others) (pp. 75–76).

One response to crime that has gained considerable momentum in the last decade is private security. That trend is not different in terms of private efforts to stem or control computer crime. The demand for those professionals skilled in cybersecurity is far greater than the supply, and both companies and government agencies (e.g., U.S. State Department, Federal Reserve) are using "innovative programs to recruit and train workers with specialized skills in information security" (Emery, 2001, pp. 1–2).

An often-forgotten "player" in the attempt to control transnational computer crime is the community of Internet users themselves. Complaint hotlines and organized, voluntary groups such as the Internet Rapid Response Team are early attempts of the user community to police its own and rid the Internet of offensive material (Wall, 1997, p. 222). Another instance is the group modeled after the Guardian Angels known as CyberAngels started in 1995. CyberAngels number about 1,300 volunteers in more than 14 countries (Karp, 2000, p. 76). The group's goal is to help out those who are stalked and harassed by, effectively, changing the hunter into the hunted. This is accomplished by teaching the victim of stalking to use his or her computer to track and research the stalker (Karp, 2000).

Huey (2002) argues that policing cyberspace will require rethinking old habits; more specifically, a habit of thinking in terms of set geography for traditional police work is simply not going to suffice in a circumstance where geography has little or no meaning. However, in Huey's view, we should not throw the baby out with the bath water, so to speak; some traditional policing methods will work, but they must be accomplished in a new environment of technology (pp. 252–253).

GLIMPSES INTO THE FUTURE?

Paul Saffo, director of the Institute for the Future, suggests, "Ask yourselves when are we going to see the first journal of bio-hacking oriented toward teenage males, so they can create molecules in their bedroom. Well, that journal came out in 1998. Be very afraid" (cited in Oakes, 2000, p. 4).

Traditional Criminology Meets the Study of Transnational Computer Crime

We all too easily become bogged down in studying the practical, legal, and economic effects (transnational) computer crime. These issues are important, of course. However, of equal importance is reflecting on the conceptual, theoretical implications of the computer revolution for the study and control of crime in the future. In this concluding section, we highlight very briefly some of these selected issues: changing notions of time, place, and identity; changing ideas about traditional family, community, and organization; changing notions of how to study computer criminals and criminality; and futuristic ideas of crime and crime fighting through robotics and telerobotics.

Social Facts, Revised?

The unique character of computer wrongdoing forces social scientists to confront a most foundational social science notion—the *social fact*. Social fact was defined by Durkheim in 1895 as

> *every way of acting, fixed or not, capable of exercising on the individual an external constraint; or again, every way of acting which is general through a given society, while at the same time existing in its own right independent of its individual manifestations.* [italics in original] (1985/1938, p. 13)

The social fact is, for the social scientist, the social "thing," on-a-par-with the rocks, billiard balls, planets, and electrons of the physical sciences; it is the bearer of our data and the subject of our "modeling" efforts. Constituent parts of that conceptual apparatus—that social fact—are *identity, place,* and *time*. These conceptual parts of the social fact become oddly problematic with the involvement of computer technology: What is the "I" or the "self" of *identity*? Where is the "here" of *place*? What is the "now" of *time* in a computer-mediated community joined by electronic devices shooting electronic packets to and fro?

Identity: What Is the "I" or the "Self" in a Computer-Mediated Community?

Among the more promising thinkers willing to deal head-on with problems of identity (see also Castells, 1997, pp. 5–67) as well as place and time in inventive ways are Gilles Deleuze and Felix Guattari (see 1983, 1987). These authors, in the context of a discussion of the meaning of the "authorship" of one of their collaborative efforts *Anti-Oedipus: Capitalism and Schizophrenia* (1983), hint at a new foundation:

> The two of us wrote *Anti-Oedipus* together. Since each of us was several, there was already quite a crowd. . . . Why have we kept our own names? Out of habit, purely out of habit. To render imperceptible, not ourselves, but what makes us act, feel, and think. Also because it's nice to talk like everybody else, to say the sun rises, when everybody knows it's only a manner of speaking. *To reach, not the point where one no longer says I, but the point where it is no longer of any importance whether one says I.* [italics added] (Deleuze & Guattari, 1987, p. 3)

The social fact, as it was framed and subsequently used in social science, never even remotely suggested a lack of importance of the "I" or the "self"; it only suggested that there was something over and above the constituent "I's" or "selves" making up groups and societies.[14] However, for Deleuze and Guattari, reflecting a postmodern approach to understanding a globalizing, computer-mediated world, these I's and selves—so important and foundational to our traditional *social facts*—may be mere manners of speaking just like the "sun rises."

Place: Where Is the "Here" in a Computer-Mediated Community?

Earlier, we introduced the strange story of Melchizedek, a fictional nation-state complete with 300+ fictional banks involved as part of criminal activity. Now the "where" of this dominion, Melchizedek, is cyberspace; *yet*, what are its specific longitudinal and latitudinal coordinates? Every *place* has coordinates. Puzzles like this abound in cyberspace, and they boggle the mind.

Another example of the paradoxical character of the "here" is the intriguingly chronicled tale told in the *Cuckoo's Egg*[15] (Stoll, 1989). Clifford Stoll, an astronomer turned computer espionage sleuth, tracks down the source of a 75-cent discrepancy on the monthly computer usage billing logs at Lawrence Berkeley Lab's computers in Berkeley, California. The journey to the source of the discrepancy takes Stoll ultimately to a hacker in Hannover, Germany, whose hacking efforts operated through many computers, including the University of Bremen; a defense contractor in McLean, Virginia; the U.S. Air Force Base in Ramstein, West Germany;[16] the Anniston Army Depot in Anniston, Alabama; the U.S. Navy Coastal Systems Computer in Panama City, Florida; and others. These connections to military-related computers were *through* the Lawrence Berkeley Lab's computers. The motivation for the German hackers—Marcus Hess and others of the hacker

group, Chaos Computer Club—was to sell information about Western technology, "including integrated circuit design, computer-aided manufacturing, and, especially, operating systems software that was under U.S. export control as well as copies of Digital Equipment's VMS operating system" (p. 366) to the East German KGB for Deutschmarks and cocaine.

In the working document, *e + Finance + Crime: A Report on Cyber-Crime and Money Laundering,* Zombori (2001) comments, in summarizing the changes caused by computing and the Internet, that "the meaning of time and space must be revisited. Living in the Internet time and cyber-space, practical implications of time and space require reconsideration" (p. 5).

Time: What Is the "Now" in a Computer-Mediated Community?

The speed of transmission of messages—or, more accurately, the constituent *packets* comprising messages—is blinding. Currently, conveyance of electronic bits, those electronic 0s and 1s that constitute the packets, over fiber-optic cables reaches 2 Gbps (gigabits per second) or 2 billion bits per second; and, "each year, transfer rates and bandwidth increase as communication companies develop new communications techniques and technologies" (Shelly et al., 1999, pp. 9.14–9.15). This kind of speed is already affecting our lives as we try to keep up—if only to delete the spam messages that arrive in our e-mail boxes hourly. Castells (1996; see his full discussion of his notion of "timeless time," pp. 429–468) argues that the networked society is characterized by random discontinuities of the sequence of phenomena or the de-sequencing of time (p. 464); he describes the "timeless landscape of computer networks and electronic media, where all expressions are either instantaneous, or without predictable sequencing" (Castells, 1998, p. 370). Moreover, the *perception* of time in the Information Age is in flux. For example, Himanen (2001) comments on the "Sundayization of Friday" as the boundaries between work and leisure break down (pp. 32–38). Linus Torvald, originator of one of the most famous hacker creations of our time, the Linux operating system (Himanen, 2001, p. xi), describes his own approach to time and work:

> Hackers optimize time to be able to have more space for playfulness: [my] way of thinking is that, in the middle of the serious work of Linux development, there always has to be time for some pool and for some programming experiments that do not have immediate goals. (quoted in Himanen, 2001, p. 32)

Some of the "painful" puzzles involved with place and time in a computer-mediated world are even more puzzling in the relation *between* the two—place and time. One way to get a feel for this problem is to think of asking the person who has just had heart surgery and is currently kept alive with pulmonary and cardiac machines (see Note 3) outside his or her body, Where *are* you? What are the coordinates describing the physical *you*? Do those coordinates of *you include* the pulmonary and cardiac machines?

Social Organization of the Future

Davis and Pease (2000) suggest that the basic motivations for computer crime remain the same as those for traditional crimes: *acquisitive*—as with theft or forgery—and *expressive*—such as violence or disorder. What will change, however, is the context for crime: It will no longer be restricted to traditional communities and families (p. 60). Davis and Pease rely on an earlier report, "Britain Towards 2010" (Scase, 1999) that predicts the decline of traditional communities, families, and social structures that have in the past acted to limit antisocial behavior. Information communication technologies will play a huge

role by way of not only increasing the speed, scale, and complexity of human interaction but increasing the isolation of people in public spaces. Davis and Pease (2000) describe a threatening, bleak life in 2010:

> There are increasing opportunities for people to be isolated in public space. Business, interpersonal and entertainment activities have moved from the social and static to the personal and mobile. People have greater choice as to who they "meet" and how. Physical society may, therefore, become a more hostile place, through which people travel rather than in which they expect to interact. In a dehumanized environment, people may become less "real" to one another, leading to more extreme reactions and interactions. (p. 61)

In addition to having different contexts, crime in this Information Age will, more than likely, also have different targets. For instance, stealing paper money will be less likely because paper money's role will be largely eliminated and replaced with electronic transactions—this trend, of course, is already well underway. That which will be valued by an Information Age thief will be more along the lines of "electronic property." For instance, valued electronic property will be electronic services such as video-on-demand, knowledge and information such as copyrights or trademarks, or identity devices such as biometric smart cards or odor profiles to gain entrance to premises, facilities, and services (Davis & Pease, 2000, pp. 62–63).

Organizational Structure: Bureaucracy or Network? Hierarchy or Horizontal?

The structure of organizations has been of interest to social scientists since Max Weber's famous *Bureaucracy* (Weber, 1925/1946). The ideal type bureaucratic organization was thought to be *the* organizational structure of the future, and many organizations from educational to governmental to corporate fell more and more in line with the seven characteristics of bureaucracy (pp. 196–198). The second of these bureaucratic characteristics— "a firmly ordered system of super- and subordination in which there is a supervision of the lower offices by the higher ones" (p. 197)—is potentially problematic in 21st-century organization. Some scholars and observers are beginning to weigh in on "horizontal organization" (see, e.g., Brooks, 1995; Miller & O'Leary, 1989). Professor Peter Drucker (1992) observes that

> because the modern organization consists of knowledge specialists, it has to be an organization of equals, of colleagues and associates. No knowledge ranks higher than another; each is judged by its contribution to the common task rather than by any inherent superiority or inferiority. Therefore, the modern organization cannot be an organization of boss and subordinate. It must be organized as a team. (p. 101)

Drucker's organization clearly violates Weber's second characteristic of the bureaucracy. The team concept of organization has yet to catch on in criminal justice organizations such as that of law enforcement. Law enforcement, in most cases, remains firmly built on a bureaucratic and military model.

Some look to a "network" model of organization such as Lipnack and Stamps (1986) describe: "Networks *decentralize decision making* through guidance by *many leaders* with *multiple layers* of intertwining connection and concerns in which people communicate as *nodes and links* that fade from view through *fuzzy boundaries*" (pp. 6–7).

The idea of a network has a familiarity and clarity that it might not have once had were it not for the Internet. People have become acquainted with the ideas of nodes and connections of computers with networks as well as networks connected with networks. The Internet may be an organizational model for the future social organization in addition to being a collection of physical and electronic machines.

Social Order: Chaos? Catastrophe?

Social order is generally thought to be the condition under which we live most of the time; it is mainly a synonym for *normal* among the general educated public. The involvement of computer technology seems to make social order a more problematic notion: The possible breakdown of power or electric or transportation grids makes us more likely to include *dis* before *order*. Alternative paradigms or conceptual perspectives are emerging that may enable adaptation to the Information Age. One candidate is chaos theory, a nonlinear, nonnormally distributed, and non-clockwork vision of nature (see two early attempts to sketch new, alternative paradigms for 21st-century social organization in Brown, 1995; Tetenbaum, 1998).[17] Such nontraditional perspectives, once thought to be the drivel of malcontents, charlatans, and others of the scientific fringe, are becoming more respectable to social science and mathematics (Liebovitch & Scheurle, 2000); however, in large part, social science and criminology continue relatively fixed in linear, normally distributed, clockwork foundational assumptions of social behavior.

SEEKING A WORKING PERSPECTIVE FOR COMPUTER HACKING

There exists no "theory of the computer hacker" to guide empirical research. Moreover, theoretical ventures into this area of human conduct are not even remotely moored to a single perspective in the sense of Kuhn's (1970) normal science "paradigm." Although it remains an open and vexing question as to how traditional positivist social science methods can be contorted to *capture* transnational computer crime, the importance of *some* guidance for empirical work is well accepted, if only to suggest what questions to ask. To that end, we draw on two general areas of thinking that might show promise as "working guides" for thinking about transnational crime, especially that part attempting to understand computer hacking: the work of Stanley Cohen (1971a, 1971b, 1973, 1988; Cohen & Taylor, 1976) and Arnold Goldstein (1996) on vandalism; and Jack Katz's (1988) *Seductions of Crime*. Both Cohen and Goldstein on vandalism and Katz incorporate nontraditional notions in their work.

Toward a Typology of Computer Hacking

Stanley Cohen and his associates worked out preliminary conceptual material on vandalism in the mid-1970s. One of the types of vandalism that Cohen (1973) elaborates is "ideological vandalism." Some of this kind of vandalism is that directed at companies or landlords or mill owners by disgruntled laborers—that is, working-class aggression toward new machines and the displacement the machines caused during the Industrial Revolution (pp. 34–41). This kind of conceptual label might work well with some hacker activities, such as those hackers who deface Department of Defense Web sites or break into Department of Defense or Central Intelligence Agency computer systems. It will, naturally, be impossible to consider all attacks of this kind as *ideological,* but the concept might help categorize some types of hacking. In addition to ideological vandalism, Cohen formulated five other types of conventional vandalism: acquisitive, tactical, vindictive, play, and malicious (pp. 41–51). Cohen strenuously disagrees with two aspects of traditional thinking about vandalism: (1) Vandalism is homogeneous, and one type of person commits all similar acts of vandalism; and (2) vandalism is meaningless, senseless behavior (pp. 41–42). Both points seem to be very much in step with current images of the malicious computer hacker.

Criminal Motivation of the Computer Hacker

It is well-known that Cohen is quite critical of traditional criminological methods (see Cohen, 1988, for the full elaboration of his views). He focuses on the process aspect of deviance, a quality broadly missed in traditional criminology where the product—the criminal act—is the main target of concern. Therefore, for Cohen, not only is the deviant's act important, but "the stages of involvement, disinvolvement, side-tracking, doubt, guilt, and commitment" (Cohen, 1971b, pp. 18–19) and all the other aspects of the deviant "context" are equally revealing. Cohen strays from a traditional notion that deviants are simply different from the "good folk" (Cohen, 1971b, pp. 20–21). Stark differences between good and evil, right and wrong, and criminal and noncriminal simply do not exist. In the case of computer hacking, for instance, many of those very qualities that we might like our own "good" children to have—intelligence, technical skill, assertiveness, rationality, love of fun, cleverness, bravery, derring-do—are characteristic of some of the very best computer hackers, malicious ones and otherwise.

Cohen offers yet one more potentially rich point of view that might help us understand computer hacking. His book *Escape Attempts* (Cohen & Taylor, 1976) is an interesting analysis of "acts of resistance" that human beings make for themselves while living with the dulling routinization, anxiety, irritation, boredom, and depression that characterizes modern, everyday life for some. One very intriguing chapter, "Free Areas, Escape Routes and Identity Sites," seems particularly useful in the exploring hacking and the hacker (pp. 94–137). Therein, Cohen argues that contemporary work and life is practically resisted by activities as such hobbies, games, gambling, and sex (pp. 97–113). The resistor avails himself or herself of new "landscapes" other than those presented to him or her in everyday life by engaging in travel, mass culture, and art (pp. 113–129). The resistor also applies new "mindscapes" for himself or herself with drugs—of both the licit and illicit kind—and therapy (pp. 129–137).

Another adventurous thinker, Jack Katz argues that the study of crime has long been occupied with "background forces" of crime to the neglect of the "often wonderful attractions within the lived experience of criminality" (Katz, 1988, p. 3). What it feels like to commit crime or what the criminal is trying to do when committing a crime are far more important questions to Katz than what causes crime (Vold, Bernard, & Snipes, 1998, p. 225).

The methods used by Katz (1988) for his investigations of, for example, "righteous slaughters" (homicide, pp. 12–51), "sneaky thrills" (petty theft, vandalism, joyriding, burglary, pp. 52–79), "street elites" (street fighting and violence, pp. 114–163) include biographies and autobiographies of the criminals as well as journalistic accounts and participant observation. For Katz, questions such as "Why did you do it?" are much less important than questions such as "How did you do that? or "And then what did you do?" These kinds of question are potentially useful when studying transnational computer crime.

Robotics and Telerobotics in Crime, and the Fight Against Crime

In the not-too-distant future, robotic cops (and robbers) may become more than mere Hollywood storylines (for example, *Robocop*) and special effects productions. Robotics are already involved in military applications, industrial production, policing, firefighting, bomb disposal, medical surgery, and many other things.

The possibilities and issues of telerobotics[18] are elaborated in *The Robot in the Garden: Telerobotics and Telepistemology in the Age of the Internet* (Goldberg, 2000b). This idea is not new; it dates back to the 1940s when telerobotic systems were needed for handling radioactive materials. More modern uses are tied to exploration, bomb disposal, and surgery (Goldberg, 2000a, p. 7); search-and-rescue efforts in urban catastrophic ruin situations (Sincell, 2000); and navigating Chernobyl following the April 26, 1986 nuclear accident (Alper, 1998). The Internet affords a rapidly growing audience for telerobotics: for example, the first Internet camera set up by Cambridge University researchers to monitor the status of a coffeepot or a digital camera and air jet on a robot arm so that anyone on the Internet could monitor and excavate artifacts in a sandbox in a lab at the University of Southern California (Goldberg, 2000a, p. 8). These "innocent" uses are potential harbingers of both *criminal* use of telerobotics and the *criminal justice system's* use: The technology is evolving.[19]

CONCLUSION

In this chapter, we have attempted to highlight a few of the many aspects of transnational computer crime. Our leaders struggle to legally define computer crime while our criminal justice system and law enforcement struggle to keep up with computer crime *and* standard-issue street crime. Although the difficulties are beginning to be addressed, there is a long way to go.

Those in professional criminal justice and criminology plod into a warp-speed future, burdened with the ways and thinking of old. We have what increasingly appear to be ossified conceptualizations tied to our long-favored notions of hierarchy, bureaucracy, and borders. We are reluctant to change; we have adopted *that* aspect of Kuhn's normal science practice, even in lieu of normal science *paradigm*. Yet like those standing on the beach watching an approaching tsunami, we *will* become involved. Computer technology will affect all that we do and think and are, both as ordinary citizens and as social scientists. Embracing that change will be the *only* possibility.

NOTES

1. Writing a chapter on computer crime is a daunting task. Although the amount of literature already accumulated is simply staggering, that mere *mass* of information is not what is daunting. Instead, it is the notion that most of that which is written is destined for the boneyard *even as it is written*. That is a very unsettling feeling. Although the reader need have little concern for how the authors feel, it is important to know that we can do little other here than flag *some* of the key issues. Chris Oakes (2000) describes a future living with computer technology in *The Year 2020, Explained*; he comments that "the hardest trick could be to stay sane amid a snowstorm of paradigm shifts" (p. 1). Our role as authors in the early run-up to 2020 may be in catching glimpses of a couple of those shifts while trying remain somewhat sane.

2. In the years since 1937 and Dr. John V. Atanasoff and Clifford Berry's first electronic digital computer (Shelly, Cashman, Vermaat, & Walker, 1999, p. 1.48), the size of the computer's main component—the silicon chip—has reduced dramatically. However, there remains one major constraining problem—heat; microprocessors with ever more increasing switching devices built into the microprocessors to ramp up the running speed are creating more and more heat to the point where supercomputers must be immersed in a liquid bath (Brown, 2000, p. 41). Some, including Brown, think this problem will be eventually addressed by quantum, atomic computing computing.

3. The computer is not *simply* a tool, however. Although it began that way, its role is changing. A tool never becomes a part of us in any sense; you simply put it back in the toolbox once its utility has been exhausted. But in the case of the computer, computer chips are already operating our hearts and the vital functions, keeping us alive; computer networks are substituting for meeting places such as bars and restaurants and boardrooms; personas developed in the course of chat room conversations are becoming a part of our total beings. In the easily foreseeable future, it will become more and more difficult to refer to computers as "they" or "it" instead of "we" and "I" (for an interesting example of a possible future, see the role of the "wearable computer," Oakes, 1999). This kind of revolution is *very* difficult to bear because it immediately forces upon us the question, "What are 'we'?" Many of us have watched the fictionalized accounts of cyborgs—part human, part machine—in films such as *Robocop*. However, Robert John Garigue (1998) describes his own ill father, the cyborg:

> During one painful period I witnessed my father turned into a Cyborg during his heart surgery. After a successful operation, looking at him recovering in the Intensive Care Unit, it was difficult to define his personal boundaries as some of his physical functions had their locus displaced outside of his body. Pulmonary and circulatory activities were under the supervision of an [sic] well-orchestrated combination of hardware, software, and heuristics—the wetware of the system—all attuned to his needs but well outside of his body. (p. 1)

4. *Network protocol* refers to the rules for data and its transmission across a network of communicating computers. That protocol is made of two parts: (1) Internet protocol (IP) and (2) transmission control protocol (TCP). Together, this protocol, the well-known TCP/IP, is *the* standard and foundation of network communication on today's Internet (Lipson, 2002, p. 5).

5. As of January 2004, there were 233,101, 481 hosts advertised in Domain Name Service (DNS) (Internet Systems Consortium at www. isc.org/index.pl?/ops/ds; last visited on April 19, 2004).

6. At that time, the term *transnational* had no juridical meaning but was strictly a criminological term. Professor Gerhard Mueller describes transnational as covering five activities:

- Crime as business, including organized crime, white-collar crime, and corruption;
- Offenses that involve works of art and cultural property;

- Criminality associated with alcoholism and drug abuse, especially illegal traffic;
- Violence having international significance;
- Criminal activity related to migration and flight from natural disasters and hostilities. (cited in Reuter & Petrie, 2000, pp. 7–8)

7. Toffler and Toffler (1993) suggest that "many of today's states are going to splinter or transform, and the resultant units may not be integrated nations at all, in the modern sense, but a variety of other entities from tribal federations to Third Wave city-states" (p. 262). Similarly, Godson and Williams (1998) comment that "states have almost become outmoded organizations: the world is attempting to deal with a twenty-first-century phenomenon [namely, transnational crime] using structures, mechanisms and instruments that are still rooted in eighteenth-and nineteenth-century concepts and organizational forms" (p. 66).

8. The 419 Fraud is so-named for the relevant section of the Nigerian criminal code (The 419 Coalition, 2003, p. 1).

9. The term *sniffer* is used to identify software programs designed to capture data and information crossing connecting wires joining computer systems (Chappell, 2001–2002, p. 1).

10. Source: InterGOV International Web crime statistics, www.web-police.org; last visited on July 14, 2003.

11. CERT was begun as a response to the first major incident on the DARPA network—the name of the original acronym ARPA was changed slightly to Defense Advanced Research Projects Agency (DARPA); the attack was the earlier-mentioned Morris worm launched in November 1988.

12. Even the term *hacking* is problematic. McClure, Scambray, and Kurtz (1999), in *Hacking Exposed,* observe,

The online community has harangued the mainstream media for years over the use of the term "hacker" as an umbrella definition for individuals who break into computer systems. Traditionally, the term "hacker" meant one who tinkers with unfamiliar systems in a selfless effort to gain insight and/or

re-engineer it for the better. "Cracker," on the other hand, has come to refer to those malicious hackers who break into systems for fun or profit.

Language evolves in its own way, and "cracker" never caught on as a mainstream colloquialism for computer criminals. Though we feel "cracker" is a bit awkward, the authors are also overwhelmingly sympathetic to the concept that "hackers" are not necessarily evil people (in fact, we consider ourselves hackers of the ethical sort), and we refrain from using "hackers" in this book to classify people who research and experiment with computer security on their own systems. (p. xxv)

13. An important, creative participant in this general discussion of the role of law in cyberspace is Lawrence Lessig. One of his intriguing notions involves the notion of "code" elaborated in his book *Code and Other Laws of Cyberspace* (Lessig, 1999a). Lessig explains,

In real space we recognize how laws regulate—through constitutions, statutes, and other legal codes. In cyberspace we must understand how code regulates— how the software and hardware that make cyberspace what it is *regulate* cyberspace as it is. As William Mitchell puts it, this code is cyberspace's "law." *Code is law.* (p. 6)

His basic notion is that cyberspace is not ruled merely by "direct" law regulating individuals through threats of punishments as "pundits, and especially lawyers thinking about regulation in this space" would have it (Lessig, 1998, pp. 10–11; 1999a; 1999b, p. 503). In addition, cyberspace is ruled indirectly by the code of the software and hardware that make cyberspace itself work. Regulation of this second kind can take the form of encryption in which governments have "keys" to allow them to enter ("backdoor" entry) as third parties on the content of encrypted communications. Another sort of regulatory method would involve un-encrypting digital signatures so as to authenticate who—in its fullest amplification—a person is by linking with government databases with the "bearer" of the signature. Control by a government of this latter kind is usually viewed independently from the first, but Lessig views them as two forms of government regulation. And in Lessig's (1999a) view, the second poses the greater threat to the liberal or civil libertarian ideals that Americans hold dear (p. 6).

14. This is, of course, a gross oversimplification of the foundations of social science. It overlooks the work of one of—if not *the*—finest social scientist, George Herbert Mead, who in the early days of American sociology wrestled mightily with the very issue of the "social self" and how it evolves (Mead, 1934). The model of Mead's creative efforts to seriously understand the bond/process between human individuals and human groups, however, may serve us well as we try to understand the computer-mediated *social fact.*

15. Stoll (1989) explains the curious title of the book:

The cuckoo lays her eggs in other birds' nests. She is a nesting parasite: some other bird will raise her young cuckoos. The survival of cuckoo chicks depends on the ignorance of other species. Our mysterious visitor [the hacker who compromised Lawrence Berkeley Lab's computers] laid an egg-program into our computer, letting the system hatch it and feed it privilege [to access system information as well privileged accounts on the computer]. (p. 27)

16. Many of the computers compromised in this hacking/espionage event were part of Milnet which is run by the U.S. Department of Defense for use by all services: Army, Navy, Air Force, and Marines (Stoll, 1989, p. 79).

17. René Thom, in a difficult, mainly mathematical book beginning with the caution "nothing disturbs a mathematician more than discontinuity" (Thom, 1975, p. 9), teases us with his *catastrophe theory* which seems to have potential to fit a computer-generated power grid attack or air traffic control attack and the like. To convey an intuitive notion of Thom's thinking, consider the following:

One of the central problems studied by mankind is the problem of the succession of form [read: morphogenesis]. . . . We perceive beings, objects, things to which we give names. These beings or things are forms or structures endowed with a degree of stability; they take up some part of space and last for some period of time. . . The method dealt with here puts emphasis above all on the morphogenesis of the process, that is, on the discontinuities of the phenomenon. A very general classification of these changes of form, called *catastrophes.* . . . [T]he model attempts to classify local accidents of morphogenesis, which we will call *elementary catastrophes*, where as the global macroscopic appearance, the form in the usual sense of the word is the result of the accumulation of many of these local accidents. (pp. 1, 8)

It should be noted that Thom himself stated explicitly that he is not at all certain his ideas would be of interest or use to those in life and social sciences (pp. 324–325).

18. A robot is generally a mechanism that can be controlled by a computer; a telerobot is a robot that can accept instructions from a distance. A human operator can perform "live actions in a distant environment and through sensors can gauge the consequences" (Goldberg, 2000a, p. 6).

19. It is arguable that telerobotics technology is too far in the future to be relevant here. In some ways, it *is* science fiction for all but the most simple applications. For example, the 17th Annual National Conference on Artificial Intelligence (AI) involved a competition between four teams of engineers each of which created a robot to perform search and rescue in a simulated urban catastrophe—basically, the four robots did very poorly. A major obstacle for AI—and these particular four robotic competitors—is "traversing a three-dimensional maze" (Sincell, 2000, p. 847). Of course, in a circumstance such as an urban catastrophe, this would be a huge impediment.

Similarly, describing the state of AI in a somewhat humorous vein, Levine and Rheingold (1987) tell of the early, heady days of AI.

In the early days of work in artificial intelligence, there were high hopes that computers soon could be used to translate between two natural languages. The idea was simply to equip a computer with a large dictionary and few rules of grammar, then turn it loose. Unfortunately, the first results of such experimentation put a damper on this enthusiasm, because an attempt to translate the English line "the spirit is willing but the flesh is weak" into Russian and back again into English yielded: "the wine is agreeable, but the meat has spoiled." (p. 21)

REFERENCES

Alper, J. (1998, May 8). Navigating Chernobyl's deadly maze. *Science, 280,* 826–829.

Brooks, S. S. (1995, June). Managing a horizontal. *HRMagazine,* pp. 52–58.

Brown, C. (1995). *Chaos and catastrophe theories.* Thousand Oaks, CA: Sage.

Brown, J. (2000). *Minds, machines, and the multiverse: The quest for the quantum computer.* New York: Simon & Schuster.

Castells, M. (1996). *The rise of the network society* (Vol. 1, Information Age: Economy, Society and Culture). Cambridge, MA: Blackwell.

Castells, M. (1997). *The power of identity* (Vol. 2, Information Age: Economy, Society and Culture). Cambridge, MA: Blackwell.

Castells, M. (1998). *End of millennium* (Vol. 3, Information Age: Economy, Society and Culture). Cambridge, MA: Blackwell.

Chappell, L. (2001–2002). *Cyber crime: It could happen to you.* Retrieved July 14, 2003, from www.crime-research.org/eng/library/cyber5.htm

Choudhury, J. N. (2001, August). International law enforcement and the United States: An outside view. *The Police Chief,* pp. 75–77.

Cohen, S. (Ed.). (1971a). *Images of deviance.* Middlesex, UK: Pelican Books.

Cohen, S. (1971b). Introduction. In S. Cohen (Ed.), *Images of deviance* (pp. 9–24). Middlesex, UK: Penguin.

Cohen, S. (1973). Property destruction: Motives and meanings. In C. Ward (Ed.), *Vandalism* (pp. 23–53). London: Architectural.

Cohen, S. (1988). *Against criminology.* New Brunswick, NJ: Transaction Books.

Cohen, S., & Taylor, L. (1976). *Escape attempts: The theory and practice of resistance in everyday life.* London: Allen Lane.

Computer Industry Almanac Inc. (2002). *USA tops 160M Internet users.* Retrieved February 8, 2003, from www.c-i-a.com/pr1202.htm

Cronin, B. (2002). International law. In (Ed.), *World at risk: A global issues sourcebook* (pp. 386–407). Washington, DC: CQ Press.

Davis, R., & Pease, K. (2000). Crime, technology and the future. *Security Journal, 13*(2), 59–64.

Deleuze, G., & Guattari, F. (1983). *Anti-Oedipus: Capitalism and schizophrenia* (R. Hurley, M. Seem, & H. R. Lane, Trans.). Minneapolis: University of Minnesota Press.

Deleuze, G., & Guattari, F. (1987). *A thousand plateaus: Capitalism and schizophrenia* (B. Massumi, Trans.). Minneapolis: University of Minnesota Press.

Drucker, P. F. (1992, September-October). The new society of organizations. *Harvard Business Review,* pp. 95–104.

Durkheim, E. (1938). *The rules of sociological method* (S. A. Solovay & J. H. Mueller, Trans., 8th ed.). New York: Free Press. (Original work published in 1895)

Emery, G. R. (2001, November 21). *No recession for cybersecurity.* Retrieved April 22, 2004, from www.washingtontechnology.com/news/1_1/daily_news/17501-1.html

Financial Action Task Force (FATF). (1999). *Financial action task force on money laundering: The forty recommendations.* Paris: Organization for Economic Co-operation and Development. Retrieved April 22, 2004 from www.oecd.org/searchResult/0,2665,en_2649_201185_1_1_1_1_1,00.html

The 419 Coalition. (2003). *The Nigerian scam defined.* Retrieved July 21, 2003, from http://home.rica.net/alphae/419coal

Gabrys, E. (2002, November-December). The international dimensions of cyber-crime, Part 2: A look at the Council of Europe's Cyber-Crime Convention and the need for an international regime to fight cyber-crime. *Information Systems Security,* pp. 24–32.

Garigue, R. J. (1998). Hacking belief systems: An agenda for the survival of humanity in cyber-society. In A. D. Campen & D. H. Dearth (Eds.), *Cyberwar 2.0: Myths, mysteries and reality* (pp. 1–7). Fairfax, VA: AFCEA International Press.

Godson, R., & Williams, P. (1998). Strengthening cooperation against transnational crime. *Survival, 40*(3), 66–88.

Goldberg, K. (2000a). Introduction: The unique phenomenon of a distance. In K. Goldberg (Ed.), *The robot in the garden: Telerobotics and telepistemology in the age of the Internet* (pp. 3–20). Cambridge: MIT Press.

Goldberg, K. (Ed.). (2000b). *The robot in the garden: Telerobotics and telepistemology in the age of the Internet.* Cambridge: MIT Press.

Goldstein, A. P. (Ed.). (1996). *The psychology of vandalism.* New York: Plenum Press.

Grabosky, P. (2001). Computer crime: A criminological overview. *Forum on Crime and Society, 1*(1), 35–53.

Grove, G. D., Goodman, S. E., & Lukasik, S. J. (2000). Cyber-attacks and international law. *Survival, 42*(3), 89–103.

Harvey, D. (1989). *The condition of postmodernity: An enquiry into the origins of cultural change.* Oxford, UK: Basil Blackwell.

Himanen, P. (2001). *The hacker ethic: A radical approach to the philosophy of business.* New York: Random House.

Householder, A., Kevin, H., & Dougherty, C. (2003). *Computer attack trends challenge Internet security.* Retrieved July 14, 2003, from www.computer.org/security/supplement1/hou

Huey, L. J. (2002). Policing the abstract: Some observations on policing cyberspace. *Canadian Journal of Criminology, 44*(3), 243–254.

Jacobson, H., & Green, R. (2002, Spring). Computer crime. *American Criminal Law Review*, pp. 274–325.

Karp, H. (2000, April). Angels online: Special report. *Reader's Digest,* pp. 74–80.

Katz, J. (1988). *Seductions of crime: Moral and sensual attractions in doing evil.* New York: Basic Books.

Kellner, D. (2002). Theorizing globalization. *Sociological Theory, 20*(3), 285–385.

Kuhn, T. S. (1970). *The structure of scientific revolutions* (2nd, enlarged ed., Vol. 2). Chicago: University of Chicago Press.

Lane, F. S., III. (2000). *Obscene profits: The entrepreneurs of pornography in the cyber age.* New York: Routledge.

Lessig, L. (1998, March). *The laws of cyberspace.* Paper presented at the Taiwan Net '98, Taipei.

Lessig, L. (1999a). *Code and other laws of cyberspace.* New York: Basic Books.

Lessig, L. (1999b). Commentaries—The law of the horse: What cyberlaw might teach. *Harvard Law Review, 113,* 501–546.

Levine, H., & Rheingold, H. (1987). *The cognitive connection: Thought and language in man and machine.* New York: Prentice Hall.

Liebovitch, L. S., & Scheurle, D. (2000). Two lessons from fractals and chaos: Changes in the way we see the world. *Complexity, 5*(4), 34–43.

Lipnack, J., & Stamps, J. (1986). *The networking book: People connecting with people.* New York: Routledge & Kegan Paul.

Lipson, H. F. (2002). *Tracking and tracing cyberattacks: Technical challenges and global policy issues* (Special Report No. CMU/SEI-2002-SR-009). Pittsburg, PA: CERT Coordination Center.

McClure, S., Scambray, J., & Kurtz, G. (1999). *Hacking exposed: Network security secrets and solutions.* Berkeley, CA: Osborne/McGraw-Hill.

Mead, G. H. (1934). *Mind, self, and society from the standpoint of a social behaviorist.* Chicago: University of Chicago Press.

Miller, P., & O'Leary, T. (1989). Hierarchies and American ideals, 1900–1940. *Academy of Management Review, 14*(2), 250–265.

Mukhtar, M. (2001). *Computer crime: The new threat.* Retrieved February 1, 2003, from www.crime-research.org/library/Mudavi1.htm

National Fraud Information Center. (2004). *Internet scams: Fraud trends, January–December 2003.* Retrieved April 17, 2004, from www.fraud.org/2003internetscams.pdf

Nemeth, C. P. (2004). *Criminal law.* Upper Saddle River, NJ: Prentice Hall.

Oakes, C. (1999). *Waiting for wearable wearables.* Retrieved July 8, 2003, from www.wired.com/news/technology/0,1282,31959,00.html

Oakes, C. (2000, July 8). *The Year 2020, explained.* Retrieved July 16, 2003, from www.wired.com/news/technology/ 0,1282,37117,00.html

Powell, K. S. (2000, August 17). Big promise in thinking small. *Los Angeles Times.*

Power, R. (2000). *Tangled web: Tales of digital crime for the shadows of cyberspace.* Indianapolis, IN: QUE.

President's Working Group. (2000). *The electronic frontier: The challenge of unlawful conduct involving the use of the Internet.* Washington, DC: U.S. Department of Justice.

Reid, S. T. (2000). *Criminal law* (5th ed.). Boston: McGraw-Hill.

Reuter, P., & Petrie, C. (Eds.). (2000). *Transnational organized crime: Summary of a workshop.* Washington, DC: National Academy of Sciences, Committee on Law and Justice, Commission on Behavioral and Social Sciences and Education, National Research Council.

Scase, R. (1999). *Britain: Towards 2010: The changing business environment.* London, UK: Department of Trade and Industry.

Schlegel, K. (2000). Transnational crime: Implications for local law enforcement. *Journal Contemporary Criminal Justice, 16*(4), 365–385.

Shelly, G. B., Cashman, T. J., Vermaat, M. E., & Walker, T. J. (1999). *Discovering computers 2000: Concepts for a connected world.* Cambridge, MA: Course Technology.

Sincell, M. (2000, August 11). Rescue droids stumble in an urban jungle. *Science, 289,* 846–850.

Speer, D. L. (2000). Redefining borders: The challenges of cybercrime. *Crime, Law & Social Change, 34,* 259–373.

Spinello, R. A. (2000). *Cyberethics: Morality and law in cyberspace.* Boston: Jones & Bartlett.

Stoll, C. (1989). *The cuckoo's egg: Track a spy through the maze of computer espionage.* New York: Doubleday.

Tan, S. T. (2002). Money laundering and e-commerce. *Journal of Financial Crime: The Official Journal of the Cambridge International Symposium on Economic Crime, 9*(3), 277–285.

Tetenbaum, T. J. (1998). Shifting paradigms: From Newton to chaos. *Organizational Dynamics, 26*(4), 21–32.

Thom, R. (1975). *Structural stability and morphogenesis: An outline of a general theory of models* (D. H. Fowler, Trans.). London: W. A. Benjamin.

Toffler, A., & Toffler, H. (1993). *War and anti-war: Survival at the dawn of the 21st century.* Boston: Little, Brown.

Torr, J. D. (Ed.). (2003a). *Current controversies: The information age.* San Diego, CA: Greenhaven Press.

Torr, J. D. (2003b). Introduction. In J. D. Torr (Ed.), *Current controversies: The information age* (pp. 12–14). San Diego, CA: Greenhaven Press.

U.S. Department of Justice (Fraud Section—Criminal Division). (2000a). *Internet fraud.* Retrieved July 14, 2003, from www.internetfraud.usdoj.gov

U.S. Department of Justice. (2000b). *Office of Justice Programs annual report to Congress: Fiscal Year 1999.* Washington DC: U.S. Department of Justice.

van Fossen, A. (2002). Financial frauds and pseudo-states in the Pacific Islands. *Crime Law and Social Change, 37,* 357–378.

Vold, G. B., Bernard, T. J., & Snipes, J. B. (1998). *Theoretical criminology* (4th ed.). New York: Oxford University Press.

Wall, D. (1997). Policing the virtual community: The Internet, cyberspace and cybercrime. In P. Francis, P. Davies, & V. Jupp (Eds.), *Policing futures: The police, law enforcement and the twenty-first century* (pp. 208–236). New York: St. Martin's.

Weber, M. (1946). Bureaucracy (H. H. Gerth & C. W. Mills, Trans.). In H. H. Gerth & C. W. Mills (Eds.), *From Max Weber: Essays in sociology* (pp. 196–244). New York: Oxford University Press. (Original work published in 1925)

Williams, P. (1999). Emerging issues: Transnational crime and its control. In G. Newman (Ed.), *Global report on crime and justice* (pp. 221–240). New York: U.N. Office for Drug Control and Crime Prevention, Center for International Crime Prevention.

Zombori, G. (2001). *e + finance + crime: A report on cyber-crime and money laundering* (Working document). Toronto: York University, Osgoode Hall Law School, Nathanson Centre for the Study of Organized Crime and Corruption.

8

Transnational Environmental Crime

RAYMOND MICHALOWSKI

KEVIN BITTEN

TRANSNATIONAL HARMS AND AMBIGUOUS CRIMES

The problem of environmental crime is inherently transnational. Unlike most other harms, toxins travel freely from one country to another, on the wind, in surface and ground water, and through the movements of humans and animals. Other environmental threats such as species extinction, ozone depletion, and global climate change are likewise felt around the world, not just in their countries of origin. Despite their transnational character, most cross-border environmental harms are not defined as crimes or regulatory violations. Moreover, attempts to do so are frequently confounded by legal systems rooted in national sovereignty and, thus, ill suited to address transborder injuries.

The bounded nature of national legal systems introduces a significant ambiguity into the study of transnational environmental crime. From a juridical standpoint, only a small proportion of the environmental harms that occur across borders are subject to legal control, as either crimes or treaty violations. The release of a toxic substance in Country A that harms the health of people in Country B, for instance, falls outside legal control unless one of the following conditions applies. One, A and B are signatories to a treaty that would authorize the government or citizens of Country B to seek redress from responsible parties in Country A. Two, a treaty between A and B authorizes law enforcers in Country B to take action against responsible parties in Country A or requires legal authorities in Country A to prosecute their own citizens for causing harm in Country B. Three, the event falls under the jurisdiction of an international body such as the International Atomic Energy Agency or International Whaling Commission that can initiate enforcement actions against Country A or responsible parties within it. In reality, most transnational environmental harms fall outside these conditions.

The ambiguous juridical character of transnational environmental harms is further complicated by the power differentials associated with uneven patterns of national development. The corporations, governments, and consumption practices of highly developed nations are responsible for a disproportionately large share of environmental harm. By virtue of their economic and political power, however, highly developed countries— particularly the United States, the European Union, China, and Japan—enjoy substantial leverage in framing the international treaties that govern environmental harms. In addition, powerful transnational corporations and the governments of their home countries are frequently able to influence the formation of *domestic* environmental law in developing countries where these corporations will operate (Michalowski & Kramer, 1987).

Current international environmental law is a product of international geopolitics more than of straightforward concerns to minimize the harmful consequences of environmental hazards reaching from one nation to another. Thus, a serious consideration of transnational environmental crime must include a broader range of harms than those currently under direct legal control. For this reason, we use the term *transnational environmental crime* to mean any action that causes environmental harm outside its country of its origin, whether or not its victims or some other entity have been given legal standing to punish wrongdoers or seek redress for damages. This approach is comparable to that taken by those concerned with human rights violations in countries where the acts involved are not defined as crimes under the authority committing them. Both cases point to the need to make the political intricacies behind international law part of what we study rather

than simply studying the operations of international law while ignoring the political forces that determine its content.

THE TRANSBORDER FLOW OF ENVIRONMENTAL HARM

The transnational dimensions of environmental crime are shaped by three interrelated mechanisms: (a) Transborder flows of toxic substances, (b) transborder flows of economic decisions, and (c) transborder projections of power, particularly war.

Transborder Flows of Toxic Substances

The transborder flow of toxic substances occurs when pollutants that originate within one nation-state spread to neighboring or distant countries through natural ecological processes such as the movement of streams, rivers, air currents, and living organisms or through deliberate transportation.

Most legal jurisdictions are closed systems, largely circumscribed by a nation's borders.[1] By contrast, ecosystems are open systems, governed by biological, chemical, and geological boundaries, not political ones. Environmental toxins spread throughout ecosystems, routinely exceeding the reach of closed legal systems. Rivers and streams contaminated with toxins cross national borders. The jet stream and other prevailing wind systems girdle the globe, spreading pollution from smokestacks and vehicles well beyond the countries in which they originate. Migratory animals bearing environmentally caused diseases cross national borders, damaging the biosphere as they move. Meanwhile, the destruction of wildlife habitat and species extinction in one nation (or in international waters) can have destructive environmental, economic, and aesthetic impacts on places far removed from the source of the problem.

Ecosystems are just that—*systems*. This means that each part is connected, however distantly, to every other part and damage to any part will eventually harm the whole. In recent years, the scientific recognition of worldwide environmental threats such as ozone depletion and global warming have made the systemic and transborder nature of environmental problems increasingly apparent. The political boundaries of national legal systems, however, pose significant barriers to controlling free-flowing toxins and other far-reaching forms of environmental damage.

A good example of the limits that nation-states place on transborder control of environmental hazards is found in the controversy created by the problem of acid rain in Canada. Throughout the 1970s and 1980s, water, soil, and plants in both the United States and Canada were showing increasing damage due to acid rain. The Canadian environment, however, was more sensitive to acid damage. Thus, Canada suffered more from U.S. smokestack emissions than the United States suffered from Canadian pollution. As much as 50% of the acid rain falling in Canada was a product of U.S. emissions, whereas only 15% to 25% of the acid rain falling in the United States was caused by Canadian emissions. Despite clear evidence that the U.S. failure to limit toxic emissions had a profound impact on the health of the Canadian environment, debate on the issue took place in the context of the dramatic differential in the political and economic power between these nations. Due to Canada's limited ability to exert influence over its much more powerful neighbor to the south, 12 years passed before the U.S. government agreed to sign a watered-down treaty to control cross-border smokestack emissions. Eight of those 12 years were marked by deliberate foot-dragging on the part of the Reagan administration as it pursued its promise to reduce rather than increase the regulation of American corporations. The treaty that was eventually signed by the subsequent administration did not go beyond any existing controls over acid rain precursors. By this time, however, domestic air

quality problems had led to increased control of emission in each nation, with some reduction in cross-border production of acid rain. That it took 12 years to produce a treaty that, in the end, gave Canada very little power to control acid rain precursor produced in the United States is characteristic of the geopolitical complexity of controlling cross-border flows of toxins (Cataldo, 1992).

Transborder Flows of Economic Decisions

Like environmental toxins, economic decisions that originate in one country can have devastating and often criminal consequences for the environment and people in another country. Since the late 1400s, the pursuit of economic growth has increasingly bound the world into a single global economic system (Gunder-Frank, 1978). For 500 years, powerful economic institutions from Europe—and later the United States—have pursued profit-making strategies that have often been detrimental to the well-being of the people and environments of less-developed nations, frequently doing so with the assistance of the military and political power of their home country.

The initial colonization of Africa, India, and the Western Hemisphere by England and Europe began a grand global flow of economic decisions across borders. From the 15th through the early 20th century, European colonization strategies based on direct political and military control ensured that the land and resources of subordinated peoples would be used to advance the economic interests of the colonizers. This transborder flow of economic decisions was not a gentle process. Over the centuries, unknown millions of people in less-developed regions were killed, enslaved, or had the environment on which they depended for their way of life destroyed to fulfill the economic desires of people in more powerful parts of the world.

The transborder flow of economic decisions did not cease with the end of formal colonization in the late 20th century. As nations withdrew or lost political and military control over former colonies, a new framework for economic domination emerged. Variously termed *neocolonialism, neoliberalism,* or *globalization,* these new strategies revolve around direct foreign investments by transnational corporations (TNCs). Backed by powerful financial institutions such as the World Bank, the International Monetary Fund, and the U.S. Overseas Investment Bank and protected by the political and military power of their home countries, the increasing penetration of TNCs into less-developed nations ensures that economic interests outside these subordinated countries will continue to shape economic development and resource usage within them, often with damaging environmental consequences.

Historically, TNCs have more often promoted the exploitation rather than the preservation and development of the human and biological environments of their "host" nations. As anthropologist John Bodley (1976) noted, when decisions are made by people who do not have to live with the consequences of these decisions, far less care is taken to minimize their destructive impact on the natural and the cultural environment. An ongoing example of the consequence of this can be found in the controversies surrounding the operations of Shell, Mobil, and other petroleum companies in the Niger Delta. The Niger Delta is one of the largest wetlands in the world, covering approximately 27,000 square miles. In 1956, Shell Petroleum discovered oil there, and in 1961 extensive oil fields were located off the coast of Nigeria by Mobil Corporation. From then until the present, efforts to extract this oil have resulted in significant damage to the delta's sensitive ecosystem. Almost every aspect of the oil industry—drilling, transportation, the elimination of waste, the flaring off of natural gas—harms the environmental health of the Niger Delta. The burning of "waste" natural gas alone adds 526.6 billion standard cubic feet

of pollutants into the atmosphere over the delta. Spilled oil and destruction of habitat to make room for oil production has led to a disappearance of the mud skippers, crabs, periwinkles, and shrimp that were formerly common in the delta's waters (Okoji, 2000).

The people of the Niger Delta, the Ogoni, have seen their way of life devastated by the environmental catastrophe resulting from the oil wells. In 1995, Ken Saro-Wiwa, an environmental and human rights activist, Nobel Peace Prize Nominee, and 1995 recipient of the Goldman Environmental Prize, was executed by the military government of Nigeria for charges related to his activities as the founder and leader of the Movement for the Survival of the Ogoni People (MOSOP). MOSOP sought to force TNCs extracting petroleum from the delta to repair the extensive environmental damage they had done to the delta ecosystem, the traditional source of livelihood for the Ogoni people (Daniels, 2000).

The oil industry executives whose decisions led to the cumulative ecological destruction of the Niger River Delta do not depend on the waters and rainforest of the delta region for their livelihood or for the continuation of their Euro-American cultural practices. Nor does the environmental destruction of the Niger Delta have any obvious consequences for most stockholders who benefit annually from oil industry profits generated by Nigerian oil. Because oil revenues play an important part in financing the Nigerian government, and in keeping many Nigerian businesses solvent, local elites are willing to support military repression of the tribal peoples struggling to avoid "cultural death" at the hands of oil company policy. Similar conflicts between local needs and external economic interests are ongoing in the rainforests of South America, the mountains of Tibet, the Maharashtra state of India, and in many other locales where those who must live with the environmental consequences of foreign development decisions struggle to gain a measure of control over those decisions (Roy, 2001).

Transborder flows of economic decisions accelerated rapidly in the years after World War II. Consumer economies expanded dramatically in the developed world, and manufacturing corporations initially located in the United States, Britain, Europe, and Japan increasingly sought cheaper labor and new markets in less-developed nations. In the two decades between 1960 and 1980 alone, the revenue of TNCs grew tenfold, from $199 billion to $2,155 billion (Cavenaugh & Clairmonte, 1983). Overall, the combined revenues of the Fortune 500 companies have grown for 43 of the 49 years between 1954 and 2002, clear evidence of the continuing growth of TNCs (Harrington, 2002). A significant proportion of this growth resulted from increasing relocation of manufacturing facilities from developed nations, such as the United States, to less-developed ones such as Mexico, Guatemala, Malaysia, and Singapore. As early as 1975, over three fourths of all U.S. corporations with sales of $100 million had manufacturing facilities in other countries (Blake & Walters, 1976). By 2002, nearly all had overseas operations (Hertz, 2003).

As TNCs expanded their industrial operations in developing nations, many of the environmental dangers associated with industrial production were relocated from developed nations that were beginning to formulate environmental protection laws, to less-developed ones where the political leadership was unprepared, unwilling, or unable to address these new hazards. In some instances, it was this lack of environmental controls that made certain developing countries attractive sites for industrial relocation.

Corporate decision makers recognize that differences in the pollution control standards among nations can affect operating costs and profits, and this awareness plays a role in decisions to relocate industries to countries with less stringent environmental laws. Early recognition of this trend was signaled by President Carter's chief trade negotiator, Robert Strauss, who warned in 1978 that there was an emerging "pattern of flight" as U.S. companies were being drawn toward developing nations with less costly pollution control laws. Another analyst of corporate relocation patterns noted that "hazard export is emerging as a driving force in new plant investment in many hazardous and polluting industries" (Castleman, 1978, p. 8). In some cases, entire industries involving highly toxic substances such as asbestos, arsenic, mercury, and benzene dyes were relocated to developing nations such as Korea, Mexico, Brazil, India, and Ireland to avoid the costs of meeting U.S. environmental regulations (Leonard & Duerksen, 1980).

This variability in environmental law is one of the key problems in understanding and controlling transnational environmental crime. In the 1980s, for instance, Mexican law allowed companies to emit more parts-per-million of arsenic or benzene into that country's waters than did U.S. environmental law. From a juridical standpoint, an American company that took advantage of these less stringent regulations committed no environmental crime. From a substantive perspective, however, the release of these larger quantities of toxins were as harmful to Mexicans as they had been judged to be to Americans, even though they were now legal.

Transborder Projections of Power

In addition to transborder flows of economic decisions, environments are also harmed by transborder projections of power in the form of military force. This problem is endemic in a world system where nation-states continue to rely on military power to pursue economic and political goals beyond their borders. Both war and the preparation for war, whether offensive or defensive, pose serious threats to the health of ecosystems.

Military power plays an important role in magnifying the harms resulting from economic differentials among nation-states. Environmental harms resulting from disproportionate economic power are often compounded when that power imbalance is obtained or preserved through the use of military power, creating a kind of "double jeopardy" for the environments of less-powerful nations. Nation-states are not the only purveyors of armed violence. Revolutionaries and terrorists who lack nation-state authority to legitimize their violence have also caused environmental harm through the use of force. The environmental consequences, particularly air pollution, resulting from the September 11, 2001, attack on the World Trade Center were substantial (Nordgren, Goldstein, & Izeman, 2002). Nevertheless, nation-states remain the greatest military threat to the environment. With rare exceptions, nonstate actors cannot match the resources, firepower, or global reach of powerful national militaries.[2]

The scale of environmental harm resulting from violent projections of power, particularly state power, is enormous. According to the Science for Peace Institute at the University of Toronto, military actions account for an estimated 20% to 30% of all environmental degradation on the planet (Du Nann Winter, 1998). Part of this damage is the unintentional consequence of creating and using military hardware.

On a per-machine basis, military vehicles demand far more fossil fuels than do domestic ones. In only 1 hour, an F-16 fighter jet burns approximately 850 gallons of fuel, the equivalent of driving nine automobiles from Los Angeles to New York City. The M-1 A-1 Abrams Battle Tank, used prominently in the 2003 U.S. invasion of Iraq, consumes 19 gallons of fuel *per mile*—150 times more fuel per mile than the average domestic automobile. Simply keeping this machinery supplied poses significant environmental risks. At the Ramstein air base in Germany, for instance, 300,000 gallons of jet fuel leaked into the aquifer that supplies the drinking water for the city of Frankfurt (Singer & Keating, 1999).

The production of military weaponry also involves the extensive use of toxic materials that are difficult to refine and use safely, including titanium, beryllium, germanium, and depleted uranium. One study of the consequences of reducing military production in Norway concluded that commercial industry was far less harmful to the environment than equivalent military production (Singer & Keating, 199, p. 330). One of the most significant environmental threats associated with military production has been the creation of nuclear arsenals. The production of nuclear weapons in the United States has been rife with violations of environmental regulations and accidental releases of radioactive material into the environment. A total of 423 atmospheric tests and about 1,400 underground tests of nuclear weapons worldwide resulted in widely dispersed releases of radioactive elements strontium-90, cesium-137, plutonium-329, and carbon-14 into the environment (Kauzlarich & Kramer, 1998; Leaning & McCally, 2000).

The production and testing of weapons, particularly nuclear ones, is not only hazardous to the environment, it is typically shrouded in secrecy. This concealment, sometimes even from other branches of government, shields these operations from public scrutiny, thereby increasing the likelihood of environmental violations in the absence of accountability or likelihood of detection.

Environmental damage does not occur only as a "side effect" of military projections of power. Warring nations have often used environmental damage as military strategy. The classic use of the environment as a weapon are "scorched earth" military campaigns, whether Sherman's "march to the sea," or the World War II destruction of 17% of Dutch farmland by Nazi forces through deliberate flooding by salt water (Du Nann Winter, 1998). In Vietnam, American forces used the chemical defoliant Agent Orange in an attempt to deny the North Vietnamese and Viet Cong cover and sustenance. As recently as 2003, areas that once held American bases of operation in Vietnam remained contaminated with dioxins from the spraying, and high levels of birth defects continued to be recorded among nearby populations. Intentional environmental damage is particularly likely in conflicts where one belligerent is markedly superior in its fighting power. In these "asymmetrical" wars, weaker powers are more likely to resort to using the environment as a weapon. During the 1992 Gulf War, Iraqi forces set fire to over 600 oil wells and deliberately spilled millions of barrels of oil directly into the Persian Gulf, an act that the conventionally arrayed forces could do little to prevent (Du Nann Winter, 1998, p. 418). During the 2003 U.S. invasion of Iraq, Iraqi forces fired oil-filled trenches to confuse coalition forces and aircraft by filling the air with toxic petroleum smoke.

Protecting natural ecosystems during war is particularly difficult because the treaties and accords between belligerents traditionally have been considered null and void at the outbreak of hostilities. Silja Vöneky (2000) has argued, however, that there is precedent under international law to support enforcement of environmental agreements and their accompanying sanctions even at times of war because environmental law exists for the good of the world community as a whole. Vöneky further argues that environmental law is comparable to treaties and accords governing human rights and humanitarian issues. Just as these apply, by design, during wartime, so should environmental agreements.

In addition to the case for applying peacetime environmental agreements during wartime, in the last decades of the 20th century several international laws specifically addressed the environmental conduct of warring parties. The first Protocol Additional to the Geneva Conventions, adopted in 1977, addressed the unlawful nature of environmental warfare.

Article 35, paragraph 3, states: "It is prohibited to employ methods or means of warfare which are intended, or may be expected, to cause widespread, long-term and severe damage to the natural environment" (quoted in Kiss, 2001, p. 225). The standard for violation of this passage is relatively high due to the use of the conjunctive "and," requiring that all three conditions (widespread, long-term, and severe) be present before a violation can be charged. In contrast, the 1977 Convention on the Prohibition of Military or other Hostile use of Environmental Techniques (ENMOD), replaced *and* with *or*, thus requiring only one of the conditions to produce a violation. Developed in response to the use of defoliants in Vietnam, ENMOD was limited to "deliberate manipulation of 'natural processes,'" limiting its scope. Under ENMOD, the firing of oil wells in Kuwait in 1992, for instance, could not be considered an international environmental crime because oil wells are not a "natural process" (Burhenne, 1997).

TURNING TRANSBORDER HARMS INTO TRANSNATIONAL CRIMES

A *social problem* is a harmful condition that comes to be understood as both caused and correctable by human action. Social problems emerge when organized movements bring emergent problems to the attention of the public and political decision makers (Blumer, 1969). The movement of international environmental harms from barely recognized to political center stage to the basis for new laws is typically the result of the efforts of nongovernmental organizations, or NGOs. NGOs are nonprofit, value-based private organizations supported primarily through charitable donations and voluntary service. Typically, activists form NGOs around some issue in order to provide services and expertise in service of the NGO's preferred outcomes. The central goal of most NGOs is to influence the formation of policy at national and international levels through compiling data, monitoring government activity, and mobilizing public and political advocacy for change (Yamin, 2001).

The role of NGOs in international environmental policy is clearly demonstrated by the struggle during the 1970s and 1980s to "save the whales." The rapid decline of whale populations due to 19th- and 20th-century whaling practices was not a broadly recognized problem until groups such as Greenpeace brought it to public consciousness. Using a variety of high-profile tactics, they transformed an environmental harm with relatively little political significance into an international social problem and eventually into a worldwide moratorium on commercial whaling imposed by the International Whaling Commission (IWC) in 1982. In the face of extensive grassroots pressure, the IWC underwent a fundamental philosophical shift in its mission, from preserving the commercial whaling industry through conservation to protection of whales at the expense of the industry. NGOs represent a form of political influence that frequently seeks to circumvent or disrupt established power structures, much to the displeasure of those who benefit from status quo power arrangements. In this vein, the IWC's whaling ban led some advocates of the whaling industry to complain that the IWC had been "hijacked" by environmental NGOs (von Zharen, 1999).

NGOs have been central to the environmental movement since its inception. Historically, businesses and governments have had little internal motivation to protect the environment. The logic of growth through profit maximization and economic competition means that corporations must continually search for the least costly ways to extract raw materials from the environment, transform them into finished products, and create expanding markets for their goods. Environmental protection typically increases the costs of production, distribution, and marketing

and, thus, threatens profits—at least in the short run. It is cheaper to ignore oil spills than to clean them up, and cleaning up oil spills is cheaper than redesigning all the ships and pipelines that carry oil to ensure that spills are unlikely to occur. Similarly, it is cheaper to release pollutants such as sulfur dioxide and nitrous oxide into the air than it is to clean up smokestack and vehicle emission.

The incentive for corporations to be proactive in environmental protection is further reduced by the migratory ways of environmental hazards. Environmental toxins will often have significant effects outside the legal jurisdiction of their initial release. Varying standards for culpability and varying abilities for investigation across jurisdictions reduce the likelihood of transnational polluters being identified or, if identified, being prosecuted. Even when the source of a toxin can be determined, it is difficult and often impossible to determine the actual effect a specific toxin on the environment or public health. This is especially true where environmental damage results from multiple sources. The complexity of legal jurisdiction over transnational environmental harms means that corporations are often able to *externalize* the cost of these harms. Rather than requiring corporations to pay for environmental damage and human disease caused by their transborder pollution, in most cases the current legal environment permits them to pass these costs on to those whom they have harmed.

Because there are relatively few inherent incentives for profit-seeking institutions to protect the environment, and many incentives to externalize the costs of environmental damage, the development of international environmental protection laws has depended heavily on the actions of environmental NGOs. NGOs such as Greenpeace, Friends of the Earth, the Environmental Defense Fund, Physicians for Social Responsibility, Earth Council, the Rainforest Action Network, Women's Environment and Development

Organization, and thousands of other citizen action groups have played a crucial role in bringing the international dimensions of environmental protection to worldwide attention. In doing so, they have created an emerging structure of international environmental law.

INTERNATIONAL ENVIRONMENTAL FRAMEWORKS

In the last half of the 20th century, a number of environmental issues emerged that highlighted both the global nature of many environmental problems and the need for international responses to them. Although some concern for global environmental problems existed prior to World War II, two events in 1946 played crucial roles in galvanizing movements for environmental protection at the international level.

The first was the detonation of atomic bombs over the cities of Hiroshima and Nagasaki in the final days of World War II. The second was the establishment of the United Nations. The radioactive fallout from the atomic attacks on Japan, along with continued nuclear testing in the United States, and later the Soviet Union, increased worldwide public awareness of how readily toxins released into the atmosphere could disperse around the globe. Fear of "radioactive fallout" became the most prominent international environmental issue of the early postwar years. Widespread fear of nuclear fallout led NGOs and many governments to begin working for international controls over atmospheric testing of nuclear weapons. Most of this activity was motivated by the threat posed by radioactive fallout for human health rather than by a concern for overall environmental protection. Nevertheless, the issues raised by the threat of nuclear weapons were a powerful catalyst for the eventual development of more broad-based movements for the protection of the global environment (Matthew & Gaulin, 2002).

The establishment of the United Nations near the end of World War II also played an important role in the movement for international environmental controls. The United Nations provided a forum toward which nations, scientists, and NGOs concerned about international environmental problems could direct their efforts. In August of 1963, the United Nations approved the multilateral Treaty Banning Nuclear Weapon Tests in the Atmosphere, in Outer Space, and Under Water. This was not the first multilateral treaty dealing with environmental issues sponsored by the United Nations. There had been a few earlier environmental treaties, mostly addressing marine issues. The ban on atmospheric testing of nuclear weapons, however, represented a major step toward addressing the global dimension of environmental issues and in shaping the United Nations as a mechanism through which NGOs and other entities could begin to address these problems.[3]

It was also the first formal treaty addressing the need to control what today are called "weapons of mass destruction" and recognizing that their use, even in a testing situation, represents a serious threat to the environment.

From the 1960s onward, the movement for international environmental protection grew substantially. The earliest environmental issues addressed by the United Nations were fairly specific in their focus. Atmospheric nuclear testing, protection of specific bodies of water such as the Mediterranean and the North Atlantic from oil spills, controlling overfishing in particular areas, and environmental protection of Antarctica were typical of the narrowly targeted treaties ratified by the United Nations from the late 1940s to the early 1970s. During the last quarter of the 20th century, the discussion of global environmental issues began to take on a different character. Increasing scientific documentation of global environmental problems, intensification of industrial damage to the ecosystems of both developed and developing nations, acceleration of the rate of species loss, and emerging demands from poorer nations for a more equitable distribution of the earth's wealth led to the incorporation of many separate and specific environmental problems issues under the umbrella of three major issue areas: (1) *protecting biodiversity,* (2) *global warming and climate change,* and (3) *sustainable development.* By the 1990s, these three issue areas had come to dominate the debate over international environmental protection.

In addition to these three explicitly environmental foci, the overall goal of the United Nations to promote peaceful rather than military solutions to international disputes can be seen as having significant environmental impact by working to limit the environmental damage caused by war.

Protecting Biodiversity

Biological diversity refers to the variability among and within species of plants, animals, microorganisms, and marine life and also the variability among entire ecosystems. Biodiversity is threatened whenever a network of living organisms, and the nonliving environment that sustains them as a functional unit, is altered in ways that lead to extinction of one or more life forms in that network.

In recent years, considerable energy has been directed by NGOs, governments, and businesses toward protecting biodiversity. The movement to protect biodiversity comes from a number of directions. One source is individuals and groups who believe that biodiversity is *intrinsically* valuable. From this perspective, strategies to protect biodiversity and the overall ecological well-being of the planet must take precedence over any benefits that humans might derive from altering its ecological makeup. This planet-first approach is sometimes referred to as *deep ecology* (Devall & Sessions, 1985; List, 1993; Manes, 1990). For many others, the reason to protect biodiversity is for its benefits to human populations. The

importance of biodiversity for human life has been framed in a number of ways: (a) as necessary for the evolutionary processes that sustain human life; (b) as critical to preserving the way of life for indigenous peoples and communities that would be harmed by the extinction of species on which they depend; (c) as essential stock for future development of medicines, crops, and genetic engineering; and (d) as a critical component of the aesthetic and recreational value people derive from natural settings.

The most obvious example of human threats to biodiversity is the elimination of species of animals or fish from ecosystems through hunting, fishing, or destruction of habitat. Because ecosystems are systems, the consequences of these direct extinctions are far more damaging than the loss of a single species from that ecosystem. In the high desert of southwestern United States, for instance, the virtual elimination of the mountain lion, one of the only predators that controlled the population of porcupine, resulted in widespread damage to piñon trees whose bark happens to be a favorite porcupine food. As the trees are lost, so is habitat for many species of birds and nutrition for the many animals for whom piñon nuts is an important food source. Species extinction or damage to the species composition of an ecosystem also occurs in indirect ways. Dramatic changes or destruction of terrestrial or marine habitats through deforestation, damming of rivers, acidification of lakes and streams, or draining of wetlands can deprive a number of cohabiting species of sustaining environments. Similarly, the introduction of species of plants or animals that are not native to a given ecosystem can dramatically change species composition within an ecosystem by eliminating native plants or animals from that ecosystem. The introduction, for instance, of kudzu in Southeastern United States and the tamarisk tree, commonly known as the "salt cedar," in Southwestern riparian environments has resulted in the disappearance or near disappearance of many native plants from those ecosystems.

Because the greatest current threats to biodiversity come from human activity, efforts to protect biodiversity must inevitably confront a complex web of social, economic, and political interests. The growing demand for more consumer goods, more land for crops and human settlement, more plastics and petrochemical products, more electricity, more fuel for vehicles, and more electronic devices and the increased desire of economic institutions for more profits derived from stimulating and meeting these consumer demands represent a growing threat to biodiversity. Thus, widespread acceptance of the general truth that we need to protect biodiversity often falters in the face of specific demands for the right to exploit the environment for human benefit. In the United States during the 1990s, for instance, neoconservative politicians mounted a powerful effort to weaken the Endangered Species Act on the grounds that protecting species such as birds and aquatic life by prohibiting or limiting exploitation of forests and wetlands was fundamentally wrongheaded because it put the needs of animals ahead of the needs of humans. A similar battle has been waged for years over the protection of rainforests in South America and elsewhere (Rehmke, 1991). Thus, the international interest in creating legal structures that would protect biodiversity on a global basis must address a complex of local interests, including those of developing nations to use their resources for economic growth.

Global Climate Change

Concern for global warming and climate change emerged in the 1970s as a highly controversial part of the international environmental debate. By the mid-1980s, however, climatological data increasingly confirmed that the earth's temperature was rising. Scientific data and computer modeling also pointed toward increases in the proportion of greenhouse gases in the earth's atmosphere as the most important human contribution to this warming trend. Greenhouse gases absorb higher levels of radiant energy than do other components of the atmosphere. Thus, as the proportion of greenhouse gases in the atmosphere increases so does planet temperature. Although natural biological processes can alter the level of greenhouse gases, evidence increasingly indicates that human activity is a significant contributor to the current trend in global warming. Activities such as the burning of fossil fuels and deforestation increase the levels of carbon dioxide, nitrous oxide, and methane in the atmosphere, and the introduction of chlorofluorocarbons (CFCs) from manufacturing, refrigeration, and aerosol sprays has the double impact of increasing the greenhouse gases near the earth and reducing the stratospheric ozone layer that serves to block a portion of the sun's radiant energy from reaching the earth.

It has been estimated that the average surface temperature of the globe has increased between .6 and 1.3 degrees Fahrenheit over the last 100 years. Although these numbers appear small at first glance, computer models indicate that this increase is both larger and faster than any change in the earth's temperature over the last 9,000 years (U.N. Convention on Biodiversity, 1992). A change of global temperature of this magnitude poses serious threats to ecosystems and human habitation. Rises in average sea levels due to increased melting of polar ice caps will lead to increased flooding of coastal communities and salinization of underground water supplies. Changes in patterns of rainfall and the moisture levels of soils will pose significant threats to agriculture. Entire ecosystems and the human communities that depend on them—particularly those based in subsistence agriculture—could be drastically and negatively affected if the current global warming trend continues.

Sustainable Development

The terms *sustainable development, sustainable use,* and *sustainable livelihoods* refer to strategies for production and consumption that would promote a dignified continuation of human life on the planet while simultaneously minimizing practices that degrade the environment, consume nonrenewable resources, and threaten ecosystems. The central proposition of sustainable development is that current production and consumption practices cannot continue indefinitely. From this perspective, the future well-being of humans and the other species that inhabit the planet depends on developing alternative systems for human survival that (a) use renewable energy sources, (b) do not require extensive transportation of people between work and home and of goods between producers and consumers, and (c) reduce overall levels of resource consumption while (d) equalizing disparities between rich and poor nations

The movement for sustainability promotes two controversial ideas. The first is that global environmental problems can be solved only by radical restructuring of how people live, work, and consume. The second is that achieving sustainability will require drastic reductions in the current levels of economic and political inequality between social groups and nations. Despite the wide gap between the ideals of sustainability and actual systems of production and practices of consumption, the concept of sustainability has become one of the most significant guiding principles of emerging efforts to create international legal structures for environmental protection at the international level.

LAWS FOR PROTECTING THE GLOBAL ENVIRONMENT

Creating and enforcing international law is a difficult process, particularly when dealing with environmental degradation. Nevertheless, a desire for predictable and nonviolent ways of conducting international relationships has led to the development of "rules and principles . . . dealing with [the] conduct of states and international organizations" (American Law Institute, 1986, p. 2). These rules and principles have served as the basis for a rudimentary framework for the management of transnational environmental crime.

International Agreements of Limited Scope

The primary mechanism for establishing transborder environmental controls takes the form of international treaties or accords. These agreements may be *bilateral, multilateral,* or *global* in scope.

Bilateral environmental accords are legal agreements between two neighboring nation-states that promise to undertake specified actions to reduce some transborder environmental problem. The problems most often addressed in this manner are the pollution of shared waters, the reduction of immediate transborder air pollution, and the protection of fishing grounds in common coastal waters. A typical example of a bilateral agreement is the United States–Canada Air Quality Accord of 1991. Through this accord, the governments of the United States and Canada agreed to achieve specified reductions in their respective emissions of sulfur dioxide and nitrous oxides from mobile and stationary sources, to share data about the sources of the atmospheric pollutants within their jurisdictions, and to regularly exchange information regarding emission levels, monitoring systems, and technologies for measuring and reducing the emission of pollutants. The Air Quality Accord also sets forth a system for settlement of disputes arising from implementation or nonimplementation of the various components of the treaty (*Agreement,* 1991).

Multilateral environmental accords are agreements among a group of nations seeking to alleviate some shared ecological problem. Like bilateral treaties, multilateral accords generally focus on a specific set of issues arising from some shared resource, most often water. Agreements such as the Berne (Rhine River) Accord of 1963, the Convention on the Protection of the Black Sea against Pollution, and the Regional Convention for the Conservation of the Red Sea and Gulf of Aden Environment are typical of multilateral accords. Each of these treaties requires nations bordering on particular bodies of water to reduce the pollutants discharged into them, and to take other specified actions to minimize future introduction of pollutants to the ecosystem in question.[4]

Bilateral and multilateral treaties are the most common form of legal instrument for addressing transborder environmental problems. There are over 300 bi- and multilateral treaties dealing with issues of transborder water issues alone. The strength of bilateral and multilateral treaties and accords is that the nations entering into them frequently have a clear and immediate *common* interest in protecting some shared resource.

Global Environmental Law

Global environmental treaties and accords are agreements among nations to follow specific courses of action to protect some element of the planet's overall environment. They are particularly difficult to negotiate because they tend to be far broader in scope than bi- and multilateral environmental treaties in three important ways.

First, global environmental accords typically address problems from system-wide and multidimensional perspectives. Protecting biodiversity, for instance, refers to reducing *all* threats to *all* species in *all* ecosystems rather than addressing the specific problems posed by one or two pollutants in a single ecosystem or threats to a particular species.

Second, to be truly "global," these accords must be agreed to by a significant proportion of the nations of the world, which means that

they must accommodate even more conflicting and competing sets of interests than do bilateral or multilateral treaties. The multilateral Berne Accord of 1963, for instance, required that five nations, France, Germany, Luxembourg, the Netherlands, and Switzerland, come to agreement. Although important differences exist between these nations, they also share many commonalities. All are developed European nations with high material standards of living, a common hemispheric history, and relatively similar cultures. Most important, they share an obvious common resource—the Rhine River. In contrast, global treaties must create a worldwide understanding of a problem and offer solutions to it that accommodate the interests of both developed and developing nations while incorporating understandings arising from what are often significantly different cultures and political systems.

Third, global accords typically address problems where cause and effect are often separated spatially, temporally, or distributionally. For instance, pollution or waste transported from one country to some other part of the globe may not appear as a pressing problem to people living in the country that generated the waste. The time lapse between a cause (e.g., pollutants in an ecosystem) and their effect (e.g., increased cancer rates) also makes many global environmental problems difficult to identify. These time lags also provide strong arguments for inaction or slow responses by those who benefit from the current ways of doing things because it enables them to argue that claims about the supposed "problem" are based on forecasts rather than on hard evidence of an immediate problem. The arguments put forth by the U.S. government under several administrations that global climate change is scientific theory that needs more research, not scientific fact that needs remediation, is a good example of how cause-and-effect time lags can weaken movements for global environmental treaties. Finally, the effects of global environmental threats and the consequences of controlling them are not distributed equally. This makes arriving at agreements on the importance of specific problems and the strategies for responding to them often difficult to achieve. For instance, according to current estimates, global climate change is likely to have more devastating effect on peoples and nations that depend on low-technology subsistence agriculture than on industrial nations, thus creating different levels of concern and urgency among different nations (U.N. Environmental Programme, 2003). These kinds of conflicting interests make the negotiation of global environmental agreements that will be acceptable to over 150 sovereign nations a particularly complex task.

Despite the impediments to creating global accords, recent developments in the international environmental arena suggest there is a growing worldwide recognition that many of the most serious environmental problems can be addressed only through world-scale agreements. In 1972, the United Nations held the first "Earth Summit," formally known as the Stockholm Conference on the Human Environment. This conference revealed a deep division between developed and developing nations with respect to the responsibility for global environmental protection. Developed nations sought limitations on environmentally damaging development practices of the less-developed nations such as clear-cutting of rainforests, overgrazing, soil depletion due to unmanaged land clearing and farming, and lack of controls on mining and industrial wastes. In contrast, representatives of less-developed nations argued that it was the developed nations of the world with their widespread industrialization, high levels of material consumption, and high levels of toxic industrial and military wastes that posed the gravest threats to the global environment. Moreover, developing nations argued that the costs of global environmental protection should be shouldered by the already-developed

nations, because they had benefited most from damaging the earth's environment. This conference, and the tensions within it, led to the establishment of a set of environmental principles that have shaped subsequent developments in the environmental arena. In an attempt to sidestep the tension between developing and developed nations, the conference agreed on the following:

1. Nations have a responsibility to protect the ecosystems under their jurisdiction.

2. Nations should pursue "sustainable development" plans that incorporate measures for preserving ecosystems, avoiding depletion of nonrenewable resources, and preserving the earth's ability to reproduce other resources, such as clean water, clear air, forests, and grasslands.

3. Every nation has a sovereign right to exploit its own resources, presumably in keeping with principles of environmental protection.

4. Developed nations should offer financial and technological assistance to less-developed nations to assist them in implementing strategies for sustainable development.

The principles formulated at the 1972 Earth Summit subsequently became the basis for negotiated agreements concerning the transportation of hazardous wastes, protecting the earth's ozone layer, protecting biodiversity, and reducing global warming and climate change.

Hazardous Waste Transportation

In 1989, the U.N. Environmental Programme negotiated the Basel Convention on the Control of Transboundary Movements of Hazardous Wastes and Their Disposal. The process and problems leading to this convention illustrate four issues associated with the creation and enforcement of global environmental issues: the differing interests of developed and developing nations, the possibility for corporate-state conflicts, potential governmental support for environmentally destructive but lucrative activities, and the need for governmental ratification and enforcement of environmental treaties.

Historically, developed nations have been the primary producers of hazardous waste, and developing nations have been the most common destinations for international shipments of these wastes (Vallette, 1989). As a result, delegates to the Basel conference from developing nations supported a total ban on the transboundary shipment of hazardous wastes, whereas representatives from more-developed nations sought an agreement that would not require that all developed nations dispose of their toxic wastes entirely within their own borders.

Another issue that surfaced at the conference is the relationship between international economic organizations and nation-states. Historically, hazardous waste from developed nations often has entered less-developed nations through a business arrangement between a waste-producing corporation or a company specializing in the transportation of hazardous waste and landowners or other businesses in developing countries that contract to accept that waste. Traditionally, many of these international business contracts were negotiated without government involvement. Thus, one of the issues to be negotiated was the relative autonomy of businesses versus governments. In the end, the agreement did not ban international traffic in hazardous wastes; instead, it limited it to shipments that had been agreed to by the government of the receiving nation, after having been notified by the government of the originating nation.

The provision requiring government approval enables nations opposed to accepting hazardous wastes from other countries to limit the ability of international corporations to enter into private hazardous waste agreements within their jurisdiction. On the other hand,

under the Basel convention, any government that is willing to permit landholders or businesses within its boundaries to accept hazardous waste from other countries can do so. This leaves open the possibility that some developing nations may agree to accept foreign hazardous waste as a means to obtain foreign currency for their national economy.

Finally, conventions such as the Basel agreement are applicable only in those countries that sign the agreement and ratify it through their own internal political process. By 2003, 156 nations and the European Union had ratified the Basel convention, and 3 more have signed but failed to ratify the convention: Afghanistan, the United States, and Haiti. Thus, Although the Basel agreement was an important step toward addressing the problems of transboundary shipments of hazardous wastes, there remain a number of loopholes through which international shipments of hazardous waste can still pass.

Protecting the Ozone Layer

In 1985, the Vienna Convention formally recognized the threat of ozone depletion and called on signatory nations to engage in systematic research to identify the sources and consequences of ozone-depleting chemicals, and to work "to control, limit, reduce or prevent" ozone-depleting activities within their boundaries. Two years later, the Montreal Protocol on Substances That Deplete the Ozone Layer extended the Vienna Convention by setting deadlines for specific actions to reduce ozone-depleting chemicals. The 185 nations that had ratified the Vienna convention ultimately agreed to phase out *all* production of CFCs by the year 2000. This agreement also provided a political context through which NGOs were able to effectively pressure Dupont—the largest U.S. producer of CFCs—to phase out all production of these chemicals by 1995.

The Montreal Protocol represents a concrete and potentially effective strategy to address a global environmental problem. By 2002, it had been ratified by 185 nations, and scientists predicted that if the protocol remained in effect, the earth's ozone layer would recover to pre-1980 levels by 2050. Two factors aided in the effectiveness of the Montreal protocols. First, non-ozone-depleting alternatives for CFCs were developed rapidly in response to the pending ban. Once confronted with the inevitability of the elimination of CFCs, industry made impressive strides in developing replacements that would protect profitability. Second, the 1990 London amendments established a multilateral fund to assist developing nations in complying with the Montreal protocols. The fund has paid over $1 billion of assistance since its formation and has played a major role in helping the developing world eliminate the use of CFCs from industry. The fund was especially relevant in enabling India and China to eliminate the use of CFCs, a large step in reducing worldwide production (Leaf, 2001).

Protecting Biodiversity

In 1992, a "Second Earth Summit" was held in Rio de Janeiro, Brazil. This conference, formally known as the 1992 U.N. Conference on the Environment and Development, resulted in two wide-ranging agreements—the Convention on Biological Diversity and the Framework Convention on Climate Change. These agreements are broader in scope than the hazardous waste and ozone conventions because their goals can be achieved only by simultaneously addressing multiple threats to the environment.

The Convention on Biological Diversity requires its signatories take steps to limit activities that threaten species loss and ecosystem degradation within jurisdictions under their control *and* to ensure that activities within their jurisdiction do not damage the environments beyond their national boundaries. These steps include (a) rehabilitating and

restoring degraded ecosystems, (b) preventing introduction of foreign species that threaten ecosystems and eliminating those that have been introduced, (c) creating and enforcing laws and regulations to protect threatened species, (d) establishing special areas to protect threatened species or ecosystems, (e) managing the risks associated with modified organisms resulting from biotechnology, (f) conducting environmental impact assessments of all proposed development projects, and (g) in general "to conserve and sustainably use biological diversity for the benefit of present and future generations" (U.N. Convention on Biodiversity, 1992, p. 1).

The convention also addresses the interest of developing nations in having access to new biotechnology created in developed nations and using genetic stock taken from species within developed nations, and of developed nations in having access to the genetic stock of plants and animals within developing ones. Thus, the convention grants the individual states the "authority to determine access to genetic resources" while requiring that countries "shall not impose restrictions" on access to genetic stock unless it violates other components of the treaty.

The Convention on Biological Diversity represents a significant step toward creating a worldwide commitment to defining the maximization of species as an important component of sustainable development. Like other international environmental treaties, however, it could be negotiated only by recognizing the sovereignty of nations. Thus, the convention affirms that "economic and social development and poverty eradication are the first and overriding priorities of developing countries" (U.N. Convention on Biological Diversity, 1992, p. 1) and that "States have . . . the sovereign right to exploit their own resources [according to] their own environmental policies" (U.N. Convention on Biological Diversity, 1992, Art. 3). These components of the treaty mean that steps to protect biodiversity will continue to be limited by other development priorities within the individual nations.

Addressing Climate Change

The Framework Convention on Climate Change is designed to limit the worldwide emission of greenhouse gases. Because industrialized nations represent the largest source of greenhouse gas emissions, the treaty established different and higher standards for these nations than for developing ones. During treaty negotiations, the United States was the only industrialized nation that refused to accept *binding* rules for the reduction of greenhouse gases, and the U.S. delegation eventually succeeded in obtaining treaty language that made compliance with greenhouse gas reduction goals voluntary. In 1994, President Clinton reversed the policy of George H. Bush's administration, and announced that the United States would comply with the treaty goals of reducing greenhouse gas emissions to 1990 levels.

On December of 1997, delegates from 170 nations met in Kyoto, Japan, to again address global climate change at the third conference of the parties to the Framework Convention on Climate Change. This meeting resulted in the Kyoto Protocol—a multilateral agreement on legally binding targets for the reduction of greenhouse gas emissions. The Kyoto Protocol mandated a 5% reduction of greenhouse gases by 2012, with the United States agreeing to cut emissions by 7%, the European Union committed to 8% reductions, and Japan committed to 6% reductions. Achieving these goals would require that the United States and other developed countries reduce pollution and consumption in key areas by as much as 30% (Yamin, 1998). In recognition of the difficulty developing nations would have in modernizing their economies while simultaneously reducing greenhouse gases, no binding targets or timetables were set for developing nations (Leaf, 2001, p. 1218).

The protocol included several novel legal mechanisms to facilitate compliance, one of which was the trading of greenhouse gas reduction credits between states. Under this part of the protocol, a state that had exceeded its goal in reduction could offset the greenhouse gases produced by a state that had failed to meet its goal through the trading of emission reduction credits in an international market. The unanimous adoption of legally binding controls of greenhouse gases at the Kyoto conference represented a historic milestone in the development of multilateral environmental treaties, and emotions ran high as chairman of the conference Raul Estrada-Oyuela suggested that December 10 might come to be recognized as an international "day of the atmosphere" in commemoration of the signing (Yamin, 1998).

The Kyoto Protocol would become legally binding on the United States only after its ratification by the U.S. Senate. Just prior to the Kyoto conference in 1997, the U.S. Senate indicated it would *not* ratify any climate change protocol that failed to impose legally binding standards for reduction of greenhouse gas emissions on the developing world or that would "cause serious economic harm to the United States." Facing rejection of the treaty, the Clinton administration elected not to submit the protocol to the Senate for ratification. Clinton stated that he would not do so until there was "meaningful participation" in greenhouse gas reductions in "key developing countries" (Leaf, 2001, p. 1219).

Due to gridlock on this issue, the Kyoto Protocol was not ratified during the remainder of the Clinton administration. In March 2001, the administration of George W. Bush formally withdrew the United States from the Kyoto Protocol. In June of 2001, the administration introduced a series of unilateral initiatives on climate change, which included funding for further research on the issue and several unilateral moves to reduce greenhouse gas emissions, such as selling cleaner-burning

U.S. technology to the developing world and voluntary energy efficiency programs for U.S. consumers. These, however, did not include any binding targets or timetables for the reduction of U.S. emissions (Leaf, 2001).

Development and Trade Versus Environmental Protection

During the last two decades of the 20th century, a growing recognition of the global nature of environmental problems promoted a search for a legal framework of international environmental protection. This has led to the negotiation of global conventions governing hazardous waste transportation, biodiversity, ozone depletion, and climate change, as well as numerous bi- and multilateral treaties of more limited scope. Unlike most legal control exerted over social harms, these treaties constituted *voluntary* agreements among potential offenders with limited enforcement potential. Consequently, national self-interest in protecting the biosphere and the pressure of world opinion still remain the primary forces for ensuring compliance with international agreements to protect the global environment.

There are also powerful forces running counter to the protection of the global environment. These are continued demand for increased standards of living, growth and expansion of TNCs, increased expansion of the free-trade movement, and continued use of military power to achieve geopolitical goals.

As citizens of both the developed world and the developing world struggle to consume ever more material goods, the strain on the world's resources, its biological diversity, and its atmosphere will intensify. It remains an open political question as to how far nations will go to restrict present growth of material consumption for a healthier environment in the future.

Increased worldwide consumerism also has the consequence of expanding both the profitability and the power of TNCs. With many TNCs already in command of greater wealth than many nations, their ability to influence the creation and enforcement of national environmental laws is likely to increase. Corporate promises of large-scale investments, or the fear they will relocate to more hospitable countries, remains an important consideration in framing environmental and labor policies in many nations, particularly (but not only) in developing ones.

An important element of the growing power of TNCs is the free-trade movement promoted by powerful Western countries such as the United States and Britain. The central idea of "free trade" is that all barriers to the international movement of capital and goods by TNCs should be eliminated. The proponents of free trade argue that unless TNCs can invest where they deem it most profitable and sell their products profitably wherever there is a market for them, they will not be able to foster development, particularly development among the poorest nations. Environmental protection laws that slow the movement of goods and capital run counter to the goals of international free-trade agreements such as the General Agreement on Trade and Tariffs (GATT) and the North American Free Trade Agreement (NAFTA) (Jackson, 1992).

The tensions between free trade and environmental protection take several forms. First, there is wide disparity among nations in the establishment and enforcement of environmental protection laws. If TNCs can easily and freely move goods from nations with lax environmental protection laws to those where such laws are more stringent, there is a strong incentive to relocate industrial facilities to nations whose legal system will ensure higher profits. Although prohibiting the importation of goods produced in nations with lax environmental laws is a potential mechanism for enforcing international agreements regarding environmental protection, free-trade agreements such as GATT and WTO frameworks expressly prohibit the exclusion of products from one nation simply because they were manufactured elsewhere in an environmentally damaging manner. Similarly, the initial draft of NAFTA provided no guarantees that both environmental and labor standards in the United States would not be driven downward to ensure economic competitiveness with products produced under the less-stringent laws of some NAFTA trading partners, particularly Mexico. In response to pressure by NGOs in the United States, several "side agreements" designed to protect against the erosion of environmental and labor laws in the United States were drafted as part of obtaining congressional approval for NAFTA. Canada and Mexico, however, have resisted allowing the United States to encroach on their sovereignty by determining the content of Canadian or Mexican environmental and labor laws.

With the end of the Cold War in the late 1980s, there was a brief hope that use or threat of military force would decline as a means of international politics. Since then, however, two U.S. wars against Iraq, the war in Kosovo, the nuclear standoff between India and Pakistan, and the rise of international terrorism suggests that the threat of environmental damage from conventional, asymmetrical, or even nuclear war remains significant.

The various international environmental protections treaties and accords established over the past 20 years constitute genuine progress in defining a variety of environmental harms as transnational violations of law. Efforts to define cross-border environmental harms as legal wrongs, however, are frequently hindered by TNCs and the national self-interest that supports them. As increasingly free-floating political entities, TNCs cannot be easily compelled to behave in socially and environmentally responsible ways. Although their actions may have consequences far more devastating than many harms currently defined and punished as transnational crimes, the likelihood of significant legal controls being exerted over transnational

corporate offenders is limited. For these reasons, the meaning of transnational environmental crime will remain an arena of conflict well into the foreseeable future.

NOTES

1. In some instances, one country may allow its citizens to sue the citizens or government of another country for damages. Such suits, however, rarely result in actual collection of damages unless resources belonging to the defendant have already been impounded in the victim's country.

2. One important exception to this would be the detonation of a nuclear device or "dirty bomb" by the weak party in an asymmetrical war.

3. See the Multilaterals Project Web site at http://fletcher.tufts.edu/multilaterals.html for a link to the Treaty Banning Nuclear Weapon Tests in the Atmosphere, in Outer Space, and Under Water.

4. See the Multilaterals Project Web site at http://fletcher.tufts.edu/multilaterals.html for a link to the Convention on the Protection of the Black Sea against Pollution.

REFERENCES

Agreement between the government of Canada and the government of the United States of America on air quality. (1991). Retrieved April 12, 2004, from http://sedac.ciesin.org/entri/texts/bi-lateral/2.1X-The-Air-Quality-Accord.html

American Law Institute. (1986). *Restatement of the law: Foreign relations law of the United States.* St. Paul, MN: Author.

Blake D., & Walters, R. (1976). *The politics of global economic relations.* Englewood Cliffs, NJ: Prentice Hall.

Blumer, H. (1969). Society as symbolic interaction. *Symbolic interactionism: Perspective and method.* Englewood Cliffs, NJ: Prentice Hall.

Bodley, J. (1976). *Anthropology and contemporary human problems.* Menlo Park, CA: Cummings.

Burhenne, W. E. (1997). The prohibition of hostile military activities in protected areas. *Environmental Policy and Law, 27,* 373–377.

Castleman, B. (1978, Fall). How we export dangerous industries. *Business and Society Review, 27,* 7–14.

Cataldo, E. (1992). Acid rain policy in the United States. *Social Science Journal, 29*(4), 207–227.

Cavenaugh, J., & Clairmonte, F. (1983, January). From corporations to conglomerates. *Multinational Monitor,* pp. 16–20.

Daniels, A. (2000). The perils of activism: Ken Saro-Wiwa. *New Criterion, 18*(5), 4–10. Retrieved April 28, 2004, from www.newcriterion.com/archive/18/jan00/sarowiwa.htm

Devall, B., & Sessions, G. (1985). *Deep ecology: Living as if nature mattered.* Salt Lake City, UT: Peregrine Smith Books.

Du Nann Winter, D. (1998). War is not healthy for children and other living things. *Peace and Conflict: Journal of Peace Psychology, 4,* 415–428.

Gunder-Frank, A. (1978). *World accumulation, 1492–1789.* New York: Monthly Review Press.

Harrington, E. (2002, April 14). Honey, I shrunk the profits. *Fortune,* pp. 191, F-26, F-59.

Hertz, N. (2003). *The silent takeover: Global capitalism and the death of democracy.* New York: Harper Business Press.

Jackson, J. (1992). World trade rules and environmental policies: Congruence or conflict. *Washington and Lee Law Review, 49,* 1227.

Kauzlarich, D., & Kramer, R. C. (1998). *Crimes of the American nuclear state: At home and abroad.* Boston: Northeastern University Press.

Kiss, A. (2001). International humanitarian law and the environment. *Environmental Policy and Law, 31,* 223–230.

Leaf, D. (2001). Managing global atmospheric change: A U.S. policy perspective. *Human and Ecological Risk Assessment, 7,* 1211–1226.

Leaning, J., & McCally, M. (2000). Environment and health: 5. Impact of war. *Canadian Medical Association Journal, 163,* 1157–1162.

Leonard, W., & Duerksen, C. (1980). Environmental regulation and the location of industry: An international perspective. *Columbia Journal of World Business, 15,* 52-68.

List, P. (1993). *Radical environmentalism: Philosophy and tactics.* Belmont, CA: Wadsworth.

Manes, C. (1990). *Green rage: Radical environmentalism and the unmaking of civilization.* Boston: Little Brown.

Matthew, R. A., & Gaulin, T. (2002). The ecology of peace. *Peace Review, 14*(1), 33–39.

Michalowski, R., & Kramer, R. (1987). The space between laws: Corporate crime in a transnational context. *Social Problems, 34*(1), 34–53.

Nordgren, M. D., Goldstein, E. A., & Izeman, M. A. (2002). *The environmental impacts of the World Trade Center attacks: A preliminary assessment.* Washington, DC: National Resources Defense Council.

Okoji, M. A. (2000). Petroleum oil and the Niger Delta environment. *International Journal of Environmental Studies: Sections A & B, 57,* 713–724.

Rehmke, G. (1991). Eliminating government support for deforestation can save rainforests. In M. Polesetsky (Ed.), *Global resources* (pp. 150–157). San Diego, CA: Greenhaven Press.

Roy, A. (2001). *Power politics.* Boston: South End Press.

Singer, D. J., & Keating, J. (1999). Military preparedness, weapon systems and the biosphere: A preliminary impact statement. *New Political Science, 21,* 325–343.

Strauss, R. (1978, July). Interview. *Environmental Reporter, 9,* 451–454.

U.N. Convention on Biological Diversity. (1992). *Preamble.* New York: United Nations. Retrieved April 28, 2004, from www.biodiv.org/convention/articles.asp?lg=0&a=cbd-00

U.N. Environmental Programme. (2003). "Growing vulnerability of countries." In *Global Environment Outlook, Year 2003.* New York: United Nations. Retrieved April 28, 2004, from www.unep.org/geo/yearbook/060.htm

Vallette, J. (1989). *The international trade in wastes: A Greenpeace inventory.* Washington, DC: Greenpeace.

von Zharen, W. M. (1999). An ecopolicy perspective for sustaining living marine species. *Ocean Development & International Law, 30*(1), 1–41.

Vöneky, S. (2000). A new shield for the environment: Peacetime treaties as legal restraints of wartime damage. *Review of European*

Community & International Environmental Law, 9(1), 20–32.

Yamin, F. (1998). The Kyoto protocol: Origins, assessment, and future challenges. *Review of European Community & International Environmental Law, 7*(2), 113–128.

Yamin, F. (2001). NGOs and international environmental law: A critical evaluation of their roles and responsibilities. *Review of European Community & International Environmental Law, 10*(2), 149–163.

9

Drug Trafficking as a Transnational Crime

SANDEEP CHAWLA

THOMAS PIETSCHMANN

DEFINITIONS[1]

One of the most typical forms of transnational crime is the illegal movement, across one or more national frontiers, of psychoactive substances controlled under three instruments of international law known as the drug control conventions. This is usually known as "trafficking in illegal drugs."[2] Although for most types of crime, the transnational dimension is still the exception rather than the rule, drug trafficking has had—from the very beginning of the international drug control system early in the 20th century—a critical transnational element. For nearly a century, illicit drugs have been trafficked from "producer" to "consumer countries," usually involving a number of criminal groups from countries along the trafficking chain. The drug trade is, of course, more than a century old, but before the 20th century, there was no distinction between legal and illegal drugs and consequently no such thing as drug trafficking. Although the distinction between producer and consumer countries noted above has blurred over the past few decades, there is no question that drug trafficking continues to exist and that it has gained in importance over the last three decades.

AUTHORS' NOTE: Sandeep Chawla is Chief, Policy Analysis and Research Branch, and Thomas Pietschmann is Research Officer, at the U.N. Office on Drugs and Crime, Vienna. The views expressed in this chapter are those of the authors and do not represent the views of the United Nations.

The substances under international control, as well as the degree of control exercised over each substance, are laid down in the international drug conventions. The conventions were developed through a multilateral process and can be amended through such a process. Parties to the conventions (member states of the United Nations) may decide to include or exclude particular drugs from the control system or to strengthen or relax the degree of control over a particular drug. The Single Convention on Narcotic Drugs, 1961,[3] provides for the control of the production, distribution, and use of opium, heroin, various other synthetic opiates, coca bush/cocaine and related substances, and cannabis. The Convention on Psychotropic Substances, 1971, covers the control of hallucinogens such as LSD, stimulants such as amphetamines, and sedative-hypnotics such as barbiturates or benzodiazepines. The U.N. Convention against Illicit Traffic in Narcotic Drugs and Psychotropic Substances, 1988, provides for the control of a number of chemicals that are frequently used in the manufacture of drugs (also called "precursor chemicals") such as ephedrine (used to manufacture methamphetamine), P-2-P (1-phenyl-2-propanone, to manufacture amphetamine), potassium permanganate (to manufacture cocaine), and 3,4-MDP-2-P (3,4-methylenedioxyphenyl-2-propanone, also known as BMK, or benzylmethylketone, to manufacture ecstasy).

This chapter focuses on the four main groups of illicit drugs: cannabis, cocaine, opiates, and amphetamine-type stimulants (ATS, such as amphetamine, methamphetamine, and ecstasy).

HISTORY

Although limited drug control efforts at the local level date back more than a century, the evolution of an international drug control system didn't begin until the Shanghai Opium Conference of 1909. This led to the first drug control treaty, the International Opium Convention, signed at The Hague in 1912. The background of these first attempts at international drug control was the rapidly growing opium trade from India (then a part of the British Empire) to China, which had a devastating social and economic impact on the latter country. Chinese attempts to ban the import of opium in the 19th century were abortive. The opium wars and the unequal treaties imposed on China forced the country to accept "free trade" in opium. A huge trade deficit developed, and to counter it, the Chinese State allowed domestic production of opium from 1880. This alleviated the immediate problem of the trade deficit but exacerbated the problem of opium addiction. By the end of the 19th century, there was a full-fledged opium epidemic in the country.

The International Opium Convention of 1912—which included the control of not only the opium trade but also the trade in heroin and cocaine—was the beginning of the multilateral drug control system and the division of psychoactive drugs into legal and illegal ones. World War I interrupted implementation of the Opium Convention, but it was eventually incorporated into the peace treaties concluding the war. The international drug control system then developed further under the auspices of the League of Nations. Three drug control conventions were drafted in the interwar period: the Second Opium Convention of 1925, which established a system of import certificates and export authorizations and extended the scope of control to cannabis as well; the Convention for Limiting the Manufacture and Regulating the Distribution of Narcotic Drugs of 1931, which introduced a compulsory estimates system and provided controls for the manufacture of drugs; and the Convention for the Suppression of the Illicit Traffic in Dangerous Drugs of 1936, which called for the punishment of drug traffickers.

After World War II, the United Nations assumed the drug control functions and responsibilities of the League of Nations. Under the Protocol of 1948, a number of synthetic opiates, developed during the war, were added to the list of controlled drugs. The Opium Protocol of 1953 introduced a system to limit the number of countries that were legally permitted to produce opium. In 1961, all the drug control instruments were consolidated under the Single Convention on Narcotic Drugs. Control was extended to the cultivation of the plants (opium poppy, coca bush, and the cannabis plant), from which the drugs were derived. The Convention on Psychotropic Substances, 1971, extended drug control to a number of synthetically produced substances such as hallucinogens (LSD), stimulants (amphetamine, methamphetamine, etc.), and sedative-hypnotics, such as barbiturates or benzodiazepines. The 1988 U.N. Convention against Illicit Traffic in Narcotic Drugs and Psychotropic Substances tackled the transnational character of drug trafficking. It sought to criminalize drug trafficking, deprive drug traffickers of their financial gains, and establish international cooperation (such as extradition of traffickers, mutual legal assistance between countries on drug-related investigations, and preventing money laundering) to secure such outcomes. The scope of control was also extended to include a number of chemicals used in the manufacture of drugs. In June 1998, a Special Session of the General Assembly of the United Nations adopted a Political Declaration, a Declaration on Guiding Principles of Drug Demand Reduction, and a number of Action Plans on (a) controlling amphetamine-type stimulants and precursors, (b) measures to promote judicial cooperation, (c) strengthening anti-money-laundering activities, and (d) international cooperation for the eradication of illicit drug crops and alternative development.

It is not easy to judge the impact of this international drug control system, which has grown ever more elaborate over the better part of 100 years. Available data suggest that after the system was put in place at the beginning of the 20th century, the global drug trade declined substantially over subsequent decades. In parallel to the decline of the licit trade in drugs, however, illegal drug-trafficking activities emerged and gained in importance. Up until World War II, the net effect of these opposing trends seems to have been positive: Global production and addiction levels were falling. During the war, there was a drastic reduction in world trade; the drug trade consequently declined further. In the first decade after the war, the positive trend appears to have continued. Global addiction and production levels continued to decline, mainly due to major crackdowns in a number of countries. The most notable of these were the solution of the opium problem in China and the controlling of a methamphetamine epidemic in Japan.

From the 1960s, however, world drug production and consumption began to increase, fueled by the rise of transnational drug trafficking and facilitated by growing world trade and improved means of transport and communication. There was a "demand pull" from youth populations in the developed countries. The "supply push" was provided by the economic difficulties of a number of producer countries and the discovery of the lucrative illegal drug trade by various warlords, insurgency groups, and organized crime circles. More production and trafficking increased availability of drugs, in developed countries as well as in transit countries, thus contributing to an overall spread and expansion of demand. In transit countries, the problem often spills over to the local population because service providers to the illicit drug industry (such as groups that organize transporting the drugs) are often paid in kind. Without connections to the main market outlets in the developed countries, many of these groups have to sell the drugs locally to convert them into cash. The increase in both demand and

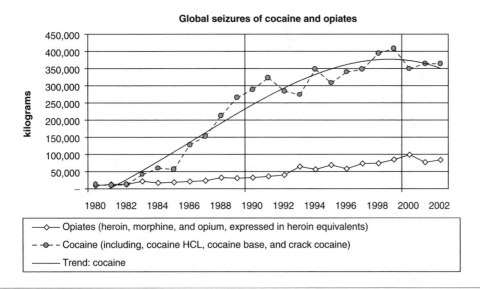

Figure 9.1   Global Seizures of Cocaine and Opiates, 1980–2002
SOURCE: U.N. Office on Drugs and Crime.

supply of drugs was thus made possible due to ever more efficient transnational drug-trafficking networks constituting the link between demand and supply. The increases were most pronounced in the 1970s and the 1980s (see Figure 9.1). In the 1990s and in the first years of the 21st century, however, global growth rates for the main problem drugs—heroin and cocaine—either decelerated or declined. World production estimates and seizure figures, as well as consumption trends of a number of countries (mainly developed ones), point in this direction. This can be interpreted as a positive outcome of the 1988 Convention against Illicit Traffic in Narcotic Drugs and Psychotropic Substances and the 1998 Special Session of the General Assembly, which gave a stronger focus to international cooperation against what is a manifestly global problem.

It is also interesting to note that global production of opium, the raw material for the manufacture of heroin, the world's main problem drug, is today significantly lower than at the beginning of the 20th century. Opium production in 2002 was one sixth the size of production in 1907–1908 (see Figure 9.2).

Even if poppy straw production is included in the calculation and the comparison is expressed in heroin equivalents, production today is some 60% less than what it was at the beginning of the century (see Figure 9.3).

This reflects the massive overall decline in the licit production and trade of opium since the beginning of the 20th century, offsetting the increases in the illicit production and trafficking of opium and heroin over the last four decades.

EXTENT AND TRENDS IN THE PAST DECADE

Overview

In 2002, the latest year for which comprehensive seizure data are available, nearly 1.1 million seizure cases were reported in the world. This represents a considerable increase from the 300,000 cases reported in 1992. The increase reflects not only more trafficking but also greater law enforcement efforts as well as improvements in reporting.

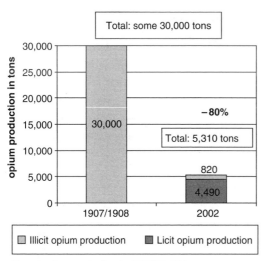

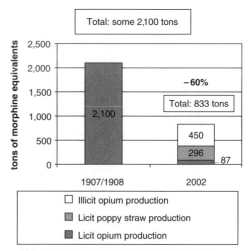

*Legal opium production in 1907/08: China:
22,200 tons, India 5,100 tons, Indochina 1200 tons,
Persia 600 tons, Turkey 560 tons.

*Using a reported 6% morphine content of opium
produced in China and assuming a 10% morphine
content for opium produced in other countries
in 1907/08.

Figure 9.2   Opiate Production in 1907/1908
                   and 2002 (excluding poppy straw)

SOURCES: International Opium Commission, Shanghai
1909; U.N. Office on Drugs and Crime, *Global Illicit
Drug Trends 2003*; and International Narcotics Control
Board, *2002 Narcotic Drugs*, New York, 2003.

Figure 9.3   Opium Production in 1907/1908
                   and Opium and Poppy Straw
                   Production in 2001/2002,
                   Expressed in Morphine
                   Equivalents

SOURCES: International Opium Commission, Shanghai
1909; U.N. Office on Drugs and Crime, *Global Illicit
Drug Trends 2003*; and International Narcotics Control
Board, *2002 Narcotic Drugs*, New York, 2003.

As Figure 9.4 shows, by far the largest traffic, in volume terms, is cannabis herb (marijuana), of which nearly 5,000 tons were seized in 2002. This is followed by cannabis resin (hashish). The next largest volumes of drugs seized are cocaine-related substances, opiates (opium, morphine, heroin), and amphetamine-type stimulants (ATS) (i.e., amphetamines and ecstasy).

The strongest increases in drug trafficking over the past decade were reported for synthetic drugs, notably ATS (see Figure 9.5). Among these, ecstasy seizures grew most rapidly, followed by methamphetamine. Trafficking increases for the two main problem drugs, opiates and cocaine, were less pronounced.

Regional Characteristics

Cannabis

Cannabis herb. Cannabis is the most widely produced and consumed illicit drug. More than 160 million people, 3.4% of the global population aged 15 and above, use cannabis, mostly in the form of marijuana.[4] Seizure data clearly reflect the fact that cannabis herb is produced, trafficked, and consumed worldwide. Concentrations can, however, be identified for North America (58% of global seizures in 2002 according to preliminary estimates, notably Mexico and the United States) and for Africa (20%). South America (including the Caribbean and Central America) accounted for 11% of global cannabis herb seizures, Asia for 6%, and Europe for 5%. Over the past few years, cannabis herb seizures appear to have stabilized, although at fairly high levels. They increased through the 1990s but are still at lower levels than in several single years during the early 1980s (see Figure 9.6).

**Global seizures in metric tons
(based on weight equivalents) 2002**

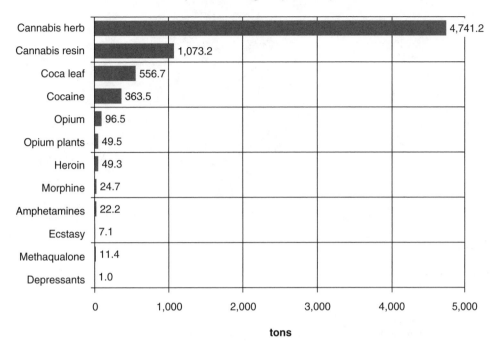

Figure 9.4   Global Seizures in Metric Tons (based on weight equivalents), 2002
SOURCE: U.N. Office on Drugs and Crime.

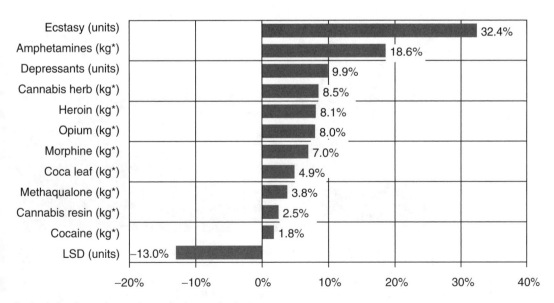

*calculation based on seizures in kg-equivalents

Figure 9.5   Average Annual Growth of Drug Seizures, 1991/1992–2001/2002
SOURCE: U.N. Office on Drugs and Crime.

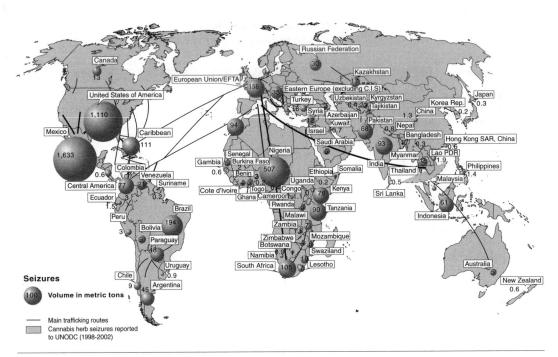

Figure 9.6a   Cannabis Herb Trafficking, 2001–2002:
Extent and Trends (countries reporting seizures of more than 0.1 tons [100 kg])

NOTE: The boundaries and names shown and the designations used on this map do not imply official endorsement or acceptance by the United Nations.

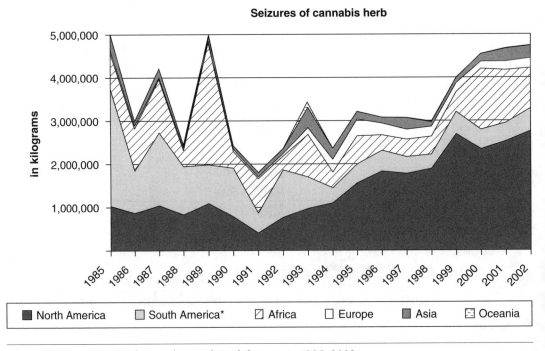

Figure 9.6b   Seizures of Cannabis Herb (in kilograms), 1985–2002

SOURCE: U.N. Office on Drugs and Crime.

Cannabis resin. With regard to cannabis resin (hashish), trafficking concentrations are more pronounced. Morocco, Afghanistan, Pakistan, and Central Asia are the main sources. Europe is the main market: Close to 70% of global cannabis resin seizures were made in Europe in 2002. More than 50% of global or more than three quarters of all European cannabis resin seizures were made in Spain, reflecting the country's strategic location between Morocco and other European hashish markets. The next two largest cannabis resin seizures were reported by Pakistan (8% of global cannabis resin seizures) and Morocco (6%). The Near and Middle East/Southwest Asia region accounted for 22% of world hashish seizures in 2002. Cannabis resin seizures showed an upward trend over the past two decades, although the last few years have witnessed the first signs of some stabilization at these high levels (see Figure 9.7).

Cocaine

More than 14 million people worldwide, 0.3% of the global population aged 15 and above, are estimated to use cocaine.[5] In terms of regional distribution, seizure data show a clear concentration of cocaine trafficking in the Americas (87% of global seizures in 2002). The main exit country for cocaine produced in the Andean region is Colombia. The countries of North America (Canada, Mexico, the United States) accounted for 32% of global cocaine seizures in 2002. The single largest cocaine market is the United States. Cocaine is mainly shipped to the United States through the Caribbean region, Mexico, or both. Cocaine is also transported directly from Colombia to the United States by air. Because of better controls, however, such direct shipments have lost importance over the past decade.

The most significant increases in cocaine trafficking over the last decade were reported from Western Europe. Only 2% of global cocaine seizures were made in Western Europe

in 1985; by 2002, this proportion had increased to 13%. The main points of entry of cocaine into Europe are Spain and the Netherlands. In addition, cocaine transits through a number of West African and South African countries. Increases in cocaine trafficking were also reported for the Oceania region, notably Australia. There is some cocaine trafficked to Asian countries, but it is only of minor importance. Global cocaine seizures are showing signs of stabilization and even moderate decline in recent years (see Figure 9.8).

Opiates

About 15 million people, 0.3% of the global population aged 15 and above, use opiates worldwide.[6] There is a concentration of trafficking in opiates (opium, morphine, heroin) in Southwest and Central Asia—that is, in the countries bordering Afghanistan, which alone accounted for 76% of global opium production in 2002. According to data submitted to UNODC, 49% of global opiate seizures took place in Southwest and Central Asia in 2002. Iran alone was responsible for 25% of global opiate seizures in 2002; Pakistan was responsible for 16% and Central Asia for 6%.

Europe accounted for 28% of global seizures of opiates. Nearly 90% of heroin in Western Europe probably originates from opium produced in Afghanistan. Although the bulk of opiates is still transported through Pakistan, Iran, Turkey, and the Balkan region to Western Europe, a new trend over the past decade was the rising importance of trafficking through Central Asia and other CIS (Commonwealth of Independent States) countries. This also reflected the emergence of the Russian Federation as a major market for Afghan opiates. In addition, direct shipments by air from Pakistan to the United Kingdom regained importance. Although the volumes are not large, some opiates continue to be

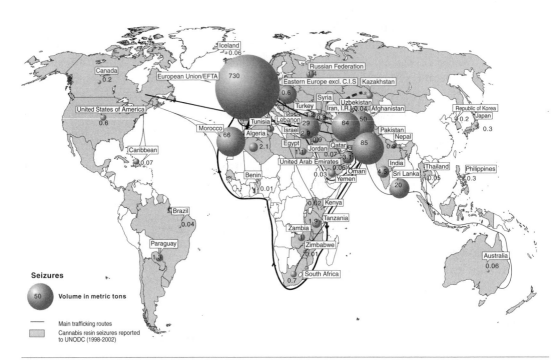

Figure 9.7a   Cannabis Resin Trafficking, 2001–2002:
                    Extent and Trends (countries reporting seizures of more than 0.1 tons [100 kg])

NOTE: The boundaries and names shown and the designations used on this map do not imply official endorsement or acceptance by the United Nations.

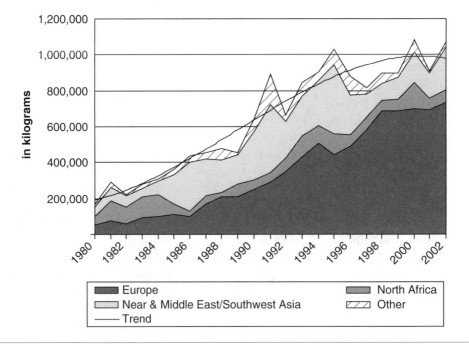

Figure 9.7b   Seizures of Cannabis Resin (in kilograms), 1980–2002

SOURCE: U.N. Office on Drugs and Crime.

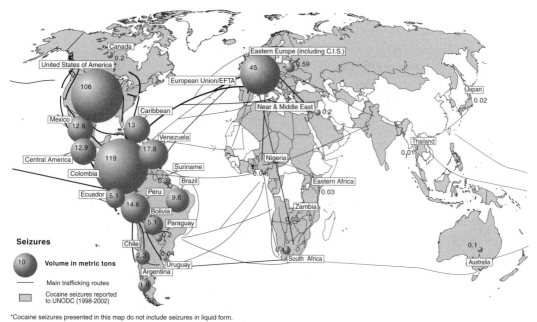

Figure 9.8a Cocaine* Trafficking, 2001–2002:
Extent and Trends (countries reporting seizures of more than 0.01 tons [10 kg])

*Cocaine seizures presented in this map do not include seizures in liquid form.

NOTE: The boundaries and names shown and the designations used on this map do not imply official endorsement or acceptance by the United Nations.

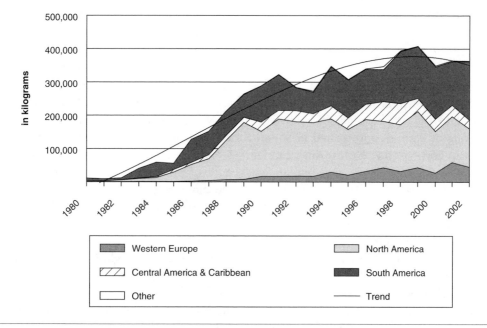

Figure 9.8b Seizures of Cocaine (in kilograms), 1980–2002

SOURCE: U.N. Office on Drugs and Crime.

trafficked, by air or container, to Western Europe through several African countries.

The world's second largest opium producing and trafficking center is the Golden Triangle (Myanmar, Laos PDR, and Thailand). Southeast Asia was responsible for 21% of global opium production in 2002, with Myanmar alone accounting for 18%. Of global opiate seizures in 2002, 14% were made in East and Southeast Asia. Most of the opiates produced in Southeast Asia are today consumed within the region. Small amounts are exported to the Oceania region, North America, and to a lesser extent, Europe, often through Africa.

North America accounted for 4% of global opiate seizures in 2002. The main source of supply for the countries in North America are opiates produced in Mexico and Colombia, although some also originate in Southeast and Southwest Asia. Shipments of opiates from the Americas to other continents are very rare.

Opiate seizures grew in the 1980s and more rapidly in the 1990s. They dropped in 2001, but increased again in 2002, reflecting the resumption of Afghan opium production. However, they are still slightly below the peak reached in 2000 (see Figure 9.9).

Amphetamine-Type Stimulants

Amphetamines. About 34 million people, 0.6% of the population aged 15 and above are estimated to use amphetamines worldwide.[7] Trafficking of ATS is concentrated in Southeast Asia, Europe, and North America. In addition, the Oceania region gained in importance in recent years. In 2002, 64% of global seizures of amphetamines (i.e., ATS, excluding ecstasy) took place in East and Southeast Asia. The world's largest ATS seizures in 2002 were reported from Thailand (39%) and China (14%).

The massive increase in the 1990s and the subsequent decline of methamphetamine seizures in East and Southeast Asia in 2001 and 2002 was mainly due to China, a reflection of

rising production in the 1990s and lower domestic production over the last few years (see Figure 9.10).

The most lucrative market for methamphetamine produced in China is Japan. In addition, Japanese authorities have recently reported increasing illegal imports of methamphetamine from North Korea. Thailand continues to be affected by large-scale production of methamphetamine in neighboring Myanmar. The main precursor chemical for the manufacture of methamphetamine, ephedrine, used to originate over the past decade almost exclusively in China. In recent years, however, authorities in Myanmar reported that ephedrine of Chinese origin was partly substituted by ephedrine produced in India, apparently reflecting improved controls introduced by the Chinese authorities in recent years.

Of global amphetamines seizures, 18% took place in Europe in 2002. These seizures are primarily of amphetamine. Methamphetamine manufacture within Europe is largely limited to just one country, the Czech Republic, which until the mid 1990s was an important producer of ephedrine. Central locations for the manufacture of amphetamine are the Netherlands, Belgium, and increasingly, Poland. In most of these countries the main "raw material" for the manufacture of amphetamine is P-2-P (1-phenyl-2 propanone), also known as BMK (benzylmethylketone).

North America accounted for 16% of global amphetamines seizures in 2002. Although there is some local manufacture of amphetamine, most of the seizures in North America are of the more potent methamphetamine. Most of the methamphetamine in the United States and Canada is nowadays produced from pseudoephedrine, which is often smuggled into the United States through Canada. In addition, Mexico plays an important role as a transshipment location for ephedrine. Criminal Mexican groups are known to be involved in the manufacture of methamphetamine, both in Mexico and in the United States.

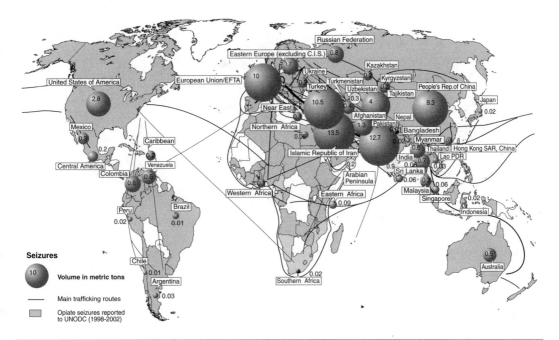

Figure 9.9a   Heroin and Morphine Trafficking, 2001–2002:
Extent and Trends (countries reporting seizures of more than 0.01 tons [10 kg])

NOTE: The boundaries and names shown and the designations used on this map do not imply official endorsement or acceptance by the United Nations.

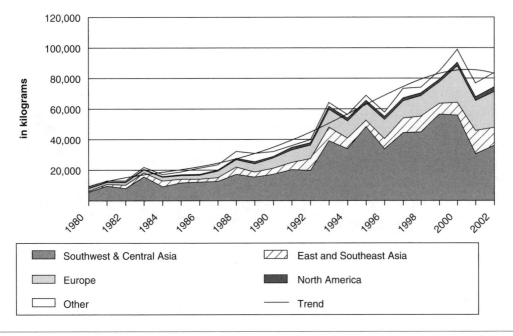

Figure 9.9b   Seizures of Opiates (opium, morphine, heroine—in kilograms of heroine equivalents), 1980–2002

SOURCE: U.N. Office on Drugs and Crime.

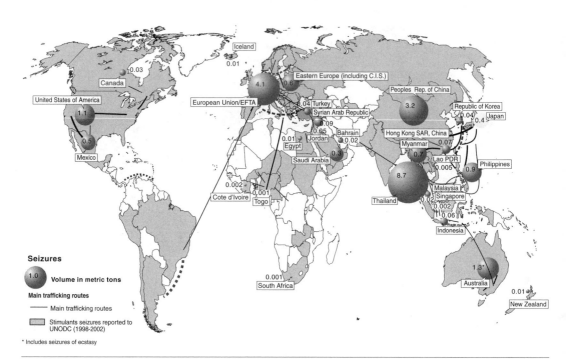

Figure 9.10a   Trafficking of Amphetamine-Type Stimulants (excluding ecstasy): Extent and Trends, 2002–2002 (countries reporting seizures of more than 0.01 tons [10 kg])

*Includes seizures of ecstasy.

NOTE: The boundaries and names shown and the designations used on this map do not imply official endorsement or acceptance by the United Nations.

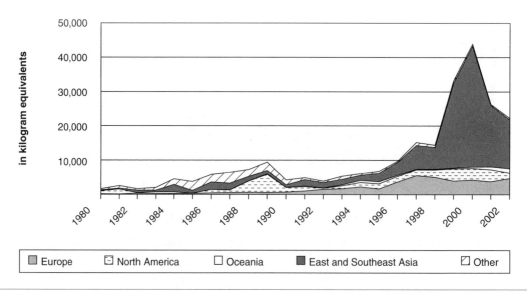

Figure 9.10b   Seizures of Amphetamine-Type Stimulates (excluding ecstasy—in kilogram equivalents), 1980–2002

SOURCE: U.N. Office on Drugs and Crime.

Ecstasy

Ecstasy is consumed worldwide by about 8 million people, or 0.2% of the population aged 15 and above.[8] The largest seizures of ecstasy (MDMA) over the past decade were made in Europe (66% of global seizures in 2002) followed by North America (12%). Increasingly, however, trafficking in ecstasy is emerging as a global phenomenon affecting countries in Europe, North America, Oceania, Central America, the Caribbean, South America, East and Southeast Asia, the Near and Middle East, and Southern Africa. The main production centers are the Netherlands and Belgium, although in recent years, production has also started to spread to a number of other countries in Europe, North and South America, Southeast Asia, and Oceania.

Ecstasy seizures showed a strong upward trend over the last decade (see Figure 9.11). The most frequently encountered chemicals among the MDMA precursors are 3,4-MDP-2-P (3,4-methylenedioxyphenyl-2-propanone), also known as PMK (piperonyl methyl ketone), followed by safrole (often in the form of sassafras oil) and piperonal, both precursors for the manufacture of 3,4-MDP-2-P. Although 3,4-MDP-2-P is the main ecstasy precursor used in Europe, safrole, in the form of sassafras oil, is the main ecstasy precursor used in North America.

Trafficking Patterns

Cannabis (Herb and Resin)

The trafficking of cannabis herb is fairly decentralized. Most of it is trafficked locally, although established international trafficking routes continue to exist and some of the trafficking can be characterized as being well organized. Most of the cannabis herb (77% on average) is trafficked by road, followed by trafficking by boat. There are a number of cases of marijuana trafficking networks expanding their activities to other drugs as well. This was the case, for instance, with several criminal groups from Western Africa that started out in cannabis herb trafficking and later expanded to shipping opiates from Southwest or Southeast Asia to Europe and North America or to trafficking cocaine from South America to Europe.

Cannabis resin production is more concentrated and confined to just a few countries: Morocco, Afghanistan, Pakistan, and Central Asia. Trafficking occurs mainly to neighboring countries and to Europe. Most of the hashish is trafficked by road (70% on average), followed by trafficking by sea.

Cocaine

The main change in the organization of cocaine trafficking over the past decade was the end of cartelization. This followed the dismantling of the Medellin and the Cali cartels in the first half of the 1990s. The operations of the cartels were increasingly taken over by a large number of decentralized trafficking groups. Production of coca leaf, which used to take place mainly in Peru (and to a lesser extent in Bolivia), shifted to Colombia, closer to the cocaine laboratories, following successful operations to break the air bridge linking Peru and Columbia in the mid 1990s. One negative side effect was that cocaine manufacturing capacities also started to develop in Peru. The bulk of the cocaine production, however, continues to take place in Colombia. Despite this, the role of Colombia as the center for the international cocaine trade declined in recent years. In addition to Colombian groups, which had almost monopolized the cocaine trade in the 1980s and the early 1990s, a number of other groups emerged over the past decade, including trafficking groups from neighboring countries as well as a number of Mexican groups, which now dominate the cocaine trade from Mexico to the western and central parts of the United States. Colombian groups continue to dominate the

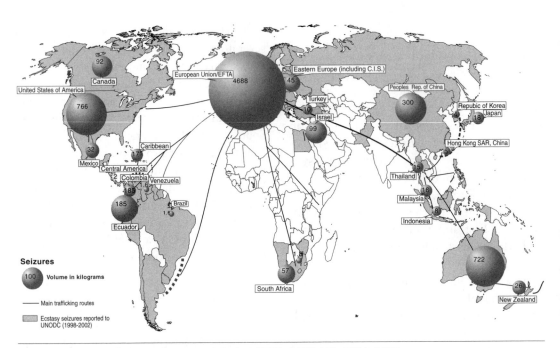

Figure 9.11a   Trafficking of Ecstasy (MDA, MDEA, MDMA), 2001–2002:
Extent and Trends (countries reporting seizures of more than 0.01 tons [10 kg])

NOTE: The boundaries and names shown and the designations used on this map do not imply official endorsement or acceptance by the United Nations.

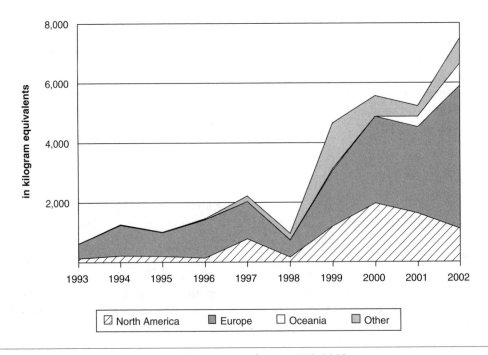

Figure 9.11b   Seizures of Ecstasy (in kilogram equivalents), 1993–2002

SOURCE: U.N. Office on Drugs and Crime.

trade to Florida, to the east coast of the United States, and to Spain. The cocaine trade to the United Kingdom is dominated by criminal groups from the Caribbean region. Over the past decade, a number of West African groups have become active in smuggling cocaine within Western Europe.

Although vertically integrated trafficking networks are less prevalent now, the average volume of a typical cocaine seizure remains significantly larger than that of opiates or ATS. This reflects the fact that cocaine shipments tend to be larger and that the cocaine trade is still more hierarchically organized than trafficking in other drugs. In 2002, the average size of a cocaine seizure amounted to 2.4 kg (ranging from less than 0.1 kg to more than 11 tons); the average size of a heroin seizure was 0.4 kg and the average size of an ATS seizure was 0.1 kg. Expressed in dosage equivalents, the average size of a cocaine seizure is also larger than the average size of a cannabis seizure. Based on individual seizure cases reported to UNODC, more than 50% of the cocaine was seized in 2002 from ships, 18% on the road (cars/trucks), and 10% from aircraft. The most cocaine seizure cases, however, were made from tourists traveling by air (66%).

Opiates

The main trafficking route of opiates is from Afghanistan to Europe; the second largest is from Myanmar and the Lao PDR (People's Democratic Republic) to China and Thailand and the third largest from Colombia and Mexico to the United States. One general trend over the past decade has been a shift of manufacturing capacities closer to the areas of opium production. Although in the early 1990s the bulk of the heroin destined for the European market was still manufactured in Turkey (and to a lesser extent in Pakistan), in recent years, heroin production capacities within Afghanistan have increased significantly.

The opiate trafficking chains are rather complex. Individual criminal groups generally transport opiates over shorter distances than for the typical trafficking in cocaine. Opiate trafficking is often organized along ethnic lines. Typically, Pashtun traders sell the opium to operators of clandestine laboratories in Afghanistan. The opium or heroin is then sold to other Pashtun or Baluch traders who smuggle the opium/heroin across the border from Afghanistan to Pakistan or Iran, or to Afghan Tajiks who ship the heroin across the border to Tajikistan. Tajik groups from Tajikistan are then frequently involved in smuggling the heroin to major Russian towns. From there, criminal Russian groups take over the business. In another parallel route, criminal Pakistani groups transport the heroin either by air or by sea to Europe or, by road, to neighboring Iran. Iranian groups then ship the heroin across the country to eastern Turkey. Criminal Kurdish/Turkish groups transport the heroin across Turkey to Istanbul. Kurdish/Turkish groups—and, increasingly, also Albanian ones (from Kosovo, the Former Yugoslav Republic of Macedonia, and partly also from Albania)—then smuggle the heroin to wholesalers in Western Europe. Finally, various West African and North African criminal groups then often take charge of retail distribution.

In 2002, 70% of the heroin seized was being transported in trucks and cars. The next most common modes of transport were by air and by sea. Heroin trafficking by rail seems to be the most common form of transport in the countries of Central Asia and in the Russian Federation.

ATS (Amphetamines, Ecstasy)

Production and consumption of ATS are, in general, less geographically separated than is the case of the other illicit drugs. One consequence of this is that trafficking in amphetamines (although not ecstasy) is mainly intraregional, not interregional. The possibilities of seizing large ATS deliveries while in transit are thus more limited than for cocaine or opiates. In contrast, ATS precursors are increasingly being trafficked interregionally—partly a consequence of better controls of precursor chemicals in developed countries.

Amphetamines. In the case of "amphetamines" (ATS excluding ecstasy) more than 80% were seized on the road in 2002. The next most frequently used form of transport was by ship. In East and Southeast Asia, countries reported, on average, that 65% of the methamphetamine discovered was seized while still on ships.

The degree of the involvement of organized crime groups in ATS production and trafficking differs from region to region. In Europe, a professional ATS manufacturing and trafficking sector seems to exist in tandem with a significant number of amateurs, producing relatively small amounts for themselves and for their friends. The involvement of organized crime groups is far more pronounced in East and Southeast Asia. In particular, the Japanese Yakuza (Japanese mafia) has for years been heavily involved in the organization of illegal methamphetamine imports into Japan and their distribution at the local level. In Myanmar, several of the paramilitary ethnic groups that used to control the opiate business have recently diversified into methamphetamine production and distribution. In the United States, criminal groups, often operating out of Mexico, have been involved in setting up domestic production and distribution of methamphetamine, partly taking over this business from the biker gangs that used to control it in the 1980s.

Ecstasy. In the case of ecstasy, the traditional pattern of drugs moving from developing to developed countries has been reversed. Ecstasy is still mainly produced in Europe while consumption has spread from Europe to many countries beyond, including North and South America, Oceania, Asia, and Africa. Dutch and Israeli criminal groups have been heavily involved in setting up distribution networks outside Europe. In addition, a large number of individuals have begun to engage in small-scale ecstasy trafficking.

Over the past few years, there have been a number of attempts to produce ecstasy in developing countries as well, notably in Southeast Asia and, to a lesser extent, in Central and South America and Southern Africa. More than 70% of the ecstasy was seized in road traffic in 2002, followed by seizures from aircraft. If ecstasy trafficking among European countries is excluded, more than 70% of the ecstasy seizures in the rest of the world were made from aircraft, reflecting the increasingly international character of trafficking.

INTERNATIONAL ACTION AGAINST DRUG TRAFFICKING

Measures against drug trafficking have been in place in a number of countries since the beginning of the 20th century. Most of the measures, however, were mainly "national" in character. This is not surprising given that the international drug control system was originally geared primarily toward controlling the licit trade in drugs. The Single Convention on Narcotic Drugs of 1961, for instance, obliged member states to limit production, trade, and possession of drugs to medical and scientific purposes (Article 4) and under Action against the Illicit Traffic (Article 35) urged member states to improve coordination and international cooperation, basically by expediting the exchange of information. Under Penal Provisions (Article 36) member states were urged to introduce adequate punishments for serious offenses such as drug trafficking.

The focus on fighting international drug trafficking, however, was not highlighted until the 1988 Convention against Illicit Traffic in

Narcotic Drugs and Psychotropic Substances.[9] The basic philosophy of the 1988 Convention was to reduce incentives for drug trafficking by increasing the risk involved (e.g., imprisonment) as well as by reducing the potential benefits (e.g., confiscation of the proceeds of drug trafficking).

The 1988 Convention obliges member states to establish as a criminal offense (Article 3) illicit traffic in drugs (including the cultivation of narcotic plants), the manufacture and distribution of equipment and precursor chemicals, and the conversion or transfer of property derived from drug trafficking (money laundering). In addition, it also foresees

- Mutual legal assistance in investigations, prosecutions and judicial proceedings (Article 7)
- Extradition (Article 6)
- Controlled deliveries (Article 11)
- Action against money laundering and the confiscation of criminal assets (Article 5)
- Action against precursors (Article 12)

Each measure has been proven useful in dismantling drug-trafficking groups, which are increasingly transnational in nature. This is not only true for *mutual assistance in investigations* but also for *extraditions* (notably of criminals who could otherwise count on the weaknesses in local judicial systems) and for *controlled deliveries,* which have proven to be particularly powerful instruments against trafficking networks. Much work still needs to be done in a number of countries to include controlled deliveries among the achievement indicators for police forces. Otherwise, there is a danger that national police forces may not be inclined to participate in such international operations, which draw resources away from other activities.

Another important field of cooperation is the struggle *against money laundering* and provisions for *confiscating illegally acquired fortunes.* Indeed, most drug trafficking is done

for profit, and nothing hurts drug traffickers more than losing their illegally acquired fortunes. International agreements in this area are crucial to prevent local pressure on politicians to close their eyes to such matters in the interest of domestic investment or employment. In this regard, the link between fighting money laundering and local authorities to confiscate the proceeds of drug trafficking is important. Article 5 of the 1998 Convention[10] states that "each Party shall adopt such measures as may be necessary to enable its competent authorities to identify, trace, and freeze or seize proceeds" and property derived from drug-trafficking activities (para 2), further stating that "a Party shall not decline to act under the provision of this paragraph on the ground of bank secrecy" (para 3)[11] and that "each Party may consider ensuring that the onus of proof be reversed regarding the lawful origin of alleged proceeds or other property liable to confiscation" (para 7), thus raising the chances of confiscating criminal assets.

Measures against the diversion of a number of identified *precursor chemicals* are another crucial element of the 1988 Convention, which have helped to identify a number of clandestine laboratories and prevent the illegal manufacture of drugs in a number of cases. The underlying problem is that many of these chemicals have many legitimate uses. Unless properly monitored, however, they can be diverted for illegal uses. Precursor control is an important element of drug control, particularly for synthetic drugs such as ATS. It is the main supply reduction measure for ATS, similar to controlling the cultivation of opium poppy or coca leaf. Without an effective international system of precursor control, it would be very difficult to explain to the chemical industry of any specific country why it should not fulfill the orders of particular clients, and thus forgo income opportunities, when companies from other countries would supply the chemical.

At the operational level, close cooperation among the various law enforcement bodies—both within countries and among countries—has proven to be a sine qua non of effective drug control. In order to implement this, an international framework for such cooperation has been established through the creation of the U.N. Commission on Narcotic Drugs (CND) and its law enforcement subcommittees, known as the HONLEA meetings (i.e., the meetings of the Heads of National Law Enforcement Agencies), which discuss topics of common interest. More important than the formal meetings as such is the possibility of ongoing informal information exchange, created through the personal contacts and networks emerging among participants of these meetings.

A further important element of operational activities developed in recent years is the creation of *international antitrafficking operations* such as Operation Purple (for potassium permanganate, the main cocaine precursor), Operation Topaz (for acetic anhydride, a key precursor used to manufacture heroin), and Operation Prism (which targets the main ATS precursors). These operations, organized by a number of key law enforcement agencies, in cooperation with the International Narcotics Control Board and other interested parties, have been successful in stopping a significant number of deliveries of precursor chemicals that were likely to have been diverted to illicit channels for illegal drug manufacture.

A new impetus for strengthening drug control and antitrafficking efforts emerged from the 1998 Special Session of the U.N. General Assembly, Devoted to Countering the Drug Problem Together. At this session the U.N. General Assembly passed a Political Declaration as well as number of Action Plans and/ or Measures to Enhance International Cooperation to Counter the World Drug Problem. The most important of these regarding aspects of drug trafficking concern the following:

- ATS
- Precursors
- Judicial cooperation
- Money laundering
- Eradication

New measures foreseen in the Action Plan against Illicit Manufacture, Trafficking and Abuse of Amphetamine-Type Stimulants and their Precursors with regard to the prevention of ATS manufacture and trafficking were, inter alia, (a) the promotion of close cooperation with industry to establish measures or a code of conduct governing the trade in precursors for ATS, (b) greater use of pre-export notifications, and (c) improved monitoring of nonscheduled precursors and the establishment of an international special surveillance list of such substances (Article 18). With regard to the ATS end products, the Action Plan foresees the introduction of the "know your customer" principle in transactions involving ATS (Article 23, h), the introduction of a new system to identify and assess new ATS found on illicit markets more rapidly (Article 23, a), and various measures to bring new ATS more rapidly under control if necessary (Article 23, b). The Action Plan also urges countries to improve their data collection systems on issues such as the size of clandestine laboratories, manufacturing methods, precursors used, prices, purities, and sources of ATS (Article 23, e).

The measures to prevent the diversion of *precursors* foresee, inter alia, the establishment of a system of control and licensing of all of the enterprises and persons engaged in the manufacture and distribution of Table I and Table II substances (precursor chemicals) of the 1998 Convention, a system for monitoring the international trade in precursors to detect suspicious shipments (Article 4, a), improvement of information exchange (Article 5), and the "know your customer" principle for those who manufacture or market precursor chemicals (Article 9, c), thus giving the seller the responsibility to investigate whether the potential purchaser indeed has a legitimate use for such chemicals.

Under the *measures to promote judicial cooperation,* the issues of extradition, mutual legal assistance, transfer of proceedings, controlled deliveries, illicit traffic by sea, and cooperation and training are addressed, basically refining the measures already foreseen under the 1988 Convention and taking technological progress into account. Thus, telephone and video link technology, for instance, is to be considered for obtaining witness statements and testimony, to accelerate judicial proceedings and save costs.

The measures to *counter money laundering* largely followed the provisions already contained in the 1988 Convention, such as the criminalization of the laundering of money derived from serious crimes (such as drug trafficking); the identification, freezing, seizure, and confiscation of the proceeds of such crime; and the requirement of international cooperation and mutual legal assistance in cases involving money laundering (Article 2, a). More specifically, governments are also requested to establish an effective financial and regulatory regime to deny criminals and their illicit funds access to the national and international financial system, inter alia, through customer identification and verification requirements, applying the know your customer principle, mandatory reporting of suspicious activities, and removal of bank secrecy impediments (Article 2, b). More important, in the preamble, a resolution passed by the U.N. CND 2 years earlier (Resolution 5 of 24 April 1996) was recalled (and thus became part of these measures as well), which declared the 40 recommendations of the Financial Action Task Force, established by the industrialized countries, as the standard by which the measures against money laundering adopted by concerned states should be judged.

Finally, the Action Plan on International Cooperation on the Eradication of Illicit Drug Crops and on Alternative Development obliges states to "develop national strategies for the reduction and elimination of illicit crops. . . . National drug crop reduction and elimination strategies should include comprehensive measures such as programmes in alternative development, law enforcement and eradication" (Article 4).

The Action Plan also introduces, for the first time, *clear guidelines on the concrete measures to be taken to eliminate the cultivation of illicit crops* and thus eliminate the very basis for drug trafficking: "In cases of low-income production structures among peasants, alternative development is more sustainable and socially and economically more appropriate than forced eradication" (Article 7). "In areas where viable alternative programmes have not yet created viable alternative income opportunities, the application of forced eradication might endanger the success of alternative development programmes" (Article 31). In contrast, "when there is organized criminal involvement in illicit drug crop cultivation and drug production, the measures, such as eradication, destruction of illicit drug crops and arrests, called for in the 1961 Convention . . . and the 1988 Convention are particularly appropriate" (Article 29). The Action Plan also underlines the role of law enforcement measures in this context: "Law enforcement measures are required as a complement to alternative development programmes in order to tackle other illicit activities such as the operation of illicit drug laboratories, the diversion of precursors, trafficking, money laundering and related form of organized crime" (Article 28, a). "Comprehensive law enforcement programmes can affect the profitability of illicitly cultivated drug crops and, in so doing, make alternative sources of legal income more competitive and attractive" (Article 28, b). "In areas where viable alternative sources of income already exist, law enforcement measures are required against persistent illicit cultivation of narcotic crops" (Article 30).

All these measures cannot, of course, stop drug trafficking entirely. But they seem at least to have led to a certain stabilization or perhaps even first signs of a decline of drug trafficking during the past few years, which can be regarded as progress if viewed against the background of decades of ongoing increases. The U.N. Office on Drugs and Crime (UNODC) advocates the need for a balanced approach, aiming at a reduction of both demand and supply of drugs. Fighting drug trafficking is an important component within this strategy because it reduces both demand (through higher drug prices in consumer markets) and supply of illicit drugs in the producer countries (through lower farm gate prices). One important precondition for further success, however, is better cooperation among the various law enforcement bodies, both within and among countries, to counteract the globalizing tendencies of drug-trafficking groups. Much progress has been made over the past few years. More is still needed. The international framework for cooperation exists. It merely needs more concrete efforts to make it bite.

NOTES

1. All the data in the present chapter, unless stated otherwise, are drawn from the Annual Reports Questionnaire (ARQ), which all member states return to the United Nations every year. The ARQ data are entered into the Database for Estimates and Long-term Trend Analysis (DELTA), and published annually by the U.N. Office on Drugs and Crime (UNODC), in a series of statistical publications titled *Global Illicit Drug Trends* (www.unodc.org/unodc/en/global_illicit_drug_trends.html).

2. The term *illicit/illegal drugs* is, strictly speaking, incorrect. What is illegal is not the substances as such but their production, manufacture, distribution, or possession in violation of the international drug control conventions. The conventions stipulate that the production, manufacture, distribution, and possession of controlled drugs are permitted only for "medical" or "scientific purposes" (Article 4, para c, Single Convention and Article 5, Convention on Psychotropic Substances).

3. United Nations, Single Convention on Narcotic Drugs, 1961, as amended by the 1972 Protocol Amending the Single Convention on Narcotic Drugs, 1961.

4. U.N. Office on Drugs and Crime, *Global Illicit Drug Trends 2003*.

5. U.N. Office on Drugs and Crime, *Global Illicit Drug Trends 2003*.

6. U.N. Office on Drugs and Crime, *Global Illicit Drug Trends 2003*.

7. U.N. Office on Drugs and Crime, *Global Illicit Drug Trends 2003*.

8. U.N. Office on Drugs and Crime, *Global Illicit Drug Trends 2003*.

9. The 1936 Convention for the Suppression of the Illicit Traffic in Dangerous Drugs addressed the issue for the first time, calling for severe punishment of illicit drug traffickers; however, given the outbreak of World War II a few years later, it was ratified and implemented by only a limited number of countries.

10. Special Session of the General Assembly Devoted to Countering the World Drug Problem Together June 8-10, 1998; Political Declaration, Guiding Principles of Drug Demand Reduction and Measures to Enhance International Cooperation to Counter the World Drug Problem.

11. Similarly, Article 7—Mutual Legal Assistance—para 2 extends the areas of mutual legal assistance to "providing original or certified copies of relevant documents and records, including bank, financial, corporate or business records; identifying or tracing proceeds property . . . for evidentiary purposes" and states that "a Party shall not decline to render mutual legal assistance under this article on the ground of bank secrecy" (Article 7, para 5).

10

Trafficking in Human Beings and Smuggling of Migrants

ANDREA DI NICOLA

Homo homini lupus, wrote Hobbes citing Plautus. The dictum seems even more appropriate today. Hobbes argued that, in order to protect their natural rights against the cruelty of others, all human beings are ready to sacrifice some of their freedom and to give it to the sovereign, who endeavours to ensure a safer society for all. In today's globalised society, to which "international sovereign" should victims of trafficking and smuggling transfer some of their natural rights in order to receive protection? And—above all—do they have any rights?

—Flathman & Johnston, 1997, pp. 70–71

Migration is not a new phenomenon; it is as ancient as humanity itself. More recent, on the contrary, are the illegal organization of migration and the exploitation of migrants in destination countries by organized criminal groups. These represent a new form of transnational offense. During the past decade, in fact, immigration has become a profitable area for organized criminals, who have started to provide migration services for people from less-developed regions of the world seeking to reach richer countries. The

AUTHOR'S NOTE: The author is grateful to Adrian Belton for his valuable assistance in editing the text. Mr. Belton works as a freelance translator/editor and teaches English at the University of Trento, Italy.

intervening variable in (illegal) migratory processes is therefore organized crime. What has happened? Thousands of people (Africans, Asians, South Americans, citizens of the former Soviet Union) have fled their birthplaces to make better lives for themselves in wealthier countries. Yet today, amid growing unemployment, developed countries increasingly respond to this pressure by closing their gates and tightening their migration policies. Given that the need for emigration remains unchanged and given that would-be migrants are confronted by tighter migration policies and border controls, the result is ever-greater demand for highly professional illegal migration services. Organized criminals have recognized the opportunities for business and moved in.

The smuggling of migrants is a continuously evolving transnational criminal activity. The organized criminal groups involved exploit legislative loopholes and regulatory asymmetries among countries to maximize their profits and reduce their risks. Throughout the world, this illicit activity has acquired stable organizational complexity and relies on the protection of public officers and collusion among different criminal organizations in different areas of the world. The increase in the criminally organized supply of illegal migration has also accentuated the exploitation of migrants in destination countries, where they are set to work in deviant markets such as drug pushing, begging, prostitution, and illegal or untaxed labor. And it has given rise to the phenomenon of trafficking in human beings for the purpose of exploitation.

This chapter—which deals with the forms of transnational offense constituted by trafficking in human beings for the purpose of exploitation and by the smuggling of migrants—seeks to answer the following questions:

- What criminal activities constitute trafficking in human beings and smuggling of migrants? Are there internationally accepted definitions that can be used?

- How are these two criminal activities undertaken? Specifically, what are the characteristics of these illicit phenomena, of the criminals, and of the victims? What are the organized crime groups involved, and what form do their modi operandi take? What routes are most widely used?
- What is the impact of these crimes? How many victims are there? Is it possible to estimate the number of victims and the turnover of traffickers and smugglers in different areas of the world?
- What efforts have been made to combat these crimes at the national and international levels? Is there a strategy that can be used to tackle them?
- What will happen in the near future in the field of trafficking in human beings and smuggling of migrants? Is it possible to foresee likely scenarios?

We cannot proceed further without using a common language or a protocol—without, that is, giving terms the same referents. Let us therefore start with the definitions of *trafficking* and *smuggling*.

DEFINING CONCEPTS AT THE INTERNATIONAL LEVEL

The international community has been slow to produce normative definitions of *human trafficking* and the *smuggling of migrants* or *alien smuggling*. The need for definitions that distinguish between these two phenomena has arisen for several reasons that relate to the practice of law enforcement, criminological and victimological factors, and policy perspectives:

- At the level of domestic investigative competencies, the two illicit activities have often fallen within the remits of different bodies.
- The criminal groups engaged in one or the other of the two activities may be different; they may be independent from each other, and they may have different modi operandi.
- The characteristics of the victims of human trafficking, and their relationships with the

criminals, differ from those of the victims of smuggling.

- Trafficking and smuggling have had different political significances over time. Whereas illegal immigration has always been a national and international priority, as a problem of security and public order, trafficking in human beings has only recently come to the attention of national governments and international organizations.

During the 1990s, the distinction consolidated in a de facto manner until it was definitively formalized, in 2000, by the two protocols supplementing the U.N. Convention against Transnational Organized Crime.[1]

The first of these two protocols—the Protocol to Prevent, Suppress and Punish Trafficking in Persons, Especially Women and Children, supplementing the U.N. Convention against Transnational Organized Crime— deals with the trade in human beings for the purpose of exploitation. The second—the Protocol against the Smuggling of Migrants by Land, Air and Sea, supplementing the U.N. Convention against Transnational Organized Crime—concentrates on illegal immigration organized by criminal groups. These protocols were intended to fill gaps in the international legal regime, and among their various objectives was the harmonization of criminal legislation by the states parties to combat the criminal activities in question.

The definition of trafficking in persons is contained in Article 3 (a) of the relative protocol. *Trafficking in persons* is the activity that consists in the "recruitment, transportation, transfer, harbouring or receipt of persons, by means of the threat or use of force or other forms of coercion, of abduction, of fraud, of deception, of the abuse of power or of a position of vulnerability or of the giving or receiving of payments or benefits to achieve the consent of a person having control over another person, for the purpose of exploitation." This article also defines what must be considered exploitation, specifying the types

of illicit market into which a person may be forced and then exploited: "Exploitation shall include, at a minimum, the exploitation of the prostitution of others or other forms of sexual exploitation, forced labour or services, slavery or practices similar to slavery, servitude or the removal of organs."

According to Article 5 of the protocol, the states parties undertake to criminalize the forms of conduct falling within the above definition. The description of the modes and means of coercion is deliberately left very broad so that it includes a wide range of behaviors aimed at trafficking for the purpose of exploitation. Article 3, subparagraph (b), also states the irrelevance of the consent given at any time by the victim in all cases in which one of the means set out in subparagraph (a) has been used.

We may say that trafficking in persons concerns all cases where human beings are exploited by organized crime groups and where there is an element of duress involved, as well as a transnational aspect such as the movement of people across borders or their exploitation within a country by a transnational organized crime group.

According to Article 3 of the Protocol against the Smuggling of Migrants by Land, Air and Sea, supplementing the U.N. Convention against Transnational Organized Crime, the smuggling of migrants consists in "the procurement, in order to obtain, directly or indirectly, a financial or other material benefit, of the illegal entry of a person into a state party of which the person is not a national or a permanent resident." Subparagraph (b) of the same article defines illegal entry as "crossing borders without complying with the necessary requirements for legal entry into the receiving State."

A further defining feature of the smuggling of migrants is the intention to obtain a benefit, either financial or material. The profit motive is therefore necessary. Unlike the protocol on trafficking outlined above, this protocol's definition of smuggling makes no reference to the migrant as a victim and states no provisions regarding his or her consent to the criminal activity. This choice—namely, not to consider a person who voluntarily uses smugglers as a victim—is justified if one considers the role played by the would-be migrant, which is not passive but active. The would-be migrant wants to migrate and invests his or her capital to do so. Almost all smuggling operations are based on a contractual relationship between the would-be migrants and the smugglers. The former buy a service (transport across the borders of a given foreign country); the latter gain by using their migratory skills and expertise to provide the service.

The trafficking protocol entered into force on December 25, 2003. As of April 2004, this protocol was signed by 117 countries and ratified by 52. The smuggling protocol came into force on January 28, 2004. As of April 2004, it was signed by 112 states and ratified by 46 (U.N. Office on Drugs and Crime, n.d.).

The above international definitions may be considered the normative standards in this particular field. Countries are already incorporating them into their legislations: If we consider a regional context like that of the European Union (E.U.), for instance, the definitions of trafficking and smuggling set out in E.U. legislation replicate those of the U.N. protocols.

Now that we know what kinds of phenomena we are dealing with, the next step is to consider why these criminal activities happen, how traffickers and smugglers organize their criminal businesses in concrete, and who their victims are.

TRAFFICKING IN HUMAN BEINGS AND SMUGGLING OF MIGRANTS AS FORMS OF TRANSNATIONAL ORGANIZED CRIME

Causes

Why are there people in the world who fall prey to traffickers and smugglers? The two criminal activities often have common origins.

We may start with the ones shared by both human smuggling and trafficking and then concentrate on those typical of the latter.

As a general rule, traffickers and smugglers exploit impoverished and vulnerable individuals seeking a better life (U.S. Department of State, 2003, p. 6). That is to say, the differences of well-being among the countries of the world, and perceptions of those differences, are the main factors responsible not only for emigration but also for the criminal activities of migrant smuggling and trafficking in human beings. Some recent data highlight these differences (U.N. Development Programme, 2002, pp. 10–11, 13–61).

- In 1999, 2.8 billion people—about half the world's population—lived on less than $2 a day, and 1.2 billion of them—about a quarter of the world population—survived on less than $1 a day. Because of population growth, between 1990 and 1999, the proportion of the world's population living in extreme poverty dropped only slightly, from 29% to 23%.

- The gap between per capita incomes in the industrialized and developing countries is still very wide. The richest 5% of the world's population have incomes 114 times higher those of the poorest 5%. During the 1990s, the number of extremely poor inhabitants of Sub-Saharan Africa rose from 242 million to 300 million.

- Every day, more than 30,000 children around the world die from preventable causes, and every year, more than 500,000 women lose their lives as a consequence of pregnancy and childbirth.

- In 50 countries comprising almost 40% of the world population, 1 in 5 children under the age of 5 is underweight. At the present rate, it will take 130 years to eliminate hunger from the world.

- In 1998, 113 million of the 680 million children of primary school age were not at school—97% of them were in developing countries.

- Seventy-three countries, accounting for 42% of the world population, still do not have free and fair elections, and 106 governments around the world do not respect civil and political freedoms.

- Since 1990, 3.6 million people have died as a result of civil wars and ethnic violence, a number 16 times higher than that of people killed in wars between countries.

More systematically, there are two categories of factors influencing the criminal activities under scrutiny (see Europol, 2002b): (1) those that force people to leave a country and to resort to trafficking or smuggling services (push factors) and (2) those that make the final destination countries attractive for those people (pull factors). Push factors (for a detailed analysis see, e.g., Bales, 1999) comprise the dissolution and disintegration of multicultural states, accompanied by religious and ethnic conflicts, natural disasters, discrimination, political instability and civil wars, economic situation, uncontrollable population growth, vast differences in population and economic growth, and impoverishment. Pull factors, by contrast, are the ones that render richer countries desirable to would-be migrants. They include a shortage of manpower, comprehensive social security, a positive economic situation, democratic systems of government, political and social stability, historical links between the countries, common languages, existing communities, and expectations.

Among the specific causes of human trafficking for exploitation, the International Organization for Migration (IOM) cites the globalization of transport, markets and labor, especially with reference to the exploitation of women in sexual markets, and the socioeconomic inequality of women in their origin countries (IOM, 2002, p. 23). All these factors relate to the supply side. However, some authors maintain that it is, instead, demand that plays the primary role (Keeler & Jyrkinen 1999; O'Connell Davidson & Sanchez Taylor, 2001).

In many destination countries, commercial sexual exploitation and the demand for inexpensive labor have increased over the last several decades. Many traffickers who are part of criminal networks involved in other transnational crimes have recognized that they can profit greatly by supplying people to fill these demands. (U.S. Department of State, 2002, p. 2)

At this point, if the above-mentioned factors are the causes of trafficking in women and children, one may inquire as to why in East and Southeast Asia there is also large-scale trafficking in women and children for sexual exploitation to countries that are not particularly wealthy and are hard to imagine as attractive, at least compared with Western countries. For instance, women and children are trafficked from Burma/Myanmar, Cambodia, and Vietnam to India, Malaysia, Pakistan, and Thailand, countries in precarious economic circumstances (Ministry for Foreign Affairs, 2001, pp. 16–22). At least two explanations can be provided for this phenomenon. First, the factor that induces people to resort to traffickers is a well-being differential between countries, and this may arise even in a very poor region. That is to say, the concept of the well-being differential is a relative one. Second, some of the destination countries in East and Southeast Asia have good tourist relations and connections with Western countries, and they have become centers of sex tourism. In this case, demand indeed plays a specific role in shaping the phenomenon (O'Connell Davidson, 2001, pp. 25–28).

A Spectrum of the Organized Crime Groups Involved

Trafficking and smuggling activities affect almost all the countries in the world—classified as those of origin, transit, or destination—but the level of involvement by criminal organizations varies a great deal.

By organizing themselves to commit crime, offenders are able to maximize expected gains and minimize the risks of punishment

(McIntosh, 1975, p. 14), and it is a process similar to the conduct of any legal entrepreneurial activity (see, for instance, Hatch, 1997). The trafficking and smuggling of humans can be straightforwardly interpreted on the basis of a business model (Aronowitz, 2001; Salt, 2000, p. 49; Salt & Stein, 1997). This also aids understanding of why individually run enterprises are not particularly common in these markets, which are almost entirely composed of organized crime groups, of different type and form and often cooperating with each other. This "business metaphor" can be used to describe the criminal groups involved in trafficking and smuggling across a spectrum that ranges from less to more transnational and organized.

Individual entrepreneurs (so-called amateur smugglers or traffickers). This category includes individuals who traffic one or two children or women and exploit them on a private basis or those who provide a single service to migrants (such as transport for a border crossing or locating employers willing to employ illegal migrants in destination countries). The latter are occasional smugglers who gain small sums by supplying national and international transportation. They are usually the owners of taxis, small boats, or trucks used to transport small groups of people departing from secluded coastal areas, effecting short sea passages, and crossing insufficiently guarded frontiers. This activity is not the main source of income for these individual entrepreneurs: It falls under the heading of spontaneous illegal nonorganized and unsophisticated trafficking and smuggling. Very often, these criminals are merely those who do the "dirty work." Bigger and more sophisticated criminal syndicates may rely on them to undertake particularly risky parts of trafficking or smuggling operations, treating them as hired labor. In many criminal investigations and prosecutions around the world, it is these persons who get caught, but they are only the last link in the chain, and they can be easily replaced. Examples of this category are individual criminals trafficking women to countries of the E.U. or the *passeurs* who smuggle migrants into Italy or the coyotes who hide migrants in the back of trucks and smuggle them across the U.S.-Mexican border.

From homemade businesses to small enterprises. The groups in this category range from those that display very rudimentary forms of organization through loose trafficking groups with a small number of affiliates to small illegal groups composed of well-organized criminals specializing in the transport of migrants from one specific country to another using tried and tested routes. Although all these criminal groups are more specialized than occasional smugglers, their influence is limited to a small number of countries, usually only two. This is the case of certain "alien smugglers" in Central America, which, because they are not large-scale organizations, can be better described as independent smugglers cooperating in loosely linked networks. They operate as regional subcontractors with associates in Asia, South America, and the United States, covering a limited area (one or two countries) from where they pass the migrants on to other smugglers or guides (U.S. Government, 2000, p. 115). A similar system operates in Europe, where numerous small and loosely connected gangs traffic women to be exploited in the prostitution markets of the E.U. countries. During their journeys, the women are repeatedly sold on, at different prices, from one small group to another until they at last reach their destinations and their final "owner-exploiters." It is worth noting that the closer they get to the final destination, the higher their price becomes (Transcrime, 2002, pp. 178–192). Generally speaking, numerous gangs throughout the world engaged in trafficking for sexual exploitation fit this position on the spectrum.

Medium and large enterprises. This category comprises very well-organized transnational groups, more highly structured, sometimes involved in a variety of criminal activities, with high levels of expertise, run on a broader geographical (regional or interregional) basis, and invariably operating in more than two countries. Fitting this description, for instance, are Albanian smugglers and traffickers, certain Eastern European groups, the Turkish Mafia, and Nigerian criminal organizations (Richard, 2000, pp. 57–51; U.S. Government, 2000). With reference to Eastern European groups in particular, an example of a medium enterprise is provided by a well-structured Slovenian criminal group that trafficked women from Russia, Moldova, and Ukraine, through Hungary, the Republic of Serbia and Montenegro, Croatia, and Slovenia to Italy. The group was also involved in the smuggling, along the same route, of people from China and Bangladesh on behalf of Asian criminal syndicates, which subcontracted the intermediate part of the journey to the group (Di Nicola, 2003, p. 113).

The Turkish Mafia—which smuggles Kurds, but also Iranians and Afghans, from Turkey to Italy and Germany—is well structured and hierarchical. A *cupola* (the main board of the criminal organization) supervises the entire operation, and the organization comprises a variety of different roles: from those of its members who recruit migrants, gather them together, and load them onto boats to those who escort migrants during the journey and contact people in the destination countries (Transcrime, 2003).

Nigerian criminal groups traffic their nationals for sexual exploitation, especially in Italy and Spain. These groups consist of recruiters and exploiters, all of them of Nigerian nationality, the former operating in Nigeria and the latter in the destination country (Transcrime, 2002, pp. 178–194). Nigerian groups "also facilitate illegal immigration of Nigerian nationals to metropolitan areas around the world" (U.S. Government, 2000, p. 104).

Multinational enterprises (international networks). This last category includes only the multinationals of trafficking and smuggling: organizations able to transport their migrants and trafficking victims over thousands of miles, often through several countries and continents, and with logistical bases in various nations. Most noteworthy among these criminal syndicates are Chinese Triads and Japanese Yakuza groups (Richard, 2000), which smuggle or traffic their conationals around the world. These groups, too, can be described as networks in which only the key roles are covered by nationals who use the assistance of other criminal groups.

In the light of the above spectrum, current trends can be summarized as follows:

1. The greater the distance to be covered and the more countries to be passed through from the origin to the destination, the more sophisticated and the better organized are the criminal groups involved.

2. Migrant smuggling and human trafficking for the purpose of labor exploitation require a larger number of actors and a higher level of expertise than does trafficking in human beings for other purposes. Consequently, criminal organizations engaged in migrant smuggling and human trafficking for the purpose of labor exploitation are usually more sophisticated and more complex.

3. Loose networks are increasingly common in this area of criminal enterprise. They consist of networks of individuals or of criminal groups, and they display considerable dynamism and fluidity. Hence every attempt to give them static definition—such as the one made above—is in danger of distorting the reality. Those that have been called "individual entrepreneurs," "small and medium/large enterprises," and "multinationals" may work together for specific and contingent

purposes, with each group furnishing its specific expertise and acting as just one node in a wider network. Of course, there are also individual large syndicates, but they are frequently not monolithic and hierarchical but flexible in their structure.

4. Smuggling enterprises are usually specialized and nonopportunistic, a feature that may differentiate them from trafficking groups. That is, they do not display a tendency, like certain criminals do, to shift from one illicit activity to another, diversifying their operational sectors on the basis of mere opportunism alone. This may instead be the case of criminal organizations trafficking in human beings for sexual exploitation.

The Trafficking/Smuggling Businesses

How do criminals organize their businesses to move people across borders and, sometimes, to exploit them once they reach their destinations? That is, how do they run their businesses? To answer the question, this section starts with a description of the various phases of the criminal activities under scrutiny and of some routes selected to traffic and smuggle people. It then illustrates some of the basic rules applied by criminals in the organization of their enterprises.

The Stages

People smuggling divides into at least three phases: recruitment, transfer, and entrance into the destination country. Human trafficking involves a further stage—exploitation (Di Nicola, 2003, pp. 112–116; Europol, 2002a; Salt & Stein, 1997), which may take place in a variety of markets operating in the destination countries.

Recruitment usually takes place in the origin countries of the would-be migrants or trafficked victims. A sharp distinction must be drawn here between persons who are trafficked and those who are smuggled. The latter always choose voluntarily to use the smugglers' services. They must pay (often in advance) a fee to be transported to the selected destination, where they are left to their own devices. The methods used by the smugglers to recruit customers may vary according to their origin. Amongst the most common are the following:

Legal or semilegal "travel agencies," which organize the transport of migrants. This may be the case of Turkish organized crime, for instance.

Spreading word among acquaintances and relatives. This method is typically used by smugglers in China, where organized criminals take advantage of ethnic factors and common geographic origin to recruit migrants.

Advertisements in local newspapers and on the Internet that publicize the contact details of "travel agencies" (a method in addition to the first one above) or those of intermediaries/smugglers.

Some of these methods are also used when people are recruited to be exploited in destination countries. In this case, recruitment may take the following forms (International Helsinki Federation for Human Rights, 2000; IOM, 2001b, p. 51; Transcrime, 2002, 2003):

Direct contact with members of the criminal organization. For instance, in the case of exploitation in the black economy, recruiters may be given the task of finding people who want to work abroad. In the case of sexual exploitation, contacts may be made with women already working as prostitutes in nightclubs.

Employment and travel agencies or model/casting/talent agencies, depending on the type of exploitation. These exploiters usually advertise in local newspapers. When the prime aim is to exploit prostitutes, the advertisements usually state specific requirements with respect to appearance, social status, and age. Some exploiters also ask for photographs. The women may be offered work as au pairs, dancers, models, housemaids, waitresses, or air hostesses.

Direct and/or indirect knowledge of the victims.

Violence and, in extreme cases, kidnapping, which is perpetrated in many areas of the world on children and women, who are the most vulnerable subjects.

Sentimental attachments and false promises of marriage in the case of sexual exploitation. The criminals get engaged to the girls before they leave the country in order to reassure them.

The transport stage may be long and complex, especially when the trafficked/smuggled persons come from countries very distant from their destinations and several countries have to be crossed. The persons trafficked/smuggled may stay for months in relatively safe "assembly" countries before they move on. Different means of transport may be used: planes, cars, trains, boats and motorboats (in various combinations). Traffickers/smugglers may rely on the help of compliant public officials or of individuals who provide food and lodging for the victims. Counterfeited documents may be used during the journey. The nature of the transport process varies according to the organized groups involved, the origin of the people trafficked/smuggled, the destination, the price, and the route selected.

Entry into the destination state may be legal or illegal. A tourist visa may be used to enter legally, or a legal work permit can be obtained with the help of cooperating citizens or compliant employers. The latter may provide fictitious work contracts for the traffickers and their victims so that they can acquire legal work permits and live in and move freely around the country. In this case, the document is valid: The illegality resides in the conditions on the basis of which the document is issued. Another legal means to enter a country is claiming political asylum on arrival at its borders. Illegal entry can take place in two ways: with or without border checks. The similarities with the smuggling of goods are evident. In the case of illegal entry without border checks, the migrant may have to cross mountain or coastal borders with the help of *passeurs* or expert guides. Examples are provided by Mexico or the Asian countries, where traffickers and smugglers are able to take advantage of scant border controls. In the case of illegal entry with border checks, fake identity documents are used, often with the collusion of corrupt customs officials—quite common when trafficking/smuggling victims enter their destination countries through airports.

Once this stage has been completed, if the migrants have been smuggled, they are now abandoned to their fates, and it is highly likely that, given the conditions of marginality in which they will now live in the host country, they will fall victim to other criminal groups or unscrupulous employers or they will commit crimes in order to earn a living (Di Nicola, 2001, p. 65). If the migrants have instead been trafficked, their exploitation begins in the host country, although some of them may have already been exploited during the journey (IOM, 2002, pp. 34–36). Exploitation may consist, for example, in forced labor, prostitution, or begging (usually children). The use of violence, deprivation of freedom of movement, and threats against the victims and sometimes their relatives are very common at this stage, whatever form the exploitation activity takes and wherever it occurs. The victims cannot keep any of the money earned from their work because they must now pay the traffickers for their migration. Exploitation of this kind is reported in all regions of the world: migrants exploited as laborers in the construction industries of Western Europe; women enslaved to work in the sweatshops of the industrialized countries or to sell their bodies in Western cities or the brothels of Asian towns; children compelled to beg in the rich countries or to work as camel jockeys in Asia—these are only some sad examples (see U.S. Department of State, 2003, pp. 5–12).

The Routes

What routes are selected to traffic human beings and smuggle migrants? Criminals seem to abide by the following rules:

Already-tested routes. Criminal organizations may engage in more than one illegal activity at the same time, and they use old routes for new criminal activities. It may happen that a

> criminal enterprise . . . relies on the particular expertise, skills and means acquired in a specific illicit sector to expand its criminal activities, changing into new criminal circuits. In practice, a criminal group with already-trained personnel, already-acquired means, *already-tested trafficking routes,* already-displaced corruption networks, and already-existing contacts in different countries of the world, will move into new illicit markets (adding new activities to the ones in which it already specialises). . . . One thinks, for example, of the connections established between drug trafficking and alien smuggling operations by Albanian groups transporting both nationals and drugs across the Adriatic Sea. The same applies to the organised crime groups of Asiatic origin which move illegal immigrants across the Canada-US border, utilising the routes, means and methods already developed for the smuggling of cigarettes. (Adamoli, Di Nicola, Savona, & Zoffi, 1998, p. 17)

Less risky countries and borders. Several countries have thousands of miles of seacoasts or mountain borders, which are difficult to patrol. Others have merely inadequate border controls or regard the security of their frontiers as the least of their problems. Yet others have loopholes in their criminal law provisions or visa law regulations mixed with high levels of corruption among public officials. These are the first countries of choice for traffickers/smugglers, who use them as transit hubs or establish their bases in them.

Opportunistic criteria. Traffickers/smugglers can be very flexible; new routes are opened when old ones are closed by contingent events, such as war or a change of policy. The ease of journey from countries of origin to countries of destination and facility of access to ports or land/sea borders are among the main variables influencing the selection of a particular route.

Some examples are trafficking and smuggling routes to the European Union, the United States, and Australia. This is not to imply, of course, that these are the only geographic areas touched by the problem, for unfortunately, almost all the continents and countries of the world are affected (see Figure 10.1) (Protection Project, 2002; Schloenhardt, 2001, pp. 343–351; U.S. Department of State, 2003).

The following routes are used principally to traffic human beings and smuggle migrants into the European Union:

> The *Baltic route,* which starts in Asian countries, passes through Russia and the Baltic states, reaches the Scandinavian countries by ferry, and from there continues to the heart of the E.U. (Di Nicola, 2001, pp. 67–68).

> Especially with regard to trafficking, the *Northern route* which stretches from Eastern Europe, through Poland, Hungary, and the Czech Republic into Germany and then Scandinavia. It is also used as the final part of the journey for people coming by plane from the Far East, Africa, and South America (Europol, 2002a).

> The *Central European route,* which passes through the central European countries and then usually enters Austria and Northern Italy (Europol, 2002a). This route may be an intermediate stage for migrants from the Asian region traveling through the southern CIS (Commonwealth of Independent States) countries (Kazakhstan, Kyrgyzstan, Uzbekistan, Tajikistan, and Turkmenistan) to Russia, and from there through Ukraine and the Slovakian and Czech Republics to Western European countries or even further to the United States and Canada (Interpol, n.d.). The route is also

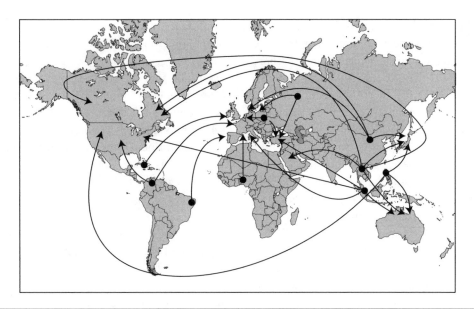

Figure 10.1　　Routes Used Around the World to Traffic Human Beings

SOURCE: Prepared from data provided by the U.N. Office on Drugs and Crime.

used by migrants from China, Sri Lanka, and other Asian countries (Transcrime, 2003).

The *Balkan route,* which crosses Turkey and the Balkan countries and usually terminates in Germany. It has several variants. From Bulgaria, migrants may travel through Romania and Hungary to Germany, or they may enter Macedonia or Albania and from there make their way to Italy, where they may remain or continue the journey to the Federal Republic of Germany or other Western European countries (Di Nicola, 2001, pp. 66–67; Transcrime, 2002).

The *East Mediterranean route* across the Mediterranean from Turkey to Italy, sometimes with a stopover in Greece or Albania (Transcrime, 2003).

The *North African route* From West Africa through Algeria and Morocco, across the Straits of Gibraltar by ship, and from there into Portugal and Spain. This route is also used as the final leg of the journey for migrants arriving by plane from the Far East, Africa, and South America (Europol, 2002a).

In addition to the above (land and sea) routes to Western Europe, there are numerous other direct connections by plane: For instance, people are trafficked into Europe by air from Central and South American countries and from Africa (Protection Project, 2002).

The traffickers of human beings (especially women and children) into the United States also make much use of air travel. The airports of New York, Miami, Chicago, Los Angeles, and San Francisco are major gateways for the trafficking of women and children into the United States. The people trafficked arrive from all over the world but especially from South America, Africa, Eastern Europe, and the East (Protection Project, 2002). New entry hubs are Atlanta, Cleveland, Houston, Orlando, and Washington Dulles. It has been reported, for instance, that Atlanta's airport was chosen as the sole entry point for a Thai trafficker who brought in some 90 women in 2 years (1994–1995). He believed that, amid preparations for the Olympic Games, the Thai women would blend in with the multitude of ethnic nationalities arriving in the city at the time. Atlanta was also a good choice because the city had only a few ethnic Asian immigration officials (Richard, 2000, p. 11).

Other traffickers fly with their victims into Toronto and Vancouver and then transport them overland into the United States (Richard, 2000, p. 11). Trafficked or smuggled human beings also arrive by boat, mainly on the West Coast, even though arrivals by this means have decreased considerably (Interpol, n.d.). However, the most popular route to the United States for Chinese, South Americans, and South Asians is still the one through Central America and Mexico. "Central America has emerged as the primary gateway for US-bound illegal migrants from all over the world" (U.S. Government, 2000, p. 25).

Given its geographic nature, Australia can be entered only by sea or air. A prime sea route starts from Cambodia and Vietnam, being used mainly for Chinese, Vietnamese, and Cambodian nationals (Schloenhardt, 1999, p. 106). Other evidence suggests that migrants from various Middle Eastern countries (especially Afghanistan, Pakistan, Iraq, and Bangladesh) are assembled in Indonesia as the final staging post before they are moved by boat to the northwestern Australian shores, and boats arriving directly from China land on Australia's eastern coasts (Schloenhardt, 1999, p. 106; 2001, pp. 347–349; Tailby, 2001, pp. 3–4). Of course, airports are major entry points as well, with traffickers/smugglers using commercial airlines (Schloenhardt, 1999, p. 107). The majority of women entering Australia to be employed in sex markets are recruited in Southeast Asia and fly into the country using tourist visas (Brockett & Murrey, 1994). Cases of trafficking for exploitation (from West to East) have also been reported from South Africa, Zambia, Turkey, Sri Lanka, Bangladesh, Malaysia, Thailand, Philippines, and Fiji (Protection Project, 2002).

Organizing a Trafficking/Smuggling Enterprise: Basic Principles

Organized crime groups operating in the trafficking/smuggling of human beings act in accordance with an organizational rationale. The manner in which they organize their businesses by seeking out and combining resources essential for the trafficking/smuggling of human beings (Ekblom & Tilley, 2000, p. 382) is governed by a rational logic of risk reduction while maximizing economic results. Among the basic principles applied by criminal organizations as they undertake these criminal activities are the following:

Networks/Alliances and outsourcing. As we have seen, the organized crime groups operating in the field can be most aptly described as *networks.* The term may mean two things: that an individual group consists of a loose network of individuals or that an entire smuggling/trafficking operation is carried out by an articulated network of crime groups linked by alliances. If one of the criminal groups maintains the leading role, the best way to describe the relationship is *outsourcing.* In this case, a central unit with numerous subunits provides specific services. The outsourcing of individual tasks to other criminal organizations or individuals is often essential for the management of trafficking/smuggling activities, and it occurs when human or material resources or both are drawn from outside the main criminal group. It frequently happens that the criminal enterprise retains the core business and allocates some parts of the activity to other more skilled or less risk-averse criminals. Outsourcing is used especially during the transfer and entry phases, but it is not uncommon during the other phases as well (Di Nicola, 2003, p. 118).

Division of labor. Like all serious legal enterprises, criminal groups seek to increase their efficiency by differentiating the roles to be assigned within the organization. "Separating tasks and filling functional positions with qualified members protects the organization as a whole" (Schloenhardt, 2001, p. 341). Possible roles within a trafficking/smuggling criminal organization may be the following: arranger/investor, recruiter, transporter, corrupt public official or protector, informer, guide and crew member, enforcer, supporting personnel and specialists, debt collector, and money launderer (Schloenhardt, 1999, pp. 93–95). When criminal organizations look for people to fill these positions, it is likely that they will find some of them within the legitimate sphere. Thus, *using the assistance of individuals from the legitimate sphere in the recruitment, transportation, entrance, and exploitation phases* is an extremely common feature of trafficking/ smuggling groups. As seen above, contacts with victims and would-be migrants are established during the recruitment phase mainly by word of mouth, advertisements in local newspapers, and the use of travel and employment agencies. The more sophisticated these techniques, the more the supply of human beings will be constant and wide. The complexity of the method is indicative of the specialization of a criminal group. The second factor to be emphasized is the connivance and help received by traffickers/ smugglers from taxi drivers, the owners and/or managers of hotels, the landlords of houses and apartments, and the owners of legal commercial establishments. These "legal facilitators" work for profit and turn a blind eye to the criminal activity, thereby aiding and abetting it. Some are occasionally convicted, but they are more frequently charged and then acquitted for lack of evidence. These phenomena require careful study, because they are dangerous forms of crime and they are essential if traffickers/smugglers are to minimize their risks and develop their criminal activities. There is no doubt that if these services were not available, the entire organization of the trade would be much more complicated (Di Nicola, 2003, p. 117).

Horizontal interdependencies among criminal activities (diversification). Some crime groups, especially if they are medium to large enterprises and are involved in trafficking for exploitation, may engage in other criminal activities as well (especially drugs and arms trafficking), using organizational skills and tools developed in other sectors to move into new sectors. When this happens, the crime group is endeavoring to diversify its criminal activities in much the same way as an investor diversifies his or her investments to reduce risks and earn higher profits.

Vertical interdependencies among crimes (specializations of criminal activities). The transfer and entry phases of the trafficking/smuggling chain may involve a vertical interdependence among crimes. This occurs when organized criminals commit an offense but also perpetrate a series of intermediate or instrumental crimes as they do so. The commission of a crime of particular importance (in terms of effects or gains) is thus flanked by a chain of concomitant offences. In the case of trafficking in human beings for sexual exploitation, a series of crimes are committed and linked together to profit from the exploitation. They include, for instance, the counterfeiting of documents, the corruption of public officials, the use of compliant individuals who aid and abet traffickers by providing food and lodging for the women trafficked, and breaches of the law on legal immigration. All this displays a pattern of specialization: The more criminal groups commit interdependent offenses, the more they are specialized and the more they reduce their risks of being caught, imprisoned, and having their goods confiscated (Adamoli et al., 1998, pp. 16–18).

Using control devices during the exploitation phase. To minimize their risks, the traffickers of human beings for exploitation exert various forms of control over their victims (in the exploitation phase or during the journey). Seizure of victims' identity documents is a first control device. After the victims have been deprived of their documents, they may be provided with false ones, and new identities may be given to them as well, these being changed from time to time to avoid recognition by the police during checks. Violence and menace are common because they undermine the victims' self-confidence. This is especially the case of women forced into prostitution, where the accommodation system also enables the exploiters to keep control over them: Even when the victims are not locked inside houses or rooms, the exploiters are able to monitor their movements. Exploiters of women resort to other devices as well, such as driving the victims to their workplaces, protecting them while working, fixing the prices of services, and giving the women an exact number of condoms. These stratagems ensure close control over the victims. For example, the method of fixed prices and a given number of condoms enables the exploiters/controllers to determine whether the women's daily income corresponds to the number of sexual services provided, and to detect any theft of the money earned during the day by the prostitutes. The role of the controllers is crucial, because they are in constant contact with the victims by mobile phone and warn them of problems (e.g., the presence of the police). They also collect all the women's daily earnings.

The Victims

The lowest common denominator of all trafficking and smuggling victims is their vulnerability, which may depend on a set of variables deriving from the fact that a person has no physical, material, social, or psychological resources with which to resist the blandishments of traffickers/smugglers. Such vulnerable persons are desperate to escape from dire socioeconomic and sociopolitical circumstances, and they have no means of knowing that the help of traffickers/smugglers is illegal and may deprive them of their basic human rights. Hence, the concept of vulnerability may assist the prediction of which individuals will become victims and in which geographical areas. It is for this reason, for instance, that traffickers prefer to

supply women and children from the rural areas of underdeveloped countries.

The human typology of victims is diverse. It comprises the poverty-stricken, the extremely uneducated, and common criminals but also intellectuals and political dissidents. Persons already working as prostitutes may sometimes become the victims of traffickers for sexual exploitation. The Europol Report 2002 (Europol, 2002a) distinguishes among three types of victim according to the methods employed to recruit them: exploited victims, deceived victims, and kidnapped victims. The first group (exploited victims) comprises those who have worked in the sex industry in their home country and are recruited for similar work in the destination country. Only on their arrival do they realize that they have been duped into working in conditions similar to slavery. The second group (deceived victims) consists of women recruited to work in the service or entertainment industries of the destination country, with no mention being made of their likely prostitution. The third group is made up of women who have been kidnapped and are therefore unwilling victims from the outset.

THE SCALE OF THE PROBLEM

Estimating the Scale of the Phenomenon

The U.S. government estimates that 500,000 illegal aliens are brought into the country annually by alien smuggling networks. It also estimates that in 1999 Chinese smugglers helped 30,000 to 40,000 Chinese to enter the United States (U.S. Government, 2000, p. 22). Other recent estimates are very difficult to find, however. An early and widely cited survey was conducted by the International Centre for Migration Policy Development (ICMPD, 1994) for 1993 and estimated that between 100,000 and 220,000 migrants had used the help of smuggling syndicates, in one or several phases of the transfer, to reach a Western European country in that year. The ICMPD estimate was based on the assumption that between 15% and 30% of the immigrants (250,000–300,000) entering Europe illegally had used traffickers, and that between 20% and 40% of those requesting asylum without genuine entitlement (estimated at 300,000) had done so as well (Widgren, 1994).

In regard to trafficking, according to government and nongovernmental experts in the field, between 700,000 and 2 million women and children are trafficked globally each year (Richard, 2000, p. 3). A recent U.S. government estimate—which includes men, women, and children trafficked into forced labor and sexual exploitation and does not include internal trafficking movements—indicates that about 800,000 to 900,000 people are annually trafficked across international borders in the world, with 18,000 to 20,000 of them having the United States as their final destination (U.S. Department of State, 2003, p. 7). Yet it has also been reported that some years previously, in 1997, according to U.S. government estimates, 45,000 to 50,000 women and children were trafficked into the United States in that year alone, which was 6% to 7% of the world total (U.S. Government, 2000, p. 25). Approximately 30,000 women and children were being trafficked into the United States annually from Southeast Asia, 10,000 from Latin America, 4,000 from the Newly Independent States and Eastern Europe, and 1,000 from other regions (Richard, 2000, p. 3). It is evident, therefore, that official estimates suffer from some inconsistencies.

The IOM (2001a) has reported that until recently an estimated 500,000 women had been trafficked from Bangladesh to India to work in the sex industry and that every year, 5,000 women and girls from Nepal are forced into prostitution in India.

Are Estimates Reliable?

The above-mentioned figures notwithstanding, it should be stressed that estimating hidden phenomena such as trafficking and smuggling in humans is very difficult and that every estimate runs the risk of becoming a "guesstimate." Research may either overestimate or underestimate the phenomenon. For instance, in Europe (as elsewhere), there are few studies that estimate the number of persons trafficked for the purpose of sexual exploitation to a given area and explain the methodology used to produce their data (Bruinsma & Meershoek, 1999; Carchedi, Picciolini, Mottura, & Campani, 2000; IOM, 1996; Kelly & Regan, 2000; see also International Organization for Migration, 2000). An example of a study that does so has been conducted by PARSEC (a Rome-based social research organization) (Carchedi et al., 2000), which has shown that the number of trafficked women can be estimated by extrapolating a subset of the population of foreign prostitutes calculated on the basis of empirical surveys. The number of trafficked women estimated by PARSEC ranged from 1,453 to 1,858 (min.) to 1,942 to 2,216 (max.) for 1996 and from 1,103 (min.) and 1,446 (max.) for 1998. Again on the basis of an empirical survey, a U.K. research study, for 1998, estimated trafficked women at between 142 and 1,420 (Kelly & Regan, 2000). In general, regarding all existing research, "Where data on specific aspects of trafficking are quoted they are more likely than not to be derived from small-scale surveys or from sources such as police records which cannot be scientifically representative"(IOM, 2001b).

Another method to estimate trafficking uses the official figures on trafficked victims who have contacted the investigative and judicial authorities. Consequently, improvements in the collection of investigative and judicial statistical data on victims may yield much more reliable estimates of the number of trafficked people and the monetary turnover of traffickers/exploiters. If these figures were available, it would then be necessary only to calculate, with the help of experts, the ratio between the victims who report their traffickers and/or contact the judicial authorities and those who do not (i.e., the "dark" number of victims). That is to say, it would thus be possible to make an estimate on the basis of a reasonable (and agreed on by experts) definition of that ratio.

This approach has already been used by an IOM study of trafficking in women in Austria (IOM, 1996), a country in which (a) the crime of trafficking in women is envisaged by the Criminal Code and (b) data are collected on the offense and on victims. This research reported that in the period considered (1990–1994), the victims trafficked and then induced into prostitution and recorded by official statistics amounted to 751. The research report added, however, that "the real number therefore may be many times higher than shown in the statistics" (p. 32). That is to say, the officially recorded number of victims represents only the tip of the iceberg, but it is certainly a useful basis for calculation of the part of the iceberg that remains submerged.

Recent research by Transcrime (2002) also applied this method and produced the following estimates for Spain and Italy: (a) the yearly number of victims, (b) the yearly maximum monetary turnover from the sale of trafficked people to exploiters (i.e., the profits of criminals who transfer foreign persons from one country to another to procure prostitutes for exploiters in the destination countries) (TT, or turnover from trafficking), and (c) the yearly maximum turnover from the sexual exploitation of trafficked people (TE, or turnover from exploitation).

In Spain, the estimated total population of victims trafficked for sexual exploitation ranged from 4,120 (min.) to 8,240 (max.) for 1999 and from 3,920 (min.) to 7,840 (max) for 2000. The estimated TT for 1999 ranged from € 29,664,000–59,328,000 to 123,600,000–247,200,000 and, for 2000, from 28, 224,000–56,448,000 to 117,600,000–235,200,000. The estimated TE for 1999 ranged from € 177,984,000–355,968,000 to 889,920,000–1,779,840,000 and, for 2000, from €169,344,000–338,688,000 to 846,720,000– 1,693,440,000.[2]

In Italy, the estimated total number of victims trafficked for sexual exploitation in the period between March 6, 1998 to December 31, 2000, ranged from 7,260 (min.) to 14,520 (max.). The yearly estimated average of victims (for 1999 and 2000) ranged from 2,640 (min.) to 5,280 (max.). The yearly estimated TT for 1999 and for 2000 ranged from € 2,640,000–5,280,000 to 36,960,000– 73,920,000, and the estimated TE for 1999 and for 2000 from € 380,160,000– 760,320,000 to 475,200,000–950,400,000.

ACTIONS TAKEN AT THE INTERNATIONAL AND NATIONAL LEVEL

What International Instruments Ask Countries to Do

The international community has become aware that a three-pillar approach is needed to tackle trafficking in human beings and the smuggling of migrants. The three pillars are repression, prevention, and protection of and assistance to victims. All the recent international instruments enacted on trafficking/smuggling matters consider these three sets of polices.

Repression

The Trafficking Protocol to the Palermo Convention calls for the parties to enact new laws to criminalize trafficking in persons, especially women and children, and to ensure that persons attempting to commit the crime, participating in its commission, or organizing and directing other persons in order to commit it are punished (Article 5). Governments, the protocol continues, should also adopt new measures to tighten border controls by means of stricter identity checks, as well as by inspecting and seizing vehicles (Article 11). The Smuggling Protocol to the Palermo Convention envisages the elimination of safe havens for migrant smugglers and the fast-track prosecution of offenders, requesting that nations adopt laws making the smuggling of migrants (together with the attempt, participation, and organization/direction) a criminal offense. Behaviors to be criminalized include producing a fraudulent travel or identity document and procuring, providing, or possessing such a document for the purpose of migrant smuggling (Article 6).

With regard to the EU, two recent provisions should be mentioned in particular: the Council Framework Decision of July 19, 2002, on combating trafficking in human beings (2002/629/JHA) and the Council Directive of November 28, 2002 on defining the facilitation of unauthorized entry, transit, and residence (Council Directive 2002/90/EC).

The Council Framework Decision establishes the offenses concerning trafficking in human beings for the purposes of labor exploitation or sexual exploitation in the E.U. and calls on E.U. member states to take the necessary measures to ensure that instigating of, aiding, abetting, or attempting to commit such an offense is punishable by effective, proportionate, and dissuasive criminal penalties, which may entail extradition (Articles 1, 2, and 3). Each member state shall also take the necessary measures to ensure the liability of legal persons for the offense of trafficking in human beings for the purposes of labor exploitation or sexual exploitation if the offense was committed for a legal person's benefit by any person, acting either individually or as part of an organ of the legal person, who has a leading position within the legal person (Article 4). In this case, effective, proportionate, and dissuasive penalties may include criminal or noncriminal fines or other sanctions (Article 5).

The Council Directive refers to the smuggling of migrants (although the term used is "facilitation of unauthorised entry, transit and residence"). According to Article 1, each

Member State shall adopt appropriate sanctions on: (a) any person who intentionally assists a person who is not a national of a Member State to enter, or transit across, the territory of a Member State in breach of the laws of the State concerned on the entry or transit of aliens; (b) any person who, for financial gain, intentionally assists a person who is not a national of a Member State to reside within the territory of a Member State in breach of the laws of the State concerned on the residence of aliens.

Sanctions should be effective, proportionate, and dissuasive (Article 3).

Prevention

The Trafficking Protocol emphasizes that governments should seek to prevent trafficking with various measures. Information campaigns should be drafted and implemented and should be focused on informing potential victims of the causes and consequences of trafficking, the penalties for trafficking, and the risks they may face. States parties are then required to take steps, also through bilateral or multilateral cooperation, to reduce the vulnerability of persons, especially women and children, to trafficking (e.g., poverty, underdevelopment). States parties shall also adopt or strengthen legislative or other measures, such as educational, social, or cultural measures, to discourage the demand for all forms of exploitation of persons that leads to trafficking (Article 9). This protocol also envisages a form of situational prevention with reference to identity documents. Member states should ensure that their travel or identity documents are of such quality that they cannot easily be misused and cannot readily be falsified, altered, replicated, or issued; they should also ensure the integrity and security of these documents issued by or on behalf of the state party and prevent their unlawful creation, issuance, and use (Article 12).

Similar action on identity documents is requested by the Smuggling Protocol (Articles 12, 13), which also calls for closer attention to be paid to border controls as a means to prevent smuggling (Article 11). The protocol also asks countries to adopt public information campaigns to prevent potential migrants from falling victim to organized criminal groups, and programs to combat the root socio-economic causes of the smuggling of migrants (Article 15).

Preventive measures against trafficking and smuggling are also set out in the Comprehensive Plan to Combat Illegal Immigration and Trafficking of Human Beings in the European Union adopted by the E.U. Council of Ministers on February 28, 2002. With reference to prevention, among the various actions proposed, the plan describes a series of measures to be adopted prior to the crossing of borders in and with the countries of origin. Among them are (a) cooperation with states of origin in combating trafficking in human beings and inducing them to assume their readmission obligations, with technical and financial assistance; (b) awareness campaigns on the risks of illegal immigration; (c) prevention of corruption; (d) improvement of the security of identity documents.

Protection and Assistance

The Trafficking (Articles 6, 7, and 8) and the Smuggling (Article 16) Protocols mandate state parties to assist and protect smuggled persons and victims of traffic. Countries should do the following:

Protect the basic rights of migrants and protect migrants against violence

Assist migrants endangered by the smuggling process, with special attention to women and children

Allow trafficked victims to remain on their territory, temporarily or permanently

Provide for the physical, psychological, and social recovery of victims

Facilitate, without delay, the return of trafficked victims who are nationals or residents in the country

Inform victims about relevant court and other proceedings against offenders and ensure victims' privacy

Enable victims to seek compensation for damages, including fines, penalties, or forfeited proceeds as well as restitution from offenders

Moreover, the European Commission has recently formulated a proposal for a Council Directive (European Commission, 2002, 71) submitted on February 11, 2002 on short-term stay permits issued to victims of action to facilitate illegal immigration or trafficking in human beings who cooperate with the competent authorities. Although this temporary stay permit is issued to victims in exchange for their cooperation with the investigative and judicial authorities—and is thus mainly a tool in the fight against human traffickers and migrant smugglers—it is a normative device that also affords protection to victims.

What Countries Are Doing

Numerous countries around the world have committed themselves to the fight against human trafficking and migrant smuggling of migrants, and they have recently undertaken legislative reforms to strengthen their normative instruments. Nevertheless, there is still a great deal to be done; the efforts made thus far are not uniformly distributed around the world—as evidenced by the results of the recent *Trafficking in Persons Report* of the U.S. Department of State (2003). This report, issued to Congress as required by the Trafficking Victims Protection Act, attempts to group the world's countries according to their variance from the act's "minimum standards for the elimination of trafficking." The Trafficking Victims and Protection Act of October 2000 was intended to combat trafficking by ensuring the effective punishment of traffickers, enhancing protection for victims, and creating significant mandates for the Departments of State, Justice, Labor, and Health and Human Services and the U.S. Agency for International Development. It has proved an effective legislative instrument against trafficking.

According to the act's "minimum standards for the elimination of trafficking," governments should (1) prohibit trafficking and punish acts of trafficking; (2) prescribe punishment commensurate with that for grave crimes, such as forcible sexual assault, for the knowing commission of trafficking in some of its most reprehensible forms (trafficking for sexual purposes, involving rape or kidnapping, or that causes a death); (3) prescribe punishment that is sufficiently stringent to deter and that adequately reflects the offense's heinous nature for the knowing commission of any act of trafficking; and (4) make serious and sustained efforts to eliminate trafficking (U.S. Department of State, 2003, p. 15). In particular, the act states seven criteria that may be considered as proving "serious and sustained efforts to eliminate trafficking" (Point 4 above):

1. Whether the government vigorously investigates and prosecutes acts of trafficking within its territory

2. Whether the government protects victims of trafficking, encourages victims' assistance in investigation and prosecution, provides victims with legal alternatives to their removal to countries where they would face retribution or hardship, and ensures that victims are not inappropriately penalized solely for unlawful acts as a direct result of being trafficked

3. Whether the government has adopted measures, such as public education, to prevent trafficking

4. Whether the government cooperates with other governments in investigating and prosecuting trafficking

5. Whether the government extradites persons charged with trafficking as it does with other serious crimes

6. Whether the government monitors immigration and emigration patterns for evidence of trafficking and whether law enforcement agencies respond appropriately to such evidence

7. Whether the government vigorously investigates and prosecutes public officials who participate in or facilitate trafficking and takes all appropriate measures against officials who condone trafficking (U.S. Department of State, 2003, p. 15)

Countries that comply with the minimum standards are classified in Tier 1; countries whose governments do not fully comply with them but are making significant efforts to bring themselves in line with those standards are placed in Tier 2; countries whose governments do not fully comply with the minimum standards and are not making significant efforts to do so are allocated to Tier 3. As shown in Figure 10.2, in 2003 there were numerous nations in the world still widely at variance with normative standards that allow the effective repression and prevention of trafficking in human beings and the protection and assistance of victims. The problem is even greater when one considers progress made in the field of policies against smuggling of human beings.

LIKELY SCENARIOS

The criminal problems discussed in this chapter result from a set of intractable variables, as follows:

First, differentials in well-being among the countries of the world. A two-speed split between West and East and North and South (i.e., a split between two worlds—rich and poor, two worlds evolving at different speeds) has developed, and it continues to grow apace.

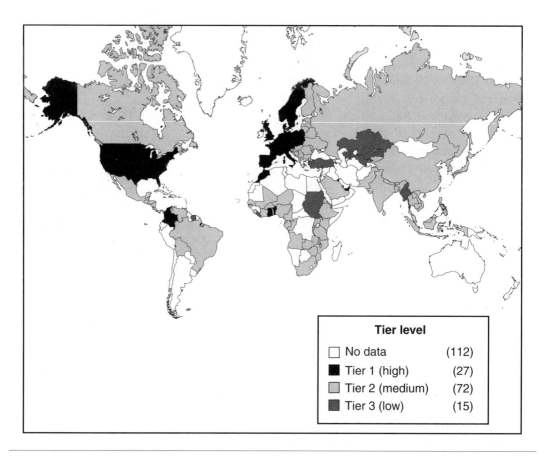

Figure 10.2   Anti-Trafficking in Human Beings Efforts, Countries' Tier Level 2002

SOURCE: Prepared from data provided by the U.S. Department of State (2003).

Second, the almost unconditional closure of their borders by rich countries and their general lack of coherent policies for the integration of newcomers.

Third, the continuing absence of a tough criminal law framework against smugglers and traffickers and the difficulty of effective investigative and judicial cooperation.

Fourth, the insufficient harmonization of migration policies, visa regimes, crime prevention, and crime control policies across the countries of the world.

All these variables influence the balance between opportunities and risks that rational criminals weigh before undertaking a new criminal activity. As long as there are easy opportunities (with high profits) and low risks, the trafficking and smuggling of humans as organized crime businesses will flourish. Transnational organized criminals will use their entrepreneurial skills, their flexibility in adapting to new and changing environments, and the ease with which they move across borders to take advantage of criminal markets.

The level of trafficking/smuggling can be reduced by working on the above variables, and the actions taken should be harmonized, global, and agreed on by several countries cooperating to achieve a common goal. Every weak link in the network is an opportunity for criminals, because it gives them a loophole to exploit. A single country working alone is bound to fail. The crucial problem is persuading the wealthier countries to surrender some of their privileges and to reduce unconditional restrictions to legal immigration, and persuading the poorest countries to admit their responsibilities and make their needs more explicit. In short, legislative measures should be tough on criminals and their illicitly acquired wealth, and a global network should be built. Some positive steps forward have been taken, but more concrete action is now necessary. The longer it takes to achieve this pact among the largest number possible of countries in the world, the more likely it becomes that future scenarios will be little different from the present situation.

NOTES

1. The United Nations Convention Against Transnational Organized Crime and the two protocols on trafficking and smuggling were adopted by the Ad Hoc Committee on the Elaboration of a Convention Against Transnational Organized Crime on October 28, 2000. They were subsequently approved by the U.N. General Assembly and opened for signature at the High-level Political Signing Conference held in Palermo from December 12–15, 2000. For further analysis of the U.N. Palermo Convention and the Trafficking and Smuggling Protocols see Vlassis (2002), Blackell (2002), and Jordan (2002).

2. In 1999, the euro € was worth about $0.93, and in 2000 the average conversion rate was about $1.08. Please visit www.x-rates.com/d/EUR/USD/hist2003.html for current and historical conversion rates.

REFERENCES

Adamoli, S., Di Nicola, A., Savona, E. U., & Zoffi, P. (1998). *Organised crime around the world* (Publication Series No. 31). Helsinki, Finland: European Institute for Crime Prevention and Control, affiliated with the United Nations (HEUNI).

Aronowitz, A. A. (2001). Smuggling and trafficking in human beings: The phenomenon, the markets that drive it and the organisations that promote it. *European Journal of Criminal Policy and Research, 9*(2), 163–195.

Bales, M. (1999, October). *What predicts global trafficking?* Paper presented at the UNICRI International Conference on New Frontiers of Crime: Trafficking in Human Beings and New Forms of Slavery, Verona, Italy.

Blackell, G. (2002). The protocols on trafficking in persons and smuggling in migrants. In International Centre for Criminal Law Reform and Criminal Justice Policy (Ed.), *The changing face of international criminal law: Selected papers* (pp. 105–124). Vancouver, BC: International Centre for Criminal Law Reform and Criminal Justice Policy (ICCLR& CJP).

Brockett, L., & Murrey, A. (1994). Thai sex workers in Sidney. In P. Perkins, G. Prestage, & R. Sharp (Eds.), *Sex work and sex workers in Australia*. Sidney: University of New South Wales Press.

Bruinsma, G. J. N., & Meershoek, G. (1999). Organised crime and trafficking in women from Eastern Europe in the Netherlands. In P. Williams (Ed.), *Illegal immigration and commercial sex: The new slave trade* (pp. 105– 118). London: Frank Cass.

Carchedi, F., Picciolini, A., Mottura, G., & Campani, G. (2000). *I colori della notte. Migrazioni, sfruttamento sessuale, esperienze di intervento sociale* [The colors of the night. Migrations, sexual exploitation and experiences of social intervention]. Milan, Italy: Franco Angeli.

Di Nicola, A. (2001). Trafficking in migrants: A European perspective. In P. C. van Duyne, V. Ruggiero, M. Scheinost, & W. Valkenburg (Eds.), *Cross-border crime in a changing Europe* (pp. 63–73). Huntington, NY: Nova Science.

Di Nicola, A. (2003). Trafficking in women for the purpose of sexual exploitation: Knowledge-based preventative strategies from Italy. In M. Gill (Ed.), *Managing security* (pp. 109–124). Leicester, UK: Perpetuity Press.

Ekblom, P., & Tilley, N. (2000). Going equipped: Criminology, situational crime prevention and the resourceful offender. *British Journal of Criminology, 40*(3), 376–398.

European Commission. (2002). *Short-term residence permit issued to victims of action to facilitate* illegal immigration or trafficking in human beings who cooperate with the competent authorities. Retrieved June 23, 2004, from http://europa.eu. int/scadplus/leg/en/lvb/133187.htm

Europol. (2002a). *Crime assessment: Trafficking of human beings into the European Union.* Retrieved August 8, 2003, from www.europol.eu.int/index.asp?page=publ_crimeassessment THB

Europol. (2002b). *Organised illegal immigration into the European Union.* Retrieved August 8, 2003, from www.europol.eu.int/index.asp?page=publ_illegalimmigration

Flathman, R. E., & Johnston, D. (Eds.). (1997). *Leviathan: Authoritative text, backgrounds, interpretations.* New York: Norton.

Hatch, M. J. (1997). *Organization theory and theorizing: Modern, symbolic-interpretive and postmodern perspectives.* Oxford, UK: Oxford University Press.

International Centre for Migration Policy Development. (1994). *The key to Europe: A comparative analysis of entry and asylum policies in Western countries.* Stockholm: Immigrant and Refugee Commission, Ministry of Culture.

International Helsinki Federation for Human Rights. (2000). *A form of slavery: Trafficking in women in OCSE Member States.* Vienna: Author.

International Organization for Migration, Migration Information Programme. (1996). *Trafficking in women to Austria for sexual exploitation.* Geneva, Switzerland: Author.

International Organization for Migration. (2000). *Migrant trafficking and human smuggling in Europe: A review of the evidence with case studies from Hungary, Poland and Ukraine.* Geneva, Switzerland: Author.

International Organization for Migration. (2001a). New IOM figures on global scale of trafficking. *Trafficking in Migrants: Quarterly Bulletin, 23.*

International Organization for Migration. (2001b). *Victims of trafficking in the Balkans: A study of trafficking in women and children for sexual exploitation to, through and from the Balkan Region.* Geneva, Switzerland: Author.

International Organization for Migration. (2002). *Journeys of jeopardy: A review of research on trafficking in women and children in Europe.* Geneva, Switzerland: Author.

Interpol (n.d.). *People smuggling.* Retrieved August 8, 2003, from www.interpol.int/Public/THB/PeopleSmuggling/Default.asp

Jordan, A. D. (2002). *The annotated guide to the complete UN trafficking protocol.* Washington DC: International Human Rights Law Group.

Keeler, L., & Jyrkinen, M. (Eds.). (1999). *Who's buying: The clients of prostitution.* Helsinki, Finland: Council for Equality, Ministry of Social Affairs and Health.

Kelly, L., & Regan, L. (2000). *Stopping traffic: Exploring the extent of, and responses to, trafficking in women for sexual exploitation in the UK* (Police Research Series, Paper 125). London: Home Office.

McIntosh, M. (1975). *The organisation of crime.* London: Macmillan.

Ministry for Foreign Affairs. (2001). *Trafficking in women and children in Asia and Europe.* Stockholm, Sweden: Ministry of Foreign Affairs.

O'Connell Davidson, J. (2001, December). *The sex exploiter.* Theme paper for the 2nd World Congress against Commercial Sexual Exploitation of Children, Yokohama, Japan.

O'Connell Davidson, J., & Sanchez Taylor, J. E. (2001). *The informal tourist economy in the Caribbean: Gender, race and age* (Final Report to the Economic and Social Research Council). Swindon, UK: Economic and Social Research Council.

Protection Project. (2002). *Human rights report on trafficking in persons, especially women and children: A country by country report on a contemporary form of slavery* (2nd ed.). Washington, DC: Johns Hopkins University, School of Advanced International Studies.

Richard, A. O'Neill. (2000). *International trafficking in women to the United States: A contemporary manifestation of slavery and organized crime.* Washington, DC: U.S. Department of State, Center for the Study of Intelligence.

Salt, J. (2000). Trafficking and human smuggling: A European perspective. *International Migration, 38*(3), 31–56.

Salt, J., & Stein, J. (1997). Migration as a business: The case of trafficking. *International Migration, 35*(4), 467–494.

Schloenhardt, A. (1999). The business of migration: Organised crime and illegal migration in

Australia and the Asia-Pacific region. *Adelaide Law Review, 21*(1), 81–114.

Schloenhardt, A. (2001). Trafficking in migrants: Illegal migration and organized crime in the Asia Pacific region. *International Journal of the Sociology of Law, 9*, 331–378.

Tailby, R. (2001). *Organised crime and people smuggling/trafficking to Australia* (Trends & Issues in Crime and Criminal Justice, No. 208). Canberra: Australian Institute of Criminology. Retrieved April 16, 2004, from www.aic.gov.au/publications/tandi/ti208.pdf

Transcrime. (2002). *MON-EU-TRAF: A pilot study on three European Union key immigration points for monitoring the trafficking of human beings for the purpose of sexual exploitation across the European Unio*n (Final Report). Trento, Italy: Author.

Transcrime. (2003). *Tratta di persone e traffico di migranti* [Trafficking in human beings and smuggling of migrants]. Trento, Italy: Author.

U.N. Development Programme. (2002). *Human development report 2002.* Retrieved June 23, 2004, from http://hdr.undp.org/reports/global/2002/en/

U.N. Office on Drugs and Crime. (n.d.). *Signatories to the UN Convention against Transnational Crime and Its Protocols.* Retrieved April 24, 2004, from www.unodc.org/unodc/crime_cicp_signatures.html

U.S. Department of State. (2002). *Trafficking in persons report.* Washington DC: Author.

U.S. Department of State. (2003). *Trafficking in persons report.* Washington DC: Author.

U.S. Government. (2000). *International crime threat assessment.* Washington DC: Author.

Vlassis, D. (2002). The United Nations Convention against Transnational Organised Crime and its protocols: A new era in international cooperation. In International Centre for Criminal Law Reform and Criminal Justice Policy (Ed.), *The changing face of international criminal law: Selected papers* (pp. 75–103). Vancouver, BC: International Centre for Criminal Law Reform and Criminal Justice Policy (ICCLR&CJP).

Widgren, J. (1994, October). *Multilateral cooperation to combat trafficking in migrants and the role of international organizations.* Paper presented at the 11th IOM Seminar on International Response to Trafficking in Migrants and the Safeguarding of Migrant Rights, Geneva, Switzerland.

11

War Crimes, Crimes Against
Humanity, and Genocide in
International Criminal Law

GRANT NIEMANN

Criminal law is often thought of as a means of maintaining human order within the confines of a specific community. The courts apply the criminal law according to a specific geographical area that they refer to as their "jurisdiction."[1] However, notions of what constitutes the boundaries of a community are relative and have changed over time.[2]

Universal recognition and acceptance of a body of law referred to as "international criminal law" is not without its detractors.[3] It is a question of how it is viewed. If international criminal law is seen as merely an extension or part of national law, then it is not a separate law at all. Those who subscribe to this view argue that international customary law cannot conflict with state law, because state law is supreme.[4] They argue that insofar as their own citizens are concerned, they can validly make laws that are inconsistent with international law and that the courts will enforce those inconsistent laws. With respect to "treaty law," such laws would not be regarded by state courts as having any application unless such international laws are made part of state law by state legislation.[5]

The alternative view is that international criminal law is a separate and distinct body of law. International criminal law may or may not be part of national law, but at least insofar as an international criminal law has achieved *jus cogens* status, then such a law would be binding on the legislature of that state. With respect to treaty law, if it is intended to be "self-executing," then on ratification of the treaty, such a law would be supreme.[6]

Neither view has achieved universal acceptance. Prior to World War II, the situation was clearer; generally, national law applied to "individuals," and international law applied to "states." However, in the period from World War II to the present, more and more, international criminal law applies to individuals. Consequently, it cannot now be safely said that state courts can simply ignore international criminal law, at least insofar as such laws have achieved *jus cogens* status. Thus, a law of a state that permitted genocide or even apartheid could now be held to be illegal by a national court, because such a law would be beyond the state legislature's competence.

Furthermore, international criminal law has been referred to as a branch of "international humanitarian law."[7] International criminal law has expanded significantly since the Nuremberg trial of 1946. However, it is fair to say that it has not reached the status of a fully self-sufficient coherent body of law; in other words, it is still emerging, and opinions may differ widely as to its interpretation and application.[8] This does not mean, however, that there is not a fundamental "core" of basic international laws that are universally accepted as binding on all humankind.

The secretary-general of the United Nations was keen to identify such laws when setting up the International Criminal Tribunal for the former Yugoslavia. He was able to conclude with some degree of certainty that the grave breaches of the Geneva Conventions of 1949, the violation of the Laws and Customs of War and of Crimes against Humanity and Genocide were undoubtedly in this category. The secretary-general was anxious to select only those crimes that he considered would be uncontroversial, lest the principle of *nullem crimen sine lege*[9] should operate to defeat any prosecutions undertaken by the fledgling tribunal.[10]

Accordingly, modern international criminal law has, for the moment, two main sources: (1) the Laws and Customs of War and (2) Crimes against Humanity and Genocide.[11]

A significant omission here is the crime of aggression. Initially recognized as an international crime by the League of Nations in 1922,[12] it was the centerpiece of the Kellogg-Briand Pact 1928 (although not expressed as a crime as such).[13] It was then inserted in the Charter of the Nuremberg Tribunal and titled "Crimes against Peace."[14] The Nuremberg crime of aggression involved the planning and waging of a war of aggression or in violation of international treaties.

The International Military Tribunal at Nuremberg held that to initiate a war of aggression "is the supreme international crime differing only from other war crimes in that it contains within itself the accumulated evil of the whole."[15] This crime was significantly omitted from the Statute of the International Criminal Tribunals for the former Yugoslavia and Rwanda and included in the Statute of the Permanent International Criminal Court only on the basis that it would not apply until states "could agree upon a suitable definition."[16]

The definition of "a crime of aggression" as proposed by the International Law Commission in July 1991 provided that a "leader organizer or individual" who orders an act of aggression would be guilty of a crime. The commission defined "aggression" as the use of armed force by a state against the sovereignty, territorial integrity, or political independence of another state or in any manner inconsistent with the Charter of the United Nations. It was also an act of aggression for one state to allow its territory to be placed at the disposal of another state so that the latter state could commit an act of aggression.[17] This definition (although legally correct) was not accepted by states for incorporation into the Statute of the Permanent International Criminal Court.

With respect to the Laws and Customs of War, these laws are mostly concerned with regulating the means of warfare and human conduct during the course of armed conflict, and they have as their central focus the participants of battle.[18]

Crimes against Humanity are not restricted to periods of armed conflict and have as their central focus the victims of such crimes.[19]

For the most part, these laws have evolved during the course of the 19th and 20th centuries, although the laws of war go back to earlier times. International criminal law is still in its emergence, but it has developed more since World War II than at any previous time in history.[20]

As human intercourse and communication has moved from the primitive printing press to satellite-conveyed television images and cyberspace, so too has the concept of what constitutes the community. Instead of criminal law being the exclusive business of a local community such as a region, town, city, or state, as human activity and concern have extended beyond the nation-state, the question of regulating human conduct, including conduct beyond the nation-state, becomes an issue.[21]

Community support for the international rule of law progressively increased because of a perceived need to regulate and control the conduct of persons whose acts had repercussions beyond the boundaries of their nation-states.[22]

WAR CRIMES

A war crime is the violation of the laws of warfare (usages or customs of war) committed by any persons military or civilian. There is a distinction to be made between the rules of warfare and war crimes. H. Lauterpacht defines war crimes as offenses against the laws of war that are criminal in the ordinary and accepted sense of the word. They are to be distinguished from traditional criminal laws by reason of their heinousness, their brutality, their ruthless disregard for the sanctity of human life, and their wanton interference with rights of property unrelated to reasonably conceived requirements of military necessity.[23]

National Codes

National war crimes codes regulating the conduct of armies have existed for centuries. The first significant national modern war crimes code that went beyond matters of strict military discipline was drafted by Francis Lieber. In 1863, President Lincoln set in train a promulgation by the War Department to settle a series of instructions for the U.S. Army to use in the field of battle. These instructions were prepared by Francis Lieber, a German veteran of the Napoleon wars who had immigrated to the United States and became a professor of law and political science at Columbia University. The instructions comprised some 159 articles covering matters such as "military necessity," punishment of crimes against the inhabitants of hostile countries, prisoners of war, and spies.[24]

Lieber drafted his code for use in the American Civil War, and parts of it are still to be found in the U.S. military code.[25] Although national codes are not a part of international criminal law, they have contributed to customary international law and constitute evidence of customary law.[26] Furthermore, the expressed opinion of states, particularly in cases where such opinion is generally accepted by other states, not only evidences the existence of customary international law but also demonstrates a change in what was previously accepted as customary international law.[27]

The Hague Law

At around the same time that Lieber was drafting his code, in Europe, Czar Alexander II of Russia proposed the idea of holding an international conference to ban the use of lightweight bullets, which exploded on contact with human flesh. As a consequence, the Declaration of St. Petersburg in 1868 prohibited the use of explosive projectiles under 400 grams in weight. This was the first international convention in modern times to prohibit the use of a particular weapon of war, although it must be said that crossbows and the like had been prohibited in earlier times.[28]

The St. Petersburg Declaration provided that the "only legitimate objective which states should endeavor to accomplish during war is to weaken the military forces of the enemy and that the unnecessary use of weapons which uselessly aggravate suffering were contrary to the laws of humanity."[29]

In 1899, Czar Nicholas II of Russia proposed another conference, this time in The Hague, Netherlands. The purpose of the conference was to consider banning the dropping of bombs from balloons, the use of poisonous gases, and the use of expanding bullets, known as "dumdum" bullets, during war.[30] The Hague Convention II of 1899, which was the result of this conference, adopted these prohibitions but significantly also introduced the first comprehensive set of regulations on the Laws and Customs of War on Land. The Laws and Customs of War (further modified in 1907) provided for the care of prisoners of war, flags of truce, and the treatment of the inhabitants and property of occupied territories and prohibited rape and pillage.[31] The 1907 Hague Conventions and regulation Article 1 apply the laws to armies as well as militia. Chapter II is concerned with the treatment of prisoners of war; Article 23 limits who may be killed under certain circumstances and the use of poison and weapons that cause unnecessary suffering—the principle of proportionality.

The 1899 and 1907 Convention on the Laws and Customs of War expressly recognized that they were not exhaustive of this area of law and provided for the development of further laws according to "usages established among civilized peoples, from the laws of humanity, and the dictates of the public conscience."[32]

Other conventions settled on at The Hague in 1907 included Convention V Respecting the Rights and Duties of Neutral Powers and Persons in Case of War on Land,[33] Convention VI Relating to the Status of Enemy Merchant Ships at the Outbreak of Hostilities,[34] Convention VII Relating to the Conversion of Merchant Ships into War-Ships,[35] Convention VIII Relating to the Laying of Automatic Submarine Contact Mines,[36] Convention IX Concerning Bombardment by Naval Forces.[37]

The prohibition on the dropping of bombs from balloons still applies but unfortunately has only limited practical application.[38] Controversy surrounds the application of 1899 Hague Declaration, relating to dumdum bullets, as a means of prohibiting the development and use of much more devastating ammunition.[39] Poisonous gases were used extensively during the course of the 20th century.[40]

Although often more recognized in their breach than their observance, the Laws and Customs of War settled on at The Hague Peace Conferences of 1899 and 1907 have now been embodied as customary international rules of war applicable to this day.[41] Thus, the killing of innocent civilians, the use of poisonous weapons, killing the enemy after they have laid down their arms, declaring that no quarter be given, sentence without trial, employing weapons causing unnecessary suffering (principle of proportionality); mistreatment of prisoners of war, and deceptive use of flags of truce or distinctive emblems are all prohibited.[42] Articles 44 to 56 restrict what an occupying force or state may do on occupied territories to the inhabitants of the occupied territory. For example, a citizen of an occupied territory cannot be compelled by a belligerent occupier to furnish information about the inhabitants' army or be compelled to swear allegiance to the occupying power.

This attempt to contain the use of excessively destructive weapons of war spurred a proliferation of similar such conventions and declarations throughout the course of the 20th century, including the Geneva Gas Protocol 1925, which banned the used of poisonous gases as a weapon of war.[43] This protocol was replaced by the Biological Weapons

Convention of 1972. Other arms control conventions included the Conventional Weapons Convention of 1980 and the additional protocols of 1995 and 1996, The Chemical Warfare Convention of 1993, and the 1997 Ottawa Treaty banning the use of antipersonnel land mines.

The laws of war prohibiting the use of excessively destructive weapons during armed conflict (gas, bombs, bullets) and the conduct of soldiers (rape, murder, and pillage) were not originally intended to apply to individuals but only to the responsible state as a basis of claiming compensation or reparation. Thus, although the conduct was prohibited, the laws did not give rise to individual criminal responsibility at the international level.[44] The Hague Protocol of 1954 for the Protection of Cultural Property in the event of armed conflict was designed to safeguard cultural property during the event of an armed conflict, but during the Yugoslav conflict, it was frequently breached.

The Hague Laws are generally referred to as the laws of war, whereas the Geneva Laws are known as the international humanitarian laws.[45]

Geneva Law

Again in the middle of the 19th century, Henry Dunant, a Swiss banker, observed the cruelty of war firsthand at Solferino in northern Italy. This was a war between France, Italy, and Austria. There were about 40,000 casualties in the conflict, and what struck Dunant most was the total lack of regulation concerning removal of the dead and wounded after the battle. He returned to Switzerland and in 1862 wrote *Memory of Solferino*. The book suggested that neutral "relief societies" should be formed to care for the sick and wounded in times of war. He further suggested that an international conference should be held to enable representatives of different countries to consider and adopt an international agreement on how to care for the soldiers wounded in battle.[46]

In 1864, such a conference was held in Geneva, Switzerland, and was attended by the representatives of 16 countries. The international conference concluded by agreeing on a short convention that focused on providing a means by which medical attention could be provided to the soldiers wounded in battle. It also saw the creation of the Red Cross Society, with its distinctive Red Cross emblem, and enshrined the Red Cross principles of neutrality, humanity, impartiality, and respect for the individual.

The Geneva Conventions first proposed by Henry Dunant of Switzerland were modified and updated throughout the course of the 20th century. The Geneva Conventions of 1906 made greater provision for the care of wounded and sick soldiers.

After World War I, the Geneva Conventions of 1929 (1) Relative to the Treatment of Prisoners of War and (2) For the Amelioration of the Condition of the Wounded and Sick in Armies in the Field were updated to include provision for the protection of medical aircraft and the adoption of red crescent and red lion emblems for Muslim countries.[47]

Following the horrors of World War II, the Geneva Conventions were again extensively overhauled at a conference in 1949. As a result of this conference, four new Geneva Conventions were adopted, each dealing with a specific subject area: (1) wounded and sick in armed forces, (2) wounded and sick at sea, (3) treatment of prisoners of war, and (4) treatment of civilians. However, because World War II was an international armed conflict, the 1949 Geneva Conventions were primarily directed at the regulation of conduct in the course of an international armed conflict.[48]

This limitation on the application of the 1949 Geneva Conventions was modified in 1977 to cater for the greater protection of civilians in both internal and international armed conflict. Thus, the 1977 additional protocols (regarding international armed conflict and internal armed conflict) when coupled with the 1949 conventions now constitute the most important source of Geneva law.[49]

Sovereign Immunity

The notion that the state could be held responsible in terms of its collective guilt and be ordered to pay reparations for the states' wrongdoings rarely did anything to redress the pain and suffering caused to the victims of such atrocities. Reparation payments went to the injured state, not to the individuals concerned.[50]

Nor were international laws of war originally meant to make the head of state criminally liable for the breach of the laws and customs of war by their armies. The sovereign head of government viewed himself or herself as above the law. They were the manifestation of the law itself. Accordingly, he or she was not bound by the criminal law.[51]

The position of the sovereign evolved into the sovereign state, and this immunity from criminal liability passed on to sovereign state itself. Accordingly, sovereign states and their human representatives were immune from the criminal law at both national and international levels when carrying out an act of state. The head of a sovereign state could not be brought to trial for domestic or international crimes, no matter how egregious his or her crimes might have been.[52]

Prior to the 20th century, there were occasional international trials for war crimes, but at no time was a sovereign head of state seriously considered as a candidate for war crimes prosecutions.[53]

After World War I, Kaiser Wilhelm II of Germany was supposed to be tried by an international tribunal for the atrocities his armies committed during World War I, but this call for prosecution action soon passed when ironically the Kaiser took asylum in the Netherlands (now the seat of the new International Criminal Court), and no prosecutions ever followed.[54]

The state of the law on individual responsibility and sovereign immunity at the international level was to change after World War II due to the extensive violation of the laws of war. The Nuremberg Charter of 1945 for the first time introduced the concept of individual criminal responsibility for violation of the Laws and Customs of War and ensured that sovereign heads of state could not shelter behind sovereign immunity.[55]

Although the Nuremberg Charter and the Charter for the International Military Tribunal for the Far East (the Tokyo Tribunal) abolished sovereign immunity, such abolition did not ensure that the sovereign Emperor of Japan, Hirohito, was prosecuted for war crimes. Indeed, no sovereign head was prosecuted following World War II, because the other contender, Adolph Hitler, was dead.[56]

Hence, the principle of sovereign immunity was to remain relatively untested until 1998 when General Augusto Pinochet went to London for medical treatment. Pinochet was entitled to assume, based on past practice, that he would not have to defend himself from a Spanish extradition warrant for his arrest for committing crimes against humanity in his native Chile. The British House of Lords after two hearings accepted the argument that for crimes against humanity, which attracted universal jurisdiction, there can be no immunity from prosecution.[57]

One can expect that the successful prosecution of other heads of state, now charged with crimes against humanity, such as Slobodan Milosevic, will finally put to rest any lingering uncertainty about the disappearance of sovereign immunity, at least at the international level.

International Armed Conflict

States are careful about intervening in the internal conflicts of another state. The trigger mechanism for a state to intervene for war crimes is the classification of the conflict as "international."[58] Determining international armed conflict can at times be difficult. For example, the conflict in the former Yugoslavia was at first viewed as the disintegration of a federal state. As with most federations, if there is a dispute involving armed conflict between the states, then this is viewed, at least prima facie, as an internal conflict or civil war, not as an international armed conflict.[59]

In the case of the former Yugoslavia, Serbia, Croatia, Slovenia, and Bosnia-Herzegovina were all states in the federation of Yugoslavia. What the International Criminal Tribunal for the former Yugoslavia (ICTY) had to decide early on was whether a war between the former states of, say, Serbia and Croatia was an international armed conflict. An even more difficult problem was the status of the war between the Bosnian Serbs, the Bosnian Croats, and the Bosniacs (initially, mostly Muslims). Was this an international armed conflict?

In the case of the conflict between Serbia and Croatia, it was a question of whether by the time of the conflict either state had achieved the status of an independent state.[60] Whether a state is an independent state depends on whether (a) it has a population, (b) it governs a particular territory, (c) it has declared itself independent, (d) other countries recognize it as an independent state, and (e) the United Nations recognizes it as an independent state.[61]

Things that militate against its being an independent state include the reverse of the above principles, such as, does the entity control its own borders, does it have its own independent army, does it control its own customs, does it depend on any other state for governance.

With Bosnia, the conflict was between the Bosnian Serbs, the Bosniacs, and the Bosnian Croats. Both Serbia and Croatia were assisting in the conflict by supplying arms and other military support.[62] In the case of Serbia, it assisted the Bosnian Serbs by leaving behind what was left of the Yugoslav People's Army (the JNA). However, to confuse the issue,

Milosevic withdrew most of the Serbian component of the JNA. He did this so that he could argue (to the international community) that the conflict in Bosnia was only an internal armed conflict and that Serbia was not involved. This Serbian withdrawal took place on May 4, 1992. The Federal Republic of Yugoslavia (FRY) publicly ordered its troops out of Bosnia. The Bosnian Republic of Srpska under General Mladic and President Karadiz then allegedly carried on the battle alone.[63]

For prosecutors to persuade the Tribunal that there continued to exist an international armed conflict in Bosnia, despite the withdrawal of FRY troops, it had to mount a complex argument that because the FRY was leaving behind a fully equipped army, this "unfriendly act" was sufficient to assert that that the FRY continued to be a party to the conflict, thus making it international. In other words, the FRY was in Bosnia before May 1992; it then (ostensibly) left. There still remained a fully equipped army, albeit that command had passed to some (but not all) of the Bosnian Serbs. Some Serb soldiers were allowed to return to Serbia. However, the prosecution pointed to evidence that showed that Mladic and Karadiz were still in effect subordinate to the FRY and further that not all Serbian and Montenegrin troops had left Bosnia. Ultimately, the tribunal saw through the ruse created by Milosevic and declared the conflict international.[64]

Similarly, Croatia supplied weapons and advisers to the Bosnian Croats. Interestingly, they were a little more open than the Serbs; hence, there was more evidence of their direct involvement, including having actual command of Bosnian Croat troops in Bosnia.[65]

The determination of the status of the conflict was important—first because it resolved the vexed issue of whether or not the grave breach provisions of the 1949 Geneva Conventions applied, but perhaps more important, it legitimized international participation in the conflict.

State Nexus?

War crimes tend to be committed by persons linked to one side of the armed conflict against neutral citizens or combatants of a belligerent party on the other side of the conflict. The armed conflict may be international or internal in nature.[66]

Crimes against humanity can be carried out against any civilian population, provided the attack is widespread or systematic. A crime against humanity—persecution—must be carried out pursuant to a policy of persecution on political, racial, or religious grounds, but no such policy is required for a war crime. For an accused to be found guilty of a crime against humanity, there is no obligation on the prosecution to prove that the accused actually intended to persecute the particular group, provided it is proved that the crime was committed as part of a widespread or systematic attack directed against a civilian population and that the accused knew that his or her acts fit into this pattern.[67]

A war crime is committed during or linked to an armed conflict, but there is no such requirement for a crime against humanity.[68]

If a soldier kills a prisoner of war, he or she commits a war crime whether or not the act is carried out on his or her own initiative or as a result of state policy, but there must be some linkage to the belligerent state. Many crimes may be committed during the course of armed conflict, but not all are war crimes.

In the Essen Lynching case,[69] a British war crimes court found some German civilians guilty of war crimes for acting as a lynch mob in the murder of a British airman. There was no evidence of any "military" or "command" link between the citizens and the Nazi German State, but clearly, they were on the side of Germany and their actions "benefited" the German state in dealing with the airman in this way. There was no question that the victims were linked to the other side of the conflict and were entitled to be treated as prisoners of war,

which in the circumstances of this case was held to be sufficient.

The proof of links becomes even more complex where the offenders are from the same side of the conflict as the victims. For example, in the Belsen Trial,[70] a number of concentration camp inmates were employed by the Nazi Germans as minor functionaries. But the court was satisfied in this case that the inmates were working for the Germans, which in the circumstances was sufficient to establish a linkage.

In a relatively modern case, the Lebanese militia massacred Palestinians in the Subra and Chattila refugee camps in 1982. These militia were trained, equipped, and under some level of control by the Israeli army. This link with Israel was sufficient for the authors of the Khan Report to find that the Israeli officers were, at least in part, responsible for the massacre.[71]

Command Responsibility

Military commanders and persons occupying positions of superior authority may be held criminally responsible for the unlawful conduct of their subordinates. The criminal liability may arise out of the superior's positive acts (direct command responsibility) or from the superior's culpable omissions (indirect command responsibility). Thus, the superior can be responsible for ordering, instigating, or planning the criminal acts carried out by his or her subordinates or by failing to take measures to prevent or repress the unlawful conduct of his or her subordinates.[72]

The 1907 Hague Convention IV Article 1 (1) provides the "roots of command responsibility" when it declares that the laws of war apply not only to armies but also to militia and volunteer corps, which must be "commanded by a person responsible for his subordinates."[73] Although the principle of command responsibility was not expressly stated in the Nuremberg Charter or Far East Charter, it appeared in a number of the military manuals of states. However, it was recognized and applied by the Nuremberg and Tokyo Tribunals and numerous tribunals after World War II. For example, the Medical Case,[74] the Hostage Case,[75] and the High Command Case[76] all recognized the existence of the principle of command responsibility.

Perhaps the most notorious command responsibility case was that of Yamashita.[77] The trial of General Tomoyuki Yamashita took place before a U.S. Military Commission in Manila between October 8 and December 7, 1945. The commission heard 286 witnesses, read 423 exhibits, and created over 4,055 pages of transcript. Yamishita was charged with unlawfully discharging or failing to lawfully perform his duty as commander to control the acts of members of his command and by permitting them to commit war crimes. The war crimes alleged were widespread acts of murder and rape. In one province alone—namely, Batangas province—25,000 men woman and children, all unarmed civilians, were killed or otherwise brutally mistreated without cause or military necessity. Other similar massacres and rapes were also alleged in the indictment.

The defense case was based on the fact that there was no evidence that the general neglected his duty or that he ever permitted the commission of the crimes alleged. The defense argued that this amounted not to an allegation that the general did or failed to do something but that he was guilty because he "was" something—namely, the commander. The defense argued that there was no crime known to law for which a commander is responsible simply because troops under his command committed war crimes.

The prosecution countered that the crimes committed were so widespread and brutal that they must have been known to the accused if he were making any effort at all to meet the responsibilities of his command. If he did not know, it was because he took affirmative action not to know.

Although this was the principle accepted by the commission as the basis of Yamashita's liability, a closer reading of the case will show that there was at least some evidence (albeit disputed) that Yamashita had ordered one Philippine general, who was collaborating with the Japanese, Antremioi Ricarte, that "all the commanders of the military posts in the Philippines Islands were to wipe out the whole Philippines population and to destroy Manila, since everyone on the Island were guerrillas or active supporters of guerrillas."[78]

One curious aspect of the defense was that Yamashita could not have gone out and properly supervised his troops because the constant bombardment by the Americans had made his job so difficult that he spent all his time and energy trying to defend his military position. This appeared to carry little weight with the commission.[79]

The principle of command responsibility was incorporated in the Statute of the Tribunal for the former Yugoslavia. In the tribunal statute, the principle was extended to include "superiors" who included political as well as military commanders. The secretary-general said "superior authority" not only included responsibility for "giving the order" but for failure to "prevent or deter." The secretary-general went on to say that this "imputed responsibility or criminal negligence" is engaged if the superior knew or had reason to know that subordinates were about to commit a crime or, if subsequently discovering the commission of a crime by the subordinates, failed to take action to punish.[80]

In *Delalic*[81] (in regard to allegations of war crimes in Bosnia) the prosecution argued that the evidence showed that Delalic had acted as if he had authority over the Celibici camp, even though there was no specific formal documentary or other evidence of this position of authority. At the time, the Bosniacs were cut off from Sarajevo, and there were no lines of communication; it amounted to "self-help." Delalic had not been a soldier before the war;

he was a businessman. The Bosniacs of the area resorted to self-help; there was no real organization. The defense used this state of disarray to their advantage to demonstrate that Delalic had no command over the prison camp. They admitted that he had control over troops, but the troops had not been charged with committing war crimes. The charges related only to crimes that had been committed in the Celibici camp. The prosecution argued that command responsibility could attach by means of de facto as well as de jure command. The tribunal accepted that this could be so, but still found that there was insufficient evidence to prove that Delalic was in command of the camp or that he had the power to prevent the crimes from being committed.

Proving the *mens rea* in command responsibility cases can be difficult. In *Delalic,* the prosecution argued the Yamashita principle—that if the acts were sufficiently widespread and notorious, then knowledge could be presumed. However, this was rejected by the tribunal, which held that knowledge has to be proved by either direct evidence or inferred from circumstantial evidence. In Celibici, it found that no such inference was reasonably open on the evidence.[82]

The Statute of the Permanent International Criminal Court draws a clear distinction between "military commanders" and "superiors," which includes political superiors. With respect to military commanders, the person must be shown to be an actual military commander or "effectively acting as a military commander." With respect to a superior, responsibility attaches only if the prosecution demonstrates that the superior had effective responsibility and control.[83]

Crimes Against Humanity

A crime against humanity is an international crime and is distinguished from a domestic crime on the basis that its breach is of concern to the whole of the international community and as a consequence invokes international jurisdiction. It is the concept of humanity as the victim, rather than just the individual victim, that essentially characterizes crimes against humanity.[84] A crime against humanity is defined as murder, extermination, enslavement, deportation, imprisonment, torture, rape, persecution on political, racial, or religious grounds, or other inhumane acts.

Crimes against humanity have their geneses in the laws of war. The "Martens" Clause of the 1907 Hague Convention (discussed earlier) first spoke of "laws of humanity" in the context of developing international customary law. Although spoken of in terms of conflicts around the time of World War I, it was not until the end of World War II that these vague and undefined references were crystallized into a new species of international criminal law.[85]

The Charter of the International Military Tribunal for Nuremberg expressly created crimes against humanity and provided a sanction for their breach. The crimes were to attract individual criminal liability for the perpetrator.[86]

Links to Armed Conflict?

The drafters of the Nuremberg Charter had to grapple with the then-applicable but outmoded principle of international law, which provided that international law had no application to events that occurred internally within the national borders of a country. In other words, international law applied only to events that had occurred during the course of an international armed conflict. This meant that the atrocious crimes committed by the Nazis against their own people, the Jews of Germany, could not be punished by an international tribunal if this principle were to apply.[87]

Fortunately, the law was changed, and the Nazi criminals were tried and punished for the crimes they had committed against the German Jewish people.[88]

The Nuremberg Charter included "crimes against humanity," "crimes against peace," and "war crimes" having been committed during the course of World War II, which in turn restricted crimes against humanity to offenses committed during the course of an armed conflict.[89] Other than the fact that the International Military Tribunal at Nuremberg was concerned with events that occurred during the course of World War II, there was no reason to restrict crimes against humanity to events that occurred during armed conflict. This restriction was not placed on crimes against humanity in Control Council Law No. 10[90] or the International Law Commissions Draft Code of 1954.[91] The Genocide Convention[92] and the Apartheid Convention[93] were not restricted to periods of armed conflict.

In the ICTY statute, there is added the additional requirement that the offense must be "committed in armed conflict."[94] This is not a requirement of other statutes such as the Statute of the International Criminal Tribunal for Rwanda or the Rome Statute of the Permanent International Criminal Court.[95] It has now been held that under customary international law, there is no need to establish a nexus with armed conflict.[96] When the secretary-general drafted the ICTY statute, he wanted to include in the statute only crimes that were "beyond doubt part of customary law."[97] Interestingly, however, the secretary-general, in his report on the statute, expressly stated that crimes against humanity are prohibited "regardless of whether they are committed in armed conflict."[98] This apparent state of confusion was resolved by the Appeals Chamber in the *Tadic* jurisdiction appeal, when the Appeals Chamber declared that it was "now a settled rule of customary international law that crimes against humanity do not require a connection to . . . armed conflict."[99] In the final *Tadic* Appeal Judgment, the Appeals Chamber essentially disposed of the matter altogether when it held that the "armed conflict requirement is a *jurisdictional*

element, not a substantive element of the *mens rea* of crimes against humanity (i.e., not a legal ingredient of the subjective element of the crime)."[100]

Widespread or Systematic Attack

For a crime to be a crime against humanity, it must be directed at a civilian population, specifically identified as a group by the perpetrators. There is a need for the crime to exhibit the characteristics of system or organization and to be of a certain scale and gravity.[101] Although if "scale" is present, the gravity may be in the acts of scale rather than in the individual acts themselves.[102]

Although the crime cannot be the work of an isolated individual acting alone, there is no requirement that the crime be carried out pursuant to the policy of a state.[103]

The perpetrator of a crime against humanity must know that his or her act is part of a widespread or systematic attack against the civilian population.[104] Nothing prevents a perpetrator from carrying out the act for purely personal motives.[105] The widespread or systematic attack is to be distinguished from random acts of violence unconnected to any system or organization.[106] Although the prosecution need only prove that the attack was widespread or systematic, not both, often the proof of one might be the proof of the other.[107] In other words, proof that an act of violence was systematic may be demonstrated by the fact that it has occurred systematically in a geographically widespread area. The term *widespread* has been defined as massive, frequent, large-scale action carried out collectively with considerable seriousness and directed against a multiplicity of victims.[108] *Systematic* is something that is thoroughly organized and follows a regular pattern on the basis of common policy involving substantial public or private resources. There is no requirement that the policy must be adopted formally as a policy of state. There must however be some preconceived plan or policy.[109]

The "attack" may be one or more of the enumerated acts such as murder, enslavement, rape, or torture, or it may be a nonviolent act such as apartheid.[110] The enumerated acts are not exhaustive and may include any inhumane act, provided the other elements are met.[111] Crimes against humanity can also include acts of terrorism. That terrorism is a crime against humanity has been recognized at least since 1948 and has been reaffirmed as good law as recently as 1997. In *The Prosecutor v. Erdemovic*[112] in the joint judgment of Judges McDonald and Vohrah, their Honors cite with approval the *Albrecht Case*,[113] where the court held in relation to crimes against humanity that

> crimes of this category are characterized either by their seriousness and their savagery, or by their magnitude, or by the circumstance that they were part of a system of terrorist acts, or that they were a link in a deliberately pursued policy against certain groups of the population.

It would be wrong to characterize crimes against humanity as consisting only of a multiplicity of different criminal acts committed by the same perpetrator at different times and places. Invariably, offenders are charged with individual acts that form part of a widespread or systematic attack, there being a link to the policy. However, a single act can be a crime against humanity, particularly if the one act is carried out pursuant to an organized policy. The bombing of Hiroshima and Nagasaki were single acts but part of an attack directed at the civilian population. Similarly, the attack on the Twin Towers in New York on September 11, 2001, were attacks directed against the civilian population and forming part of an organized and systematic plan. Having regard to the other attacks in the United States on that day, these acts were also widespread.

In the *Vukovar* case, the court considered that the one act of taking some 200 wounded and sick from a hospital and shooting them at a mass grave was a crime against humanity. The court held:

> Clearly, a single act by a perpetrator taken within the context of a widespread or systematic attack against a civilian population entails individual criminal responsibility and an individual perpetrator need not commit numerous offences to be liable. Although it is correct that isolated random acts should not be included in the definition of crimes against humanity, that is the purpose of requiring that the acts be directed against a civilian population and thus "[e]ven an isolated act can constitute a crime against humanity if it is the product of a political system based on terror or persecution."[114]

Discriminatory Intent

A crime against humanity includes persecution of the targeted civilian population based on political, racial, and religious grounds. When introducing the ICTY statute, the secretary-general said,

> Crimes against humanity refer to inhumane acts of a very serious nature, such as willful killing, torture or rape, committed as part of a widespread or systematic attack against any civilian population on national, political, ethnic racial or religious grounds.[115]

Because the secretary-general attached "on national political, ethnic, racial, and religious grounds" to all the enumerated acts such as murder, rape, and torture, the early decisions of the ICTY concluded that discriminatory intent had to be proved in all the enumerated acts, not just paragraph (h)—"persecution." This interpretation was contrary to an ordinary reading of Article 5 of the statute.[116]

When this matter was subsequently considered by the Appeals Chamber, the Appeals

Chamber noted that discriminatory attacks on the civilian population based on "national, political, ethnic, racial or religious grounds" for all of the enumerated acts, including persecution, was not a requirement of the Nuremberg Charter or Control Law No. 10, nor was it part of customary international law. The Appeals Chamber noted the importance of the *Report of the Secretary-General* but said that his comments should not prevail over the clear words of the statute, and where possible (unless some very clear contrary intention is expressed), the tribunal should interpret the statute in a manner consistent with customary international law. The Appeals Chamber observed that there was no justifiable basis to restrict the ambit of crimes against humanity in this way. The Appeals Chamber went on to say,

> For example, a discriminatory intent requirement would prevent the penalization of random and indiscriminate violence intended to spread terror among a civilian population as a crime against humanity. A *fortiori*, the object and purpose of Article 5 (Crimes against Humanity provision) would be thwarted were it to be suggested that the discriminatory grounds required are limited to the five grounds put forth by the Secretary-General in his Report.[117]

Crimes Against Humanity and Terrorism

Clearly, acts of terrorism are considered by the intentional tribunals as coming within the definition of crimes against humanity. Unlike crimes against humanity that attract universal jurisdiction and have achieved the status of *jus cogens,* it is fair to say that there does not exist a universally recognized definition of terrorism. It is indeed true that "one man's terrorist is another man's freedom fighter,"[118] which paradox has clouded the debate on who should and should not be defined as a terrorist.[119]

The difficulty with reaching universal agreement on what is an appropriate definition of terrorism is that it depends on the point of view one takes. For example, the struggle for independence of the emerging United States from the clutches of the British caused George Washington to be seen in the eyes of Americans as a national hero, but he was regarded by the colonizers as a terrorist. In modern times, the same can be said of the IRA, of the Tamils, of the Barques, and even al Qaeda, just to mention a few. Terrorism in the name of a state is also given different labels; the persecution orchestrated by the Nazis against the Jews was not seen as terrorism by the Nazis, but it was seen as such by the victims. The sinking of the *Rainbow Warrior* in Auckland Harbor was, to a New Zealander, a terrorist act, but it was viewed differently by the French.

This inability to reach international consensus on what terrorism is deprives it of legitimacy as an international crime. If the definition of what it is cannot be settled, then the legitimacy of its prohibition is tarnished.[120] One of the fundamental principles of international humanitarian law, *nullem crimen sine lege,* dictates that there be certainty in international crimes before persons are tried for their breach. It is indeed this very controversy over the definition that led to the Nazi criminals being tried for crimes against humanity.

After the French Statesman Jean-Louis Barthou and King Alexander of Yugoslavia were assassinated by a Croatian "terrorist" in 1934, the international community endeavored to introduce a convention on terrorism, which came with its own intentional criminal tribunal. Unfortunately, the convention was ratified only by India, which at the time had not achieved independence from Britain.[121]

It has not been for want of trying that an acceptable definition has not been found. Numerous conventions have been drafted under the auspices of the United Nations since its inception, mostly in response to some international catastrophic event.[122] Nor have nation-states been slow in drafting their own definitions of what they consider to be acts of terrorism.[123]

The problem is that there is no real consistency between states as to the definition of terrorism such that *opinio juris* can emerge on what we are speaking of when we use the term *terrorism*.[124] The one possible exception to this is with respect to aviation terrorism. Because aviation is of such importance to the international community, some progress has been made in reaching consensus on this topic, but this is more the exception than the rule. Furthermore, only in the area of "aviation terrorism" has any real progress been made in reducing international crime.[125]

Because the international prosecution of a terrorist offense is most likely to be a controversial affair and unlikely to be universally accepted, it is far better to prosecute a terrorist offense as a crime against humanity, provided the evidence would support such a prosecution. If terrorism included the use of politically motivated violence to create public fear, then a terrorist act may or may not be a crime against humanity. For example, a political activist may commit a terrorist act by detonating a small explosive device in a crowded picture theater, and calling out "bomb." The explosion may not kill or even seriously injure anyone, but it could still be a terrorist act. If the size of the bomb is increased such that it kills a large number of the theater patrons, then this may be a crime against humanity.

If the preceding scenario were to be considered for the purposes of launching a prosecution for a crime against humanity under the Rome Statute (Statute of the Permanent International Criminal Court) (Article 7), the prosecutor would need to examine the evidence against each element of the offense. Perhaps the first question the prosecutor would ask is, "Was the attack directed against the civilian population?" Unless the prosecutor was considering crimes against humanity—persecution—it would not be necessary for the prosecutor to go further than settle the issue that the theatergoers were indeed civilian, as opposed, for example, to military

personnel, because it is now settled law that proof of discriminatory intent is not a required element of proof in crimes against humanity, except for persecution.[126]

The next step would be to determine which of the enumerated acts can be proved in relation to the particular act. If it can be shown that people were killed, then, of course, murder would be perhaps one of the first considerations. The prosecutor would then consider other "inhumane acts" of a similar character intentionally causing great suffering or serious injury to body or mental or physical health.

The prosecutor would then need to consider the question of "widespread or systematic." This is done by looking at the perpetrators themselves. It is important if they are associated with a larger group or whether the acts were carried out pursuant to the policy of the group. If the prosecutor can demonstrate a connection to a particular organization, the next matter is to see if that organization has carried out similar acts in the past or at least attempted to carry out similar acts in the past. If this can be answered in the affirmative, it does not matter that the previous acts have been carried out against differently constituted members of the civilian population. For example, if the act under consideration was directed against a large number of foreign tourists at a popular holiday resort, it does not matter that previous acts or attempted acts were carried out against civilians who were or are of the same nationality as the perpetrators.

The prosecutor would want to establish what the perpetrators were trying to achieve by their acts, because this would be evidence of their policy. It also goes to the proof of "system." Although a crime against humanity can be established even if the victims were not killed or perhaps not even injured, it is easier to prove if the crime is of a character that offends humanity. Multiple murders invariably fall into this category.

A question arises if the act in question is the first serious crime committed by the organization with which the perpetrators are associated. Can such an act satisfy the "course of conduct" requirement of the Rome Statute? Article 7 (2) (a) of the International Criminal Court statute provides that

> attack directed against any civilian population means a course of conduct involving the multiple commission of acts referred to in paragraph 1 against any civilian population, pursuant to or in furtherance of a state or organisational policy to commit such act.

The first thing that needs to be set aside is that the attack is not limited to attacks carried out by a state but can include nonstate actors such as organizations. Second, the multiple acts referred to in Paragraph 1 of Article 7 could mean that more than one murder would satisfy this requirement. It does not have to be multiple murders committed at different times and places for it to be a crime against humanity. This makes sense because it would always mean that the first act could not be charged as a crime against humanity, but the second act could. If it were not for this, Hiroshima would not be a crime against humanity, but Nagasaki would.

By way of example, in relation to the Bali Bombings of 2002, so far as Australia is concerned, the Permanent International Criminal Tribunal in The Hague could have tried these offenses assuming the evidence was available to prove each element of the offence. How the court could have exercised jurisdiction would have depended on the cooperation of the government of Indonesia. Australia had ratified the Rome Treaty before the Bali Bombings occurred; accordingly, Article 11 of the statute was satisfied so far as Australia was concerned.

Indonesia has not ratified the Rome Treaty. The offense was committed on Indonesian territory, and it would seem that the persons accused of the crime are likely to be nationals of Indonesia. Accordingly, the court could not automatically exercise jurisdiction because the crime was committed on the territory of a nonstate party by the nationals of a nonstate party (see Article 12 (2) (a) & (b)).

However, this is not the end of the matter, because there are ways in which these jurisdictional obstacles can be overcome. For the court to have exercised jurisdiction, one of three possibilities applies:

1. Indonesia could have agreed to accept jurisdiction just for the purposes of the Bali Bombing trial and nothing else (Article 12 (3)). This would, of course, require the cooperation of Indonesia but may have been acceptable, because it was an isolated case and would not bind Indonesia in relation to any other matter.

2. Australia could have requested the Security Council of the United Nations to refer the matter acting under Chapter VII of the U.N. Charter, pursuant to Article 13 (b) of the Rome statute.

3. The prosecutor could have initiated a prosecution *proprio moto*.

The most efficient and effective course would have been Option 1 above; this would require goodwill from Indonesia and Australia. It has advantages for Indonesia because it still gives Indonesia some control over the process, which is less likely to occur if the Security Council took action under Chapter VII. The least effective method would have been a prosecutor-initiated investigation.

What is clear is that Indonesia could well face significant division in the community over this prosecution, which could affect the success or otherwise of the trial. It is more than just a possibility that at the end of the day, the trial may either stall or be a sham. Australia will want the perpetrators prosecuted, and certainly the victims will demand justice by way of a proper criminal trial. They are not likely to allow the matter to be simply swept under the carpet. Australia cannot seize the perpetrators from Indonesia, in some Eichmann fashion[127] and try them on Australian soil, so it would have been better to have the trial at the permanent court in The Hague.

Genocide

The Genocide Convention of 1948 was celebrated as one of the most significant steps in the development of international humanitarian law. Prior to 1948, international law did not prohibit genocide in peacetime. The term *genocide* itself was coined only prior to World War II,[128] although the act of genocide existed in practice well before that date.

Genocide is the intentional destruction of a national ethnic, racial, or religious group of people. The crime can be committed by killing, seriously harming (bodily or mental), or inflicting conditions of life calculated to bring about the whole or partial destruction of the group; by imposing measures intended to prevent births; or by forcibly transferring children from the group, with the intention of completely or partially destroying the targeted group of people.[129]

Essentially, genocide is concerned with the persecution of one group by another group, in circumstances where (at least) the persecuting group sees itself as different from the persecuted group. Sometimes both groups see themselves as different. All human beings are born with the ability to distinguish difference and "modernity thrives on the essentialization of difference."[130] Modern examples of the exploitation of difference include the treatment of indigenous persons by European imperialists. But perhaps the most dangerous and potentially genocidal entity is the nation-state.

Genocide and the Nation-State

The nation-state, and its policy by-product "nationalism," is predicated on the need to achieve homogeneity. Diversity and the nation-state do not make happy bedfellows. When confronted with social, religious, and cultural diversity, the nation-state has sought to achieve uniformity by annihilation or assimilation. In the end, the result is the same, but not everyone would call it genocide. The anthropologist or sociologist is perhaps more likely to brand assimilation policies as genocide, whereas the lawyer may not do so.[131] The nation-state's dependence on homogeneity as its lifeblood is kept healthy by ingesting large quantities of nation-building products such as the national anthem, the national flag, and national holidays. These rallying symbols of national unity also serve to highlight differences within the community, especially when certain groups do not identify with the national anthem, the national flag, or national holidays.[132] This could not be better illustrated than in the case of Australia. The Australian flag has for most of the life of the nation had contained within it the British Union Jack, which by definition must exclude indigenous Australians. The Australian Constitution did not recognize indigenous Australians until 1963; the Australian national anthem was for the most part of the 20th century "God Save the (British) Queen" and the "British Queen" still is Australia's head of state.

There is a fundamental inconsistency in nominating nation-states as the guardian of international human rights and the prevention of abuses. Nation-states insist on their own sovereign rights and refrain from interfering in the affairs of other states in recognition of the unifying nature of reciprocity.[133] After all, in most cases, it is the official organs of the state, such as the military and the police, who are generally directly or indirectly responsible for the implementation of policies of genocide.[134]

Some of the worst genocides have been committed in the name of the state, especially where borders have been drawn by colonial powers and are relatively meaningless to the indigenous populations—Bosnia-Herzegovina, Pakistan-India, Afghanistan-Pakistan, Israel-Palestine, to mention a few.

Cultural Genocide

Cultural genocide, which consists of destroying specific characteristics of the group, such as language, literature, learning, religion, and art,[135] was expressly excluded from the Genocide Convention because it was considered to be an unjustified extension of the concept of genocide.[136] Although the concept of cultural genocide was supposed to exclude attempted assimilation policies,[137] there is no escaping the fact that the implementation of assimilation policies did in fact bring about the partial physical destruction of the group. It is hard to see why such assimilation policies would not offend the prohibition on "inflicting measures on the group calculated to bring about its physical destruction."

Certainly, "forcibly transferring children from one group to another" as practiced on indigenous children in Australia must suggest a genocidal expectation that by so doing the full-blooded Aboriginal group would die out. Fortunately, if given the opportunity, it is unlikely that an international court would now interpret the provisions of the Genocide Convention so narrowly as to exclude liability for cultural genocide such as that which was practiced in Australia against its indigenous peoples.[138]

Colonial indigenous genocide is often characterized by intermittent genocidal massacres rather than a prolonged and sustained genocidal act such as that committed by the Nazis over the Jews of Europe. The intermittent nature of the crime gives it an appearance of being less serious than other massive genocidal acts. Therefore, indigenous genocide is somehow seen as less horrible then nonindigenous genocide; rather, it is seen as "the savages making way for civilization." In Tasmania, the land was literally swept clean of the indigenous population, as one might clear the land of "vermin."[139] Yet the killing of Aboriginal people in Australia has yet to be officially recognized as the genocide that it was.[140]

Australia was not alone in terms of committing indigenous genocide. Genocide has been committed on every continent on earth, with the exception of Antarctica. In the Congo, some 40 million people lost their lives in genocidal massacres following European occupation.[141] Indigenous genocide is a "slow and insidious form of genocide."[142]

What Makes the Crime Genocide?

Historically, there were two schools of thought about genocide. Some saw it as a unique event, such as the Holocaust; others said it has a much broader base. The narrow view could operate to exclude many victims of mass killings and would freeze the crime as an event in history. Fortunately, the narrow view has not prevailed.[143] However, the existence of the narrow view can be illustrated by the initial reluctance of the ICTY to accept various incidents in Bosnia-Herzegovina as amounting to genocide.[144] The wider view is premised on the fact that elements of genocide can be identified in all instances of life, including urban violence.

There is a need to strike a middle ground; some conflicts in which many thousands of people are killed may not be genocidal as such. The Allies in World War II for the most part had no intention of killing the Germans on racial, religious, or ethnic grounds. Genocide, unlike domestic crime, however, is a "relatively open crime"; the motives are open and so, too, is the carrying out of the crime itself. The reason for the killing based on racial, religious, or ethnic grounds is clearly articulated.[145]

In the *Akayesu* case, the Rwanda Tribunal spoke of the four protected groups—national, ethnic, racial, or religious—then opined that in circumstances where a group did not strictly fit the definition, the convention should apply to any stable and permanent group whose membership is determined by birth. By so doing, the tribunal extended protection to the Tutsi of Rwanda, which would otherwise have been excluded, by a narrow reading of the convention.[146] The question now is whether this extension by the trial chamber might also include other groups, such as homosexuals and the mentally and physically impaired.[147]

Although the Genocide Convention does not specifically refer to rape, the trial chamber in *Akayesu,* relying on the enumerated act of causing "serious bodily and mental harm," concluded that rape and sexual violence were part of this enumerated act.[148]

Genocide is now generally recognized as a norm of *jus cogens;* in other words, it forms part of customary international law binding on all states.[149] Tragically, acts of genocide are not limited to what occurred in Europe during the course of World War II; genocidal crimes have been found to have been committed in Rwanda and Bosnia as well.[150]

The Causes of Genocide

Genocide does not just happen. The community needs to be well prepared for the commission of the genocidal act—"genocidal priming."[151] Generally, some politico-socio-economic calamity sparks off the genocidal fire in a volatile population "primed for ignition." The priming is achieved by a prolonged period of state-sponsored racist propaganda against the victim group. Examples of igniting the spark abound—the Treaty of Versailles and subsequent severe economic depression with respect to Nazi Germany; the death of Tito with respect to the former Yugoslavia, the death of President Habyarimana with respect to Rwanda. In each case, there followed a period of state-sponsored propaganda.

The cause of the volatility of the population is a much deeper issue. Often, the target population in these circumstances has arrived in the country later than the victim population. With respect to German Jewish people when they arrived in what is now Germany, Christian Germans in an agrarian society denied them the right of land ownership. This

exclusion impoverished German Jews until the arrival of the industrial revolution, which presented fresh nonagrarian opportunities in finance and commerce. In a sense, the German Jews occupied the vacuum of commerce and finance that was part and parcel of the industrial revolution. This had the effect of placing German Jews in positions of financial control when the German depression of the 1920s arrived. This position of control was much resented by Christian Germans, even though it was of their own making. Because German Jews were seen as "outsiders," hatred toward them was, in the circumstances, relatively easy to muster by the use of targeted propaganda.

Similarly, in the case of the former Yugoslavia, the Muslim Bosniacs were also seen as outsiders who had seized control of Bosnia-Herzegovina during the rule of the Ottoman Empire. This occupation was much resented by the Orthodox Serbs and Catholic Croats who asserted original ownership of the land.[152] In the case of Rwanda, the Tutsi were viewed by the Hutu as "foreigners from Abyssinia."[153]

Generally, the community can function effectively notwithstanding underlying ethnic hatreds, but if persons in authority stir up these community hatreds and if political and economic instability occurs, then genocide can follow. It has been argued that the cause of genocide in Bosnia-Herzegovina was triggered by the collapsing political and economic structures. With the disappearance of life as it was previously known, insecurity and fear, especially if fanned by propaganda, cause people to divide into "we groups" where qualification and entry is determined by birthright and ethnicity. If persecution, assaults, and violence are heaped on those other forces of disunification, hatred is directed toward the victim group.[154] Clearly, responsibility for the genocide in the Balkans lay at the feet of the political leadership, aided and abetted by the media that they controlled. By dwelling on past atrocities committed by the "other group," this manipulation of fear is the most important tool in the nationalist armory.[155]

Propaganda employed to promote genocide is not limited to words alone. The use of music, the arts, and dance is also part of the genocidal conquest. In the case of Kampuchea, songs and dance were used to promote Angkor as the rallying point of the Khmer Rouge. Specific songs were directed at driving the "reactionary imperialists from Kampuchea." Catchphrases such a "blood avenges blood" were used to rally the people to carry out the genocide. Singers and dances associated with the old regime were especially targeted and eliminated. This was not so much because they were part of the old regime, but because the aim was to expunge the dance itself.[156] Elements of this can be seen in other genocidal events—the Nazi youth songs, Hitler's passion for Wagner; Rwanda, Serbia, both had their songs. Serbs sang of the glory of Serbia— "Who says Serbia is small?"[157] The Hutu sang about the Tutsi "cockroaches."[158]

Accepting Responsibility

Often, the consequences of genocide carried out by one generation have to be dealt with by subsequent generations. This can take various forms. In the case of Germany, German youth in the 1960s saw the Holocaust as something that punished future German generations.[159] German parents immediately after the war dutifully continued the tradition of rigid "moral conformism." This conformism was rejected by subsequent generations who considered themselves "victims" and in so doing identified themselves with the Jews. One of the most powerful manifestations of this rebellion was nudism. The naked body was seen in stark contrast to the authoritarian patterns of conformism. Public nudism was a "sign of liberation."[160]

The alternative approach was to ignore the genocide altogether. In many cases, the genocide carried out against indigenous populations in many countries was not taught in

schools until recent times, if at all.[161] In Australia, the reconciliation movement, which amounted to a citizen-led groundswell of support for the plight of indigenous people, really did not take place until the 1990s.[162]

A feature of genocide is the tendency for apologists to explain away genocide as some terrible biologically determined event. Horrific but natural, something that could not be prevented, and something that simply had to run its course[163]—Nazi cleansing the German blood, the pure Aryan race; the Hutu expelling the "cockroach"; the Serbs removing the Islamic fundamentalist threat. Nazi genocide has been described as a horrific experiment in modernity. Mass death was "facilitated by modern processes" of science technology and bureaucracy. Social engineering so as to create a new pure order required the extermination of those who "did not fit the new mould."[164]

There is a danger in asserting that one particular community or nation-state is immune from committing genocide. Genocide has been committed by the poor, the rich, the ignorant, the educated, the black, the white, and in the name of many different religions. However, it is no doubt correct that a society can condition itself against the possibility of genocide; for example, genocide does not usually occur in societies where (a) racial, religious, or ethnic differences are insignificant or are not a source of deadly conflict; (b) there is tolerance and preparedness to share between the dominant and minority groups; (c) minority rights are legally guaranteed; (d) social relations or voluntary groups cut across racial religious or ethnic differences; or (e) there is a balanced accommodation between groups, such as a willingness to share power.[165]

It is not as though genocide is something born of the 20th century. Although the term *genocide* is relatively new, instances of genocide have been with humankind since very early times. Even the Bible contains examples of God-endorsed genocide—the destruction of human life by flood (with the exception of

Noah and his animals), King Herod's decrees ordering the destruction of the firstborn infant sons of Judea. Genocide has occurred throughout the ages—the Crusades, the destruction of witches during the Inquisition, and the colonial genocides against the indigenous people of the Americas, Africa, and Australia.

THE FUTURE

International criminal law is still very much in the developmental stage. In some cases, crimes such as torture and slavery, which are the subject of their own international conventions, are picked up and applied in the interpretation of traditional crimes against humanity. This has been especially so with respect to sexual assaults, including rape and sexual slavery during armed conflict, which has been characterized as both sexual slavery and torture.[166] As customary international law develops alongside or in addition to statute or treaty law, it is likely that other crimes will ultimately form part of the body of international criminal law in their own right.

Following the formation of the United Nations in 1945, aspirations ran high that international criminal law, as a body of universally recognized and enforced laws, would become a permanent feature of the international legal landscape. The International Law Commission (ILC) was given the responsibility of formulating principles of international law, including a code of offenses against the peace and security of humankind. Sadly, the Cold War delayed much of this work by the ILC.

After 50 tortuous years, from 1947 to 1996, the ILC did eventually produce a code that incorporated general principles of international criminal law.[167] Unfortunately, the ILC excluded crimes that did not have a political element or that were not concerned with international peace or security.[168] The effect of this process of self-censorship meant that important transnational crimes, such as trafficking in drugs and children, money laundering, fraud,

counterfeiting money and the like, were excluded.

As a consequence, the ILC code covered much of the same territory as the traditional international criminal laws discussed earlier. What makes the ILC code of some importance is that what it did cover is now considered as norms of customary international law.[169]

With the ever-increasing number of transnational issues affecting the world as a single global community, international criminal law will inevitably have to expand to address new questions that extend beyond the borders of any one sovereign state. Such issues may well include illegal international financial manipulation—globalization of the world economy, global environmental vandalism (the greenhouse effect), and the international drug trade, to mention a few.[170]

Crimes such as these can threaten the peace and security of humankind as much as war threatens human peace and security. Unfortunately, the process of development of international criminal law is slow and intermittent, often moving forward only after some catastrophic international event. For so long as state sovereignty has ascendancy over the rights of humanity, this process will continue to be slow.

At least the international criminal laws that we do have are a good start. The international community may come to depend very heavily on international criminal law as a means of preserving the global community in much the same way as traditional national criminal law protects the society of the nation-state.

As international criminal law gains strength and acceptability, the process of expansion of international criminal law to include other transnational crimes will inevitably follow. Global democratization is the engine that drives the development of international laws protecting the welfare of humankind. With the expansion of democratization, international laws, especially those protecting human rights, will ultimately gain ascendancy over sovereign interests, and the state will be subordinate to humanity—its servant rather than its master.

CONCLUSION

Today, the Laws and Customs of War and Crimes against Humanity and Genocide are the mainstay of international criminal law. These laws are no longer separate and distinct crimes as such but form part of a package of laws, referred to variously as international humanitarian law or international criminal law.[171] The effect of the Nuremberg Charter was to incorporate all these laws in one article of the charter and make them criminal.[172] This method of presentation was carried on in the criminal provisions of the Statute for the International Criminal Tribunal for the former Yugoslavia, the Statute for the International Criminal Tribunal for Rwanda, and the Statute of the Permanent International Criminal Court. These international crimes are collectively referred to as breaches of international human-itarian law, for which a criminal sanction applies.[173] These laws are now undoubtedly part of international customary law, and their existence cannot be ignored by anyone or anything, including the sovereign state.

NOTES

1. M. D. Kirby, "Criminal Law: The Global Dimension." Keynote Address to International Society for Reform of the Criminal Law Conference, Canberra, Australia, August 27, 2001, p. 3. "In no field of law was jurisdiction more important than the criminal law. The apho-rism, criminal law is local persisted in Australia even until very recent times" (ILC/9 [c]).

2. D. Farrier, N. Weisbrot, D. Brown, S. Egger, and L. McNamara, *Criminal Laws,* 3d ed. (Annandale, Australia: Federation Press, 2001), 266.

3. G. Schwarzenberger, "The Problem of an International Criminal Law," in *International Criminal Law and Procedure,* eds. J. Dugard and C. Wyngart, pp. 3-36 (Brookfield, VT: Dartmouth, 1996), 4.

4. *Polites v. The Commonwealth* 70 CLR 60 (1945).

5. *Chow Hung Ching v. R* 77 CLR 449, 477 (1949).

6. *Sei Fujii v. The State of California* 38 Cal 2d 718 (Cal Sup Ct) (1952).

7. *The Prosecutor v. Tadic* (Jurisdictional Appeal) IT-94-I-AR72 App. Ch. October 2, 1995 para. 87.

8. L. S. Sunga, *The Emerging System of International Criminal Law* (The Hague, Netherlands: Kluwer Law International, 1997), 2–9.

9. "There can be no crime without a law."

10. *Report of the Secretary-General pursuant to paragraph 2 of Security Council Resolution 808(1993) (relating to the establishment of the International Criminal Tribunal for the former Yugoslavia).* Presented May 3, 1993 (S/25704) para. 34. Available online at www.un.org/icty/basic/statut/S25704.htm.

11. *Report of the Secretary-General,* para. 35.

12. On September 27, 1922, The League of Nations directed the Advisory Committee to pro-pose a draft treaty dealing with the issue of "wars of aggression" (Sunga, *The Emerging System,* p. 25).

13. *International Treaty for the Renunciation of War as an Instrument of National Policy,* concluded in Paris on August 27, 1928.

14. *Charter of the International Military Tribunal at Nuremberg Annexed to the Agreement for the Prosecution and Punishment of Major War Criminals of the European Axis* (The London Agreement), *U.N. Treaty Series* 8: 270, Article 6 (a).

15. "International Military Tribunal (Nurem-berg): Judgment and Sentences," *American Journal of International Law* 41 (1947): 186.

16. *Rome Statute of the International Criminal Court,* Article 5 (2). Available online at www.un.org/law/icc/statute/romefra.htm.

17. *Draft Code of Crimes against Peace and Security of Mankind.* UN Doc. A/CN.4/L.464/Add.4, July 1991, Article 15.

18. Per decision of Judge Sidhwa, *Tadic* (Jurisdictional Appeal), paras. 113 to 116, "The Laws and Customs of war . . . have two sources . . . the laws of war and the customs of war . . . the laws of war are the rules and regulations setting forth the

norms constituting the modes, methods and conduct of warfare and prohibitions connected therewith. They include [1] treaties, conventions, agreements, declarations and protocols, [2] constitutions and statutes of international tribunals, [3] decisions of international tribunals. The customs of war are those which arise out of State practices extending over a period of time, coupled with *opinio juris.*"

19. *Report of Secretary-General,* para 47.

20. Sunga, *The Emerging System,* 2.

21. Kirby, "Criminal Law," 4.

22. *Report of Secretary-General,* paras. 12 to 14.

23. H. Lauterpacht, "The Laws of Nations and the Punishment of War Crimes," *British Yearbook of International Law* 15 (1944): 79.

24. R. Piotrowicz and S. Kaye, *Human Rights: In International and Australian Law* (Sydney, Australia: Butterworths, 2000), 97–98.

25. Piotrowicz and Kay, *Human Rights.*

26. Per Judge Sidhwa, *Tadic* (Jurisdictional Appeal), para. 113.

27. *Tadic* (Jurisdictional Appeal), para. 83.

28. A. Roberts and R. Guelff, *Documents on the Laws of War,* 2d ed. (Oxford, UK: Oxford University Press, 1989), 29. Opened for signature December 11, 1868, LXIV UKPP (1869) 659. Entry into force, December 11, 1868.

29. Roberts and Guelff, *Documents on the Laws of War,* 28.

30. Roberts and Guelff, *Documents on the Laws of War,* 35.

31. Roberts and Guelff, *Documents on the Laws of War,* 44.

32. Roberts and Guelff, *Documents on the Laws of War,* 45. Referred to as the "Martens Clause" after the Russian Foreign Minister, this clause has become a common provision in international treaties and conventions, because it facilitates the development of international customary law.

33. Roberts and Guelff, *Documents on the Laws of War,* 63.

34. Roberts and Guelff, *Documents on the Laws of War,* 72.

35. Roberts and Guelff, *Documents on the Laws of War,* 80.

36. Roberts and Guelff, *Documents on the Laws of War,* 86.

37. Roberts and Guelff, *Documents on the Laws of War,* 94.

38. Roberts and Guelff, *Documents on the Laws of War,* 121.

39. Roberts and Guelff, *Documents on the Laws of War,* 40.

40. Roberts and Guelff, *Documents on the Laws of War,* 138.

41. *Report of the Secretary-General,* para. 41.

42. Roberts and Guelff, *Documents on the Laws of War,* 44–69.

43. Roberts and Guelff, *Documents on the Laws of War,* 139.

44. K. Kittichaisaree, *International Criminal Law* (Oxford, UK: Oxford University Press, 2001), 7.

45. G. Kewley, *Even Wars Have Limits,* 2nd ed. (Victoria, Australia: Australian Red Cross, 2000), 35.

46. Kewley, *Even Wars Have Limits,* 16–19.

47. Kewley, *Even Wars Have Limits,* 32.

48. Kewley, *Even Wars Have Limits,* 33.

49. Kewley, *Even Wars Have Limits,* 35.

50. Piotrowicz and Kaye, *Human Rights,* 160.

51. G. Robertson, *Crimes Against Humanity: The Struggle for Global Justice* (London: Penguin, 1999), 197.

52. Robertson, *Crimes Against Humanity,* 351.

53. Robertson, *Crimes Against Humanity,* 51.

54. Robertson, *Crimes Against Humanity,* 197.

55. *Charter of the International Military Tribunal at Nuremberg,* Article 6.

56. Robertson, *Crimes Against Humanity,* 347.

57. Robertson, *Crimes Against Humanity,* 347.

58. *Tadic* (Jurisdictional Appeal), para. 80.

59. *Tadic* (Jurisdictional Appeal), para. 72.

60. *The Prosecutor v. Delalic and others* (Trial) IT-96-21-T (1998), ICTY Trial Chamber paras. 96 to 108.

61. I. A. Shearer, *Starke's International Law,* 11th ed. (London: Butterworths, 1994), 85 ff.

62. *Delalic,* 60.

63. *Delalic,* at para. 116 and following.

64. *Prosecutor v. Tadic* (Appeal Judgment) IT-94-1-A, ICTY App Ch July 15, 1999 paras. 68–162.

65. *Delalic,* para 118.

66. *Tadic* (Jurisdictional Appeal), para. 94.

67. *Tadic* (Appeal Judgment),para. 255.

68. *Tadic* (Jurisdictional Appeal), para. 141. In *Tadic,* the court found that there was a jurisdictional requirement of proving the existence of

an "armed conflict," but this was restricted to the ICTY Statute only (Kittichaisaree, *International Criminal Law,* appendix 1). No such requirement exists in the ICTR (International Criminal Tribunal for Rwanda) Statute (Kittichaisaree, *International Criminal Law,* 2).

69. *In re Heyer & Others (Essen Lynching Case)* British Military Court, Essen Germany, December 22, 1995. Annotated Digest (1946): 287. Also reported in *Law Reports of the Trials of War Criminals.* Vol. 1. The United Nations War Crimes Commission, Case No. 8 (London: Her Majesty's Stationery Office, 1947).

70. "The Belsen Trial" in *Law Reports of the Trials of War Criminals,* Vol. 1, 88.

71. "The Report of the Commission of Inquiry Into the Events at the Refugee Camps in Beirut (The Kahan Report), February 7, 1983," *International Legal Materials* 22: 473.

72. *Report of the Secretary-General,* paras. 55 to 59, Article 7 (2) & (3).

73. Roberts and Guelff, *Documents on the Laws of War.*

74. *USA v. Karl Brandt* ("Doctor's Trial"), in *Law Reports of the Trials of War Criminals,* Vol. 2, 212.

75. *USA v. Wilhelm List,* in *Law Reports of the Trials of War Criminals,* Vol. 8 (1949).

76. *USA v. Wilhelm von Leeb,* in *Law Reports of the Trials of War Criminals,* Vol. 12 (1951).

77. *In the Matter of the Application of General Tomoyuki Yamashita: General Tomoyuki Yamashita v. Lt. General Wilhelm D. Styer–General United States Army Forces, Western Pacific* 327 US 1-81 (1945).

78. *Yamashita,* 14.

79. *Yamashita.*

80. *Report of the Secretary-General,* para. 56; see also Additional Protocol 1 & A 7 (3) of ICTY Statute.

81. *Delalic.*

82. *Delalic,* para. 384.

83. *Rome Statute of the International Criminal Court,* Article 28.

84. *Prosecutor v. Erdemovic* (Hearing) IT-96-22-T 29, ICTY Trial Chamber, November 1996, paras. 27–28.

85. Kittichaisaree, *International Criminal Law,* 85–89.

86. *Charter of the International Military Tribunal at Nuremberg.*

87. K. D. Askin, *War Crimes Against Women* (The Hague, Netherlands: Martinus-Nijhoff, 1998), 107.

88. Askin, *War Crimes Against Women,* 87.

89. Sunga, *The Emerging System,* 8.

90. "Control Council Law No. 10," 36 *ILR* 31 (1945), was a law adopted by the Allied Powers following the end of World War II and the surrender of Germany. It provided for the trial by the Allied powers of war crimes and crimes against humanity committed by offenders captured in their particular occupied zones. The relevant article is 2(1c).

91. Sunga, *The Emerging System,* 161.

92. Sunga, *The Emerging System,* 8.

93. Sunga, *The Emerging System,* 8.

94. Kittichaisaree, *International Criminal Law* 44, annex. 1, Art. 5 of the Statute of the International criminal Tribunal for the Former Yugoslavia.

95. Kittichaisaree, *International Criminal Law* 44, annex. 2, Art. 3 of the Statute of the International Criminal Tribunal for Rwanda; Art. 7 of the Rome Statute of the International Criminal Court (annex. 3).

96. *Tadic* (Jurisdictional Appeal), para. 78.

97. *Report of the Secretary-General,* para. 34.

98. *Report of the Secretary-General,* para. 47.

99. *Tadic* (Jurisdictional Appeal), para. 141.

100. *Tadic* (Appeal Judgment), para. 249.

101. *The Nickolic Indictment* (Rule 61 Hearing) IT-95-2-R61 ICTY, October 20, 1995, para. 26.

102. Note, for example, the "political denunciation" cases committed as part of the persecution of the Jews in Nazi Germany. The prosecutions under Control Law No. 10 invariably involved one person informing the Gestapo that certain persons were Jews. Individually, each crime was not so serious, but the court held that a crime against humanity had been committed due to the scale of the persecution. See discussion in *Tadic* (Appeal Judgment), paras. 255–263.

103. *Nikolic,* para. 26.

104. *Prosecutor v. Erdemovic* (Appeal judgment) IT-96-22A October 1997, paras. 21–23.

105. *Tadic* (Appeal Judgment), para. 248.

106. *Prosecutor v. Akayesu* (Hearing) ICTR-96-4-t Trial Ch. 1., September 2, 1998.

107. *Akayesu,* para. 579.

108. *Akayesu,* para. 580.

109. *Akayesu,* para. 580.

110. *Akayesu,* para. 581.

111. *Akayesu,* para. 585.

112. *Erdemovic,* para. 23.

113. *Albrecht Case,* Special Court of Cessation in the Netherlands, April 11, 1949, Nederlandse Jurisprudentie (1949) No. 425, p. 747.

114. *Vukovar Case* (Rule 61 Hearing) IT-95-13-R61 ICTY, April 3, 1966, para. 649.

115. *Report of Secretary-General,* para. 48.

116. *Prosecutor v. Tadic* (Judgment of the Trial Chamber) IT-94-I-T ICTY, May 7, 1997, para. 649.

117. *Tadic* (Appeal Judgement), para. 285.

118. Barry Kellman, "An Introduction to Terrorism and Business," in "Symposium, Terrorism and Business," special issue, *De Paul Business Law Journal* 12 (Fall/Spring 1999/2000): 21.

119. J. A. Carberry, "Terrorism: A Global Phenomenon Mandating a Unified International Response," *Indiana Journal of Global Studies* 6, no. 2 (1999): 687.

120. M. Cherif Bassiouni, "Assessing Terrorism into the New Millennium," in "Symposium, Terrorism and Business," special issue, *DePaul Business Law Journal* 12 (Fall/Spring 1999/2000): 9.

121. *League of Nations Convention for the Prevention and Punishment of Terrorism,* O.J. 19 at 23 (1938), League of Nations Doc. C 546 (I). M 383 (I) 1937–1938.

122. The following U.N. conventions all touch on terrorism in one or more of its many manifestations: aviation—Convention on Offences and Certain Other Acts Committed on Board Aircraft (Tokyo Convention, 1963); aircraft hijackings—Convention for the Suppression of Unlawful Seizure of Aircraft (Hague Convention, 1970); aviation sabotage—Convention for the Suppression of Unlawful Acts against the Safety of Civil Aviation (Montreal Convention, 1971); the Convention on the Prevention and Punishment of Crimes against Internationally Protected Persons (1973) protects government officials and diplomats; the Convention on the Physical Protection of Nuclear Material (Nuclear Materials Convention, 1979) has to do with unlawful taking and use of nuclear material; the International Convention against the Taking of Hostages (Hostages Convention, 1979); terrorist acts at airports serving international civil aviation—Protocol for the Suppression of Unlawful Acts of Violence at Airports Serving International Civil Aviation (1988); terrorist activities on ships—Convention for the Suppression of Unlawful Acts against the Safety of Maritime Navigation (1988); terrorist activities on fixed offshore platforms—Protocol for the Suppression of Unlawful Acts against the Safety of Fixed Platforms Located on the Continental Shelf (1988); plastic explosives—Convention on the Marking of Plastic Explosives for the Purpose of Identification (1991); international cooperation in the investigation, prosecution, and extradition of persons who engage in terrorist bombings—International Convention for the Suppression of Terrorist Bombing (1997); International Convention for the Suppression of the Financing of Terrorism (New York, December 1999).

123. The following are some examples of the definitions of terrorism as contained in national legislation:

British Prevention of Terrorism Act, s. 20: Terrorism is "the use of violence for political ends and includes any use of violence for the purpose of putting the public or any section of the public in fear."

United States—US Law 100-204 of 1987, s. 901: "The term *terrorist activity* means the organizing or participating in a wanton or indiscriminate act of violence with extreme indifference to the risk of causing death or serious bodily harm to individuals not taking part in armed hostilities."

Further (US Law 104 302 of 1996), a "federal crime of terrorism" is a crime "calculated to influence or affect the conduct of government by intimidation or coercion, or to retaliate against government conduct."

Australia—the Australian Security Intelligence Organisation Act 1979 s 4 provides that "terrorism" includes

(a) acts of violence for the purpose of achieving a political objective in Australia or in a foreign country (including acts of violence for the purpose of influencing the policy or acts of a government in Australia or in a foreign country);

(b) training, planning, preparations, or other activities for the purposes of violent subversion in a foreign country or for the purposes of the commission in a foreign country of other acts of violence of a kind referred to in paragraph (a).

124. Carberry, "Terrorism," 687.

125. Convention on Offences and Certain Other Acts Committed on Board Aircraft ("The Tokyo Convention"), opened for signature on September 14, 1963, 704, U.N. Treaty Series 219; Convention for the Suppression of Unlawful Seizure of Aircraft, opened for signature on December 16, 1970, 860, U.N. Treaty Series 105; Convention on the Suppression of Unlawful Acts against the Safety of Civil Aviation, opened for signature on September 23, 1971, 974, U.N. Treaty Series 177; Protocol for the Suppression of Unlawful Acts of Violence at Airport Serving Civil Aviation, International Civil Aviation Organization Doc. 9518.

126. *Tadic* (Appeal Judgment), 135.

127. *Attorney General for Israel v. Adolf Eichmann*, ILR 5 (1961). Israeli agents "kidnapped" Eichmann in Argentina and forced him to go to Israel to face trial.

128. R. Lemkin, *Axis Rule in Occupied Europe* (Washington, DC: Carnegie Endowment for International Peace, 1944), 79.

129. *Convention on the Prevention and Punishment of the Crime of Genocide of 1948*, 78 U.N. Treaty Series 277, Article II.

130. A. L. Hinton, "The Dark Side of Modernity: Toward an Anthropology of Genocide," in *Annihilating Difference: The Anthropology of Genocide*, ed. A. L. Hinton, 1–40 (Berkeley: University of California Press, 2002), 12.

131. Hinton, "The Dark Side of Modernity," 13. This is to be contrasted with the lawyer's perspective; see *Kruger v. Commonwealth of Australia*, 146 ALR 126 (1997).

132. Hinton, "The Dark Side of Modernity," 13.

133. Carole Nagengast, "Inoculations of Evil in the US-Mexican Border Region: Reflections on the Genocidal Potential of Symbolic Violence," in *Annihilating Difference*, ed. A. L. Hinton, 325–347 (Berkeley: University of California Press, 2002), 327.

134. Nagengast, "Inoculations of Evil," 338.

135. *Commentary by the UN Secretary General on the Draft Genocide Convention*, UN Doc. E/477 (1947), note 71, pp. 6–7.

136. M. Lippman, "The 1948 Convention on the Prevention and Punishment of the Crime of Genocide Forty-Five Years Later," *Temple International and Comparative Law Journal* 8 (1994): 37.

137. Lippman, "The 1948 Convention."

138. *Akayesu*, paras. 509–524.

139. D. Maybury-Lewis. "Genocide Against Indigenous Peoples" in *Annihilating Difference*, ed. A. L. Hinton, 43–53 (Berkeley: University of California Press, 2002), 45.

140. *Nulyarimma v. Thompson* 165 ALR 621 (1999).

141. Maybury-Lewis. "Genocide Against Indigenous Peoples," 47.

142. Maybury-Lewis. "Genocide Against Indigenous Peoples," 49.

143. Nancy Scheper-Hughes, "Coming to our Senses: Anthropology of Genocide," in *Annihilating Difference*, ed. A. L. Hinton, 348–381 (Berkeley: University of California Press, 2002), 369.

144. *The Prosecutor v. Jelisic* (Hearing) IT-95-10-T ICTY, December 14, 1999, para. 59 ff.

145. J. R. Bowen, "Culture, Genocide and a Public Anthropology," in *Annihilating Difference*, ed. A. L. Hinton, 382–395 (Berkeley: University of California Press, 2002), 382.

146. Paul F. Magnarella, "Recent Developments in the International Law of Genocide: An Anthropological Perspective on the International Criminal Tribunal for Rwanda," in *Annihilating Difference*, ed. A. L. Hinton, 310–322 (Berkeley: University of California Press, 2002), 317. See also *Akayesu*, para. 516.

147. Magnarella, "Recent Developments," 317.

148. Magnarella, "Recent Developments," 319.

149. Jordan J. Paust, "Congress and Genocide: They're Not Going to Get Away With It," *Michigan Journal of International Law* 11 (1989): 92; also, *Belgium v. Spain* (Barcelona Traction Case) 1970 ICJ Reports 3 at 32, although the court did not expressly state that genocide was a norm of *jus cogens*, evidence of *opinio juris* and general state practice, support the conclusion that the rule against genocide is part of customary international law and most probably *jus cogens* as well. However, in *Jelisic* ICTY Trial Chamber, at para. 60, did make this conclusion.

150. *Karadzic and Mladic* (Rule 61 Hearing) IT-95-5-R61 ICTY, para. 95.

151. Hinton, "The Dark Side of Modernity," 29.

152. *Tadic* (Judgment of the Trial Chamber), paras. 55 ff.

153. *Akayesu,* para. 120.

154. Tone Bringa, "Averted Gaze: Genocide in Bosnia-Herzegovina 1992–1995" in *Annihilating Difference,* ed. A. L. Hinton, 194–225 (Berkeley: University of California Press, 2002), 212.

155. Bringa, "Averted Gaze," 216.

156. Toni Shapiro-Phim, "Dance Music and the Nature of Terror in Democratic Kampuchea," in *Annihilating Difference,* ed. A. L. Hinton, 179–193 (Berkeley: University of California Press, 2002), 186.

157. *Tadic* (Judgment of the Trial Chamber), para. 467.

158. *Akayesu,* para. 118.

159. Hinton, "The Dark Side of Modernity," 26.

160. Uli Linke, "Archives of Violence: The Holocaust and the German Politics of Memory," in *Annihilating Difference,* ed. A. L. Hinton (Berkeley: University of California Press, 2002), 235.

161. Samuel Totten, William S. Parsons, and Robert K. Hitchcock, "Confronting Genocide and Ethnocide of Indigenous Peoples: An Inter-disciplinary Approach to Definition, Intervention, Prevention and Advocacy," in *Annihilating Difference,* ed. A. L. Hinton, 54–91 (Berkeley: University of California Press, 2002), 82.

162. This followed the decisions of the High Court in *Marbo v. Queensland* 175 CLR 1 (1992), which had a significant effect on public opinion. Contrary to widespread public opinion in favor of "reconciliation," the conservative Prime Minister John Howard still refused to apologize on behalf of the Australian people for what had happened to Australia's indigenous people.

163. Bringa, "Averted Gaze," 202.

164. Linke, "Archives of Violence, 262.

165. Linke, "Archives of Violence," 342.

166. *Delalic,* paras. 475–497.

167. European Law Students' Association, *Handbook on the International Criminal Court,* 2d ed. (Brussels, Belgium: ELSA, 1997), 3–6.

168. Sunga, *The Emerging System,* 4.

169. Sunga, *The Emerging System,* 14.

170. Kirby, "Criminal Law," 1.

171. Kittichaisaree, *International Criminal Law,* appendix 1, Article 1 of the Statute of the Tribunal for the former Yugoslavia.

172. *Charter of the International Military Tribunal,* Article 6.

173. Sunga, *The Emerging System.*

PART III

Cross-National and International Efforts to Combat Transnational Crime

In facing global crime we are not powerless. The tools to fight it exist; they have to be adapted and applied.

—André Bossard (former Secretary-General of ICPO-Interpol)

In the face of crime's globalization, Bossard's statement provides a note of optimism when confronting the daunting task of combating that crime. Although each country may try to counteract transnational crime on its own, it seems more prudent to rely on transnational cooperation. The alternative of relying on a single nation to be the world's police, court, and punisher would have limited effectiveness. Chapters in Part III provide examples of how that cooperation is being achieved at the start of the 21st century.

Mitchel Roth (Chapter 12) begins Part III with his overview of how the primary components of justice systems (i.e., policing, courts, and corrections) have coordinated their efforts to combat transnational crime. He accomplishes this by noting the variation in how countries structure each component, identifying some of the challenges to achieving that cooperation among countries, then providing examples of instances where national, regional, and international cooperation has been successful. Roth's overview provides the base for the specific coverage given to policing, courts, and corrections in Chapters 14, 15, and 16.

It is true that cooperative efforts to combat transnational crime can be structured around informal agreements among interested countries. More realistically, those efforts require formal agreements to be successful. In Chapter 13, Matti Joutsen explains the need for formal international instruments that provide rules for effective international cooperation. After describing the evolution of those agreements, Joutsen explains the primary subject matter of these agreements: extradition, mutual legal assistance, transfer of proceedings, recognition of judgments, and the transfer of prisoners. His chapter provides a necessary background to discussions in the remaining chapters in Part III.

Collaboration among countries attempting to investigate crimes and arrest suspects is one of the earliest examples of international cooperation. The importance of cooperation among police agencies is reflected in Part III, with two chapters devoted to the topic. In Chapter 14, Mathieu Deflem provides an historical context by reviewing the origins of Interpol. He shows how 19th-century efforts to control anarchism and white slavery provided the impetus for 20th-century international police cooperation. The examples of anti-anarchist measures and of international accords on white slavery are fascinating in themselves, but they also provide interesting insight into the sometimes unexpected consequences of political maneuverings.

Discussion of Interpol continues in Chapter 15, where Maki Haberfeld and William McDonald explain how that organization operates today. They provide specific information on Interpol's efforts at combating crimes such as terrorism, trafficking in humans, and money laundering. Also discussed in Chapter 15 is Europol, the premier example of regional police cooperation among countries. As they do with Interpol, Haberfeld and McDonald explain Europol's organizational structure and provide examples of cases where European police resources are shared in the investigation of crimes. The chapter concludes with a description of various international police task forces.

Examples of international cooperation in adjudicating transnational offenders are not as easily found as are examples of cooperative policing. In Chapter 16, Frank Höpfel and Claudia Angermaier explain that the enforcement of international criminal law (which they carefully define) remains a decentralized process. Individual nations identify international crimes as violations of their country's criminal law, prosecute those violations, and enforce the punishment. The only centralized (and therefore truly international) examples of adjudicating international crimes have been the Nuremberg and Tokyo Military Tribunals. The International Criminal Tribunals for the former Yugoslavia and Rwanda and the newly established International Criminal Court provide contemporary examples that may be instances of adjudicating international crimes and criminals, but even those rely on the cooperation of nations for enforcement issues such as the execution of prison sentences. As a result, they directly enforce international criminal law only in part. Yet these contemporary examples are likely the forerunners to any international cooperative efforts at adjudicating transnational offenders and should be understood as such. Höpfel and Angermaier provide a fascinating and complete review especially of the International Criminal Court, but they also explain the role of the International Court of Justice, the European Court of Human Rights, the European

Court of Justice, and internationalized courts such as the special courts in Sierra Leone and East Timor.

Part III concludes with Chapter 17, wherein Robert Weiss provides a provocative analysis of what he dubs "transnational correctional concerns." As with adjudication of transnational offenders, there is no truly universal example of punishing those offenders. There are, in other words, no versions of probation, prison, or parole that operate under a supranational authority responsible for punishing persons convicted of transnational or international crimes. It is possible, however, to anticipate a punishment system that reflects international standards. Should there ever be an agreed-on punishment system for transnational criminals who are adjudicated by an international court, that system should follow a universal standard of penal treatment. Weiss identifies four stages (anticolonial, Western imperialist, postcolonial, and neocolonial) through which transnational correctional concerns have progressed (or maybe regressed). His indictment of the primacy given to or taken by the United States in setting a standard for penal treatment warns us of the dangers of hegemony and implies that any reasonable standard for humane treatment of offenders (those committing either traditional or transnational crimes) is not in the foreseeable future.

REFERENCE

Bossard, A. (2003). Crime and globalization. *Crime & Justice International, 19*(71), 38.

12

Comparative Overview of Policing, Courts, and Corrections

MITCHEL ROTH

Elements of criminal justice systems such as the police, courts and prisons are found in almost all countries, albeit their names may be different.

—Mukherjee and Reichel (1999, p. 65)

All countries have the three primary parts of the modern criminal justice system: police, courts and prisons.

—Newman (1999, p. xv)

In the summer of 1966, 3 years before astronauts landed on the moon, a U.N. sub-committee examined the "Peaceful Uses of Outer Space." Among the committee's recommendations was that "All nations must help one another in emergencies involving inter-planetary travel or travelers" (Chang, 1976, p. 51). From today's vantage point, the whole notion of interplanetary cooperation between nations seems naïve if not delusory, particularly in an era in which nations are still striving to cooperate on the planet Earth itself. The specter of law enforcement cooperation in outer space seems rather far-fetched as we live in a 21st-century world where inner space is still cleaved by international conflict.

It is beyond the scope of any book chapter, let alone this one, to offer a comprehensive examination of international police, courts, and corrections. The primary purpose of this chapter is to identify certain themes that demonstrate and perhaps explain how variations and similarities in criminal justice procedures in the aforestated areas of study can either hamper or help achieve international cooperation.

HISTORICAL ROOTS OF INTERNATIONAL COOPERATION

International cooperation between unique criminal justice systems is not a new phenomenon. As early as the 19th century, Paris police were keeping a photographic identification file. Scholars have noted that by the end of the 1800s, prescient police officers from countries as diverse as Argentina, Belgium, Austria, France, Germany, and the United States recognized the distinctive features of "transnational crimes and offenders." Characteristics included "multiple appearances, effective planning, great mobility, and the creation and utilization of masking and dissembling methods" (Fooner, 1989, pp. 29–30). Most countries soon created "rogue's galleries" replete with photos and Bertillon information and, eventually, fingerprints. By the beginning of the 20th century, photography and fingerprinting were easing modern police forces toward "internationalization." Both methods of identification provided a "universal language" for identifying criminals, despite their attempts to conceal their true identities.

In the first decades of the new century, a distinctive group of police administrators recognized the emerging problem posed by criminals who could cross at will the rigid jurisdictional boundaries that hindered police cooperation. In 1914, hundreds of police delegates representing more than a dozen nations convened at the First International Criminal Police Congress in Monaco. The remarkable turnout at the first meeting of police professionals discussing international crime boasted attendees from Europe and as far away as Central America, North Africa, and the Near East. However, representatives from North America, England, and the Far East were absent. With the outbreak of World War I, only 4 months later, all this became moot, stopping this effort in its tracks.

In 1923, Vienna hosted the Second International Criminal Police Congress, leading to the formation of the International Criminal Police Commission. By the 1940s, this organization was known as Interpol, usually credited as the first step in multinational police cooperation against transnational criminals.

POLICING

The first people to conceive of law enforcement at the international level were undoubtedly those who negotiated, drafted and signed the many extradition treaties between various countries— some of which, in fact, have linked certain European countries since the nineteenth century.

—Former Interpol
Secretary-General Jean Nepote
(quoted in Fooner, 1989, p. 138)

According to one pioneer in comparative police studies, "Police come in a bewildering variety of forms" (Bayley, 1985, p. 7). This can lead to confusion when trying to elaborate on the similarities and differences of international police forces. For example, can scholars examine the Los Angeles Police Department, Soviet political police, and Islamic religious police using the same criteria? Every culture has its own distinctive system of establishing justice.

The primary obligation of the state is to maintain peace and order. As Fairchild and Dammer (2001) have noted, modern police forces are organized to perform "civil order control and deviance control" (p. 96). Countries as diverse as Germany, France, China, Japan, and Saudi Arabia use different divisions within a larger organization to accomplish these goals. On the other hand, regular street police perform both functions in Great Britain and the United States. All these differences make sense when one examines historical developments in these countries.

Due to the high degree of centralization of governmental structure in many nations, most countries have developed centralized police forces. But although this may be true in most countries in Europe, Africa, Asia, and South America, the United States stands apart with a decentralized system composed of almost 20,000 different police forces. American policing is cleaved by jurisdictional disputes that are unavoidable in a decentralized system. Jurisdictional problems in cooperative efforts in the United States mirror the international jurisdictional issues facing global law enforcement. Diversity of forces can lead to lack of coordination.

Due to the nature of world history and politics, police forces vary widely within some geographical regions. To the untrained eye, Japanese policing may seem similar to other Asian police forces, but the Japanese police system of today has been largely derived from the West. However, that Japanese police often remove their shoes before kicking in a door on a police raid demonstrates their cultural uniqueness. Since the end of World War II, despite the ever-present language barrier, the Japanese criminal justice system can be understood in terms of Western antecedents. So on one level, we can find Anglo-American and European legal foundations. But further examination reveals a system rooted in feudalistic traditions deeply ingrained in Japanese society. This would explain in part the public's rather detached view toward the government's handling of criminal justice issues. This harkens back to the widely adopted mantra

of the Tokugawa Shogunate, which endeavored to "keep the public uninformed and dependent."

Most historical examinations of police organizations begin with the origins of the London Metropolitan Police in 1829. Focusing on this particular system and its impact on police systems around the world, however, often leads to the impression that it is the dominant strand in policing. But according to Mawby (1999), alluding to the conventional "Anglo-American policing tradition" (p. 28), "not only are there marked differences between Britain and North America, but within Britain there are also considerable variations, with the police systems of Scotland, Northern Ireland and the Channel Islands quite distinctive" (p. 23).

British policing has therefore had its most direct impact on former English colonies such as Australia, Canada, New Zealand, the United States, and some Caribbean nations. An examination of these systems reveals instantly identifiable similarities. Differences on the other hand demand a more detailed examination. One need look no further than China, North Korea, and Saudi Arabia to understand that other traditions of criminal justice demand other systems of policing.

The recent surge in interest in comparative justice has led to a number of publications chronicling at least some of the conventional differences between various styles of policing. Contemporary challenges to transnational policing have made the cooperation between police forces increasingly crucial. To understand how forces can work better, it is important to note the similarities and then detail how differences can be barriers to cooperation. It is hoped that a better understanding of these differences can lead to an understanding of transnational crime and crime fighting. For the purposes of this chapter, I will rely on David Bayley's (1985) definition, which considers police as "people authorized by a group to regulate interpersonal relations within the group through the application of force" (p. 7).

Transnational crime is a phenomenon touching every nation to one degree or another. As transnational crime becomes more complex, the demand for police services from different nations to cooperate has become increasingly important. Unfortunately, the growth of international law enforcement has been paralleled by the rise of a criminal element that has taken advantage of rapid and cheap transportation, easy movement across borders, miniature explosive devices, and transnational corporate movements of information (i.e., electronic fund transfers). In an era when criminals know no real boundaries, the single most significant factor in policing is the need for formal cooperation and strategic alliances between international agencies.

When criminal activity crosses national boundaries, a number of complications arise for law enforcement officials. Barriers to cooperation can be related to different notions of criminality and customs, political instability, language, variations in legal systems, different police practices, technological issues, cultural uniqueness, and even simple geography. All these factors can determine how an international investigation is conducted and resolved.

One cannot examine the differences and similarities of police forces without recognizing issues such as civil rights of citizens and powers endowed to police. A number of police practices in various countries can be compared and contrasted. Researchers can examine (a) police-to-population ratios in diverse societies, (b) duties required of police in different cultures, (c) relationships between the police and other public agencies, (d) cross-cultural investigation of the public's attitude toward police, (e) comparison of police power with the efficiency of government, (f) crime clearance rates, and (g) who carries out police functions such as prevention, investigation, and apprehension.

Respecting the Sovereignty of Nations

Problems often ensue when neighboring countries cooperating in various treaties or agreements vary significantly in economic and military power. This often forces one of the countries into a subordinate position, creating concerns about protecting its sovereignty, as in the case of the United States and Mexico. It often seems that American authorities take a more arrogant attitude toward their counterparts in Mexican criminal justice. Recent transnational criminal cases that have brought Mexican and American authorities into conflict have included the imprisonment of Americans (sometimes unaware of laws regarding cross-border transport of ammunition) for carrying ammunition across the border; arrests of Mexican nationals fleeing across the border to evade the death penalty (which Mexico has abolished); and acts of enforcement by American officers, bounty hunters, and the like, who pose a threat to Mexican sovereignty. According to one scholar, the "relative strength of U.S. personnel, equipment, technology, and technical know-how" often leads the stronger country "to take the lead in law enforcement efforts" (Reichel, 2002, p. 7).

A number of studies have indicated that when nations share a national boundary, such as the one that exists between the United States and Mexico, "a criminal subculture is facilitated" (Resendiz & Neal, 2000, p. 8). When cars are stolen from Texas destined for Mexico, the process is not very different from car theft within the United States and other nations. However, the process becomes more complicated because the motor vehicles have to cross one of the international bridges to gain entry into Mexico. The only way this can be facilitated is by bribing custom officers who man the border checkpoints (Miller, 1987). Once the final checkpoint is crossed into Mexico, American police cannot arrest the thief until the identified individual crosses back to the States.

Challenges to International Cooperation at the Highest Levels

Transnational crime is able to flourish in every type of political or economic environment. This type of crime is assisted by inefficient law enforcement measures at home that allow criminals to exploit banking and investment laws among nations.

One of the most difficult challenges facing law enforcement is in the prevention of transnational money laundering. Little can be accomplished at the lower levels of policing, and as a result, money laundering "can have devastating economic consequences" for the international community." The act of "money laundering . . . was not criminalized until 1986" (Pontell & Frid, 2000, p. 40). But by the late 1980s, steps were taken toward international cooperation in combating the crime through the actions of the 1988 U.N. Vienna Convention.

In the 1990s, a number of accomplishments were achieved after the inauguration of the Financial Action Task Force. Under the Clinton administration, transnational crime was fought at the highest levels of government and policing. One method of ensuring international cooperation was to punish nations that disregarded the international efforts to suppress money laundering, by imposing sanctions that could prevent the transgressors from conducting business in the United States, including making electronic transfers of money through American banks (Pontell & Frid, 2000). However, these decisions on withholding certification of countries that disregard international legislation are not made without "political and economic motivations as well as the general relationship between the United States and the country facing certification" (Pontell & Frid, 2000, p. 41).

Two of the biggest obstacles to cooperation are in the realms of financial offenses and political crimes. Despite the best efforts of policing at the highest levels of government, the time required to develop and implement effective policies against money laundering are hampered by ever-present issues of national sovereignty. This is particularly true not just in underdeveloped nations but also in countries in transition such as Russia and other former Soviet republics. In the process of making the transition from socialism to capitalism, the emerging market economy has provided new avenues for investing illicit proceeds. Indeed, according to some scholars, "Many countries have insufficient technology to counteract the technology employed by organized traffickers" (quoted in Pontell & Frid, 2000, p. 42).

Regional Approaches to Police Cooperation

In an age of transnational crime and terrorism, international law enforcement cooperation is of manifest importance. Police cooperation can take a variety of forms. Typically, agreements are influenced by social and cultural traditions. For countries with similar legal traditions, cultures, language families, political environment, and crime problems, it is advantageous to enter bilateral, multinational, and multilateral global agreements.

Europe has developed a variety of cooperative schemes over the years, including Interpol, TREVI, the Schengen System, and Europol. But there are so many different systems of judicial or police cooperation, it can complicate the procedure of international cooperation even through Interpol. This is especially true now that there are several systems of police control in Europe. The two most important systems have been the Schengen Agreements (beginning in 1995) and Europol (which replaced the TREVI group in 1976).

In Africa, police cooperation ventures have sparked innovations such as the East African Sub-Regional Bureau, headquartered in Nairobi, Kenya. In a poorly capitalized part of the world, East African countries hope to spur advances in the development and sharing of information technology and communications. In addition, it is hoped that these innovations will also facilitate the development of regional policy for international cooperation among regional police forces. One of the bureau's members, Tanzania, has entered into police cooperation arrangements with neighboring nations in Southern, Eastern, and Central Africa. In 2001, it was reported that 12 heads of state had signed a protocol to fight drug trafficking through the Southern African Development Community region. This agreement, like most others, is designed with the intention of improving efficiency and ensuring legality while bypassing traditional diplomatic channels required in political exchanges.

Formerly, there was little control of transnational crimes in the Southern African countries. Countries as diverse as Angola, Botswana, Lesotho, Malawi, Mozambique, Namibia, South Africa, Swaziland, Tanzania, Zambia, and Zimbabwe have had more success of late in cooperating in suppressing drugs, and arms- and human-smuggling syndicates. The establishment of the Southern African Regional Police Chiefs Cooperation Organization (SARPCCO) in 1995 is considered a major step in galvanizing cooperation in these 11 Southern African states (also members of Interpol). The member states have addressed in several conferences many of the principles that have hindered police cooperation. The organization adopted a number of principles that have afflicted police cooperation in the past. The principles of SARPCCO include (a) equality of police forces and services, (b) nonpolitical professionalism, (c) nondiscrimination and flexibility of working methods, (d) mutual benefits to all members, (e) observance of human rights, (f) respect for national sovereignty, and (g) amicable settlement of differences (Bruce, 1998).

Other issues addressed by SARPCCO that have a particular resonance for similar geographical efforts involve extradition, a uniform curriculum for specialized training for investigation on a regional basis, the lifting of visa requirements for police officers

conducting investigations, establishment of a crime intelligence database, and the installation of modern technology for effective and immediate communication (Bruce, 1998).

Challenges to Police Cooperation at the Regional Level

International cooperative ventures in policing have confronted a number of obstacles. Problems include financial constraints, geographic factors such as large porous borders, cultural and linguistic complexities, and the lack of professional police standards, often resulting in police corruption.

Challenges to police cooperation can result from civil and internal disturbances that lead to the demise of civil society (e.g., in Liberia, Rwanda, Congo, Angola). Some countries lack laws relating to organized crime, extradition, passports, and other matters, often leading to a lack of trust in police organizations.

Historical issues have on occasion created rifts between traditional foes such as the distrust between the Irish and the English or between the American and Mexican police. This, in turn, has hampered the cooperation in suppressing crimes such as drug trafficking, money laundering, illegal immigration, and other forms of transnational crime.

A number of problems have been encountered as nations resolve to achieve effective international police cooperation. Regional strife and civil wars within countries have impeded efforts to establish collaborative efforts as well.

A major obstacle to police cooperation has been the attempt to reconcile principles of national sovereignty with joint efforts at international police cooperation. Conflict can ensue when some countries become hesitant about ceding their sovereign authority to strengthen the collaborative fight against transnational crime. These concerns have led some countries to refrain from supporting diverse conventions, agreements, and protocols. As a result, bilateral and multilateral agreements are out of the question with these nations. Also difficult in such scenarios has been the extradition of offenders and collection of evidence (witness Saudi Arabian lack of cooperation with the FBI after the Khobar Tower bombing).

The variety of legal traditions in use today can present problems ranging from frustration to inability to cooperate meaningfully. Europol and Schengen are restricted by their geographical limitations and continue to be reliant on Interpol's role in ensuring cooperation between Europe and the rest of the world.

Extradition Treaties

Because transnational crime is dominated by international crimes involving drugs, terrorism, and financial offenses, extradition has emerged as a critical issue in international policing. In many cases, individuals captured in various countries have been able to thumb their noses at powerful nations where they committed their original crimes. One such incident occurred in October 1985, when hijackers seized the Italian cruise ship *Achille Lauro*, killing American passenger Leon Klinghoffer and holding the crew and passengers for ransom. The U.S. government tried to capture the hijackers through military channels to bring them to justice. But the rescue plan failed because of intervention by the Italian government, within whose territory the capture was almost made. In this episode, the U.S. government also filed formal criminal charges against the hijackers for violations of U.S. criminal law and requested Italy to extradite them for prosecution. The Italian government refused to honor the request and instead prosecuted the hijackers under Italian law. This is considered the first time the United States used the extradition process in a terrorism case.

There are a number of barriers to efficient extradition practice, none more important than ideological differences that sometimes lead detractors to point to extradition's conflict with traditional policies of asylum and hospitality for oppressed strangers. Extradition practices around the world are determined by the hundreds of bilateral treaties that have amassed since the late 1800s.

Other Barriers

Police corruption. Police corruption can occur at any level. However, when it occurs at the highest levels, it presents one of the greatest barriers to transnational police cooperation. Nations will be reticent to enter into cooperative ventures if they know a country's police force is corrupt.

Geographical. International police cooperation is challenged on a number of fronts. From a geographical vantage point, nations with long borders punctuated by deserts, mountains, and water sources, are usually plagued by lack of manpower.

Police structure and styles. Differences in police force structures around the world make it difficult for officials in one country to know which department in another country has authority to handle a particular case or share information.

Because law enforcement styles vary from region to region, some police forces use interrogation techniques that violate what other nations would consider civil liberties, although these protections might not exist in all countries.

Police forces in transition. A wide range of assistance has been required to help in the police system transition and transformation of Eastern European police forces over the past 20 years. Under the communist regimes in Russia and Eastern Europe, police systems served the ruling elites and severely controlled police contacts in Western Europe. With many of the political barriers to police cooperation removed by the end of the Cold War, the police systems of Eastern and Western Europe have developed a number of linkages. These connections have included the recent bilateral UK/Russian Federation Memorandum of Understanding on Serious Crime. Other linkages have been multilateral and region specific, such as the connections between the Baltic States. However, prior to September 11, 2001 (9/11), Interpol was virtually the only bond that offered the former communist nations access to European and worldwide contacts. Interpol has played an important role in promoting dialogue between the police systems of Eastern and Western Europe.

Sharing information. One area of cooperation that continues to be the "Achilles heel" for police forces has been information and intelligence sharing. Sensitive information is often restricted because of national, political, and ideological concerns; however, this is often overstated. Just witness the recent intelligence-sharing fiasco among American police systems prior to 9/11. In Europe, several questions have arisen as to whether sensitive information sharing should be a "relevant concept" within Interpol and Europol. Should exchanges of information be accomplished nonelectronically?

Language. The use of different languages can become a challenging barrier to communication in even the wealthiest nations on earth. One need look no further than the lack of Arabic speakers in U.S. policing and intelligence prior to the 9/11 terrorist attack. Inability to communicate can discourage and even interfere with communication.

COURTS

Like police forces and correctional systems, courts come in all manner of forms. In some nations, the court and the police apparatus operate side by side. In others, police can be subordinated to the court (Chang, 1976).

According to most sources, to function correctly, courts should be characterized by judicial independence and impartiality (Fairchild, 1993). Designed to settle disputes according to established legal protocol, courts reflect the norms of a society and assure citizens that a measure of impartial justice can be expected by all. In addition, courts play a role in educating a society as to the laws and standards of a particular government.

Criminal codes are highly specialized, the product of centuries of evolution. Although many criminal laws are the product of cultural diversity, crimes such as murder with intent, incest, and rape have been almost universally prohibited. Virtually all countries have adopted legal punishments ranging from fines to imprisonment to capital punishment as ways to correct criminal behaviors. Of these, imprisonment is the most universal penal sanction.

The particular structure and operation of a court reflects the political structure of a country (e.g., socialist, democratic). Most national penal codes are influenced by a particular type of legal tradition. However, in some nations, judges have the discretion to choose between several legal traditions. For example, the early Iranian penal code is rooted in Islamic law. Beginning in 1906, the country incorporated the French Penal Code of 1810. It took a number of years "to overtake the religious courts" (Newman, 1976, p. 218). During the reign of the Shah, a highly developed court system handled most criminal matters. Major revisions were adopted following the overthrow of the Shah in the late 1970s, leading to a recrudescence of Islamic law.

When teaching a class on comparative criminal justice from an historical perspective, I am usually able to motivate meaningful discussion by asking the students, "If you committed a murder or a sexual offense or theft, under which criminal justice procedures employed in history would you want to be tried and which would you prefer to avoid?" This evokes reference to a comparative scholar who quipped, "If he were innocent he would prefer to be tried in a civil law court, but if he were guilty he would rather be tried by a common law court" (quoted in Reichel, 2002, p. 203).

One needs more than a passing understanding of legal traditions and criminal justice systems to get beyond the typical knee-jerk responses toward unique court systems that usually include some reference to hand amputation and stoning under Islamic law. Obviously, court systems vary tremendously around the world. This can be a detriment to international cooperation, or it can sometimes furnish a system with better methods of court procedures than what already exists.

For example, many Western nations are rediscovering shaming techniques as an alternative for a variety of offenses. Shaming techniques vary widely and are controversial for reasons such as the belief by some that punishments should be neither degrading nor humiliating. But shaming is not a new punishment. It has a long tradition in Japanese society, and its use can be traced back in America to the first English colonists in the 17th century. But with the revival of alternative sanctions, shaming has enjoyed a revival as an inexpensive response to criminal recidivism.

Two scholars have recently suggested that Islamic procedural law may have some "potential uses" in the West (Holscher & Mahmood, 2000). These authors have pointed to the successful adoption of the German and English "fee-shifting" technique in the United States (which forces individuals to think before litigating) as a way that cultures borrow legal procedures from other cultures. This form of resolution is in turn linked to some of the neighborhood-based dispute resolution programs popular in Africa and Asia.

In a post-9/11 world, it is a daunting task to convince Westerners, let alone North Americans, to pursue the idea that Islamic law may includes aspects of potential use in western legal systems. A major barrier is the rampant stereotyping that often distorts Islamic law.

Another challenge has been the syncretic nature of Islam, where there is no central doctrine, allowing unique Muslim countries to interpret the Koran as it befits their particular culture and place in the world.

With little homogeneity in the practice of the Muslim faith, it has led to tremendous differences in its practice around the world. It should not then be unexpected that a number of misunderstandings have occurred between Islamic and Western nations and regions. Some countries follow traditional Islam (e.g., Saudi Arabia). Turkey abolished the Shariah courts (1924), recently prohibited the wearing of Islamic head scarves, and eschews Koranic law in the contemporary era, whereas in Iran, female students must wear head scarves. But for most Muslims living in the Middle and Near East, laws are arbitrated under Western European systems rather than the Shariah.

It has been suggested that procedural Islamic law could offer a useful model in the process used for determining major sanctions for Western nations such as the United States that still use the death penalty or are moving more toward mandatory sentencing (e.g., three-strikes legislation). Although Islamic courts do not use the jury system, there is more emphasis on the use of procedural safeguards and standards of proof. This is illustrated best by examining the procedures for testimony, which are numerous, including (a) defendants cannot be convicted on the basis of circumstantial evidence, (b) witnesses must have direct knowledge of a crime (having witnessed it in most cases), (c) defendants can raise circumstantial evidence to help their own case, (d) four witnesses are required to prove a case of fornication, (e) defendants have the right to retract testimony to ensure against coercion, (f) false accusations are severely punished, (g) all witnesses are required to be above reproach and of good character (versus the Western use of jailhouse informants and snitches), (h) those testifying can never have been convicted of a serious crime, and (i) those testifying must be mature and sane at the time of the offenses and at the time of testimony (Holscher & Mahmood, 2000; Lippman, McConville, & Yerushalmi, 1988; Souryal, Potts, & Alobied, 1994).

Due Process

"Is one criminal justice system more just than another?" Which is fairer, the presumption of guilt or a presumption of innocence? Under the former Soviet regime, "law was subordinate to policy." By placing "ideology over public safety," even more constraints were placed on law enforcement efforts. In the 1970s and 1980s, a series of murders by Andrei Chikatilo was kept under wraps. Before Chikatilo was arrested (in the post-Soviet era 1990s), an innocent man had already been mistakenly executed for his crimes. With residents unaware of the serial killings for 5 years, a number of safety precautions went unheeded. What liability issues might have arisen if a visiting citizen from a different legal system was among the victims due to the poor Soviet/ Russian police work?

One of the peculiarities of comparative criminal justice is finding any meaningful definition for *due process*, an important part of any penal system. All legal systems offer some incarnation of due process. Under Islamic law, it takes four witnesses to prove a case of adultery. Likewise, at least two witnesses are needed to go the distance in a capital case. However, in the United States, it is not uncommon for an individual to be executed in the 21st century on the words of *one* witness (e.g., Gary Graham in Texas in 2000). Conventional wisdom led most scholars to infer that the United States "gave greater weight to due process than did the inquisitory processes of Western Europe" (Tonry, 2001a, p. 4). However, Michael Tonry suggests that this is no longer true, citing the influence of the European Human Rights Convention on European due process as it becomes less influential in America. Tonry reports that one former director of the Max Planck Institute for International and Comparative Penal Law was disappointed that in the 1980s and 1990s, American lawmakers retracted many due process values that were greatly admired by post–World War II policymakers in Germany. Most criticism rests on the assumption that America is more committed to crime control than due process values, citing concerns for capital punishment (Tonry, 2001a).

Americans are long used to the protections afforded by the Bill of Rights and more recent protections under state law, such as the right to an attorney. Try demanding such protection in a nation without common law. According to Reichel (2002), in some Islamic countries "parties in legal disputes are infrequently represented by counsel" (p. 190).

In 1994, an American teenager named Michael Fay was convicted of vandalizing a car in Singapore with graffiti. His sentence included a 90-day jail term and 24 lashes with a cane. Naturally, an uproar arose in the United States over such a punitive sentence. Many critics ascribed it to the "primitivity" of Asian society. However, any research into this punishment would find that the punishment of caning was introduced by British colonial administrators in the previous century. In the United States and most other common law countries, the punishment given Michael Fay probably would have included probation, a warning, or some type of financial reparation. Several issues arise over such an incident. On one side are apologists who cite the low crime rates and lack of graffiti in Singapore that would make introducing community policing a moot issue. Others would point to the many American and European cities that are awash in graffiti and plagued by property crime and perhaps on reflection might consider that a more punitive system would deter such behavior. But the question that remains is what happens to a member of one society's criminal justice system when he or she violates a law without an analogue at home? What should be the punishment? Would a better resolution involve deportation, having the trial in the offender's country, or convincing the victim's country to reduce the severity of the penalty?

One of the most vexing questions facing international criminal justicians is whether there is any possibility of creating international standards for sentencing and punishment. Today there is a movement toward international standards or limits for domestic criminal justice systems. A number of U.N. conventions and human rights conventions have espoused limits involving "criminal trials, limits on criminalization and punishment, and standards for implementation of punishments" (Kurki, 2001, p. 331). Other criminal justice standards have been adopted involving various aspects of arrest, police powers, pretrial detention, fair trial or due process requirements, prohibited forms of punishment, and prison conditions.

Soering v. the United Kingdom

There is no shortage of cases that could be used to illustrate how criminal justice systems cooperate when a foreign national is caught between systems. One is *Soering v. the United Kingdom* (European Court of Human Rights, 1/89/161/217). In 1989, an 18-year-old German killed his girlfriend's parents in Virginia. The murder was planned by both individuals, who then fled to Europe. Following their arrest in England, Virginia requested their return to the state for trial. When this case came first before the European Court of Human Rights, questions arose as to whether the European convention protected individuals from being extradited to a third country where they may face inhuman treatment. According to European standards, the special circumstances that constituted inhumane treatment included the average length of time an individual spent on death row (6–8 years) and his age at time of crime (18). However, in the United States, court cases at the federal and state levels have declined to agree that long delays were cruel or

unusual or that an 18-year-old should be exempted. After much deliberation, the Virginia state prosecutor guaranteed that the German national would not face the death penalty, and Soering was subsequently extradited to the United States. Currently, states belonging to the Council of Europe allow extradition to countries with the death penalty only after receiving guarantees that it will not be imposed (see also the Ira Einhorn case involving France and Pennsylvania).

Other death penalty issues hinge on the execution of juveniles and the mentally impaired. But although the U.N. safeguards require that capital punishment be imposed with a minimum possible of suffering, this protection is routinely flouted around the world. Some Arabic countries allow stoning to death, and several American states still allow electrocution, the gas chamber, hanging, and firing squads.

What measures can be used to compare the differences and similarities of international court systems? Scholars have used any number of ways to compare court systems. Some focus on institutions in different countries established to bring a defendant to justice (variations in legal training, prosecution, defense, court organization, and adjudication). Others focus on the litigiousness of some societies or the tendency to take cases to court. Several pioneering comparative scholars have examined the patterns of decision making by judges, recruitment and training of judicial personnel, or how court cases move through certain courts to contrast the reality of justice in various systems.

Court systems differ markedly in terms of punishment. There is great variation in what constitutes cruel and unusual punishment. Some countries and cultures use the death penalty; others do not. Extradition and sentencing become complicated when an individual is sentenced to death for a certain crime, such as drug smuggling, which is not a capital offense in most secular countries. In Thailand, Saudi Arabia, and other countries, this is the case. How do countries cooperate when one country uses the death penalty while another is adamantly opposed? How would this affect extradition?

Some countries have different notions of criminality. Blasphemy is a capital crime in some Islamic countries; in other countries criminal negligence is. Are these to be considered extraditable offenses? Some nations use different court procedures. Who defends the defendant (public defender or privately paid lawyer)? What is the role of the victim in the process; does the victim have the right to be heard and to actively participate? Who decides on the question of guilt and on the sentence? What types of sanctions can be imposed?

Comparing Court Systems

Making meaningful comparisons is probably easiest within legal traditions and geographical/cultural units. For example, it is much easier to compare court systems in Denmark and Sweden than, say, Denmark and Nigeria. Extending the parameters of the comparison to take into account legal tradition, comparing the United States and Great Britain would be easier than comparing the United States and Saudi Arabia. However, comparisons can be dicey even within geographical regions, especially if one compares the court system of Islamic Saudi Arabia with other Arabic countries.

Virtually every court system has a lower judicial agency, sometimes staffed by laypersons, that doles out justice in minor cases. Some countries do not offer an appeals process (Shariah courts in Saudi Arabia). For example, in Western nations, appeals courts ensure that the trial at the lower level was fair and according to law and guard against the possibility of disparate interpretations of law at lower court levels. In comparison, the Islamic societies, such as Saudi Arabia and Iran, that rely on Koranic principles do not use appeals courts (although modern Islamic justice does).

There can be major differences in judicial procedures even when comparing within similar legal traditions. For example, the voir dire process in the United States by which jury members are questioned by defense and prosecution does not exist in England. In addition, a unanimous verdict is not necessary for conviction in the United Kingdom. If at least 10 of 12 jurors believe guilt beyond a reasonable doubt has been determined, the accused can be convicted.

Although there are great variations in court structure and procedures in world legal systems, there are more similarities than differences (Fairchild, 1993). According to Reichel (2002), the similarities in courts systems stem from a nearly universal court organization that includes "lowest-level, mid-level, and highest-level courts" (Reichel, 2002, p. 216).

Differences usually hinge on the legal systems in operation, whether influenced by common law or civil law, Islamic law or socialist law. There is no consensus by comparative legal scholars on the number of legal systems that exist today. What is a legal system? One definition suggests that a legal system "refers to attitudes, values and norms regarding the nature and role of law, including rules and practices for processing and functioning" (Mukherjee & Reichel, 1999, p. 65). Whatever the definition, there is little argument that legal traditions are based on historical traditions deeply ingrained in cultures.

CORRECTIONS

In early June 2003, a Cuban dissident's wife smuggled out her husband's diary, offering a rare firsthand glimpse into a Cuban prison. According to Manuel Vazquez Portal, he lived in a 5-foot by 10-foot cell. His cell was bordered with a barred door partially covered by a steel plate. With only bars on the windows to protect him, Portal was at the mercy of the "sun's rays, the rain, [and] the insects" (Rodriguez, 2003, p. 28A). A journalist and critic of the Castro regime, he was among 75 activists arrested during a crackdown on dissidents and was subsequently sentenced to 18 years.

At first glance, it is easy to make certain assumptions about Cuban corrections from reading Manuel Portal's diary. But it would be impossible to place Cuba into either the socialist or Caribbean island models of corrections. An examination of these diverse systems reveals major differences between prisons, even in the same geographical region, leading one to surmise that there is an almost inexhaustible variety of correctional models. Even the former colonies of Europe (many British) that have made the transition to independence have taken divergent paths into the new century. Some have thrived economically, whereas others have lagged behind, plagued by economic hardship.

Reaching back in time, cultures have used banishment, exile, and more draconian modes of punishment prior to the advent of the penitentiary. Since the inauguration of the penitentiary in the 18th century, a number of alternatives to imprisonment have evolved. But most countries cling to the traditional methods of imprisonment, leading in many cases to the warehousing of prisoners.

The history of corrections is also a history of experimentation. But few methods of punishment have surpassed the almost universal popularity of incarceration. For hundreds of years, prisoners have been incarcerated in dungeons, on fetid prison hulks, in gulags and concentration camps, at boot camps, on deserted islands, and most recently, in penitentiaries. Although involuntary confinement is the most familiar characteristic of corrections, countries around the world have made increasing inroads on finding alternatives to the warehousing of inmates.

According to the fifth U.N. Survey of Crime Trends and Operations of Criminal Justice Systems, the main categories of official punishment in use today include life imprisonment, corporal punishment, deprivation of liberty (incarceration), control in freedom (probation), warnings or admonition, fines, and community service orders.

In the majority of countries, most serious crimes are punished with prison sentences regardless of legal system or level of development. However, within the global community, there are wide variations in the imprisonment rates of nations, with many measuring enormous differences.

Prison incarceration rates vary widely around the world (see International Centre for Prison Studies, 2004), with imprisonment rates highest in the United States (715 per 100,000) and Russia (584), and lowest in such countries as India (29), Iceland (40), and Japan (54).

By the late 1990s, the United States was imprisoning almost 5 times as many people as it did in 1970 (150 per 100,000) (Pastore & Maguire, 2000). One thing that confounds many international penologists is the American resistance to alternatives to incarceration. One strategy used by criminologists to study comparative corrections is to use the United States as a "frame of reference" due to its position as one of the most extreme examples of correctional policy (Frase, 2001). However, the United States has not been alone in resorting to unprecedented imprisonment rates. More draconian sentencing has been a major factor in causing imprisonment rates to soar around the world in the first years of the 21st century. The number of prisoners has increased in Holland, England, Italy, Portugal, France, Germany, and Australia (Tonry, 2001a).

For much of the modern era, it was fashionable to argue that America surpassed its European counterparts in its emphasis on due process. But recent evidence suggests this is no longer true. A number of academics have cited the influence of the European Human Rights Convention on the inquisitorial processes of Western Europe. On the other hand, in the 1970s and 1980s, the United States placed increased emphasis on mandatory sentencing policies over due process values. Tonry (2001a) suggests that "the United States is a country committed more to crime control and less to due process values in 2001 than any Western European or other major English-speaking country" (p. 5), citing areas such as capital punishment, incarceration, defendants' procedural protections, and acceptance of international human rights standards.

In recent years, more countries have reported increases rather than decreases in prison admissions and populations. A number of countries report that prison populations exceed capacity. Developing countries tend to have more prisoners awaiting trial than do developed countries (one reason for disagreement over international cooperation). Noncustodial sanctions are used less in the regions of Africa, Latin America, and Asia. But it should be noted that many developing nations use noncustodial sanctions without reporting this in official statistics. In developing countries and countries in transition, the public prefers prison as a mode of punishment for more serious crimes (Shinkai & Zvekic, 1999, p. 120).

Comparing Correctional Systems

Compared with the United States, which has the most punitive crime policies in the Western world, Scandinavian countries have the lowest percentage of incarcerated offenders in the world. Denmark is a nation with low rates of interpersonal victimization and interpersonal violence; most crimes are property crimes. Prison policies supported by the government are very liberal. Imprisonment is more humane and lenient, featuring short prison sentences. Most prisoners are sentenced to "open" prisons, with the tacit understanding that they will be transferred to closed prisons for rule violations. However, pretrial detention is very restrictive, favoring a lengthy pretrial detention, with total isolation of the defendant to keep evidence "pure" (Umbreit, 1980, 27).

Danes apparently place more value on education and rehabilitative treatment instead of emphasizing punishment. According to Henriques (1996), "Ordinary imprisonment and lenient imprisonment are the most common incarcerative sanctions used in Denmark" (p. 59).

However, what probably helps best explain the Danish affinity for civility is the fact that Denmark has a high standard of living with a small and rather homogeneous population. These societal features are becoming increasingly rare in the world today. One archetype of prison popular in Scandinavian nations "is a full wage prison—a 'factory with a fence'" (Morris & Rothman, 1998, p. xi) according to an American Supreme Court Justice who favors this policy. In this way, the prisoner can earn almost as much as in the free world, allowing the inmate to pay a number of expenses, including board and food; compensate crime victims; support dependents; and save for his or her release.

In Brazil, there are almost 5,000 penal institutions (Henriques, 1996, p. 62). In stark contrast to Danish prisons, most Brazilian institutions are plagued by extensive overcrowding, leading to frequent citations by human rights monitors. Prison riots, brutality, poor sanitation and medical care, and murder are common. Women's prisons, on the other hand, are operated by religious orders and are not called prisons. Here, small children are allowed to live with their mothers, and conjugal visits are permitted.

Although many former colonies of England have adopted similar methods of incarceration, "The prison system is alien to African nations, and contrary to Africans' traditional beliefs in reintegration" (Ebbe, 1996, p. 65). However, within Africa itself, prisons run the gamut from overcrowding to being almost nonexistent. In former British West Africa, prisons are more punitive and retributive, lacking treatment and counseling facilities, resulting in high recidivism rates. There is little institutional support for prison reform.

In Sierra Leone, another former British colony in West Africa, rehabilitation is emphasized through vocational training opportunities, while at the same time focusing on restorative justice in sentencing practices. Inmates must either work or learn basic skills and attain a modicum of literacy; also, they are taught trades such as carpentry, tailoring, and shoemaking.

Japan has one of the lowest incarceration rates among industrialized countries. During the past 40 years, it has not experienced overcrowding. With low crime rates, few offenders are imprisoned, demonstrating less reliance on this method than other industrialized nations, opting instead in favor of financial compensation and suspended sentences. Most offenders are "either diverted from the criminal justice system or placed under treatment in the community" (Hamai, 2001, p. 201). Prison sentences are short term, averaging less than 20 months. Many factors limit incarceration as a penalty in Japan, including decisions of public prosecutors and sentencing judges. The fact that more than 90% of defendants plead guilty allows judges more sentencing discretion. According to 1996 prison surveys, "more than 80% of prisoners thought they had gained something positive from their imprisonment" (Hamai, 2001, p. 205), demonstrating that the Japanese prison system has the confidence of the public and inmates.

Human Rights and Prisons

How does the researcher come up with a viable objective method of evaluating human rights practices in world prison systems? Which rights are fundamental human rights? Should prisons at least reflect the living conditions of countries where they are located? Can prisons in underdeveloped countries such as Nepal and Guinea be expected to maintain standards equivalent to more prosperous nations? Or is it fair that prisoners should face conditions not much different from free citizens (Wright & Cingranelli, 1985)?

The end of World War II was followed by a shift in attitudes concerning human rights. Nowhere was this more apparent than in the world's prison systems, particularly after the war revealed the extent of the abuses in the concentration camps (Neier, 1998). The adoption of the U.N. Charter in 1945 committed the organization to promote "universal respect for, and observance of, human rights," committing the member states to pursue the mutual goal promoting human rights. Since the adoption of the Universal Declaration of Human Rights in 1948, the first global instrument to define and protect fundamental human rights, there has been no lack of human rights instruments promulgated under the aegis of the United Nations.

Human rights, particularly in corrections, did not become a focus for major public attention until the last years of the 1970s as the Chinese Cultural revolution came to a close. According to one explanation, during the Cold War era, the human rights cause was exploited on a partisan level by superpowers to denounce the practices of their adversaries behind the Iron Curtain. According to Neier (1998), most international human rights campaigns originated and enjoyed the greatest support in the United States and Western Europe.

Until relatively recent times, countries such as China and Indonesia were too remote and unfamiliar to the West for much attention to be paid to human rights and possible violation of those rights. With few Indonesian exiles in the West to arouse interest in their plight, little attention was directed to the faraway archipelago. China, too, was far away, "with a language difficult if not unpronounceable to Westerners" (Neier, 1998, p. 371). But following its opening in the 1970s, rather than concentrating on human rights abuses in Chinese prisons, the West became infatuated with all things Chinese.

In the 1980s, Turkey was targeted for confining substantial numbers of political prisoners. But this was a partial success story; although it bowed to pressure from a number of directions, not least of all from the Council of Europe, Turkey made strides to reduce political imprisonment rates by the end of the

1980s. However, the 1990s saw a recrudescence in political imprisonment in Turkey. Regardless, the drop in political imprisonment demonstrated the impact a concerted regional effort can have on the direction taken by the criminal justice apparatus.

But political imprisonment is not always hampered by international pressure. One needs look no farther than Myanmar. In 1962, General Ne Win seized control of what was then Burma. Despite receiving the Nobel Peace Prize in 1991, the nation's best-known dissenter, Aung San Suu Kyi, has been held under house arrest as the military state's opposition to dissent continues unabated. However, Myanmar has recently had a change in heart, announcing that Suu Kyi will be freed from house arrest sometime before May 17, 2004, and her National League for Democracy party will be allowed to attend a constitutional convention.

Following the adoption of various landmark agreements to respect human rights, many countries have practiced mass political imprisonment—a partial list includes the following: Africa—Ethiopia, Sudan, Uganda, Guinea, Zaire, and South Africa; Asia—China, Indonesia, India, Afghanistan, Burma, Cambodia, and Vietnam; Middle East—Iraq, Syria, Iran, Israel, Egypt, and Morocco; Latin America—Argentina, Chile, Uruguay, Brazil, Haiti, and Cuba; Europe—Soviet Union, Poland, Turkey, Greece, and Yugoslavia (Neier, 1998, p. 368). Political criminals continue to thrive in the human rights era, often due to the economic, military, and political relationships between countries.

The European Court of Human Rights has examined most dimensions of issues revolving around sentencing and punishments. The court has weighed in on which offenses should be criminalized by national laws, what may not be criminalized, and what forms of punishment are prohibited. The European Court enumerates penalties for criminal offenses that should be charged, including marital rape and any corporal punishment of children that leaves visible bruises, swelling, or mark.

Today, in more advanced nations, there is little productive work for prisoners. One factor has been the opposition of organized labor and organized business to competing with prison labor.

Correctional Standards

The European Court of Human Rights is faced with another challenge to implementation of any correctional standards. A number of questions arise whenever two or more nations cooperate in the criminal justice process. Who decides if a suspect should be taken into custody and then kept in custody? Under what circumstances should a suspect be held or released, and should that decision be made by the police, a prosecutor, or a judge?

Almost all nations have problems with prison overcrowding. Some governments have adopted programs to expand capacity by building new prisons or adapting other institutions for correctional use. Constructing new prisons is a costly endeavor.

Many governments have scarce resources, making prison construction a lower priority than transportation, education, health care, and other concerns.

The United States has experienced what has been referred to as an "incarceration binge." As far back as the 1980s, American courts incarcerated 10 times more people than did Holland, 4 times more than Australia, and 3 times more than the United Kingdom, West Germany, and France (Braithwaite, 1988, pp. 54–55). At the beginning of the 21st century, the United States continues to imprison its citizens at a higher rate than does any other country in the world.

Searching for Alternatives

Imprisonment has long been justified as the cornerstone in a punishment system that desires retribution, deterrence, rehabilitation, or incapacitation. Western nations have employed similar responses to the crime problem since the 18th century. Most of these responses are rooted in a "widespread commitment to democratic values and Enlightenment ideals" (Tonry, 2001b, p. 3). Most recently, Richard S. Frase (2001) has suggested that "despite differences in language, laws, culture, and traditions, there is a substantial degree of similarity in the sentencing purposes, procedures, and alternatives currently employed in Western countries" (p. 261).

One alternative gaining increasing currency around the world today is a movement toward restorative justice, an attempt to make the victim and the community "whole again" by restoring things to the way they were before the crime was committed. In comparison, traditional noncustodial alternatives have usually included fines, conditional or suspended sentences, probation, and work release. The most popular basic sanctions used to keep first-time prisoners out of prison have been probation and other forms of community supervision. However, when crime increases, the public criticizes the system as being too lenient. Hence, community-based programs are seen as therapeutic, not punitive.

The disparity of prevailing beliefs among policymakers about the causes of crime helps explain the variance in correctional practice and theory across the map. For example, in the United States, England, and parts of Australia, policymakers suggest that crime is the result of personal decisions made by individual criminals. Eschewing for the most part other explanations (such as inadequate socialization and criminogenic conditions), it has become popular to turn to incapacitation and more restrictive punishment to suppress criminal activity (Tonry, 2001b).

Challenges to International Cooperation

One of the biggest barriers to international cooperation in the sphere of criminal justice is the variation of treatment in corrections systems. One of the biggest impediments is the poor conditions found in prisons and other correctional institutions around the world. Although a number of agencies are lobbying on behalf of corrections reform, they have little power to change conditions, outside of publicizing reports so that governments can make decisions as to cooperating with nations that fail to recognize certain human rights. Among these groups is the Human Rights Watch Project, which issues periodic reports on prison conditions around the world.

Chief among the findings presented by Human Rights Watch (1993) is that "the conditions of pretrial detention are much worse than those of long-term incarceration" (p. xxi). This is often the result of interrogation tactics and physical intimidation used by authorities when prisoners are in predetainment and a case is still under investigation.

Overcrowding and inadequate physical conditions are not confined to underdeveloped nations—conditions often characterized by inadequate clothing, cell furnishings, plumbing, and light and by extremes of heat and cold. Although conditions have been updated and improved, as late as 1991, Human Rights Watch reported that almost 40% of British cells lacked plumbing, resulting in conditions similar to Egypt and Jamaica, where buckets served as the main toilet facilities.

The disparity in prison conditions around the world continues to be a major barrier to the adjudication of cases that result in the imprisonment of foreign nationals in facilities that are considered inhumane. Of course, the entertainment and news media have not helped in ameliorating the prejudice that exists between the West and other cultures. One only needs to watch the 1970s depiction of Turkish prisons in the movie *Midnight Express*.

The United Nations and other international organizations have few sanctions or rewards at their disposal to ensure human rights. Developed countries such as the United States have taken the lead by attaching certain conditions to financial assistance. During the past decade, the United States has enacted several public laws that make foreign assistance available only on evidence of improving human rights practices. This can result in the United States withdrawing military and economic assistance or voting against loans from multilateral agencies.

CONCLUSION

Suppressing transnational crime is the greatest challenge to modern law enforcement. Richer countries need to assist developing countries with technology and training. Transnational crime appears in many guises—drugs, weapons, and human trafficking; motor vehicle theft; money laundering; cybercrime; and terrorism. Criminals play by no rules. But the criminal justice systems of the world must follow a set of rules designed to protect the due process rights of citizens of each country. Unfortunately, the rule of law can also protect international criminals and syndicates by limiting the cooperation between criminal justice systems.

Today, a number of terrorist groups operate under the disguise of religious activism. Millions of individuals around the world may subscribe to beliefs similar to those held by such terrorists. This may hamper the crime enforcement strategies of nations that are less ideologically organized.

A number of regional initiatives have been taken within the framework of various international organizations. Internationally coordinated laws and strategic law enforcement cooperation are more important than ever. To maintain peace and order on a transnational level, the various arms of the criminal justice system must be willing to adopt new strategies.

International cooperation is hindered on a variety of levels. Most important, nations have to respect the cultural and political sovereignty of all nations. A major obstacle to international cooperation "derives from the defense of political sovereignty which is very much identified with independent national systems of criminal law and procedure" (Nelken, 1994, p. 221).

Joint efforts such as multinational police investigations and task forces to fight drug smuggling and terrorism have become a reality only after government officials are aware of the complexities of other societies. To do this, policymakers must be aware that there will always be cultural variation in the definition of punishment, manifested in cultural variation in the degree of seriousness, "measured by severity of punishment" (Beirne, 1983). Assumptions that punishment should be the same across cultures can destroy any attempt at cooperation. For example, in Japan, suicide is accepted as an honorable choice following military defeat, whereas in contemporary cultures, the ramifications of suicide are considered criminal.

Whether it is the oil company executive arrested for drinking whiskey in Saudi Arabia or the foreign sex worker accused of prostitution, the question usually arises as to which system the individual belongs to and whether ignorance can be an excuse before the law. As countries make the transition from one legal system to another or decide under which system to choose punishment, this issue becomes even more complex when foreign nationals are caught up in the intricacies of alien criminal justice cultures.

The Council of Europe and the United Nations may have passed standard guidelines for the use of the death penalty, treatment of prisoners, noncustodial community sanctions, sentencing laws and structures, protection of juveniles, and so forth, but without binding treaties and with lack of law enforcement, there is little bite in the bark of these agreements. What member states can do is to refuse to extradite offenders unless the receiving state guarantees that certain sanctions, including the death penalty (recently, Cuba promised not to execute hijackers extradited back by the United States), will not be imposed.

REFERENCES

Bayley, D. H. (1985). *Patterns of policing: A comparative international analysis.* New Brunswick, NJ: Rutgers University Press.

Beirne, P. (1983). Cultural relativism and comparative criminology. *Contemporary Crises, 7,* 371–391.

Braithwaite, J. (1988). The future of prisons: A Canadian view. In D. Biles (Ed.), *Current international trends in corrections: Selected papers from the Australian Bicentennial International Congress on Corrective Services* (pp. 51–61). Sydney, Australia: Federation Press.

Bruce, D. J. M. (1998). Regional approaches to international police cooperation: The role and achievements of the South African Regional Police Chiefs Co-Operation Organization. In *Interpol: 75 Years of Police Co-Operation* (pp. 52–55). Kensington, UK: Kensington.

Chang, D. H. (1976). *Criminology: A cross-cultural perspective* (2 Vols.). Durham, NC: Carolina Academic Press.

Ebbe, O. (Ed.). (1996). *Comparative and international criminal justice systems: Policing, judiciary and corrections.* Boston: Butterworth- Heinemann.

Fairchild, E. (1993). *Comparative criminal justice systems.* Belmont, CA: Wadsworth.

Fairchild, E., & Dammer, H. (2001). *Comparative criminal justice systems* (2nd ed). Belmont, CA: Wadsworth.

Fooner, M. (1989). *Interpol: Issues in world crime and international criminal justice.* New York: Plenum.

Frase, R. S. (2001). Comparative perspectives on sentencing policy and research. In M. Tonry & R. S. Frase (Eds.), *Sentencing and sanctions in Western countries* (pp. 259–292). New York: Oxford University Press.

Hamai, K. (2001). Prison population in Japan stable for 30 years. In M. Tonry (Ed.), *Penal reform in overcrowded times* (pp. 197–205). New York: Oxford University Press.

Henriques, Z. (1996). Treatment of offenders in Denmark and Brazil. In O. Ebbe (Ed.), *Comparative and international criminal justice systems* (pp. 57–63). Boston: Butterworth-Heinemann.

Holscher, L. M., & Mahmood, R. (2000). Borrowing from the Shariah: The potential uses of procedural Islamic law in the West. In D. Rounds (Ed.), *International criminal justice* (pp. 82–96). Boston: Allyn & Bacon.

Human Rights Watch global report on prisons. (1993). New York: Human Rights Watch.

International Centre for Prison Studies. (2004, January). *World prison brief.* Retrieved June 25, 2004, from http://www.kcl.ac.uk/depsta/rel/icps/worldbrief/world_brief.html

Kurki, L. (2001). International standards for sentencing and punishment. In M. Tonry & R. S. Frase (Eds.), *Sentencing and sanctions in Western countries* (pp. 331–378). New York: Oxford University Press.

Lippman, M., McConville, S., & Yerushalmi, M. (1988). *Islamic criminal justice procedures.* New York: Praeger.

Mawby, R. I. (1999). *Policing across the world: Issues for the twenty-first century.* London: UCL Press.

Miller, M. V. (1987). Vehicle theft along the Texas-Mexico border. *Journal of Borderlands Studies, 2*(2), 12–32.

Morris, N., & Rothman, D. J. (Eds.). (1998). *The Oxford history of the prison: The practice of punishment in Western society.* New York: Oxford University Press.

Mukherjee, S., & Reichel, P. L. (1999). Bringing to justice. In G. R. Newman (Ed.), *Global report on crime and justice* (pp. 65–88). New York: Oxford University Press.

Neier, A. (1998). Confining dissent: The political prison. In N. Morris & D. Rothman (Eds.), *The Oxford history of the prison* (pp. 350–380). New York: Oxford University Press.

Nelken, D. (1994). Whom can you trust? The future of comparative criminology. In D. Nelken (Ed.), *The futures of criminology* (pp. 220–243). London: Sage.

Newman, G. (1976). *Comparative deviance: Perception and law in six cultures.* New York: Elsevier Scientific.

Newman, G. (Ed.). (1999). *Global report on crime and justice.* New York: Oxford University Press.

Pastore, A., & Maguire, K. (2000). *Sourcebook of criminal justice statistics 2000.* Washington, DC: U.S. Department of Justice.

Pontell, H. N., & Frid, A. (2000). International financial fraud: Emerging trends and issues. In D. Rounds (Ed.), *International criminal justice* (pp. 32–47). Boston: Allyn & Bacon.

Reichel, P. L. (2002). *Comparative criminal justice systems: A topical approach* (3rd ed.). Upper Saddle River, NJ: Prentice Hall.

Resendiz, R., & Neal, D. M. (2000). International auto theft: The illegal export of American vehicles to Mexico. In D. Rounds (Ed.), *International criminal justice* (pp. 7–18). Boston: Allyn & Bacon.

Rodriguez, A. (2003, June 6). Dissident's secret diary details life in Cuban prison. *Houston Chronicle*, p. 28A.

Shinkai, H., & Zvekic, U. (1999). Punishment. In G. Newman (Ed.), *Global report on crime and justice* (pp. 89–120). New York: Oxford University Press.

Souryal, S., Potts, D. W., & Alobied, I. (1994). The penalty of hand amputation for theft in Islamic justice. *Journal of Criminal Justice, 22*(3), 249–265.

Tonry, M. (Ed). (2001a). *Penal reform in overcrowded times*. New York: Oxford University Press.

Tonry, M. (2001b). Punishment policies and patterns in Western countries. In M. Tonry & R. S. Frase (Eds.), *Sentencing and sanctions in Western countries* (pp. 3–28). New York: Oxford University Press.

Umbreit, M. (1980). Danish use of prisons and community alternatives. *Federal Probation, 44*(2), 24–28.

Wright, K. N., & Cingranelli, D. L. (1985). Inhumane, cruel, and degrading treatment of criminal prisoners throughout the world. *Justice Quarterly, 2*(3), 345–362.

13

International Instruments on Cooperation in Responding to Transnational Crime

MATTI JOUTSEN

International instruments provide the rules needed for effective international cooperation. This chapter examines (a) the concept of international instruments and how they supplant less formal forms of international cooperation and (b) how international instruments have evolved. The chapter also examines the main form of cooperation under these international instruments—(c) extradition, (d) mutual legal assistance, (e) the transfer of proceedings, (f) recognition of judgments, and (g) the transfer of prisoners. The final section summarizes the development of international instruments.

THE CONCEPT OF INTERNATIONAL INSTRUMENTS

International instruments (treaties) are the cornerstone of international law and of international criminal justice. They can be defined as formally signed and ratified international agreements between two or more states or other international entities.

International instruments may deal with substantive or procedural issues. In criminal law instruments, the substantive provisions almost invariably deal with the definition of certain crimes. The procedural provisions may deal with the exercise of jurisdiction—in other words, with which state has the right or duty to place offenders on trial. The procedural provisions may also deal with the right or duty of signatory states to extradite suspected or convicted offenders to another state for trial or with what mutual legal assistance[1] (such as the hearing of witnesses or the service of summons) may or should be extended among the signatories. More rarely, international instruments may deal with issues such as the transfer of proceedings, the recognition of foreign judgments, cooperation in enforcement, and the transfer of convicted persons. Increasingly, international criminal law instruments also contain provisions that seek to protect certain fundamental human rights.

The earliest international instruments were *bilateral*; in other words, they were signed between two states. The advantage of bilateral agreements is that they can be tailored to the specific needs of the states in question and can be expanded, amended, or (if necessary) terminated relatively easily. They are adaptable to the specific interests of the two states, which is a particular concern if differences between legal systems must be overcome. On the down side, they are very resource-intensive to negotiate, especially for smaller or developing states that cannot afford an extensive international negotiating program.

Multilateral agreements (conventions) have several signatories. They are more difficult than bilateral agreements to draft, amend, and terminate. The implementation of some multilateral agreements may require a permanent infrastructure (e.g., a secretariat), which requires, in turn, the investment of additional resources. At the same time, however, multilateral agreements provide a greater degree of stability to international cooperation. The parties to multilateral conventions are signaling their intention to establish lasting rules and institutions based on mutual solidarity and shared responsibilities. Moreover, accession to a multilateral agreement relieves the state in question of the need to enter into a number of different bilateral agreements, each of which may require different procedures. Finally, the extension of the geographical scope of multilateral agreements on cooperation in crime prevention and criminal justice lessens the possibility that offenders can evade justice by operating in or from, or escaping to, states that are not parties to such agreements.

At present there are no truly *universal* criminal law instruments, global conventions that have been ratified by every state around the world. It is unlikely that such instruments will ever be developed, due largely to the differences in legal systems and in political priorities. The heated discussions, for example, on terrorism have illustrated a third difficulty in drafting universal instruments—differences in the definition of the issue that is being addressed.

International instruments are binding on the signatory states and are subject to international law. In some rare cases, widely ratified international instruments that define certain crimes may contribute to the evolution of customary international law, as defined by Article 38 of the Statute of the International Court of Justice. Once the definition of a crime becomes part of such customary international law, it is binding on all states (thus, at the same time, eliminating much of the need for developing universal instruments on such crimes). Even persons from states that have not signed any of the relevant international instruments may be convicted by the courts of any other state that claims jurisdiction or by an international tribunal that exercises jurisdiction. Although there are different views on which international crimes have moved from the status of being based (solely) on international agreements to becoming part of customary international law, the prevailing view is that this is the case at least with war crimes, crimes against peace, crimes against humanity, genocide, piracy, slavery, and torture.

One offense conspicuously absent from the list of international crimes is terrorism. No single definition of terrorism has yet gained universal acceptance, although a number of conventions have entered into force on specific features of terrorism.

International cooperation need not be based on formal agreements between states. Domestic law may allow the authorities to engage in various forms of cooperation. Moreover, where the authorities of two states have worked in close contact with one another (e.g., because of extradition cases, requests for mutual assistance, or general concerns about transnational crime), they generally build up a relationship of trust. This often leads to *less formal* forms of bilateral cooperation between the central authorities (such as officials at departments or ministries of justice or of the interior) or, for example, between the local authorities on both sides of the border (in particular, police and customs authorities). Such forms of cooperation may in time be guided by bilateral executive agreements between the agencies involved.

Examples of less formal multilateral arrangements among states for cooperation in criminal law issues include the cooperation carried out within the framework of the Commonwealth, the French-speaking states, the Economic Community of West African States, the Council of Europe, the Nordic Council, the African Union (formerly the Organization of African Unity), the Southern African states, the Organization of American States, and the Mercosur structure (Argentina, Brazil, Paraguay, and Uruguay). Such arrangements, for example, provide the participating states with a framework for aligning their policy on topical issues, agreeing on matters such as technical assistance and the exchange of personnel, and where necessary, agreeing on the drafting of formal international instruments. The close and effective cooperation overseen by the International Criminal Police Association (Interpol) is not based on any international instrument; instead, the criminal police of each participating state have simply decided to cooperate with one another within the framework of Interpol.

The European Union provides a unique framework for rapidly deepening cooperation among its member states. This cooperation ranges from networking among officials and the funding of joint projects to the drafting of so-called framework decisions that directly affect the domestic legislative process all the way to the mutual recognition of decisions and judgments and the establishment of formal bodies that have a mandate to act on behalf of all the member states. For example, Europol serves as a body for cooperation among the police forces of the European Union and is taking on increasing duties in, for example, the analysis of crime data and the provision of technical expertise to national police forces.

Over the years, several multilateral treaties have been drafted that deal with international cooperation. In addition, many states have entered into bilateral treaties with other states. As a result, two or more treaties may be applicable to the same facts. Because there are almost inevitably differences between these treaties (e.g., in relation to the conditions under which cooperation may or should be provided or the procedure used), the question arises of which treaty should be applied.

General conflicts between treaties can be decided on the basis of the 1969 Vienna Convention on the Law of Treaties. Among the principles applied are that, other things being equal, a later treaty replaces an earlier one, and a treaty dealing with a specific issue replaces a treaty dealing only with general issues.

In addition, some new treaties contain specific provisions on the resolution of possible conflicts between treaties. For example, Article 18(6) of the U.N. Convention against Transnational Organized Crime (known as the Palermo Convention) provides that "the provisions of this article shall not affect the obligations under any other treaty, bilateral or multilateral, that governs or will govern, in whole or in part, mutual legal assistance." This provision means in practice that obligations under other agreements remain in force. The practitioner should examine the agreements side by side and identify which provisions of the different agreements would, in combination, result in the highest possible level of cooperation.

THE EVOLUTION OF INTERNATIONAL INSTRUMENTS

As long as crime was regarded as (and, in most respects, actually was) a local or, at most, a national issue, criminal law remained almost wholly territorial, concerned only with acts or omissions committed in the territory of the forum state. This was the approach taken in particular by the common law states: Offenses committed abroad were not their concern, and their authorities tended to be unwilling to assist the authorities of another state in bringing offenders to justice.

Where formal cooperation in criminal cases is impossible, informal cooperation may arise. Such informal cooperation began to emerge in *law enforcement* during the 1700s and early 1800s, when the major international law enforcement concerns were related to piracy, the slave trade, smuggling, and cross-border forays by bandits. At that time, the tendency was for states to take unilateral action to make arrests and bring the offenders to justice. This could take the form of blatant incursions into foreign territory (with or without the support of law enforcement colleagues on the other side of the border). Examples were seizures of suspected pirate or slave trade ships even when they lay in the territorial waters of a foreign state or the posses that rode across the Rio Grande from the United States to Mexico in pursuit of bank robbers or cattle rustlers.

Such informal and unilateral actions—colorful as they may be—were an unsatisfactory response to a growing problem. Unilateral action can create unnecessary tensions between nations. Under international law, states may not intervene in the domestic affairs of other states. In particular,

> A party has no right to undertake law enforcement action in the territory of another party without the prior consent of that party. The principle of non-intervention excludes all kinds of territorial encroachment, including temporary or limited operations (so-called "in-and-out operations"). It also prohibits the exertion of pressure in a manner inconsistent with international law in order to obtain from a party the subordination of the exercise of its sovereign rights.[2]

Judicial cooperation in criminal matters was slower to emerge than was cooperation in law enforcement. A few bilateral instruments were developed during the late 1800s. Two early efforts to develop a multilateral instrument, the 1928 draft developed within the framework of the League of Nations and the 1939 Harvard Draft Convention, never entered into force (McClean, 1992, p. 125). In respect to extradition, the first multilateral instrument did not emerge until 1933. This was the Convention on Extradition prepared within the framework of the Organization of American States.[3] In respect of mutual assistance in criminal matters, even more years had to pass until a multilateral instrument entered into force: the 1959 Convention on Mutual Assistance in Criminal Matters, prepared within the framework of the Council of Europe.

On substantive issues, the first international instruments tended to deal with the definition of drug offences. The International Opium Convention was completed in 1912, and a second convention on this subject appeared in 1925. This was followed, in 1931, by the Convention for Limiting the Manufacture and Regulating the Distribution of Narcotic Drugs,[4] and in 1953 by the Protocol Limiting and Regulating the Cultivation of the Poppy Plant, the Production of, International and Wholesale Trade in, and Use of Opium.

Bringing these multilateral treaties up to the present, the 1961 Single Convention established new mechanisms and obligations. It assigned certain functions to the Commission on Narcotic Drugs and to an International Narcotics Control Board. It also required states to provide annual estimates of drugs used for various purposes; to abide by restrictions on manufacture, production, and import; and to criminalize the possession, supply, and transport of drugs and make them extraditable offences.

The main drug treaty today is the U.N. Convention against Illicit Traffic in Narcotic Drugs and Psychotropic Substances of 1988, which entered into force in 1990. The 1988 Convention calls for criminalization of a range of criminal offenses, including the organization, management, or financing of drug offenses and the laundering of the proceeds of drug offences (Article 3). According to Article 6, the offenses criminalized by the 1988 Convention are by definition extraditable offenses, and the convention itself can be regarded as providing the necessary legal basis for extradition and mutual assistance. Article 5 contains provisions on confiscation, Article 7 on mutual assistance,[5] Article 8 on the transfer of proceedings, and Article 11 on controlled delivery.

Aside from the topic of drugs, before the Palermo Convention was opened for signature at the end of 2000, there were almost no multilateral treaties that would have defined an offense.[6] During the 1970s, in response to a rash of skyjacking and other hostage taking, treaties were signed on this topic.[7] In 1980, a convention was completed on the physical protection of nuclear material; 10 years later the Council of Europe completed the Convention on Laundering, Search, Seizure and Confiscation of the Proceeds From Crime, and in 1996 the Inter-American Convention against Corruption was completed. As the following examples show, it has taken a long time for the world to realize the need for agreeing on the rules for international cooperation in responding to crime.

EXTRADITION

The Concept of Extradition

Extradition is the process by which a person charged with an offense is forcibly transferred to a state for trial, or a person convicted of an offense is forcibly returned for the enforcement of punishment (see, e.g., *Restatement of the law third*, 1990, pp. 556–557).

For a long time, no provisions or international treaties existed on the conditions for extradition or on the procedure that should be followed. Extradition was largely a matter of either courtesy or subservience, applied in the rare cases where not only did a case have international dimensions but also the requesting and the requested states were prepared to cooperate. In practice, extradition was rarely required, more rarely requested, and even more rarely still granted.

Bilateral extradition treaties did not begin to emerge until the 1800s. In particular the common law states have made wide use of bilateral treaties. The first multilateral convention on this topic was the Organization of American States Convention on Extradition in 1933.[8] It was followed 20 years later by the Arab Extradition Agreement in 1952 and then by the influential European Convention on Extradition in 1957 and the 1966 Commonwealth scheme for the rendition of fugitives.[9] The most recent multilateral treaties have been the 1995 European Union Convention on simplified extradition within the European Union and the 1996 European Union Convention on the substantive requirements for extradition within the European Union.

To promote new extradition treaties and to provide guidance in their drafting, the U.N. prepared a Model Treaty on Extradition (General Assembly Resolution 45/116 of December 14, 1990).

In addition to these general treaties on extradition, provisions on extradition have also been included in several international conventions that deal with specific subjects. Perhaps the best-known example is the 1988 U.N. Convention against Illicit Traffic in Narcotic Drugs and Psychotropic Substances, Article 6 of which deals with extradition. The extradition provisions in the Palermo Convention were largely drafted on the basis of this 1988 Convention.

The Conditions for Extradition

Among the common conditions included in international instruments dealing with extradition are the double criminality requirement (generally accompanied by the definition of the level of seriousness required of the offense before a state will extradite), a refusal to extradite nationals, and the political offense exception.

The principle of double criminality (dual criminality). The great majority of extradition treaties require that the offense in question be criminal in both the requesting and the requested state and, often, that it is subject to a certain minimum punishment, such as imprisonment for at least 1 year. Even where a state allows extradition in the absence of an extradition treaty, this principle of double criminality is generally applied.

The double criminality principle may cause legal and practical difficulties. Legal difficulties may arise if the requested state expects more or less similar wording of the provisions, which is often an unrealistic expectation, in particular if the two states represent different legal traditions. Practical difficulties may arise when the requesting state seeks to ascertain how the offense in question is defined in the requested state.

Double criminality can be assessed both in the abstract and in the concrete. In the abstract, what is required is that the offense is deemed to constitute a punishable offense in the requested state. In the concrete, the offense will be deemed extraditable only if the constituent elements of the offense in both states correspond with each other. The present tendency (as supported for example by Article 2(2)(a) of the U.N. Model Treaty on Extradition) is to favor the simpler approach, an assessment in the abstract.

In practice, it is possible that extradition is sought for several separate offenses, and some of these do not fulfill the conditions of double criminality. The general rule expressed in Article 2(2)(a) of the U.N. Model Treaty on Extradition and Article 2(2) of the Council of Europe Extradition Convention is that the offenses in question must be criminal in both states; however, the condition of the minimum punishment can be waived for part of the offenses. Thus, for example, if extradition is sought for a bank robbery as well as for several less serious offenses for which the minimum punishment would not otherwise meet the conditions for extradition, all of them can nonetheless be included in the request.

Recent trends in extradition have attempted to ease difficulties with double criminality by inserting general provisions into agreements, either listing acts and requiring only that they be punished as crimes or offenses by the laws of both states or simply allowing extradition for *any* conduct criminalized to a certain degree by each state (Blakesley & Lagodny, 1992, pp. 87–88).

The rule of speciality. The so-called rule of speciality stipulates that the requesting state may not, without the consent of the requested state, try or punish the suspect for an offense not referred to in the extradition request and committed before he or she was extradited.

This rule does not prevent an amendment of the charges, if the facts of the case warrant a reassessment of the charges. For example, even if a person has been extradited for fraud, he or she may be prosecuted for embezzlement as long as the facts of the case are the ones referred to in the request for extradition.

If, following extradition, the person in question is released in the territory of the requesting state, he or she may not be prosecuted for an offense that had been committed before the extradition took place until after he or she has had a reasonable opportunity to depart from this state.

The nonextradition of nationals. As a rule, states have long been willing to extradite nationals of the requesting state or nationals of a third state. When it comes to extraditing their own citizens, however, most states have traditionally been of the opinion that such extradition is not possible. Some states have even incorporated such a prohibition into their constitution. Furthermore, the principle of the nonextradition of nationals is often expressly provided for in international instruments. The rationale for such a view is a mixture of the obligation of a state to protect its citizens, a lack of confidence in the fairness of foreign legal proceedings, the many disadvantages that defendants face when defending themselves in a foreign legal system, and the many disadvantages of being in custody in a foreign state (Nadelmann, 1993, p. 427).

The United States, the United Kingdom, and most other common law states have been prepared to extradite their own nationals. This may have been due in part to the fact that these states have been less likely than, for example, civil law states to assert jurisdiction over offenses committed by their citizens abroad—and thus, failing extradition, the offender could not have been brought to justice at all. The common law states have also stressed the advantages of trying the suspect in the place where the offense was alleged to have been committed. There is, for example, the greater ease with which evidence and testimony can be obtained in the *forum delicti* and the difficulties in submitting evidence obtained in one state to the courts of another state.

In cases where the requested state does in fact refuse to extradite on the grounds that the fugitive is its own national, the state is generally seen to have an obligation to bring the person to trial. This is an illustration of the principle of *aut dedere aut judicare*—"extradite or prosecute," "extradite or adjudicate."[10]

The reluctance to extradite one's own nationals appears to be lessening in many states. The recent Palermo Convention incorporates a provision that reflects this development. According to Article 16(11),

> Whenever a State Party is permitted under its domestic law to extradite or otherwise surrender one of its nationals only upon the condition that the person will be returned to that State Party to serve the sentence imposed as a result of the trial or proceedings for which the extradition or surrender of the person was sought and that State Party and the State Party seeking the extradition of the person agree with this option and other terms that they may deem appropriate, such a conditional extradition or surrender shall be sufficient to discharge the obligation set forth in paragraph 10 of this article.

Thus, under the Palermo Convention a national can be extradited on condition that he or she be returned to serve out the possible sentence.

The political offense exception. During the 1700s and the early 1800s, extradition was used very much on an ad hoc basis primarily in the case of political revolutionaries who had sought refuge abroad (*Restatement of the law third*, 1990, p. 558). However, during the 1830s, the view developed in France and Belgium that suspects should not be extradited for politically motivated offenses (Nadelmann, 1993, p. 419).

There is no universally accepted definition of what constitutes a "political offense." In deciding whether an offense qualifies as political, reference is generally made to the motive and purpose of the offense, the circumstances in which it was committed, and the character of the offense as treason or sedition under domestic law. One of the leading cases internationally is *In re Castione* ([1891] 1 Q.B. 149), where the refusal to extradite the suspect was based on the view that alleged offenses that had been committed in the course of, or incident to, a revolution or uprising are political (cited in Nadelmann, 1993, p. 420).[11]

Recent developments suggest that attempts are being made to restrict its scope or even abolish it. The recent Palermo Convention does not make specific reference to political offenses as grounds for refusal, even though the U.N. Model Treaty on Extradition, adopted only 10 years earlier, had clearly included this as a *mandatory* ground for refusal. On the other hand, Article 16(7) of the Palermo Convention provides states parties with a built-in escape clause. It states that

> extradition shall be subject to the conditions provided for by the domestic law of the requested State Party or by applicable extradition treaties, including, *inter alia*, . . . the grounds upon which the requested State Party may refuse extradition.

Thus, if the domestic law of the requested state allows for the possibility of the political offense exception (as would almost inevitably be the case), this option remains, even if not specifically mentioned in the Palermo Convention.

One factor behind the restriction or abolition of the political offense exception is the growth of terrorism. A distinction is commonly made between "pure" political offenses (such as unlawful speech and assembly) and politically motivated violence (*Restatement of the law third, 1990*, p. 558). If the offense is serious—such as murder, political terrorism and genocide—courts in different states have (to varying degrees) tended not to apply the political offense exception. Examples include the extradition from the United States of several persons suspected of being Nazi war criminals or IRA terrorists (Nadelmann, 1993, pp. 421, 424). Violation of international conventions is one criterion in determining such seriousness; a case in point is the readiness of many states to extradite persons suspected of skyjacking.

The refusal to extradite on the grounds of the danger of persecution or unfair trial, or of the expected punishment. Originally, extradition treaties between states were seen to be just that, treaties between sovereign and equal states as parties. According to this approach, other parties, in particular the fugitive in question, had no standing to intervene in the process, nor was the nature of the proceedings or expected treatment in the requesting state a significant factor. Recently, however, the individual has also been increasingly regarded as a subject of international law. This has perhaps been most evident in extradition proceedings. Democratic states have been increasingly reluctant to extend full cooperation to states that do not share the same democratic values— for example, on the grounds that the political organization of the latter states is undemocratic or because their judicial system does not afford sufficient protection to the prosecuted or convicted individual (Gully-Hart, 1992, p. 249).

In line with this reassessment in the light of the strengthening of international human rights law, many of the more recently concluded treaties pay particular attention to the nature of the proceedings or the expected treatment in the requesting state. States will generally refuse to extradite if there are grounds to believe that the request has been made for the purpose of persecution of the person in question or that the person would not otherwise receive a fair trial (Gully-Hart, 1992, pp. 249–251, 257).

Refusal on the grounds of expected persecution is dealt with in, for example, Article 16(14) of the Palermo Convention:

> Nothing in this Convention shall be interpreted as imposing an obligation to extradite if the requested State Party has substantial grounds for believing that the request has been made for the purpose of prosecuting or punishing a person on account of that person's sex, race, religion, nationality, ethnic origin or political opinions or that compliance with the request would cause prejudice to that person's position for any one of these reasons.[12]

The question of fair trial and treatment is in principle distinct from the question of persecution. Article 3(f) of the U.N. Model Treaty on Extradition gives as a mandatory ground for refusal the possibility that the person in question would be subjected to torture or cruel, inhuman or degrading treatment or punishment, or the absence of the minimum guarantees in criminal proceedings, as contained in Article 14 of the International Covenant on Civil and Political Rights.[13]

The issue of fair trial and treatment is dealt with in Article 16(13) of the Palermo Convention:

> Any person regarding whom proceedings are being carried out in connection with any of the offences to which this article applies shall be guaranteed fair treatment at all stages of the proceedings, including enjoyment of all the rights and guarantees provided by the domestic law of the State Party in the territory of which that person is present.

This provision is a new one in U.N. conventions. No similar provisions are to be found in the 1988 Convention or in the U.N. Model Treaty on Extradition.

Perhaps the most notable and influential case concerning fair treatment is the transatlantic case of *Soering v. the United Kingdom* (European Court of Human Rights, 1/89/161/217). Soering had been charged with murder in Virginia, where murder was a capital offense. Following a request for extradition from the United States, he was arrested in the United Kingdom and his extradition was prepared. He appealed the extradition decision. Article 3 of the European Convention for the Protection of Human Rights and Fundamental Freedoms prohibits torture or inhuman and degrading treatment or punishment. The European Court of Human Rights unanimously found that extradition would be a violation of this, since circumstances on death row—6 to 8 years of isolation, stress, fruitless appeals, separation from family, and other damaging experiences—would be inhuman and degrading. (The follow-up to this case is that Soering was extradited, after the attorney general had promised not to seek the death penalty.)

Following the adoption in 1983 of Protocol No. 6 to the European Convention for the Protection of Human Rights and Fundamental Freedoms, which abolished the death penalty, European states have been reluctant to extradite suspects to states where the death penalty might be imposed.[14] One common resolution to this difficulty is that, as in the *Soering* case, the requesting state agrees to waive the death penalty or, if this is imposed by the court, the requesting state agrees to ensure that it is not enforced. Another option is to agree that the suspect, if convicted, will be returned to the requested state for enforcement of the sentence (and where capital punishment would be commuted to long-term imprisonment).

Other grounds for refusal to extradite. One of the fundamental legal principles of the rule of law is that no one should be subjected to double jeopardy (*non bis in idem*). Consequently, extradition will generally be refused if the person requested has already been prosecuted in the requested state for the acts on the basis of which extradition is requested, regardless of whether the prosecution ended in conviction or acquittal (*Restatement of the law third, 1990* p. 568). According to Article 3(d) of the U.N. Model Treaty on Extradition, extradition shall not be granted "if there has been a final judgment rendered against the person in the requested State in respect of the offence for which the person's extradition is requested."

Some states may also deny extradition if the person in question has been prosecuted in the requesting state or in a third state (*Restatement of the law third, 1990* p. 568). The U.N. Model Treaty on Extradition also includes, as a mandatory grounds for refusal, the fact that "the person whose extradition is requested has, under the law of either Party, become immune from prosecution or punishment for any reason, including lapse of time or amnesty."

MUTUAL LEGAL ASSISTANCE

The Concept of Mutual Legal Assistance

The purpose of mutual legal assistance is to get a foreign state to assist in the judicial process—for example, by securing the testimony of possible victims, witnesses, or expert witnesses; by taking other forms of evidence; or by checking judicial or other official records.

Over the years, some multilateral instruments have been drafted that deal with specific offenses. These instruments generally include extensive provisions on mutual legal assistance as well as on extradition. The sets of provisions included in some of these agreements are so extensive that they have been referred to as "minitreaties" on mutual legal assistance.

Such is the case, for instance, with the following conventions:

- The Convention for the Suppression of Unlawful Seizure of Aircraft of December 16, 1970 (Article 10)
- The Convention for the Suppression of Unlawful Acts against the Safety of Civil Aviation of September 23, 1971 (Article 11)
- The Convention for the Suppression of Unlawful Acts against the Safety of Maritime Navigation and the Protocol for the Suppression of Unlawful Acts against the Safety of Fixed Platforms Located on the Continental Shelf, of March 10, 1988
- The U.N. Convention against Illicit Traffic in Narcotic Drugs and Psychotropic Substances of December 19, 1988 (Article 7)
- The International Convention against the Taking of Hostages of December 17, 1979 (Article 11)
- The Palermo Convention, opened for signature on December 12, 2000 (Article 18)

In addition, two influential multilateral arrangements apply to a wide spectrum of offenses, a convention prepared by the Council of Europe and an instrument applied within the context of the British Commonwealth (the so-called Harare Scheme).

The oldest, most widely applied and arguably most influential is the Council of Europe Convention on Mutual Assistance in Criminal Matters. This was opened for signature in 1959 and entered into force in 1962.

The Council of Europe Convention focuses on assistance in judicial matters (as opposed to investigative and prosecutorial matters). Furthermore, because it has been in force for over 40 years, it has in some respects been bypassed by practice. To improve the effectiveness of the convention, the European Union prepared its own Mutual Assistance Convention of May 29, 2000. This supplements the 1959 Council of Europe convention and its protocol in order to reflect the emergence of "good practices" over the past 40 years.

The Commonwealth Scheme for Mutual Assistance in Criminal Matters does not create binding international obligations; instead, it represents more an agreed set of recommendations (McClean, 1992, p. 151).[15] It deals with identifying and locating persons, serving documents, examining witnesses, search and seizure, obtaining evidence, facilitating the personal appearance of witnesses, effecting a temporary transfer of persons in custody to appear as a witness, obtaining production of judicial or official records, and tracing, seizing, and confiscating the proceeds or instrumentalities of crime. A model bill to assist states in preparing legislation has been developed by the Commonwealth Secretariat.

The Commonwealth scheme extends to both "criminal proceedings that have been instituted in a court" and when "there is reasonable cause to believe that an offence in respect of which such proceedings could be instituted have been committed." Thus, it effectively also allows mutual assistance when certain serious offenses, such as terrorism, could potentially be prevented.

The U.N., in turn, has prepared a Model Treaty on Mutual Assistance in Criminal Matters (General Assembly Resolution 45/117 of December 14, 1990). The purpose of the Model Treaty is to provide a suitable basis for negotiations between states that do not have such a treaty. The Model Treaty is by no means a binding template. The states can freely decide on any changes, deletions, and additions. However, the Model Treaty does represent a distillation of the international experience gained with the implementation of such mutual legal assistance treaties, in particular between states representing different legal systems.

The Scope of Mutual Legal Assistance

The earliest international instruments on mutual legal assistance referred primarily to the hearing of witnesses and other taking of evidence. The scope has been constantly expanded. The listing in Article 18(1) of the Palermo Convention illustrates what types of measures are envisaged under more modern instruments:

a. Taking evidence or statements from persons

b. Effecting service of judicial documents

c. Executing searches and seizures, and freezing; examining objects and sites

d. Providing information, evidentiary items, and expert evaluations; providing originals or certified copies of relevant documents and records, including government, bank, financial, corporate, or business records

e. Identifying or tracing proceeds of crime, property, instrumentalities, or other things for evidentiary purposes

f. Facilitating the voluntary appearance of persons in the requesting state party

g. Any other type of assistance that is not contrary to the domestic law of the requested state party

Most of the items on the above list are familiar from Article 7(2) of the 1988 Convention, Article (2) of the U.N. Model Treaty and paragraph 1 of the Commonwealth Scheme, as well as from many bilateral instruments. The Palermo Convention, however, allows several forms of assistance that were not envisaged under most earlier instruments. Examples include the freezing of assets (under Point c), video conferences (Article 18(18)), and what is known as the "spontaneous transmission of information," whereby the authorities are allowed, even without a prior request, to pass on information to the competent authorities of another state.

Grounds for Refusal of a Request for Mutual Legal Assistance

There are several basic common grounds for refusal to grant a request for mutual legal assistance:

- The absence of double criminality
- The offense is regarded as a political offense
- The offense is regarded as a fiscal offense
- The granting of mutual legal assistance would be counter to the vital interests (*ordre public*) of the requested state[16]

Absence of double criminality. A longstanding rule in international instruments has been that a state may decline mutual legal assistance if the offense in question is not an offense under its laws. More recent instruments, however, give the requested state the discretionary option of providing the assistance even if the act in question is not an offense under its laws.

Political offenses. In respect to extradition, the political nature of the offense is generally a mandatory cause for refusal. In respect to mutual legal assistance, in turn, this is generally only an optional reason for refusing cooperation. Moreover, over the years the possibility or obligation to refuse assistance in such conditions has in general been curtailed, in particular with a view toward the need to combat terrorism (see, e.g., Article 2 of the 1959 Council of Europe Convention, when read together with Article 8 of the European Convention on the Suppression of Terrorism of January 27, 1977).

Fiscal offenses. Under the 1959 Council of Europe Convention, mutual legal assistance may be refused where the requested state considers the offense to be a fiscal offense. To restrict the scope of these grounds of refusal, an additional protocol to the European Convention was drawn up at the same time, in 1959. Signatories to this additional protocol undertake not to refuse assistance on the grounds that the offense in question is a fiscal offense.

According to Article 18(22) of the Palermo Convention, states parties may *not* refuse a request for mutual legal assistance on the sole ground that the offense is also considered to involve fiscal matters.

Violation of the vital interests of the requested state (ordre public). Generally speaking, conventions on mutual legal assistance on criminal matters provide that the requested state can refuse assistance that it deems might endanger its sovereignty, security, law and order, or other vital interests (see, e.g., Article 18(21)(b) of the Palermo Convention).

Conflict with the laws of the requested state. Since the procedural laws of states differ, it is possible that some measure requested by a state (such as electronic surveillance of a suspect) is not allowed by the laws of the requested state. International instruments generally specify such a conflict to be grounds for refusal (see, e.g., Article 18(21) of the Palermo Convention).

Bank secrecy. One relatively common ground for refusal is that granting the request would be contrary to bank secrecy. The scope of this ground for refusal has been restricted during recent years. In line with this development, Article 7(5) of the 1988 Convention and Article 18(8) of the Palermo Convention stipulate that states parties shall *not* decline to render mutual legal assistance on the ground of bank secrecy.

The need to indicate the ground for refusals. Good practice in mutual legal assistance requires that the requested state, if it refuses to grant assistance, should indicate the grounds for such refusal (see, e.g., Article 18(23) of the Palermo Convention, Article 19 of the 1959 Council of Europe Convention, and paragraph 6(3) of the Commonwealth Scheme).

The Mutual Legal Assistance Procedure

Letters rogatory. The traditional tool of mutual legal assistance has been *letters rogatory,* a formal mandate from the judicial authority of one state to a judicial authority of another state to perform one or more specified actions in the place of the first judicial authority (see, e.g., 1959 Council of Europe Convention, chap. 2). The concept of letters rogatory had been taken from civil procedure and focuses on judicial action in the taking of evidence. More recent international instruments simply refer to "requests."

In international practice, letters rogatory have typically been transmitted through diplomatic channels. The request for evidence, almost always originating from the prosecutor, is authenticated by the competent national court in the requesting state and then passed on by that state's foreign ministry to the embassy of the requested state. The embassy sends it on to the competent judicial authorities of the requested state, generally through the foreign ministry in the capital. Once the request has been fulfilled, the chain is reversed.

Central authorities or direct contacts? Increasingly, treaties require that states parties designate a central authority (generally, the ministry of justice) to whom the requests can be sent, thus providing an alternative to diplomatic channels. The judicial authorities of the requesting state can then contact the central authority directly. Today, to an increasing degree, even more direct channels are being used, in that an official in the requesting state sends the request directly to the appropriate official in the other state.[17]

Direct requests may also be possible under some instruments in case of emergency. For example, Article 15(1) of the 1959 Council of Europe Convention allows the judicial authority of the requesting state to send the letter of request directly to the competent judicial authority of the requested state. Article 18(13) of the Palermo Convention allows the possibility that, in urgent cases and when the states in question agree, the request can be made through the International Criminal Police Organization, if possible.

Execution of the Request
for Mutual Legal Assistance

Law governing the execution. The procedural laws of states differ considerably. The requesting state may require special procedures (such as notarized affidavits) that are not recognized under the law of the requested state. Traditionally, the almost immutable principle has been that the requested state should follow its own procedural law.

This principle has led to difficulties, in particular when the requesting and the requested state represent different legal traditions. For example, the evidence transmitted from the requested state may be in the form prescribed by the laws of this state, but such evidence may be unacceptable under the procedural law of the requesting state.

The 1959 Council of Europe Convention is one international instrument that has been drafted to apply to states representing two quite different legal traditions, the common law and the continental law systems. Although

Article 3(1) of this convention follows the traditional principle referred to above, the commentary notes that the requesting state can ask that witnesses and experts be examined under oath, as long as this is not prohibited in the requested state.[18]

According to Article 7(12) of the 1988 Convention, a request shall be executed in accordance with the domestic law of the requested state and, to the extent not contrary to the domestic law of the requested state and where possible, in accordance with the procedures specified in the request. Thus, although the 1988 Convention does not go so far as to *require* that the requested state comply with the procedural form required by the requesting state, it does clearly exhort the requested state to do so. This same provision was taken verbatim into Article 18(17) of the Palermo Convention.

Promptness in fulfilling the request. One of the major problems in mutual legal assistance worldwide is that the requested state is often slow in replying, and suspects must be freed due to absence of evidence. There are many understandable reasons for the slowness: a shortage of trained staff, linguistic difficulties, differences in procedure that complicate responding, and so on. Nonetheless, it can be frustrating to find that a case must be abandoned because even a simple request is not fulfilled in time.

The 1988 Convention does not make any explicit reference to an obligation on the part of the requested state to be prompt in its reply. The 1990 U.N. Model Treaty (Article 6) does state that requests for assistance "shall be carried out promptly." Paragraph (1) of the Commonwealth Scheme calls for the requested state to grant the assistance requested as expeditiously as practicable.

The Palermo Convention is even more emphatic about the importance of promptness, and makes the point in two separate provisions. Article 8(13) of the Palermo Convention provides that if the central authority itself responds to the request, it should ensure speedy and prompt execution. If the central authority transmits the request on to, for example, the competent court, the central authority is required to encourage the speedy and proper execution of the request. Article 18(24) provides that the request is to be executed "as soon as possible" and that the requested state is to take "as full account as possible of any deadlines suggested by the requesting State Party and for which reasons are given."

Good practice in execution. Other elements of "good practice" in mutual legal assistance also worked their way into the Palermo Convention, making the life of the practitioner easier than under, for example, the 1988 Convention. According to Article 18(24) of the Palermo Convention:[19]

- the requested state should not only execute the request as soon as possible but also "take as full account as possible of any deadlines suggested by the requesting State Party";
- the requested state should respond to reasonable requests by the requesting state for information on progress of its handling of the request; and
- the requesting state should promptly inform the requested state when the assistance sought is no longer required.

Article 18(25) of the Palermo Convention states that mutual legal assistance may be postponed by the requested state party on the ground that it interferes with an ongoing investigation, prosecution, or judicial proceeding. Article 7(17) of the 1988 Convention is in this respect similar.

Article 18(26) of the Palermo Convention states that before refusing a request for mutual legal assistance or postponing its execution, the requested state should consult with the requesting state to consider whether assistance may be granted subject to such terms and conditions as it deems necessary. (The 1988 Convention provides that if the central authority itself

(Article 7(18)) called for consultations only in the case of postponements, not refusals.) The model for the wider formulation used in the Palermo Convention was taken from Article 4(4) of the 1990 U.N. Model Treaty.

Confidentiality of information and the rule of speciality. Once the information has been sent by the requested state to the requesting state, how can it be used?

The requested state may ask that any information provided be kept confidential except to the extent necessary to execute the request (this is provided, for example, in Article 18(5) and 18(20) of the Palermo Convention). However, the situation may arise that the information received in respect of one offense or suspect at the same time exculpates another suspect in a completely separate procedure. To address this potential problem, Article 18(20) of the Palermo Convention goes on to provide that the state receiving the information is not prevented from disclosing it in its proceedings if this information is exculpatory to an accused person. (The provision also deals with the necessity to inform and, if requested, consult with the other state prior to such disclosure.)

Article 18(19) of the Palermo Convention embodies the rule of speciality: The state receiving information may not transmit or use it for investigations, prosecutions, or judicial proceedings other than those stated in the request without the prior consent of the requested state party. Again, however, exculpatory information may be disclosed.

Costs. According to Article 18(28) of the Palermo Convention, the ordinary costs of executing a request shall be borne by the requested state party, unless otherwise agreed by the states parties concerned. If expenses of a substantial or extraordinary nature are or will be required to fulfill the request, the states parties shall consult to determine the terms and conditions under which the request will be executed, as well as the manner in which the costs shall be borne. This latter provision has been modeled on, for example, Article 8(3) of the Canadian-U.S. treaty and paragraph 12(3) of the Commonwealth Scheme.[20]

TRANSFER OF PROCEEDINGS

A relatively new option in international criminal justice is for the state in which the offense took place to transfer proceedings to another state, often the state in which the suspect is found. This would be an appropriate solution in cases where this other state appears to be in a better position to conduct the proceedings or the defendant has closer ties to this state—for example, because the defendant is a citizen of this state.

One multilateral convention has been adopted on the transfer of proceedings. Within the framework of the Council of Europe, the European Convention on the Transfer of Proceedings in Criminal Matters was signed in 1972 and entered into force in 1978. It has not been widely ratified, however; of the 45 member states of the Council of Europe, only 19 states are currently parties (as of May 4, 2004).

The convention in itself is complicated, but the underlying concept is simple: When a person is suspected of having committed an offense under the law of one state party, that state may request another state party to take action on its behalf in accordance with the convention, and the latter would prosecute it under its own law. The convention requires double criminality.

The U.N. has sought to promote the development of bilateral and multilateral agreements on this subject, by preparing a Model Treaty on the Transfer of Proceedings in Criminal Matters (1990). This is only a framework treaty, which has to be adapted to the specific requirements of the two or more states that are negotiating such a treaty.

RECOGNITION OF JUDGMENT

For a variety of reasons, states may want judgments passed by criminal courts in one state to be carried out in another. There are two general mechanisms for this. One, which applies to all types of judgments (including imprisonment, fines, confiscation, and disqualification from certain rights), is that of *recognition of judgment*. The other relates specifically to the *transfer of sentenced persons* from one state to another. Both mechanisms are designed for use primarily when the offender has closer ties to the state where the enforcement of the judgment is desired rather than to the state where the judgment was passed. (For example, the offender may be a resident in the state in question.)

In 1970, the Council of Europe adopted a convention on the international validity of criminal judgments. This was followed by a spate of bilateral instruments on the same topic—for example, between France and several African states.

The process outlined by the 1970 Convention is that the state where the judgment was passed requests a second state to take over the enforcement of the judgment. If the requested state is prepared to act, this request will then be brought before a court (or, optionally, an authority) in the requested state (Articles 37–52). This court is charged with ensuring that the conditions laid out in the convention are met and with "translating" the judgment into one that is recognized by the laws of that jurisdiction. The court is bound by the findings as to the facts in the case.

The convention can be invoked only by the state where the judgment was passed (Article 3(2)). Thus, it cannot formally be invoked by the state where the judgment would be enforced, much less by the offender. (Nonetheless, the convention provides the offender with some rights to intervene in the process. In the case of judgments in absentia and "ordonnance penal," the offender is provided some rights of intervening, under Article 24 ff. More important, the offender is to be heard by the court in the requested state regarding the enforcement, under Article 39.)

According to the convention, the conditions for recognition of judgment include double criminality (Article 4). Considerations of *ordre public* and related concerns of justice may be taken into account (Articles 6 and 7).[21] The convention also notes the principle of *ne bis in idem*—in other words, the prohibition of double jeopardy (Article 53).

Once the judgment has been recognized under the convention, the enforcement is to be governed only by the law of the requested state. As a result, questions of conditional release and correctional treatment and the like are decided by this latter state. One exception is made: Also the requesting state can exercise the right of amnesty or pardon (Articles 10 and 12).

In October 1999, the European Union agreed on the importance of mutual recognition of decisions and judgments, which, in its view, "should become the cornerstone of judicial co-operation in both civil and criminal matters within the Union." The argument was that already today, the member states of the European Union share fundamental values and legal principles. The authorities of a member state should have confidence in the operation of the legal system of the other states and (much as is done within the United States on the basis of Article 4(1) of the Constitution) should therefore be prepared to give full faith and credence to any decision or judgment handed down in other states.

Work proceeded slowly. For a time, it seemed as if work on mutual recognition would be buried by the many technical problems involved. The terrorist attacks on September 11, 2001 changed the situation dramatically. Within only a few months, agreement was reached on an E.U. arrest warrant. Simply put, the new decision in fact replaces extradition among the E.U. member states with a new system whereby suspects and convicted offenders are "surrendered" to the requesting state. The process no longer needs to go through the central authorities. An arrest warrant issued by a court in one state will be recognized as valid throughout the European Union and is to be enforced.

A European arrest warrant may be issued for offenses punishable by the law of the issuing member state by a custodial sentence or a detention order for a maximum period of at least 12 months or, where a sentence has been passed or a detention order has been made, for punishments of at least 4 months. In some cases, the requested state must refuse to surrender the person in question. These are cases where the offense is covered by an amnesty in the requested state, *ne bis in idem* (double jeopardy), and the lack of criminal responsibility due to age.

Subsequently, the European Union adopted a second decision on mutual recognition, related to orders on the freezing of assets and evidence. In effect, a court decision in one member state to freeze the assets of a suspect (such as ban accounts) or evidence will immediately enter force throughout the European Union.

TRANSFER OF CONVICTED PERSONS

International instruments on the transfer of convicted persons are assuming increasing importance. This is due largely to the increasing number of foreign suspects and convicted offenders to be found in pretrial detention and prisons. Among the benefits seen of the transfer of prisoners are (a) the strong state interest in how its citizens are treated abroad and in the future behavior of its citizens, (b) the increased probability of rehabilitation, (c) the improvement of bilateral relations, (d) the interest of law enforcement, (e) humanitarian consideration, and (f) administrative savings (Plachta, 1993, pp. 164–167).

The first U.S. treaty in which the transfer of prisoners was covered was with the Republic of Korea (ROK) in 1954: The Status of Forces Agreement provided that the ROK would give "sympathetic consideration" to any U.S. request for custody of American citizens sentenced by Korean courts (Plachta, 1993, pp. 143–144). In the 1951 NATO Transfer of Forces Agreement, this was reversed: The agreement provides that the authorities of the receiving state shall give "sympathetic consideration" to a request from the authorities of a sending state for assistance in carrying out a sentence of imprisonment pronounced by the authorities of the sending state within the territory of the receiving state.

In 1995, the U.N. General Assembly approved the U.N Model Agreement on the Transfer of Foreign Prisoners.

The various instruments tend to raise the same issues. The sentence should be final and enforceable (see, e.g., Article 3(1) of the Council of Europe Convention and Article 10 of the U.N. Model Agreement). There should be a certain minimum period left in the sentence (Article 3(1) of the Council of Europe Convention and Article 10 of the U.N. Model Agreement). The double criminality condition should be met (Article 6 of the Council of Europe Convention and Article 3 of the U.N. Model Agreement).

The offender should be a national of the enforcing state (Article 3(1) of the Council of Europe Convention). In the arrangements among the five Nordic States, permanent residents will also be considered; some other bilateral instruments may contain similar exceptions.

The request may emanate from either state concerned (Article 2(3) of the Council of Europe Convention, Article 4 of the U.N. Model Agreement). Both the Council of Europe Convention (Article 2(2)) and the U.N. Model Agreement (Article 4) also allow the prisoner (and the latter, even close relatives of the prisoner) a limited right of initiation. The consent of the prisoner is required (Article 7 of the Council of Europe Convention and

Articles 5 through 7 and 9 of the U.N. Model Agreement). In particular, in some of the older bilateral instruments, consent was not a requisite; it was generally enough that the prisoner be heard regarding the request.

The administering state is entitled to adapt the sentence according to its national law (Articles 9 and 11 of the Council of Europe Convention and Article 6 of the U.N. Model Agreement) but is bound by the findings as to the facts (Article 11 of the Council of Europe Convention and Article 17 of the U.N. Model Agreement). This process of adaptation (recognition and conversion) is referred to as *exequatur*. Also in the bilateral U.S. treaties, the sentencing state has exclusive jurisdiction over proceedings intended to challenge convictions or sentences handed down by its courts, and the transferee is required to waive his or her rights to judicial review in the enforcing state as a precondition to transfer.

Either the sentencing or administering state may grant pardon and amnesty (Article 12 of the Council of Europe Convention and Article 22 of the U.N. Model Agreement).

CONCLUSION

With the increase in international travel, the improvement in technology and communications, the greater likelihood that a crime can have an impact beyond national borders, and the increased profits that can be made from organized crime, the need to obtain assistance from other states in bringing offenders to justice has expanded rapidly. The basic tools that can be used—in particular extradition and mutual legal assistance in criminal matters— have regrettably not evolved to keep pace with developments in crime.

Much of the everyday practice of extradition and mutual assistance continues to be based on bilateral and multilateral instruments that have been drafted many years ago. The transfer of proceedings, mutual recognition of judgments, and the transfer of prisoners remain rarities. Moreover, many states that are parties to instruments on these issues still do not have the necessary legislation or resources to respond to requests for extradition or mutual assistance. The following represent some of the problems commonly encountered:

Requests are often transmitted through diplomatic channels or from government to government, and the resulting delays may cause a carefully assembled case to collapse in the hands of the prosecutor.

The requesting state may misunderstand the formal requirements in the requested state as to the presentation and contents of the request. For example, the requesting state may not realize that, under some treaties, it must present documentation that the double criminality requirement is met, that the offense is extraditable, and that execution is consistent with the law of the requested party.

The requested state, in turn, may not always demonstrate flexibility in demanding more details about the offense and the offender. Often, very specific information may be difficult to provide if the investigation is still underway.

Nonetheless, some developments have taken place to strengthen the importance of international instruments in practice, in particular over the past 10 years.

Bilateral instruments are being increasingly replaced by *multilateral instruments*. Although bilateral instruments have been preferred, for example, by the common law states, the simultaneous existence of many international instruments complicates the work of the practitioner. For this and other reasons, the common law states are seeing the advantages of multilateral instruments that have a wide scope of application.

The earliest international instruments were based on lists of offenses. If an offense was not included in the list, extradition or mutual legal assistance could not be granted. More recent instruments tend to be generic, in that they apply to a *broad scope of offenses*.

Because courts have traditionally been cautious in applying coercive measures, the courts, in particular in common law states, have required prima facie evidence that the suspect had indeed committed the offense in question before a request for extradition would be granted. Because of the differences in the law of evidence and in criminal procedure in different states, such prima facie evidence was often difficult to provide. More recent instruments have generally regarded it as sufficient that the requesting state (at least if it belongs to a select group of states) produce a valid *arrest warrant*.

One of the most cherished principles in extradition law has been that states will not extradite their own nationals and will, at most, undertake to bring them to trial in their own courts. Today, more and more states are *allowing extradition of their own nationals*, although some conditions may be placed, such as that the national, if convicted, should be returned to his or her own state to serve the sentence.

The range of measures offered under mutual legal assistance instruments (and domestic laws in many states) has expanded. At first, the focus was on service of summons. Today, a *wide range of measures* are offered.

There is currently a clear trend toward *elimination of the many grounds for refusal* to extradite or grant a request for mutual legal assistance, such as the elimination of the political offense exception.

There is a trend toward granting *greater rights to the person in question* as an object (as opposed to subject) of the process and to greater consideration of how he or she would be treated or punished in the requesting state. Consideration can be given, for example, to the possibility of persecution on the grounds of sex, race, religion, nationality, ethnic origin or political opinions, the possibility of unfair trial, and the possibility of punishment that, in the requested state, is deemed inhumane.

Another trend is toward *less rigid procedural requirements*, including direct communications and simplified procedure.

During the years after World War II, international cooperation in responding to transnational crime has expanded and deepened. International instruments have provided the main building blocks for this development. The pace of development has clearly quickened during the 1990s and the beginning of the new millennium. The 1988 U.N. "Drug Convention" and the 2000 U.N. Convention against Transnational Organized Crime are clear signs that multilateral instruments are assuming increasing importance. More such globally applicable instruments will undoubtedly be drafted. At the same time, however, states will continue to enter into bilateral arrangements with those states with which they share particular concerns and interests.

Along with the spread of transnational crime, these multilateral and bilateral instruments will also assume increasing importance. Law enforcement authorities, prosecutors, defense counsels, and judges will find that cases no longer have solely domestic connections; they must turn to their colleagues in other countries for assistance. Without international instruments, such assistance would be difficult if not impossible to obtain.

NOTES

1. The terms *mutual assistance, mutual legal assistance,* and *mutual assistance in criminal matters* are often used interchangeably.

2. *Commentary on the United Nations Convention against Illicit Traffic in Narcotic Drugs and Psychotropic Substances, 1988,* para. 2.17. The *Commentary* cites as authority the Declaration on Principles of International Law concerning Friendly Relations and Co-operation among States in accordance with the Charter of the United Nations (General Assembly Resolution 2625 (25), annex) and the principle concerning the duty not to intervene in matters within the domestic jurisdiction of any state, contained in para. 2 of the Charter.

3. This has subsequently been replaced by the 1981 Inter-American Convention on Extradition.

4. The 1925 convention has subsequently been amended many times with protocols.

5. One notable aspect of the 1988 convention is that a state party may not refuse to render mutual legal assistance on the grounds of bank secrecy.

6. Among the few exceptions are treaties on the slave trade, the trade in women and children, the forgery of currency, and terrorism.

7. The 1970 Convention for the Suppression of Unlawful Seizure of Aircraft, the 1971 Convention for the Suppression of Unlawful Acts against the Safety of Civil Aviation, the 1973 Convention on the Prevention and Punishment of Crimes against Internationally Protected Persons including Diplomatic Agents, and the 1979 International Convention against the Taking of Hostages. In 1988, the Convention for the Suppression of Unlawful Acts against the Safety of Maritime Navigation was completed.

8. This has subsequently been replaced by the 1981 Inter-American Convention on Extradition.

9. As amended in 1990. The Commonwealth scheme, although not a formal treaty, has been unanimously approved by all members of the Commonwealth.

10. See, for example, Article 4 of the U.N. Model Treaty on Extradition, Article 16(10) of the Palermo Convention, and Article 6(9)(a) of the 1988 convention. The principle of *aut dedere aut judicare* can, of course, be applied also to other cases where the requested state refuses extradition.

11. In respect to the United States, Nadelmann (1993, p. 426) sees two trends: One trend is toward a narrower definition of the political offense exception, and another, somewhat opposing, trend is toward greater consideration of foreign policy interests and its bilateral relationship with the requesting government.

12. This wording is taken from Article 3(b) of the U.N. Model Treaty on Extradition (see also the U.N. Convention Relating to the Status of Refugees).

13. Furthermore, Article 3(g) of the U.N. Model Treaty on Extradition cites as mandatory grounds for refusal the rendering of the judgment of the requesting state *in absentia*, the failure of the convicted person to receive sufficient notice of the trial or the opportunity to arrange for his or

her defense, and the failure to allow him or her the opportunity to have the case retried in his or her presence.

14. See also Article 4(d) of the U.N. Model Treaty on Extradition.

15. The Harare Scheme was originally adopted in 1983. It has been amended most recently in 1999.

16. Article 4(c)-(d) of the U.N. Model Treaty on Mutual Assistance in Criminal Matters and para. 7(1)(d) and 7(2)(b) of the Commonwealth Scheme provide as additional optional grounds for the refusal of assistance the presence of substantial grounds for believing that the request for assistance may lead to prosecution or punishment, or cause prejudice, on account of, for example, race, religion, nationality, or political opinions, or that the prosecution in the requesting state would lead to double jeopardy. The U.N. Model Treaty adds as a further optional ground the fact that the offense is already under investigation or prosecution in the requested state.

17. One of the earliest bilateral treaties to allow for direct contacts was the additional protocol to the 1959 Council of Europe Convention drawn up by France and Germany on October 24, 1974. The 1990 Schengen agreement in the framework of the European Union specifically allows the use of direct contacts between judicial authorities (Article 53). The same concept is embodied in the even more recent European Union 2000 Convention on Mutual Legal Assistance.

18. Explanatory Report to the 1959 Convention, p. 14.

19. Cf. Article 4 of the 2000 European Union Convention.

20. In 1999, the Law Ministers of the Commonwealth adopted guidelines on the apportionment of costs incurred in providing mutual assistance in criminal matters.

21. The concept of *ordre public* essentially covers the protection of public security and the physical integrity of individuals as part of society.

REFERENCES

Blakesley, C., & Lagodny, O. (1992). Competing national laws: Network or jungle? In A. Eser & O. Lagodny (Eds.), *Principles and procedures for a new transnational criminal law: Documentation of an international workshop, 1991* (pp. 47–100). Freiburg, Germany: Max Planck Institute for Foreign and International Criminal Law.

Commentary on the United Nations Convention against Illicit Traffic in Narcotic Drugs and Psychotropic Substances, 1988 (E/CN.7/590). (1998). New York: United Nations.

Gully-Hart, P. (1992). Loss of time through formal and procedural requirements in international co-operation. In A. Eser & O. Lagodny *Principles and procedures for a new transnational criminal law: Documentation of an international workshop, 1991* (pp. 245–266). Freiburg, Germany: Max Planck Institute for Foreign and International Criminal Law.

McClean, D. (1992). *International judicial assistance.* Oxford, UK: Clarendon.

Nadelmann, E. A. (1993). *Cops across borders: The internationalization of U.S. criminal law enforcement.* University Park: Pennsylvania State University Press.

Plachta, M. (1993). *Transfer of prisoners under international instruments and domestic legislation: A comparative study* (Vol. 39). Freiburg, Germany: Max Planck Institute for Foreign and International Criminal Law.

Restatement of the law third, foreign relations law of the United States (2 Vols.). (1990). St. Paul, MN: American Law Institute.

14

"Wild Beasts Without Nationality"

The Uncertain Origins of Interpol, 1898–1910

MATHIEU DEFLEM

I n recent years, scholars of criminal justice and policing have devoted much attention to the growing impact of the interconnectedness of nations on the control and management of crime. A considerable literature now exists on the structures and processes of how police institutions and other agents of social control define and respond to the flow of criminal activities across national borders (e.g., Deflem, 2001; Koenig & Das, 2001; McDonald, 1997; Nadelmann, 1993; Passas, 1999; Sheptycki, 2000). International patterns of policing have historical foundations that date back to at least the 19th-century development of national states, when police and government authorities began to recognize the need for police cooperation across the boundaries of national jurisdictions (Deflem, 1996, 2000, 2002a, 2002b). Among the historical antecedents of

international police cooperation were various efforts, especially on the European continent, to control the international spread of people and organizations that were held to be opponents of established political systems, such as socialists, democrats, liberals, and anarchists. It is the most striking development of international police cooperation from the latter part of the 19th century onward that police institutions gradually began to abandon the political objectives of early cooperation efforts to focus on enforcement of laws prohibiting acts of a distinctly criminal nature. It would, however, be incorrect to conclude that the shift toward criminal police cooperation involved a radical break from earlier political cooperation efforts. On the contrary, as shown in this chapter, available historical evidence indicates that the development and growth of international police cooperation for criminal enforcement duties was facilitated by prior practices of cooperation that had been initiated for political reasons.

Drawing on archival data on the history of international police cooperation from the mid-19th century onward, in this chapter I will analyze two case studies of police cooperation planned at the intergovernmental level of international law concerning matters of the control of anarchism and white slavery. These cases will serve to substantiate the argument that the political nature of early efforts to foster police cooperation paradoxically enabled the elaboration of international police cooperation for criminal enforcement duties, because they promoted a process of bureaucratization that led police institutions to independently develop the means and objectives of cooperation across national borders. I will first situate the case studies of the policing of anarchism and white slavery in its proper historical context.

THE AGE OF INTERNATIONAL POLICE COOPERATION

At the beginning of the 20th century, international police cooperation was not yet structured on a broad international scale, such as is the case today with the International Criminal Police Organization (Interpol) (Deflem, 2002a). In the United States, police duties with international dimensions were mostly related to specifically American circumstances associated with slavery, immigration, and the creation of national borders on the North American continent. Collaboration with European and other police located outside the United States occurred only on sporadic occasions. In Europe, international police practices were, from the middle of the 19th century onward, comparatively much more developed, yet they were organized on a rather limited basis with appeal to police institutions of a relatively small number of nations. Most European police cooperation until the early 20th century also concerned political tasks related to the

protection of established conservative rule from suspected subversive political activities. Such was most clearly the case with the Police Union of German States, an international police organization that was active from 1851 until 1866 to suppress the political opposition from liberals, democrats, and socialists (Deflem, 1996, 2002a, pp. 45–62). The Police Union was able to attract cooperation from police of only seven German-language nations that were ideologically closely akin and politically united in a common federal union. Other efforts to formalize cross-border police collaboration in the 19th century likewise remained too closely tied to the political conditions within and among national states to garner broad international support.

Throughout the 19th century, attempts to promote international police cooperation on a broad multilateral scale were mostly organized at the level of international law rather than at the administrative level of police institutions. An expansion of international law was established through formal agreements reached between the governments of national states, but typically, such intergovernmental accords failed to be a basis for practical cooperation between police. At best, such agreements served as catalysts for the development of international policing if the formal provisions of international law were accompanied by informal arrangements separately worked out among police officials. International police collaboration on political matters and cooperation efforts instituted at the level of intergovernmental treaties share the characteristic that they will unavoidably mirror the political conditions of international affairs among national states and the characteristics of their diverse systems of law. Therefore, such political and legal forms of cooperation plans pose severe limitations to the scope of their international potential and do not allow participating police to move beyond the jurisdictional authority sanctioned by their respective governments.

However, even though international legal agreements remained without much consequence for practical police cooperation, toward the close of the 19th century there was a distinct trend noticeable in international police cooperation practices to focus away from political crimes toward more distinctly criminal police duties. Theoretically, this development can be conceptualized in terms of a bureaucratization process that has historically influenced police institutions to gain institutional independence from the governments of their respective states to develop and share knowledge systems of international crimes that need to be responded to through cooperation (Deflem, 2002a, pp. 12–34). The influence of police bureaucratization on international cooperation was clearly, albeit negatively, revealed in 1914, when the First Congress of International Criminal Police was held in Monaco (Deflem, 2002a, pp. 102–110). Although the meeting specifically aspired to foster international police cooperation on criminal matters, the attempt failed because it was still framed in terms of the provisions of international law rather than the bureaucratic model that police institutions had by then come to adopt. Not until the formation of the organization today known as Interpol, the International Criminal Police Commission in 1923, was international police cooperation successfully organized on a more permanent basis. The commission was oriented toward criminal enforcement duties and was independently established by the representatives of police institutions rather than their nations' political authorities.

An increasing bureaucratization of police institutions had in the decades preceding the formation of the International Criminal Police Commission already begun to inspire new forms of international police cooperation that did not rely on principles of international law and that did not focus on political crimes. It may come as somewhat of a surprise, then, that an important multilateral effort to establish European-wide police cooperation would be attempted on a highly political issue, when as late as 1898 an international conference was held in Rome, Italy, to coordinate police measures against anarchism. Unveiling the causes and implications of the anti-anarchist conference will help explain this paradoxical development and bring out the ironic finding that international police cooperation for purposes of criminal enforcement, such as they continue to exist until this day, have origins in distinctly political efforts.

THE ANTI-ANARCHIST CONFERENCE OF ROME, 1898

In the final decade of the 19th century, violent incidents inspired by radical political ideas shook the foundations of established autocratic regimes in Europe and accelerated international police activities with political objectives. It was partly in response to this "Decade of Regicide," to borrow a term from historian Richard Jensen (2001, p. 16), that new attempts were made to establish international police cooperation with wide international representation in a form that would overcome difficulties relating to national sovereignty. Although in most respects these attempts were to be unsuccessful, they also signaled an important transformation in the history of international police cooperation, the impact of which would become clear during the first half of the 20th century.

The 1890s witnessed a revival of anarchist activities and, in response, police actions directed at suppressing them (Jensen, 2001; Liang, 1992, pp. 155–163). In the course of the decade, alleged anarchist incidents led to 60 killings and the wounding of some 200 people. Between March 1892 and June 1894, 11 bombing incidents killed 9 people in Paris alone. In 1893, police from France intercepted news about plans to assassinate Emperor Wilhelm II and Chancellor Caprivi of the German Empire and passed the information on to Berlin police. That same year, following bombings in Paris and Barcelona, negotiations were held between the French and Spanish governments to establish an international police organization against anarchism. But although authorities from England, Austria, and the German Empire indicated interest in joining the plan, it never came to fruition. Other anti-anarchist police measures were restricted to bilateral agreements. In 1898, for instance, French and Italian police exchanged information through their respective consulates about the possible connections between a bombing in Milan, a bank robbery in Paris, and a case of dynamite theft in Switzerland. On September 10, 1898, Empress Elisabeth of Austria was murdered by the Italian anarchist Luigi Lucheni, further intensifying concerns over the anarchist menace. A week after the assassination, the Austrian foreign minister, Goluchowsky, proposed to his Swiss colleague to form an anti-anarchist "international police league." The Austrian-Swiss plan remained unexecuted, but a few weeks later, on September 29, 1898, the Italian government sent out invitations for an international conference to be held in Rome to organize the fight against anarchism.

The International Conference of Rome for the Social Defense Against Anarchists was held from November 24 to December 21, 1898, and was attended by 54 delegates from no less than 21 European countries, including all major powers, such as Great Britain, the German Empire, France, and Austria-Hungary (see Fijnaut, 1979, pp. 930–933; Jensen, 1981; Liang, 1992, pp. 163–169). The gathering was mostly attended by government representatives, but also present were police officials from the participating countries. The conference delegates discussed the formulation of an appropriate concept of anarchism, legislative measures against anarchism, and the development of international anti-anarchist police measures. The British government was the sole dissenter in signing a final protocol that was drafted at the meeting (U.K. Public Record Office [PRO], FO 881/7372). In the protocol, anarchism was defined as any act "having as its aim the destruction, through violent means, of all social organization" (PRO, FO 45/784). The protocol's other resolutions included the introduction of legislation in the participating countries to prohibit the illegitimate possession and use of explosives, membership in anarchist organizations, the distribution of anarchist propaganda, and the rendering of assistance to anarchists. It was also agreed that governments should try to limit press coverage of anarchist activities and that the death penalty should be mandatory punishment for all assassinations of heads of state.

On matters of practical policing, the protocol from the Rome Conference included provisions to encourage participating governments to have police keep watch over anarchists, to establish in every participating country a specialized surveillance agency to achieve this goal, and to organize a system of information exchange among these national agencies. Furthermore, the countries that signed the final conference protocol agreed to adopt the *portrait parlé* method of criminal identification. A more sophisticated version of the bertillonage system invented by Alphonse Bertillon, the *portrait parlé* (spoken picture) was a method of identification that classified criminal suspects on the basis of measurements of parts of their head and body. Bertillonage measurements were expressed in numbers, which could be transmitted across nations by means of telephone and telegraph. In addition, the conference also approved a provision to extradite persons who had attempted to kill or kidnap a sovereign or head of state. The provision was referred to as the *attentat* (assassination) clause or Belgian clause and had first been introduced in Belgium in 1856 following a failed attempt to murder Napoleon III in 1854.

In November 1901, Russian authorities used the assassination of U.S. President McKinley by an anarchist in September of that year as a basis to revive the anti-anarchist program of the Rome Conference. Cosponsored by the

German government, Russian officials sent out a memorandum to hold an international meeting on anarchism to the governments of various European countries as well as the United States. The initiative led to a second anti-anarchist meeting, held in March 1904 in St. Petersburg, then the capital of Russia, where the representatives of 10 countries, including Germany, Austria-Hungary, and Denmark, agreed on a Secret Protocol for the International War on Anarchism (Jensen, 1981, 2001). The agreement was later also adhered to by the governments of Portugal and Spain. Although France and Great Britain did not sign the St. Petersburg Protocol, the authorities of these countries did express their willingness to provide assistance with other states on police matters relating to anarchism. The U.S. government did not participate in the St. Petersburg meeting and declined to follow its provisions, although President Theodore Roosevelt had called for an international treatise to combat anarchism after the assassination of his predecessor.

THE DEPOLITICIZATION OF INTERNATIONAL POLICING

The anti-anarchist meetings of Rome and St. Petersburg occurred at a time when international police cooperation for political purposes had slowly but steadily been in decline (Deflem, 2002a, pp. 65–77). To explain this paradoxical situation, one must consider more precisely the manner in which the topic of anarchism was treated at the intergovernmental level and the actual consequences of the intergovernmental treaties in terms of legislation and police practice.

The fight against anarchism was evidently a matter of a decidedly political nature, especially when it included policies reaching beyond the control of criminal incidents inspired by anarchist motives. Aware of the politically sensitive nature of anarchism, the anti-anarchist meetings in Rome and St. Petersburg

purposely conceived of anarchism as a strictly criminal matter, the enforcement of which was to be handled at the administrative level by police institutions. The Italian government's invitation to the meeting downplayed the delicate and divisive issues involved with drawing up appropriate legislation and instead emphasized the practical police aspects involved, for which reason the invitation explicitly stated that "technical and administrative staff" would also be invited to the meeting (cited in Liang, 1992, p. 162). After the delegates at the Rome Conference had spent considerable time discussing a proper definition of anarchism, they ultimately settled on a broad and imprecise concept that sought to avoid any associations with political ideology. In the final protocol of the Rome Conference, it was stated that anarchism had "nothing in common with politics" and was not "under any circumstance to be regarded as a political doctrine" (PRO, FO 45/784).

However, although anarchism was formally depoliticized in order to accommodate many politically diverse national states and although the conference attendants promised to enact in their respective countries appropriate legislation, only a few countries actually passed new legislation based on the provisions of the Rome and St. Petersburg protocols. The aspiration to treat anarchism as a criminal matter could not be maintained at the level of the various national governments where the international treaties had to be ratified, because there the initiatives were injected into the ideological battles of intranational politics and their international implications. The official response from the French government to the Rome Conference, for instance, declined to approve any intergovernmental accord sanctioning international police cooperation on anarchism because of stated difficulties "from the political point of view" (quoted in Jensen, 1981, p. 345). In the French case, new legislation on anarchism was also redundant because France in many instances already had such legislation in place. Likewise indicating the political limitations of intergovernmental treaties, the main reason why the U.S. government did not participate in the international accord of the St. Petersburg meeting was the political animosity that existed among U.S. officials against Germany and Russia because of those countries' perceived imperialist tendencies.

Next to the failure of the Rome and St. Petersburg treaties to influence anti-anarchist legislation in the various participating states, ideological divisions in international political affairs also posed certain limits to international police cooperation plans developed in function of those treaties. Most clearly, the participants of the Rome and St. Petersburg meetings could not agree on the creation of a central anti-anarchist intelligence bureau through which the exchange between the various national bureaus could be coordinated. Nationalist sentiments in Europe were too intense to accept the creation of a central bureau that would put the one country in which it was to be located at a marked advantage; the central bureau would be in the advantageous position of being the only office that would be connected with all other national bureaus. Instead, only a system of direct facilitation exchange between the various participating states was agreed on. In the case of the United States, even this system was too ambitious in the early 20th century because no federal U.S. police existed that would be sufficiently equipped to participate in such a cooperative arrangement (Deflem, 2002a, pp. 78–96; Jensen, 2001; Nadelmann, 1993).

Thus, ideological-political differences among the governmental powers of Europe prevented anti-anarchist legislation from being passed at the national levels and restricted the practical implications of related plans to foster international police cooperation. It is therefore correct to state that the international anti-anarchist treaties failed to influence legislation in the states that signed the accord because

"national self-interests and rivalries edged out international concerns" (Jensen, 1981, p. 340). Yet it is equally important to observe how the Rome and St. Petersburg meetings did contribute to enhance practices of direct police communications across nations, the necessity of which was widely recognized. It is typical, for instance, that although the British government did not sign the Rome protocol, one of the British representatives at the conference, Howard Vincent, the former head of the Criminal Investigations Division at Scotland Yard, also acknowledged that direct police communications were beneficial "if only by forming reciprocal friendships leading to greater cooperation" (quoted in Jensen, 1981, p. 332). Among the agreements reached at the meetings was the establishing of anti-anarchist intelligence bureaus in several of the participating states. Police of Italy and Greece, for example, had such systems of information exchange up and running until the eve of World War I.

The relative success of the international anti-anarchist treaties in matters of international police practices is explained by the fact that the suggested system of information exchange was to be instituted and coordinated at the administrative level by police agencies. These provisions were conceived in technical and bureaucratic terms and not coined in the legal language of most of the other provisions. This was no coincidence, for while the delegates at the Rome and St. Petersburg meetings were mostly diplomats and other government representatives who negotiated with one another in a language of formal systems of law rooted in jurisdictional authority, the anti-anarchist methods of information exchange that had successfully been worked out had been decided on by police officials meeting separately in informal gatherings on several days when the conference took place (PRO, FO 881/7179). The success of the administrative means of the international fight against anarchism, in other words, was possible because of the attained level of expertise and professionalism in police institutions rather than because of any willingness on the part of the governments of national states to legislate anti-anarchist policies.

Further indicating that international anti-anarchist intelligence work was influenced more by established international police culture than by intergovernmental legality is that the two provisions of the Rome Conference that applied to all crimes and not only to anarchism—the *portrait parlé* system of identification and the Belgian clause of extradition—were among the few conference proposals that were effectively put into law in several European countries in the years following the meeting (Jensen, 1981, pp. 331–333). Legislation on these international police measures was successfully accomplished because of developments in matters of international police organization and police technique that had already begun many years before. Whether focused on anarchism or not, police institutions had indeed been exchanging information on a regular basis throughout the 19th century and has thus *de facto* forged a network of international police experts (Deflem, 2002a, pp. 70–77). That practical police measures were effectively legislated in the aftermath of intergovernmental accords shows that police authorities sometimes succeeded in having their activities perceived by their respective national governments as purely administrative in nature. The Rome and St. Petersburg treaties, therefore, promoted the expansion of international police practices that had already been set up and developed by police institutions.

The anti-anarchist conference of Rome in 1898 and its follow-up meeting in St. Petersburg in 1904 represent remarkable threshold cases in the history of international policing. On one hand, these efforts clearly have a foot in the 19th century in that they remained largely framed in a politically sensitive framework of international law. On the other hand, they also reveal the growing influence of a developing police culture that was moving in the direction of instituting international police practices on the basis of professional expertise. It is for this reason appropriate to consider international treaties on white slavery during the early 20th century in the same context as the anti-anarchist accords.

THE SOCIAL DEFENSE AGAINST WHITE SLAVERY

Anarchism and white slavery share the characteristic that they were perceived by government and police authorities to be problems of an international nature. When, after the assassination of Empress Elisabeth of Austria, the Austrian foreign minister called for the establishment of an international police league, he referred to anarchists as "wild beasts without nationality," who were a menace "to all persons" (cited in Liang, 1992, p. 160). The broad international representation at the Rome Conference, with countries as diverse in ideological persuasion as France, England, the German Empire, and Switzerland, reveals the extent to which the notion of anarchism's internationality was accepted. The problem of white slavery, likewise, was perceived by police and government representatives from the viewpoint of its international dimensions (Decker, 1979; Petrow, 1994). The very terms *white slavery* and *white slave trade* are meant to indicate that "movement between brothels was at the very heart of the system" (Bristow, 1983, p. 29). Regular clientele demanded variety in supply; venereal diseases caused unemployment and required replacement; and the deliberate removal of women from their familiar surroundings strengthened the control powers of their employers. During the 19th century, the traffic in prostitutes had increasingly assumed an international scope, within Europe as well as beyond, especially toward South America (Decker, 1979, pp. 63–66).

As the president of the Austrian League for the Suppression of White Slavery stated in 1904, "There exists an international organization which in many places of the earth has its general terminals; the export is so regulated that women of particular countries of origin are always sent to those centers where they are especially appreciated" (quoted in Schmitz, 1927, p. 13). The trafficking in prostitutes was recognized to have become an international business that had to be tackled internationally.

The international implications of white slavery occupied private groups, governments, and police institutions at national and international levels for some time in the second half of the 19th century (Bristow, 1983; Decker, 1979; Petrow, 1994). As early as 1869, Austrian authorities requested information from a number of European governments about their laws regarding the transportation of prostitutes across national borders. The request aimed to harmonize antiprostitution laws in Europe, but the attempt was not successful. Subsequent privately planned international efforts to control prostitution included the International Congress on the White Slave Traffic organized by the National Vigilance Association in London in 1899. The meeting led to the creation of an International Bureau for the Suppression of White Slavery in London, and produced a follow-up meeting, the Second International Congress on the International Fight Against the White Slave Traffic, held in Frankfurt, Germany, in 1902.

At the intergovernmental level of states, an important antiprostitution initiative was taken when an international conference on white slavery was organized by the French authorities in Paris on July 15, 1902 (League of Nations, 1927; Palitzsch, 1926). The participants of the Paris meeting agreed on a final protocol that criminalized prostitution and specified extradition treaties and several administrative arrangements on the matter. The recommended police measures included

government-authorized observations of procurers and suspicious foreigners in railway stations and ports (Petrow, 1994, pp. 163–164). At a follow-up meeting in Paris in 1904, the International Agreement for the Suppression of White Slave Traffic was signed by the governments of 12 European countries, including France, Germany, Great Britain, and Russia. Some non-European states, among them Brazil, China, India, and the United States, did not sign the accord but nonetheless agreed to adhere to its provisions (League of Nations, 1927, p. 197). The nine-article agreement specified, among other things, that governments should police all persons involved with prostitution at railway stations and ports. It was also decided to create intelligence bureaus on prostitution in all participating countries and for these bureaus to be in direct contact with one another. Furthermore, the Paris Agreement provided that governments should arrange to report foreign prostitutes residing in their respective countries to the authorities of the prostitutes' country of origin and to repatriate them on request from foreign authorities.

At a subsequent meeting in Paris on May 4, 1910, the International Convention for the Suppression of the White Slave Traffic was signed by 13 nations, including most of the countries that signed the 1904 Agreement, as well as Austria-Hungary and Brazil. The United States was among the countries that no longer adhered to the new treaty (League of Nations, 1927, pp. 197–200). The convention reaffirmed the provisions of the 1904 Agreement, additionally regulating a system of information exchange between the participating states. Specifically, international police communications on prostitution were recommended to be conducted either through diplomatic channels or directly between the appropriate police authorities.

Although the international agreements on white slavery dealt with a nonpolitical issue, the agreements reached in Paris were, like those on anarchism, decided on at the intergovernmental level and framed in the language of formal international law. Yet unlike the Rome Conference on anarchism, the international meetings on white slavery had no police authorities separately working on issues of practical control but, instead, subsumed all policy measures, legislative and administrative, under one accord of international law. In consequence, the white slavery accords did not significantly influence the course and outcome of international police strategies and other practical aspects of prostitution policy. Instead, police activities in the area of white slavery developed as part of national policies and on the basis of the international networks police institutions had established outside the context of intergovernmental agreements (Decker, 1979). Efforts to control the trafficking of prostitutes into the United States, for example, were largely conducted on the basis of national U.S. legislation. In 1908, the U.S. Immigration Commission conducted an investigation on the Importation and Harboring of Women for Immoral Purposes, which led to changes in U.S. immigration laws and the passing of the White Slave Traffic Act on June 23, 1910 (League of Nations, 1927, p. 7). Introduced in Congress by Republican Representative James Robert Mann of Illinois, the federal law came to be known as the Mann Act, and its enforcement was assigned to the Justice Department's Bureau of Investigation.

CONCLUSION

The bureaucratization theory of international police cooperation holds that police institutions need to be sufficiently autonomous from the political dictates of their sanctioning governments to independently devise the objectives of and the means for international police work (Deflem, 2002a, pp. 17–23). Relying on professional knowledge systems on international crime problems and the appropriate measures for their control, police institutions

can then establish international cooperation arrangements with wide international appeal. Over the course of history, these conditions were gradually met in more successful ways as international police cooperation increasingly moved beyond the formal legal systems of national states on the basis of professional standards of efficient policing. The relevance of the professionalism that was shared among bureaucratic police institutions would be manifested most clearly in 1923 when the International Criminal Police Commission, the organization today known as Interpol, was formed as the most ambitious international police organization on a wide multilateral scale. Despite several ups and downs in the course of its 80-year history, the organization has continued to exist as the most successful exponent of the trend toward the internationalization of the police function. The 19th-century antecedents of Interpol, however, concerned international police activities that were largely driven by the political dictates of national governments and framed in the language of international law. The international developments concerning anarchism and prostitution discussed in this chapter, therefore, need to be seen in terms of the complex dynamics between intergovernmental arrangements, on one hand, and international police practices, on the other.

Sociopolitical conditions at the turn of the 20th century prevented broad support for intergovernmental agreements that attempted to formalize international police cooperation at the level of international law and also set boundaries to the scope of police objectives that remained too closely tied up with the political directives of national governments. Accomplishments in effective practical police cooperation, even when cooperation was achieved in the wake of formal intergovernmental treaties, was not governed top-down by governments and the treaties they had been able to agree on but was worked out from the bottom up at the level of a developing cross-national police culture of experts. Although the Rome and St. Petersburg meetings could not effectively dictate the international police response against anarchism, they did provide an arena for heads of police to formalize developments of international cooperation in practical police methods that had already begun many years earlier. In contrast, the international treaties on white slavery dealt with a distinctly criminal matter but did not take into account achieved accomplishments in police professionalization and bureaucratization (Deflem, 2002a, pp. 23–26).

The ironic conclusion to the impact of the anti-anarchist measures is that an elaboration of international police practices was achieved on criminal matters although they had originally been conceived in relation to the political issue of anarchism. Equally ironic is that the white slavery agreements were unsuccessful in fostering international police cooperation, although they concerned a clearly nonpolitical crime. The reason is that the international accords on white slavery were planned by the political authorities of national states at the level of international law without much regard for practical issues of policing. With respect to fostering international police relations, the white slavery treaties were less important than the anarchist accords and cannot be regarded as a critical antecedent of international police cooperation. In terms of the enforcement of the international laws on anarchism and white slavery, attention should go to the relative success of the Rome Conference in a manner that was depoliticized and the relative failure of the anti–white slavery initiatives despite their concern for a criminal issue.

REFERENCES

Bristow, E. J. (1983). *Prostitution and prejudice: The Jewish fight against white slavery, 1870–1939*. New York: Schocken Books.

Decker, J. F. (1979). *Prostitution: Regulation and control*. Littleton, CO: Rothman.

Deflem, M. (1996). International policing in 19th-century Europe: The police union of German states, 1851–1866. *International Criminal Justice Review, 6*, 36–57.

Deflem, M. (2000). Bureaucratization and social control: Historical foundations of international policing. *Law & Society Review, 34*(3), 601–640.

Deflem, M. (2001). International police cooperation in North America. In D. J. Koenig & D. K. Das (Eds.), *International police cooperation: A world perspective* (pp. 71–98). Lanham, MD: Lexington Books.

Deflem, M. (2002a). *Policing world society: Historical foundations of international police cooperation*. New York: Oxford University Press.

Deflem, M. (2002b). Technology and the internationalization of policing: A comparative-historical perspective. *Justice Quarterly, 19*(3), 453–475.

Fijnaut, C. (1979). *Opdat de Macht een Toevlucht Zij? Een Historische Studie van het Politieapparaaat als een Politieke Instelling* [So that power be a sanctuary: A historical study of the police as a political institution] (2 Vols.). Antwerp, Belgium: Kluwer.

Jensen, R. B. (1981). The International Anti-Anarchist Conference of 1898 and the origins of Interpol. *Journal of Contemporary History, 16*(2), 323–347.

Jensen, R. B. (2001). The United States, international policing and the war against anarchist terrorism, 1900–1914. *Terrorism and Political Violence, 13*(1), 15–46.

Koenig, D. J., & Das, D. K. (Eds.). (2001). *International police cooperation: A world perspective*. Lanham, MD: Lexington Books.

League of Nations. (1927). *Report of the special body of experts on traffic in women and children: Part one*. Geneva, Switzerland: Author.

Liang, H-H. (1992). *The rise of the modern police and the European state system from Metternich to the Second World War*. New York: Cambridge University Press.

McDonald, W. F. (Ed.). (1997). *Crime and law enforcement in the global village*. Cincinnati, OH: Anderson.

Nadelmann, E. A. (1993). *Cops across borders: The internationalization of U.S. criminal law enforcement.* University Park: Pennsylvania State University Press.

Palitzsch, H. (1926). *Die bekämpfung des internationalen verbrechertums* [The fight against international criminality]. Hamburg, Germany: Otto Meissners Verlag.

Passas, N. (Ed.). (1999). *Transnational crime.* Aldershot, UK: Ashgate.

Petrow, S. (1994). *Policing morals: The metropolitan police and the home office, 1870–1914.* Oxford, UK: Clarendon Press.

Schmitz, H. (1927). *Das internationale Verbrechertum und seine Bekämfung* [International criminality and its control]. Inaugural doctoral dissertation, University of Cologne.

Sheptycki, J. (Ed.). (2000). *Issues in transnational policing.* London: Routledge.

United Kingdom. Public Record Office. Records created and inherited by the Foreign Office. FO 45/784. General Correspondence before 1906, Italy, Sir P. Currie, 1898.

United Kingdom. Public Record Office. Correspondence respecting the Anti-Anarchist Conference Held in Rome in 1898. FO 881/7179.

United Kingdom. Public Record Office. Further Correspondence respecting the Anti-Anarchist Conference Held at Rome, 1899. FO 881/7372.

15

International Cooperation in Policing

MARIA (MAKI) HABERFELD

WILLIAM H. McDONALD

THE CONCEPT OF INTERNATIONAL POLICE COOPERATION

The concept of international police cooperation, both formal and informal, has quite an extensive history. This chapter provides an overview of the two most prominent organizations embodying cooperation in international policing, Interpol and Europol. An overview of their history, missions, goals, and activities will familiarize the reader with the basic tenets of the global exchange of information on issues related to law enforcement.

As we become of necessity more and more global in our attempts to thwart the sophisticated groups of criminals, the urgent need for international police cooperation becomes increasingly apparent. Its clear relevance could not have been more clearly illustrated than in the aftermath of the September 11, 2001

(9/11) terrorist attacks on the World Trade Center in New York City and the Pentagon in Washington, D.C. The only practical and efficient way to combat terrorist actions, and the entire host of its spin-off activities such as money laundering and trafficking in weapons of mass destruction, is through mutual cooperation among law enforcement agencies around the world.

The feasibility of such cooperation in operational matters will be illustrated at the end of this chapter by an overview of the role of police in peacekeeping missions. Such cooperation, although limited in scope and authority, provides a baseline for creative solutions in areas subject to a variety of disasters. Whether one looks at the Balkans or, more recently, at Iraq, it is quite clear that international police cooperation cannot be confined to clearinghouse (exchange of information) type of operations only. We have reached the stage at which a proactive and reactive global law enforcement response is the only way to address the international nature of crime. The global nature of crime, transcending as it does borders, cultures, languages, and legal systems, must be met with an effective response. The organizations and task forces overviewed in this chapter seek to assist in providing such a response.

The information provided herein is based on a compilation of available data, primarily downloaded from the Internet, without any content analysis of the sources. The official Web sites of Interpol, Europol, and the United Nations provide the most valuable source of information for research on international police cooperation. The final part of this chapter provides some critical analysis of the effectiveness and perceived efficiency of these organizations and entities.

INTERPOL

Interpol is the byname of the International Criminal Police Organization, an organization established to promote international criminal police cooperation. The name Interpol, once the telegraphic address of the organization, was officially incorporated into the new name adopted in 1956: International Criminal Police Organization-Interpol (abbreviated to ICPO-Interpol or, more frequently, Interpol).

History

The history of Interpol goes back to the 1920s. After World War I, Europe underwent a relatively new phenomenon, a great increase in crime. One of the countries most affected was Austria, which in 1923 hosted a meeting of the representatives of the criminal police of 20 nations to discuss the problems facing them. This meeting led to the establishment that same year of the International Police Commission (Interpol's predecessor), which had its headquarters in Vienna. From 1923 until 1938, the commission flourished. However, in 1938, Austria became part of Nazi Germany, and the commission with all its records was moved to Berlin.

The outbreak of World War II brought the activities of the commission to a standstill. After World War II, the French government offered the International Police Commission new headquarters in Paris, together with the services of a number of French police officials to form the general secretariat. This offer was gratefully accepted, and the commission was thus revived, although its complete reorganization was necessary because all its prewar records had been lost or destroyed. The commission again became very active, and by 1955, the number of affiliated countries had increased from 19 to 55.

A modern and complete constitution for the organization was ratified in 1956. At the same time, its name was changed to the International Criminal Police Organization-Interpol (Interpol, n.d.).

Member Countries

In 2004, Interpol was the second largest international organization in terms of membership after the United Nations, with 181 member countries (as of April 2004), from Afghanistan to Zimbabwe, spread over five continents. Among the member countries (see the complete list at www.interpol.int/Public/Icpo/Members/default.asp) are, for example, the People's Republic of China, Cuba, and Vietnam; all the Arab nations, including Libya and Iraq; and all the former Soviet republics with the exception of Tadjikistan and Turkmenistan. North Korea is one of the few countries that are not members of Interpol. Affiliated with Interpol are, among others, India, Indonesia, the Russian Federation, and the United States as well as small such countries as Aruba, Monaco, and the Seychelles.

Every member country has an Interpol office called a National Central Bureau, which is staffed with the country's own police officers. This bureau is the single point of contact for foreign governments requiring assistance with overseas investigations and information on the different police structures in other countries.

Contrary to popular belief, Interpol officers do not travel around the world investigating cases in different countries. Each member country employs its own officers to operate on its own territory and in accordance with its own national laws. Each member country can also send officers to serve a tour of duty at Interpol Headquarters in Lyon, France.

Mission

Interpol's official Web site states that its mission is "to be the world's pre-eminent police organization in support of all organizations, authorities, and services whose mission is preventing, detecting and suppressing crime" (Interpol, 2004h, col. 2). Interpol seeks to achieve this by providing both a global perspective and a regional focus; exchanging information that is timely, accurate, relevant, and complete; facilitating international cooperation; coordinating operational activities of the member countries; and making available know-how, expertise, and good practice.

Interpol offers three core services as it attempts to achieve its mission: (1) a unique global police communication system, (2) a range of criminal databases and analytical services, and (3) proactive support for police operations throughout the world (Interpol, 2004g).

Because of the politically neutral role Interpol must play, its constitution prohibits any involvement in the investigation of crimes that do not affect several member countries or engage in any activity of a political, military, religious, or racial character. Interpol's work focuses primarily on public safety and terrorism, organized crime, illicit drug production and trafficking, weapons smuggling, human trafficking, money laundering, financial and high-tech crime, and corruption (Interpol, 2004f).

Organizational Structure

Interpol has two interrelated governing bodies—the General Assembly and the Executive Committee (see Figure 15.1). Major decisions on the policy, budget, working methods, finances, and program of activities of Interpol are made by its General Assembly, which meets annually. It is composed of delegates appointed by the governments of member countries. Each member country represented has one vote.

The Executive Committee supervises the execution of the decisions of the General Assembly and the work of the secretary general. The committee has 13 members: the president (who chairs the committee), 4 vice presidents, and 8 delegates. The members are elected by the General Assembly and should represent different countries. The president and the four vice presidents must come from different continents. The president is elected for 4 years and the vice presidents for 3.

Decisions and recommendations adopted by the two governing bodies are implemented by the General Secretariat. The current (serving until 2005) Secretary-General, Ronald K. Noble, is the first non-European and the first American to hold the position. A native New Yorker and long-serving prosecutor, he has held senior law enforcement positions in the U.S. Treasury and Justice Departments and, most recently, was a professor of criminal law at New York University (Interpol, 2004f).

Financing

Interpol is financed by the annual contributions paid by the governments of its 181 member countries. These contributions are calculated on a sliding scale according to the gross national product of the member countries. Interpol is taking on a multibillion-dollar crime problem with an annual budget

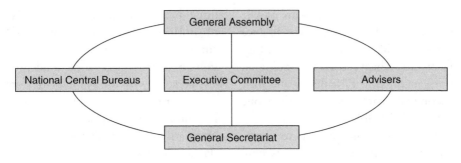

Figure 15.1   Structure of Interpol
SOURCE: www.interpol.int/Public/icpo/governance/default.asp

of only 32.8 million euros (about \$39 million in 2004). Efficiency requires Interpol to use its limited resources and technology as well as the support of its member countries to the best advantage (Interpol, 2004f).

Fighting Terrorism

Terrorists often seek to justify their acts on ideological, political, or religious grounds. That might seem to place terrorism outside of Interpol's reach because, as noted earlier, Interpol does not become involved in acts of political, military, religious, or racial character. However, Interpol does respond to acts of terrorism because those acts—regardless of their motivation—constitute a serious threat to individual lives and freedom.

Interpol's role in fighting terrorism is twofold: to prevent acts of international terrorism and, if such acts are carried out, to ensure that the perpetrators are brought to justice. It does this by exchanging information with its member countries through its secure messaging system and by arranging meetings of experts to address the subject. Interpol collects, stores, analyzes, and disseminates intelligence about suspect individuals and groups and their activities. These data are provided by its member countries and are obtained from public and other sources of information that Interpol monitors. All terrorist-related information has to be shared in a systematic, timely, and accurate manner. The veracity and

timeliness of the information are often directly proportional to its usefulness to the specialized officers within Interpol's Public Safety and Terrorism Branch, who are tasked with assessing the threat and issuing alerts and warnings.

To help member countries report on suspect individuals, Interpol has issued a number of practical guidelines to its member countries on the type of information needed. This includes information about suspect individuals and groups, modus operandi, evidence from scenes of the crime, and the use of new technologies by terrorist groups.

As an example of these antiterrorist activities, following the attacks on 9/11 Interpol has issued 55 so-called red notices (notices are explained in more detail below) regarding terrorists suspected of having committed or been connected to these global terrorist attacks. Interpol is also increasing its circulation of so-called blue notices (requests for information/location of a suspect), of which 19 have already been issued for the presumed hijackers (Deridder, 2001, October).

Fugitive Investigations

One of the most important fields of activity of the global law enforcement community today is the apprehension of fugitives. First of all, fugitives attempting to evade capture by crossing international borders should be apprehended and returned, already in the interests of justice. Moreover, as a result of their criminal activity, fugitives pose a pervasive threat to public safety worldwide. Fugitives are mobile and opportunistic. They frequently finance their continued flight from the law by further criminal activities, which respect no traditional political or geographical boundaries and may result in criminal charges in more than one country (Interpol, 2004b).

Interpol's activities in respect to international fugitives have been part of its core business since the creation of the organization. At the request of its member countries, Interpol electronically circulates on an international basis notices containing identification details and judicial information about wanted criminals. A number of countries have given Interpol's red notices legal status as a basis for provisional arrest.

The General Secretariat of Interpol offers its member countries direct automatic search facilities and responds to queries concerning wanted persons. Although these are important tools in the hunt for fugitives, they are not sufficient. Interpol believes that its member countries need a proactive approach in locating and hunting fugitives at the international level. That is why, in an effort to further assist its member countries in apprehending fugitives, the secretary general has established a new investigative service at the General Secretariat, which deals exclusively with matters related to fugitives. The Fugitive Investigative Support Sub-Directorate, as it is known, actively encourages the international search for and arrest of fugitive offenders wherever they may hide, coordinates and enhances international cooperation in the field, collects and disseminates best practice and expert knowledge, offers direct investigative support and specialized knowledge, and develops and promotes best practice and training (Interpol, 2004b).

The International Notices System

One of Interpol's most important functions is to help the police of its member countries in communicating critical crime-related information to one another. In practice, this is done primarily through Interpol's system of notices, which help the world's law enforcement community exchange information about missing persons, unidentified bodies, persons who are wanted for committing serious crimes, and criminal modus operandi. In addition, Interpol notices are used by the International Tribunals for the Former Yugoslavia and Rwanda to seek persons wanted for serious violations of international human rights law (Interpol, 2003).

Each notice gives full details of the individual concerned, the relevant national arrest warrant or court order, and specifically requests that the fugitive be traced and arrested or detained with a view to extradition.

Interpol issues five types of notices: (1) Red notices, based on a national arrest warrant, are used to seek the arrest and extradition of suspects. (2) Blue notices are used to seek information on the identity of persons or on their illegal activities related to a criminal matter. Such blue notices are used primarily for tracing and locating offenders when the decision to seek to extradite them has not yet been made and for locating witnesses to crimes. (3) Green notices are used to provide warnings and criminal intelligence about persons who have committed criminal offenses and who are likely to repeat these crimes in other countries. (4) Yellow notices are used to help locate missing persons, including children, or to help people (such as persons suffering from amnesia) to identify themselves. Finally, (5) black notices are used to determine the identity of deceased persons (Interpol, 2003).

Interpol notices often concern fugitives, terrorists, and violent criminals who pose an imminent danger to people throughout the world, as well as perpetrators of other forms of serious crime with an international dimension. For this reason, Interpol notices should be processed quickly by the General Secretariat and responded to quickly by the National Central Bureaus. To minimize delays in exchanging information on notices, to make it less labor-intensive, and in general to improve efficiency, Interpol's General Secretariat introduced a more rapid and cost-efficient procedure for requesting and issuing notices. The previous paper-based system was converted into an electronic system at the disposal of member countries with the necessary technical equipment. This new system allows all member countries a secure, speedy, and efficient possibility of requesting and receiving notices in an electronic format. The faster circulation of notices from and to the National Central Bureaus coincided with the introduction at the General Secretariat of a new 72–hour production deadline for high-priority notices, such as notices regarding terrorists (Interpol, 2003).

All new notices are now published on Interpol's restricted-access Web site. This allows all member countries having the necessary electronic capability to access them directly and to print copies where needed. In addition, Interpol is seeking to publish all red, yellow, and black notices on Interpol's public Web site unless a member country directly concerned requests otherwise. Public knowledge of an arrest warrant is often of great value to law enforcement agencies in their efforts to obtain information that is important to their work (Interpol, 2003).

Children and Human Trafficking

In 1989, the U.N. Convention on the Rights of the Child was adopted. The convention has the highest number of signatories ever, 190 countries. The purpose of the convention is to protect all children from all forms of abuse. The convention requires its signatories to take all appropriate measures to prevent child prostitution and the production of child pornography.

Interpol's involvement in the investigation of offenses against children began in 1989, following the adoption of the U.N. convention. A specialized Trafficking of Human Beings Sub-Directorate was set up at Interpol Headquarters, and the combating of crimes against children became Interpol's highest priority. Furthermore, Interpol's Specialist Group on Crimes against Children (formerly known as the Standing Working Party on Offences against Minors) brings together law enforcement officers from every continent to exchange information, develop working relationships, and agree on and implement operational matters. These semiannual meetings now attract more than 100 police officers from some 40 countries. The Specialist Group deals with child prostitution, child pornography, missing children, and trafficking in children and has recently taken on the issue of the management of sex offenders, which reflects the reality that to protect children, known sex offenders need to be prevented from reoffending. The Specialist Group has also produced the *Interpol Handbook of Good Practice for Specialized Officers Dealing With Crimes Against Children*. This handbook has been circulated to all member countries (Cameron-Waller, 2001).

Interpol is also deeply engaged in combating the increasing amount of child pornography, especially that distributed over the Internet. Interpol's General Secretariat has set up an automated image comparison database that is capable of linking series of images to provide investigators with the tools necessary to rapidly analyze data seized from persons suspected of involvement in child pornography. In recent years, Interpol has coordinated a number of international operations that have been initiated by individual member countries and that have led to significant successes in identifying and prosecuting those who are active in child pornography (Cameron-Waller, 2001).

Interpol maintains a database on missing and abducted children on behalf of the 181 member countries. The only children appearing on this Web site are those on whom the respective law enforcement authorities have requested that Interpol circulate information on an international basis, which is why, out of the very large number of children who go missing, only a few hundred appear in the database (Interpol, 2004i).

In June 1999, Interpol's General Secretariat, at the request of member countries, initiated Project Bridge to facilitate more effective and efficient collection of information on organized crime groups and associations involved in the smuggling of immigrants and to improve the combating of this form of crime by undertaking adequate prevention and investigative measures (Interpol, 2004k).

Drug Control

Interpol's Criminal Organizations and Drug Sub-Directorate is located within the Criminal Intelligence Directorate of its General Secretariat. This subdirectorate is the central repository of professional and technical expertise in drug control within the Interpol framework and provides assistance, for example, to National Central Bureaus. Essentially, it acts as a clearinghouse for the collection, collation, analysis, and dissemination of drug-related information. It also monitors the drug situation on a global basis, seeks to identify international drug trafficking organizations, coordinates international investigations, and maintains liaison with the United Nations, its specialized agencies, and other international and regional organizations involved in drug control activities.

Interpol's Criminal Organizations and Drug Sub-Directorate seeks to enhance cooperation among member countries and to stimulate the exchange of information among all national and international enforcement bodies concerned with countering the illicit production, traffic, and use of narcotic drugs and psychotropic substances. In addition to responding to international drug investigation inquiries and coordinating international drug investigations where at least two member countries are involved, the subdirectorate

organizes working meetings involving two or more countries where common links have been identified in cases being investigated in those member countries. The subdirectorate also organizes either regional or worldwide meetings on specific drug topics, on an annual or ad hoc basis. The aims of these meetings on specific topics include assessing the extent of the drug problem in question, exchanging information on the latest methods of investigative techniques, and further strengthening cooperation within the law enforcement communities.

With its worldwide membership, Interpol is able to follow developments around the world in relation to drug trafficking. This offers the possibility of making links between drug cases being conducted by national administrations, links that would otherwise seem unrelated. When it is clearly established that there is good potential for developing a substantial case, this case is given an operational name. As the case is developed, a working meeting of the concerned countries can be organized to bring together all of the case officers concerned to discuss all aspects of the case and devise future strategy (Interpol, 1999).

Financial Crime

Some transnational crimes are clearly financial in nature (e.g., money laundering), but even those without an obvious link will likely involve illicit financial transactions as an integral aspect of the crime. In its capacity of facilitating the cooperative efforts of police, international institutions, and the private sector, Interpol has an important role in responding to financial crime.

Payment Cards

Interpol assumed responsibility for counterfeit currency as a result of an international treaty, the 1929 International Convention for the Suppression of Counterfeiting Currency (known as the 1929 Geneva Convention), but there are no similar arrangements for counterfeit payment cards, and it is unlikely that there will be such arrangements in the near future. Payment cards are increasingly being used as a substitute for cash. With the growth of debit card activity and emergence of electronic applications, the trend is likely to increase rather than diminish. Although it is difficult to be specific about the quantity of counterfeit currency in circulation, which varies considerably from country to country, its monetary value is thought to be far less than the millions of dollars in losses a year as a result of payment card counterfeiting (Interpol, 2004j).

Money Laundering

The international police community is aware that there is a need to achieve major results in the struggle against the financial criminal activities related to organized criminal groups. During the past 20 years, Interpol's General Assembly has passed a number of resolutions that have called on member countries to concentrate their investigative resources on identifying, tracing, and seizing the assets of criminal enterprises.

These resolutions have also called on member countries to increase the exchange of information in this field and encourage governments to adopt laws and regulations that would allow access by the police to the financial records of criminal organizations and would also allow the confiscation of proceeds gained by criminal activity. A concise working definition of money laundering was adopted by Interpol's General Assembly in 1995: It is defined as any act or attempted act to conceal or disguise the identity or illegally obtained proceeds so that they appear to have originated from legitimate sources.

On September 17, 2001, a Financial and High Tech Crime Sub-Directorate was established within the Specialised Crimes Directorate of ICPO-Interpol. Police officers

in the subdirectorate also deal with offenses relating to money laundering, counterfeit currency, payment cards, and intellectual property. The subdirectorate seeks to provide National Central Bureaus with expertise in specialized areas and enhance partnerships with relevant organizations, develop and coordinate best practices, and increase the flow and exchange of information related to these forms of crime (Interpol, 2004c).

Intellectual Property Crime

This particular area of crime covers an array of offenses from trademark and patent right infringements to software piracy and affects a vast range of products from medicines to aircraft and vehicle spare parts, from clothing to music CDs and computer software. The total losses caused by this form of crime add up to hundred of billions of U.S. dollars globally every year. Interpol has recognized the extensive involvement of organized crime and terrorist groups in intellectual property crime. In 2000, the Interpol General Assembly mandated the Interpol General Secretariat to take action not only to raise awareness of the problem but also to provide a strategic plan in close cooperation with private industry (Interpol, 2004d).

Interpol's first international conference on intellectual property crime (Lyon, France, November 15–16, 2001) led to the establishment of a Group of Experts on Intellectual Property Crime, bringing together representatives of all the key stakeholders, including custom authorities, international agencies, and the private sector. The Group of Experts functions as a forum for the exchange of information and facilitation of investigations into intellectual property offenses and will also offer support through tailored training programs. The group will be multi-agency, drawing its membership from public and private sectors (Interpol, 2004d).

Corruption

Interpol's International Group of Experts on Corruption (IGEC) was established in 1998. Its membership consists of law enforcement representatives from eight countries (including the United States), a representative of Interpol's General Secretariat, and seven other persons representing a variety of international organizations, the international financial services community, and academia. This group was mandated to develop and implement an anticorruption strategy, with the objective of not only raising awareness of the major issues but also, and in particular, improving the capacity and effectiveness of law enforcement in the fight against corruption (Interpol, 2004a).

The original concept and structure of the group was, in essence, that it should be made up in equal numbers of representatives of the Interpol regions—namely, Africa, the Americas, Asia, and Europe. This would allow for coordination and harmonization of the different national and regional approaches to combating corruption. In addition, an advisory group was set up, consisting of a variety of other international stakeholders in anticorruption efforts. The purpose behind the proposal for such a group was to enable law enforcement to combat corruption (as a phenomenon) holistically, in cooperation with all major stakeholders and the community at large.[1]

Among its activities, the IGEC has prepared a code of ethics and code of conduct (subsequently adopted by Interpol's General Assembly in 1999), a survey of police integrity in its 181 member countries, and global standards to combat corruption in police forces and services (adopted by Interpol's General Assembly in 2002).

The global standards referred to consist of several principles and numerous measures designed to improve the integrity of police forces and services, as well as efficacy in combating corruption, and to represent an ideal toward which the Interpol member countries should strive. These standards have been well received by the international law enforcement community and mark the beginning of a proactive approach for law enforcement in combating corruption (Interpol, 2004a).

Publications

Interpol's primary publications include the *International Criminal Police Review* and *International Crime Statistics*. The *International Criminal Police Review*, which was published between 1946 and 2001, is not currently in production as Interpol reassesses the publication's role. However, sample articles since 1998 are available at the publication's Web site (www.interpol.int/Public/Publications/ICPR/default.asp) and the interested reader will find information on subjects such as investigation techniques, forensic science, and international crime.

Interpol has published *International Crime Statistics* every 2 years since 1950 and every year since 1993. Since 2000, the publication has been available electronically on a country-by-country basis (free of charge) and in four languages (Arabic, English, French, and Spanish).

The statistics relate to the following major categories of offenses brought to the attention of the police: murder, sexual offenses (including rape), serious assault, theft (e.g., aggravated theft, robbery and violent theft, breaking and entering, theft of motor cars), fraud, counterfeit currency offenses, drug offenses, and the total number of offenses contained in national crime statistics.

The data are provided by the National Central Bureaus, and Interpol publishes them as submitted, without any attempt to process them. Due primarily to the legal and procedural differences in the different countries and the differences in statistical methods, the statistics cannot be used for comparative purposes. Police statistics reflect only reported crimes, which represent only a fraction of the "real" level of crime. Furthermore, the volume of crime reported to the police depends, to a certain extent, on the action of police and can vary with time, as well as from country to country. Consequently, the data published in the current set of statistics should be interpreted with caution (Interpol, 2004e).

Regional Activities

In 2001, the Interpol General Secretariat set up the Directorate for Regional and National Police Services. It comprises five subdirectorates—Africa, Americas, Asia and South Pacific, Europe, Middle East and North Africa—and a Sub-Regional Co-ordination Bureau. Underlying the establishment of the directorate was the realization that practical law enforcement needs in each region vary to some extent. By promoting a network of regional institutions and developing effective strategic alliances with other institutions, Interpol seeks to provide better-tailored assistance through its National Central Bureaus. In time, the bureau of each region will have the same facilities as the General Secretariat.

To illustrate the work of the regional subdirectorates, the Sub-Directorate for the Americas can be examined more closely (see Interpol, 2004l). Its primary mission is to support regional and national crime-fighting activities in the Americas by providing a wide range of operational and administrative services.

The subdirectorate covers 37 member countries and seven sub-bureaus, servicing a total area of more than 15 million square miles and a population of more than 800 million. For management purposes, the region has been divided into four subregions: North America, Central America, South America, and the Caribbean. All the Interpol National Bureaus in the Americas are linked by computer, enabling them to exchange information bilaterally with other National Bureaus and with the General Secretariat in Lyon.

The objectives of this and other subdirectorates are to address regional crime issues,

increase the flow and exchange of information on priority crime issues, increase the exchange of information with regions, make information available on regional basis, and provide adequate support at the regional and national level. The staff of the subdirectorate analyzes crime reports prepared in the region to identify emerging crime trends and to prepare adequate responses. It also assists in specific cases—for example, by monitoring and helping to coordinate complicated ongoing criminal investigations and by organizing and supporting ad hoc working groups on specific cases. The subdirectorate seeks to provide backup support to individual National Central Bureaus by identifying problems and assisting the bureaus in overcoming difficulties. More generally, the subdirectorate seeks to improve the quantity and quality of information entered into the Interpol databases, promotes the relevant training programs in the region, pursues and promotes agreements with regional law enforcement organizations and other potential Interpol partners, and provides secretariat support for Interpol activities in the Americas, such as the American Regional Conference and other meetings organized by Interpol in the region (Interpol, 2004l).

EUROPOL

History

The European Union was originally established largely to promote the economic integration of its member states. Economic integration, however, brings with it new opportunities for offenders, above all the ease with which they can transcend national borders. Because crime was being increasingly organized at a European level rather than on a national or local level, politicians agreed that an organization was needed that could coordinate the law enforcement resources of member states to effectively tackle crime on a pan-European level (a level that as of May 1,

2004, encompasses 25 countries).[2] In 1992, the Maastricht Treaty established Europol's predecessor, the European Drugs Unit. It formally began operations on January 3, 1994. The European Drugs Unit had a rather limited mandate; it was focused on supporting each member state's fight against drugs and the associated money laundering.

The Convention on the Establishment of a European Police Office (the Europol Convention) was adopted on July 26, 1995, and by 1998 had been ratified by all the member states. On July 1, 1999, Europol formally took over the work of the European Drugs Unit. It is based in The Hague, in the Netherlands. Its remit has grown from drugs policing to include areas of serious crime as diverse as terrorism, drug trafficking, trafficking in human beings, illegal immigration, trafficking in radioactive and nuclear substances, trafficking in stolen motor vehicles, counterfeiting of the euro, and money laundering associated with international criminal activities (British Broadcasting Corporation [BBC], 2003; Europol, 2004).

Mission

As is the case with Interpol, Europol is (at least at present) not an operational entity in that Europol staff members do not have police powers in the individual member states. Thus, they do not, for example, investigate offenses or question suspects. Instead, Europol seeks to support the law enforcement agencies of all its member states primarily by gathering and analyzing information and intelligence specifically about people who are members or possible members of criminal organizations that operate internationally. This information is received from a variety of sources, such as the national police forces as well as other international crime-fighting organizations (such as Interpol), and is entered into computers for processing and analysis. When Europol identifies information that requires action by the national law enforcement agencies, such as connections identified between criminal offenses, it notifies the competent authorities without delay of information concerning them. Europol is also charged with the task of developing expertise in certain fields of crime and making this expertise available to the member states when needed (Europol, 2002c, 2004). Europol thus serves as a link between the law enforcement agencies of the member states of the European Union. On October 16, 1999, an essentially parallel unit called Eurojust was created to serve the same function among the prosecution authorities of the member states. To foster close cooperation between Eurojust and Europol—necessary in particular because of the key role that the prosecutors have in many member states in guiding the course of police investigations—Eurojust also has its headquarters in The Hague, in the Netherlands (Eurojust, n.d.).

Organizational Structure, Management, and Control

Europol is above all a body for the coordination of international law enforcement. The police officers working at Europol fall into two categories: regular staff members and liaison officers. The regular staff members (some 391 as of January 2004) take care of the joint activities, such as planning and analysis. The liaison officers (some 60 as of January 2004) represent a variety of national law enforcement agencies: the police, customs, gendarmerie, immigration services, and so on. Their function is largely to work together on individual cases that affect their national law enforcement interests. For example, if an analysis of data shows that a case may have connections with Germany and Spain, the German and Spanish liaison officers will meet together to discuss how to deal with the case. They will then liaise with the competent national or local law enforcement authorities to ensure follow-through.

Europol is accountable to the European Union Council of Ministers for Justice and Home Affairs (Europol, 2002d). The council is responsible for the main control and guidance function of Europol. It appoints the director and deputy directors and adopts the budget. It also adopts a number of important implementing regulations related to Europol's work. Each year, the council forwards a special report to the European Parliament on the work of Europol. The European Parliament is also consulted if the Europol Convention or other Europol regulations are amended.

Europol's Management Board is composed of one representative of each member state. Each member has one vote. The Commission of the European Communities is also invited to attend the meetings of the Management Board with nonvoting status. The Management Board meets at least twice a year to discuss a wide range of Europol issues that relate to its current activities and its future developments. It also unanimously adopts a general report on Europol's activities during the previous year. The Management Board also adopts a report on Europol's future activities, taking into account the operational requirements of member states as well as the budgetary and staffing implications for Europol. These reports are submitted to the Council of Ministers of Justice and Home Affairs for approval (Europol, 2002d).

Europol is headed by a director appointed by the council acting unanimously, after obtaining the opinion of the Management Board, for a 5-year period. The director's mandate may be renewed once for a further period of 4 years. The director is responsible for the day-to-day administration of Europol, the performance of its tasks, the personnel management, and other tasks assigned to him or her by the Europol Convention or by the Management Board. The director is assisted by deputy directors, also appointed by the council, for a 4-year period, renewable once.

After the events of 9/11, the Interpol Directorate was partially restructured. The three departments—Investigation Support, Intelligence Analysis, and Organized Crime—were combined into one single department called Serious Crime (as shown in Figure 15.2), thus combining information exchange, analysis, and expertise.

Cooperation With Third Countries and International Organizations

Europol has improved its international law enforcement cooperation by signing bilateral agreements with the following non-EU countries and international organizations: Iceland, Norway, and the United States, and the European Central Bank, the European Monitoring Centre on Drug and Drug Addiction, Interpol, and the World Custom Organization. Furthermore, Europol opened a Liaison Office in Washington D.C. (Europol, 2004).

The Europol Computer System

The Europol Convention calls on Europol to establish and maintain a computerized system to allow input, access, and analysis data. The convention lays down a strict framework for human rights and data protection, control, supervision, and security. The Europol Computer System (TECS) will have three principal components: an information system, an analysis system, and an index system (Europol, 2004).

The analysis and index systems are already in place. A provisional version of the information system became operational on January 1, 2002. More advanced versions that will eventually connect all member states are under development.

Because of the strict data protection legislation in many member states of the European Union, the Europol Convention set up a special body to ensure compliance with such legislation: the Joint Supervisory Body. This body is composed of two representatives of each

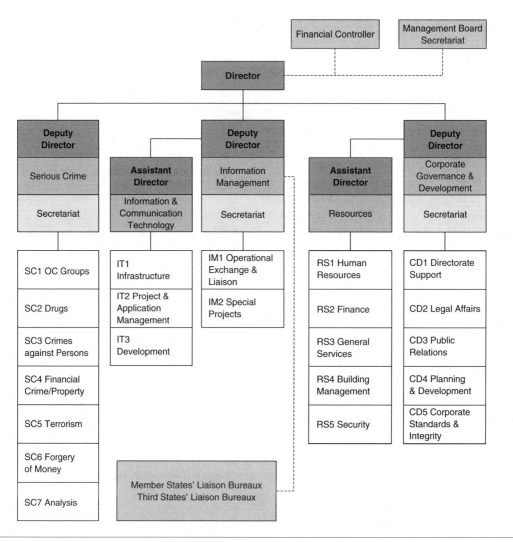

Figure 15.2 Europol Organization Chart
SOURCE: www.europol.eu.int.

of the national Supervisory Bodies, appointed for 5 years by each member state. Each delegation has one vote. Its task is to review the activities of Europol to ensure that the rights of the individual are not violated by the storage, processing, and use of the data held by Europol. It also monitors the permissibility of the transmission of data originating from Europol. Each individual has the right to request the Joint Supervisory Body to ensure that the manner in which his or her personal data have been collected, stored, processed, and used by Europol is lawful and accurate (Europol, 2002d).

Financing

Europol is funded by contributions from the member states, calculated on the basis of their gross national product. The budget for 2003 was 55.5 million euros (approximately $68 million). The annual accounts of

Europol are subject to an audit, which is carried out by the Joint Audit Committee (Europol, 2004).

Activities

Europol is deeply involved in combating all kinds of major crimes taking place in the member states. The results of its activities are published in detail in the *Europol Annual Reports.* The following is a presentation of selected Europol activities based on its annual reports for 2001 and 2002 (Europol, 2002a, 2002b).

Combating Terrorism

Following the events of 9/11 and the subsequent decisions taken by the EU Council of Justice and Home Affairs Ministers on September 20, 2001, Europol together with the member states set up a Counter-Terrorism Task Force (CTTF) to implement a comprehensive set of measures. The CTTF consists of experts and liaison officers from the police forces and services of member states, as well as intelligence services in an unprecedented exercise of cooperation and collaboration.

In addition to the creation of the CTTF, Europol provided several products and services related to counterterrorism. The exchange of counterterrorist information between member states by way of the Europol liaison officers and the network of national units expanded. A special conference on terrorism was held in Madrid (January 29–February 2, 2002). Several directories were updated—for example, on the counterterrorism responsibilities on the national level within each member state, counterterrorism legislation in member states, and the counterterrorism competencies/centers of excellence in the member states.

The *Open Source Digest* on terrorism-related activity is disseminated to the member states on a weekly basis. Also updated was the *Glossary of Terrorist Groups,* containing

basic details about their origins, ideology/objectives, leadership, and activities.

Periodical trends and situation reports are provided on topics related to terrorism, based on open sources information that is reported by member states to Europol.

Financial Crimes and Other Crimes Against Property and Public Goods, Including Fraud

In the area of financial and property crime, Europol's activities currently focus on providing strategic support, while preparing for more operational activities in the immediate future. In the field of money laundering, Europol began to systematically collect information on suspicious transactions that were identified by the law enforcement and judicial authorities of the member states. Further strategic support included the issuing of information bulletins on specific matters related to financial investigations, and assistance in an initiative to create a *European Manual on Money Laundering.* An E.U. "Situation Report" was elaborated in the area of combating credit card fraud. The result of this work will be used to define a common E.U. strategy to fight this phenomenon.

The Financial Crime Information Centre was further developed with a view to providing member states with access through a secure Web site. This Web site includes a library of information related to financial matters and various technical subjects related to financial investigations.

As for stolen vehicles, Europol was involved in 2001 in three operations concerning trafficking in stolen motor vehicles in Europe. Europol supported these operations by providing analytical support, coordinating the international cooperation, and coordinating the information exchange. To give a flavor of the clear operational results of these activities, one investigation resulted in the identification of 705 stolen vehicles and 130 suspects, and another operation led to 10 arrests of suspects and the issuing of 5 international arrest warrants. An investigation of the re-registration of secondhand cars identified 216 vehicles stolen in E.U. member states and re-registered in third countries. Europol initiated several bilateral investigations between third countries and member states.

In cooperation with the German and Austrian authorities, Europol developed the international European Vehicle Identification Database. This database was developed and translated by Europol and is now available in German, English, and French. Europol also developed the Blanco Documents Database containing stolen blank vehicle registration documents of various countries.

Combating Drug-Related Criminality

Europol has supported operational projects against, for example, Turkish, Latin American, and indigenous criminal groups. There has been an improvement in both the quality and quantity of information supplied to Europol. This has led to the identification of criminals, new common targets, and links between investigations, as well as improvement in cooperation among the member states based on intelligence and analysis supplied by Europol.

During 2001, Europol assisted law enforcement teams in three member states in the dismantling of nine illicit laboratories and the collection of evidence, thus contributing to seizures of synthetic drugs and precursors and to the arrests of several suspects. Currently, there are two expert systems related to drugs in place at Europol: the Ecstasy Logo System and the Cocaine Logo System. These systems improve law enforcement cooperation in member states through the identification of the links between seizures of ecstasy tablets and cocaine, primarily based on certain partic-ularities of the seized drugs.

Following a ban on opium poppy cultivation in Afghanistan and the 9/11 events, Europol also drafted a report on the situation of opium production in this country, the world's largest producer of opium. In the framework of the Joint Action on New Synthetic Drugs, Europol, together with the European Monitoring Centre for Drugs and Drugs Addiction (EMCDDA), drafted joint progress reports on GHB (gamma-hydroxybutyrate, a "rape drug"), ketamine, and PMMA (polymethylmethacrylate). As a direct result of the E.U. Action Plan on Drugs 2000–2004, a Collection Model for drug seizure statistics was drafted by Europol, in close coop-eration with experts from member states and the EMCDDA.

A Model of Parameters for the Assessment of the European Drugs Strategy, drafted by Europol in cooperation with experts from member states and the EMCDDA, has been adopted by the Horizontal Working Party on Drugs and was implemented in 2002.

Under the PHARE (Poland and Hungary: Action for the Restructuring of the Economy) Synthetic Drug Assistance Programme, during 2001, Europol organized and gave training courses on the dismantling of illicit laboratories to law enforcement officers, forensic scientists, and public prosecutors from several East European countries. In addition, training was provided to specialist teams in the Nether-lands. Europol also assisted French authori-ties in a joint training program on synthetic drugs and precursors for law enforcement staff from Latin American countries.

INTERNATIONAL POLICE TASK FORCES

Peacekeeping Operations: The Police Component

From 1948 up to the present, more than 65 international peacekeeping missions or operations have been established worldwide,[3] primarily, but not exclusively, under the flag of the United Nations. All these operations have included the contribution of law enforce-ment agencies, which so far have come from a total of 89 countries. Nonetheless, the main components of these peacekeeping forces have been military units, and the police component usually played only a minor part.

A few examples illustrate the role of the police in peacekeeping operations. The United Nations peacekeeping operation in the territory of the former Yugoslavia (the U.N. Protection Force), which lasted from 1992 to 1995, involved 37,795 military personnel and only 803 police officers.[4] The U.N. peacekeeping operation in Cyprus, which began in 1964 and continues at present, has involved 1,373 military personnel and only 35 police officers.

This ratio of military to police was more in favor of the police component in the peacekeeping operation in Namibia, from April 1989 through March 1990. The operation involved 4,493 military personnel and 1,500 police officers.[5] The very recent U.N. peacekeeping operation in East Timor, which began on May 20, 2002, is being carried out by a contingent of 5,000 troops and 1,250 police officers from 33 countries.[6]

In the following, the peacekeeping operations that have involved a sizable police force component are examined more closely, in chronological order.

The U.N. International Police Task Force in Bosnia and Herzegovina

The first peacekeeping operation involving a sizable police force component followed the work of the U.N. Protection Force mentioned above. This was the U.N. Mission in Bosnia and Herzegovina (UNMIBH), which included the U.N. International Police Task Force. UNMIBH began in January 1995 and continued until the European Union took over the responsibility from the United Nations in January 2003 (in the form of the E.U. Police Mission in Bosnia and Herzegovina).

Since the International Police Task Force (IPTF) was an organic component of UNMIBH,

understanding the place and role of the IPTF requires a description of the organizational structure, the scope of the mission, and the other components of UNMIBH.[7]

Background

In 1946, the Socialist Republic of Bosnia and Herzegovina (BiH) became part of the Federal People's Republic of Yugoslavia. The population of the republic (almost 4 million) is ethnically diverse. According to the 1991 census, 44% of the population were Muslims, 31% were Serbs, and 17% were Croats. For many years, a seemingly endless conflict had been carried out among these ethnic groups in the fields of religious, economic, cultural, and political life. As long as Yugoslavia was under Communist rule, under the leadership of Marshall Tito, these conflicts were "hidden under the cover." The post-Tito regime in Yugoslavia was not able to deal with these and other, no less important, conflicts, which beset all six federal republics. As a result of growing tensions in Bosnia and Herzegovina, on April 7, 1992, a civil war broke out. Serb paramilitary forces started firing on Sarajevo, and the bombardment of the city by heavy artillery began soon thereafter.

During this war, which spread to all the parts of the territory of BiH (about 20,000 square miles) and lasted until November 1995, approximately 200,000 people died and more than 2 million were driven from their homes.[8]

The member states of the United Nations were unable to agree on military intervention, although the United Nations did send troops to facilitate the delivery of humanitarian aid. This mandate was later extended to the protection of a number of territories declared by the United Nations as "safe areas." A cease-fire negotiated in December 1994 generally held until mid-March 1995.

In May 1995, North Atlantic Treaty Organization (NATO) forces launched air strikes on Serb targets (70% of the territory of BiH was then under Serb control), after the Serb military refused to comply with a U.N. ultimatum to remove all heavy weapons from a 12-mile exclusion zone around Sarajevo. Further NATO air strikes against Serb targets and a new offensive by the BiH and Croatian military helped to bring about U.S.-sponsored peace talks in Dayton, Ohio, in November 1995. Formalized in Paris in December of the same year, the agreement called for a federalized BiH in which 51% of the land would constitute the Croat-Bosnian federation and 49% would constitute the Serb Republic (Republika Srpska).[9] The Dayton-Paris Agreement,[10] which contained 15 detailed articles and 11 annexes, covered a broad range of issues, from the military aspects of the peace settlement and the delineation of a boundary between the Federation of Bosnia and Herzegovina and the Republika Srpska to the holding of democratic elections, the protection of human rights, and assistance to refugees. Part of the Dayton-Paris Agreement called for the withdrawal of the U.N. Protection Force and the deployment of the NATO-led multinational Implementation Force (IFOR), and in this connection also the establishment of the IPTF.

On December 20, 1995, IFOR replaced the U.N. Protection Force. On the next day, December 21, the U.N. Security Council set up the IPTF and the U.N. Civil Affairs office, brought together as the UNMIBH, originally for a period of 1 year. The Security Council renewed the UNMIBH mandate on several occasions, the last one extending the mandate to December 31, 2002, at which time UNMIBH was terminated (U.N. Peace and Security Section, 2003a).

UNMIBH's mandate was to contribute to the establishment of the rule of law in Bosnia and Herzegovina, assist in reforming and restructuring the local police, monitoring and auditing the performance of the police and others involved in the maintenance of law order, and monitor and investigate police compliance with human rights (U.N. Peace and Security Section, 2003b).

To implement this, UNMIBH

monitored, observed and inspected law enforcement activities and facilities,

advised law enforcement personnel and forces,

facilitated the law enforcement activities of the parties[11] within the IPTF mission of assistance,

trained law enforcement personnel,

assessed threats to the public and advised on the capability of law enforcement agencies to deal with such threats,

advised authorities in BiH on the organization of effective civilian law enforcement agencies, and

assisted by accompanying the local law enforcement personnel as they carried out their responsibilities.

Components

The main components of the UNMIBH were the IPTF, the Civil Affairs unit and the Division of Administration, which included the work of the U.N. Trust Funds (three separate trust funds were established by the U.N. secretary-general: the Restoration of Essential Public Services in Sarajevo in March 1994, the Police Assistance Programme in December 1995, and the Emergency Assistance Trust Projects outside Sarajevo in 2001). UNMIBH had a nationwide presence with regional headquarters in Banja Luca, Bihac, Doboj, Mostar, and Tuzla and a district headquarters in Brcko (U.N. Peace and Security Section, 2003a).

Personnel

The IPTF had an authorized strength of 2,057 police officers representing 43 countries, approximately 336 international civilian staff members from around 48 countries, and 1,575 locally recruited staff members. In October 2002, as the IPTF was nearing the end of its mandate, the United States and Jordan were providing the greatest number of police officers. Other countries contributing large numbers of officers included Bulgaria, Egypt, France, Ghana, India, Ireland, the Netherlands, Pakistan, Poland, Portugal, the Russian Federation, Sweden, Turkey, Ukraine, and the United Kingdom. During the 7 years that the IPTF was in existence, due to the rotation of police officers, more than 8,000 police officers from 43 countries took part (U.N. Security Council, 2002).

Mandate Implementation Plan, 2000–2002

The Mandate Implementation Plan (MIP) was a consolidated strategic and operational framework for the completion of UNMIBH's core mandate in Bosnia and Herzegovina. On the basis of the relevant Security Council resolutions, the MIP identified the objectives of the mission and the programs and modalities used to achieve those objectives. With the full cooperation of the parties[12] and the support of international partners, UNMIBH's assessed that the following goals could be met during its mandate (see, e.g., UNMIBH Public Affairs, n.d.):

All law enforcement personnel meet internationally determined standards of professional competence and personal integrity.

All civilian law enforcement agencies meet internationally determined standards of organizational capability and institutional integrity while progressively meeting the benchmarks for multiethnic representation.

The institutional, legislative, and operational requirements for effective civilian police and judicial cooperation in law enforcement are in place.

The State Border Service is fully established, and there is effective cooperation between law enforcement institutions at inter-entity, state, and international levels.

The public and the police know their respective rights and duties and how to exercise them.

BiH is supported in playing a full role as a member state of the United Nations.

The Police Component (The International Police Task Force)

Overall Goal

The IPTF monitored and advised local police with the objective of changing the primary focus of the police from the security of the state to the protection of the individual. In so doing, IPTF was helping to restructure and reform the local police to create democratic and professional police forces that should be multiethnic, effective, transparent, impartial, accountable, and representative of the society they serve and that will facilitate the return of refugees and displaced persons.

Police Reform

IPTF aimed to create a professional police force that met international standards and accurately reflected the ethnic composition of the population according to the 1991 census in the federation and the 1997 election results in the Republika Srpska and by encouraging female recruitment. IPTF registered some 25,278 local police personnel.

Special Trafficking Operations Program (STOP)

This program was established in June 2001 to address the issue of the trafficking of women and girls for prostitution in Bosnia and Herzegovina. STOP teams (IPTF staff together with the local police) throughout the country actively coordinated their efforts with the relevant entity and cantonal authorities to ensure that all establishments determined to be involved in using trafficked woman and girls for prostitution were closed and that traffickers and brothel owners were brought to justice (Bureau for International Narcotics and Law Enforcement Affairs, 2003; U.N. U.N. Mission in Bosnia and Herzegovina, 2002).

The End of the Mandate

On December 31, 2002, the mandate of the UNMBIH, including its police component (the IPTF), was successfully completed. This mission and the IPTF made up the most extensive police reform and restructuring mission ever undertaken by the United Nations.

On a global scale, when we take into consideration the approximately 8,000 police officers from 43 different countries who served in the IPTF during the 7 years of its existence, the task force was unprecedented. The service of so many police officers in the BiH was quite fruitful. The UNBMIH and its main component, the IPTF, leave behind a legacy of democratic law enforcement, ensuring a secure environment for returning refugees. Independent local police structures have been established in the country, with approximately 16,000 law enforcement officers certified after a comprehensive verification process. All local police officers have been trained in basic standards of democratic policing. Progress has been made on minority recruitment and gender balance through the two police academies established by the UNMIBH and the IPTF.

It is highly symbolic that, among other police forces from various countries that are presently serving in the U.N. Mission of Support in East Timor (UNMISET), there is also a team of police officers from Bosnia and Herzegovina, who have developed under the help and supervision of the IPTF in that country (U.N. Mission of Support in East Timor, 2002).

The IPTF in BiH assisted not only in healing the wounds left by the tragic massacre of the 1992–1994 war but also in enlarging the scope of peace building and in laying the foundations for recovery. Bosnia and Herzegovina now has a "police force fit for Europe," firmly based on international standards of democratic policing and in the service of all citizens of BiH. It represents a major stride forward toward European integration. The foundation for a secure and stable environment in Bosnia and Herzegovina has been laid.[13]

The U.N. Liaison Office in Sarajevo

The U.N. Liaison Office in Sarajevo was established in January 2003. Its main task is to ensure a seamless transition from the UNMBIH and its IPTF, which completed their mandate on December 31, 2002, to the European Union Police Mission (EUPM).

The U.N. Liaison Office assists the EUPM in the implementation of its mandate. The aim is to preserve and build on the achievements of the UNMIBH in police reform and restructuring. The Liaison Office provides the institutional memory of the UNMIBH mission to EUPM to ensure continuity in the democratization process of law enforcement agencies.

Another task of the Liaison Office is to maintain close contact and continue the political dialogue with the authorities of Bosnia and Herzegovina on the state and entity levels. In addition, the office continues communication and close liaison with the Office of the High Representative, the Organization for Security Cooperation in Europe, the Office of the United Nations High Commissioner for Refugees and other international organizations.

The U.N. Trust Fund, after the successful implementation of its projects to equip the local police, continues with the implementation of a number of projects in Bosnia-Herzegovina aimed at the rehabilitation of the devastated infrastructure and the restoration of essential public services. The Liaison Office assumes the role of observing the implementation of U.N. Trust Fund projects and organizes media coverage on project completion (U.N. Liaison Office Sarajevo, 2002).

The European Union Police Mission in Bosnia and Herzegovina

The establishment of the European Union Police Mission (EUPM) has been endorsed by both the Peace Implementation Council Steering Board and the United Nations Security Council (Resolution 1396). The mission is established for a period of 3 years. Its annual budget is 38 million euros, of which 20 million euros come from the community budget.

EUPM began operations on January 1, 2003. It follows on from the U.N.'s IPTF. The mission is part of a broad approach followed by the E.U. and other actors, with activities addressing the whole range of rule of law aspects.

In line with the general objectives of the Dayton-Paris Agreement, the EUPM seeks to establish sustainable policing arrangements under BiH ownership in accordance with best European and international practice. It does so in particular through monitoring, mentoring, and inspection activities. Five hundred police officers from more than 30 countries make up the mission, coming from 15 E.U. member states as well as 18 other countries (EUPM, 2003).

The Kosovo Force's Multinational Police Specialized Unit

Kosovo lies in southern Serbia and has a mixed population, of whom the majority are ethnic Albanians. Until 1989, the region enjoyed a high degree of autonomy within the former Yugoslavia. In 1989, the Serbian leader Slobodan Milosevich altered the status of the region, removing autonomy and bringing the region under the direct control of Belgrade, the Serbian capital. The Kosovar Albanians strenuously opposed the move.

Military and paramilitary forces from the Federal Republic of Yugoslavia and the Kosovo Liberation Army were fighting day and night. Ethnic tensions were at their highest and claimed the lives of many. More than 1,500 Kosovar Albanians were killed. Nearly 1 million people had fled Kosovo to seek refuge.

Under the U.N. Security Council mandate (Resolution 1244 of June 10, 1999) the peace enforcement Kosovo Force (KFOR) was set up. The objectives of KFOR were to establish and maintain a secure environment in Kosovo, including public safety and order; monitor, verify, and when necessary, enforce compliance with the agreements that ended the conflict; and provide assistance to the U.N. Mission in Kosovo (NATO, 2003, 2004).

KFOR has two main components: the military component, consisting of five multinational brigades, and the police component, the Multinational Specialized Unit (MSU). In total, the KFOR troops come from 30 NATO and non-NATO nations.

The MSU is a police force with military status, with an overall police capability. It consists of a regiment of the Italian carabinieri (police), a contingent of the French gendarmerie (militarized police), and a platoon of the Estonian Army.

The MSU has substantial experience in combating organized crime and terrorism. It possesses the human resources and dedicated investigative tools needed to analyze the structure of subversive and criminal organizations. It also provides prevention and repression resources to be used as KFOR assets.

The MSU conducts general patrolling operations to maintain a regular presence within KFOR. Such operations are in support of KFOR routine patrol activity and allow the MSU to interact with the local community while deepening their overall knowledge of evolving criminal and security threats in each area. Each detachment in KFOR has a different strength depending on the public order and security situation of the area.

The primary tasks of the MSU are to maintain a secure environment and establish a presence through patrolling, attend to law enforcement in close cooperation with the U.N. Mission in Kosovo, gather information, police civil disturbances, gather and analyze criminal intelligence on organized crime, conduct antiterrorism and VIP escort operations, and investigate crimes related to military security (Bureau for International Narcotics and Law Enforcement Affairs, 2003; NATO, 2003, n.d.).

The Next Steps

The deployment of the police in peacekeeping missions originally occurred, exclusively, under the auspices of the United Nations and the European Union, and continues to recognize the primacy of the U.N. Security Council for the maintenance of internal security. Increasingly, however, the United Nations calls on regional organizations to take over responsibility for civilian crisis management in trouble spots closest to them. In June 2000, at a meeting of the European Council at Santa Maria da Feira, the member states of the European Union agreed that by 2003 they should be able to provide up to 5,000 police officers for international missions across the range of crisis prevention and crisis management operations. Within this goal, member states also took upon themselves the task of identifying and deploying up to 1,000 police officers as part of a so-called Rapid Reaction Police Force, when the need arises (within 30 days).[14]

The unexpected mass looting in Baghdad, Basra, and other Iraqi towns in April 2003 placed a new and very urgent task on the agenda of the police forces: preparing and setting up new well-armed and specialized antilooting police detachments. According to the Geneva Convention, in wartime the armed forces are responsible for the safety and security of hospitals, museums, banks, and the like in operational areas. The lessons from the recent war in Iraq are that the army alone is not capable of effectively preventing and combating mass looting. It should be supported with well-trained and highly specialized antilooting police units acting, where possible, in cooperation with the local police forces. Until now, police force detachments that participated in

war operations were not brought into action until some time had passed since the liberation of towns. However, in Baghdad, organized gangs of looters broke into the National Archaeological Museum, some other museums, libraries, banks, and even some hospitals almost simultaneously with the arrival of U.S. tanks and troops. Thus, in the future, police antilooting detachments should be prepared for action already with forward combat detachments. This is a very new, and not easy, task for the police, which, undoubtedly, must prepare some of its units for such work in the very near future (UNB Saint John Ward Chipman Library, 2002).

FUTURE TRENDS

The future of international police cooperation can and should be evaluated from the perspective of the assessment of the two supranational law enforcement organizations, Interpol and Europol, which despite their quite impressive geographical mandate remain nonoperational and serve more as clearinghouses for the exchange of information rather than as fully operational entities. To fully assess the potential of those two organizations, we must also look at the hybrid creation, referred to in this chapter as international police task forces, which, at this point, represent the only actively operational solution to law enforcement–related problems around the world.

We have established from the beginning of this chapter that to target, effectively and efficiently, transnational criminal activity, which appears to be on the constant rise, we need to identify operational mechanisms of response. Despite the fact that both Interpol and Europol are not operational in the traditional sense of this word, they can clearly serve as a very important backup system for operational agencies around the world. The key word, however, is *can*.

At this point, based on the overview of their capabilities and capacities, it is rather obvious that a number of problems emerge as an outcome of such multinational cooperation. First, to borrow from the terminology used in the literature dealing with terrorism, "One person's terrorist is another's freedom fighter." The membership, especially of Interpol, is open to virtually all existing countries, give or take a few. Among those members, one can find many countries that are not on friendly relations with one another on a variety of issues. Sharing information about potential terrorist threats with a country that harbors terrorism might prove to be quite challenging. Sharing information with the police force of a country that is well-known to be infiltrated by organized crime doesn't seem prudent, either. Finally, making sense of statistical data that are grouped and defined in a somewhat archaic manner won't contribute to much of an efficient response to the particular crime. For example, for statistical purposes, Interpol still groups murder and attempted murder in the same category.

To conclude, we would like to identify a number of recommendations for the future with regard to international police cooperation. First, the need for an efficient and effective operational force, such as an international police task force, is clearly a priority, especially given the recent developments in Iraq and Afghanistan. Such a task force needs a well-developed support system in the form of valid intelligence, and this could and must be supplied by organizations such as Interpol or Europol. However, the composition of such a task force has to be very carefully defined, and it remains to be seen who could be put in charge of such a decision-making process. Second, the existence of numerous international law enforcement academies, not discussed in this chapter, will further some informal cooperation among law enforcement agencies around the world, and this type of cooperation is frequently more valuable than a reliance on formal entities. Finally, the exchange of police representatives among allied countries such as was established by the New York Police Department after the 9/11 attack will certainly facilitate this formal and informal cooperation.

What we need in the future is some sort of a clearly defined policy with regard to international police cooperation, both on the level of exchange of information and operational assistance. The answer to the question of who will be in charge of this initiative remains open for now.

NOTES

1. The terms of reference of the group were discussed in January 2003 (see www.icac.org.hk/conference).

2. At the time of the establishment of Europol, in 1999, the European Union consisted of 15 countries: Austria, Belgium, Denmark, Finland, France, Germany, Greece, Ireland, Italy, Luxembourg, the Netherlands, Portugal, Spain, Sweden, and the United Kingdom. The new member states as of May 1, 2004, are Cyprus, the Czech Republic, Estonia, Hungary, Latvia, Lithuania, Malta, Poland, Slovakia, and Slovenia. Already in advance of the accession of these new member states to the European Union, agreements were drafted on cooperation. An early example of such an agreement was signed on September 27, 2001, with Estonia (Europol, 2001).

3. See, for example, the *European Foreign and Security Policy Newsletter,* Issue 9, April 2002, page 9, which lists 20 U.N. peacekeeping missions in which the Irish Garda (the Irish police force) has participated. For a full list of the total of 55 U.N. peacekeeping operations from 1948 to 2002, see www.un.org/Depts/dpko/dpko/home.shtml.

4. For more about this operation, see www.un.org/Depts/dpko/missions.

5. See www.un.org/Depts/dpko/missions.

6. See www.un.org/Depts/dpko/missions/unmiset/mandate.html.

7. All information about the UNMIBH and the IPTF, unless not specified otherwise, is taken from the UNMIBH official Web site at www.un.org/Depts/dpko/dpko/home.shtml.

8. Excellent general descriptions of the war in Bosnia and Herzegovina can be found for example in *The World Almanac and Book of Facts 2000* (New York: World Almanac Books, 2002), p. 776, and *Encyclopedia Britannica* 2000, the online version (subscription required at www.britannica.com).

9. This Serb Republic in the territory of Bosnia and Herzegovina should not be confused with the Serb (Belgrad) and Montenegro Republic, which recently officially replaced the former Socialist Federal Republic of Yugoslavia.

10. The full text of the Dayton-Paris Peace Agreement is available at www.oscebih.org/essentials/gfap/eng/home.asp.

11. The parties are the Republic of Bosnia and Herzegovina (Muslims), the Federation of Bosnia and Herzegovina (Croats), and Republika Serpska (Serbs).

12. See www.oscebih.org/essentials/gfap/eng/annex11.asp.

13. However, such glowing views of peacekeeping missions, which are based on official U.N. reports and publications on the achievements of the UNMIBH and IPTF, are not shared by all. For example, the independent International Crisis Group (ICG), based in Brussels, gave a quite critical assessment of the results of their mission (A Report of the International Crisis Group, Sarajevo/Brussels, page 1, May 10, 2002, www.intl-crisis-group.org/projects/showreport.cfm?reportid=6440; URL no longer active).

14. *European Foreign and Security Policy Newsletter*. (2002, April). No. 9, pp. 1–2.

REFERENCES

British Broadcasting Corporation. (2003, December 2). *Crime fighters: Policing—Europol*. Retrieved May 3, 2004, from www.bbc.co.uk/crime/fighters/europol.shtml

Bureau for International Narcotics and Law Enforcement Affairs. (2003, January 10). *United States participation in international police (CIVPOL) missions*. Retrieved April 18, 2003, from www.state.gov/g/inl/rls/fs/ 16554.htm

Cameron-Waller, S. (2001, December 17). *Interpol statement: Second world conference on commercial exploitation of children*. Retrieved March 21, 2003, from www.interpol.int/ Public/Icpo/speeches/20011219.asp

Deridder, W. (2001, October). *16th annual Interpol symposium on terrorism*. Retrieved May 5, 2004, from www.interpol.int/public/nICPO/ speeches/20011022b.asp

Eurojust. (n.d.). *Welcome to Eurojust's website*. Retrieved May 3, 2004, from www.eurojust.eu.int/index.htm

European Union Police Mission. (2003). *European Union police mission in Bosnia and Herzegovina*. Retrieved May 7, 2004, from www.eupm.org/index.html

Europol. (2001). *Europol and Estonia establish a co-operation agreement in fighting organised crime*. Retrieved June 25, 2004, from http://www.europol.eu.int/

Europol. (2002a). *Annual report 2001*. Retrieved May 3, 2004, from www.europol.eu.int/index.asp?page=publar2001

Europol. (2002b). *Annual report 2002*. Retrieved May 3, 2004, from www.europol.eu.int/index.asp?page=publar2002

Europol. (2002c). *Frequently asked questions*. Retrieved May 3, 2004, from www.europol.eu.int/index.asp?page=faq&language=en

Europol. (2002d). *Management and control*. Retrieved May 3, 2004, from www.europol .eu.int/index.asp?page=mgmtcontrol&language=en

Europol. (2004, January). *Fact sheet on Europol*. Retrieved May 3, 2004, from www.europol.eu.int/index.asp?page=facts&language=en

Interpol. (1999, February 17). *Drug control*. Retrieved May 5, 2004 from www.interpol.int/Public/drugs/Default.asp

Interpol. (2003, March). *Interpol's international notices system*. Retrieved May 5, 2004, from www.interpol.int/Public/Wanted/Fugitives/Default.asp

Interpol. (2004a). *Corruption: Interpol group of experts on corruption*. Retrieved May 5, 2004, from www.interpol.int/Public/Corruption/IGEC/Default.asp

Interpol. (2004b). *Fugitive investigations: Interpol and fugitives*. Retrieved May 5, 2004, from www.interpol.int/Public/Wanted/Fugitives/Default.asp

Interpol. (2004c). *Funds derived from criminal activities*. Retrieved May 5, 2004, from www.

interpol.int/Public/FinancialCrime/Money Laundering/default.asp

Interpol. (2004d). *Intellectual property crime.* Retrieved May 5, 2004, from www.interpol.int/Public/FinancialCrime/IntellectualProperty/Default.asp

Interpol. (2004e). *International crime statistics.* Retrieved May 5, 2004, from www.interpol.int/Public/Statistics/ICS/default.asp

Interpol. (2004f, April). *Interpol: An overview.* Retrieved May 3, 2004, from www.interpol. int/Public/Icpo/FactSheets/FS200101.asp

Interpol. (2004g). *Interpol: Core functions.* Retrieved May 3, 2004, from www.interpol.int/Public/Icpo/default.asp

Interpol. (2004h). *Interpol: Mission.* Retrieved May 3, 2004, from www.interpol.int/Public/Icpo/Members/default.asp

Interpol. (2004i). *Missing children.* Retrieved May 5, 2004, from www.interpol.int/Public/Children/Missing/Default.asp

Interpol. (2004j). *Payment cards.* Retrieved May 5, 2004, from www.interpol.int/Public/CreditCards/Default.asp

Interpol. (2004k). *Project bridge.* Retrieved May 5, 2004, from www.interpol.int/Public/THB/PeopleSmuggling/Bridge/Default.asp

Interpol. (2004l). *Regional activities: Americas.* Retrieved May 5, 2004, from www.interpol.int/Public/Region/Americas/ Default.asp

Interpol. (n.d.). *Brief history of Interpol.* Retrieved May 3, 2004, from www.interpol.int/public/ICPO/history.asp

NATO. (2003, November). *KFOR information.* Retrieved April 14, 2003, from www.nato.int/kfor/kfor/about.htm

NATO. (2004). *Kosovo force.* Retrieved May 7, 2004, from www.nato.int/kfor/welcome.html

NATO. (n.d.). *Multinational specialized unit.* Retrieved April 17, 2003, from www.nato.int/kfor/kfor/msu.htm

UNB Saint John Ward Chipman Library. (2002). *Peace keeping and related operations.* Retrieved April 18, 2003, from www.unbsj.ca/library/subject/peace1.htm

U.N. Liaison Office Sarajevo. (2002, December 31). *About us.* Retrieved April 17, 2003, from web.archive.org/web/20030622024527/http://www.unlos-bih.org

U.N. Mission in Bosnia and Herzegovina. (n.d.). *Building a better future together: December 1995–June 2002.* Retrieved May 16, 2004, from www.un.org/Depts/DPKO/Missions/unmibh/Achiv.pdf

U.N. Mission of Support in East Timor. (2002, May 20). *East Timor UNMISET: Facts and figures.* Retrieved April 18, 2003, from http://un.org/Depts/dpko/missions/unmiset/ facts.html

U.N. Peace and Security Section. (2003a). *Bosnia and Herzegovina: UNMIBH—Background.* Retrieved May 7, 2004, from www.un.org/Depts/dpko/missions/unmibh/background.html

U.N. Peace and Security Section. (2003b). *Bosnia and Herzegovina: UNMIBH—Mandate.* Retrieved May 7, 2004, from www.un.org/Depts/dpko/missions/unmibh/mandate.html

U.N. Security Council. (2002, June 5). *Report of the Secretary-General on the United Nations mission in Bosnia and Herzegovina.* Retrieved on May 18, 2004, from http://216.239.51.104/search?q=cache:ZjDRIz7mTTcJ:www.womenwarpeace.org/bosnia/docs/sgreptosc 5jun02.pdf+iptf+hana&hl=en

16

Adjudicating International Crimes

FRANK HÖPFEL

CLAUDIA ANGERMAIER

International criminal law merges two legal disciplines that are fundamentally different in their focus: (1) international law, which deals with the legal duties and rights of equal sovereign states and (2) criminal law, where the focus is on the criminal responsibility of individuals.[1] Although the notion of individuals as subjects with certain rights under international law has a longer tradition in various humanitarian and human rights instruments,[2] individual criminal responsibility under international law is quite a recent phenomenon. Its roots can be traced back to the Treaty of Versailles of 1919 after World War I, which established the right of the Allied Powers to try to punish individuals responsible for "violations of the laws and customs of war."[3] On the basis of this treaty, attempts were made to submit Kaiser Wilhelm II to an allied military tribunal. It was only after World War II that trials of individuals before an international tribunal for crimes against international law took place. These were conducted before the Nuremberg and Tokyo Military Tribunals.[4] In its judgment, the Nuremberg Tribunal espoused the principle of international individual criminal responsibility contained in Article 6 of the Nuremberg Charter with the famous statement: "Crimes against international law are committed by men, not by abstract entities, and only by punishing individuals who commit such crimes can the provisions of international law be enforced."[5] The General Assembly of the United Nations in 1946 affirmed this principle for the crime of aggression, war crimes, and crimes against humanity.[6] Half a century later, the Statutes of the International Criminal Tribunals for the former Yugoslavia and Rwanda (ICTY and ICTR)[7] adopted under Chapter VII of the U.N. Charter reinforced the idea of individual criminal liability under international law for gross violations of international humanitarian law, and it is again reflected in Article 2 of the 1996 Draft Code of Crimes Against the Peace and Security of Mankind.[8] With the 1998 Rome Statute of the International Criminal Court (ICC), the principle of individual criminal responsibility under international law for aggression, genocide, war crimes, and crimes against humanity was firmly established.[9] Individuals can therefore be held directly accountable under international law for these crimes by international tribunals or national courts, irrespective of whether the crimes are punishable under domestic legislation.

The principles of *nullum crimen sine lege* and the concomitant *nullum poene sine lege,* which can be found in most national legal orders, dictate that no one can be held criminally accountable and punished for behavior that has not been declared criminal by law. The point of reference for domestic courts may be national or international law depending on whether states follow a dualist or monist conception of the relationship between international rules and the domestic legal order, but also depending on the degree of specificity required by states to satisfy the principle of legality. Adjudicating individuals for international crimes[10] thus presupposes the criminalization of certain behavior under international law or national law. Although proscriptions under international criminal law can be found in various international instruments as well as customary international law, these are not always transposed into national legislations. Some 20 categories of international crimes can be distinguished, most notably, aggression; genocide; crimes against humanity; war crimes; apartheid; slavery and slave-related practices; unlawful traffic in drugs and related drug offenses; destruction and theft of cultural heritage; unlawful

possession, use, and emplacement of weapons; theft of nuclear materials; unlawful human experimentation; unlawful acts against certain internationally protected elements of the environment; international traffic in obscene materials; piracy; aircraft hijacking; and torture and other forms of cruel, inhuman, or degrading treatment.[11] Bassiouni identifies four factors that determine states' policy of defining certain acts as international crimes:

(a) the prohibited conduct affects a significant international interest (including threats to peace and security);

(b) the prohibited conduct constitutes an egregious conduct deemed offensive to the commonly shared values of the world community (including conduct shocking to the conscience of humanity);

(c) the prohibited conduct involves more than one state (transnational implications) in its planning, preparation or commission either through the diversity of nationality of its perpetrators or victims, or because the means employed transcend national boundaries;

(d) the conduct bears upon an internationally protected interest which does not rise to the level required by (a) or (b) but which cannot be prevented or controlled without its international criminalization.[12]

Hence, transnational crimes constitute international crimes. International crimes do not, however, necessarily presuppose a transnational element;[13] indeed some of the most heinous crimes are committed within a state's territory by its own nationals. Although all these crimes are international crimes, the enforcement systems available for each of these crimes vary considerably.

The enforcement of international criminal law has traditionally been and still is to a large extent a decentralized system, relying on individual states to prosecute international crimes and execute the punishment. For the effective functioning of this system,[14] states in principle have to (1) proscribe international crimes under their national laws, (2) provide for jurisdiction over these crimes, and (3) actually assert their jurisdiction or, alternatively, extradite to a state that is willing to exercise its jurisdiction over the international crime. Customary international law and international treaties provide a framework in which states may decide to what extent they will assert their jurisdiction over specific crimes. Some international conventions do not leave such discretion to the state parties but oblige them to enact legislation with regard to international crimes. The content of these obligations varies: States may be obliged to criminalize certain behavior in their national laws, but often treaties also contain an obligation for states to enact rules that allow them to assert criminal jurisdiction when certain conditions are met. A centralized enforcement system of international criminal law entails the arrest, prosecution, adjudication, and the enforcement of the punishment by an international tribunal. The only examples of such a system were the Nuremberg and Tokyo Military Tribunals.[15] The ICTY and ICTR as well as the recently established ICC also prosecute and adjudicate certain international crimes but have to rely on the cooperation of states for the other aspects of enforcement, such as the arrest of suspects and the execution of prison sentences. As such, they only in part directly enforce international criminal law.[16]

The purpose of this chapter is to explore a specific aspect of enforcement—namely, the prosecution and adjudication of perpetrators of international crimes. In light of continuing criticism of the ICC and the Security Council Resolutions providing for the immunity of U.N. peacekeepers from adjudication by the ICC, it will be particularly important to discuss the role of national courts and the ICC in the adjudication of international crimes. We will provide a short overview of other tribunals that have jurisdiction over international crimes, such as the ad hoc tribunals and

internationalized courts. These courts need to be distinguished from international courts such as the International Court of Justice and the European Court of Human Rights, which do not have the competence to determine the criminal responsibility of individuals.

NATIONAL COURTS ADJUDICATING INTERNATIONAL CRIMES

In prosecuting conduct that constitutes a crime under international law, states do not necessarily invoke the fact that a crime under international law has been committed to justify their jurisdiction but, rather, proceed in accordance with their respective domestic legislation: first determining whether the conduct in question is proscribed under their domestic law and then whether there is a legal basis in their domestic legal order for asserting jurisdiction. Thus, it does not suffice that specific conduct is punishable under the domestic law of a state; the state must also be able to assert jurisdiction over the conduct in question. The rules governing the criminal jurisdiction of a state are primarily found in domestic legislation. International law only delimits the boundaries within which states may exercise their domestic jurisdiction. These boundaries are embodied in the so-called principles of jurisdiction, the most important of which are (a) the principle of territoriality (the crime was committed in the territory of the state), (b) the active personality principle (the perpetrator is a national of the state), (c) the protective principle (the crime violates essential interests of the state), (d) the passive personality principle (the victim is a national of the state), and (e) the universality principle (certain crimes can be adjudicated by any state, no matter where and by whom they were committed).[17] It is important to note that these principles are not all equally accepted and states may combine various principles when defining the extent of their criminal jurisdiction over a specific offense. Therefore, discrete categories such as territory and nationality are not necessarily invoked by states to justify their criminal jurisdiction over a specific incident. It has been argued that the overarching principle of international law that justifies a state in exercising jurisdiction is the existence of a *meaningful link* between the forum state and the specific criminal conduct.[18]

A distinction is often made between the jurisdiction to prescribe, to adjudicate, and to enforce.[19] Some commentators differentiate only between prescriptive and enforcement jurisdiction, where adjudication is taken to be a part of the enforcement of legal rules.[20] However, it is arguable that the distinction between prescriptive and enforcement jurisdiction is merely one of degree: There is a presumption that the enactment of rules is followed by their enforcement in the future.[21] In the following sections, the various principles under international law that allow a forum to assert jurisdiction, and thus give the state the *right* to prosecute crimes, will be discussed. This must be kept separate from the question of how far states are *obliged* to prosecute certain crimes. Last, we explore the effect of the Rome Statute on this existing decentralized enforcement system with reference to some national implementing legislation.

Traditional Bases for Asserting Jurisdiction

Territoriality

Territorial jurisdiction is the most uncontested principle of jurisdiction because it is closely related to the notion of sovereignty:[22] States may prosecute any person who commits an offense in whole or in part in their territory. It can be distinguished generally from extraterritorial jurisdiction, which does not flow from the idea of sovereignty but is tied rather to concrete state interests. This seemingly clear distinction has become blurred by broad conceptions of the *locus delicti* (the place where an offense was committed). For example, if an anthrax letter is posted in Austria and is intended for a person living in Vienna who receives the letter and dies from the contents, the offense of murder was committed in whole in the territory of Austria. However, if the same letter was posted in Germany, the offense was committed in part in German and in part in Austrian territory. Both the Austrian and German criminal code enable their courts to assert jurisdiction when only part of the offense took place in their territory: The *locus delicti* is defined as the place where the perpetrator acted or where the effect of the crime occurred or was intended to occur.[23] This means, in the second scenario, that both Austria and Germany can assert jurisdiction based on their respective national legal provisions, because the perpetrator acted in Germany and the effect of the crime took place in Austria. If, however, the letter was intercepted at the border before reaching its destination in Vienna, both Austrian and German courts would still be able to assert jurisdiction over the incident, because the Austrian criminal code also defines the *locus delicti* as that place where the effect of the crime was intended to take place. Therefore, the principle of territoriality in the Austrian and German criminal code covers also inchoate offenses.[24] U.S. courts have similarly asserted their jurisdiction based on the principle of territoriality in conspiracies in drug trafficking, based on the fact that drugs were intended to be trafficked to the United States.[25] Under Austrian law, conspiracy is defined as an independent criminal offense[26] and not merely as a material element of another crime such as drug trafficking, which is the reason why Austrian courts have not applied the principle of territoriality to thwarted conspiracies outside Austrian territory.[27] These examples illustrate that the definition of the material elements of a crime as well as the definition of the *locus delicti* in domestic legislation determines whether a state can assert jurisdiction over a specific criminal conduct based on the principle of territoriality. From the above it is clear that, especially in the case of transnational crimes involving different states, all these states could have concurrent territorial jurisdiction.[28]

Although it is accepted under international law that territorial jurisdiction can be established when the effect of the criminal act occurs in the territory of the forum state, the "effects doctrine," which allows states to assert jurisdiction over acts that have a significant effect in their territory,[29] is by no means generally accepted. In the case of the former, the effect of the act is a material element of the crime, whereas in the latter case, the effect is merely the vague concept of a general consequence of the conduct in question. The controversy has arisen mainly with regard to United States antitrust legislation, which, many affected states have argued, goes beyond what is permissible under international law.[30]

Nationality

The principle of nationality, which is often combined with the principle of domicile or residence, is based on the idea that citizens owe their state allegiance. They thus have to respect the laws of their state of nationality even when they leave its territory. States may punish their nationals under their own domestic law, independently of whether the behavior is punishable under the law of the state in whose territory the crime was committed.[31] In practice, states seem to assert such jurisdiction only in the case of grave offenses.[32] For example, the Austrian penal code establishes the jurisdiction of Austrian courts for statutory rape on the basis of nationality in conjunction with the principle of domicile, to combat the phenomenon of sex tourism.[33] Furthermore, the principle of nationality may also be invoked to assert jurisdiction over persons whose behavior is punishable under the laws of the territorial state and the state of nationality.[34] Traditionally, the principle of nationality has been favored by civil law countries and can be seen as a corollary to the constitutional prohibition of extraditing their own nationals.[35]

Protective and Passive Personality

On the basis of the protective principle, states may exercise their jurisdiction over criminal behavior that threatens the security of the state or other important public interests.[36] The principle of passive personality, allowing states to exercise jurisdiction on the basis of the nationality of the victim, is not as widely accepted by states as the other traditional principles of jurisdiction. Although continental systems often apply the principle of passive personality in conjunction with the principle of protection of state interests,[37] the United States has traditionally been a strong opponent of this principle.[38] U.S. Congress enacted legislation that accords U.S. courts jurisdiction over certain violent acts committed against American citizens.[39] However, this act requires that there must be an intention to harm the government or civilian population, thereby relying primarily on the protective principle.[40] In *United States v. Yunis*,[41] where the only link between the United States forum and the crime was the nationality of two passengers that had remained unharmed, U.S. courts were willing to assert their jurisdiction over the crime.[42] This could be seen as an acceptance of the principle of passive personality or universality, but not an application of the protective principle, because the action was not directed against U.S. interests. There is thus some marginal support for the passive personality principle.

The Principle of Universality

Overview

The principle of universality is the most controversial principle of jurisdiction.[43] As a principle of jurisdiction based solely on the nature of the crime, independent of notions of nationality, territoriality, and other important state interests, it does not fit the traditional framework outlined above under which states can assert jurisdiction when there is a meaningful connection with the crime. One can broadly distinguish between an absolute notion and a more restrictive notion of universal jurisdiction. Under the former view, states may assert their jurisdiction independently of whether the alleged offender is present in their territory, whereas the latter view ties universal jurisdiction to the presence of the accused in the territory of the forum state.[44]

As with all principles of jurisdiction, the source of justification under international law for applying universal jurisdiction to a specific crime may be found in international treaties as well as customary international law. International treaties that espouse universal jurisdiction only do so in the narrow sense[45] but generally also contain provisions that allow states to enact farther-reaching criminal jurisdiction.[46] Although many commentators and, most notably, human right groups have argued that customary international law allows for universal jurisdiction in the broad sense over certain serious international crimes, this may be only a desired state of affairs and not entirely reflect the extent to which such a broad notion is accepted by states.[47] Moreover, there is by no means agreement about which crimes are subject to universal jurisdiction.

The Princeton Project on Universal Jurisdiction brought together a group of leading international legal experts to formulate a set of guidelines for states to apply the universality principle in their courts and thus to increase accountability for certain serious crimes under international law. The Princeton Principles essentially advocate a broad notion of universal jurisdiction for piracy, slavery, crimes against peace (e.g., crimes of aggression), war crimes, crimes against humanity, genocide, and torture.[48] The presence of the alleged offender in the territory of the forum state is not a prerequisite for asserting universal jurisdiction:

The jurisdiction over these crimes is inherent and can form the basis of an extradition request.[49]

Another important issue is whether universal jurisdiction provides the asserting state with an equally strong claim to jurisdiction as a state whose jurisdiction is based on a traditional principle of jurisdiction. It is useful to look at the origins of the notion of universal jurisdiction. Piracy is regarded as the first crime for which states accepted universal jurisdiction. However, again there are two views on the precise rationale of the jurisdiction of states over pirates: The one view points to the jurisdictional vacuum because the high seas constituted so-called *terra nullius,* and the other view focuses on the specific gravity of the crime that designates pirates as enemies of mankind.[50] The second rationale has lead to the expansion of the principle to other grave crimes, such as genocide and war crimes. The state prosecuting the perpetrator of these crimes is thus primarily acting in the interest of the world community. The first rationale supports the idea that universal jurisdiction is merely a subsidiary form of jurisdiction and can be exercised only if other states with a more traditional link to the crime are not bringing perpetrators to book. When states having a traditional basis for jurisdiction do not exercise that jurisdiction, the crime is perpetrated in a de facto jurisdictional vacuum. These two rationales have been combined to form a theory of subsidiary universal jurisdiction for serious international crimes. The intolerability in the eyes of humankind of letting certain offenses go unpunished establishes a subsidiary link of all states to the crime. A state is empowered to assert its criminal jurisdiction where it can be assumed that no other state with a traditional jurisdictional link to the crime will prosecute.[51]

We have illustrated some of the different theories that have been advocated with regard to universal jurisdiction. Earlier, we made the distinction between a broad and more restrictive notion of universal jurisdiction based on whether the presence of the accused in the territory of the forum state is seen as a precondition to the exercise of universal jurisdiction. Another issue subject to different interpretations is whether universal jurisdiction allows states to exercise concurrent jurisdiction over a crime or whether it is merely a subsidiary form of jurisdiction with regard to jurisdiction based on the traditional principles. Although many states have enacted laws that establish a broad notion of universality, some of these states have subsequently repealed such provisions and limited the scope of universal jurisdiction, as was the case in Belgium, or their domestic courts have taken a restrictive interpretation and required additional conditions for the application of universal jurisdiction, as illustrated by the latest Spanish cases.

The Belgian Law on Universal Jurisdiction

Probably the most far-reaching national legislation with regard to establishing universal jurisdiction over international crimes was the 1993 Act Concerning Grave Breaches of International Humanitarian Law as amended by the Act of 1999.[52] Article 7 of this law provides that Belgian courts are competent to assert universal jurisdiction over war crimes, crimes against humanity and genocide, even if the alleged offender is not present in Belgian territory. On the basis of Article 7, an extradition may be requested and in case such an extradition is impossible, the trial may be conducted *in absentia*. In principle, the Belgian criminal justice system is based on prosecutorial discretion, and with regard to the exercise of extraterritorial jurisdiction, Belgian law stipulates certain additional requirements, such as official denunciation by foreign public authorities or a formal complaint by the foreign victim or his or her relatives. The 1993 law, however, seems to establish mandatory prosecution for genocide, crimes against humanity, and war crimes. On the basis of this law, numerous applications

were brought before Belgian courts, mostly by victims of the alleged crimes. Among others were the cases against four Rwandan citizens for war crimes and against the former President of Chad, Hissène Habre, for torture and crimes against humanity.[53]

In the *Arrest Warrant* case[54] before the International Court of Justice (ICJ) the Democratic Republic of Congo objected to the issuing of an international arrest warrant *in absentia* by a Belgian court against the incumbent minister of foreign affairs of the Congo, which alleged grave breaches of the Geneva Conventions of 1949 and of the Additional Protocol thereto as well as crimes against humanity. The Congo argued that the Belgian law that entitled courts to assert universal jurisdiction even where the alleged offender was not present in Belgian territory violated international law and that the circulation of the arrest warrant through Interpol contravened a rule of customary international law concerning the inviolability and immunity from criminal process of an incumbent minister of foreign affairs. The ICJ forfeited the opportunity of settling the issue of universal jurisdiction by confining itself to the second question and held in its judgment that the issue of the arrest warrant indeed violated the immunity of a minister of foreign affairs under international law.

With its recent investigations against Ariel Sharon, Colin Powell, and George Bush, Sr., Belgium increasingly found itself in diplomatic hot water. When the United States threatened to remove the NATO headquarters from Brussels, the Belgian parliament drastically reduced the scope of the statute, allowing for universal jurisdiction only where there exists a link to Belgium, such as the nationality or residence of the accused or the victims.[55]

The Pinochet Case

In 1999, the British House of Lords had to consider an extradition request of the Spanish authorities for General Augusto Pinochet of

Chile who at the time was undergoing medical treatment in Britain. A Spanish court had issued an indictment against Pinochet for acts of torture, among others, and based its jurisdiction on the principle of universality that is encoded in Spanish law.[56] While the House of Lords judgment[57] mainly focused on the immunity of former heads of states, the issue of universal jurisdiction was important in deciding whether the principle of "double criminality" required under British extradition law was satisfied. The Court maintained that the principle of double criminality required that the act be punishable in the requesting and requested state at the date of commission. In its final judgment, the Court held that Pinochet could not be extradited for acts of torture committed in Chile because British courts acquired extraterritorial jurisdiction over this crime only after the Criminal Justice Act of 1988 entered into force on September 29, 1988.

It is important to note that English courts can base their jurisdiction on domestic common law as well as on customary international law. Thus, the exercise of criminal jurisdiction over the crime of torture does not require a domestic law if such criminal jurisdiction is legitimated by international law. Lord Millet argued that national courts may exercise universal jurisdiction over a crime once the prohibition of this crime has the status of *jus cogens* and when it reaches such a scale and gravity that it can be seen as an attack on the international legal order. He maintained that the prohibition of torture had risen to the status of *jus cogens* well before 1984[58] and that the crimes committed by Pinochet in Chile from 1973 onward were of such a gravity and scale as to allow other states to exercise universal jurisdiction. As a result, British courts had extraterritorial jurisdiction even over acts of torture committed prior to the enactment of the Criminal Justice Act of 1988.[59] Although not all judges agreed on the exact time when torture constituted a violation of a peremptory

norm of international law, they did endorse, in principle, the exercise of universal jurisdiction in cases where the prohibition of the crimes in question has risen to the status of *jus cogens*.[60]

The Spanish extradition request for General Pinochet based the criminal jurisdiction of Spanish courts on Article 23(4) of the *1985 Organic Law of the Judicial Power,* which provides for universal jurisdiction of Spanish courts over the specific crimes such as genocide and terrorism, as well as any other crime that by international treaty or convention should be prosecuted in Spain. There is no added requirement for the exercise of universal jurisdiction in Spanish law. Thus, this provision can be regarded as embodying the principle of universal jurisdiction in its broad form. In contrast to Britain, Spanish courts can assert criminal jurisdiction only on the basis of a domestic legal provision. The Criminal Appeals Chamber of the *Audiencia Nacional* affirmed that Spain had universal jurisdiction over the acts committed in Chile and that such jurisdiction did not contravene Article 2 of the U.N. Charter, which enshrines the principle of sovereign equality of states.[61] However, in February 2003 in the *Guatemala Genocide* case,[62] the Spanish Supreme court held that universal jurisdiction interferes with the principles of nonintervention and sovereign equality of states as provided in Article 2 of the U.N. Charter, unless there is a point of connection with Spain, such as the involvement of important national interests or the nationality of the perpetrator or the victims. With regard to nonnationals, the Court maintained that the presence of the perpetrator in the territory of Spain was a precondition to exercise of universal jurisdiction.

The recent Spanish Supreme Court judgment and the amendment of the Belgian law on universal jurisdiction seem to suggest that states are becoming more reticent to apply universal jurisdiction in its pure form but, rather, require that some additional condition be met. In her dissenting opinion in the *Arrest*

Warrant Case, Judge Van den Wyngaert examined the scope of the principle of universality under international law.[63] She argued that although many national courts and national legislation require for the exercise of universal jurisdiction an additional link to the crime, such negative state practice with respect to universal jurisdiction constitutes evidence of *opinio juris* under international law only if the abstinence was based on a conscious decision of the respective states that they were conforming to a rule of international law. It seems, however, that most states restrict the exercise of universal jurisdiction merely for political or practical reasons rather than from a conviction that they are acting in accordance with a rule of customary international law. Judges Higgins, Kooijmans, and Buergenthal in their joint separate opinion also maintain that state practice is neutral in this regard.

It is clear that the abrogation of the Belgian law resulted from intense political pressure by the United States rather than a conviction that a broad notion of jurisdiction contravenes international law. Interestingly, the position of U.S. courts is in favor of universal jurisdiction for genocide, war crimes, and crimes against humanity as was demonstrated in the *Demjanjuk* case and more recently in the case of *Yousef and others*.[64] Moreover, the German Parliament recently explicitly rejected the restrictive stance of its courts, which had required a legitimizing link for the exercise of universal jurisdiction, by enacting a broad version of universal jurisdiction for genocide, crimes against humanity, and war crimes.[65] Although universal jurisdiction is a viable avenue for addressing the prevailing impunity in many countries for serious international crimes, its precise scope under customary international law is not yet settled,[66] and thus, as the Spanish Supreme Court decision and the House of Lords decision in the *Pinochet* case demonstrate, many states seem to be hesitant to exercise universal jurisdiction based solely on customary international law.

Aut Dedere aut Judicare *and* Vicarious Administration of Justice

Clauses in international conventions relating to the jurisdiction of a state must be distinguished from prosecution clauses, expressing the rule of *aut dedere aut judicare*.[67] This rule is contained in many multilateral treaties on international crimes and establishes an obligation on states to extradite or prosecute the alleged offender. Clearly, states would be able to prosecute only if their national laws foresee jurisdiction in such cases. Thus, the principle of *aut dedere aut judicare* presupposes that states can assert jurisdiction over the relevant crime but does not in itself confer jurisdiction on the state.

The principle of *aut dedere aut judicare* often is equated with the jurisdictional principle of vicarious administration of justice,[68] contained in some legal systems such as Austria and Germany.[69] Under the principle of vicarious administration of justice, the jurisdiction of a state is dependent on the following circumstances: (1) The perpetrator is in the custody of the state; (2) he or she cannot be extradited, either because no such request was made by other states or because an extradition is prohibited for reasons other than the nature of the crime; (3) the criminal conduct amounts to an extraditable offense; and (4) the conduct is subject to punishment both in the state of territoriality and the state of custody. These conditions are at the same time necessary and sufficient for the exercise of jurisdiction: If these conditions are fulfilled, the state acquires jurisdiction over the crime, although no inherent jurisdictional link based on nationality, territoriality, or protection exists. It is therefore a derived form of jurisdiction and only subsidiary because it arises when states having inherent jurisdiction over the crime cannot or will not exercise their jurisdiction.

In a sense, the principle of vicarious administration of justice combines the idea behind *aut dedere aut judicare*, which is to ensure that states do not become safe havens for criminals, with a jurisdictional clause.[70] Jurisdiction on the basis of vicarious administration of justice can go further than universal jurisdiction, because it is not limited to specific grave international crimes.[71] Austrian courts relied on this principle in the case of Dusko C.[72] to assert their jurisdiction over the crime of genocide. Because the crime of genocide was contained in the criminal codes of both the state of territoriality (Bosnia-Herzegovina) and the state of custody (Austria), and extradition was not possible due to the ongoing war in Bosnia-Herzegovina, Austrian courts became competent to judge the case based on the provision in the Austrian code that enshrines the principle of vicarious administration of justice. In contrast, universal jurisdiction provides states with an inherent jurisdiction over certain international crimes and, in the case of the broad notion of universality, can itself be the basis of an extradition request.

Obligation to Prosecute International Crimes?

International law not only defines the legal limits in which states may extend their extraterritorial jurisdiction but in some cases may even oblige states to prosecute certain offenses. That there is a duty of states to uphold the rule of law in their own countries with regard to crimes committed in their own territory has been reiterated by various monitoring bodies in the field of human rights.[73] However, to what extent states have a duty to prosecute offenses committed outside their own territory is a controversial issue, especially with regard to the duty to exercise universal jurisdiction. Most international treaties on international crimes establish an obligation for state parties to enact domestic legislation proscribing these crimes under their national laws.[74] Some international treaties oblige states to provide for jurisdiction over the relevant crimes,[75] and some treaties explicitly require states to prosecute offenders for these crimes and thus exercise their jurisdiction. The obligation to prosecute an international crime is established by the principle of *aut dedere aut judicare*, which gives states the choice to either extradite or prosecute offenders located in its territory.[76] Thus, insofar as one can speak of an obligation under international law for states to prosecute international crimes that were committed outside their territory, the obligation is never absolute: First, the offender must be located in the territory of the forum state; second, an obligation to prosecute only arises if states do not extradite; and third, such an obligation applies only to state parties of the relevant treaty.[77] Common law countries have been reluctant to introduce universal jurisdiction—even in a limited form—into their systems, whereas civil law states often did not provide for the imprescriptibility of war crimes, crimes against humanity, and genocide in their domestic laws.[78] However, it seems that the Rome Statute of the International Criminal Court[79] has provided new impetus for states to enact legislation proscribing international crimes and establishing broader extraterritorial criminal jurisdiction.

The Implementation of the Rome Statute

State Parties to the Rome Statute of the International Criminal Court have taken different approaches in adopting implementing legislation. Although the Rome Statute does not oblige state parties to proscribe or prosecute the crimes listed in the statute, many states have incorporated the substantive provisions of the statute into their domestic legislation and extended their extraterritorial jurisdiction. Germany enacted a Code of Crimes against International Law (CCIL)[80] in which the provisions of the Rome Statute with regard to genocide, war crimes, and crimes against humanity have to a large extent been copied. However, the CCIL must be regarded as an independent codification of these crimes, because it includes norms that are part of customary international law but that have not been reflected in the ICC Statute.[81] Furthermore, it contains some modifications to satisfy the constitutional requirement of legal certainty[82] and differentiates between serious crimes and less serious crimes against international law. With regard to the serious crimes, the CCIL provides for imprescriptibility and universal jurisdiction, which is mandatory because the CCIL refers to the general rule of obligatory prosecution (*Legalitätsprinzip*) contained in many civil law countries.[83] Section 153f of the Code of Criminal Procedure provides for some exceptions to this rule and therefore allows the prosecutor a certain amount of discretion, most notably, in the case where the crime was committed by a nonnational against a nonnational abroad and the alleged offender is not located in nor expected to enter German territory.[84]

In Canada, the implementation of the Rome Statute also sparked a legislative reform of the substantive provisions on genocide, war crimes, and crimes against humanity. The Crimes Against Humanity and War Crimes Act[85] defines these crimes broadly, primarily referring to the customary or conventional international law that applied at the time and place of commission but also clarifying that these provisions reflect the substantive part of the Rome Statute.[86] The extraterritorial jurisdiction of Canada over these crimes is based on the active and passive personality principle as well as universal jurisdiction, whereby for the exercise of the latter, the only requirement is the presence of the offender in Canadian territory.[87] Canada has thus extended its jurisdictional regime over extraterritorial international crimes, thereby ensuring that effective domestic prosecution may take place.[88]

Quite a different approach has been taken by Austria in implementing the Rome Statute into its domestic legal order. Austria generally takes a minimalist stance with regard to transposing the substantive provisions of international treaties. With the exception of genocide,[89] Austria does not explicitly proscribe international crimes, relying on its existing penal provisions. Arguably, the gravity of these specific crimes is not sufficiently reflected in traditional domestic offenses. Thereby, Austrian courts can rely only to a limited degree on jurisprudence of international judicial bodies with regard to crimes against humanity and war crimes. It is unfortunate that Austria did not take the opportunity when implementing the Rome Statute to develop its substantive criminal law on international crimes.[90] With regard to jurisdiction, Section 64, paragraph 1, subparagraph 6 of the Austrian Criminal Code provide that its substantive provisions apply to extraterritorial crimes, whenever an international treaty contains an obligation to prosecute those crimes.[91] The Rome Statute only obliges states to enact domestic legislation enabling them to cooperate effectively with the ICC.[92] Thus, Austria limited itself to passing legislation on cooperation with the ICC with regard to assistance during proceedings and enforcement of sentences.[93] It should be noted that there are no statutory exceptions to the Austrian principle of mandatory prosecution (*Legalitätsprinzip*)[94] with regard to serious crimes committed abroad. Thus, if Austrian courts have jurisdiction over these crimes, the prosecutor is obliged to take up investigations, unless this would contravene the principle of *ne bis in idem*.

ADJUDICATION BY THE ICC

Following years of preparation and various draft proposals, the ICC was established by a multilateral treaty, which was adopted on July 17, 1998, and entered into force on July 1, 2002.[95] As a permanent international criminal tribunal situated in The Hague, it is competent to investigate and prosecute serious violations of international human rights law that occurred after July 1, 2002. The ICC is premised on the principle of complementarity, which allows the Court to give due deference to states that are willing and able to prosecute international crimes while at the same time ensuring that these crimes do not go unpunished when political or practical considerations render their prosecution unfeasible for an individual state. In the words of the newly elected prosecutor of the ICC, Luis Moreno Ocampo, "The absence of trials before this Court, as a consequence of the regular functioning of national institutions, would be a major success."[96] The ICC has been criticized repeatedly for providing the possibility of politically motivated prosecutions and not being truly complementary.[97] When evaluating the ICC, it is important to consider not only the international framework in which the ICC is embedded but also that it merges different legal traditions, most notably common law and civil law, and therefore must not be criticized with reference to a specific legal tradition but with reference to its own legal framework defined by the ICC Statute, the "Rules of Procedure and Evidence"[98] and the "Elements of Crimes."[99] In this section, we provide an overview of the jurisdictional scope of the ICC and the procedural safeguards that ensure that the prosecution before the ICC is based on legal considerations.

Substantive Scope of the Court's Jurisdiction

Article 5 of the ICC Statute stipulates that the Court has jurisdiction with respect to genocide, crimes against humanity, war crimes, and the crime of aggression. Thus, by no means is the Court called on to adjudicate all international crimes but is limited to these four categories of crimes, which constitute "the most serious crimes of concern to the international community as a whole."[100] The crime of genocide, crimes against humanity, and war crimes are respectively defined "for the purpose of this Statute"[101] in Articles 6 to 8.[102] According to Article 9(1), the interpretation

of these crimes is subject to the "Elements of Crimes," which were adopted at the first session of the Assembly of State Parties in September 2002.[103] The Court will be able to exercise its jurisdiction over the crime of aggression only once this crime has been defined.[104] Given the highly political nature of this crime and the years of fruitless negotiations to arrive at a common definition on the international level, it is unlikely that a consensus in this regard will be reached in the near future. Furthermore, a definition of the crime would constitute an amendment of the statute, which may only occur 7 years from the date of entry into force and in accordance with the rules laid down in Articles 121 and 123.[105]

Even though the main impetus for restarting negotiations on the establishment of a permanent ICC came from a coalition of 16 Caribbean and Latin American nations, who saw such a court as an effective way of dealing with drug crimes,[106] the Rome Statute does not provide for the jurisdiction of the Court over drug trafficking.[107] Furthermore, the Court does not have jurisdiction over acts of terrorism. The main reasons for the exclusion of this crime from the Court's jurisdiction was the lack of an internationally accepted definition and the opinion of many states that the Court would have become too politicized if the crime were included.[108] In a sense, the same arguments could apply to the crime of aggression; however, this crime was included at least *de jure,* even if *de facto* the Court is not able to exercise its jurisdiction over this crime.

Temporal Jurisdiction

According to Article 11(1), the Court does not have retroactive jurisdiction over crimes that occurred before the entry into force of the statute on July 1, 2002.[109] Under Article 11(2), the jurisdiction of the Court over crimes committed by nationals or in the territory of states that acceded to the statute only after this date is limited to crimes that were committed after the statute entered into force for that state.[110] The principle of nonretroactivity is reinforced by Article 24(1), which stipulates that no person shall be held liable under this statute for conduct committed prior to the entry into force of the statute.

Natural Persons

Article 25(1) of the ICC Statute limits the Court's jurisdiction *ratione personae* to natural persons. Although the French delegation pushed for the inclusion of legal persons under the jurisdiction of the Court, the proposal was finally rejected given the evidentiary difficulties involved and the fact that corporate criminal liability is not yet an established element in most national criminal justice systems.[111] The minimum age of the alleged perpetrator is 18 years at the time of the commission of the crime.[112]

Trigger Mechanisms

The Court's jurisdiction over crimes listed in Article 5 is triggered in three ways: (1) by a referral of a situation by a state party, (2) by the Security Council, or (3) by a *proprio motu* investigation of the prosecutor.[113] Any state party, not only the states concerned, may refer a situation to the Court and request that the prosecutor initiate an investigation.[114] Second, the Security Council can adopt a resolution under Chapter 7 of the United Nations Charter[115] and refer a situation to the Court. Last, the prosecutor can initiate investigations on his or her own motion. There are, however, a number of safeguards that ensure that the prosecutor bases his or her decisions on objective criteria and is not led by political motives. If the prosecutor decides that there is a reasonable basis to proceed with the investigation, thus to start a formal investigation, he or she has to file a request with the Pre-Trial Chamber for authorization of such an investigation. The Pre-Trial Chamber has to

authorize an investigation if it finds that there is a reasonable basis to investigate the situation. Such a finding of the chamber does not, however, prejudice subsequent decisions of the Court with regard to admissibility and jurisdiction.[116] Should the Pre-Trial Chamber refuse to authorize an investigation, the Prosecutor may resubmit a request only if it is based on new facts and evidence.[117]

Preconditions to the Exercise of Jurisdiction

The Court has automatic jurisdiction over the crimes listed in Article 5 of the statute. Thus, the ratification of the treaty and the acceptance of jurisdiction by the Court are not two distinct processes, but the state already accepts the Court's jurisdiction when it ratifies or accedes to the Rome Statute.[118] This is a clear refusal of a jurisdiction à la carte, which would have been the result if alternate proposals advocating an opt-in or case-by-case consent of states had been accepted.[119] By limiting the instances in which the consent of state parties is required for the Court to perform its functions, the Court is able to function more effectively. In principle, the ICC Statute does not allow for reservations of state parties; however, a 7-year opt-out clause with regard to war crimes has been included in Article 124. On becoming a party to the statute, a state can reject the jurisdiction of the Court over war crimes allegedly committed in its territory or by its nationals for a period of 7 years, taking effect after the statute entered into force for that state.[120]

When the jurisdiction of the Court is triggered by a state party referral or by the prosecutor acting *proprio motu*, the Court may only exercise its jurisdiction if the crimes allegedly were committed either in the territory of a state party or by a national of a state party.[121] Thus, the automatic jurisdiction of the Court is tied to two different principles of jurisdiction: the territoriality principle and the nationality principle. On the basis of these principles, national courts can also assert their jurisdiction over crimes proscribed in their national legal orders.[122] Furthermore, the Court can exercise its jurisdiction if the state of nationality or territoriality is not a party to the statute but accepts the jurisdiction of the Court with respect to the crime, by lodging a declaration with the Registrar.[123]

The well-received proposal of the Korean delegation,[124] which provided for two additional jurisdictional links—namely the state of nationality of the victim and the custodial state[125]—was cut short to accommodate the United States to some degree[126] and thus gain its support for the statute. It is unfortunate that such a weakening of the Court did not pay off in the end, although it is arguable that this brought many other states on board and thus accelerated the overall ratification process. Nevertheless, the effectiveness of the Court in deterring offenders has been severely hampered. Individuals committing genocide, war crimes, and crimes against humanity against their own people, as is often the case with dictators, will not be subject to the jurisdiction of the Court, if these states are not parties to the statute.

On the other hand, it is still possible that the U.N. Security Council refers the situation to the Court under Chapter 7 of the UN Charter. Such a referral is not bound to the preconditions laid down in Article 12. Thus, no matter where or by whom the crime was committed, the offender may be prosecuted by the Court, subject to a Security Council Resolution under Chapter 7. However, considering that the Security Council is a highly politicized body, it will be political expediency and not the rule of law that dictates when such a situation is referred to the Court. In the words of one of the judges at the Court, Article 12 creates a "Janus-headed double court with a double sword," where "one court is potentially very strong and universal and has a sharp jurisdictional sword with a long

outreach," while "the other court is quite weak and has only a jurisdictional sword which is cumbersome and short."[127]

Deferral by the Security Council

Article 16 provides for the possibility of the Security Council intervening in the functioning of the Court. Where an investigation or prosecution by the ICC would run contrary to the maintenance or restoration of international peace and security, the Security Council may adopt a resolution under Chapter 7 of the U.N. Charter requesting that the Court not commence or proceed with an investigation or prosecution for the period of 1 year. At the end of this period, the Security Council may renew its request "under the same conditions."[128] Thus, if after 1 year, criminal proceedings before the ICC would still run contrary to the maintenance or restoration of international peace and security, the Security Council may adopt another resolution, in which it renews its request that the Court not undertake any actions.

Commentators have criticized this provision for allowing the Security Council to exert political control over a judiciary body, which is unprecedented: The Security Council cannot defer proceedings before the ICJ[129] and national courts dealing with crimes that arise out of situations that the Security Council can deal with under Chapter 7. Seeing that the Court mainly deals with crimes arising from situations that fall under the agenda of Chapter 7, there is a strong possibility that the Security Council adopts a resolution to defer proceedings before the Court. This would be a blow to the independence of the Court.[130] However, because the Security Council can adopt a resolution under Chapter 7 only to "maintain or restore international peace and security," a deferral would mean an implicit acknowledgment that investigations and proceedings before the Court are a threat to international peace and security. If the Security Council too often makes use of its power to defer, it risks loosing its credibility. Furthermore, the Security Council has to garner nine votes from its members in order to adopt such a resolution. In such highly sensitive matters, it is likely that consensus will be reached easily. Although Article 16 therefore opens up the possibility of political interference with the Court, it constitutes a necessary compromise between (a) recognizing the role of the Security Council as the primary body responsible for the maintenance of the peace and security of mankind and (b) eliminating all political influence on the Court's function. In this sense, the provision is meant to allow for a compromise between peace and justice.[131]

These theoretical considerations put aside, a Security Council resolution was adopted on July 12, 2002, only a few days after the ICC Statute entered into force, requesting the Court to defer proceedings against nationals of non-state parties taking part in U.N. or U.N. authorized operations.[132] Resolution 1422 was taken after the United States stated that it would veto a resolution to renew the U.N. peacekeeping operations in Bosnia-Herzegovina.[133] It is, however, questionable how far the Security Council has the power to defer proceedings against certain persons a priori, considering that the wording and drafting history of Article 16 indicates that such a deferral must be with reference to a specific situation that is being investigated by the ICC. The resolution is based explicitly on Article 16, and it is arguable that the ICC is thus ultimately called on to determine its validity under the ICC Statute.[134]

The Principle of Complementarity

The ICC Statute repeatedly emphasizes the complementary nature of the Court's jurisdiction.[135] The Court is not meant to substitute its jurisdiction for that of the national courts, but merely to be a safety net, should the national criminal justice system not be able or willing to adjudicate offenders of the crimes under the jurisdiction of the Court. Thus, this principle is a way to ensure that "the most serious crimes of concern to the international community as a whole must not go unpunished."[136]

Article 17 defines three scenarios in which the Court must declare a case inadmissible on the basis of this principle:

- A state is already investigating or prosecuting the case
- A state has investigated the case and decided not to prosecute
- A state has already tried the person concerned before its own courts[137]

However, if the states are either unable or unwilling to genuinely prosecute the case, the Court may declare the case admissible, thus not giving precedence to the national courts. Although "inability" is a fairly objective criterion,[138] the notion of "unwillingness" may be subject to wide interpretation. The ICC Statute[139] defines three factors that the Court has to take into account when determining whether a state is "unwilling" to prosecute: (1) The proceedings are undertaken for the purpose of shielding a person from the jurisdiction of the ICC; (2) there is an unjustified delay in proceedings that is contrary to the intent to bring the person to justice; and (3) the proceedings are not carried out impartially or independently and are conducted in a manner inconsistent with an intent to bring the alleged perpetrator to justice.[140]

The principle of complementarity obliges the Court to give deference to states if they are capable and willing to bring the person concerned to justice. It is the Court and not the states who decides whether the states meet the criteria laid down in Article 17. If there were no such review of national enforcement, the function of the ICC in combating impunity would be hampered: States not wanting certain cases to be prosecuted by the Court would simply have to commence proceedings against the person concerned and thus prevent the

Court from exercising its jurisdiction. This would de facto result in a case-by-case consent of states and thus undermine the automatic jurisdiction of the Court as laid down in Article 12(1). However, at the same time, the onus of proof is on the Court. It might be virtually impossible to demonstrate the requisite intent that national proceedings were initiated for the "purpose of shielding the person."[141] More realistic are the requirements that the delay or the manner in which proceedings are or were conducted is, in the circumstances, "inconsistent with an intent to bring the person concerned to justice." If the onus of proof is too high, the system of automatic jurisdiction would be overridden in favor of a "jurisdiction à la carte." On the other hand, it is arguable that the mere fact that another Court has the power to review national decisions runs contrary to traditional concepts of state sovereignty. The principle of complementarity thus tries to find a balance between ensuring the prosecution of grave crimes and giving due deference to a state's sovereign power to prosecute and punish offenders.

Procedural Safeguards

The ICC Statute contains special procedural provisions that ensure that the Court gives due deference to states that are willing and able to investigate and prosecute a certain case. It is important to note that these safeguards in general apply to state parties as well as nonstate parties. First, the prosecutor must consider national investigations or prosecutions when determining whether there is a reasonable basis to start an investigation. Second, once the prosecutor makes a decision to investigate a situation, he or she must notify all state parties as well as those states that would normally exercise jurisdiction of the crimes at issue. States that would normally exercise jurisdiction over the matter can request the prosecutor to defer to their

investigations into the case.[142] A deferral to the state's investigation is subject to a review by the prosecutor after 6 months or at any time when a state's unwillingness or inability to genuinely investigate the matter becomes apparent. The prosecutor may ask the Pre-Trial Chamber to authorize necessary investigative steps for preserving evidence[143] and request the states to inform him or her on the process of the investigation.[144] Should the prosecutor decide not to defer to the requesting state and the Pre-Trial Chamber authorizes the investigation by the prosecutor, states can lodge an appeal with the Appeals Chamber.

Third, states have the possibility at a later stage to challenge the admissibility of a case on the grounds of Article 17 as well as to challenge the jurisdiction of the Court.[145] In principle, such a challenge may be brought forward only once and prior to or at the commencement of the trial.[146] The prosecutor has to suspend his or her investigation if a challenge is brought forward by a state. Pending a ruling by the Court on a challenge to its jurisdiction or the admissibility of the case, the prosecutor may, however, request the Court to authorize him or her to pursue necessary investigative steps, take the testimony of a witness, complete the gathering and evaluation of evidence that had begun prior to the challenge, or prevent the absconding of persons for whom an arrest warrant had been requested. The prosecutor may also, having regard for the principle of complementarity, defer the investigations to the state and request the state to inform him or her on the process of the investigation. Should the prosecutor take up investigations again, he or she has to inform the state of this fact.

Thus, even before an investigation has been started, the principle of complementarity can already take effect, by giving precedence to states in investigating a matter. Furthermore, states have at least two possibilities to request a deferral to their national proceedings and may appeal against decisions of the Pre-Trial

Chamber to the Appeals Chamber. However, the deferral to a state or the suspension of proceedings pending a decision by the Pre-Trial Chamber can lead to a loss of important evidence. Without the possibility of preserving necessary evidence as provided for in the statute, the crimes might go unpunished.

Jurisdictional Overreach?

When evaluating the jurisdictional regime of the ICC as a whole, it becomes clear that the Court by no means can exercise its jurisdiction over all incidents of genocide, crimes against humanity and war crimes. First of all, the Court is bound to a jurisdictional link with the state of nationality or state of territoriality, if the situation was referred to the Court by a state party or if the prosecutor initiated an investigation on his or her own motion. Second, where this jurisdictional link cannot be established because the state of nationality or territoriality is either not a state party or does not consent ad hoc to the jurisdiction of the Court, the Court may exercise jurisdiction over the crimes only on the basis of a Chapter 7 resolution by the Security Council. Last, under the principle of complementarity, the Court must give precedence to states that are willing and able to prosecute crimes that fall within their jurisdiction. Several procedural safeguards exist that ensure that states have the possibility to challenge the jurisdiction of the Court and the admissibility of a case. Thus, the legal regime of the ICC constitutes a balance between respecting the states' sovereign right to prosecute crimes within their jurisdiction and ensuring that crimes are effectively prosecuted. Considering that the Court is dependent on the cooperation of states in fulfilling these functions and its limited jurisdictional scope, it seems more likely that the Court could be accused of falling short of its goal of combating impunity for international crimes rather than of a jurisdictional overreach.

THE AD HOC TRIBUNALS

The ICTY and ICTR were established by Security Council Resolutions under Chapter 7 of the Charter of the United Nations.[147] The main purpose of the ad hoc tribunals is to ensure some measure of justice in a postconflict situation where the local judicial infrastructure has been destroyed and it cannot be expected that domestic courts will perform a politically independent and effective prosecution of such serious crimes. It was the first time that a judicial body was created as a "measure to maintain or restore international peace and security, following the requisite determination of the existence of a threat to the peace, breach to the peace or act of aggression."[148] The ICTY has jurisdiction over the territory of the former Socialist Federal Republic of Yugoslavia for crimes committed in the period starting with January 1, 1991,[149] and the ICTR is competent for crimes committed by Rwandan citizens in the territory of Rwanda and neighboring states in the period between January 1 and December 31, 1994.[150] The jurisdiction *ratione materiae* of both tribunals is limited to genocide, war crimes, and crimes against humanity.

Although the ICC and the ad hoc tribunals essentially deal with the same crimes, the purpose of these institutions is fundamentally different: The ad hoc tribunals, in principle, focus on past atrocities and are envisaged to function for a limited period of time, whereas the ICC is a permanent institution that can exercise jurisdiction only over crimes committed after July 1, 2002, primarily aiming to prevent such atrocities from being committed. The ex post facto jurisdiction of the tribunals does not violate the principle of *nullum crimen sine lege* or the principle of nonretroactivity of criminal laws, because the crimes within the jurisdiction of the tribunal were already firmly established as crimes under customary international law.[151] The tribunals, thus, merely provide a framework in which these crimes can be adjudicated. Their jurisdiction is concurrent with that of domestic courts but having primacy if the tribunal decides to take over a case pending before a national court. The obligation of states to cooperate with the tribunals is based on the statutes[152] and applies to all states by virtue of the U.N. Charter.[153] The cutoff date for crimes under the jurisdiction of the ICTY has not been defined, which means that the ICTY will also have jurisdiction over crimes that might still occur in the territory of the former Yugoslavia. Its function is thus also to deter such atrocities from being committed and thereby to ensure stability and peace in the region.[154] In this sense, its approach is similar to the ICC, and a concurrent jurisdiction of these two institutions is conceivable. However, the U.N. member states must give precedence to their obligations under the U.N. Charter[155] and would therefore have to cooperate primarily with the ICTY. Furthermore, the primacy of the jurisdiction of the ICTY might also be derived on the grounds of speciality.[156] These considerations will probably remain hypothetical because the ICTY and ICTR have both been called on by the Security Council to complete all investigations by the end of 2004 and finish trials by the end of 2008, which will enable the tribunals to complete all their work by 2010.[157] These completion strategies are predicated on a division of the caseload between the tribunals and the domestic courts in the former Yugoslavia and Rwanda, respectively: The prosecution of those most responsible will be undertaken by the tribunals, and the other cases will be referred to the competent national courts. For this purpose, a specialized War Crimes Chamber will be established within the State Court of Bosnia and Herzegovina (BiH).[158]

The tribunals are subsidiary organs of the Security Council, whereas the ICC was established by a multilateral treaty and is a wholly independent institution. In the *Tadić* case[159] the Trial Chamber 2 of the ICTY stated that it "must interpret its provisions within its own legal context and not rely in its application on interpretations made by other judicial bodies." In the same case, it reiterated that the competence of the tribunal is determined by its statute.[160] Thus, although the tribunals rely on various U.N. bodies for administrative and financial support, their judicial function is exercised independently of other institutions. This became clear when the prosecutor established a Review Committee to ascertain whether there were reasonable grounds to proceed with an investigation against nationals of the Allied Forces concerning the NATO bombings of the then Federal Republic of Yugoslavia in 1999.[161] Although the prosecutor on the basis of the report of the Review Committee decided not to proceed with investigations into the matter, this still shows that even nationals of the permanent members of the Security Council are not a priori immune from prosecution by an ad hoc tribunal created under the auspices of the United Nations.[162]

INTERNATIONALIZED COURTS

Sierra Leone

In recent discussions on how to deal with the past atrocities in transitional societies, such as in the case of Iraq, references have been made to special models of justice employed in countries such as Sierra Leone and East Timor. These models can be regarded as a middle path between a purely national and international approach. The prime example is the Special Court in Sierra Leone created in January 2002 by an agreement between the United Nations and the Sierra Leone government to deal with the atrocities committed in Sierra Leone in the 1990s.[163] This international treaty body is not a subsidiary organ of the United Nations. It is independent of the domestic legal system as well as of the U.N. Mission in Sierra Leone. The Special Court has jurisdiction over crimes against humanity, grave breaches of the Geneva Conventions, and other serious violations of international humanitarian law, but it is also competent to apply certain rules of domestic law pertaining to the abuse of girls and damage of property.[164] Just like the ad hoc tribunals, the Special Court and domestic courts have concurrent jurisdiction over these crimes, but the former has primacy over the latter.[165] Furthermore, a Truth and Reconciliation Commission (TRC)[166] has been set up in accordance with the Lomé Peace Agreement,[167] which provides a platform for the victims and perpetrators to come forward to further the reconciliation process. The TRC has no powers to prosecute and punish; this will be left to the Special Court. Nevertheless, the exact relationship to the Special Court, especially with regard to the use of evidence brought before the TRC, is still unclear.[168] On March 10, 2003, the Prosecutor of the Special Court announced the indictment of seven individuals for war crimes, crimes against humanity, and violations of international humanitarian law, among them Foday Sankoh, former leader of the Revolutionary United Front.[169]

Cambodia

The approach used in Cambodia, East Timor, BiH, and Kosovo is less radical, providing merely for special chambers or panels of judges within the existing judicial system to deal with grave crimes, some of which constitute crimes under international law. In Cambodia, an agreement between the United Nations and the Cambodian government, which was signed on June 6, 2003, in Phnom Penh,[170] foresees the establishment of "Extraordinary Chambers" within the Cambodian courts in accordance with the Cambodian law on the Establishment of Extraordinary Chambers of August 2001.[171] This law stipulates that the Extraordinary Chambers shall be composed of Cambodian and international judges and have jurisdiction to try genocide, crimes against humanity, war crimes, torture,

and other serious crimes committed during the Khmer Rouge regime between 1975 and 1979.[172] Only the definition of crimes against humanity in the Cambodian law follows the definition in the Rome Statute.[173]

A point of controversy in the long process of negotiations between the United Nations and the Cambodian government was the complicated organizational structure of the Extraordinary Chambers, which could easily lead to cumbersome and inefficient trials and thus undermine the credibility of these Chambers.[174] The Cambodian law originally provided for a three-tier structure within the Extraordinary Chambers and a majority of Cambodian judges as well as co-prosecutors and co-investigating judges. In his report to the General Assembly of March 2003, the secretary-general repeatedly emphasized the lack of independence of the judiciary and the absence of fair trial guarantees in Cambodian courts. Thus, it appears that a stronger role of the international judges and prosecutors would have been imperative to ensure the efficacy and credibility of the Extraordinary Chambers. However, there seems to have been pressure from important member states such as the United States and France to conclude the draft agreement without proposing substantial changes to the existing Cambodian law.[175] As a result the agreement initialed on March 17, 2003, and signed on June 6, 2003, only replaces the three-tier structure of the Extraordinary Chambers by a two-tier structure, leaving the rest of the organization as provided for in the Cambodian law intact. Although the establishment of such Extraordinary Chambers for the crimes committed by the Khmer Rouge is in principle a positive step toward ending impunity, the independence of these Chambers is not sufficiently guaranteed. The international community has a measure of control insofar as the agreement stipulates that any deviation of the Cambodian government from its obligations under the agreement would result in the withdrawal of cooperation and assistance by the United Nations to the Extraordinary Chambers.[176]

East Timor

The U.N. Transitional Administration in East Timor established Special Panels within the Dili District Court to deal with the crimes committed in the time of the referendum on the independence of East Timor from Indonesia in 1999.[177] These Special Panels, consisting of East Timorese and international judges, have exclusive jurisdiction over crimes against humanity, genocide, and war crimes, as well as torture, murder, and sexual offenses that were committed in the period between January 1 and October 25, 1999.[178] With the independence of East Timor from Indonesia, there is the difficulty that the principal instigators and leaders of the atrocities are located in Indonesia. Although the Special Panels have universal jurisdiction over these cases,[179] they have to rely on the extradition of the defendants from Indonesia, which has proven very difficult. Unfortunately, limited resources have further hampered the effective functioning of the panels. On the Indonesian side, there have also been efforts to bring the perpetrators to justice.[180] The Rome Statute was incorporated into Indonesian law[181] enabling an ad hoc tribunal[182] to apply its substantive provisions to the offenses committed in East Timor immediately following the referendum. The ad hoc tribunal was created specially for this purpose and is a purely domestic court dealing with specific international crimes. Although it is laudable that the Indonesian government took steps to bring those responsible to justice, the tribunal has been criticized for only indicting persons who were lower in command and not high-ranking individuals such as General Wiranto.[183]

Bosnia and Herzegovina/Kosovo

The approach taken in BiH is similar to the model employed in East Timor and Cambodia:

A specialized War Crimes Chamber is to be established under the auspices of the High Representative[184] within the State Court of BiH and a concomitant War Crimes Department within the Prosecutors Office.[185] The War Crimes Chamber is envisaged to deal primarily with war crime cases concerning lower- and intermediate-rank accused. The ICTY, as part of its completion strategy,[186] will refer these cases to the Chamber, which will temporarily include a component of international judges and prosecutors.

In Kosovo, a slightly different approach has been taken by the U.N. Interim Administration Mission in Kosovo (UNMIK) with regard to the prosecution of war crimes committed during the 1998–1999 armed conflict in the region of Kosovo. Although the mandate of UNMIK does not specifically include the prosecution of war crimes,[187] a number of UNMIK regulations enable the Special Representative of the Secretary General (SRSG) to appoint international judges and prosecutors to local courts to strengthen the independence and impartiality of the judiciary. UNMIK Regulation 2000/6[188] regulates for the appointment of international judges and prosecutors by the SRSG, and UNMIK Regulation 2000/64[189] stipulates that the Department of Judicial Affairs may submit a recommendation to the SRSG for the assignment of international judges or prosecutors to specific cases on its own motion or at the request of the prosecution, the accused, or defense counsel. The SRSG can accept or reject the motion. On the basis of such a motion, a panel of judges consisting of two international judges and one local judge can be designated to a case where there are doubts that the local judge can perform his or her function impartially. These panels of judges do not have exclusive jurisdiction over serious crimes but operate within the Kosovo judicial system and may pronounce on any criminal matter to which they are assigned. The internationalized panels and international prosecutors in Kosovo have been criticized for making little use of international jurisprudence and for prosecuting few cases of war crimes, thus not making any significant contribution toward ending impunity for these international crimes.[190] The establishment of a Kosovo War and Ethnic Crimes Court that had been envisaged by the international community in the year 2000 was put on hold. These plans may, however, be taken up again within the context of the ICTY Completion Strategy.[191]

The Lockerbie Trial

The Lockerbie trial can be regarded as another form of internationalized adjudication. The trial of two Libyan nationals was conducted in the Netherlands before a Scottish panel of judges applying Scottish law. On December 21, 1988, a bomb exploded on the Pan Am Flight 103 killing all passengers as well as some residents of the town of Lockerbie where the Boeing crashed. Libya had refused to extradite the two suspects, both Libyan nationals, to the United States and the United Kingdom, maintaining that a fair trial could not be expected in these countries due to the strong public interest in finding the accused guilty. Following the imposition of economic sanctions and embargoes on oil and military production equipment by Security Council Resolution 883 in 1993, Libya declared in 1994 that it would agree to a trial before a Scottish court provided it was located in a neutral country. It was only in 1998 that the United States and the United Kingdom agreed to this proposal and the suspects were surrendered to the Netherlands in April 1999 for trial before a Scottish panel of judges sitting at Camp Zeist, a former U.S. military base that for the duration of the trial was declared Scottish territory by an agreement between the United Kingdom and the Netherlands. In January 2001, one of the accused, al-Megrahi, was convicted of murder and sentenced to life imprisonment to be served in Barlinnie prison

in Glasgow under U.N. supervision. The other accused, Fhima, was acquitted due to inconclusive evidence. Although the Lockerbie Trial was conducted before a national court applying national law, there was a strong involvement of various states as well as the United Nations.[192]

OTHER INTERNATIONAL COURTS

The International Court of Justice

The International Court of Justice (ICJ) established in 1945 by the Charter of the United Nations as the successor to the Permanent International Court, which was established in 1922 by the League of Nations, is competent to adjudicate on any question of international law and on the interpretation of treaties. Article 34 of the ICJ Statute[193] stipulates that only states may be parties before the ICJ subject to their consent to the jurisdiction of the Court under Article 36. Therefore, the ICJ is not competent to pronounce criminal judgments over individuals, although its decisions may affect whether individuals will be prosecuted for international crimes.[194] In the *Lockerbie* cases,[195] the ICJ has been called on by Libya to decide that the United States and the United Kingdom are in breach of their obligations under the Montreal Hijacking Convention by not accepting the criminal jurisdiction of Libya over its nationals for the Lockerbie incident. The ICJ has also generally decided on issues relating to international humanitarian law, such as in its Advisory Opinion on the Legality of the Threat or Use of Nuclear Weapons[196] or in its two orders on provisional measures in the case concerning Application of the Convention on the Prevention and Punishment of the Crime of Genocide.[197] With regard to the ICC, the ICJ may play a role in settling a dispute between state parties over the interpretation of the Rome Statute, which does not relate to the judicial function of the ICC.[198] However, the practical importance of this provision may be very limited, because the primary body for settling disputes in these matters is the Assembly of State Parties.[199]

Human Rights Courts

The European Court of Human Rights was established as a permanent court under the auspices of the Council of Europe in Strasbourg to ensure that the state parties to the Convention for the Protection of Human Rights and Fundamental Freedoms[200] honor their obligations under this convention. Its decisions are binding only on states and do not concern the criminal responsibility of individuals. Individuals as well as states may, however, submit complaints to the Court. Similarly to the Inter-American Court of Human Rights, this Court is merely a regional human rights instrument and does not adjudicate individuals for crimes under international law.[201]

The European Court of Justice

The European Court of Justice (ECJ) in Luxembourg is the judicial organ of the European Union and is competent to decide in matters concerning the interpretation of the founding treaties of the European Union. It acts as a control mechanism over activities of the European Council, European Parliament, and European Commission, ensuring that they keep within the powers transferred to them by the member states. Furthermore, the Court determines whether states find themselves in breach of the E.U. treaties. The Court of First Instance mainly serves to relieve some of the burden on the ECJ, especially in cases brought forward by individuals and legal entities and in staff cases concerning employment issues. In the area of criminal justice, the European Union is still far from being a centralized system and mainly provides a framework for close interstate cooperation.[202] The ECJ

therefore does not have the competence to hold individuals criminally liable.[203]

CONCLUSION

This chapter provided an overview of the various adjudication models that exist in a complex network of international and national rules. Although international law permits states to assert their jurisdiction over international crimes based on nationality, territoriality, passive personality, the protective principle, and the universality principle, states do not always legislate up to the full scope provided by international law. Were we to take state practice as an indication of an obligation to ensure the effective prosecution of crimes under international law, we would have to say that states have merely a moral duty to bring these perpetrators to justice. However, various international treaties impose certain obligations on states with regard to the enactment of legislation and the prosecution or extradition of offenders. These obligations, it seems, are often not taken seriously. We may well ask ourselves, whether the rule of law is an unrealistic goal when we enter the international arena. Is it too much to ask states to abide by those rules that they commonly agreed to, to honor their obligations? It is precisely the fact that states will act in their own interest, that the Rome Statute is a milestone in enforcing the rule of law: If states are not willing to prosecute offenders, the ICC will ensure that perpetrators are brought to justice. The Rome Statute has already provided an impetus for states to enact domestic legislation allowing them to assert criminal jurisdiction over war crimes, crimes against humanity, and genocide. Moreover, proceedings before the ICC follow the highest human rights standards.[204] Without this latter aspect, the system of the ICC would fall short of its goal of establishing global justice for these crimes.

Nevertheless, it is important to realize that no single model can provide an effective solution to all forms of international crime. A centralized system of enforcement such as the ICC may not be the best way to combat international crimes with a strong transnational character, such as drug trafficking or trafficking in human beings. Here, it is more effective to strengthen the cooperation mechanisms between states and to facilitate training programs and proper resource allocation within states. Furthermore, crimes that do not fall within the temporal scope of the Rome Statute, or for which no jurisdictional nexus exists with state parties of the ICC, can be adjudicated by ad hoc tribunals or internationalized courts. Where these are not established, individual states are called on to ensure that egregious crimes of concern to the international community as a whole do not go unpunished.

NOTES

1. For a detailed discussion of the origins and definition of International Criminal Law, see Chapter 11 of this volume on International Criminal Law; and M. C. Bassiouni, "The Sources and Content of International Criminal Law: A Theoretical Framework," in M. C. Bassiouni (ed.), *International Criminal Law* (2nd ed.), Vol. 1, Transnational Publishers, Ardsley, NY (1999), pp. 3–125.

2. See F. Newman and D. Weissbrodt, *International Human Rights: Law, Policy and Process* (2nd ed.), Anderson, Cincinnati, OH (1996), pp. 1–17; T. Buergenthal, "The Human Rights Revolution," *St. Mary's Law Journal*, 23 (1991), pp. 3–10; J. P. Humphrey, "The International Law of Human Rights in the Middle Twentieth Century," in R. B. Lillich, *International Human Rights: Problems of Law, Policy, and Practice* (2nd ed.), Little, Brown, Boston (1991), pp. 1–13.

3. See Article 228 of the Treaty of Versailles, in *The Treaties of Peace 1919–1923*, Vol. 1, Carnegie Endowment for International Peace, Washington, DC (1924). Similarly, Article 230 of the Treaty of Sèvres of 1920 (reprinted in *American Journal of International Law* 15 (1921), Suppl. 179) between the Allied Forces and Turkey

contains a reference to an international tribunal. This treaty never came into force.

4. See *Agreement for the Prosecution and Punishment of the Major War Criminals of the European Axis,* London, August 8, 1945, 82 U. N. T. S. 279 ("London Agreement"), to which the "Charter of the International Military Tribunal" ("Nuremberg Charter") was annexed; *Special Proclamation by the Supreme Commander for the Allied Powers at Tokyo,* January 19, 1946, T. I. A. S. No. 1589, to which the "Charter of the International Military Tribunal for the Far East" ("Tokyo Charter") was annexed. To provide a uniform legal basis for the trials of war criminals in Germany other than those dealt with by the Nuremberg Tribunal, the Control Council Law No. 10 was passed on December 20, 1945.

5. "Trial of the Major War Criminals," Judgment of October 1, 1946, reprinted in G. K. McDonald and O. Swaak-Goldman (eds.), *Substantive and Procedural Aspects of International Criminal Law: The Experience of International and National Courts, Vol. 2, Part 2: Documents and Cases,* Kluwer Law International, The Hague (2000), p. 660.

6. See *Affirmation of the Principles of International Law Recognized by the Charter of the Nuremberg Tribunal,* GA Res. 95 (1), U.N.Doc. A/236 (1946), and, for the subsequent codification of the principles, International Law Commission, "Principles of International Law Recognized in the Charter of the Nuremberg Tribunal and in the Judgment of the Tribunal," in *Yearbook of the International Law Commission* (1950), Vol. 2 (text and commentary). The report of the International Law Commission confirms that these principles are part of customary international law.

7. See Articles 7(1) and 23(1) of the ICTY Statute and Articles 6(1) and 22(1) of the ICTR Statute, *infra* note 147.

8. International Law Commission, "Draft Code of Crimes Against the Peace and Security of Mankind," *Report of the International Law Commission on the Work of Its Forty-eighth Session,* U.N.Doc. A/51/10 (1996).

9. See Article 25 of the ICC Statute, *infra* note 95. For a more detailed overview of the historical and legal development of individual criminal responsibility in international law, see

E. Greppi, "The Evolution of Individual Criminal Responsibility Under International Law," *International Review of the Red Cross* No. 835 (1990), pp. 531–553; K. Ambos, *Der Allgemeine Teil des Völkerstrafrechts: Ansätze einer Dogmatisierung* [The General Part of International Criminal Law], Duncker & Humblot, Berlin (2002). For a discussion on the issue of criminal responsibility of organizations, states, and nonstate actors under international criminal law, see Bassiouni, *supra* note 1, pp. 24–31. Although the issue of criminal responsibility of organizations is especially important in the realm of organized crime, we will focus, following the competence of the ICC *ratione personae,* on natural persons.

10. The terminology is not consistent: Werle distinguishes between "crimes under international law" or "core crimes," which are directly punishable under international law irrespective of domestic legislation, and "treaty-based crimes," which require states to proscribe such crimes in their domestic legal system in order for them to be punishable. The category of "international crimes" comprises both these sets of crimes. See G. Werle, *Völkerstrafrecht,* Mohr Siebeck, Tübingen (2003) p. 98 *et seq.* The Restatement of U.S. Foreign Relations Law speaks of "offenses of universal concern" when referring to some of the crimes that may constitute an offense under international law. However, the definition of the restatement is jurisdictional in nature, asserting that only those crimes that are subject to universal jurisdiction independently of other jurisdictional links can constitute a "crime of universal concern." Arguably, this is a specific subcategory of international crimes, and the concept of offenses of universal concern is thus more narrow than that of "international crimes." See R. S. Clark, "Offence of International Concern: Multilateral State Treaty Practice in the Forty Years since Nuremberg," *Nordic Journal of International Law* 48 (1988), p. 51; see also American Law Institute, *Restatement of the Law (Third), The Foreign Relations Law of the United States,* American Law Institute, Washington, DC (1987), § 404. The notion of "crime under international law" is not identical to that of "crime of universal concern": The latter is broader because it refers to those crimes for which customary international law allows states to exercise universal jurisdiction, but these crimes are not necessarily

all directly punishable under international law. It is important to note that there is no clear consensus on the exact content of these various categories. With the establishment of the International Criminal Court there is, however, no doubt that genocide, war crimes, crimes against humanity, and aggression (once it is defined) are crimes under international law and therefore entail individual criminal responsibility under international law.

11. For an extensive analysis, see M. C. Bassiouni, *International Criminal Conventions and Their Penal Provisions,* Transnational Publishers, Ardsley, NY (1997). See also Chapter 11 of this volume for a detailed discussion of the crime of aggression, genocide, war crimes, and crimes against humanity. For a discussion of environmental crimes, see F. Höpfel, "Die Internationale Dimension des Umweltstrafrechts," K. Schmoller (ed.), *Festschrift für Otto Triffterer zum 65. Geburtstag* [Liber Amicorum for Otto Triffterer], Springer, Berlin (1996), pp. 425–435.

12. Bassiouni, *supra* note 1, p. 33.

13. For a definition of *transnational* see Article 3(2) of the *United Nations Convention against Transnational Organized Crime (2001),* U.N.Doc.A/Res/55/25.

14. See also Bassiouni, *supra* note 1, p. 5 *et seq.* He distinguishes between direct and indirect enforcement.

15. *Ibid.*, p. 6.

16. *Ibid.*

17. For a general overview of these principles, see Harvard Research on International Law, "Draft Convention on Jurisdiction with Respect to Crime," *American Journal of International Law* 29 (1935), Supplement 1, pp. 435–651, p. 480 *et seq.* See Jescheck and Weigend, *Lehrbuch des Strafrechts: Allgemeiner Teil* [Criminal Law Textbook: General Part] (5th ed.), Duncker & Humblot, Berlin (1996), p. 163 *et seq.*; I. Brownlie, *infra* note 18, p. 303 *et seq.*; R. Jennings and A. Watts (eds.), *Oppenheim's International Law* (9th ed.), Vol. 1, Longman, London (1996). See also C. L. Blakesley, "Extraterritorial Jurisdiction," in M. C. Bassiouni (ed.), *International Criminal Law* (2nd ed.), Vol. 2, Transnational Publishers, Ardsley, NY (1999), pp. 33–105; *Restatement of the Law (Third), supra,* note 10, §§ 402–404.

18. See H.-H. Jescheck and T. Weigend, *supra* note 17, p. 167; *Oppenheim's, supra* note 17, §136; C. L. Blakesley and O. Lagodny, "Competing National Laws: Network or Jungle?" in A. Eser and O. Lagodny (eds.), *Principles and Procedures for a New Transnational Criminal Law: Documentation of an International Workshop in Freiburg, May 1991*, Beiträge und Materialien aus dem Max-Planck-Institut für Ausländisches und Internationales Strafrecht, Freiburg i. Br. (1992), Vol. S 33, pp. 47–100, p. 95. Compare also I. Brownlie, *Principles of Public International Law* (5th ed.), Clarendon Press, Oxford, UK (1998), p. 309; R. Wolfrum, "The Decentralized Prosecution of International Offences Through National Courts, "in Y. Dinstein and M. Tabory (eds.), *War Crimes in International Law*, Kluwer Law International, The Hague (1996), pp. 233–249, p. 233 *et seq.*

19. See, for example, *Restatement of the Law (Third), supra* note 10, Part IV, Chapters 1–3.

20. See M. Dixon, *Textbook on International Law* (4th ed.), Blackstone Press, London (2000), p. 134.

21. See A. Bianchi, "Comments on H. G. Maier, Jurisdictional Rules in Customary International Law," in K. L. Meessen (ed.), *Extraterritorial Jurisdiction in Theory and Practice*, Kluwer Law International, The Hague (1996), pp. 64–102, 78. The Helms-Burton Act and D'Amato Act imposed penalities on individuals investing in countries that were subject to a U.S. embargo. The strong opposition to these acts by the European Union and subsequent agreements limiting their application illustrate that in practice there is no strict distinction between prescriptive and enforcement jurisdiction.

22. See *Lotus* (France v. Turkey), 1927 Permanent Court of International Justice, Judgement No. 9 of September 7, 1927, Series A, No. 10; Brownlie, *supra* note 18, p. 303.

23. See Section 67(2) of the Austrian Penal Code; Section 9(1) of the German Penal Code; and Article 7(2) of the Swiss Penal Code.

24. Blakesley (*supra* note 17) maintains that European jurisprudence clearly also rejects the application of the territoriality principle to inchoate offenses. However, he merely refers to French jurisprudence. The application to inchoate offenses intended to be consummated in the territory of the forum state is stipulated in the German, Austrian, and Swiss Code. See supra note 23.

25. Blakesley, *supra* note 17, p. 52.

26. Section 277 *et seq.* of the Austrian Penal Code.

27. Supreme Court Decision of October 2, 1997, 15 Os 104/97; see also U. Kathrein, commentary on § 67, margin no. 10, in F. Höpfel and E. Ratz (eds.), *Wiener Kommentar zum Strafges etzbuch* [Vienna Commentary to the Criminal Code] (2nd ed.), Manz, Vienna, Issue 21 (2000).

28. See also Brownlie, *supra* note 18, p. 303 (states do not have exclusive jurisdiction on the basis of the principle of territoriality). The principle of *ne bis in idem* (the prohibition of double jeopardy), which plays an essential role in domestic systems, has developed into a rule that can also apply between states. Thus, if a state has already adjudicated a case, the other state having concurrent jurisdiction cannot assert its jurisdiction over the same case. See, for example, Article 54 of the Schengen Agreement, which foresees *ne bis in idem* for many European States.

29. See Restatement (Third), *supra* note 10, § 401(1)(c).

30. See Oppenheim, *supra* note 18, §139.

31. Brownlie, *supra* note 18, p. 306.

32. *Ibid.*

33. Section 64 (1) (4a) of the Austrian Penal Code; Section 5 (8) of the German Penal Code.

34. See Section 65 (1) (1) of the Austrian Penal Code; Section 7 (2) (1) of the German Penal Code.

35. See Blakesley, *supra* note 17, p. 62.

36. The "effects doctrine" goes beyond the protective principle, not being limited to national or public interests. It can be found in U.S. antitrust legislation and has been severely criticized for its wide application to cases where the agreements did not even intend to affect U.S. commerce. See *supra* note 29 and corresponding text.

37. This has a long tradition in German and Austrian Law. For example, Section 64 (1) subpara. 2 of the Austrian Penal Code stipulates that Austrian courts have jurisdiction over a crime committed against an Austrian public official in connection with his or her duties.

38. See Cutting Case, Moore, *Digest of International Law*, Vol. 2, 1887 For. Rel. 751 (1888).

39. Section 1202 Omnibus Diplomatic Security and Antiterrorism Act of 1986, 18 U.S.C. s. 2231.

40. See Blakesley, *supra* note 17, p. 70.

41. *United States v. Yunis,* 681 F.Supp 896 (D.D.C. 1988), affirmed *United States v. Yunis,* 924 F.2d 1086 (D.C. Cir. 1991).

42. A separate issue was the acceptance of jurisdiction in spite of the abduction of the defendant by U.S. officials, in violation of international law. For U.S. practice in this regard, see also *U.S. v. Alvarez-Machain* (1992), 31 ILM 902.

43. For an overview of legal writing on universal jurisdiction, see A. Hays Butler, "The Doctrine of Universal Jurisdiction: A Review of the Literature," *Criminal Law Forum* 11 (1999), pp. 353–373.

44. See A. Cassese, *International Criminal Law,* Oxford University Press, Oxford (2003), p. 285 *et seq.*

45. See Article 5(2) of the Torture Convention; Article 4(2) of The Hague Hijacking Convention; Article 5(2) of the Montreal Hijacking Convention; Article 3(2) of the Convention on the Prevention and Punishment of Crimes against Internationally Protected Persons; Article IV (a) of the Apartheid Convention; Article 4 (2) (b) of the Drug Trafficking Convention.

46. See, for instance, Article 5(3) of the *Convention against Torture and Other Cruel, Inhuman or Degrading Treatment or Punishment* (1984), ILM 1984, 1027 with changes in ILM, 1985, 535 (Torture Convention), Article 3(3) of the *Convention on Offences and Certain Other Acts Committed on Board Aircraft (1963),* 704 U.N.T.S. 219; Article 4(3) of the *Convention for the Suppression of Unlawful Seizure of Aircraft* (1970), ILM 1971, 133 (Hague Hijacking Convention). The Genocide Convention does not contain such a clause. It could be argued, however, that customary international law allows for universal jurisdiction over the crime of genocide. In the *Eichmann Case* (A-G of *Israel v. Eichmann,* 1961, 36 ILR 5) it was argued that the Genocide Convention does not prohibit the exercise of universal jurisdiction. See also *Application of the Convention on the Prevention and Punishment of the Crime of Genocide (Bosnia and Herzegovina v. Yugoslavia),* ICJ, Judgment, July 11, 1996, para. 31. The Court maintains that the obligation to prevent and punish genocide is not limited to state of territoriality.

47. See, generally, S. W. Becker, "Universal Jurisdiction: How Universal Is It? A Study of Competing Theories," *Palestine Yearbook of International Law,* Vol. 12, Kluwer, London (forthcoming).

48. Princeton Project on Universal Jurisdiction, *The Princeton Principles on Universal Jurisdiction,* July 23, 2001 (www.princeton. edu/~lapa, Princeton Principle 2(1). The ILC Draft Code of Crimes against the Peace and Security of Mankind only suggests that genocide, crimes against humanity, war crimes, and crimes against the United Nations and associated personnel are subject to universal jurisdiction (Commentary of the ILC on Article 8 of the ILC Draft Code of Crimes Against the Peace and Security of Mankind, *Report of the International Law Commission on Its Forty-eighth Session,* U.N.Doc. A/51/10 (1996). Brownlie considers piracy, hijacking, and offenses related to traffic in narcotics to be subject to universal jurisdiction, and Dixon maintains that genocide, crimes against humanity, war crimes, torture, piracy, and perhaps hostage taking and hijacking are offenses for which customary international law allows states to exercise universal jurisdiction (Brownlie, *supra* note 18, p. 308; M. Dixon, *supra* note 20, p. 139).

49. Princeton Principle 1(3). Principle 1(2) must thus not be read as establishing a condition for the exercise of universal jurisdiction.

50. See Butler, *supra* note 43, p. 355.

51. This idea is similar to the notion that the state is acting as a surrogate for the international community (M. C. Bassiouni, "Universal Jurisdiction for International Crimes: Historical Perspectives and Contemporary Practice," *Virginia Journal of International Law* 42 (2001), pp. 83–156, p. 96) or is substituting for the "defaulting territorial or national state" (Cassese, *supra* note 44, p. 285).

52. *Loi du 16 juin 1993 relative à la répression des infractions graves aux Conventions internationales de Genève du 12 août 1949 et aux Protocoles I et II du 8 juin 1977, additionnels à ces Conventions, et de la loi du 10 février 1999 modifiant cette loi,* Moniteur Belge. For a general overview see L. Reydams, "Universal Criminal Jurisdiction: The Belgian State of Affairs," *Criminal Law Forum* 11 (2000), pp. 183–216.

53. See, generally, Reydams, *supra* note 52. The four Rwandans were convicted on June 8,

2001, but the case against Hissène Habre is still pending.

54. *Case Concerning the Arrest Warrant of 11 April 2000 (Democratic Republic of the Congo v. Belgium)* ICJ, Judgement, February 14, 2002.

55. *Loi relative aux violations graves du droit international humanitaire* of August 5, 2003. Under the new Article 6, Belgian courts can assert such jurisdiction even when the accused or victim became a citizen or resident after the date of the commission of the crime. For a more detailed discussion, see L. Reydams, "Belgium Reneges on Universality: The 5 August 2003 Act on Grave Breaches of International Humanitarian Law," *Journal of International Criminal Justice* 1 (2003), pp. 679–689.

56. Article 23(4) of the 1985 *Organic Law of the Judicial Power.*

57. *R. v. Bow Street Metropolitan Stipendiary Magistrate & others, ex parte Pinochet Ugarte* (Amnesty International & others intervening), No. 3 (1999) 2 All ER 97 (HR).

58. Lord Browne-Wilkinson also maintained that torture is a *jus cogens* crime, which justifies states in exerting universal jurisdiction, but he did not draw the logical conclusion that British courts had jurisdiction based on customary international law and independently of a statutory authorization.

59. See J. D. Van der Vyver, "Universal Jurisdiction in International Criminal Law," *South African Yearbook of International Law* 24 (1999), pp. 107–132, at 120 *et seq.*

60. Some judges questioned whether universal jurisdiction could be exercised in cases not covered by an international convention.

61. *Auto de la Sala de lo Penal de la Audiencia Nacional confirmando la jurisdicción de España para conocer de los crímenes de genocidio y terrorismo cometidos durante la dictadura chilena,* Audiencia Nacional (1998). With regard to the alleged acts of torture, the Court argued that these acts were part of the alleged genocide and thus dealt only with the question of whether Spain had universal jurisdiction over acts of genocide committed in Chile. See also N. Roth-Arriaza, "The Pinochet Precedent and Universal Jurisdiction," *New England Law Review* 35, No. 2 (2001), p. 313.

62. *Sentencia del Tribunal Supremo sobre el caso Guatemala por genocidio,* Tribunal Supremo, Sala de lo Penal, Decision No. 327/2003.

63. *Case Concerning the Arrest Warrant of 11 April 2000 (Democratic Republic of the Congo v. Belgium)* 2002 ICJ, Dissenting Opinion of Judge Van den Wyngaert, paras. 48–67.

64. *Demjanjuk v. Petrovsky et al.,* 776 F. 2d 571, 582 (6th Cir. 1985). This case concerned the extradition of a Nazi collaborator to Israel. In the case of *U.S. v. Ramzi Ahmed Yousuf and others,* 327 F 3d 56 (2nd Cir. 2003), the Court of Appeals rejected universal jurisdiction for the crime of terrorism because there did not exist a precise definition of it. However, it reaffirmed that universal jurisdiction for piracy, war crimes, and crimes against humanity, including genocide, is accepted under customary international law.

65. See *infra* note 80 and accompanying text.

66. It will be interesting to see how the ICJ decides in the case of *Certain Criminal Proceedings in France (Republic of the Congo v. France,* 2002), which concerns investigation and prosecution measures taken by French authorities in response to complaints of crimes against humanity and torture against the president of the Republic of Congo and other high-ranking individuals, including ministers and generals. The ICJ will probably have to deal with the issue of universal jurisdiction at least with regard to the generals, because they arguably do not enjoy immunity under international law. The request of the Congo for the indication of provisional measures was denied by Order of June 17, 2003.

67. See Van den Wyngaert, *supra* note 63, paras. 60–62.

68. For a detailed discussion of this principle, see J. Meyer, "The Vicarious Administration of Justice: An Overlooked Basis of Jurisdiction," *Harvard International Law Journal* 31, No. 1 (1990) pp. 108–116; C. Pappas, *Stellvertretende Strafrechtspflege: Zugleich ein Beitrag zur Ausdehnung Deutscher Strafgewalt Nach § 7 Abs. 2 Nr. 2 StGB,* Max Planck Institute for Foreign and International Criminal Law, Freiburg, Germany (1996), Vol. S 58. See also Blakesley and Lagodny, *supra* note 18, p. 66.

69. See Section 65(1)(2) of the Austrian Criminal Code; Section 7(2)(2) of the German Criminal Code.

70. The Austrian and German criminal justice systems are based on the principle of mandatory

prosecution. Thus, if jurisdiction over a crime exists, the prosecutor must initiate investigations. In this sense, there is also an obligation to prosecute if a person cannot be extradited, but at the same time, nonextradition gives rise to criminal jurisdiction of the state of custody. *Aut dedere aut judicare*, however, only establishes an obligation to prosecute without conferring jurisdiction on the state of custody.

71. See, for example, the *Hamadei* Case, Bundesgerichtshof [German Federal Supreme Court], *Neue Juristische Wochenschrift* 44 (1991), p. 3104, where German courts asserted their jurisdiction over the crime of murder on the basis of vicarious administration of justice. A discussion of the case is also found in Pappas, see *supra* note 68, and with reference to questions on extradition, in D. Kennedy et al., "The Extradition of Mohammed Hamadei," *Harvard International Law Journal* 31, No. 1 (1990), pp. 5–36.

72. Oberster Gerichtshof [Supreme Court of Austria], July 13, 1994, 15 Os 99/94. The Austrian Criminal Code does not provide for universal jurisdiction. The provision that might be relied on is Section 64 (6) of the Austrian Criminal Code, which stipulates that Austrian Courts have jurisdiction over such crimes, for which Austria has an obligation to prosecute. Because the Genocide Convention does not contain an explicit obligation for nonterritorial states to prosecute (but see note 46), Austrian courts must rely on the principle of vicarious administration of justice to adjudicate the crime of genocide. See also note 91 and corresponding text.

73. For a more detailed analysis of this interface between human rights protection and criminal law, see C. Tomuschat, "The Duty to Prosecute International Crimes Committed by Individuals," in H.-J. Cremer et al. (eds.), *Tradition und Weltoffenheit des Rechts: Festschrift für Helmut Steinberger* [Liber Amicorum for Helmut Steinberger., Vol. 152, Springer, Berlin (2002]; M. Nowak, "Strafrechtspflege und Menschenrecht: Gedanken zu einer lebendigen Schnittstellenproblematik," [Criminal law and Human Rights], in *Strafverfahren-Menschenrechte-Effektivität: Vorträge Gehalten bei der Richterwoche 2001 in Wels*, Schriftenreihe des Bundesministeriums für Justiz [Publication of Austrian Judges Week], Vol. 106 (2001), pp. 1–61.

74. See Articles 5, 6, 8, and 23 of the *U.N. Convention against Transnational Organised Crime*; Article 4 of the Torture Convention; Article 4 of the *Convention on the Prevention and Suppression of the Crime of Genocide* (1948), 78 U.N.T.S. 277 (Genocide Convention); Articles 49 and 54 of the *Convention for the Amelioration of the Condition of the Wounded and Sick in Armed Forces in the Field* (1949), 75 U.N.T.S. 31 (Geneva Convention I); Article 50 of the *Convention for the Amelioration of the Condition of the Wounded, Sick, and Shipwrecked Members of the Armed Forces at Sea* (1949), 75 U.N.T.S. 85 (Geneva Convention II); Article 129 of the *Convention Relative to the Treatment of Prisoners of War* (1949), 75 U.N.T.S. 135 (Geneva Convention III) and Article 146 of the *Convention Relative to the Protection of Civilian Persons in Time of War* (1949), 75 U.N.T.S. 287 (Geneva Convention IV); Article 4 (a) of the *International Convention on the Suppression and Punishment of the Crime of Apartheid* (1973), ILM 1974, 50; Article 2 of the *Convention for the Suppression of Unlawful Seizure of Aircraft* (1970), ILM 1971, 133 (The Hague Hijacking Convention); Article 3 of the *Convention for the Suppression of Unlawful Acts against the Safety of Civil Aviation* (1971), 974 U.N.T.S. 177 (Montreal Hijacking Convention); Article 2 (1) and (2) of the *Convention on the Prevention and Punishment of Crimes against Internationally Protected Persons, Including Diplomatic Agents* (1973), 1035 U.N.T.S. 167 (Convention on Internationally Protected Persons); Article 4 of the *Convention on the Prohibition of the Development, Production and Stockpiling of Bacteriological (Biological) and Toxin Weapons and on Their Destruction* (1972), 1015 U.N.T.S. 163; Article 3 of the *United Nations Convention against Illicit Traffic in Narcotic Drugs and Psychotropic Substances* (1988), ILM (1989) 493 (Drug Trafficking Convention). For a more detailed list of treaty obligations to criminalize certain behavior, see Bassiouni, *supra* note 11.

75. Where there is an obligation to establish universal jurisdiction over international crimes, this is never couched in absolute terms. See Article 5(2) of the Torture Convention; Article 4(2) of The Hague Hijacking Convention; Article 5(2) of the Montreal Hijacking Convention; Article 3(2) of the Convention on the Prevention and Punishment

of Crimes against Internationally Protected Persons; Article IV (a) of the Apartheid Convention; and Article 4 (2) (b) of the Drug Trafficking Convention.

76. See Article 49 of Geneva Convention I; Article 50 of Geneva Convention II; Article 129 of Geneva Convention III; Article 146 of Geneva Convention IV; Article 5 of the Apartheid Convention; and Article 7 of the Torture Convention. Article 6 of the Genocide Convention establishes such an obligation only for the state of territoriality but also provides for the alternative possibility of surrendering the alleged offender to an international tribunal. For a detailed discussion of the principle of *aut dedere aut judicare*, see Bassiouni and E. M. Wise, *Aut Dedere aut Judicare: The Duty to Extradite or Prosecute in International Law*, Nijhoff, Dordrecht (1995). According to the Commentary of the ILC to Article 9 of the Draft Code of Crimes Against the Peace and Security of Mankind, *Report of the International Law Commission on Its Forty-eighth Session*, U.N.Doc. A/51/10 (1996) the principle of *aut dedere aut judicare* does not give priority to either course of action. However, the Geneva Conventions seem to provide for a stronger obligation on states to prosecute grave breaches, which may be expressed as *primo prosequi, secundo dedere* (see Van den Wyngaert, *supra* note 63, para. 62).

77. See International Law Association (Committee on International Human Rights Law and Practice), *Final Report on the Exercise of Universal Jurisdiction in Respect of Gross Human Rights Offences*, 2000, p. 21, stipulating an obligation for state parties of the Geneva Conventions and Torture Convention to exercise universal jurisdiction in respect of grave breaches and torture. Tomuschat (*supra* note 73, p. 328) maintains that the obligation to prosecute international crimes on the basis of universal jurisdiction must be founded in conventions. The ILC commentary to Article 9 states that the duty to prosecute prohibits the exercise of prosecutorial discretion to the effect of conferring immunity to alleged offenders in exchange for giving evidence or assisting in the prosecution. Some commentators have argued that the principle of *aut dedere aut judicare* has become a rule of customary international law, which must be applied to all international crimes

(see, e.g., C. Enache and A. Fried, "Universal Crime, Jurisdiction and Duty: The Obligation of Aut Dedere Aut Judicare in International Law," *McGill Law Journal* 43 [1998], pp. 613–633).

78. Prescription led to the acquittal by Italian courts of Priepke in 1996, who had admitted to the massacre of several hundred civilians. Extradition of Menten was refused because the alleged war crimes had prescribed under Swiss law. The *United Nations Convention on the Non-Applicability of Statutes of Limitation to War Crimes and Crimes against Humanity (1968)*, ILM 1969, 68, was not signed by many states because they viewed it as being incompatible with the rule of nonretroactivity. Although the principle of nonretroactivity applies only to substantive provisions of criminal law, states differ on the categorization of jurisdiction and prescription, seeing them as part of either substantive or procedural law. For a more detailed discussion of state practice with regard to war crimes, genocide, and crimes against humanity, see C. Van den Wyngaert, "War Crimes, Genocide and Crimes against Humanity: Are States Taking National Prosecutions Seriously?" in M. C. Bassiouni (ed.), *International Criminal Law* (2nd ed.), Vol. 3, Transnational Publishers, Ardsley, NY (1999), pp. 227–238.

79. See *infra* note 95.

80. *Völkerstrafgesetzbuch* [Code of Crimes Against International Law] Federal Gazette I (2002), p. 2254. An English translation can be found annexed to the article by G. Werle and F. Jessberger, "International Criminal Justice Is Coming Home: The New German Code of Crimes Against International Law," *Criminal Law Forum* 13 (2002), p. 191 *et seq.*

81. Persecution is an independent offense under customary international law, although the ICC Statute requires a link to another crime against humanity or to genocide or war crimes (see Article 7(1)(h) of ICC Statute, *infra* note 95).

82. See, for example, Article 7(1)k of the ICC Statute, *infra* note 95.

83. For example, Greece, Italy, Portugal, Spain, Austria, and Germany. See C. Van den Wyngaert (ed.), *Criminal Procedure Systems in the European Community*, Butterworths, London (1993).

84. For a more detailed discussion of the CCIL see Werle and Jessberger, *supra* note 80.

85. Crimes Against Humanity and War Crimes Act, S. C. 2000, c. 24.

86. *Ibid.*, Sections 4(4) and 6(4).

87. *Ibid.*, Section 8. The principle of prosecutorial discretion, however, still applies.

88. For a general overview of the Crimes Against Humanity and War Crimes Act, see M. Rosenberg, "Canadian Legislation Against Crimes Against Humanity and War Crimes," in *The Changing Face of International Criminal Law: Selected Papers*, The International Centre for Criminal Law Reform and Criminal Justice Policy (2002), pp. 229–236.

89. See Section 321 of the Austrian Criminal Code.

90. Little thought was given to this aspect during the Parliamentary discussions on the implementation of the ICC Statute. See Stenographic Records of the Nationalrat, 21st term, 110th Session, July 10, 2002, p. 271 *et seq.*

91. Compare I. Gartner, "Implementation of the ICC Statute in Austria," in C. Kress and F. Lattanzi (eds.), *The Rome Statute and Domestic Legal Orders Volume I: General Aspects and Constitutional Issues*, Nomos, Baden-Baden (2000), pp. 51–63. Jurisdiction is established by an enabling clause. The principle of vicarious administration of justice may provide a further basis of jurisdiction, see *supra* note 68 and corresponding text.

92. See H. Duffy and J. Huston, "Implementation of the ICC Statute: International Obligations and Constitutional Considerations," in C. Kress and F. Lattanzi (eds.), *The Rome Statute and Domestic Legal Orders Volume I: General Aspects and Constitutional Issues*, Nomos, Baden-Baden (2000), pp. 29–49.

93. Bundesgesetz über die Zusammenarbeit mit dem Internationalen Strafgerichtshof [Law on Cooperation with the International Criminal Court], Federal Gazette I (2002), No. 135.

94. Section 34 of the Austrian Code of Criminal Procedure.

95. Rome Statute of the International Criminal Court, U.N.Doc. A/CONF.183/9 [ICC Statute]. At the time of writing, 139 states had signed and 94 states had ratified the statute. For a historical overview of the ICC, see M. C. Bassiouni, "Historical Survey: 1919–1998," in Bassiouni, *supra* note 78, Vol. 3, pp. 597–635;

M. Scharf, "The Draft Statute for an International Criminal Court," in Bassiouni, *supra* note 78, Vol. 3, pp. 637–653. For a compilation of the preparatory documents for the establishment of the ICC, see M. C. Bassiouni, *The Statute of the International Criminal Court: A Documentary History*, Transnational Publishers, Ardsley, NY (1998). An in-depth analysis of the ICC Statute and its drafting history is provided by O. Triffterer (ed.), *Commentary on the Rome Statute of the International Criminal Court: Observers' Notes, Article by Article*, Nomos Verlagsgesellschaft, Baden-Baden (1999); A. Cassese et al., *The Rome Statute of the International Criminal Court: a Commentary*, Vols. 1 and 2, Oxford University Press, Oxford, UK (2002). For an overview of the Court, see W. A. Schabas, *An Introduction to the International Criminal Court*, Cambridge University Press, Cambridge, UK (2001); L. Sadat Wexler, "A First Look at the 1998 Rome Statute for a Permanent International Criminal Court: Jurisdiction, Definition of Crimes, Structure and Referrals to the Court," in Bassiouni, *supra* note 78, Vol. 3, pp. 355–391; B. Broomhall, "The International Criminal Court: Overview, and Cooperation with States," in Association Internationale de Droit Penal, *Nouvelles Etudes Penales: ICC Ratification and National Implementing Legislation*, Érès (1999), pp. 45–91; A. Cassese, "The Statute of the International Criminal Court: Some Preliminary Reflections," *European Journal of International Law* 10 (1999), pp. 144–171.

96. Statement of Mr. Luis Moreno Ocampo at the *Ceremony for the solemn undertaking of the Chief Prosecutor of the International Criminal Court*, June 16, 2003, The Peace Palace, The Hague, The Netherlands.

97. Such criticism has mainly been voiced by the United States, which has repeatedly made it clear that in its view the ICC is fundamentally flawed. Although taking an active role during the Rome Conference, the United States "unsigned" the Rome Statute on May 6, 2002, in a letter to U.N. Secretary-General Kofi Annan. The United States has subsequently adopted the American Servicemembers' Protection Act (ASPA, Pub. L. No. 107–206, 116 Stat. 899 (2002), enacting H.R. 4775 (S. 2551)), which bars U.S. military assistance to states after July 1, 2003, if these states did not conclude bilateral agreements with the United

States prohibiting them from surrendering U.S. nationals or other persons acting on behalf of the U.S. military to the ICC. At the time of writing, 75 countries had signed such agreements based on Article 98(2) of the Rome Statute. The United States has also pushed for Security Council Resolution 1422, exempting peacekeepers of non-state parties from the jurisdiction of the ICC. For the European Union position on Article 98 agreements, see *Council Conclusions on the International Criminal Court (30/09/2002)* and the *EU Guiding Principles Concerning Arrangements between a State Party to the Rome Statute of the International Criminal Court and the United States Regarding the Conditions to Surrender of Persons to the Court* annexed thereto; ACP-EU Joint Parliamentary Assembly, Resolution on the International Criminal Court, April 3, 2003, Brazzaville. See also Parliamentary Assembly of the Council of Europe, Resolution 1300 on Risks for the Integrity of the Statute of the International Criminal Court, September 24, 2002. For a general discussion of the U.S. position on the ICC, see R. Wedgwood, "The International Criminal Court: An American View" *European Journal of International Law* 10 (1999), pp. 93–107; G. Hafner et al., "a Response to the American View as Presented by Ruth Wedgwood," *European Journal of International Law* 10 (1999), pp. 108–123; S. B. Sewall and C. Kaysen (eds.), *The United States and the International Criminal Court: National Security and International Law*, American Academy of Arts and Sciences, Cambridge, MA (2000); D. J. Scheffer, "Staying the Course with the International Criminal Court," *Cornell International Law Journal* 35 (Nov. 2001–Feb. 2002), pp. 47–100; J. Gurulé, "United States Opposition to the 1998 Rome Statute Establishing an International Criminal Court: Is the Court's Jurisdiction Truly Complementary to National Criminal Jurisdictions?" *Cornell International Law Journal* 35 (Nov. 2001–Feb. 2002), pp. 1–45; C. C. Joyner and C. C. Posteraro, "The United States and the International Criminal Court: Rethinking the Struggle between National Interests and International Justice," *Criminal Law Forum* 10 (1999), pp. 359–385. For continuous updated information, see the Web site of the Coalition for the International Criminal Court (www.iccnow.org,

last access: June 11, 2003) and the Washington Working Group on the International Criminal Court (www.wfa.org/issues/wicc/wicc.html, last access: June 11, 2003).

98. Official Records of the Assembly of States Parties to the Rome Statute of the International Criminal Court, First Session of the Assembly of State Parties (September 3–10, 2002), ICC-ASP/1/3, pp. 10–107.

99. Official Records of the Assembly of States Parties, *supra* note 98, pp. 108–155.

100. Article 5(1), first sentence of the ICC Statute; further references are found in para. 9 of the Preamble and Article 1 of the ICC Statute.

101. The statute does not purport to be a codification of international criminal or humanitarian law (see Wexler, *supra* note 95, p. 661). Article 10 of the ICC Statute reiterates this point.

102. For a more detailed discussion of these crimes, see Chapter 11 of this volume.

103. For a more detailed discussion on whether this satisfies the principle of legality, see E. Gadirov, in O. Triffterer, *supra* note 95, Article 9.

104. See Article 5(2) of the statute.

105. An amendment must be accepted by a two-thirds majority vote (Article 121(3)). The Court may not exercise jurisdiction over such a crime if it was committed by a national or in the territory of a state that did not accept such an amendment (Article 121(5)). If accepted by seven-eighths of the state parties, a dissenting state may withdraw from the treaty.

106. See *International Criminal Responsibility of Individuals and Entities Engaged in Illicit Trafficking in Narcotic Drugs across National Frontiers and Other Transnational Criminal Activities: Establishment of an International Criminal Court with Jurisdiction over Such Crimes*, U.N.Doc. A/Res/44/49.

107. Proposals to this effect were rejected by the majority of the delegates on the basis that drug-related crimes do not reach the gravity requirement as implied by the "most serious crimes of concern to the international community as a whole" and that the Court would be swamped with drug-related cases (see A. Zimmermann, in O. Triffterer, *supra* note 95, Article 5, margin Nos. 5–6).

108. *Ibid.*, margin Nos. 3–4.

109. Although this provision is in accordance with Article 28 of the Vienna Convention on the

Law of Treaties, retroactive jurisdiction of the Court would not necessarily be in conflict with the principle of *nullum crimen sine lege*, if the conduct was already proscribed under international law at the time of its commission. See S. A. Williams, in O. Triffterer, *supra* note 95, Article 11, margin Nos. 1–2. In the Eichmann case, Israel argued that the genocide committed prior to the existence of the State of Israel was punishable before Israeli courts because at the time of commission, it was already a crime under international law.

110. See Article 126(2) of the ICC Statute.

111. See K. Ambos, in O. Triffterer, *supra* note 95, Article 25, margin No. 4.

112. See Article 26 of the ICC Statute.

113. See Article 13 of the ICC Statute.

114. See Article 14 of the ICC Statute.

115. See Article 39 of the Charter of the United Nations, which stipulates that the Security Council may adopt necessary measures "to maintain and restore international peace and security." That such a measure may be of an adjudicatory nature has been developed through the Security Council Resolutions establishing the ad hoc Tribunals for the former Yugoslavia and Rwanda (see *infra* section under the heading "The *Ad Hoc* Tribunals").

116. See Article 15(4) of the ICC Statute.

117. See Article 15(5) of the ICC Statute.

118. See Article 12(1) of the ICC Statute.

119. For the drafting history see S. A. Williams, in O. Triffterer, *supra* note 95, Article 12, margin Nos. 1–12.

120. It was mostly the permanent members of the Security Council who wanted an opt-out clause for crimes against humanity and war crimes. The exact legal effect of a declaration that the state does not accept the jurisdiction of the Court is unclear from the wording alone: Such a declaration could either generally bar the Court from exercising its jurisdiction in such cases, thus having an effect similar to a Security Council deferral under Article 16 (see *infra*), or it could have the effect that such a state would have the status of a nonparty state, meaning that the Court could still exercise its jurisdiction if another jurisdictional link is provided. The drafting history shows, however, that it was the intention of those states who advocated such a clause to categorically bar the Court from exercising its jurisdiction in these cases. See

A. Zimmermann, in O. Triffterer, *supra* note 95, Article 124, margin Nos. 1–7.

121. See Article 12(2) of the ICC Statute.

122. See *supra* section under the heading "Traditional Bases for Asserting Jurisdiction." For a discussion on whether the Court has inherent jurisdiction or conferred jurisdiction, see M. Inazumi, "The Meaning of the State Consent Precondition in Article 12(2) of the Rome Statute of the International Criminal Court: A Theoretical Analysis of the Source of International Criminal Jurisdiction," in *Netherlands International Law Review* 49 (2002), pp. 159–193.

123. See Article 12(2) and (3) of the ICC Statute.

124. Proposal of the Republic of Korea, U.N.Doc. A/CONF.183/C.1/L6, June 18, 1998.

125. The Korean Proposal followed a German proposal (U.N.Doc. A/AC.249/1998/DP.2), which had advocated a universal jurisdiction of the Court over the crimes listed in Article 5. The German delegation argued that if the contracting states are able to assert universal jurisdiction over these crimes, the Court should have the same capacity because its jurisdiction is derived from that of the party states. Many delegations, however, felt that such a jurisdictional regime gave the Court too much power. See Williams, *supra* note 109; H.-P. Kaul, "Preconditions to the Exercise of Jurisdiction," in Cassese et al., *supra* note 95, pp. 583–616, p. 596 *et seq.*

126. The U.S. delegation wanted the consent of the state of nationality to be a precondition to the exercise of the court's jurisdiction, when triggered by a state complaint or a *proprio motu* investigation of the prosecutor. See Williams, *supra* note 109; margin No. 10; Kaul, *supra* note 125, p. 600.

127. H.-P. Kaul, "The International Criminal Court: Jurisdiction, Trigger Mechanism and Relationship to National Jurisdictions," in M. Politi and G. Nesi (eds.), *The Rome Statute of the International Criminal Court*, Ashgate, Aldershot, UK (2002), pp. 59–62, p. 60, 61.

128. The wording of this article does not imply any limit on the number of times that the Security Council may renew such a request.

129. On the relationship between the ICJ and the Security Council, see the *Corfu Channel case, Aegean Sea, Teheran Hostages, Military and*

Paramilitary Activities in and against Nicaragua, and the *Lockerbie* case.

130. M. Bergsmo and J. Pejic, in O. Triffterer, *supra* note 95, Article 16, margin No. 10.

131. For the drafting history, see Bergsmo and Pejic, *supra* note 130, margin Nos. 1–10; L. Condorelli and S. Villalpando, "Referral and Deferral by the Security Council," in Cassese et al., *supra* note 95, pp. 627–655, p. 644 *et seq.*

132. Security Council Resolution 1422, U.N.Doc. S/Res/1422 (2002).

133. Normally, a Security Council resolution under Chapter 7 is adopted to sanction a state whose behavior constitutes a threat to the peace and security of mankind. In this case, the Security Council gave into the demands of a state whose lack of cooperation would have undermined the peacekeeping operation in Bosnia-Herzegovina and thus indirectly threaten the peace in the region.

134. On June 12, 2003, the resolution was renewed for another 12 months by Security Council Resolution 1487. Where the first resolution was adopted unanimously, Resolution 1487 was adopted with 12 votes, Germany, France, and Syria abstaining. U.N. Secretary-General Kofi Annan maintained that such a resolution was not necessary because no peacekeeper has ever been accused of the kind of crimes that fall into the jurisdiction of the Court. He voiced his concern that the renewal should not become an annual routine because this would undermine the authority of the Security Council and the ICC. For a discussion of Resolution 1422, see Z. Deen-Racsmány, "The ICC, Peacekeepers and Resolution 1422: Will the Court Defer to the Council?" *Netherlands International Law Review* 49 (2002), pp. 353–388; S. Zappalà, "The Reaction of the US to the Entry into Force of the ICC Statute: Comments on UN SC Resolution 1422 (2002) and Article 98 Agreements," *Journal of International Criminal Justice* 1 (2003), pp. 114–134.

135. See para. 10 of the preamble, Articles 1 and 17 of the ICC Statute.

136. Paragraph 4 of the Preamble of the ICC Statute.

137. The principle of *ne bis in idem* is generally defined in Article 20 of the ICC Statute.

138. Article 17(3) defines inability as a breakdown of the judicial system of the state that renders national enforcement authorities incapable of carrying out their tasks properly.

139. See Article 17(2).

140. The threshold for the Court asserting its jurisdiction when the person has already been tried, thus overriding the principle of *ne bis in idem*, is higher: "Unwillingness" can be determined only by referring to "the purpose of shielding" and "the lack of independence or impartiality." See Article 20(3) of the ICC Statute.

141. See S. A. Williams, in O. Triffterer, *supra* note 95, Article 17, margin No. 27.

142. See Article 18 of the ICC Statute.

143. See Article 18(6).

144. See Article 18(5). From the wording "State Parties," it is clear that only state parties are obliged to respond to such a request. This is in keeping with Article 86, which obliges state parties to cooperate with the Court. A state investigating and prosecuting international crimes does so on behalf of the international community and thus should be held accountable to some degree over its actions. See D. Ntanda Nsereko, in O. Triffterer, *supra* note 95, Article 18, margin. No. 24.

145. See Article 19 of the ICC Statute. Challenges may also be made by an accused or person who has been summoned before the Court or for whom an arrest warrant exists under Article 58. Article 19(2) further defines the grounds on which such a challenge may be based.

146. If exceptional circumstances apply, the Court may allow for more than one challenge or that the challenge can be made at a later stage. Challenges to admissibility brought forward at commencement of the trial or at a later stage, with leave of the Court, may be based only on the fact that the case has already been tried by a national court and is thus inadmissible under the principle of *ne bis in idem.*

147. U.N. Security Council Resolution 808 (1993), U.N.Doc. S/Res/808 (1993), adopted on February 22, 1993; U.N. Security Council Resolution 827 (1993), U.N.Doc. S/Res/827 (1993), adopted on May 25, 1993, *Report of the Secretary-General Pursuant to Paragraph 2 of Security Council Resolution 808* (1993), U.N.Doc. S/25704, May 3, 1993; U.N. Security Council Resolution 955 (1994), U.N. Doc. S/Res/955 (1994).

148. Secretary-General's report, *supra* note 147, para. 22. See U.N. Charter, Articles 39, 41, 42.

For a more detailed discussion of the legal basis for the ICTY and ICTR, see *Prosecutor v. Tadić*, IT-94-1-AR72, Appeals Chamber, Decision on the Defence Motion for Interlocutory Appeal on Jurisdiction, October 2, 1995, paras. 26–48 and *Prosecutor v. Kanyabashi*, ICTR-96-15-1, Trial Chamber II, Decision on the Defence Motion on Jurisdiction, paras. 9–29. For a commentary on the Tadić decision, see H. Fischer, in A. Klip and G. Sluiter (eds.), *Annotated Leading Cases of International Criminal Tribunals: The International Criminal Tribunal for the Former Yugoslavia 1993–1998*, Intersentia, Antwerp, Belgium (1999), pp. 140–142.

149. Article 8 of the ICTY Statute.

150. Article 7 of the ICTR Statute.

151. Therefore, the Secretary General's report emphasizes that only such rules of international humanitarian law should be applied by the ICTY that are beyond any doubt part of customary international law (para. 34). See also *Prosecutor v. Delalić et al.,* IT-96-21-T, Appeal Chamber, Decision on Application for Leave to Appeal, October 15, 1996, paras. 26, 27, and in the same case the final judgment rendered by the Trial Chamber on November 16, 1998, at paras. 402, 417. The same does not seem to apply to all crimes within the jurisdiction of the ICTR, where Protocol 2 of the 1949 Geneva Conventions is also applied, which cannot be regarded as part of customary international law. However, because the ICTR primarily deals with genocide, the issue might not be as relevant.

152. See Article 29 of the ICTY Statute and Article 28 of the ICTR Statute.

153. See Articles 24, 25, 39, and 41 of the U.N. Charter. With regard to the ICTY, the Dayton-Peace Agreement (initialed in Dayton on November 21, 1995, and signed in Paris on December 14, 1995) provides a further basis for such an obligation.

154. See *Report of the International Tribunal for the Prosecution of Persons Responsible for Serious Violations of International Humanitarian Law Committed in the Territory of the former Yugoslavia since 1991*, U.N. Doc. A/49/342, S/1994/1007, paras. 13, 14.

155. See Article 103 of the U.N. Charter.

156. See M. Bohlander, "Possible Conflicts of Jurisdiction with the *Ad Hoc* International Tribunals," in Cassese et al., *supra* note 95, pp. 687–691.

157. U.N. Security Council Resolution 1503 (2003), U.N. Doc. S/Res/1503(2003), adopted on August 15, 2003, para. 7.

158. See *infra*, section under the heading "Bosnia and Herzegovina/Kosovo."

159. *Prosecutor v. Tadić*, IT-94-1-T, Appeals Chamber, Decision on the Prosecutor's Motion Requesting Protective Measures for Victims and Witnesses, August 10, 1995, para. 27.

160. *Prosecutor v. Tadić*, IT-94-1-T, Trial Chamber II, Opinion and Judgement, May 7, 1997, para. 558.

161. *Final Report to the Prosecutor by the Committee Established to Review the NATO Bombing Campaign Against the Federal Republic of Yugoslavia*, published on the Web site of the ICTY (www.un.org/icty/pressreal/nato061300. htm, last access: June 19, 2003).

162. For a detailed discussion and criticism of the Report of the Review Committee, see P. Benvenuti, "The ICTY Prosecutor and the Review of the NATO Bombing Campaign against the Federal Republic of Yugoslavia," *European Journal of International Law* 12, No. 3(2001), pp. 503–529.

163. Agreement between the United Nations and the Government of Sierra Leone on the Establishment of a Special Court for Sierra Leone, January 16, 2002, to which the Statute of the Special Court for Sierra Leone is annexed.

164. Articles 2–5 of the Special Court Statute.

165. *Ibid.*, Article 8.

166. The Truth and Reconciliation Commission Act of 2000, February 22, 2000.

167. Peace agreement between the government of Sierra Leone and the Revolutionary United Front of Sierra Leone (RUF/SL), Lomé, Togo, July 7, 1999, Article 26.

168. See S. de Bertodano, "Current Developments in Internationalized Courts," *Journal of International Criminal Justice* 1 (2003), 226–244, 242; A. McDonald, "Sierra Leone's Shoestring Special Court," *International Review of the Red Cross* 84 (2002), No. 845, pp. 121–142; A. Tejan-Cole, "The Complementary and Conflicting Relationship between the Special Court for Sierra Leone and the Truth and Reconciliation Commission," *Yale Human Rights and Development Law*

Journal 6 (2003), pp. 139–159; Office of the Attorney General and Ministry of Justice Special Court Task Force, *Briefing Paper on Relationship between the Special Court and the Truth and Reconciliation Commission: Legal Analysis and Policy Considerations of the Government of Sierra Leone for the Special Court Planning Mission*, Planning Mission Briefing Series, January 7–18, 2002. In this regard, it is interesting to note that the Trial Chamber rejected a request by the TRC to conduct a hearing with Samuel Hinga Norman, who had been indicted by the Special Court, on the grounds that such a hearing would prejudice the presumption of innocence and the accused right to a fair trial. See *Decision on the Request by the Truth and Reconciliation Commission of Sierra Leone to Conduct a Public Hearing with Samuel Hinga Norman*, SCSL-2003-08-PT, October 29, 2003, paras. 10–16.

169. See *Seventeenth Report of the Secretary-General on the United Nations Mission in Sierra Leone*, March 17, 2003, U.N.Doc. S/2003/321.

170. The Draft Agreement between the United Nations and the Royal Government of Cambodia Concerning the Prosecution under Cambodian Law of Crimes Committed during the Period of Democratic Kampuchea (henceforth, the Agreement), which was accepted by the General Assembly on May 2, 2003, is annexed to the General Assembly Resolution on the Khmer Rouge Trials, U.N.Doc. A/Res/57/228.B.

171. Law on the Establishment of Extraordinary Chambers in the Courts of Cambodia for the Prosecution of Crimes Committed during the Period of Democratic Kampuchea, August 10, 2001, reproduced in K. Ambos and M. Othman (eds.), *New Approaches in International Criminal Justice: Kosovo, East Timor, Sierra Leone and Cambodia*, Max Planck Institute for Foreign and International Criminal Law, Freiburg, Germany (2003), p. 267.

172. *Ibid.*, Articles 2–8, including crimes under the 1954 Hague Convention for the Protection of Cultural Property and under the 1961 Vienna Convention on Diplomatic Relations.

173. *Ibid.* Article 5. See also Article 9 of the agreement. Cambodia has ratified and signed the Rome Statute.

174. See *Report of the Secretary General on Khmer Rouge Trials*, U.N. Doc. A/57/769, March 31, 2003, paras. 15 *et seq.*

175. *Ibid.*, paras. 20 and 21. See also Human Rights Watch, *Briefing Paper of 30 April 2003*, available at http://hrw.org/backgrounder/asia/cambodia043003-bck.pdf [last access: November 15, 2003].

176. Article 28 of the agreement.

177. U.N. Transitional Administration for East Timor (UNTAET) *Regulation No. 2000/15 of 6 June 2000 on the Establishment of Panels with Exclusive Jurisdiction over Serious Criminal Offences*, UNTAET/REG/2000/15.

178. *Ibid.*, Section 1.

179. *Ibid.*, Section 2.

180. See S. de Bertodano, *supra* note 168, p. 230.

181. Law No. 26/2000.

182. Decision 53/2001 by President Wahid of Indonesia.

183. See de Bertodano, *supra* note 168, p. 234; S. Linton, "Cambodia, East Timor and Sierra Leone: Experiments in International Justice," *Criminal Law Forum* 12 (2001), p. 202 *et seq.*

184. The High Representative is charged with overseeing the implementation of the provisions of the Dayton Peace Agreement of December 14, 1995 in Bosnia and Herzegovina.

185. See *Press Release of the Office of the High Representative and the ICTY*, October 30, 2003, OM/P.I.S./797e.

186. See *supra* note 158 and corresponding text.

187. See U.N. Security Council Resolution 1244(1999), U.N.Doc. S/Res/1244(1999), adopted on June 10, 1999.

188. U.N. Interim Administration Mission in Kosovo (UNMIK) Regulation No. 2000/6, On the Appointment and Removal from Office of International Judges and International Prosecutors, as amended by UNMIK Regulation No. 2000/34 and UNMIK Regulation No. 2001/2.

189. U.N. Interim Administration Mission in Kosovo (UNMIK) Regulation No. 2000/64, On Assignment of International Judges/Prosecutors and/or Change of Venue.

190. See Organization for Security and Co-Operation in Europe (OSCE) Mission in Kosovo, *Kosovo War Crimes Trials: A Review*, September 2002, as cited by de Bertodano, *supra* note 173, p. 240/1, at notes 77 and 78.

191. See *supra* note 158 and corresponding text. See also M. Bohlander, "Kosovo: The Legal Framework of the Prosecution and the Courts," in Ambos and Othman, *supra* note 171, pp. 21–59, p. 32.

192. See Y. Beigbeder, *Judging Criminal Leaders: The Slow Erosion of Impunity*, Kluwer Law International, The Hague (2002), p. 199 *et seq.*

193. Statute of the International Court of Justice, annexed to the Charter of the United Nations, June 26, 1945.

194. In the *Arrest Warrant* case (see *supra* note 54), it held that the issue of the arrest warrant against the incumbent minister of foreign affairs of the Congo infringed on the immunity from criminal jurisdiction he enjoyed under international law.

195. *Questions of Interpretation and Application of the 1971 Montreal Convention Arising from the Aerial Incident at Lockerbie* (*Libyan Arab Jamahiriya v. United Kingdom, Libyan Arab Jamahiriya v. United States*), 1992 ICJ (Applications of March 3, 1992, instituting proceedings).

196. Request of the General Assembly (49/75 K), 1996 ICJ, Advisory Opinion, July 8, 1996.

197. *Bosnia-Herzegovina v. Yugoslavia*, 1993 ICJ, Orders of April 8 and September 13, 1993.

198. See Article 119(2) of the ICC Statute.

199. For general remarks on the relationship between the ICC and the ICJ, see R. Higgins, "The Relationship between the International Criminal Court and the International Court of Justice," in H. Hebel et al. (eds.), *Reflections on the International Criminal Court*, T.M.C. Asser Press, The Hague (1999), pp. 163–172.

200. Council of Europe, ETS No. 005, as amended by Protocol 11 of May 11, 1994 (44 ratifications with Serbia and Montenegro being the 45th signatory state).

201. For a general overview of these two courts, see R. S. MacDonald et al. (eds.), *The European System for the Protection of Human Rights in Europe*, Nijhoff, Dordrecht (1995);

R. Bernhardt, "Reform of the Control Machinery under the European Convention on Human Rights," *American Journal of International Law* 89 (1995), p. 145 *et seq.*; M. Pasqualucci, The *Practice and Procedure of the Inter-American Court of Human Rights*, Cambridge University Press, Cambridge, UK (2003); T. Buergenthal and D. Shelton, *Protecting Human Rights in the Americas*, 4th rev. ed., International Institute of Human Rights, Strasbourg (1995).

202. In a recent decision on the interpretation of Article 54 of the convention implementing the Schengen Agreement of June 14, 1985 (signed on June 19, 1990, OJ 2000 L 239, p. 19) the European Court of Justice (ECJ) held that the principle of *ne bis in idem* applies between the state parties also with respect to diversional measures of the public prosecutor by which further prosecution is barred (ECJ, Joined Cases C-187/01 and C-385/01, Judgment, February 11, 2003). This judgment thus affects whether an individual may be held criminally responsible in another state. In general, there is a strong development within the European Union toward a principle of mutual recognition of decisions in criminal matters (this principle being a "cornerstone" of future cooperation between the member states, see Conclusions of the European Council at Tampere, October 15 and 16, 1999). For more details, see Chapter 13 of this volume on international instruments of cooperation.

203. For an introduction to the European Union and its institutions, see P. Craig and G. de Búrca, *EU Law: Text, Cases and Materials*, 2nd ed., Oxford University Press, Oxford, UK (1998). A detailed overview of the functions of the European Court of Justice can be found in L. N. Brown and T. Kennedy, *The Court of Justice of the European Communities*, 5th ed., Sweet & Maxwell, London (2000).

204. This includes the issue of punishments: The maximum sentence is life imprisonment.

17

From Anticolonialism to Neocolonialism

A Brief Political-Economic History
of Transnational Concern About Corrections

ROBERT P. WEISS

> *In other times, the police served an economic system that needed abundant docile*
> *labor. The justice system punished vagrants by forcing them into factories at bayo-*
> *net point. That's how European society industrialized the peasantry and managed*
> *to impose the work ethic in its cities. But today the question is how to impose the*
> *unemployment ethic. What mandatory obedience techniques are there to manage*
> *the growing multitudes who have no work or hope of ever getting any? What can*
> *be done to keep all those who have fallen overboard from trying to climb back in*
> *and capsizing the ship?*
>
> —Eduardo Galeano (2000, p. 91)

This chapter surveys the history of transnational correctional concern (TNCC) from the birth of the penitentiary to the present,[1] with special attention given to the role of the United States as a key actor. In a display of Enlightenment-like reflexivity, the Philadelphia Society for Alleviating the Miseries of Public Prisons was founded in 1787—only 3 years after the construction of the Walnut Street Jail. International interest in penal reform took hold soon after the Walnut Street jail added a penitentiary house in 1790, and by 1846, an international conference of prison reformers had gathered in Germany to discuss the purpose of imprisonment and consider resolutions regarding separate confinement, education, labor, and religious instruction. Using the activity of international congresses devoted to prison reform as a measure of TNCC and considering legislative achievements and policy decisions influenced by their recommendations, four periods of intense TNCC can be identified:

1. *Anticolonial*—from the opening of the world's first penitentiary at the Walnut Street Jail, to the first international penal reform congress, at London, in 1872

2. *Western imperialist*—extending from 1878 Stockholm Congress to the 1910 meetings in Washington, during which Brazil, Argentina, Japan, and China adopted the penitentiary design as symbols of modernity and entry into the world economy

Period 2 was followed by an interwar period of relative inactivity and lack of accomplishment.

3. A *postcolonial* period that began at the end of World War II with the efforts of the United Nations and extended through the prisoners' rights movement of the 1960s and early 1970s

4. Since the 1980s, a *neocolonial* period of reactionary crime control policies and extreme penal severity

From its inception in the late 18th century, concern for the welfare of prisoners was linked to the rise of national citizenship based on democratic inclusion. *Anticolonial* and *postcolonial* refer to discourses, ideologies, constructs, and practices that expose, reject, and condemn domination, oppression, and exploitation. *Colonial* and *imperial* refer to domination, oppression, and coercion of—and hegemony over—individuals, groups, countries, or regions. Colonialism can take the form of one nation or bloc of nations dominating another; colonialism can also be exercised within nations ("internal colonialism").

It is very clear from the outset that the lofty ideas discussed at the international penal meetings seldom connected with the action of governments. The concept of reformative incarceration was the intellectual product of several 18th-century cultures, and the idea of the penitentiary traveled widely around the world over the next century. Correctional concern was transnational from the beginning,[2] and international congresses tried to establish an international standard of treatment. But each country that adopted the penitentiary did so as an amalgam of Western and indigenous ideas.[3] They established systems of social control that reflected their own social structural realities, many of which were authoritarian, and penitentiary reform was adopted in countries that were neither industrializing nor capitalistic (Dikötter, 2002; Salvatore & Aguirre, 1996). There is, however, at least one constant and universal penal characteristic, regardless of social structure: The welfare of prisoners has been contingent on the general welfare of free society, particularly in regard to labor rights. Everywhere, social, economic, and cultural conditions external to the prison set limits to benevolence and determined the specific meaning of the penitentiary as social control. One common denominator could be expressed as Jeremy Bentham's "less eligibility" principle.[4] Less eligibility shaped penality everywhere. In industrializing economies, the welfare of prisoners was strongly influenced by the vicissitudes of the labor market and swings in the business cycle. Thus, a sound assessment of correctional reform activity must temper the history of ideas with the realities of political economy. A high international standard of penal treatment requires widespread economic security, the prospects of which seem to be dimming with the advent of "neoliberal globalization."[5]

The high point of a progressive TNCC came after World War II. The postwar political economy of "corporate liberalism" and the management ideology of "Fordism" reduced inequality and stabilized the (comparatively) low U.S. imprisonment rate of the 1950s and 1960s. Forced by the Great Depression to develop "import substitution" and develop state-protected enterprises and placate urban unions, Latin America entered a period of relative prosperity and low crime and imprisonment rates. All of those gains began reversing in the last quarter of the 20th century, with the class divide everywhere widening to a chasm: Fully entitled citizens at one social extreme today confront a large marginalized contingent workforce with diminished citizenship. Increasing inequality in Brazil, China, the Middle East, Africa, and the countries of the former Soviet Union have generated an enormous alienated population surviving outside the legitimate labor market, many of whom circulate through the world's prison systems. Eager to obtain global capital investment, developing nations are pressured by business interests to privatize, deregulate, and impose stringent fiscal austerity to compete for foreign investment. At the same time, neoliberal states must be viewed as "safe" from crime and revolutionary activity, so they turn increasingly to physical repression to maintain social order. In many countries around the world, official repression has popular support, and vigilantism is common. The fearful emulate their oppressors, supporting "polyarchies,"[6] "coercive democracies," and "illiberal democracies," all of which mock liberal democracy with their oppressive penal systems as abusive as any of the *fin-de-siècle* imperial empires.

FOUR PERIODS OF TRANSNATIONAL CORRECTIONAL CONCERN

Anticolonial Beginnings: From Revolution to Frustration

The formative period of TNCC commences with the birth of the modern prison in the late 18th century and extends through a series of international congresses from the 1840s through the 1872 meeting of the First International Penal and Penitentiary Congress (IPPC).[7] The founding inspiration for the IPPC

and the chief organizer for the 1872 meetings in London was Enoch C. Wines, who attended the event with a U.S. government commission tendered to him by President Grant. Later congresses reported that national penal codes were reformed and prison discipline eased as a result of the London Congress. We have designated this period "anticolonial," in that the penitentiary movement was strongly associated with revolution in France and America, and its spread elsewhere in the world was connected to revolution and the rise of the nation-state and modernization. The modern prison first appeared in France after its 1789 revolution; the fall of the Bastille was its preeminent symbol. In the wake of revolutionary political changes in America in 1790, intellectual and social elites of the 19th and early 20th centuries spread the idea of reformative incarceration to Russia in 1863, Brazil in 1834, Japan in 1868, and China in 1905.

The Quakers of Pennsylvania extended human rights to convicts by creating a merciful and proportionate alternative to capital and corporal punishments. The penitentiary was a reformative sanction based on a faith in human equality. Although the penitentiary sprang from humanitarian sentiments, it had materialist underpinnings: Prisoners were expected to help defray the costs of their incarceration, and prisoners were an economic resource in labor-hungry industrializing America. Citizenship in a democracy was predicated on gainful employment. Prison labor was the essence and ultimate justification of reformative incarceration, so at Cherry Hill, handicraft work was a central feature of the solitary regime. The architectural antithesis, New York's Auburn congregate prison, created a factory model prison industry designed to inculcate labor discipline in its immigrant wards. The rival Auburn and Pennsylvania models of the American penitentiary gained immediate international attention and passionate debate among wardens, chaplains, judges, lawyers, and humanitarians of the early 19th century. The Cherry Hill and Auburn designs inspired 19th- and early 20th-century penitentiary architecture in Europe, Latin America, China, India, Russia, and Japan, albeit with regional and national variations in penal discourse and practice (Grünhut, 1972; Teeters, 1946). A coterie of reformers encouraged international standards of treatment, making punishment one of the oldest major social problems to gain international attention. Beginning in 1816, Elizabeth Fry visited women confined in Newgate Prison in London and established an association to improve the treatment of children, which inspired reform societies in Canada. In 1866, the Howard League for Penal Reform was established, an organization active today on behalf of penal reform internationally. Through the indefatigable efforts of Dr. Enoch Cobb Wines, the dream of a world organization to promote the reformation of criminals in an ideal prison inspired American and European colleagues to establish a lasting world organization to improve penal conditions.[8]

The first National Conference on Penitentiary and Reformatory Discipline in the United States met in Cincinnati, Ohio, in 1870 to discuss reformation and building self-respect through education, religion, and industrial training. Under the presidency of Governor Rutherford B. Hayes of Ohio, more than 130 delegates from 24 countries attended, including representatives from Canada and South America. Zebulon Brockway presented an address urging nonpolitical governance of prisons and the creation of intermediate reformatories for young men and women. The "Declaration of Principles" they adopted renounced vindictiveness in favor of reformation based on rewarding good conduct and self-discipline. Special training, religion, and education are the vital forces inspiring self-respect, the declaration held. At Cincinnati, Wines gathered charter members to the newly created National Prison Association, and the conferees adopted a resolution to invite the nations of the world to an international congress on prison reform to meet in London in 1872 (Wines, 1871). Twenty-two nations sent 400 delegates to their first opportunity to meet professional counterparts from around the world, creating a stimulating interchange of ideas. But reformers were soon frustrated, their resolutions and proclamations overwhelmed by political turbulence and labor strife surrounding the international depression of the mid-1870s that left legislatures in little mood to reform prison policy.[9] This was to be a pattern: The lofty ideas presented at the 100 or so international prison congresses since 1846 have failed to have much impact on policy.

Western Imperialism

The second period of TNCC commenced with the 1878 meetings of the Second IPPC and extended through the Eighth IPPC in 1910, during which the focal concerns of the congressional delegates shifted from the nature of punishment and the discipline of hard labor regimes to the indeterminate sentence and reformation through education and religion. But the theories and reports and legislative recommendations rarely translated into penal practice, in the United States and elsewhere. The penitentiary form was adopted abroad, but a stubborn localism changed the spirit of reform. In Latin America, prison reform was "predicated upon nondemocratic conceptions of the political order," and was employed to marginalize the Indian population even more. The penitentiary served as "an instrument of social differentiation and control" in Latin America (Salvatore & Aguirre, 1996, p. 2). Although American reformers—led by Wines and Brockway—were early leaders in global penal reform, the U.S. Congress refused to endorse any of the many penal resolutions passed by the international congresses, for fear that they would be binding. This is a difference between an anticolonial power and a growing *imperial* power. Federal interest lay dormant for over 20 years after Wines's 1872 presidential commission, finally revived with the appointment of Samuel J. Barrows as the U.S. commissioner of the Fifth International Prison Commission of 1895 in Paris. One of the most contentious issues debated at the Paris conference concerned the right of prisoners to a wage (Teeters, 1949). At the behest of the United States, the congress resolved that prisoners had no right to a wage—even though wages were accepted practice in much of Europe at the time. China preferred to call their system of compensation "pecuniary reward" (as Japan would later). The congress nevertheless concluded, "It was seen that the concession of the prisoners' rights to wages would carry with it a good many other rights which the Congress was not prepared to concede and which it might be dangerous to affirm."[10] Among the rights implied (but they dared not express) was prisoner unionization. After all, back in the United States, free workers themselves had few labor rights by law and, in practice, workers were in a fierce battle with state and private police over fair wages and unionization.

By the 1880s and early 1890s, IPPC delegates were emphasizing classification for special treatment approaches and indeterminate sentencing. Although these reforms had progressive potential, not much materialized in practice—and what did, for example, in the United States, was in the service of separating children and other categories of the "competent" from the "born criminal" and "moral and mental defectives," with a large concentration of low-class immigrants in the latter category. Progressive Era reforms of parole, probation, juvenile court, and indeterminate sentencing were U.S. innovations that gained international interest, but they also had the effect of net widening. Parole and probation expanded social control more than they substituted for imprisonment, and prisons and jails greatly increased their populations between 1880 and the early 1920s.[11] Europeans favored the indeterminate sentence only for the youthful offender and "moral degenerates," the latter case so they could incarcerate indefinitely those "criminal by nature." The Progressive aspiration to individualize and democratize the prison did move most institutions away from the Auburn-style lockstep conformity and regimentation, but the prevalence of custody overcame the rehabilitative programs envisioned by reformers. The European laboring classes experienced vast improvements in living standards with the expansion of industry during the imperialist era. Increasing prosperity from the last quarter of the 19th century until World War I coincided with decreasing crime and declining imprisonment rates on the Continent (Rusche & Kirchheimer, 2003, pp. 138–155). For their part, prisoners during this period enjoyed a substantial improvement in their treatment because the threshold of less-eligibility had been raised.

The depression of the 1890s led to a globalization backlash in the United States that lasted from 1914 to 1975, during which organized labor forced protectionist measures and was able to restrict foreign immigration.[12] Heightened international competition required greater within-nation interdependence, which took hold during the Progressive Era. At the start of the 20th century, the recently renamed American Prison Association (changed from National Prison Association in 1908) set out to promote reformatory ideology abroad. Buoyed by a period of moderate, although uneven prosperity and diminishing inequality, Progressive Era penal reformers advocated a spirit of "compassionateness," urging the Germans, for instance, to discard the old Auburn regime in favor of rehabilitation through education (McKelvey, 1977, p. 237). But there was much debate over the merits of American principles promoting the reformatory versus the Italian, German, and French deterministic theories of crime causation. Few nations adopted the American program, including the reformatory; actually, these reforms were petering out in the United States, except for the short-lived but dramatic experiment in inmate self-government at Auburn in 1913 and Sing Sing in 1914 by Thomas Mott Osborne. The Europeans placed their belief in the born criminal. "Yankee Imperialism" had greater effect elsewhere, notably in China and with the Meiji reformers in Japan, who undertook the modernization of its social and legal institutions to strengthen its capacity to resist Western imperialism. Japan's penitentiary was based on the French version of the Auburn model. Japan's treaties of 1902 and 1903 with the United States and Britain supported legal reforms. The Penal Code of 1907, based on the German model, reflected this cultural borrowing and adaptation to avoid extraterritoriality.

The former Central and Allied Powers confronted many serious social problems in the post–World War I decade. Rising crime and juvenile delinquency overcrowded their deteriorated prisons. In the United States, black incarceration increased dramatically, particularly in midwestern state prisons. Blacks were migrating *en masse* from the South to the northern ghettos, replenishing the low-wage labor pool drained by the termination of foreign immigration after World War I. As free labor battled capital in one of the most intense eras of anti-union warfare (called the "Age of Industrial Violence"), workers were able to exert sufficient political pressure to abolish the contract system of prison industry in most states. This was a symbolic victory against capital inasmuch as private contracting had been waning anyway.[13] The diminution of prison industry left the mass of prisoners idle, and the loss of revenue led to program reduction and cuts in education. Prison violence increased, with the 1920s ending in a dozen major prison riots. Not surprisingly, the interwar years were fallow to regressive in terms of prison reform globally. The rise in recidivism and the growing failure of treatment programs discouraged even the hard-core idealist (McKelvey, 1977, p. 267). Many of the disillusioned penologists from the United States

were attracted to neoclassical theory and "soft determinism," closing somewhat the earlier split with Europe on the issue of free will. Interwar bright spots in prison reform include Howard Gill's Norfolk Prison Colony in Massachusetts, in the late 1920s and early 1930s, based on individualized treatment, and the League of Nations. The U.S. Congress failed to ratify the League of Nations, but the League's model rules influenced republican China, which adopted the League's 1934 minimum standards for the treatment of prisoners, including health, clothing, and corporal punishment provisions (Dikötter, 2002, pp. 226–227). The two IPPCs that met in the interwar years were reactionary. The most notable achievement of the 1930 Prague Congress was to vote for the inclusion of the word, *penal*, in the name of the commission. The next congress met in Berlin in 1935 and, not surprisingly, it was outright fascist— preoccupied with draconian and barbaric anticrime measures. Called by its contemporary critics, the "Congress in Chains," 425 Nazi delegates dominated the voting and passed a measure approving the castration of criminals (Teeters, 1944, pp. 98–99).

The Human Rights Era and American Hegemony

Period 3 began toward the end of World War II, with the formation of the United Nations to promote peace, security, and economic development. The treatment of prisoners would obviously be a central concern to an organization that tries to foster and safeguard "fundamental human rights." This would be a tough assignment, because the basic nature of imprisonment—the routine application of legitimated force on dehumanized subjects— invites abuse in even the most democratic and egalitarian of countries. The rules and principles of humane treatment are in practice subject to the less-eligibility principle, and the postwar economy and polity were favorable to the prisoner. The working class enjoyed a new balance of power in its relations to capital. Immigration was throttled, and an enormous consumer demand had built up during the war. The United States emerged from war with a strong and undamaged industrial infrastructure. Oligopolistic enterprises—led by the auto, steel, glass, and tire industries and home appliance manufacturers—were willing to grant the wage-and-hour demands of union bosses in exchange for the latter's guarantee of a disciplined rank and file. Corporations in the monopoly sector were able to pass the cost of wage-and-benefit increases on to the increasingly affluent consumer. And the federal government, following Keynesian principles, intervened aggressively to avert postwar depression and high unemployment among returning war veterans. The GI Bill of Rights, passed by Congress in 1944, subsidized the education and training of war veterans in a massive program that sent 2.25 million veterans to college, 3.5 million to other schools, and 1.5 million to job training. Home and business loans were also federally guaranteed for GIs. The New Deal Welfare State was in place to help the poor. And blue-collar wages were high enough to finance a great expansion of the middle class. Western European nations strengthened their welfare states. Strong worker protections were brokered. Throughout the Western world, conditions were favorable for an extremely progressive agenda of correctional concern and general human rights.[14] Elsewhere after the war, colonial possessions were gaining independence, and many of the new governments turned immediately to revamping their legal and criminal justice systems.

The human rights era was led by the United Nations, whose 1945 charter reaffirmed faith in "human rights" and the dignity of all persons. The Section on Social Defense was dedicated to eradicating fascist penal policy and creating punishment that emphasized rehabilitative justice, with greater rights of the individual. The Universal Declaration of Human Rights in 1948 specifically addressed the treatment of prisoners, establishing minimum standards for their treatment. Decolonization and the experience of the Holocaust inspired the United Nations to issue a series of documents seeking to outline humane principles and prohibitions of prisoner mistreatment, including rules concerning women, juveniles, medical care, outside contact, and work (the latter ignited considerable controversy), backed with international monitoring and complaint mechanisms. One result was the Standard Minimum Rules for the Treatment of Prisoners, adopted August 30, 1955, by the U.N.'s First United Nations Congress on the Prevention of Crime and the Treatment of Offenders. U.N. rules were not intended as a detailed model system of penal institutions; rather, they were to be essential elements for an "adequate" system meeting general consensus. They did not expect the same standard of progress on even the standard minimum rules that called for registering, identifying, and providing reasons for commitment; and classification on the basis of age, sex, criminal record, and nature of sentence. U.N. rules further specified the essential physical accommodations and hygiene requirements and set rules concerning food, clothing, and exercise.[15]

The drafters of the U.N. rules understood the challenge, given the "great variety of legal, social, economic and geographical conditions of the world." U.N. officials say that these rules had considerable influence among African nations and in Asia. Others are not so sanguine. Although the international community embraced the new rules in theory, Human Rights Watch (2003) notes that U.N. members failed to adopt U.N. standards in practice because they were not bound by treaty. To this day, the rules have been largely ignored by the United States, China, and Japan. But there are reform optimists. The Tenth U.N. Congress on the Prevention of Crime and the Treatment of Offenders, meeting at Vienna in April 2000, endorsed treatment approaches based on restorative justice "accountability and fairness to offenders and victims in the justice process" (p. 2).[16]

Regional Instruments and NGOs

In May of 1949, one of the first examples of regional associations dedicated to human rights was created, the Council of Europe, with representatives from France, Belgium, Denmark, Italy, Ireland, Norway, Sweden, and the Netherlands. In 1950, the European Convention for the Protection of Human Rights and Fundamental Freedoms was established, which today has 40 countries as signatories. Its European Prison Rules were modeled after the United Nations but reflected the better treatment accorded Western European nations. The rules are now proving problematic for countries of the former Soviet bloc, however (Morgan, 2001). The council also has the European Convention for the Prevention of Torture and Inhuman or Degrading Treatment or Punishment. The Council of Europe has been a reasonably effective mechanism of enforcing humane standards in a large and diverse array of countries (Maguire, Vagg, & Margan, 1985). In the Americas, there is the American Convention on Human Rights, under the auspices of the Organization of American States, which is far less accomplished. The African (Banjul) Charter on Human and Peoples' Rights, adopted by the Organization of African Unity in June of 1981, is an extensive but general listing of articles regarding the "freedom, equality, justice and dignity" for all African people. This is a valiant effort to establish basic humane penal policy in extremely difficult material and political circumstances.

Nongovernmental organizations (NGOs) have been the most aggressive in pursuit of humane treatment of prisoners worldwide. Perhaps most well-known is Amnesty International, founded in 1961. Their 1999 Report, "Brazil: No One Here Sleeps," is typical in its detailed account of human rights violation in prisons—in this case, cataloguing numerous acts of cruelty and indifference to convicts and suspects held in unsanitary and dangerous conditions. Another highly influential NGO is Human Rights Watch (HRW), started in 1978 to monitor Soviet compliance with the 1975 Helsinki Accords, which has played major monitoring functions. With offices in major cities on three continents, the HRW promotes international justice and monitors prisons through its U.S.-based Prison Project, founded in 1987. Its *Global Report on Prisons* surveys prison conditions and issues an annual World Report that receives considerable press coverage. But while annoying to officials in Washington, the various reports placing the United States on lists of human rights violators appear to have had little practical effect at the state and federal levels. HRW's April 1999 *Report on Human Rights Violations in the United States,* "Red Onion State Prison"[17] reports of the extensive use of unnecessary and excessive force and degrading treatment at Virginia's new "supermax" prison. Isolated 23 hours a day, prisoners are denied all treatment, educational, vocational, work, and religious programs.

Physicians for Human Rights investigates human rights abuses, especially those regarding the medical profession. They occasionally team up with other human rights organizations, as in the report undertaken with HRW in the publication of the monograph *Cold Storage: Super-Maximum Security Confinement in Indiana.*[18] This is a detailed study of two Indiana prisons—typical of scores of others nationwide—that engage in degrading and cruel treatment of emotionally disturbed, low-IQ, and mentally ill prisoners. Studies this exhaustive can be financed only with private money from small donors and from foundations such as the Edna McConnell Clark Foundation and the Open Society Institute. In addition, university-based organizations monitor prison conditions, most notably the International Center for Prison Studies at King's College, University of London. The United Kingdom has been a most important origin for TNCC organizations, including Penal Reform International, founded in London in 1989, and the Howard League for Penal Reform, founded in 1866.

Discussion of postwar human rights and prison reform would not be complete without mention of the prisoners' rights movement, which originated in the United States in the early 1960s and, during its apogee, spread throughout the West and to Australia and New Zealand. Prior to the 1960s, prisoners had practically no rights in law (the Thirteenth Amendment makes them slaves of the state), and courts would not intervene on the basis of the "hands-off" doctrine. In a few isolated and extreme cases, the Eighth Amendment's prohibition of cruel and unusual punishment formed the basis for a handful of decisions in the 1940s and 1950s, such as the *Johnson v. Dye* (1949) decision involving a Georgia chain gang. Prisoners used two main legal devices: the writ of habeas corpus and the Civil Rights Act. The group most responsible for the expansion of prisoners' rights in the early years was the Black Muslims. As the prisoners' movement joined the black liberation and civil rights movements, the scope of legal rights expanded to cover medical treatment, mail censorship, disciplinary procedures, visitation, and proper use of force. Prisoners' rights were part of a general postwar democratization involving numerous other marginalized groups, notably gays, women, children, blacks, and the mentally ill, all of whom pressed for admission to full citizenship. Prisoners' rights was promoted in academic and policy circles in Western Europe, Australia, Canada, as well as in the United States by a school subscribing to the "justice-as-fairness" model (Fogel, 1975) that rejected the prevailing "coercive cure" of the rehabilitative ethic. The advocates of the justice model pursued the "normalization" of prison environments and rejected the rehabilitation school of the 1950s and 1960s (Richardson, 1985). According to this view, prisoners are rational decision makers who should retain most of the rights of free individuals and be entitled to have the greatest liberty as consonant with prison safety.

Postcolonialism and Changing Power Relations

Extending from the late 1940s through the prisoners' rights movement of the 1960s and early 1970s, we designate the third period of TNCC "postcolonial" in that there was a real expansion of minority rights. At the peak of the black civil rights movement, the United States assumed world leadership in tolerance and respect for the rights of oppressed groups—including prisoners. As in the 1790 to 1830 anticolonial period of reform, the 1960s and early 1970s was an age of optimism and high ideals. Postcolonial reforms of the latter period rode on the crest of 20 years of general prosperity for workers, with upward mobility, shrinking inequality, and expansion of general well-being, reversing a century-and-a-half trend of rising inequality within industrializing countries (Bourguignon & Morrisson, 2002).[19] Capital income shrank relative to labor income, and transfer income increased, leading to a diminution of power differences between the socioeconomic classes and greater democratization. This was a time when the competitive nation-state required interdependency *within* states and capital depended on organized labor and politicians on average citizens (Wilterdink, 1995, p. 11). Rising labor incomes, full employment, and comprehensive welfare policies decreased inequality, providing the necessary security for increased social cooperation and the lessening of less eligibility.

The downward trend in inequality that began in 1950 reversed sharply after the early 1970s. Rising unemployment, post-Fordist labor policies ("flexible accumulation," including downsizing, just-in-time manufacturing, outsourcing, and subcontracting), wage freezes, pay cuts, and concerted anti-unionism from Washington shifted power relations fundamentally. The anticolonial and postcolonial periods of correctional concern, separated by a century and a half, were socially *inclusive*. Today, neoliberal globalization requires intensified transnational relations of interdependence that increase inequality and weaken domestic interdependence. The prison systems of free-market nations are called on today to *exclude* and marginalize populations made redundant to the postindustrial economy of advanced capitalist nations and to control and contain those millions of dispossessed in second and third world countries attempting to make the transition from state planned and regulated economies to laissez-faire.

Neoliberal Globalization and the Return to Empire

The contemporary period of TNCC could be termed "neocolonial," as NGOs struggle with government repression and human rights violations in the United States and throughout the world. The United States has abdicated its historical leadership in TNCC. The current unilateralism and move to a permanent warfare state, its contempt for the United Nations and international alliances, its domestic assault on workers and "internal colonialism" directed at the young male African American through massive prison warehousing, coupled with the growing economic inequality within and between nations (Aghion & Williamson, 1998) auger poorly for the future of a progressive and liberal TNCC. While the United Nations and NGOs do what they can in the fight for prisoner rights, President George W. Bush has made clear his opposition to an international court, and his administration denies human rights for "illegal combatants" and others designated as "terrorists." The U.S.

embrace of the death penalty, its infatuation with ultra-high-security prisons devoid of meaningful rehabilitation programs, and the rollback of prisoners' rights since the 1980s set a deplorable example for developing nations and those countries recently liberated from Soviet domination, many of whom look to the United States for leadership on social, economic, and political issues. Elite transitions in Russia and Poland make repression a natural inclination when confronting the rampant crime generated by the "buccaneer capitalism" that replaced the command economy.

Neoliberal restructuring in Latin America— pushed over the last quarter century by the International Monetary Fund, the World Trade Organization, the World Bank, and the United States—has also greatly aggravated inequality, which in turn has increased crime enormously, undermining civilian democratic governments.[20] The HRW World Report for 2003 reports that internationally recognized labor rights are routinely violated. Brazil, which built the first Latin American penitentiary (in Rio de Janeiro in 1834), today has a horrifically overcrowded and brutal prison system that is the backbone of a grotesque socioeconomic polarity. Argentina, Colombia, Chile, Peru, and Brazil, among other Latin American nations, have been importing U.S.-style "zero-tolerance" policing that has increased "prisoners-without-sentence" (del Olmo, 1998); two thirds of prisoners in Central America are unsentenced, according to Amnesty International's 2002 *World Report*. Fortunately, the United Kingdom, Canada, Australia, New Zealand, France, and Denmark have expanded rehabilitation efforts, but they are under unrelenting pressure to adopt the U.S. standard of penal severity.

The turn away from prisoners' rights and human rights in general is not total and unequivocal, even among advanced capitalist nations. Some penologists see the glass as half-full, and the international impact of regressive U.S. policies is not total.

Vivien Stern (1998, 2001, 2002) is one of the optimists. She points to the countertrends in Canada's redirection and stubborn refusal to join the drug war, American style. The Canadian government has introduced several diversion programs that have reduced its prison population (Stern, 2001, p. 90). Africa has introduced many radical programs promoting reconciliation, most notably in Nigeria and Zimbabwe, especially at the local and village levels. There is much that the West could learn from Africa's methods of conflict resolution, Stern (2001, p. 101) contends. But most of Africa is far removed from a culture that respects human rights, a situation that would require political stability and economic growth. But the simultaneous introduction of laissez-faire capitalism and universal suffrage is disastrous, according to Amy Chua (2002), because "markets concentrate enormous wealth in the hands of an 'outsider' minority, thereby fomenting ethnic envy and hatred among the chronically poor majorities" (p. 63), a situation in which demagogues scapegoat resented minorities in the competition for votes. The human rights prescription advocated by the West, based in liberal democracy and market fundamentalism, is widely associated among African nations with the hypocrisies of Western-driven globalization. Makua Mutua (2002) argues that Africa needs a genuine international human rights corpus that avoids Eurocentric individualism and is a genuine blend of cultural, religious, and legal traditions. In Latin America, where market fundamentalism has been adopted extensively, Stern (2001) points to the case of Chile, where prison alternatives are underway. Several Latin American countries have ratified the International Criminal Court (ICC), which took effect July 1, 2002. But as Galeano (1989) observes, "For five centuries, Latin American history has been a history of continued disjunction between reality and words" (p. 119)—never more than in criminal justice reform. The prison was a cultural importation that faithfully reproduced bourgeois constitutions but without a bourgeois revolution. Rather than incorporate the indigenous people into a mercantile economy as had been the case in 18th- and early 19th-century Europe and America, the penitentiary in Latin America could be used only to marginalize and exploit them further.

Quaker Ideals Betrayed

Conceived in the milieu of political revolution and Enlightenment humanitarianism and informed by the rise of science and the notion of free will, the penitentiary (as the embodiment of correctional concern) was anticolonial in two senses: (a) as a break from English domination (symbolized by its onerous penal traditions) and (b) as a reaffirmation of the equality and "inalienable rights" for all humans (except slaves and the American Indian). This is rhetoric and discourse of a particular era, a concrete historical circumstance, and an argument can be made that Thomas Jefferson and the founding fathers did not mean for political equality and the rights of life, liberty, and the pursuit of happiness to apply to anyone else but themselves. This became apparent as the 19th century unfolded, in the labor wars of the 1870s and 1880s. Immigration helped swell the labor pool and—in concert with technological advances and changes in the organization of production—a formidable reserve army of the unemployed appeared with each deep recession. Soaring post–Civil War inequality pushed prisoners below a humane threshold. In the postbellum South, where voluntary labor was scarce, the neoslavery of the convict lease greatly diminished the moral capital of American delegations to world congresses on penal reform. The American "revolution" was merely a transfer of power from metropolis to colonists, with the ruling elite pursuing the same project of domination against the Indians. As the colonial and imperial empires developed, American delegates to the international congresses between 1870 and 1895 lacked formal diplomatic approval, official instructions, or power to strike universal agreements. America's own commitment to human rights was not firm and unambiguous: Throughout the 19th century, women, Native Americans, and African Americans did not posses full citizenship. As foreign immigration peaked in the late century, millions of Chinese and poor Eastern and Southern Europeans joined the excluded, foiling the effort to apply enlightened correctional concern to American penal practice. Other nations imitated the penitentiary form but also bent the spirit to fit local needs for social control.

TOWARD A UNIVERSAL STANDARD OF PENAL TREATMENT?

The Diplomatic Approach Thwarted by Political and Material Realities

The United States claims to be the world leader in the advancement of human rights, promoting American-style democracy (read: plutocracy) and market fundamentalism as prerequisites. Samuel Huntington (1996, p. 39), however, argues that universalism requires imperialism, either military or cultural, because democracy is inherently local and parochial. Imperialist nations cannot advance an enlightened TNCC. But some versions of imperial order are more liberal than others. The E.U. model of capitalist world order is based on enlightened legal treatment of offenders. Under the Treaty of European Union (Maastricht), member states must abide by a set of fairly progressive conditions regarding criminal justice, meet minimal standards of penal treatment, and disavow the death penalty—all in the service of creating a predictable business environment abroad. As a method to advance neoliberal principles regarding trade and commerce, the E.U.'s "collective world order project" would

anchor "the dominance of the richest capitalist countries over the globe for the twenty-first century" (Gowan, 2002, p. 24). The new world order would be coercive, imposing legal and juridical regimes on other nations. But this structure would be legitimated by legal principles and institutional models developed in the postwar liberal corporate capitalist era. When target nations bridle at economic policy goals, E.U. diplomacy can assert that E.U. human rights norms are being violated.

The trouble with the European Union's seemingly sensible (from the business perspective) version of the new world order is that it clashes head on with the U.S. idea of global dominance; it is a direct threat to U.S. hegemony. In this battle of hegemonies, the "ultra-imperialist" Europeans are pitted against the "super-imperialist" United States (Gowan, 2002, p. 25), which wants Europeans to return to their postwar protectorate status. Also, the E.U. hegemonic concept cannot accommodate the peculiarly American cultural emphases on long, retributive criminal sentences and frequent use of the death penalty. The faction within the Republican Party crucial to Bush's electoral success is particularly resistant to the prospect of U.S. conformity to E.U. norms. But American punitiveness and vindictiveness are not in the best long-term interests of transnational capital, especially given the growing mass resistance to American-style globalization.

The United States has attacked the creation of the ICC as a standard of international justice by pressing states around the world with diplomatic and economic force to enter into ICC impunity agreements regarding U.S. nationals. Not only would military personnel be exempt from ICC jurisdiction, but Washington is also concerned about the autonomy of private police and military contractors and subcontractors, including Halliburton, Bechtel, and DynCorp. The latter company, a subsidiary of the giant Computer Sciences Corporation, has been charged with developing for Iraq a criminal justice system from whole cloth: new police, courts, and prisons. In the spring of 2003, the U.S. Department of State put out a call for qualified American citizens to apply to DynCorp as sworn police, corrections officers, and "judicial experts" to serve in Iraq at handsome compensation. Under the guise of human rights—but following neoliberal principles that diminish public accountability—Iraq promises to be a template for privatizing control throughout the "arc of instability," running from the Andean region to Southeast Asia, that contains much of the world's oil lands.

National security officials and the State Department are split on whether al-Qaeda prisoners in Cuba are covered under the full weight of the Geneva Conventions. A year and a half after September 11, 2001, children as young as 13 were being held gulag-style at Guantanamo Bay without charges or legal representation. In a March 21, 2003, letter to President Bush, Leonard S. Rubenstein, Executive Director of Physicians for Human Rights, complained of a host of interrogation practices against detainees that violate the U.N. Convention Against Torture, ratified by the United States in 1994, including beatings, hours of forced kneeling, sleep deprivation, psychological pressure, withholding medical attention and painkillers to the wounded, and transferring detainees for interrogation to countries that engage in torture, such as Egypt. Much of the rest of the world sees the hypocrisy in U.S. "human rights imperialism." It is clear that America's vaunted regard for human rights does not apply to those who are not its allies, most notably the enemies of Israel.[21] Nor can the United States or the United Kingdom promote enlightened penal policies elsewhere when they repress their own citizens, as is developing in Britain's war on crime and the continued war on drugs in the United States and, now, the War on Terrorism. Throughout Western Europe, legal and illegal immigrant workers (as part of a transnational labor force) are added to

homegrown "dangerous groups" as a focus for penal repression.

Neoconservatives emulate the U.S. imperial power of the William McKinley administration at the turn of the 20th century: laissez-faire and corporate dominance domestically and foreign domination for cheap raw materials (today, oil) and labor power. The United States claims American exceptionalism to international agreements. As articulated by Richard Haass, director of policy planning in the State Department under President George W. Bush, Americans should "re-conceive their role from a traditional nation-state to an imperial power," resembling 19th-century Great Britain, with coercion and force normally a last resort.[22] Twenty-first century imperialism is not colonialism in the McKinley sense, but it is a global capitalist market system requiring increased militarism and repression to cope with and facilitate the growing inequality within and between nations and the disappearance of work everywhere. In the United States, nearly 75 million adults were out of the labor force during April 2003, in addition to the 9 million officially unemployed (Davey & Leonhardt, 2003). Worldwide, the International Labor Organization estimates over 150 million unemployed. But as U.N. Secretary-General Kofi Annan argues, this figure is a gross underestimate because it does not include the large part of the world outside of employment surveys; nor does it include the 1 billion underemployed. In China alone, an estimated 100 million peasants daily roam the countryside in search of work. In some Latin American countries, unemployment has reached half of the adult population.

Sir Leon Radzinowicz's (in "International Collaboration and Criminal Science") observation is perhaps more cogent today than when it was pronounced in 1942:

> The proper solution of penal problems in all countries alike will not only make for the welfare of each but will also be in a factor in

stabilizing international peace. The efficient and enlightened administration of criminal justice is an essential element of social and international security. (quoted in Alpers & Boren, 1972, p. 86)

And the proper solution to penal problems requires a reasonable standard of living for workers in all countries; without this security, the less-eligibility principle will smother enlightened and humane correctional sentiments.

NOTES

1. Transnational correctional concern was associated with the penitentiary through the 19th century, with parole and probation assuming an increasing importance by the late 19th century and the early 20th century.

2. The rival Pennsylvania and Auburn penitentiary models became the most influential penal institutions in world history, visited by hundreds of foreign dignitaries—most notably, Charles Dickens of England and de Beaumont and de Tocqueville of France. The current of reform ideas flowed both East and West across the Atlantic: The London and Danzig "houses of refuge" inspired Quaker "child saving institutions" in Philadelphia, Boston, and at New York City's Madison Square in 1825. The 1855 Lancaster (Ohio) "school for boys" was the first state reform school modeled after the French "family system," introduced by Frederic-Auguste Demetz at Mettray over a decade earlier. The so-called Irish system of prison administration propounded by Walter Crofton in 1853 was based in part on the mark system of Captain Maconochie in Australia; then the concept spread to the United States through Enoch C. Wines and Zebulon Brockway as a system of sentence commutation for good behavior. The American "reformatory" of the late 19th century was an amalgam of ideas from Ireland, Australia, Germany, and Spain.

3. Historians debate how prison reform ideas spread globally—whether by "cultural imperialism," slavish imitation of the dominant national powers, or clever borrowing with local adaptation. See Dikötter (2002), Dutton and Xu (1998), Salvatore and Aguirre (1996), and Jones and Newburn (2002). Not only is the manner in which the penitentiary idea spread globally debated, but so is the why of penitentiary globalization (see Weiss, 1987). The subject of how penal policy travels is worthy of full monographic treatment.

4. As a disincentive to crime, the welfare of prisoners should never exceed the living conditions of the most destitute in free society. This policy prescription was central to Rusche and Kirchheimer's (2003) thesis on punishment and comparative social structures and very much discussed in the contemporary literature regarding prison industry (Hawkins, 1983).

5. The term *neoliberalism* refers to an economic and political philosophy that came to prominence during the Thatcher and Reagan administrations, in reaction to the postwar welfare state and government regulation of business. Based on a return to 18th-century classical liberalism of enlightened self-interest and 19th-century laissez-faire social philosophy, neoliberalism is a market fundamentalism that fosters free trade; deregulation; privatization of all government functions, including much of the military and policing; and the exercise of fiscal conservatism regarding social services (stressing individual over social responsibility). Known in foreign policy circles as the "Washington consensus," this has been the orthodoxy of the International Monetary Fund and the World Bank. In the United States, neoliberal political economy was strongly promoted by the Clinton administration, but now is coupled with neoconservative political philosophy that stresses a laissez-faire approach to business activities and labor markets, but morally motivated intrusion and repression regarding the personal lives of the working class and poor.

6. "Polyarchy is neither dictatorship nor democracy. It refers to a system in which a small group actually rules, on behalf of capital, and participation in decision-making by the majority is confined to choosing among competing elites in tightly controlled electoral processes. This 'low-intensity democracy' is a form of consensual domination," according to Robinson (1996, p. 20). See also Robinson (1998/99).

7. We will use the IPPC as the principal measure of TNCC until 1950, when its functions were transferred to the United Nations.

8. Earlier congresses convened international meetings to promote prison reform, beginning with Frankfort am Main in 1846. Representatives from Germany, Switzerland, Russia, Sweden, Denmark, Italy, Poland, and Austria addressed the purposes of punishment and the effects of solitary confinement and rule of silence on the health and morale of prisoners. The next year, a second congress met in Brussels, which added new national participants (200 in all) and the first woman delegate, from France.

9. A long-wave recession in the United States, which extended from 1873 to 1897, had troughs during 1873–1879, 1883–1885, and 1893–1897 that corresponded to the rest of the industrializing world, particularly England, France, and Germany. See Fels (1959, p.62).

10. Dangerous indeed, considering that the Pennsylvania Supreme Court had ruled only a few years earlier that the striking steel workers' union had violated the individual "freedom of contract" rights of the "replacement workers" (scabs) sent to the Homestead Steel Works of Andrew Carnegie in 1892 under false pretenses and under armed escort by Pinkerton guards.

11. From 1880 to 1923, the U.S. prison population grew from 30,655 to 78,210; the rate per 100,000 went from 61.51 to 71.43, and the total jail population doubled (Sutton, 1987, p. 618).

12. As Aghion and Williamson (1998, p. 193) observe, "Immigration in labor to scarce parts of the global economy became increasingly restrictive prior to 1914, and . . . much of this retreat from open immigration was driven by a defense of the deteriorating relative economic position of the working poor in the labor-scarce New World."

13. In the United States, labor unions pressured for laws abolishing the prison contract system, which was an easy enough political concession when contracting had lost its profitability as the result of developments in mass production and a surfeit of black low-wage laborers. It is interesting to contrast the United States case with Japan, where prison industrial contracting remained a central feature of its penal regime, as a culturally preferred prison management tool as much as for economic reasons (Johnson, 1996, pp. 87–89).

14. This is not to ignore the strong counter-tendencies in the United States of McCarthyism and the FBI's Cold War repression of radical political and union movements.

15. Even at that, the rules had a number of shortcomings, neglecting women and not dealing adequately with sexual orientation.

16. See Tenth United Nations Congress on the Prevention of Crime and the Treatment of Offenders (www.uncjin.org/Documents/10th-congress/10cDocumentation/10cdocumentation.html).

17. See report at www.hrw.org/reports/1999/redonion/.

18. See report at www.hrw.org/reports/1997/usind/.

19. Global economic inequality increased after 1820, mostly within nations; for instance, in the world's industrializing countries, the Gini coefficient (with 1.0 representing maximum inequality) went from 0.5 in 1820 to 0.61 in 1914 and to 0.64 in 1950, then declined between 1950 and 1960, and leveled off from 1970 to 1992 (Bourguignon & Morrisson, 2002, p. 731).

20. In his article, "Democracies Without Citizenship," Paulo Sérgio Pinheiro (1996, p. 17) discusses the legacies of authoritarianism that burden the civilian democracies and allow the same elites to dominate the masses.

21. For instance, the United States lodged the sole "no" vote (versus 52 in favor) against a 1998 U.N. resolution regarding the human rights situation in southern Lebanon and West Bekaa, calling on Israel to refrain from holding Lebanese detainees incarcerated in its prisons as hostages for bargaining purposes.

22. As quoted in Foster (2003).

REFERENCES

Aghion, P., & Williamson, J. G. (1998). *Growth, inequality, and globalization: Theory, history, and policy.* Cambridge, UK: Cambridge University Press.

Alpers, B. S., & Boren, J. F. (1972). Crime: International agenda. *Concern and action in the prevention of crime and treatment of offenders, 1846–1972.* Lexington, MA: Lexington Books.

Amnesty International. (1999). *"No one here sleeps": Killings, torture and abuse of prisoners in Brasil.* Retrieved April 30, 2004, from

http://web.amnesty.org/library/Index/ENGAM
R190101999?open&of=ENG-380

Amnesty International. (2002). *Report 2002: Americas.* Retrieved May 12, 2004, from http://web.amnesty.org/web/ar2002.nsf/regA
MR/regAMR?OpenDocument

Bourguignon, F., & Christian Morrisson, C. (2002). Inequality among world citizens: 1820–1992. *American Economic Review, 92*(4), 727–744.

Chua, A. (2002, Autumn). A world on the edge. *Wilson Quarterly,* pp. 62–77.

Davey, M., & Leonhardt, D. (2003, April 27). Jobless and hopeless, many quit the labor force. *New York Times,* p. 1.

del Olmo, R. (1998). The state of prisons and prisoners in four countries of the Andean Region. In R. P. Weiss & N. South (Eds.), *Comparing prison systems: Toward an international and comparative penology* (pp. 115–142). Amsterdam: Gordon & Breach.

Dikötter, F. (2002). *Crime, punishment and the prison in modern China.* New York: Columbia University Press.

Dutton, M., & Xu, Z. (1998). Facing difference: Relations, change and the prison sector in contemporary China. In R. P. Weiss & N. South (Eds.), *Comparing prison systems: Toward an international and comparative penology.* Amsterdam: Gordon & Breach.

Fels, R. (1959). *American business cycles: 1865–1897.* Chapel Hill: University of North Carolina Press.

Fogel, D. (1975). *We are the living proof: The justice model for corrections.* Cincinnati, OH: Anderson.

Foster, J. B. (2003). Imperial America and war. *Monthly Review, 55*(1), 1–10.

Galeano, E. (1989). Democracy in Latin America: Best is that which best creates. *Social Justice, 16*(1), 119–126.

Galeano, E. (2000). *Upside down: A primer for the looking-glass self.* New York: Metropolitan Books.

Gowan, P. (2002). The American campaign for global sovereignty. In L. Panitch & C. Leys (Eds.), *Socialist register 2003: Fighting identities* (pp. 9–22). London: Merlin Press.

Grünhut, M. (1972). *Penal reform: A comparative study.* Montclair, NJ: Patterson Smith. (Original work published 1948)

Hawkins, G. (1983). Prison labor and prison industries. In M. Tonry & N. Morris (Eds.), *Crime and justice: An annual review of research* (Vol. 5, pp. 85–127). Chicago: University of Chicago Press.

Human Rights Watch. (1997, October). *Cold storage: Super-maximum security confinement in Indiana.* Retrieved June 25, 2004, from http://hrw.org/reports/1997/usind/

Human Rights Watch. (1999, April). *Red onion state prison.* Retrieved June 25, 2004, from http://hrw.org/reports/1999/redonion/

Human Rights Watch. (2003). *World report 2003.* New York: Author. Retrieved May 12, 2004, from www.hrw.org/wr2k3/europe13.html

Huntington, S. P. (1996). *The clash of civilizations and the remaking of world order.* New York: Simon & Schuster.

Johnson, E. H. (1996). *Japanese corrections: Managing convicted offenders in an orderly society.* Carbondale: Southern Illinois University Press.

Jones, T., & Newburn, T. (2002). Policy convergence and crime control in the USA and the UK: Streams of influence and levels of impact. *Criminal Justice, 2*(2), 173–204.

Maguire, M., Vagg, J., & Morgan, R. (1985). *Accountability and prisons.* London: Tavistock.

McKelvey, B. (1977). *American prisons: A history of good intentions.* Montclair, NJ: Patterson Smith.

Morgan, R. (2001). International controls on sentencing and punishment. In M. Tonry & R. S. Frase (Eds.), *Sentencing and sanctions in Western countries.* Oxford, UK: Oxford University Press.

Mutua, M. (2002). *Human rights: A political and cultural critique.* Philadelphia: University of Pennsylvania Press.

Pinheiro, P. S. (1996). Democracies without citizenship. *NACLA: Report on The Americas, 30*(2), 17–23.

Richardson, G. (1985). The case for prisoners' rights. In J. Vagg, R. Morgan, & M. Maguire (Eds.), *Accountability and prisons: Opening up a closed world* (pp. 185–211). London: Tavistock.

Robinson, W. I. (1996). Globalization: Nine theses on our epoch. *Race & Class, 38*(2), 13–31.

Robinson, W. I. (1998/99). Latin America and global capitalism. *Race & Class, 40*(2/3), 111–131.

Rusche, G., & Kirchheimer, O. (2003). *Punishment and social structure*. New Brunswick, NJ: Transaction Press.

Salvatore, R. D., & Aguirre, C. (1996). The birth of the penitentiary in Latin America: Toward an interpretive social history of prisons. In R. D. Salvatore & C. Aguirre (Eds.), *The birth of the penitentiary in Latin America: Essays on criminology, prison reform, and social control, 1830–1940* (pp. 1–43). Austin: University of Texas Press.

Stern, V. (1998). *A sin against the future: Imprisonment in the world*. Boston: Northeastern University Press.

Stern, V. (2001). An alternative vision: Criminal justice developments in non-Western countries. *Social Justice, 28*(3), 105–120.

Stern, V. (2002). The international impact of U.S. policies. In M. Mauer & M. Chesney-Lind (Eds.), *Invisible punishment: The collateral consequences of mass imprisonment*. New York: New Press.

Sutton, J. R. (1987). Doing time: Dynamics of imprisonment in the reformist state. *American Sociological Review, 52*, 612–630.

Teeters, N. (1944). *World penal systems: A survey*. Philadelphia: Pennsylvania Prison Society.

Teeters, N. (1946). *Penology from Panama to Cape Horn*. Philadelphia: University of Pennsylvania Press for Temple University Publications.

Teeters, N. (1949). *Deliberations of the International Penal and Penitentiary Congresses: Questions and Answers: 1872–1935*. Philadelphia: Temple University Book Store.

Weiss, R. P. (1987). Humanitarianism, labour exploitation, or social control? A critical survey of theory and research on the origin and development of prisons. *Social History, 12*(3), 331–350.

Wilterdink, N. (1995). Increasing income inequality and wealth concentration in the prosperous societies of the West. *Studies in Comparative International Development, 30*(3), 3–23.

Wines, E. C. (Ed.). (1871). *Transactions of the National Congress on Penitentiary and Reformatory Discipline*. Albany, NY: Weed, Parsons.

PART IV

Regional and Special Issues

Transnational organized crime has been likened to a cancer, spreading across the world. It can undermine democracy, disrupt free markets, drain national assets, and inhibit the development of stable societies. In doing so, national and international criminal groups threaten the security of all nations.

—*Global Issues*, 2001, August

This quote from the editors of the electronic journal *Global Issues* highlights the importance of transnational organized crime to world security. Few people would suggest it is an exaggerated statement. Noticeable by its absence in Part II, however, is a chapter in this *Handbook* devoted to transnational organized crime. This was not an easy decision to make because it clearly deserves significant attention.

The problem for the editor and the advisory board members was that most transnational crimes covered in Part II are, in fact, examples of transnational organized crime. Were Part II to have included a chapter on transnational organized crime, that chapter's material would certainly overlap with material in the specific crime chapters. Instead, authors of Part II chapters were encouraged to include organized crime topics as relevant during coverage of their particular crime. But the importance of transnational organized crime still requires independent coverage. The concept is given its due in this Part IV on regional and special issues related to transnational crime and justice.

The decision to seek contributions from authors familiar with regional issues of organized crime provided a unique opportunity for this *Handbook*. Transnational organized crime is certainly global in nature and impact, but its regional aspects are receiving increased attention. For example, the Federal Bureau of Investigation divides responsibilities of its Organized Crime Section among the following units: The La Cosa Nostra/Italian Organized Crime/Labor Racketeering Unit, the Eurasian Organized Crime Unit, and the Asian/African Criminal Enterprise Unit (Federal Bureau of Investigation, 2003). Interpol is focusing on key areas of regional organized crime (McClure, 2003), and the United Nations has undertaken two regional assessments (in West Africa and in Central Asia) of organized crime (Office on

Drugs and Crime, 2003). We believe that providing chapters on organized crime with attention to specific regions is a particularly interesting and effective way to present material on this important topic.

The chapters on regional coverage of organized crime are ordered alphabetically, but it is especially appropriate that Africa is presented first. Mark Shaw and Gail Wannenburg (Chapter 18) note that the concept of organized crime does not necessarily mean the same thing everywhere—and that is a very good point with which to begin these regional chapters. In fact, the authors of the chapters on Europe and on Latin America make the same point. Shaw and Wannenburg offer an explanation of the nature, evolution, and growth of organized crime in Africa but note that this topic is clearly understudied on the African continent.

In Chapter 19, Richard Ward and Daniel Mabrey suggest that organized crime in Asia is best understood by recognizing how varying legal structures and justice systems of different countries—particularly police, courts, and corrections—affect public order and crime control. They make their point by focusing on organized crime activities in six Asian countries chosen to reflect different political and economic systems (the People's Republic of China, Hong Kong—discussed separately because of the "one country, two systems" agreement—Japan, Cambodia, Republic of Korea, and Myanmar). Five other countries are covered more briefly (Taiwan, Singapore, the Philippines, Thailand, and Vietnam), and the end result is a very complete picture of the major organized crime groups in Asia and the activities in which they engage. Ward and Mabrey conclude their chapter with comments on the future of organized crime in Asia.

Klaus von Lampe begins his review of organized crime in Europe (Chapter 20) by noting that the term *organized crime* is of American origin, and he therefore warns that available material for Europe reveals more about the social construction of reality than about the reality of organized crime. Von Lampe's attempt to provide structure for his discussion relies on a classificatory scheme with three basic dimensions: "organized" criminal activities, structural patterns of criminal cooperation, and the systemic context of "organized" criminals, criminal structures, and criminal activities. As his discussion leads to some basic types of organized crime in Europe, von Lampe provides specific analysis of the Sicilian Mafia and the Russian Mafia.

Organized crime in Latin America is the topic of Chapter 21 wherein Mauricio Rubio and Román Ortiz add yet another interesting twist to the traditional American understanding of organized crime. Specifically, they argue that the line separating criminal organizations from insurgent groups, or terrorists, is increasingly tenuous, confused, and irrelevant for the purposes of internal security. They explain how the overlap of politically motivated violence and organized crime has given Latin America an especially politicized version of organized crime. Their chapter concludes with a review of obstacles to confronting organized crime in Latin America particularly and with comments on the U.N. Convention against Transnational Organized Crime.

Regional coverage of organized crime concludes with Chapter 22 on organized crime in North America. Jim Finckenauer and Jay Albanese explain that organized crime can be described in terms of the activities it engages in or by the groups that are involved. Although noting that there are advantages and disadvantages to either approach, Finckenauer and Albanese concentrate on the *groups* involved because the groups differ by region more so than do the *activities*. They have chosen to concentrate on five groups: Cosa Nostra groups,

Russian groups, Chinese groups, Mexican groups, and Canadian groups. The groups are described in terms of their organization structure, the criminal activities with which they are frequently linked, and their associated economic and political features. Comments on law enforcement efforts to combat the groups are also included.

Part IV and the *Handbook* conclude with two chapters on special topics. Neither topic deals specifically with transnational crime or efforts to combat it, but both topics are clearly important to the world community. In Chapter 23, John Winterdyk notes that although youth crime is not transnational by definition, it is international and exhibits cross-national concerns. Those concerns are reflected in international documents that develop guidelines and standards for handling young offenders under various justice systems. After explaining the various models of juvenile justice that exist around the world, Winterdyk describes some of the key U.N. documents relevant to youthful offenders and comments on the degree to which countries are following the guidelines. He concludes with the optimistic observation that some countries are beginning to focus on social prevention and crime prevention through an interdisciplinary and integrated approach.

Capital punishment is one of the most contentious criminal justice topics, and its continued use in the United States astonishes many people in other countries—and many Americans as well. As David Keys points out in Chapter 24, the People's Republic of China, Japan, and the United States are today the only technically sophisticated, industrialized nations to regularly use a death penalty. If for philosophical reasons only, world perceptions on the death penalty are an appropriate topic for this *Handbook*. But there are also practical reasons for the topic's inclusion here. For example, countries in the European Union—and most other countries with which the United States must cooperate in combating transnational crime— will not extradite to the United States a person who faces the death penalty should he or she be convicted of the charged offense. In addition, the execution by U.S. jurisdictions of foreign nationals strains relations between countries and inhibits cooperative efforts at combating transnational crime. Keys highlights the problems by describing how America's use of the death penalty complicates U.S.-Mexican relations (see, e.g., http://news.lawinfo. com/story/3_ds_26670.cfm) especially, but also U.S.-European relations.

REFERENCES

Federal Bureau of Investigation. (2003). *About organized crime*. Retrieved December 12, 2003, from www.fbi.gov/hq/cid/orgcrime/aboutocs.htm

From the editors. (2001, August). *Global Issues: Arresting Transnational Crime, 6*(2), 2. Retrieved May 10, 2004, from http://usinfo.state.gov/journals/itgic/0801/ijge/ijge0801.htm#note

McClure, G. (2003). *The role of Interpol in fighting organized crime*. Retrieved December 12, 2003, from www.interpol.int/Public/Publications/ICPR/ICPR481_1.asp

Office on Drugs and Crime. (2003). *Assessment of organized crime in West Africa*. United Nations. Retrieved December 12, 2003, from www.unodc.org/unodc/en/organized_crime_ assessments. html#Africa

18

Organized Crime in Africa

MARK SHAW

GAIL WANNENBURG

Organized crime is one of the most serious challenges facing African development today. It robs governments of much-needed revenue to provide basic services, undercuts democracy, directly threatens the safety of citizens, and in some extreme cases, because of environmental degradation, strips subsistence farmers of their livelihoods. However, the term *organized crime* needs to be used with great care in the African context. It is not that crime is not organized or that organized criminal groups are not active; indeed, this chapter will show the extent to which organized criminal formations have expanded rapidly over the past decade on the continent. But for most

Africans, if they have given any thought to the term at all, it is more likely to resemble the Hollywood-style mafia don and his cohorts than the complex network of individuals, sometimes with strong ties to the political establishment, that is more common in the African context. There is not, for the most part, much reference at all to the problems of organized crime in African political discourse, as there may be elsewhere in the world. This is mirrored, too, by the organization of law enforcement agencies, where specialized units dedicated to the fighting of a clearly identifiable phenomenon called "organized crime" are the exception rather than the rule. It

AUTHORS' NOTE: Mark Shaw is with the Anti-Organized Crime and Law Enforcement Unit, U.N. Office on Drugs and Crime. Gail Wannenburg is the War and Organized Crime Researcher at the South African Institute of International Affairs. The opinions expressed in this article are those of the authors and not those of the United Nations.

should be no surprise then that there is also little literature on organized crime in Africa.[1]

THE NATURE OF "ORGANIZED CRIME" IN AFRICA

Studies conducted in Africa, insufficient as they may be, suggest that serious crime in Africa may fit a particular sociological profile in which family and ethnic connections assume a particular importance. Stephen Ellis has noted that these very factors are also often important in African politics and that it suggests the existence of an important terrain for the study of serious crime in Africa that does not fit the

> classical criminological category of organized crime, but a category existing in a grey area between politics, legitimate social formation and professional crime, in which those concerned may not consider themselves as professional criminals in the same way as their counterparts in Europe or North America.[2]

The boundaries between the formal and informal economy and the licit and illicit market are consequently blurred. If organized crime in Africa is understood in this way—indeed, this chapter will show that unless this is the case, an accurate representation of the true scale and impact of the problem will escape an external observer—then it is apparent that the problem has reached serious proportions.

One metaphor used by a policeman when describing organized crime in the region of the continent where he works is useful. The officer suggested that organized crime in Africa should be understood like a large net pitched like a circus tent. The net is held up in various places by poles with the net stretched in between. The poles constitute the nodes of the network, key pillars of the criminal establishment. Around each pole is a complex network of individuals and activities that overlap and phase into the

activities of other nodes—not necessarily clear groups but a complex meshing of different individuals and their entrepreneurial activities.[3] Indeed, the term *entrepreneur* is useful in understanding the nature of organized crime in Africa. African criminal operators in interviews have described themselves as "businessmen," and indeed this is what some of them genuinely consider themselves to be.[4] Individuals have identified economic opportunities, which often happen to be criminal, and pursue them in the pursuit of profit. The fact that such activities—the smuggling of particular natural resources, for example—may not be defined as criminal in that particular country or that the groups and individuals involved may also engage in legitimate business makes the easy identification of what is criminal, what is business, and what is politics difficult.

It can also be argued that the complex network of criminal activity across the continent has consolidated to the degree that in some areas, the networks of organization are taking on the shape more clearly of criminal organizations. Even where this occurs, however, such organizations almost always retain a closer resemblance to complex networks of individuals than to strict hierarchical groups. This is because few networks have the logistical or financial capacity to manage the production, supply, and retailing of goods or services. Also, it seems that many of these networks use different suppliers and logistical networks consistently, which obviates the need for more formal relationships. Those that perform less-complex tasks within the network, such as the couriers, may be regarded as disposable and easily replaced.

Most of these networks are relatively new and owe their formation to a complex interplay of historical, socioeconomic, and political factors that have shaped the social formations and forms of governance on the continent in the post–Cold War era.

Political Crises, War, and Organized Crime

Some of the reasons for the exponential growth in organized crime in Africa are as follows:

- The weakening or implosion of state authority in areas such as the Democratic Republic of Congo (DRC) and Somalia
- The onset of a series of brutal wars since the early 1990s in areas such as Rwanda, the DRC, and Angola and the imposition of U.N. sanctions banning the trade in weapons and other resources, such as diamonds, to conflict zones, which created a market for lootable commodities and illicit war material
- The reform of centralized economies and the introduction of a free market in countries such as Mozambique and Angola, which resulted in wholesale privatization of state assets and created opportunities for organized crime
- The transition from authoritarian to democratic rule in countries in southern Africa, most notably South Africa, which ended its isolation from African and international markets when mechanisms of social control were undergoing major transformation

These issues suggest a direct link in many countries between political crisis, dysfunctional states, and the development of organized crime. Although many conflicts in Africa are underpinned by political grievances, over the past decade many protagonists have been unable to articulate any defined ideological outcome, with the result that they are characterized as simple resource wars. In turn, the accumulation of these resources serves to sustain ongoing conflicts. Resource accumulation, the desire for profit, and a breakdown between what is considered legal and illegal by state and other actors, have ensured that protagonists in conflicts are vulnerable to outside influence.

As basic services, infrastructure, and the formal economy decline, the civilian population and rebels or lower-level government forces are compelled to adopt survival strategies that may involve the extraction of alluvial diamonds or other valuable commodities for or on behalf of military and political elites who have connections with organized crime middlemen who can facilitate this trade. Legitimate business corporations also may seek to acquire mining, oil, or other concessions to exploit natural resources that may result in complex payoffs and protection fees and in an overlap between legal and criminal activity. For example, in Angola it is estimated that US$1 billion in oil revenue remained unaccounted for in 2000 while its population lives in dire poverty.[5] The situation in Angola is by no means unique on the continent.

This phenomenon is fueled by the glut of inexpensive weapons on world markets in the aftermath of the Cold War. As a review of global organized crime commissioned by President Clinton points out,

> With the substantial decline in state support [after the Cold War], many insurgencies and extremist groups reach out to criminal networks to acquire arms and supplies that cannot be obtained through more traditional or legitimate channels. Unlike insurgent groups, criminal groups are well-connected to outside gray arms merchants, transportation co-ordinators, money launderers, and other specialists who can provide the weapons and other logistics support once given by state sponsors.[6]

Criminal networks have played an important role in linking combatants with suppliers, although the two parties may seldom meet or even know who they are in business with. The difficulty of understanding the phenomenon of the connection between war and crime in Africa is confounded by the fact, as suggested in the introduction, that those involved seldom structure their operations as hierarchical (and thus more easily understandable) groups, with clear leadership and rank structures. Rather, it is increasingly recognized that the reality of organized crime on the continent more closely resembles complex networks of key individuals. To illustrate the point, the profile of one such individual is provided below.

Victor Bout, a former interpreter in a military aviation unit in Belarus, runs one of the most sophisticated criminal operations allegedly selling weapons to Africa. Bout has been implicated in supplying weaponry from the former Eastern bloc to 17 African countries and (allegedly) to the Taliban in Afghanistan and Abu Sayyaf in the Philippines. He has been implicated in all the U.N. reports on those individuals and groups flouting the ban on supplying arms to rebels in Angola, Sierra Leone, and the Liberian government. He has also been named in the U.N. expert panel reports on the illegal exploitation of natural resources in the DRC. He has used at least five aliases and owns a maze of airline, cargo, and freight forwarding companies. He maintains 60 planes that have been registered in Belgium, the United States, Liberia, South Africa, Swaziland, the United Arab Emirates, Rwanda, and the Central African Republic. When his companies are subjected to scrutiny, he moves his operations elsewhere. He is still at large, although the Belgian government has issued an international warrant of arrest for him on money-laundering charges. Bout denied all the charges against him in 2002 when he appeared on a Russian radio station.[7]

Apart from arms dealing, evidence now also exists that "trafficking in and abuse of narcotic drugs and psychotropic substances are increasingly being linked to the various civil conflicts in Africa."[8] Illicit drugs have, for example, been used to finance civil conflict, including the purchasing of arms, in Angola. In the DRC, apart from financing parts of the rebel war effort, drugs have been issued to combatants "to induce them to carry out dangerous operations with impunity."[9]

The task of rebuilding areas of conflict in which rebels and militias have held sway and bringing them under central government control and establishing civilian structures

such as local administrations, policing, and the criminal justice system is enormous. This is the case in Angola and the DRC where much of the countryside is inaccessible because of landmines or damaged infrastructure.

Fragile peace processes in some countries such as Sierra Leone and the DRC are under threat from former rebels or militia that are prepared to work as mercenaries in neighboring countries that funded these movements in the past. The presence of large numbers of firearms on the continent will continue to enhance opportunities for lawlessness in Liberia, Sierra Leone, the Democratic Republic of Congo, and their neighboring countries and increase the violence associated with lawlessness in regions such as southern Africa. Many civilian populations were militarized and armed in the conflicts on the continent. The cessation of hostilities has reawakened ancient disputes over land and resources at local levels. This is evident in areas such as Ituri in the DRC where Hema and Lendu militias have continued to fight after the signature of a peace accord.

Regional instability, therefore, including both weak and unstable states and ongoing conflicts, serves as an important driver of illicit activity in Africa. The space and opportunities made possible by those engaged in armed conflict, who seek to fund war through the exploitation of natural and other resources, are crucial in the development of criminal networks. In this process, links are established with external criminal groups, and new networks of lawful and criminal activity are forged—again, an important defining feature, as suggested above, being the crossover between legal and illegal operations.

The Vulnerability of Post-Conflict Societies to Organized Crime

Although the conduct of war itself has enhanced the opportunities for crime, it is in war's aftermath that the greatest danger lies.

Postconflict societies on the continent are likely, given the conditions spawned by wars, to be vulnerable to higher levels of crime and, in particular, violent crime. This is because war has reduced economic opportunities (or centralized them around a small elite), undermined the rule of law, weakened states with little enforcement capacity, and ensured cheap and easily accessible firearms. Parallel with these developments has been the growth, over the last decade, in global organized criminal activity able to exploit opportunities in Africa.

A number of characteristics apply to societies recovering from conflict, which make them vulnerable to higher levels of crime and disorder. These include the following:

Established Networks to Smuggle Contraband. Networks established during times of conflict to smuggle weapons or other necessities of war are easily converted into channels for the smuggling of drugs, contraband, or stolen goods. In South Africa, the apartheid government authorized the establishment of numerous covert front companies to obtain war material and other goods that were the subject of U.N. sanctions.[10] Now, cars, drugs, and other contraband are brought in along old gun-smuggling routes while the general availability of weapons and the weakness and corruptibility of the police serve as additional incentives to criminal activity.

There Are Few Opportunities for Legitimate Economic Activity. The immediate postwar environment may contain few opportunities for involvement in the formal economy, ensuring that there are few alternatives but to engage in crime.[11] Young men with guns were the principal source of most of the violence in Somalia: They had no jobs and could find cheap weapons in local markets. The best way to make up for the absence of a job was a weapon, a traditional symbol of manhood in nomadic culture and now a source of income as well. In countries undergoing reform of a centralized state-planned economy, the privatization of state assets may provide opportunities for entry of organized crime groups into the economy, in conjunction with the political elite. In Mozambique, there were insufficient systems in place in the banking sector to regulate the privatization and indigenization of business with the result that widespread corruption and penetration of the state occurred.

Former Combatants With Military Training Are Unemployed. The presence of large numbers of ex-combatants who have easy access to weapons and few skills other than the conduct of warfare provides a ready source of recruits for criminal activity. Many demobilization programs in Africa have offered one-off small payments to former soldiers or rebels, insufficient to start small businesses. In a recent survey in Mozambique, for example, it was found that ex-combatants, particularly the disabled veterans, run drug-trafficking networks.[12] Some combatants may already have been involved in criminal activities during the conflict as a means of survival or to supplement their incomes, so turning to crime is a relatively easy psychological step, particularly if they feel betrayed by their leaders.

Local Strong Men Control Distinct Geographic Areas. The immediate postconflict environment may see certain areas occupied and controlled by local groups or strong men. Such areas have the potential to become springboards for crime and are almost impenetrable to external actors. When the state is very weak or nonexistent, such areas are effectively local fiefdoms that may require the income generated by criminal acts to finance military activities. The clearest example of this is Somalia, where, in the absence of state control, local warlords assume control over specific communities and geographic entities. Ironically, the weakness of a state and its lack of resources may make it unattractive to organized crime, which makes cost-benefit calculations in the same way as legitimate business. However, local warlords who are predominant in a number of other places, particularly if they control access to valuable resources, may be a more attractive proposition.[13]

Wars and State Actions May Generate a Disrespect for the Rule of Law. Ongoing conflicts on the African continent and state involvement in criminal activities have meant that few citizens believe that the law is worth respecting. In fact, engaging in criminal activities may be seen as a right, an attempt to "redistribute" wealth from the rich to the poor. For example, Nigerian drug dealers interviewed for a recent study "view the black market [and criminal activities] as the only way to redistribute wealth from the north to the south, arguing that mainstream commercial channels are effectively occupied."[14]

The vulnerability of societies emerging from conflict to high levels of criminality has important implications for state authority in sub-Saharan Africa. The vulnerability to crime will not only affect those societies that have suffered directly from conflict but will have repercussions for others on the continent, given the porous nature of national borders and the subsequent ease of movement between states. African societies engaged in, or emerging from, war seldom have legitimate police agencies willing and able to enforce the law. Law enforcement is generally highly militarized, with the civil function often shared with the army. In some countries, such as Mozambique, former soldiers form the bulk of the police service. Policing remains inherently colonial—the provision of "firefighting" responses to problem areas rather than the maintenance of close and ongoing relations with citizens. As a U.N. report on African drug control notes,[15] "[African] law enforcement institutions must often resort to costly and inefficient 'search and seize' interventions such

as roadblock inspections, neighbourhood raids and border checks—their role as a non-present deterrent is often marginalised because of poor credibility."

Although legal instruments (implemented in many cases as a result of international pressure) have been created to fight criminal activity, including organized crime, there is often insufficient capacity within police agencies themselves. The growing sophistication of organized crime on the continent has in general not been matched by an increase in the sophistication, skill, and resources of the police. Indeed, targeting such security threats may not be the key purpose of the police at all.[16]

The management of security in at least a substantial number of African states is in practice essentially "private," in that such security as exists is designed primarily to protect the lives, power, and access to wealth of specific groups and individuals who control the state. For political elites in some African countries, therefore, effective and impartial law enforcement may be more a threat to the established order than something to be welcomed. Few serving members of African governments have been indicted for unlawful activity.

For ordinary citizens, however, police officers are the most visible extensions of the state so that inefficient and corrupt law enforcement undermines the view ordinary people have of the instruments of the state as a whole. Growing vigilantism is a measure of the insecurity and dissatisfaction felt by many ordinary citizens. The credibility and legitimacy of policing agencies is thus a key factor in ensuring their effectiveness. This remains one of the key challenges facing the police in most of the countries of sub-Saharan Africa. Ultimately, one leading analyst has concluded, the security of fragmented African societies must come from within by domestic actors creating a framework of order that allows them to survive—and with any luck develop—in some reasonably peaceful way.

THE EVOLUTION AND GROWTH OF ORGANIZED CRIME IN AFRICA

A study of the evolution and growth of organized crime in different contexts within Africa can provide a more nuanced view of its causes, consequences, and possibly, its future trajectory. The following section considers major trends in organized crime in West, South, and East Africa. In each region, although a number of important parallels can be identified, including the issues of conflict and state weakness already discussed above, particular conditions have been important in the development of organized crime. In West Africa, where the problem is particularly serious and has the highest global impact, the nature of organized crime has its origins in the breakdown of state institutions in Nigeria from the late 1970s. In South Africa, organized crime has grown rapidly since the end of apartheid, expanding not only because of the new opportunities offered by the comparative wealth of the country but also because apartheid itself bred criminalized smuggling networks well placed to take advantage of the openness that democracy would bring. Finally, East Africa, for centuries a hub of trade between the continent and Asia and Arabia, is increasingly now at the heart of a complex network of illicit trafficking up and down the east coast of the continent and expanding into its interior. As in other places in Africa, such expansion has also been accentuated by conflict, state weakness, and instability.

Crime as Business: The Evolution of West African Organized Crime

By 1990, Nigerian criminal groups were widely regarded as one of the most significant threats confronting law enforcement agencies in many countries. Nigerian groups were active across the globe, from Latin America to Asia, with particularly sophisticated operations in Europe and North America. Few businesspeople around the world have not received fraudulent letters from Nigeria promising great profits, if only an advanced fee will be paid (so-called 419 scams, named after the section of the Nigerian Penal Code that prohibits such practices). Illicit trafficking and fraud have thus become the hallmark of Nigerian criminal operations. Perhaps most important to note about such activities is that unlike, say, Colombian organized crime, the commodities that Nigerian groups smuggle, most notably heroin and cocaine, are not produced in West Africa. Nigerian criminal groups then act in the majority of criminal exchanges as transporters or middlemen; they have added value not by producing but by buying, moving, and selling. The section that follows uses the term *West African criminal networks*, given that this is the term now widely accepted to describe the phenomenon.

What is perhaps most remarkable about the emergence of West African criminal networks is how quickly they have established themselves, dominating particular sectors of the global illicit economy. Most important, the origins of criminal networks from West Africa directly parallel the decline and economic crisis of the Nigerian state in the 1980s. In contrast, the period before the decline of the country was marked by the degree to which the country's relative wealth allowed Nigerians to travel, study, and acquire interests abroad, in some cases establishing the seeds of the criminal networks that were to develop in the later crisis years. Economic mismanagement, a failed structural adjustment program, continuous political contestation, and ongoing and harsh periods of military rule marked the decline of the Nigerian state.[17]

Why should Nigeria and Nigerians be singled out immediately in a study the focus of which is organized crime originating in Africa as a whole? The extent of economic decline in the country, the size of its population (with 125 million people, the most populous state on the continent—1 in 5 sub-Saharan Africans is a Nigerian), and the degree to which oil wealth ensured an educated elite, well traveled and interconnected to the rest of the world, are all contributing factors.

Despite the extent of the problem, a detailed study of the origins of West African criminal groups must still be conducted. In fact, although most analyses of events in Nigeria refer to the criminalization of the state, few explore the extent to which Nigeria became an important exporter of criminal activity. From 1985, the unprecedented diversion of revenues depleted resources, aggravated the debt burden, and alienated important external creditors. In this period, overtly illegal activities became a major portion of Nigeria's shadow economy with more than $1 billion dollars (about 15% of government revenues) flowing through criminal networks, often with the connivance of the country's elite.[18] Although much has been staked on the civilian government that took power in 1999, significant problems remain, and the country is currently estimated to have the largest "shadow" economy (although not all of this can, of course, be attributed to illegal activities) in the world.[19]

Although these figures suggest the astonishing extent of economic activity outside the formal economic sector, they provide little indication of how criminal activities, such as drug trafficking, were spawned in the context of a declining state. Law enforcement explanations also provide little insight. For example, a U.S. Drug Enforcement Administration (DEA) briefing paper on explains that Nigerian naval officers undergoing training in India during the 1980s began trafficking heroin through Nigerian student networks to Europe and the United States. "When these students realized the potential profits to be earned from heroin trafficking, they started their own operations and heroin trafficking was gradually introduced to most Nigerian traders."[20] Of course, although such developments may certainly

have occurred, the reality of the rise of West African criminal networks is much more complex.

The dramatic increase in oil revenues after 1973 ensured the influx of millions of petrodollars that, while bringing great wealth to the Nigerian state, had important consequences for the development of criminal enterprises in the 1980s. The sudden generation of wealth unsurprisingly led to disagreements (which have yet to be resolved) about who is entitled to spend it. This was exemplified by the fact that the oil wells are situated along the coast in the south, and the country has largely been ruled by military governments based in the north.[21] Such disputes encourage a strong sense of entitlement and little compunction for citizens who steal from the state, because the state has stolen from them.

Such social dislocation has been accompanied by rapid economic decline. Although the oil windfall brought great wealth to Nigeria (even though it was concentrated in few hands), its dominance has ensured that the economy depends on fluctuations of the oil price, and the country, like Angola, suffers from the classic effect of "Dutch disease" where distortions are introduced, given the value of a single and dominant commodity to an economy. The petroleum sector produces about 40% of the country's GDP and accounts for 96% of recorded exports.[22] The presence of oil has created multiple opportunities for corruption and has ensured that control of the state is key to the accumulation of wealth. Economic decline in particular was accentuated during the Second Republic (1977–1983), the period immediately before the first increases in Nigerian involvement in illicit activities were noted by law enforcement agencies around the world.[23]

The result by the early 1990s was a highly unstable and corrupt state with significant disaffected minorities. Nigeria, and West Africa more generally, developed into the hub of a worldwide drug-trafficking web, spanning almost every part of the globe.[24]

The issue of ethnic alienation appears to be closely related to the development of criminal networks originating in Nigeria. The presence of the alienated Igbo ethnic group in southeastern Nigeria and their close involvement in organized criminal activities is a strong theme.[25] Stemming from deep resentments around the Biafran War (1967–1970), the conflict resulted in the marginalization of Igbos from the various postwar military regimes. Although the details of the war are not of concern here, it was in effect an attempt by eastern parts of the country to break away from the federation and achieve independence. The war, however, generated a strong ethnic persecution complex among Igbo-speaking people and an alienation from the institutions of governance.[26]

This dominance of Igbos in criminal networks has been attributed to their "business" or "commercial" skills.[27] Yet according to some informants, it is also possible to exaggerate their involvement. Economic and political decline have had the impact of marginalizing and impoverishing larger numbers of Nigerians than just those who live in the southeast. And multiple ethnic identities as well as tight community and familial networks ensure that illicit activities are not confined (at least not now) to a single ethnic group.

It is worth noting in the context of this discussion on the growth of organized criminal networks originating from Nigeria that many Nigerians hold the West responsible for the decline of the country. That, for many, has provided justification for their involvement in criminal activities. Engagement in crime is considered justifiable to redistribute wealth back from those who have "stolen" it. Interestingly, any social controls in respect to the prevention of criminal activity are internally rather than externally focused. Thus, studies of Nigerian criminal networks have shown that their members seldom consumed their "own product" (meaning cocaine) because they saw it as introducing unneeded dependency on a commodity used exclusively for the purpose of gaining profit.[28]

The crisis of governance that affected Nigeria has now spread throughout West Africa, having important impact in countries such as Liberia, Senegal, Ivory Coast, and Ghana. In particular, the involvement of Ghanaians and Liberians in enterprise-type crime mirrored economic decline and war in both societies.[29] Although their numbers are smaller and they are unlikely to dominate in the way of the Nigerian networks, interview evidence suggests that they have become involved in similar activity such as advance-fee fraud (419 scams), and they have developed specific criminal specializations of their own. It is possible, therefore, that police agencies around the world overestimate the extent of Nigerian involvement simply because all people from West Africa are labeled as Nigerians with little attempt made to differentiate particular nationalities.

The role of West Africans in criminal networks from the mid-1980s onward, however, cannot be explained simply by the collapse of governance and economic opportunity in their home countries. Powerful pull factors, such as the growing demand for illegal narcotics in North America and Europe that forced up the price of illegal narcotics (and therefore the profitability of drug smuggling) must also be considered. In turn, West African ethnic communities that had not been assimilated into the societies in which they lived, concentrated in various North American and European cities, provided a secure network for local distribution.[30]

The weakening and criminalization of the state in particular West African countries—notably Nigeria, Liberia, and Ghana—resulted in the heavy involvement of state actors themselves in criminal activities.[31] Paradoxically, this process of state capture and collapse was central, as we have seen, in forcing some people to leave in search of new (and often criminal) opportunities, given limited and declining economic opportunities at home while ensuring that the instruments of the state—such as the police, the diplomatic service, and various agencies responsible for the issuing of identity and travel documents—become heavily involved in criminal activity. The net result was often that the activities of the state and those of criminal groups became indistinguishable.[32]

If the negative trend of state weakness in West Africa has been responsible for the development of sophisticated criminal networks, the position in South (and by implication, southern) Africa has been different. Here, positive developments, most prominently the development of democracy in South Africa, have had the unintended consequence of promoting the development of organized crime.

Democracy's Disorder?
The Changing Nature of
Organized Crime in South Africa

What is surprising in the case of South Africa, where the state is comparatively strong, is the speed with which criminal activity grew after 1990. This has contributed to the current difficulties that government is experiencing in eradicating the problem as the instruments of the state slowly realign to confront the challenge.

The development of organized crime in South Africa has seen a complex interaction between the rise of local criminal syndicates and networks and the expansion of foreign criminal groups within the country. Before 1994, organized criminal activity (apart from the criminal activities of the state itself) were poorly developed because the country was largely cut off from the world and engaged in a low-intensity civil war. Although the apartheid government and the liberation movements used criminal organizations to smuggle weapons and disrupt

opponents' tactics, political considerations were always predominant. Nevertheless, the roots of organized criminality were bred before the transition began, were magnified in the period immediately before dramatic shifts in power occurred, and then became highly visible in the posttransition environment.[33]

According to police undercover agents, many criminal syndicates had their origins in the late 1980s. These were the result of both foreigners coming into the region to establish legitimate import-export operations and the activities of local entrepreneurs. Locals had contacts through which they could acquire a range of resource products such as cobalt, ivory, diamonds, or drugs. Foreigners provided the means through which these products could be transferred to lucrative markets. From the beginning, then, the line between the activities of legitimate and illegitimate business has often been blurred.

Investigations of the trade in ivory and rhino horn from countries in southern Africa during the 1980s and early 1990s has implicated senior individuals in the military intelligence division of the then South African Defence Force. There is a clear overlap between the destabilizing wars conducted at the time—the support of the National Union for the Total Independence of Angola in Angola and RENAMO (Mozambican National Resistance) in Mozambique—and criminal activity such as the smuggling of military supplies to the rebel groups and (in conjunction with Chinese Triads) the extraction of ivory and rhino horn to South Africa and on to the Far East.[34] A pathbreaking early study of the phenomenon concluded:

> It was clear that during the time when South Africa was fighting secret wars in Southern Africa, officers under the command of [defence intelligence] were systematically demanding from their allies payment in whatever commodities lay to hand, including hardwood, gold, diamonds, rhino horn and ivory.[35]

Former RENAMO soldiers claim that military helicopters were used to transport ivory and other goods from Mozambique to South Africa on a regular basis.[36]

By the time the wars of destabilization were scaled back, individuals in South African Military Intelligence were in possession of a strategically valuable network of contacts with both old allies and former enemies. Johannesburg developed as a trading and communications hub for the movement of illegal goods, including drugs, with the trade being controlled by a small group of insiders.

The political changes that occurred in 1994, when apartheid was replaced by a fledgling constitutional democracy, created the opportunity for both indigenous, as well as international organized crime groups, to exploit the new low-risk environment that South Africa provided for criminal activities. The country had entered a political transition, and state structures (including the police) were being transformed and therefore weakened. Border controls were relaxed, and international tourism expanded. South Africa became more accessible to the international community, including the organized crime community.

The expansion of foreign criminal groups into the country has been a noticeable phenomenon of the new democracy. South Africa has become the linchpin in the development of a regional organized crime network. The country, given its comparative wealth, is both a market and a source for criminal groups. A significant proportion of the criminal syndicates identified by the authorities as operating in South Africa have a regional focus. These organizations generally involve themselves in a multiplicity of activities—for example, the smuggling of guns, drugs, or stolen car parts. One form of commodity may be exchanged for others. Once the routes are in place (and where necessary the appropriate border officials bribed), almost any commodity can be transported.

The hijacking and theft of motor vehicles in South Africa, for example, cannot be controlled without an examination of regional factors. Crime bosses in South Africa (many of whom are themselves from outside the country) have begun to focus on "exports" of stolen or hijacked cars or parts in the same way as if these were legitimate business concerns. Mozambique, Zambia, and Zimbabwe have become markets for small delivery vans, 4 × 4s, and trucks. This is now a highly lucrative business run by increasingly sophisticated syndicates.[37]

The fluidity and flexibility of syndicates in the subregion can be illustrated by the manner in which they have seized the opportunities available due to the political crisis in Zimbabwe. Unrealistic price controls in Zimbabwe have led to a lucrative black market in basic goods such as sugar. These goods are smuggled from Zimbabwe into its neighboring countries, undermining the local industries. In turn, Zimbabwean crime networks are buying up currency in neighboring states, as the Zimbabwe dollar depreciates, and using it to buy scarce resources such as fuel in Zimbabwe, which in turn can be sold at a profit on the black market.[38]

Organized criminal activity often operates under the pretense of, or in conjunction with, legitimate commercial activity such as import-export companies or the taxi business. The need to move illicit goods has meant that the largely unregulated transport sector in the country has served as a breeding ground for organized crime. Some members of the cargo trucking industry are allegedly able to offer 50% discounts, thereby undercutting their competition by transporting illicit goods. The nature, organization, and use of violence by some groups in the taxi industry in South Africa have resulted in a complex interchange between licit and illicit activity, which fits the definition of organized crime.

A dramatic expansion in the number of minibus taxis in the 1980s, plying their trade within the larger cities and on long-distance routes, has given rise to turf wars for profitable routes as well as tightly structured taxi organizations that employ "hit squads" to eliminate potential competitors (as well as ambitious individuals in their own ranks) and actively engage in the corruption of state officials. Given that the taxi industry is poorly regulated and that there are many unregistered operators, competition for and between routes is intense. Unsurprisingly, the use of violence to protect economic interests has become a feature of the industry. The growth and consolidation of a few powerful figures in the taxi industry constitutes a classic case of the overlap between legitimate and illegitimate business and the development of organized crime. Given their capacity for mobility, taxi operators are useful partners in, and sometimes initiators of, smuggling networks across the subcontinent. In some cases, taxi associations serve as middlemen, selling weapons bought outside the country to criminal organizations in South Africa. They are also implicated in the trafficking of women and children from Mozambique and other countries to South Africa.[39] State attempts to regulate the industry are gaining pace and proving to be effective challenges to some crime leaders, but these efforts are often undercut by high levels of corruption and weak law enforcement.

All these factors illustrate the extent to which both the transition to democracy and the changes in the southern Africa region— including the end of old conflicts and the beginning of new ones—have had important effects on illicit activities. This applies to many criminal networks and organizations that operate in South Africa. There is one area of the country, however, that has its own particular characteristics—the Western Cape. This is because it is the one region where there has been a history of both gang activity and, more recently, violent community-based responses. These factors have ensured that the development of criminal organizations in the Western Cape in the postapartheid period has taken on a specific trajectory of its own.

Gang formation in Cape Town has been the survival strategy of the poor. A result of grinding poverty, social exclusion, unemployment, and the dislocation caused by apartheid-forced removals, gangs have been a powerful organizing principle for the communities of the Cape Flats. Under apartheid, gangs were often harshly and indiscriminately policed while at the same time being used to target political opponents of the state. In the last decade of apartheid, a count of gangs in 30 areas of the Cape Flats found 280 groups who labeled themselves as gangs, with the majority of gang members interviewed suggesting that their gangs were about 100 strong.[40] The hierarchy and organization of the gangs is complex and multifaceted. Organization has ranged from low-level street gangs to more organized family mafias and drug syndicates.

From the early 1990s, a number of significant developments altered the nature of the Western Cape gangs. The end of apartheid saw more relaxed border controls and the greater exposure of the country to international organized crime groups. These included the expansion of the activities of the Russian Mafia, involved particularly in money-laundering operations and in cross-border smuggling, and the role of Chinese Triads in the smuggling of abalone and the illegal trade in rhino horn and ivory, among other activities.[41] Pakistani syndicates, involved largely in the trade in "grey products" (knockoffs of popular brand names) are a growing phenomenon. The most rapid expansion of foreigners involved in crime in South Africa, however, has been the dramatic growth within a short period of time of Nigerian organized crime groups. Nigerian crime syndicates now dominate the illicit trade in crack cocaine in South Africa and are involved in sophisticated fraud scams.[42]

Before 1994, the six or seven largest crime syndicates in the Western Cape province, primarily involved in the narcotics trade, were constantly engaged in debilitating turf battles.

This made them more vulnerable to police action and provided an environment that was conducive to the recruitment by the police of informers who were then tasked with providing information on gang activities. Rival gangs also used the criminal justice system to try to neutralize their opponents by laying criminal charges against them.

With the opening up of South Africa's borders after the 1994 election and the realization that foreign crime syndicates were likely to exploit the new situation, most of these Western Cape syndicates decided to establish a cartel. Their aim was to reduce turf battles, order bulk shipments, distribute the drugs in prearranged proportions at agreed prices, and allocate distribution areas in terms of a set of agreed principles. Called "The Firm," the cartel substantially changed the nature of organized crime in the Western Cape after 1994. By 1996, enormous profits had been generated that needed to be laundered and invested. Members of The Firm started buying fixed properties in rural areas along the Cape coastline. Some of the more assertive gangs that formed part of The Firm, such as the Hard Livings, set up branches in many communities and towns and made contact with Chinese Triads and the Sicilian Mafia.[43]

Most of the local leaders of the Hard Livings were provided with seed capital and cars to run their own drug trade. The role of the leadership of the Hard Livings became one of merely collecting the money and coordinating activities. The consolidation and better coordination of activities are typical of what occurred with some criminal groups elsewhere in South Africa. It reflects a progression of a common criminal gang moving up the ladder of sophistication on its way to becoming a well-organized criminal group that thinks strategically after assessing its own strengths and weaknesses.

Notwithstanding increases in these crimes, one of the most important outcomes of these developments has been the growth of drug trafficking to South Africa, not only to satisfy growing local demand but because the country has become an important transshipment point for drugs destined for more lucrative markets.[44] Current estimates are that 60% of all drugs that reach South African shores are moved on to other destinations.[45] As already mentioned, one of the most significant developments in South Africa since 1994 has been the growth of Nigerian criminal syndicates, with important domestic implications.[46]

The use of South Africa as a transshipment point has regional dimensions. Direct flights between source and destination countries are generally avoided in favor of diversionary stops in neighboring states.[47] Law enforcement sources both inside and outside Angola, for example, have long identified the country as a source of cocaine entering Southern Africa. Originating in South America and trafficked via Brazil—with which Angola has strong historic, cultural, and language connections—powdered cocaine enters the country mainly on the weekly Angola Airways flight from Rio, according to a recent unpublished U.N. Office for Drug Control and Crime Prevention report.[48]

Trafficking routes from Latin America appear to be relatively sophisticated. Police sources suggest that Luanda serves as a "portal" into southern Africa. Smuggling routes from Luanda into the region itself are seldom direct; police records indicate that narcotics are transported by air to Windhoek or Maputo and then forwarded on to Johannesburg by road, rail, or air. In documented cases, Nigerian trafficking groups have recruited Angolan citizens to go to Brazil where they link up with other Nigerians resident there, bringing back cocaine destined for South Africa, and further afield.[49]

The role of Nigerian syndicates in the drug trade has important implications for the inner city. The center of the trade remains the high-density area of Hillbrow, Johannesburg, now dominated by Nigerian traffickers, operating out of a series of residential hotels and who also have important links to local prostitution networks.[50] These trends are also evident in Durban and, to a lesser extent, in Cape Town,[51] although the situation in these cities is not yet as serious as in Johannesburg. The level of dominance by the Nigerian syndicates of these inner-city areas is reflected by interviews with local businesses and prostitutes who regard the Nigerians as bringing order by discouraging violent street crime that might drive away customers from outside the area.[52]

As elsewhere in the world, the high profits generated by the illicit trade in drugs and other illegal commodities have ensured growing corruption of police officers. Low levels of morale, poor pay, and weak internal controls contribute to this problem. Some evidence points to active collusion between the police and drug dealers at street level.[53] Higher up the chain, the arrest of the head of the organized crime unit in Durban for corruption suggests just how serious the problem may have become.[54] These incidents both undermine public confidence in those that are meant to ensure citizens' safety and confound any attempt at concerted law enforcement.

South Africa then has become a hub for the development of organized crime, not only because of the county's comparative wealth and developed transport infrastructure but because of both the presence and the later development of sophisticated criminal operations as well as the regional instability in southern Africa, which has promoted the development of sophisticated forms of cross-border criminal activity. In southern Africa, in particular, some states, most notably Mozambique, have been badly affected by this trend. This is also partly because the east coast of Africa has long served as a trading interface between Africa, Arabia, and South Asia. Although much of this trade has been legitimate, a significant proportion has not.

The Hub of Illicit Trade: East Africa

Located on the shores of the Indian Ocean, East African countries developed trade networks connecting Central Africa, southern Africa, the Middle East, and Southwest and Southeast Asia. Indian Ocean trade brought Islamic merchants and culture to East Africa over the past 1,000 years. Countries in the region are Eritrea, Ethiopia, Kenya, Malawi, Rwanda, Sudan, Tanzania, Uganda, and Somalia. This region as a whole has been a dynamic and crucial point for commercial trade with Africa. As elsewhere in the world, regions where significant levels of commercial trade take place are also vulnerable to the development of illicit transactions. In East Africa, reflecting a theme already outlined at the beginning of this article, state weakness and conflict have been an important contributing factor in the development of this trend.

Because some East African governments lost effective control over their states in a course of escalated armed conflicts in the region, especially after the Cold War, the region has become vulnerable to illicit trade and criminal activities. Its trade network is now threatened by criminal organizations. Today, East Africa is still struggling with ongoing and long-lasting regional conflicts, which place barriers to regulating internal affairs. Existing criminal activities in the region also suggest that there is serious potential for the further growth of organized crime. A preliminary review of the development of cross-border criminal activities in the region by the U.N. Office on Drugs and Crime (UNODC) shows significant problems in human trafficking, drug smuggling, and the trafficking of firearms.

Human trafficking, especially of women and children, has been recognized throughout the region by various news sources and academic research. According to a report by the U.S. Department of State,[55] East African countries are both a source and destination for human trafficking for the purpose of commercial sexual exploitation and forced labor. In the case of sex trafficking, states in East Africa principally serve as source countries. Women and teenage girls are mainly trafficked to European countries. Middle Eastern countries such as Lebanon and some countries within Africa are also recognized as destinations for those trafficked women. In the case of forced labor, women and children are mainly sent to the Middle East, North and southern Africa, and even within East Africa itself. Most of the women and children are from poor areas; therefore, either they or their parents are easily lured by traffickers' promises, such as educational opportunities and marriage in Europe. Cultural tradition, where parents send children to wealthier relatives to care for the child, also leaves people vulnerable to child-trafficking traps.

The International Organization for Migration, which has a close partnership with the United Nations, has acknowledged in its report[56] that organized crime is widespread in the eastern and southern African regions. The report addresses a connection between Malawian business and Nigerian traffickers in sex trafficking. In Ethiopia, employment agencies, most of which are not registered, act as a key recruitment mechanism, and some collusion between traffickers and government officials have been acknowledged.[57] However, despite the significant evidence of human trafficking, there is little information on traffickers' identities in East Africa.

As for drug smuggling, East Africa is a very busy transit region. Of all the states in the region, Ethiopia, Kenya, Malawi, and Tanzania are the most critical transit hubs. In addition to its attractive location on a transit route between Asia and Europe, factors such as porous borders, poorly paid civil servants, and corruption are ideal conditions for drug smugglers. East Africa, thus, is an essential middleman in global drug trafficking. Sea and air transportation infrastructure in the region and the network of commercial and family ties on a global scale are critical in this regard. In addition, corruption in law enforcement and lack of resources for counternarcotics programs make East African ports very vulnerable to organized syndicates. A recent U.N. report

noted that Nairobi and Mombasa, the latter with the biggest commercial seaport in the region, are systematically exploited by well-organized drug traffickers.[58] Seaports in Kenya and Tanzania are particularly critical points to assess criminal syndicates in both regional and global drug trafficking.

Heroin and cocaine are the major substances that pass through the region. Most of the drugs originate in Southeast and Southwest Asia and are destined for Europe and North America. Southern Africa is another destination, although on a smaller scale. Khat, cannabis, and opium poppy are cultivated on a small scale compared with the flow of heroin and cocaine and, currently, are mainly for domestic consumption. A recent report from the UNODC[59] shows that large amounts of cannabis/marijuana in Kenya and Tanzania are increasingly trafficked to neighboring countries, especially southern Africa. It also reports a large increase of cannabis use in Africa, especially Kenya and Uganda in East Africa.

Journalists in South Africa and Mozambique have identified a drug-smuggling route that stretches from Afghanistan via Pakistan to Tanzania and Mozambique. Drugs are transported by boat from Tanzania to Pemba in Mozambique. Some of the containers are floated at sea and collected by local fishermen at night. These drugs make their way into the former military veteran housing complexes in Maputo, dubbed Little Colombia, and by road to South Africa. Buyers claim that 5 grams of heroin will sell for R700 (just under US$100).[60] This sends a warning that there are potential demands that help drug smugglers to expand their business into these countries.

Diffusion of small firearms in East Africa is now a well-recognized problem. It is apparent that there are millions of light arms in East Africa, where an AK-47 costs only 6 U.S. dollars. The proliferation of lightweight small guns is closely related to the collapse of the Soviet Union and the regional war in East Africa. The U.N. Security Council has recognized this small-arms matter in the region as key challenge for promotion of durable peace and sustainable development.

Ongoing research indicates two major patterns of light arms trafficking: regional flow and smuggling from external traffickers. Regional flow of small arms is vast. It is attributed to the regional nature of conflicts in East Africa, where the conflicts in the DRC spill over into neighboring countries. Porous borders in the region allow soldiers and rebels to flee to neighboring countries very easily, and they are always accompanied by small arms. With the spillover of the conflicts in wide areas, small arms move along and are eventually sold in the civilian market.

The current stockpiles of small arms in Africa are remnants of former wars and the Cold War security that equipped anticolonial fighters. In the DRC, for example, most of weapons are from the Congolese wars of 1996 and 1998. It is now said that 100 million small arms are in the hands of unauthorized and unqualified individuals or groups in Congo. Somalia's capital Mogadishu, with a population of 1.3 million residents, was estimated to possess over a million guns in 1999. In the confusion of ongoing armed conflicts and their aftermath, where there is weak, if any, state security, possession of a gun is a matter of survival. Therefore, today's East Africa is fertile ground for small-arms traffickers to develop their business.

Such facts illustrate the vulnerability that will be faced in countries along the East African coast in the near future. Already, and as referred to several times, Mozambique has developed a significant problem of organized criminality that will prove difficult to curb. But similar problems are present in a variety of other states, including Kenya and Uganda. In Somalia, state breakdown has developed to such a degree that the activities of criminal groups and local clans trading in a variety of items, both licit and illicit, make distinguishing between local warlords and organized criminal activity nearly impossible.

CONCLUSION

A key theme that has run through this chapter is the degree to which the development of contemporary organized criminal activity on the African continent cannot be understood separately from state weakness, collapse, and ongoing civil conflicts. There is perhaps one exception to this, that being South Africa, where although such factors have also played a part, the key driving force for the development of organized crime has been the evolution of local gangs, which had largely been kept in check (or used for controlling liberation movements) by the apartheid state, combined with the opening of the country's border to new and sophisticated criminal operators, most notably Nigerian criminal networks.

In West Africa, the problem of organized crime has now developed to the extent that West African criminal networks are renowned for their acumen in many other countries across the globe. This, combined with conflict and state collapse in some areas of the region, has ensured that the development of organized criminal activity now directly threatens the ability of states to develop both economically and politically. In East Africa, the historic position of the region as a trading hub, combined with the common feature of weak states and ongoing and past conflicts, has made the east coast vulnerable to illicit smuggling, most notably in human beings, drugs, and firearms.

What is perhaps most surprising about the overall development of organized crime in Africa is the extent to which it has not been documented in any detail. This remains an urgent and much-needed task. The definitive text on the developing problem of organized crime on the continent is yet to be written. At the moment, the story is one of fragments, with a hazy picture only now developing. This is partly because, as suggested at the beginning of the chapter, the term *organized crime* is still not widely used in Africa. Nevertheless, the past decade has seen the expansion of criminal networks across the continent, with increasing evidence that such networks have accumulated (and will continue to accumulate) profits, power, and political resources, making them a permanent feature of the African landscape. This poses significant threats to the long-term well-being of Africans. These networks threaten democratic processes, undercut economic development that benefits everybody, and have created new power centered on an already politically fragmented environment. In conclusion, it must be emphasized again that resolving such problems, given their complex political, social, and economic roots, cannot be the task of law enforcement agencies alone. Indeed, in Africa, with few exceptions, police and criminal agencies are seldom up to the tasks, and reliance must be placed on a long-term (and largely political) process that aims to strengthen institutions of peacemaking and governance on the continent as a whole.

NOTES

1. There are some recent exceptions. See Phil Williams and Douglas Brooks, "Captured, Criminal and Contested States," *South African Journal of International Affairs* 6, No. 2 (Winter 1999); Jean-Francois Bayert, Stephen Ellis, and Beatrice Hibou, *The Criminalization of the State in Africa* (London: James Currey, 1999); Mark Shaw, "West African Criminal Networks in South and Southern Africa," *African Affairs* 101, No. 404 (July 2002). A series of ongoing research projects, most notably at the Institute for Security Studies and the South African Institute of International Affairs, now focus on organized crime in southern Africa.

2. S. Ellis, *Crime in West Africa: A Bibliographical Essay* (Leiden, Netherlands: African Studies Centre), 9.

3. Interview by Mark Shaw, Johannesburg, July 2001.

4. *Crime as Business, Business as Crime: West African Criminal Networks in Southern Africa* (Johannesburg: South African Institute of International Affairs, 2003).

5. P. van Niekerk and L. Peterson, *Greasing the Skids of Corruption*, International Consortium of Investigative Journalists (November 4, 2002): www.publicintegrity.org/search.aspx?strSearch=Greasing+the+Skids+of+Corruption (accessed May 10, 2004).

6. *International Crime Threat Assessment* (December 2002), http://clinton4.nara.gov/WH/EOP/NSC/html/documents/pub45270/pub45270 index.html (accessed May 10, 2004), 11.

7. G. Wannenburg, "Catching the Middlemen Fuelling African Conflicts," in *South African Yearbook of International Affairs 2002/03* (Johannesburg: South African Institute of International Affairs, 2003), 283. Available online at http://members.lycos.co.uk/ocnewsletter/SGOC0903/wburg.pdf (accessed May 10, 2004).

8. U.N. Office for Drug Control and Crime Prevention, *The Drug Nexus in Africa* (Vienna: ODCCP Studies on Drugs and Crime, 1999), 100.

9. U.N. Office for Drug Control and Crime Prevention, *The Drug Nexus*, p. 101.

10. *Truth and Reconciliation Commission Report*, Section 3, Chapter 1, 2003. Available online at www.gov.za/reports/2003/trc (accessed May 10, 2004).

11. Andrew S. Natsios, "Humanitarian Relief Intervention in Somalia: The Economics of Chaos," *in Learning from Somalia: The Lessons of Armed Humanitarian Intervention*, eds. Walter Clarke and Jeffrey Herbst, 77–97 (Boulder, CO: Westview Press), 85.

12. U.N. Office for Drug Control and Crime Prevention, *The Drug Nexus*, p. 101.

13. For a detailed overview of the phenomenon, touching on many of the issues covered in this chapter, see P. B. Rich, "Warlords, State Fragmentation and the Dilemma of Humanitarian Intervention," *Small Wars and Insurgencies* 10, No. 1 (Spring 1999): 78–96; and A. Hills, "Warlords, Militia and Conflict in Contemporary Africa: A Re-Examination of Terms," *Small Wars and Insurgencies* 8, No. 1 (Spring 1997): 35–51.

14. T. Leggett, "The Sleazy Hotel Syndrome: Housing Vice in Durban and Johannesburg," *Crime and Conflict* 18 (Summer 1999): 16.

15. U.N. Office for Drug Control and Crime Prevention, *The Drug Nexus*, p. 96.

16. C. Clapham, "African Security Systems: Privatisation and the Scope for Mercenary Activity," in *The Privatisation of Security in Africa*, eds. G. Mills and J. Stremlau, 23–45

(Johannesburg: South African Institute of International Affairs, 1999), 24.

17. For a detailed overview see Eghosa E. Osaghae, *Crippled Giant: Nigeria since Independence* (London: Hurst, 1998).

18. Peter Lewis, "From Prebendalism to Predation: The Political Economy of Decline in Nigeria," *Journal of Modern African Studies* 34, No. 1 (1996): 97.

19. Friedrich Schneider and Dominik Enste, "Shadow Economies Around the World: Size, Cause and Consequences" (working paper, International Monetary Fund, WP/00/26, January 2003), 6.

20. Europe, Asia, Africa Unit: Strategic Intelligence Section, Drug Enforcement Administration, *Nigeria, Nigerian Criminals and the Drug Trade* (Washington, DC: U.S. Department of Justice, October 1996), 1–2.

21. Given that oil is produced in 12 of the 36 states, the country's constitution sets out a formula for how the wealth should be divided. Such intrastate divisions point to the fragility of the federation itself. For an overview of recent tensions see "Nigeria," *Africa Confidential* 42(15) (July 2001), 1–4.

22. Background information: Nigeria, Foreign and Commonwealth Office. Available online at www.fco.gov.uk.

23. See, for example, U.S. House of Representatives, *Combating International Crime in Africa, Hearing before the Subcommittee on Africa of the Committee on International Relations*, 105th Cong., 2nd Sess., July 15, 1998.

24. See map drawn from the U.S. government's *International Crime Threat Assessment* completed for President Clinton in 2000, p. 102. Available online at http://clinton4.nara.gov/WH/EOP/NSC/html/documents/pub45270/pub45270index.html (accessed May 20, 2004).

25. See, for example, Bayert, Ellis, and Hibou, *The Criminalization of the State in Africa*, p. 10.

26. This was encouraged by the presentation of the war in the east as "a genocidal one waged by the Muslims of Northern Nigeria who had declared a *jihad* to exterminate Igbos from the face of the earth." This, Osaghae concludes, is not without credence given "the massacres of Igbos in the north and the strategies of economic blockade and starvation pursued throughout the war." Osaghae, *Crippled Giant*, p. 66.

27. This is confirmed by earlier research in South Africa. See Ted Leggett, "The Sleazy Hotel Syndrome," pp. 15–16.

28. It would be difficult, however, to avoid problems of drug consumption that afflict all transit centers for illegal narcotics. See Axel Klein, "Trapped in the Traffick: Growing Problems of Drug Consumption in Lagos," *Journal of Modern African Studies* 32, No. 4 (1994).

29. For the case of Ghana, see Henry Bernstein, "Ghana's Drug Economy: Some Preliminary Data," *Review of African Political Economy* 79 (1999).

30. Axel Klein, "Nigeria and the Drugs War," *Review of African Political Economy* 79 (1999): 57.

31. For example, the involvement of the Liberian government in drug trafficking is explored by Stephen Ellis, *The Mask of Anarchy: The Destruction of Liberia and the Religious Dimensions of an African Civil War* (New York: New York University Press, 2001), 169–172.

32. Phil Williams and Douglas Brooks, "Captured, Criminal and Contested States: Organised Crime in Africa," *South African Journal of International Affairs* 6, No. 2 (Winter 1999).

33. Mark Shaw, *Crime and Policing in Transitional Societies*, Seminar Report, 2001, No 8. Johannesburg: South African Institute of International Affairs.

34. See De Wet Potgieter, *Contraband: South Africa and the International Trade in Ivory and Rhino Horn* (Cape Town: Queillerie, 1995).

35. Stephen Ellis, "Of Elephants and Men: Politics and Nature Conservation in South Africa," *Journal of Southern African Studies* 20, No. 1 (1994): 58.

36. Interview with former RENAMO commander, Ponto Do Ouro, Mozambique, 2003.

37. For a good overview, see Ferial Haffajee, "Inside the Hot Car Trade," *Financial Mail* (Johannesburg), August 11, 2000.

38. G. Wannenburg, "Organised Crime Thrives in Paradise," *Business Day*, July 11, 2003.

39. Interview with Mozambican nongovernmental organization in Maputo, September 2003.

40. Peter Gastrow, "Main Trends in the Development of South Africa's Organised Crime." Paper presented at a conference on South Africa After the Elections: Stock-taking and Future Perspectives, Wildbad Kreuth, Germany, September 22–23, 1999, p. 19.

41. Martin Booth, *The Dragon Syndicates: The Global Phenomenon of the Triads* (London: Doubleday, 1999), 354–356.

42. Gastrow, "Main Trends."

43. Wilfried Schärf and Clare Vale, "The Firm: Organised Crime Comes of Age during the Transition to Democracy" (unpublished paper, Institute of Criminology, University of Cape Town, 1996).

44. International Narcotics Control Board, *Report of the International Narcotics Control Board for 1999* (New York: United Nations, 2000), 28.

45. Glenn Oosthuysen, "South Africa in the Global Drug Network," in *The Illegal Drug Trade in Southern Africa: International Dimensions to a Local Crisis* (Johannesburg: South African Institute of International Affairs, 1998), 130.

46. Juan Grobbelaar and Rika Snyman, "Invasion from the North? West Africans and Crime," *Crime and Conflict* 17 (Spring 1999).

47. Grobbelaar and Snyman. "Invasion from the North?" p. 15.

48. Gary Lewis, *Mission Report: Angola* (Pretoria: U.N. Office for Drug Control and Crime Prevention, March 2000).

49. Lewis, *Mission Report.* See also, Mark Shaw, "Shared Regional Challenges: Economic Reform and Strategic Issues," Seminar Report, *Southern Africa and Mercosur: Reviewing the Relationship and Seeking Opportunities* (Johannesburg: Konrad-Adenauer-Stiftung, 2000). Also, interviews conducted in Luanda, Angola, by the author in September 2000.

50. Ted Leggett, "The Sleazy Hotel Syndrome." Of course, not all Nigerians living in the inner-city areas of Johannesburg are involved in crime. For an overview of the difficult lives of Nigerian newcomers to Johannesburg see Alan Morris, *Bleakness and Light: Inner-City Transition in Hillbrow, Johannesburg* (Johannesburg: Witwatersrand University Press, 1999), 307–328.

51. Jean Redpath, "The Hydra Phenomenon, Rural Sitting Ducks and Other Recent Trends in Organised Crime in the Western Cape" (unpublished report prepared for the National Director of Public Prosecutions, October 9, 2000), 12–13.

52. Leggett, "The Sleazy Hotel Syndrome," p. 18.

53. See examples in Paul Thulare, "Welcome to Hellbrow: Talking to Johannesburg's Drug Syndicates," *Crime and Conflict* 16 (Winter 1999). Also, Leggett, "The Sleazy Hotel Syndrome."

54. "Downfall of 'Durban's Biggest Gangster'" (July 23, 1999). *Mail & Guardian.* Available online at http://archive.mg.co.za (accessed May 17, 2004).

55. U.S. Department of State, *Trafficking in Persons Report 2003* (June 2003). Available online at www.state.gov/g/tip/rls/tiprpt/2003 (accessed May 17, 2004).

56. International Organization for Migration, *The Trafficking of Women and Children in the Southern Africa Region* (March 24, 2003). Available online at www.iom.int/documents/publication/en/southernafrica%5Ftrafficking.pdf (accessed May 17, 2004).

57. "Trafficking in Persons," Report 2003.

58. Mgendi, Catherine. "Corruption and Drugs in Kenya," *Africa Recovery* 12, No. 1 (1998): Box 3. Available online at www.un.org/ecosocdev/geninfo/afrec/vol12no1/drugboxs.htm#Corruption (accessed May 17, 2000).

59. U.N. Office on Drug and Crime, *Global Illicit Drug Trends 2003* (Vienna: UNODC, 2003).

60. Special assignment documentary, screened on South African Broadcasting Corporation, October 2003, and interviews with a Mozambican journalist, September 2003.

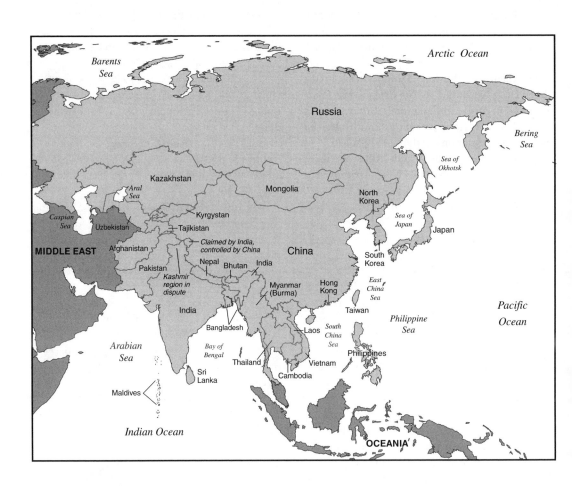

19

Organized Crime in Asia

RICHARD H. WARD

DANIEL J. MABREY

For most of the developing economies of Asia, crime in the past two decades has been a troubling issue, characterized by corruption, unstable or weak governments, and in many cases, criminal justice systems that have neither the funding nor the technology necessary to cope with increasingly sophisticated criminal activity. In many countries throughout Asia, organized criminal groups have long histories, in some cases dating back hundreds of years. In virtually all cases, these groups have been evolutionary, adapting to changing political conditions, warfare (both domestic and international), and perhaps most important, the development of technology, communications, travel, and the emergence of a global economy.

In addition to general increases in traditional criminal activity, such as robbery, burglary, theft, and assault, a number of countries have been the focus of transnational criminal activity, particularly in the areas of drug trafficking, illegal immigration, arms trafficking, the exploitation of women and children, and widespread public and private corruption. Behind most of these activities are organized and enterprising criminal groups. Some examples include the Triads and Tongs in Hong Kong and China, the Yakuza in Japan, the United Bamboo Gang in Taiwan, warlords in Myanmar, the Nam Cam Gang in Vietnam, and other ethnic entrepreneurs throughout Asia.

In many cases, there are symbiotic relationships between groups that have resulted

AUTHORS' NOTE: The authors would like to express their appreciation to Dr. Cindy Moors for her assistance in the preparation of this chapter.

in a global network of organized criminal activity. Various forms of criminal trafficking, money laundering, and illegal enterprises involving technology (e.g., cybercrime) are the most common activities of these groups. In adapting to a new world order, many criminal groups in Southeast Asia have reinvented themselves, both to evade international law enforcement efforts and to take advantage of new "markets" throughout the world.

At the heart of these criminal activities is the world market in illegal drugs, ranging from poppy production for heroin to new demands for psychotropic substances, such as methamphetamines and other forms of "designer" drugs like 3,4 methylenedioxy methylamphetamine (commonly known as ecstasy), gammahydroxybutyrate (GHB), Rohypnol, ketamine (Special K), methcathinone ("cat"), and mescaline.

With the opening of China to the West in the 1980s and the fall of the Soviet Union in December 1991, a growing market in illegal immigration and the exploitation of women and children have also become lucrative sources of income for organized crime. In addition, the technological advances of the past decade have fostered child pornography, money laundering, and Internet scams. Asian organized crime groups have become an integral part of this burgeoning international phenomenon.

It is widely assumed that organized crime cannot exist to any substantial degree in the absence of corruption, and many Asian countries find themselves facing growing levels of government, judicial, and police involvement in corrupt activities that support criminal enterprises.

This chapter examines Asian organized crime, predominantly in East and Southeast Asia, from the perspective of developing nations, industrialized countries, and democratization. Although these three variables are not mutually exclusive, they do reflect in large measure a typology that relates to criminal activity. For example, crime in developing countries is less likely to be transnational in nature, with the exception of illegal migration, exploitation of women and children, and to some degree, drug trafficking. Crime in industrial countries—democratic or autocratic—is characterized by more sophisticated criminality and organized crime. There is also likely to be more cross-border or transnational crime. Countries that have placed a greater emphasis on the rule of law and democratic freedoms have seen increases in street-level crime, such as robbery and burglary, and are more likely to be plagued by sophisticated international organized crime groups. To better understand some of these relationships, it is important to be familiar with the cultural, political, and economic environments of different countries and how they contribute to organized criminal activity. Countries in the sample include the following:[1]

- China (The People's Republic of China)
- Hong Kong
- Japan
- Republic of Korea
- Philippines
- Cambodia
- Singapore
- Taiwan (Republic of China)
- Vietnam
- Thailand
- Myanmar (formerly Burma)

To better understand organized crime in Asia, one must also recognize that different legal structures and the justice systems of different countries, particularly police, courts, and corrections, have an impact on public order and crime control. Methods of training, education, and selection of personnel in each of these areas frequently differ between countries. The following analysis is illustrative rather than exhaustive and provides a brief overview of the justice systems in select Asian countries.[2]

ASIAN CRIMINAL JUSTICE SYSTEMS

China

The People's Republic of China, with a population of more than 1 billion, is the largest country in the world and has evolved since its inception in 1949 from a relatively isolated country to a burgeoning superpower. The criminal justice system has undergone numerous changes from the time when the country opened up to the West in the late 1970s and early 1980s. Although crime in China is relatively low by Western standards, China has experienced an increasing crime problem over the past two decades, due in no small measure to a growing economy and the ability of organized crime to move more freely throughout the country. China's police service, known as Public Security, numbers more than 1.5 million personnel and is centralized under the Ministry of Public Security. Judicial and correctional services come under the Ministry of Justice. Over the past 20 years, these two ministries have undergone sweeping changes, modeled in many ways on European and American concepts of criminal justice. The criminal laws and judicial process have also undergone key revisions, although, in practice, there is a major difference between the written legal system and the actual practices of the system.

Organized crime in China is somewhat amorphous but generally takes two similar forms. The first involves criminal activity by gangs such as the Triads, frequently in cooperative ventures involving black market activities, large burglaries, thefts, and hijackings. These gangs are also involved in extortion of small businesses. Criminal syndicates make up the second form of Chinese organized crime and are involved in more sophisticated crimes such as prostitution, illegal emigration, slavery, and other organized forms of vice.

Historically, Chinese law enforcement officials maintained that organized crime was virtually eliminated under the leadership of Mao Zedong, but it is doubtful that organized crime ever left the country; rather, the Triad societies,[3] which moved to Hong Kong following the fall of the Kuomintang government,[4] maintained a clandestine presence on the mainland. In 1993, the minister of public security admitted that Triads were operating in China ("Guangdong Takes Hard Line," 1993). Although data relative to the increase of Triad activity in China are scarce, public officials acknowledge the increasing presence of Triad groups from Hong Kong (see Figures 19.1 and 19.2).

There have also been reports of Triads forming drug trafficking networks with the Bamboo Union gangs in Taiwan, the Yakuza in Japan, and even with drug cartels from Colombia. The U.S. Bureau for International Narcotics and Law Enforcement Affairs reported that China is a major transit point for illegal narcotics produced in the Golden Triangle, and the largest number of seizures of Southeast Asian heroin now occur within the country (U.S. Department of State, 2002). The southern areas of China will also continue to be major transit routes for Southeast Asian heroin. Heroin, particularly, is pouring into China from Thailand, Myanmar, and Laos. Despite death sentences for traffickers and a widespread war on drugs, the Chinese government admits that it is facing an uncontrollable crisis, especially given the reported increases in drug use by the young. China is also a major source country for precursor chemicals such as ephedrine, pseudoephedrine, and acetic anhydride and is a major producer of crystal methamphetamine (Drug Enforcement Administration [DEA], 2002b).

Official figures show the use of drugs, including ecstasy and amphetamines, up by more than 25 percent last year. The official number of addicts is 860,000 in a population of 1.2 billion. The crackdown has had a sharp effect on young club-goers, particularly in coastal cities. Many wind up in mental hospitals and are left there until a $6,500 bribe is paid. (August, 2001, p. D13)

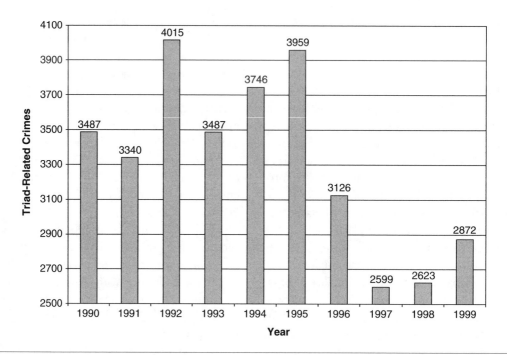

Figure 19.1   Total Number of Triad-Related Crimes in China, 1990 to 1999

SOURCE: Tat-wing (2001, p. 39).

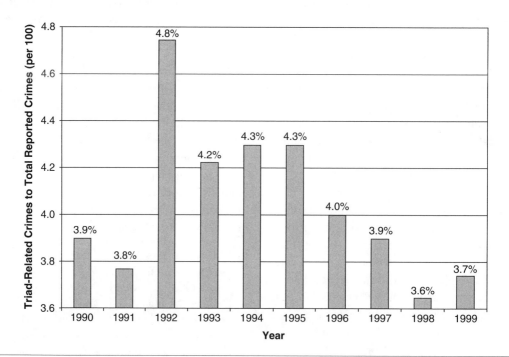

Figure 19.2   The Percentage of Triad-Related Crimes to Total Reported Crimes, 1990 to 1999

SOURCE: Tat-wing (2001, p. 39).

In 1991, there were an estimated 148,000 registered drug users, and despite a rapid increase in the number of drug rehabilitation centers, the number of users had grown to more than 900,000 by the end of 2001. Some independent reports estimate the number of drug users is about 7 million (Ching-Ching, 2003). Most drug users are under 35 and take heroin, intravenously, which leaves them vulnerable to AIDS[5] (Ching-Ching, 2003). China's nationwide "drug-free community" program resulted in some 66,000 drug addicts being sent for compulsory treatment to medical centers, and 11,000 to labor camps in 2001 (Schauble, 2001).

Drug trafficking is one of a number of crimes punishable by death in China. Unemployment, and what is commonly referred to as the "floating population," has created migration to the cities and contributes to the crime problem. In 2000, more than 36,000 people were charged with drug trafficking ("China Targets Golden Triangle," 2001).

> The ethnic Yi of southern China have been leaving home in droves, joining an avalanche of unemployed workers and idle farmers crisscrossing the land searching for a piece of the new economic miracle . . . [a]s many as 90 percent of these low skilled workers can't find jobs. Many turn to drug trafficking. A dealer can make more money in a day than a farmer makes in a year. Some of their best customers are other migrants from their villages. (Ching-Ching, 2003, E6)

The exploitation of women and children for sex and human trafficking by organized criminal groups represents another major problem for China. Yunnan, Sichuan, and Guizhou provinces are the principal areas from which many women are kidnapped and sold into slavery. Within the country, prostitution has become a major source of revenue for the poor, and as drug addiction has increased, the problem has become more widespread. In the larger cities, organized crime has taken over much of the trade, and corruption of police and others, such as hotel employees and cab drivers, has contributed to the problem.

> The pre-revolutionary custom of bride selling has returned to rural villages in China. Marriage brokers—essentially slave dealers—search the countryside, offering girls for sale to prospective husbands. The recruiters kidnap and buy women and girls. From 1991 through 1996, Chinese police freed 88,000 kidnapped women and children and arrested 143,000 people for participating in the slave trade. (Liu & Elliott, 1998, p. 48)

Illegal emigration has also become a lucrative business for organized crime, and the smuggling of individuals to all parts of the world has become commonplace. Chinese organized crime groups, especially the Triads, are deeply involved in the human trade business. Traffickers, known as "snakeheads," are part of a global network, wherein an individual may pay as much as $30,000 or more to enter the United States. Within the United States, a well-organized criminal network has been developed to foster illegal immigration. Many, if not most, of the illegal immigrants must work for years to pay off their debt and, in the case of women, many are destined to be forced into prostitution (DeStefano & Gordy, 1994).

> Chinese Triads have taken over the smuggling of illegal immigrants from smaller "mom and pop" organizations as an increasingly attractive alternative to drug trafficking because it promises multibillion dollar profits without the same severe penalties if caught. Earnings from illegal immigrant trade are estimated to total $3.2 billion per year, yet it is punishable in the United States by a maximum sentence of only five years in jail. Most who are convicted under current laws are sentenced to less than six months. (Bolz, 1995, p. 147)

The increase in drug trafficking and other organized criminal activities in China has contributed largely to government and police corruption. Despite severe penalties and a number of ongoing crackdowns, the problem has become increasingly severe. Former Minister of Public Security Jia Chunwang vowed to attack police corruption in 1999 promising to contain police corruption within 3 years. He cited bribery, abuse of power, negligence, direct involvement in illegal activities and collaboration with criminals, illegal use of weapons, and dereliction of duty while enforcing the law as the most serious violations ("Minister Vows to Further Curb," 1999).

A grassroots survey found that between 1997 and 1999, the Public Security force was identified as the most corrupt of all government bodies. The survey found that local police were involved in gambling, prostitution and drug-trafficking rackets, and shakedowns of the public, including levying fines and detaining people without authorization (Hsieh, 2001). Jia's reform efforts resulted in numerous arrests and convictions, not the least of which was the conviction of a former vice-minister of public security, Li Jizhou, who was sentenced to death for corruption. Reform efforts also resulted in a major crackdown on government and business leaders. Local procurators recovered almost 1.3 billion yuan (about $157 million) from corrupt officials over a 5-year period, from 1999 to 2003. In 2002, prosecutors instituted 62 major cases involving corruption, 79 cases involving government officials, and 27 cases involving municipal officials. According to some reports, approximately 170 million yuan (about $20.5 million) was recovered in these cases ("China: Beijing Authorities," 2003).

Beyond the Triads and sophisticated criminal syndicates, thousands of minor gangs exist throughout the country; they are involved in a wide range of illegal activities, from theft to extortion thefts and commerce violations. As they become more sophisticated and form larger criminal organizations, it is likely that they will broaden their activities and begin to cooperate with other criminal groups.

Hong Kong

In 1997, Hong Kong was returned to the People's Republic of China, ending a 100-year lease to the United Kingdom. Under the transition agreement, the Chinese government established a policy of "one country, two systems," agreeing that the former colony would continue to follow a legal system based on British common law for a period of 50 years. As one of the most successful communities in Asia, Hong Kong has one of the most advanced criminal justice systems in the world. Nevertheless, it continues to be the center of Triad activity in that part of the world.[6] One police estimate calculated as many as 50 triad societies in Hong Kong, the largest being the "Wo Sing Wo" and "14-K" (Macko, 1997).

With a police force of more than 27,000 personnel and a budget close to $HK6.7 billion, this relatively small geographic city has a population of 6,815,800 (February 2003 estimate). As previously noted, the judicial system is based on British common law that allowed a relatively independent judiciary to be adopted under Chinese control, which is exercised through an administrator appointed by the government.

Compared with mainland China, Hong Kong's crime rates are generally higher, with theft being the most significant criminal activity. However, one must recognize that Hong Kong is a densely populated city, and when compared with other large cities, the crime rate is comparable.

Unlike many of the other countries in Asia, illegal drug trafficking is not viewed as a major problem, and police place a high priority on drug suppression and the control of precursor chemicals. Drugs smuggled into Hong Kong are primarily for local consumption (U.S. Department of State, 2002).

One of the more interesting criminal justice units in Hong Kong is the Independent Commission Against Corruption (ICAC), an independent body established when Hong Kong was under British control. ICAC's reputation for fighting corruption is unparalleled, and the organization has some extraordinary powers to conduct investigations. Over the years, Hong Kong has been rated as one of the least corrupt places in the world. The Chinese government has continued to support ICAC and its activities, and in a conference in 2003 in cooperation with Interpol, officials from many countries attended to observe the anti-corruption activities in this unique city.

Japan

Japan is one of the most advanced governments in Asia, with a well-trained and organized criminal justice system. The political system has been influenced by 19th-century German and British Parliamentary models and the country's constitution was rewritten following World War II by U.S. advisers. The legal system is based largely on the legal systems of Germany and France, as well as the United States model, while facets of Oriental law continue to be imbedded in the culture (Moriyama, 1997).

In recent years, a sluggish economy and revelations about the influence of organized crime, the Yakuza or *Boryokudan*, in government and business have cast a cloud over crime control efforts.

The yakuza make millions of dollars a year through corporate extortion, and the *sokaiya* (shareholders' meeting men) are the masters of the enterprise. *Sokaiya* will buy a small number of shares in a company so that they can attend shareholders' meetings. In preparation for the meeting, the *sokaiya* gather damaging information about the company and its officers; secret mistresses, tax evasion, unsafe factory conditions, and pollution are all fodder for the *sokaiya*.

They will then contact management and threaten to disclose whatever embarrassing information they have at the shareholders' meeting unless they are "compensated.". . . In Japan, where people fear embarrassment and shame much more than physical threats, executives usually give the *sokaiya* whatever they want. (Bruno, 2003)

The Yakuza influence has infiltrated banks, real estate agencies, corporations, and government, prompting major scandals (Bremner, 1996). There are an estimated 110,000 active members who are part of as many as 2,500 "families" (Bruno, 2003). In 2001, police arrested 9,893 Yakuza members for possession of stimulants, 1,949 for extortion, and 1,398 for gambling (National Police Agency, 2002).

Given the strong presence of the Yakuza in Japan's private sector, it is not surprising then that Japan's government and police agencies have also been negatively affected by corruption. A crackdown on police corruption in 2000 resulted in disciplinary action against 525 officers, who were fired, suspended, or disciplined, in cases involving all provinces in the country. This was the highest number of corruption cases reported in 10 years ("Police Corruption Cases," 2001).

The exploitation of women by the Yakuza has been a continuing problem, largely as a result of the large number of foreigners trafficked or smuggled from the Philippines and Thailand who are involved in prostitution. The Yakuza have been known to pay between US$2,400 and US$18,000 for female Taiwanese and Filipino prostitutes. According to one report, there were more than 150,000 foreign prostitutes in Japan in 1998, most of whom entered the country legally as entertainers, a euphemism for those engaged in the booming sex industry (Coalition Against Trafficking in Women, 1998). Approximately one third of all prostitution cases in Japan involve teenagers (Hughes, Sporcic, Mendelsohn, & Chirgwin, 1999c).

Cambodia

The major transnational criminal activities in Cambodia are controlled largely by Chinese and Myanmarese organized crime groups and are closely tied to drug and human trafficking. Cambodia has been cited by the U.S. Drug Enforcement Administration (DEA) (2002a) as a source country for the growth of marijuana, which is trafficked largely in Europe, and as a transit country on the international drug market for the distribution of Southeast Asian heroin. Heroin is moved from Laos and Thailand through Phnom Penh as part of the global drug trade.

Law enforcement efforts against organized crime in Cambodia are largely ineffectual. In 2000, only 124 people were arrested for drug offenses (81 were foreign nationals), and only 1,108 kilograms of cannabis products were seized by the National Anti-Drug Unit (DEA, 2002a). Law enforcement agencies are underfunded and lack even basic training in drug control efforts, a problem that is further compounded by endemic corruption. Despite this, Cambodia was removed by the United States from the list of major drug-producing and transit countries in 2002 (U.S. Department of State, 2002).

Within the country, there has been a significant increase in the use of methamphetamines by young people, prompting the government to take an active role in working with international agencies in antidrug activities. Nevertheless, widespread corruption hampers enforcement efforts. Gambling, prostitution, and money laundering have also fostered the existence of global organized crime networks in the country.

Organized crime groups control prostitution, and the exploitation of women is a major problem within Cambodia.

Virgins, who have been sold to brothels by trafficking agents, are confined to the brothel or a hotel room until the first client comes. Due to the belief that sex with a virgin has rejuvenating properties, her first client is charged an expensive amount. Advertised as "special commodities," virgins are also attractive in that they are less likely to have AIDS or other sexually transmitted diseases. The customer pays from $300 to $400 to have sex with her for one week in a local hotel chosen by the brothel owner. (Flamm & Ngo, 1997)

Although Cambodia has no extradition or mutual legal assistance treaty with the United States, the government has cooperated with U.S. law enforcement agencies by deporting persons wanted in the United States for crimes, including narcotics. In 2001, the government signed the U.N. Convention against Transnational Organized Crime, the Protocol to Prevent, Suppress and Punish Trafficking in Persons, and the Protocol against the Smuggling of Migrants. Despite this, the country rivals Thailand as a major haven for prostitution, and unofficial estimates indicate that most of the 15,000 prostitutes (many ranging in age from 15–18) are brought into the country from China and Vietnam. Consequently, the AIDS virus is also a serious problem (Hughes et al., 1999b).

Republic of Korea

South Korea, with a population of 48 million (July 2003 estimate), employs a civil law system wherein written laws are the primary source of reference, as opposed to statutes or ordinances. The criminal law classifies crimes into five broad categories: (1) crimes that breach the national interest, (2) crimes that breach the social interest, (3) crimes of a personal nature, (4) tax-related crimes, and (5) drug crimes. Children between the ages of 14 and 20 are handled under the juvenile legal system (U.S. Department of Justice, 1997).

Organized crime in Korea has a unique history when compared to that of other Asian nations. As Korea began to modernize in the 1800s, the population swelled and began to concentrate in urban centers where unemployed

Table 19.1   Persons Arrested and Punished for Organized Crimes in Korea, 1995 to 1999

Year	1995	1996	1997	1998	1999	Total
Number arrested	1,763	1,928	2,691	2,303	2,750	11,435
Number punished	575	578	779	750	653	3,335
Percentage punished	32.6	30.0	28.9	32.6	23.7	29.2

SOURCE: Park (2001, p. 69).

young men banded together and idled about city streets. These groups of young men were called *Keondal,* meaning scamps, and they worked in places like bars, gambling houses, and construction sites. The *Keondal* were not considered criminal groups, even though they engaged in criminal activities and internecine violence, because they honored loyalty and faithfulness, and they would sometimes help the weak and the poor. Much like the Japanese Yakuza, the lives of *Keondal* are an attractive subject of movies and are admired by some Korean youth (Park, 2001).

In the 1960s, organized crime groups emerged as an influential power in entertainment districts and quickly became associated with politicians, who used them as their personal henchmen to attack political rivals. The military government in Korea at the time arrested over 13,000 members of these political gangs and temporarily stamped out organized crime in Korea.

Throughout the 1970s and 1980s, Korean organized crime groups developed into nationwide organizations, with some groups even extending their activities to foreign countries through associations with the Yakuza and other organized crime groups in the United States. This led the Korean government to officially declare a "war" against organized crime. Members could be arrested and punished for forming, joining, or even affiliating with criminal organizations. As of January 2000, the prosecutors in the Violent Crime Department (the agency charged with combating organized crime)

estimated that there were over 11,500 members in 404 organized crime families or groups in Korea, with the average criminal organization having 35 members (Park, 2001). Special surveillance is conducted on 647 members in 117 families or groups, the majority of whom are teenagers (see Table 19.1) (Park, 2001).

Drug trafficking is the main criminal enterprise for Korean organized crime, with most shipments originating in drug factories in China and Japan before being smuggled into countries throughout Asia and into the United States. According to the U.S. Department of State (2002), Korea is neither a major user nor a major producer of dangerous drugs, although drug use by young people is increasing. In 2000, there were approximately 10,000 arrests for drug violations (U.S. Department of State, 2002).

Prostitution and the exploitation of women is a common problem, due in no small measure to the presence of the large American military presence in the country. It is estimated that there are 18,000 registered and 9,000 unregistered prostitutes near military bases (Hughes et al., 1999d). According to one report, many younger children are lured into the sex trade because men prefer young girls because they believe they are less likely to contract AIDS and other sexually transmitted diseases (Hughes et al., 1999d). Russian and Korean-Chinese criminal organizations are involved in trafficking women and migrant workers. The Russian Mafiya provides job opportunities as entertainers to young Russian women and assists them in obtaining Korean tourist visas. In this process, the Russian Mafiya receives commissions from the applicants. The women who apply are sent to Korea to work in entertainment businesses as dancers or barmaids, although they eventually end up as prostitutes (Park, 2001).

Myanmar

Myanmar, formerly Burma, is a major opium-producing country, and under the leadership of a military junta, is one of the most lawless countries in Asia. The military-controlled criminal justice system is rife with corruption.

[In 2002], under the generals' protective partnering with drug lords, Burma was the source for 68 percent of the world's opium production. And methamphetamine from Burma has been flooding into Thailand. One of the crudest of the junta's human rights abuses has been its unceasing exploitation of forced labor. In November 2000, the International Labor Organization, a UN agency, took the unprecedented step of punishing the Burmese regime by invoking an article of its charter that requires all the ILO's 175 member states to review their policies toward Burma on the supposition that each would decide the most effective ways to compel the junta to end the practice of forced labor. ("Forced Labor in Burma," 2002, p. A18)

Drug production and trafficking is controlled by several "armies," which in effect are perhaps the largest organized crime groups in the world. Armed ethnic groups such as the United Wa State Army (UWSA), the Kokang Chinese, and the Myanmar National Democratic Alliance Army control the cultivation areas, refine opium into heroin, and also produce methamphetamine. These heavily armed ethnic groups have promised to eliminate opium production, and

it is believed that the Eastern Shan State Army area has eliminated opium production (DEA, 2002c).

In areas controlled by the UWSA, the government has virtually no control and has not attempted to eliminate opium production, claiming that cracking down on the Wa jeopardizes Burma's national security (U.S. Department of State, 2002).

Wei Hsueh-kang, the commander of the Southern Military Region of the UWSA, is the most significant drug trafficker in Myanmar because of his contacts in both Southeast Asia and North America. Wei was indicted in 1993 in the Eastern District of New York for conspiracy to smuggle heroin into the United States. . . .

As the largest drug-producing and trafficking group in the country, the UWSA and its leaders continue to amass millions of dollars. The UWSA has expanded geographically and militarily; its social, economic, and political influence rivals the government. (DEA, 2002c, p. 6)

Corruption is endemic within Myanmar, and between 2000 and 2002, "32 police officers have been punished for narcotics-related corruption: 17 received jail sentences; 4 have been terminated; 6 officers were forced to retire" (U.S. Department of State, 2002, pp. viii–11). At the same time, the government's war on drugs has been costly to the police, and 828 officers have been killed since 1988, with another 2,515 wounded (Wenge, Aung, Namdar, & Maiyalarp, 2000). In 1999, 24 judges were charged with taking bribes, and this increased to 28 in 2000 and 66 in 2001 ("Burmese Leader Calls for Justice," 2002).

Myanmar is also a major source of women and children who are trafficked to Pakistan and Thailand by organized criminal groups, many of whom are under the age of 18. Many of the victims are lured by job placement agencies, frequently controlled by organized crime groups, and other young girls are simply abducted from hill tribes and exported into the sex trade (Hughes et al., 1999a).

Other Asian Countries

Although this chapter focuses on the countries above, it should be noted that organized criminal groups have expanded to include most countries in Asia in one form or another.

In Taiwan, organized crime is controlled largely by the Bamboo Union Gangs. These gangs have close relationships with Triad groups in China and Hong Kong and are primarily involved in drug trafficking (methamphetamine and heroin) from mainland China (U.S. Department of State, 2002). Prostitution, controlled largely by organized crime, was outlawed in 1997, giving rise to "floating brothels" off the coast. According to one estimate there were 60,000 female child prostitutes (ages 12 to 17) in Taiwan in 1999, most of whom were sold by their parents to criminal syndicates ("Floating Brothels Popular," 1998).

In contrast to most countries in Asia, the tiny country of Singapore stands as one of the few places where strict law enforcement and strong central government impose stringent fines, extended prison sentences, and capital punishment to maintain public security. In 1973, the Misuse of Drugs Act established severe penalties for drug violations, including long prison sentences and capital punishment for trafficking and production of drugs. Despite the severe penalties, there are a number of organized criminal organizations operating in the country. In 2000, almost half of the 56 major operations conducted by the Central Narcotic Bureau were against criminal syndicates (U.S. Department of State, 2002).

The Philippines has long been a haven for the sex industry, both within the country and as part of the human export trade. Organized crime groups control virtually every aspect of the commerce in women and children. Thousands of women are sent to Japan,

Thailand, and other countries. The country is also a major provider of young children for pedophiles who travel from countries throughout the world, including the United States, on so-called sex tours (Juvida, 1997).

Thailand's sex industry is one of the most notorious in the world, and is a multibillion-dollar industry. Organized crime groups have imported an estimated 1 million women from China, Laos, and Vietnam to Thailand. An estimated 400,000 children under the age of 16 work in brothels, bars, and nightclubs (Serjeant, 1998). Global criminal networks involved in Thailand's drug trafficking, money laundering, and prostitution operate from China, Hong Kong, Japan, and Singapore.

Most of the transnational organized crime groups operating in Vietnam are from bases in other Asian countries, but there are a growing number of Vietnamese organized gangs (namely, affiliates of the Nam Cam Gang), many of which display characteristics of the more sophisticated groups in Hong Kong and China. Accordingly, corruption of public officials and the police is increasing. Vietnam is ranked by the United States among the top 26 drug-producing and -trafficking countries in the world ("Seven Vietnamese Police Officers," 2000). In 1995, the U.S. Department of State identified Vietnam as a major transit point and production entity for heroin. Heroin from Laos, Myanmar, China, and Thailand and marijuana from Cambodia are frequently moved through Vietnam by organized crime groups.

THE FUTURE OF ASIAN ORGANIZED CRIME

One need not speculate to conclude that organized crime in Asia will continue to grow well into the next decade. Despite a number of breakthroughs in major cases, the growth in transnational organized crime throughout the world sees the "fingerprints" of both traditional and nontraditional groups.

Traditional criminal enterprises include the Chinese Triads based in Hong Kong, Taiwan, and Macau, as well as the Japanese Yakuza. Nontraditional criminal enterprises include groups such as Chinese criminally influenced tongs, Triad affiliates, and other Asian street gangs situated in several continents with sizable Asian communities (Federal Bureau of Investigation, 2003, p. 16).

Within the individual countries that have spawned organized criminal activity, many groups have expanded their operations because of weak criminal justice systems and high levels of police corruption. Many of these groups have histories over several hundred years, involving "the ever expanding, hierarchical network that a person develops throughout life involving numerous reciprocal relationships and obligations to the people to whom one is bonded" (Morrison, 2003, p. 6). The strength of the Chinese Triads and the Japanese Yakuza are founded on these types of relationships in Asia.

One of the most important changes in the past two decades has been the introduction of new forms, or at least more sophisticated forms, of enterprise crime. Criminal groups are extensively involved in human smuggling and corruption, and contribute to the changing nature of the drug trade. There is evidence that many of the traditional groups in the area of human smuggling have been "replaced with small individual cells that operate independently and are motivated by financial gain rather than honor" (Mabrey, 2003, p. 8). This changing trend toward the "subcontracting" of criminal activities to street gangs and loosely tied affiliates poses a new dilemma for law enforcement in efforts to develop intelligence and clear cases. There is no effective mechanism in many of these developing countries to conduct sophisticated criminal investigations into organized crime. Many of the police and security forces lack both the training and technology necessary to carry out such investigations.

In addition to the illegal drug trade, the most common form of activity affecting countries with well-developed organized criminal syndicates is corruption. However, it is important to recognize that corruption takes many forms and may involve different levels of government as well as the private sector. In some countries, such as Japan, government corruption is tied largely to the private sector, which in turn is influenced in large measure by the Yakuza. In Singapore, there is very little corruption among government and police officials, and traditionally, this small country has been used largely as a transit point. On the other hand, low pay and low status contribute to widespread police and government corruption in Myanmar and Cambodia. Thailand, under the reform government of Prime Minister Thaksin Shinawatra, has cracked down heavily on drug trafficking, but the country remains a haven for pornography, the exploitation of women and children, and the illegal sex trade. Police corruption in the form of payoffs for overlooking the sex trade is common.

Improved international law enforcement networks have been strengthened through the efforts of the United Nations, Interpol, and other global organizations. In the private sector, groups such as the American Society of Industrial Security, which includes many members from multinational and global corporations, have also become more active in fostering cooperation and intelligence sharing. Another more recent approach has been the expansion of programs that assign law enforcement officers to other countries. Many of these officers work closely with their counterparts in the host country, focusing on the investigation of transnational organized criminal groups. The United States is the largest participant in assigning federal agents to other countries. The DEA, U.S. Customs Service, the Federal Bureau of Investigation, the Immigration and Naturalization Service, the Secret Service (responsible for controlling counterfeiting), and the U.S.

Postal Inspection Service are but some of the American agencies with representatives abroad.

The U.S.-initiated International Law Enforcement Academies (ILEA) in Budapest, Bangkok, and Gabarone have cooperative relationships with host countries to provide training to police. The ILEA in Roswell, New Mexico, has trained police officials from more than 40 countries in management and focuses on strategic approaches to controlling international crime. Likewise, exchange programs such as those offered by the Office of International Criminal Justice and colleges and universities present criminal justice practitioners and academics the opportunity to study the successes and failures of other countries. Despite these efforts, Asian criminal organizations have continued to expand their activities, in many cases teaming up with criminal enterprise groups from countries throughout the world, including the American and Italian mafia, Colombian and Mexican cartels, the Russian Mafiya, and emerging groups in Eastern Europe. Organized crime now has its hand in the global community.

NOTES

1. This is not a random sample but, rather, reflects different political and economic systems.

2. For a more comprehensive description of justice systems throughout the world see *The World Factbook of Criminal Justice Systems* at www.ojp.usdoj.gov/bjs/abstract/wfcj.htm.

3. Triad societies have their roots in 17th-century China.

4. The Kuomintang government, under the leadership of Chiang Kai-shek, moved to the island of Taiwan and formed a new country, which is in dispute today; the Chinese government maintains that Taiwan is still a province of China.

5. Official estimates indicate that there are about 1 million people in China with the human immunodeficiency virus, which can lead to AIDS. Some experts maintain that the actual number could be double this figure (Ching-Ching, 2003).

According to the Ministry of Health, between 1995 and 2001 the average infection rate among drug users rose from 0.04% to nearly 5%, with drug use being the leading cause of the rapid HIV/AIDS increase ("China Reports New HIV/AIDS Statistics," 2001).

6. With the transition to Communist rule, many of the Triad groups relocated to other parts of the world, although there continues to be a Triad presence in the former British colony.

REFERENCES

August, O. (2001, February 12). China locking addicts in mental hospitals. *London Times*, p. D13.

Bolz, J. (1995, September). Chinese organized crime and illegal alien trafficking: Humans as a commodity. *Asian Affairs: An American Review*, 22, 147.

Bremner, B. (1996, January 1). How the mob burned the banks. *Business Week*, p. 42.

Bruno, A. (2003). Unique gang organizations: The Yakuza. *Court TV: Crime Library*. Retrieved May 12, 2003, from www.crimelibrary.com/gangsters_outlaws/gang/yakuza/1.html

Burmese leader calls for justice to be administered "correctly and fairly." (2002, July 10). BBC Worldwide Monitoring. *The New Light of Myanmar*. Retrieved May 2003 from Lexis Nexis Database.

China: Beijing authorities recover millions of dollars in anti-graft crackdown. (2003, January 15). *BBC Monitoring Asia Pacific*. Retrieved May 2003 from Lexis Nexis Database.

China reports new HIV/AIDS statistics. (2001, August 24). Xinhua News Agency. Retrieved May 13, 2003, from Lexis Nexis Database.

China targets golden triangle as drug use soars. (2001, February 10). *Deutsche Presse Agentur*. International News.

Ching-Ching, N. (2003, January 24). China struggles to combat drug use: Heroin becomes a scourge in poor regions of the country where its use is soaring among her young. *Los Angeles Times*, p. E6.

Coalition Against Trafficking in Women. (1998, Winter). *CATW-Asia Pacific Newsletter*, 1.2.

DeStefano, A. M., & Gordy, M. (1994, April 6). Raids smash alien smuggling network. *Newsday.*

Drug Enforcement Administration. (2002a, March). *Drug intelligence brief: Cambodia country brief.* Washington, DC: Author.

Drug Enforcement Administration. (2002b, March). *Drug intelligence brief: China country brief.* Washington, DC: Author.

Drug Enforcement Administration. (2002c, March). *Drug intelligence brief: Myanmar country brief.* Washington, DC: Author.

Federal Bureau of Investigation. (2003, April). Organized crime: The FBI perspective. *Crime and Justice International, 19*(72), 13–16.

Flamm, M., & Ngo, K. C. (1997, February 23). Children of the dust. *Bangkok Post.*

Floating brothels popular in Taiwan. (1998, July 22). Associated Press. Retrieved May 2003 from Lexis Nexis Database.

Forced labor in Burma. (2002, March 19). *Boston Globe,* p. A18. Retrieved May 2003 from Lexis Nexis Database.

Guangdong takes hard line on Triads. (1993, May 28). *Hong Kong Standard,* p. 3.

Hsieh, D. (2001, November 22). Corruption in China's police force intolerable, says minister. *Straits Times* (Singapore), p. A2.

Hughes, D. M., Sporcic, L. J., Mendelsohn, N. Z., & Chirgwin, V. (1999a). Burma/Myanmar. *World factbook on global sexual exploitation.* Coalition Against Trafficking in Women. Retrieved May 9, 2004, from www.catwinternational.org/fb/Burma_Myanmar.html

Hughes, D. M., Sporcic, L. J., Mendelsohn, N. Z., & Chirgwin, V. (1999b). Cambodia. *World factbook on global sexual exploitation.* Coalition Against Trafficking in Women. Retrieved May 9, 2004, from www.catwinternational.org/fb/Cambodia.html

Hughes, D. M., Sporcic, L. J., Mendelsohn, N. Z., & Chirgwin, V. (1999c). Japan. *World factbook on global sexual exploitation.* Coalition Against Trafficking in Women. Retrieved May 9, 2004, from www.catwinternational.org/ fb/Japan.html

Hughes, D. M., Sporcic, L. J., Mendelsohn, N. Z., & Chirgwin, V. (1999d). Trafficking in women and prostitution in the Southeast Asia and Pacific. *World factbook on global sexual exploitation.* Coalition Against Trafficking in Women. Retrieved May 9, 2004, from www.catwinternational.org/fb/Asia_Pacific.html

Juvida, S. F. (1997, October 12). Philippines—children: Scourge of child prostitution. *IPS-Third World News.* Retrieved May 2003 from Lexis Nexis Database.

Liu B., & Elliott, D. (1998, June 29). Trying to stand on two feet [Special Report, Women]. *Newsweek,* p. 48.

Mabrey, D. J. (2003, March). Human smuggling from China. *Crime and Justice International, 19*(71), 5–11.

Macko, S. (1997, December 27). *Chinese Triads: An update.* ERRI Emergency Services Report. Retrieved May 9, 2004, from www.emergency.com/chi-tria.htm

Minister vows to further curb police misconduct. (1999, November 4). *China Business Information Network.* Retrieved May 2003 from Lexis Nexis Database.

Moriyama, T. (1997). Japan. *World factbook of criminal justice systems.* Department of Justice, Bureau of Justice Statistics. Retrieved May 12, 2003, from www.ojp.usdoj.gov/bjs/pub/ascii/wfbcjjap.txt

Morrison, S. (2003, April). Approaching organized crime: Where are we now and where are we going? *Crime and Justice International, 19*(72), 4–10.

National Police Agency. Criminal Investigation Bureau. (2002, October 10). Criminal trends. *Japan Information Network.* Retrieved May 12, 2003, from www.jinjapan.org/stat/category_14.html (URL no longer active).

Park, Y. K. (2001). *Transnational organized crime and the countermeasures in Korea* Resource Material Series No. 58 of the 116th International Training Course. U.N. Asia and Far East Institute, Harumi-cho, Fuchu, Tokyo, Japan.

Police corruption cases in Japan doubled in 2000. (2001, February 9). *Global Financial Times.* Information News Wire. Retrieved May 13, 2003, from Lexis Nexis Database.

Rinaldo, S. (2001, December 16). *China's battle against illegal drug use* [television broadcast]. CTV Television, Inc.

Schauble, J. (2001, August 28). China facing increase in drug use. *The Age* (Melbourne), p. 13.

Serjeant, J. (1998, April 1). *Asia to launch joint crackdown on child sex trade*. Reuters.

Seven Vietnamese police officers sacked for drug use. (2000, March 4). Bernama, the Malaysian News Service. Retrieved May 13, 2003, from Lexis Nexis Database.

Tat-wing, P. Y. (2001). *Triads*. Resource Material Series No. 58 of the 116th International Training Course. U.N. Asia and Far East Institute. Harumi-cho, Fuchu, Tokyo, Japan.

U.S. Department of Justice, Bureau of Justice Statistics. (1997). South Korea. *World factbook of criminal justice systems*. Retrieved May 12, 2003, from www.ojp.usdoj.gov/ bjs/pub/ascii/ wfbcjsko.txt

U.S. Department of State, Bureau for International Narcotics and Law Enforcement Affairs. (2002, March 1). *International narcotics control strategy report—March 2002*. Retrieved May 13, 2003, from www.state.gov/g/inl/rls/ nrcrpt/2001/c6085.htm

Wenge, R., Aung, T. O., Namdar, A., & Maiyalarp, Y. (2000, March 5). Anti-drug efforts lag in golden triangle [television broadcast transcript]. CNN World Report. Retrieved May 13, 2003, from www.cnn.com/TRAN SCRIPTS/0003/05/wr.03.html

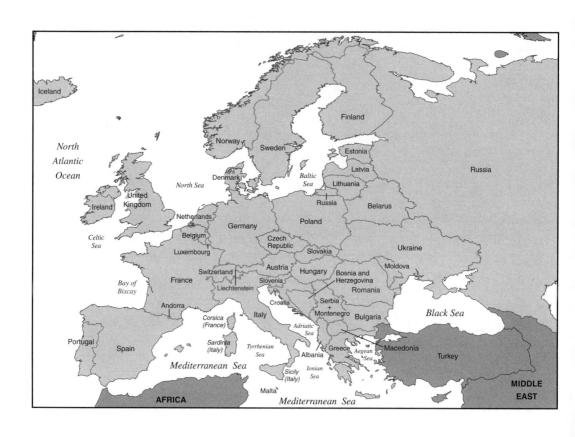

20

Organized Crime in Europe

KLAUS VON LAMPE

The concept of "organized crime" is an American invention[1] that has been superimposed on a heterogeneous European crime landscape. The overall picture is murky, fragmented, and often contradictory because of factual differences, scattered and often incompatible data, and culturally induced differences in perceptions and conceptualizations. Numerous attempts have been made in Europe to redefine the term *organized crime*. These efforts have oscillated between, on the one hand, the desire to depart from the conventional American imagery of "crime syndicates" to accommodate the specific conditions in Europe and, on the other hand, the concern not to relinquish the "emotional kick" (Levi, 1998, p. 336) the term *organized crime* has,

exactly because of the connotation of sinister crime organizations. So far, the diversity of perspectives has not been overcome by a common European approach. Even within the European Union, efforts toward a harmonization of views have not yet produced the intended results. To date, the European Union has been unable to arrive at a clear-cut definition of organized crime (Mitsilegas, 2001), and the contributions from member states to the annual E.U. Organised Crime Report continue to reflect not only different phenomena but also diverging conceptions. In some countries, for example, the focus is on the volume of certain types of "organized" crime, whereas other countries emphasize the number of "criminal groups" that operate within their

AUTHOR'S NOTE: The author would like to thank Liliya Gelemerova for her assistance in reviewing the literature used for this chapter. The author would also like to thank the following individuals for providing information and sharing their views and expertise: Mark Donovan, Petrus van Duyne, Michael Levi, Matthias Neske, Igor Osyka, Miroslav Scheinost, and Mechthild Stöhr.

borders (Europol, 2002; see also den Boer, 2001). In light of this background, it is difficult to summarize the situation of organized crime in Europe. Much of the available material reveals more about the social construction of reality than about the reality of organized crime.

THE CONCEPTUAL HISTORY OF ORGANIZED CRIME IN EUROPE: A BRIEF OVERVIEW

The phenomena that are variously lumped together under the umbrella term *organized crime* have a long tradition in Europe, some going back to preindustrial times (Egmond, 1996; Sharpe, 1996) and even all the way back to the Roman Empire (Woodiwiss, 2001). But the concept of organized crime has only recently been introduced to the European criminal policy debate (Fijnaut, 1990). The beginnings of the organized crime discourse in Europe can be traced back to the 1960s. At that time, the American public's preoccupation with "La Cosa Nostra" was approaching its climax (von Lampe, 2001a), and some observers in Western Europe began to wonder if similar problems could emerge on their side of the Atlantic.[2] These concerns, however, were not broadly shared. The notion prevailed that organized crime was an ill-fitting term for the description of the Western European crime picture. A study sponsored by the Council of Europe in 1970 found that police forces across Western Europe had little use for this concept.[3] The researchers noted a general agreement that American-style organized crime in the sense of the provision of illegal goods and services by well-organized and politically entrenched "crime syndicates" was almost nonexistent. Instead, developments in the area of predatory crime were believed to pose a much greater and far more immediate danger. In the final report of the project (Mack & Kerner, 1975), two major trends were emphasized. One perceived trend went from traditional predatory crimes to predatory

business-type crimes such as long-term fraud. The other trend involved the weakening of the traditional localized underworld milieu and the emergence of a more anonymous, nonterritorial network of individuals and clusters of individuals from different social and regional backgrounds who formed temporary teams to pool resources for the commission of specific crimes. This network of criminals, it was stressed, did not have "any elaborate collective organisation," nor was there a "Mr. Big" (Mack & Kerner, 1975, p. 54). New dimensions of organizational sophistication were seen only insofar as the degree of planning and preparation of each criminal enterprise had allegedly increased and a vertical division of labor between background organizers and frontline operators had become more common. In light of these perceived trends of committing crimes that are more distinct and business-like the spectacular, violence-prone exploits of gangland figures like the Krays and Richardsons in London[4] did not appear to be the signal for a coming era of gang rule in Europe but more an anomaly. Instead, it was the Great Train Robbery of 1963[5] that in the eyes of the contemporary observer constituted "the outstanding single criminal operation in the 1960s" (Mack & Kerner, 1975, p. 39). In fact, the Great Train Robbery was described by one British criminologist "as the most outstanding achievement in the entire history of organised crime" (quoted in Mack & Kerner, 1975, p. 171).

Although the Council of Europe study of 1970 found little evidence of "syndicated crime," it seemed at least plausible that criminal organizations could evolve out of enduring patterns of cooperation within the overall crime network (Kerner, 1973). But when in the mid-1980s two research projects once again investigated police perceptions of organized crime, these concerns had still not materialized. The two studies, which were conducted in West Germany and which can probably be taken as indicative of the situation in most of Western Europe, produced a picture very similar to the one drawn 15 years earlier (Rebscher & Vahlenkamp, 1988, 1991; Weschke & Heine-Heiss, 1990).[6] The German underworld was characterized as essentially a loose system of varying criminal alliances. It seemed that during the 1970s and early 1980s, neither the existing groups had developed into larger units nor had a concentration of power taken place in the form of a mafia-style protection monopoly. The prevailing principle appeared to be that of peaceful coexistence. There were some exceptions to the rule, but these were not seen as decisive factors. Both studies pointed to the existence of more clearly defined, hierarchical crime organizations made up of foreigners who remained on the margins of the criminal landscape, whereas other foreigners had allegedly blended into the domestic underworld circles. Yet the notion of more cohesive criminal groups, as Rebscher and Vahlenkamp (1988) self-critically pointed out, might well have been a misconception. They found that officers who conducted their investigations on a case-by-case basis tended to report the existence of criminal organizations, whereas respondents from offender-oriented units that monitored the entire range of activities of particular suspects did not. In sum, the main difference between the early 1970s and mid 1980s is probably one mainly of terminology. Although at first the organized crime label was only very hesitantly used in the European context, in the mid-1980s the network of criminally exploitable contacts within and between the urban underworlds was identified as the specific form of organized crime in Western Europe.

A major shift in the perception of organized crime did not take place until the late 1980s (van Duyne, 2004; von Lampe, 2001a). The inclusion of so-called nontraditional (i.e., non-Italian) organized crime in the official American view on organized crime at that time (President's Commission on Organized Crime, 1986), the growing migration problem in

most of Western Europe, the discussion of new police powers in the fight against drug trafficking, and finally the profound changes following the fall of the Iron Curtain can be seen as some of the factors that contributed to a revitalization of the threatening image of mafia syndicates. In contrast to the original perception of the 1960s, however, these were now believed to be a present danger. According to journalistic depictions and official reports, Europe had become a hotbed for transnational, mostly ethnically defined "mafias" (Europol, 2002; Flormann & Krevert, 2001; Freemantle, 1995; Lindlau, 1987; Sterling, 1994). Ironically, efforts on the part of the police to arrive at a common understanding of organized crime have continued to follow the opposite direction. The working definition by Germany's national police agency BKA (*Bundeskriminalamt*), for example, which since its formulation in 1990 has found some acceptance in Europe, requires little more than the cooperation of three offenders over a certain period of time (Black, Vander Beken, & De Ruyver, 2000; Levi, 1998).[7] Along these lines, in Eastern Europe yet another understanding of organized crime has evolved, one that places much more emphasis on economic crime and high-level corruption. Here, the term *mafia* applies to "the entire web of persons who profit from the new economic order" (Foglesong & Solomon, 2001, p. 33).

A CLASSIFICATORY SCHEME FOR ASSESSING ORGANIZED CRIME IN EUROPE

The brief review of the conceptual history indicates the heterogeneity of the European understanding of organized crime. To do justice to the different approaches and to capture the broad range of aspects addressed in the public and scientific debate, it seems necessary to adopt a metatheoretical conceptualization. The following analysis will be outlined by a classificatory scheme that distinguishes three basic dimensions: (a) organized criminal activities, (b) structural patterns of criminal cooperation, and (c) the systemic context of organized criminals, criminal structures, and criminal activities.

Activity Dimension

Some depictions of organized crime place more emphasis on the "crime" component than on the aspect of "organization." They treat certain modalities of the commission of crimes as distinctive or even quintessential features, linking organized crime, for example, to "serious" or "sophisticated" criminal activities. One crucial differentiation is the distinction between predatory and market-based crimes. As mentioned, in the 1960s, predatory crimes, including property crimes and fraud, tended to be regarded as a greater menace than crimes connected with illegal markets. Today, organized crime is primarily associated with the provision of illegal goods and services. Europol has named drug trafficking, illegal immigration, trafficking in human beings, and various types of financial crimes, including different kinds of fraud, as the areas of crime expected to be most important for organized criminal groups in the future (Europol, 2002). A special case is constituted by the extortion of protection payments (racketeering), which is essentially a predatory crime but may also involve the provision of services, for both legal and illegal actors—for example, the actual protection against physical harm from other criminals, the elimination of competitors, or the collection of debts. Protection rackets that extend to the legal spheres of society and offer some services to the victims have, for instance, been reported in Southern Italy (Gambetta, 1993) and Russia (Skoblikov, 1999; Varese, 2001). In Western European countries, extortion of legal businesses is believed to be confined largely to particular ethnic minority communities and subculturally embedded businesses

such as nightclubs (Europol, 2002; Fijnaut, Bovenkerk, Bruinsma, & Van de Bunt, 1998; Hobbs, Hadfield, Lister, & Winlow, 2002; Krevert, 1997).

Other potentially useful classifications within the activity dimension pertain to the methods ascribed to "organized criminals," most notably the use of violence and intimidation. It has been argued that (racketeering aside) violence may be a latent feature of all organized crime but is far less commonly applied than stereotypical imagery would suggest. Where violence erupts, it may be more a sign of disorganized crime than organized crime (Pearson & Hobbs, 2001; Zaitch, 2002).

Structural Dimension

Networks and Organizations

Central to most conceptions of organized crime is the structural dimension. Usually, patterns of criminal cooperation are ordered along a continuum from "loosely structured" networks to "tightly structured" criminal organizations. A clearer picture, however, emerges when networks and organizations are treated as two distinct analytical categories. Criminal networks are webs of criminally exploitable ties. They demarcate the social space within which a given criminal actor can operate and cooperate. The notion of criminal organization, in contrast, addresses the question of whether or not network members cooperate as autonomous partners or in the context of an overarching system of more or less persistent norms, expectations, and procedures that permit coordinated, purposeful action (von Lampe, 2003).

Recent research, especially in the area of drug trafficking but also in other areas of crime, has by and large confirmed earlier assessments that the predominant structural pattern of criminal cooperation in Europe are webs of personal relations that are flexibly used by criminals for the commission of crimes. Cooperation typically occurs either on a contractual basis, in the form of supplier-consumer or ephemeral employer-employee relations, or on a partnership basis in pairs or small groups with little overall horizontal or vertical integration (Bruinsma & Bernasco, 2004; van Duyne, 1996; Fijnaut et al., 1998; Gruppo Abele, 2003; Hobbs & Dunnighan, 1998; Johansen, 1998; Junninen & Aromaa, 2000; Kleemans & Van de Bunt, 1999; von Lampe, 2003; Paoli, 2002, 2003; Pearson & Hobbs, 2001; Ruggiero, 1996; Zaitch, 2002). Official statements at times go in the same direction but claim (not quite convincingly) that it constituted a new development that "traditional hierarchical structures are being replaced by loose networks of criminals" (Commission of the European Communities, 2001, p. 8). This does not mean that criminal organizations have ceased to exist. Criminal organizations with a complex structure have been observed, for example, in the case of criminal groups that operate from "safe haven" countries (Williams, 1999, p. 44) where they experience little or no law enforcement interference (see, e.g., Benninger, 1999). In contrast, the emergence of criminal organizations in hostile environments, marked by high levels of law enforcement pressure, is theoretically and empirically an exceptional phenomenon (von Lampe, 2003), unless the criminal structures rest on some form of legitimate structure. This is the case, for instance, where outwardly legitimate businesses are involved in VAT (value added tax) fraud (van Duyne, 1996; van Duyne, Pheijffer, Kuijl, Van Dijk, & Bakker, 2001) and E.U. subsidy fraud (Sieber, 1998); private security firms offer illegal debt collection services (Varese, 2001); or licensed casinos are used for the operation of illegal gambling (Sieber & Bögel, 1993). Finally, clandestine fraternal associations that are only indirectly involved in criminal enterprises, such as, for example, the Sicilian Cosa Nostra (Paoli, 1998), can qualify as organizations.

Functions

This point regarding the emergence of criminal organizations in hostile environments leads to another valuable distinction, apart from differentiating between networks and organizations: the distinction between various functions of criminal structures. Criminal structures can be expected to serve economic, social, or quasi-governmental purposes. Economic structures aim at material gain, such as, for example, a cigarette-smuggling ring or a gang of burglars. These have to be distinguished, analytically, from criminal structures that serve social functions. Fraternities such as the Sicilian Cosa Nostra (Paoli, 1998), outlaw motorcycle gangs (Brown, 1999; Haut, 1999; Zimmerli, 1999), and the Russian *vory v zakone* (Varese, 2001) fall into this category, but to a certain degree, so also do subcultures such as the clubbing scene (Pearson & Hobbs, 2001) or those emerging within marginalized ethnic communities (Bovenkerk, 1998). These structures support their members only indirectly in illegal economic activities—for example, by facilitating contacts, giving status, reinforcing deviant values, and providing a forum for the exchange of information (Haller, 1992). Quasi-governmental structures, in turn, support illegal economic activities in a more abstract way by establishing and enforcing rules of conduct and by settling disputes in a given territory or market (Anderson, 1979). Here, too, the Italian Mafia seems to be an appropriate example, but less formal arrangements fulfilling the same function of maintaining order among criminal actors have also been documented in other countries. For example, in Germany's red light districts, influential pimps are reported to hold "councils" to adjudicate disputes (Behr, 1985; Sieber & Bögel, 1993).

The notion of quasi-governmental criminal structures leads the discussion to a more complex level of observation, pertaining to structures that overarch the "underworld" either in the form of monopolies in illegal markets or in the form of illegal monopolies of violence over certain territories. Here, again, no clear picture can be discerned. Theoretically, monopolies can be expected to emerge in the area of systematic extortion as a precondition for doing business (Schelling, 1971). Empirically, monopolies of violence in Europe seem to exist primarily on a local level with more or less fragile agreements on territorial or sectorial exclusiveness between different racketeering groups (Gambetta, 1993; Varese, 2001). Monopolies in illegal commodity markets, on the other hand, appear to be more the exception than the rule (Besozzi, 2001), but economies of scale may lead to oligopolistic structures as, for example, on the upper levels of the cigarette black market (von Lampe, 2002b) and the production level of the synthetic drugs market (Gruppo Abele, 2003).

The three identified core functions of criminal structures are not empirically independent—that is, a criminal group may serve, for instance, both social and economic purposes. However, from a theoretical point of view—given different structural and logistical demands—it is unlikely that a particular criminal group will have both economic and quasi-governmental functions (Block, 1983; Skaperdas & Syropoulos, 1995). Often enough, it seems that the role of a particular "mafia" is misinterpreted because this distinction is not made and social and quasi-governmental structures are falsely described in terms of business enterprises (Haller, 1992).

Systemic Dimension

The third basic dimension of the organized crime concept, the systemic context, addresses two important issues: (a) the social embeddedness of organized crime and (b) the nexus between illegal and legal economic and political structures. Social embeddedness refers, in the first instance, to underlying social relations that enable or at least facilitate the emergence of criminal networks by providing participants with a common basis of trust (Kleemans & Van de Bunt, 1999). Familial, friendship, and ethnic ties are those most frequently mentioned in this regard, but legal business relations have also been found to develop into criminal relations (von Lampe & Johansen, 2004). In a more general sense, social embeddedness refers to the degree of hostility that organized criminals face with regard to recruitment, the marketability of illegal goods and services, or the securing of logistical and ideological support. It must be stressed that the social embeddedness of organized crime varies greatly in Europe from region to region and from one area of crime to an other. The same is true for the relations between criminals and representatives of the legal institutions of society. These relations may be characterized by confrontation, factual tolerance, connivance, cooperation, and integration, the latter being the case when legal actors themselves are committing "organized crimes."[8]

In sum, this means that there is not one naturally given relationship between "upperworld" and "underworld." Not all organized criminals, for example, seek to neutralize law enforcement through corruption or attempt to infiltrate legal businesses,[9] just as collusion between illegal and legal actors does not always imply an asymmetry of power in favor of the criminal side.[10] Rather, the available evidence suggests that contextual variables such as socioeconomic and cultural cleavages, the legitimacy of legal institutions, and the effectiveness of law enforcement influence the structure and operations of criminal networks and the interrelations with the immediate and broader environment.

THE CRIMINAL GEOGRAPHY OF EUROPE

Conventional descriptions tend to paint a black-and-white picture of organized crime in Europe: The countries in transition in Eastern Europe are seen to have conditions conducive to the emergence of criminal organizations, whereas the rich Western European countries, according to this view, serve primarily as markets for illegal goods and services and as easy targets for the commission of predatory crimes and the laundering of illicit profits. In a global perspective, Europe is in a similar fashion said to be an area of operation for transnational criminal groups from Latin America, Africa, and Asia. Although the East-West and North-South dichotomies are not without merit, a closer look reveals a more complex and differentiated picture. To begin with, even in the age of globalization, crime remains, to a considerable extent, a localized problem. Indigenous criminals continue to play a role (Europol, 2002), and where international ramifications have developed, organized crime seems to be characterized more by interdependent local units than by structures that operate in what would appear to be an almost metaphysical transnational sphere (Hobbs & Dunnighan, 1998). In the light of this background, the importance of Europe for crime globally, and of any country within Europe, is defined as much by domestic conditions in their own right as by the international context.

Europe in the Global Context of Organized Crime

Europe as a whole occupies a position in the global crime picture that is characterized, at the same time, by (a) significant manifestations of domestic organized crime—for example, the production and distribution of synthetic drugs (European Monitoring Centre for Drugs and Drug Addiction [EMCDDA], 2002; Gruppo Abele, 2003); (b) lucrative markets for illegal goods and services from abroad, such as agricultural drugs from Latin America, North Africa, and Asia (EMCDDA, 2002); (c) the export of illegal goods, such as embargoed weapons technology (Wamers, 1996) or child pornography (Jenkins, 2001); and (c) the operation of European criminals

outside of Europe such as fraudsters from the former Soviet Union operating in the United States (Finckenauer & Waring, 1998). Europe also functions as a transit route for illicit goods—for example, drugs going from Nigeria to the United States and Canada (Adamoli, Di Nicola, Savona, & Zoffi, 1998). The different roles Europe plays point to the interplay and overlap of various factors. That drugs like heroin and cocaine are imported rather than homegrown can be attributed to natural conditions as well as to differences in law enforcement between Europe and the main coca- and poppy-cultivating countries in Latin America and Asia. These "asymmetries" (Passas, 1998) are exploited by criminal entrepreneurs who are capable of transnational operation and cooperation—for example, through the use of legal business contacts or familial ties connecting actors in cultivation and transit countries with members of migrant communities in the countries of distribution (Bovenkerk, 1998; Tarrius, 1999). The lack of language barriers between former colonies and former colonial powers can also facilitate international criminal cooperation. This helps to explain, for example, why Spain is the main European port of entry for cocaine from Latin America (EMCDDA, 2002; see also Zaitch, 2002).

European Organized Crime and Postcommunist Transition

Within Europe, the crime picture has come to be described primarily in the context of the changes that have been set in motion by the collapse of the Soviet system. The shift from state planning to a free-market economy and the reorganization of the political and administrative framework from totalitarian control to democratic structures in the transition countries in Eastern Europe have been marked by an increase in social inequalities, the undermining of traditional values, and a weakening of formal and informal control mechanisms.[11]

Probably as a result of these and other factors, there has been a dramatic increase in reported crimes going hand in hand with decreasing clearance rates (Holyst, 1999; Levay, 2000).[12] But the postcommunist transition period has not only produced conditions conducive to crime as such. It has also created opportunities for the predatory takeover of legal institutions of society, such as politics, private enterprise, and the media, by ruthless interest groups. These actors, who come primarily from the ranks of the old communist elite and black marketeers, have been able, for example, to manipulate the privatization of formerly state owned businesses in a way that they acquired shares below market value or obtained factual control over businesses for the purpose of systematically looting company assets (Baloun & Scheinost, 2002; Osyka, 2000; Peev, 2002; Varese, 2001). Even businesses with no criminal connotation have come under the influence of criminal elements because of the inefficiency of the justice system and the resulting demand for illicit dispute settlement and debt collection services (Skoblikov, 1999; Varese, 2001). Likewise, entrepreneurs have found themselves under pressure to engage in corrupt practices to stay in business (Roberts, Adibekian, Nemiria, Tarkhnishvili, & Tholen, 1998; Varese, 2001).[13] Consequently, the boundaries between the legal and illegal spheres have become blurred, and terms such as "crony capitalism" and "criminal-syndicalist state" have become customary to characterize the economic and political situation (Gerber, 2000; Peev, 2002). Still, it would be false to generalize and to make a simple distinction between the countries of transition on the one hand and the established democratic countries in Western Europe on the other.

The Transparency International Corruption Perception Index, for example, points to substantial differences between relatively well-off countries such as Slovenia, Estonia, and Hungary with average scores between 6.0 and 4.9 and relatively corrupt countries such as Russia, Romania, and the Ukraine with scores between 2.7 and 2.4. Two transition countries, Slovenia and Estonia, even fare better than the worst-ranked Western European countries, Italy and Greece (Transparency International, 2002). Estimates on the extent of the "shadow economy" go in the same direction, showing a significant East-West difference within Europe as a whole and within Eastern Europe while at the same time, according to some calculations, the shares of unreported economic activities could well be lower in Poland, the Czech Republic, Slovenia, and Estonia, than in Italy and Greece (Schneider & Enste, 2000).

The legal and institutional framework to combat organized crime also shows important differences as well as similarities across the East-West divide. The countries in transition have not only struggled to bring their legislations in line with international standards, in some cases they have gone beyond this level to pass more far-reaching provisions (Adamoli et al., 1998; Ambos, 2002; Gropp & Huber, 2001). Thus, the problem of effective implementation aside, in some regards, conditions in Western Europe may well be more favorable to organized crime than in Eastern Europe. At the same time, efforts on the E.U. level toward legal harmonization and improved police and judicial cooperation have been slow going, so that potential criminogenic legal asymmetries have persisted in Western Europe, just as they continue to exist in Europe as a whole.[14]

Selected Areas of Crime

In light of these diverging trends and circumstances, general statements on the geography of organized crime in Europe have to be made with great caution. Looking at specific types of crime, it becomes apparent that in some cases, new threats have emerged as a result of the political changes in Eastern Europe; some crimes have received a new impetus; and in some instances, geographical distribution patterns have changed.

As has been noted earlier, the transformation from state planning to private business created numerous opportunities for embezzlement and fraud. A unique example of crime brought forth by the transition process is provided by the exploitation of currency exchange provisions that accompanied the currency union between East and West Germany in 1990. Fraud schemes involving members of the communist *nomenklatura* in various former Soviet Bloc countries resulted in several billion Euros worth of damages incurred by the German federal bank from the exchange of rubles in connection with nonexistent export deals (Schmidt, 1993).

Another type of crime closely linked to the demise of the Soviet regime, but one with more far-reaching implications, is the trafficking in nuclear material. In the early and mid-1990s, radioactive substances from nuclear facilities in the former Soviet Union were seized in Western Europe. These incidents gave rise to concerns that an illicit market for nuclear material was in the process of developing. Since then, however, cases of suspected trafficking in radioactive substances have diminished, presumably because of improved security in nuclear installations and because of poor market demand. Moreover, the market has so far not been populated by criminal organizations but, rather, "by amateur criminals, scam artists, and (on the demand side) undercover police and police decoys" (Lee, 2003, p. 101; see also Lee, 1998; Nillson, 1998).[15]

Two types of criminal activity that have undergone considerable changes since the fall of the Iron Curtain, and on which the economic differences between Eastern and Western Europe have come to bear, are illegal migration and human trafficking. Eastern European countries have become major source and transit countries for illegal migrants on their way to Western Europe (Dobovšek, 2004; Lehti & Aromaa, 2004). Moscow, for example, serves as an important hub for migrants from Asia. But in recent years, some transition countries seem to have become destination countries themselves (Okólski, 2000; Pieke, 2002). In the area of human trafficking, Eastern European countries, since the early 1990s, have replaced third world countries as the major sources of trafficked women and children for the Western European sex industry. Poverty, increasing gender inequality, sex discrimination, and ethnic discrimination in the countries of transition are believed to be the driving forces behind this development (Kelly, 2002; Vocks & Nijboer, 2000). Trafficking routes are in part determined by geographical proximity—for example, between Scandinavia and the Baltic states—and in part they appear to reflect consumer demands that are met by chains of interlocking networks of traffickers and procurers, connecting source countries in Eastern Europe with Western Europe over greater distances. At the same time, trafficking routes also exist between different countries of transition (Kelly, 2002; see also Salt, 2000). In the related field of child pornography, East-West differences in attitudes and in the intensity of law enforcement have allegedly "revolutionized" the market. The break away from communist austerity has created an atmosphere, enhanced by the weakness of the police, in which child pornographic material can be produced and distributed quite freely (Jenkins, 2001).

Similar to human trafficking and child pornography, the smuggling of excise goods—namely, cigarettes—has experienced a boost since the early 1990s. One scheme involves the large-scale procurement of cigarettes for export from the European Union to Eastern Europe. The cigarettes, for which no excise and VAT is payable within the European Union, are being reloaded and smuggled back to the European Union. Main trafficking routes stretch from the Baltic States and Poland to Germany and Great Britain, and from the Balkans to Italy. Traffickers can take advantage of the relative immunity from law enforcement in those countries where the reloading takes place and of the sheer volume of cross-border trade that makes detection of contraband difficult (van Duyne, 2003; Joossens, 1999; Joossens & Raw, 1998; von Lampe, 2002b). In some Balkan countries, smugglers even seem to have received active cooperation from governments (Hajdinjak, 2002).

As a final selected example of crime types, the trafficking in stolen motor vehicles may be used to illustrate the diverse and dynamic European criminal landscape. Within a few months of the fall of the Iron Curtain, a substantial market for stolen consumer goods, including cars, emerged in Eastern Europe (Killias & Aebi, 2000). Cars were stolen primarily in the Benelux countries, France, Italy, and Germany, to meet a huge demand for motor vehicles in the former economies of shortage (Sieber & Bögel, 1993). The opening of the borders to the East meant an overall increase in the volume of car theft in Europe, because traditional trafficking routes, most notably to the Middle East, did not cease to function (Sehr, 1995). In the early years, Poland seems to have been the main trade center for the Eastern European market, because of its geographical location and because already during the 1980s, Polish crime networks had been involved in the cross-border trafficking of stolen cars on a small scale (Rixdorf, 1993). Soon, however, offenders from other countries, such as Bulgaria and Romania, appeared on the scene, and the areas of operation for car thieves expanded in all directions, including to countries in Eastern Europe (Dobovšek, 2004). Likewise, the consumer markets shifted eastward, to the Baltic States, Russia, the Ukraine, and even farther to the Caucasus region, presumably in part as a response to the saturation of demand in countries such as Poland, which has increasingly adopted the role of a transit and source country for stolen motor vehicles (Sehr, 1995). Parallel to this development, the volume of car theft has decreased in Western Europe,

following, as one important factor, the introduction of more effective antitheft technology (Europol, 2002; Ratzel & Lippert, 2001). Trafficking in motor vehicles can serve as a case in point for the changing crime patterns in Europe. Moreover, it helps to illuminate the sometimes ambiguous nature of organized crime. A significant share of reported cases of car theft is believed to involve insurance fraud where car owners conspire with traffickers. Estimates place the figure for Germany as high as 50% (Ratzel & Lippert, 2001).[16] This means that the dividing line between offenders and victims is blurred and that, unlike conventional wisdom suggests, there is similarly no clear-cut role allocation between Eastern and Western European countries.

BASIC TYPES OF ORGANIZED CRIMINAL STRUCTURES IN EUROPE

So far, the discussion has highlighted particular aspects of the overall problem of organized crime from different angles, against the backdrop of a metatheoretical conceptualization. In the concluding section, these aspects will be dealt with in a more holistic way in connection with some basic types of organized criminal structures. Two stereotypical manifestations of organized crime will be analyzed—the Sicilian Mafia and what has come to be called the Russian Mafia. It is argued that both phenomena constitute deviant cases and that other criminal structures, also discussed below, are more characteristic of European organized crime.

The Sicilian Mafia (Cosa Nostra)

The Mafia in Sicily is often regarded as the archetype of organized crime and has been the subject of much scholarly controversy. One hotly debated issue concerns the question of whether the Mafia is a stable organization, or, rather, a cultural phenomenon, state of mind, or behavioral system that reflects certain traits of Sicilian culture (see Catanzaro, 1992; Lupo, 2002). The best answer to this question seems to be that the Mafia is both. The Mafia, or Cosa Nostra, is a secret association with a clearly defined membership. At the same time, it is a reflection of more general social and cultural conditions in southern Italy that have also produced other mafia groups in Sicily outside Cosa Nostra but with essentially the same purposes and functions (Arlacchi, 1993; Gambetta, 1993).

The basic structural unit of the Cosa Nostra is the *cosca* or family, consisting of from a handful to over 100 members under the leadership of a *capo*. Each family claims an illicit monopoly of power in a defined territory. The families, with intermittent variations over the years, are coordinated on the provincial level by a so-called *commissione* or *cupola*. Above the provincial level a *commissione interprovinciale* has been created as the supreme coordinating body of the Cosa Nostra (Gambetta, 1993). The structure, which in practice has proven to be fragile and not always effective (Hess, 1998; Lupo, 2002; Stille, 1995), is quite simple. There is a hierarchy, but no horizontal differentiation of tasks. This needs to be understood with a view to the limited functions the Cosa Nostra serves as an organization. As has been mentioned above, the Cosa Nostra is a fraternal association with both social and quasi-governmental functions, but not a business enterprise (Paoli, 1998). Therefore, it does not require, for example, elaborate arrangements for the performance of tasks in a division of labor. The aims of the Cosa Nostra are more or less limited to the protection and promotion of the legal and especially illegal economic, political, and social interests of its members and to the regulation of internal conflicts (Arlacchi, 1993). These conflicts arise quite naturally from the main occupation of mafiosi, the provision of private protection in the absence of effective regulatory institutions. The guarantee of protection necessitates the absence

of competition. This can best be secured when all providers are integrated into one centralized, hierarchical structure (Gambetta, 1993). Apart from private protection, Mafia members are involved in a variety of criminal activities, including drug trafficking (Paoli, 1999).

One of the characteristic features that set the Mafia apart from other manifestations of organized crime is the close bond mafiosi have established to representatives of the political system on the local, regional, and national levels. In fact, a number of Cosa Nostra members are said to have held public offices themselves (Arlacchi, 1993). The alliance between the Mafia and politics has its historical roots in the ability of Mafia dons to mobilize electoral support. In return, mafiosi have received political protection, and they have been allowed to share in the distribution of public benefits (Catanzaro, 1992; Stille, 1995). As such, the Mafia has become an integral component of the clientelistic political culture of Italy (Ginsborg, 2001). Since the 1980s, however, the relationship between the Mafia and politics has deteriorated. Although mafiosi have gained greater autonomy due to the financial power obtained from drug trafficking, the state has taken far-reaching legislative and administrative measures to curtail the Mafia's role in mediating political and social conflicts (Arlacchi, 1993). The confrontation has culminated in the assassinations of Magistrates Falcone and Borsellino in 1992 and the subsequent arrest and eventual conviction of numerous Mafia leaders (Paoli, 1999; Stille, 1995). In recent years, the Cosa Nostra has allegedly shifted away from violent confrontation and adopted a low-profile strategy under a new leadership (Europol, 2002; Neubacher, 2002).

The "Russian Mafia" and the *Vory v Zakone*

The so-called Russian Mafia, like its Sicilian counterpart, is linked to the territorially based provision of protection services and to alliances between upperworld and underworld (Varese, 2001). The term "Russian Mafia" variously refers to any or all of essentially three types of actors that characterize the crime picture in Russia today: (a) corrupt government officials; (b) shady business tycoons, so-called oligarchs; and (c) members of criminal gangs headed by so-called authorities (*avtoritety*) and loosely tied to each other through a criminal fraternity known as the "thieves in law" (*vory v zakone*). This three-tiered edifice first took shape in the Soviet Union during the 1960s, when government and party bureaucrats, participants of the shadow economy, and professional criminals began to establish a corrupt system of mutually beneficial relations. In the period of privatization, these three groups, because of their connections and financial power, were those best positioned to take advantage of the new opportunities and to acquire control over formerly state-owned businesses and natural resources. The new criminal entrepreneurs have been able to amass huge fortunes from the mostly illicit export of strategic raw materials such as nonferrous and rare metals, jewels, timber, and various products of the military-industrial complex (Finckenauer & Voronin, 2001; Glinkina, 1994; Varese, 2001).

The keys to understanding the crime situation in post-Soviet Russia appear to be systemic corruption and the fact that the state has lost its monopoly over coercion (Galeotti, 1998). The criminal landscape is described as populated by territorially based, hierarchically structured criminal groups with the reputation and ability to use violence. These groups offer a protective roof (*krysha*) to legal and illegal businesses. This can take on the form of pure extortion, or it may be combined with the actual protection from physical harm and the provision of services such as debt collection and the elimination of competitors (Skoblikov, 1999; Varese, 2001). The criminal gangs strive in a situation where violence is a readily available and viable option for solving

conflicts in the business world and on the political arena (Galeotti, 1998). Their influence, however, appears limited by the fact that on the one hand, private security firms and even government agencies have entered the market of private protection and, on the other hand, that some potential victims of extortion, major economic conglomerates, have established their own security forces (Varese, 2001; Volkov, 2000a, 2000b). The internalization of protection goes hand in hand with corrupt ties to political figures who offer a variety of favors, including tax concessions, protectionist measures against competitors, and exemptions from duties. In providing political protection, different branches of the state apparatus may come in conflict with each other. In those cases, the side whose "roof" is higher in the state hierarchy is said to keep the upper hand. In turn, political roofs appear to be superior to criminal roofs. Criminals reportedly refrain from entering into conflict with political protectors (Varese, 2001). So although there is evidence of alliances between criminal gangs and the political and business elites and a partial overlap between these groups, the gang element seems to be, relatively, the weakest component in the overall system of crime and corruption.

Given this caveat, it appears somewhat odd that so much emphasis is placed on the *vory v zakone*, Russia's alleged gangster elite. The thieves in law are a criminal fraternity that evolved during the 1920s in the Soviet prison system (*Gulag*). Their cultural roots supposedly go back to thieves' guilds of the 19th century and the traditional Russian village community, stressing solidarity, a sense of equality, and defiance for state authority. The internal structure is nonhierarchical, although older members reportedly wield greater moral authority. The *vory* control a communal fund (*obshchak*) to support group activities. Contributions to the *obshchak* come from extorted inmates and from criminals outside the prison (Sobolev, Rushchenko, & Volobuev, 2002;

Varese, 2001). In the post-Soviet era, *vory* have less of a prison background. Long incarceration is no longer a precondition for being inducted into the fraternity. Many young criminals are simply buying membership, whereas in other instances the title *vor v zakone* is bestowed on deserving criminals, and obtaining the title signals a promotion within the underworld (Varese, 2001). From this description follows that *vory v zakone* do not have a power base of their own. In fact, the *vory* code of conduct, unlike mafia culture in Sicily, does not emphasize the use of violence (Volkov, 2000b). Rather, the *vory*'s position of power seems to depend on their individual role within criminal gangs and on the high reputation they enjoy in criminal circles. This is no guarantee of underworld supremacy. In the Yekaterinenburg region, Russia's largest industrial center, for example, a gang led by thieves in law lost to ruthless competition with a criminal gang composed of former athletes (Finckenauer & Voronin, 2001; Volkov, 2000b).

Organized Crime European Style

The Sicilian Mafia and the Russian Mafia are characterized by the close interaction and partial overlap of criminal, economic, and political elites. In this respect, both phenomena seem to constitute deviant cases in the European crime landscape. Although there are no systematically collected data to corroborate this claim, violence-based criminal gangs appear to operate more or less separately from the legal spheres of society. Moreover, criminal networks seem to have a tendency not to stretch across social and cultural boundaries. Instead, criminal actors tend to associate with criminal actors of a similar background (Weerman, 2003). To put the Sicilian and Russian Mafias into perspective, the following classification based on differences in the social embeddedness of criminal actors (von Lampe, 2001b, 2002a) briefly highlights some manifestations of organized criminal structures that may be more characteristic of Europe in general. The typology is premised on two tentative assumptions: (a) the relative social homogeneity of criminal networks and (b) a positive correlation between the social position of criminal actors and the quality of criminal opportunities.

The typology distinguishes four basic constellations. The first type comprises criminal networks with no social support structure within the countries of operation, as in the case of burglary gangs that use home bases in Eastern Europe as a hub for crime sprees in Western Europe (Benninger, 1999). The recruitment and training of group members and the formation of teams takes place under relative immunity from law enforcement. These conditions appear to be favorable for the emergence of complex organizational structures, including a military-like hierarchy and a division of labor within and between teams. The lack of social support in the countries of operation, in turn, corresponds to the predatory nature of the crimes and to the seemingly unrestrained willingness to use violence against persons and property.

The second category refers to subculture-based crime networks. In these cases, criminal actors can rely on a social support structure that is larger than that provided by their immediate criminal network but more or less set apart from mainstream society and its institutions. An illustrative example is provided by Turkish and Kurdish drug smuggling and distribution rings embedded in migrant communities in various Western European countries. Most heroin marketed in Europe comes from the Golden Crescent area via Turkey (EMCDDA, 2002). Smuggling, storage, and distribution of heroin are typically organized through networks of familial ties. Although on one hand, the seclusion of ethnic minority communities is used to shield criminal activities from detection, on the other hand, actors are familiar enough with the infrastructure in their respective host countries—communication, business, and finances—to take advantage of it (van Duyne, 1996; Flormann & Krevert, 2001; Pearson & Hobbs, 2001).

The third constellation includes criminal networks rooted in mainstream society. These networks comprise outwardly law-abiding actors who are not restricted by any practical, cultural, or legal obstacles in taking advantage of the legitimate social infrastructure. Mainstream embedded networks are typically involved in organized business crimes such as investment fraud or health insurance fraud. In comparison with crime networks rooted in subcultures, they have a number of strategic advantages, including "natural" interaction with officeholders that may translate into crime opportunities or reduced risks of law enforcement interference. Even in the absence of outright corruptive relations, ties to public officials can prove a valuable shield against police action (van Duyne, 1997).

The fourth type pertains to networks entrenched in the power elites. In contrast to the former category, actors have direct access to socially relevant decision-making processes in politics, business, and the media. Examples are provided by a long series of scandals on the local, state, national, and supranational levels, involving the abuse or misuse of competencies for profit, power, or protection from criminal prosecution for other crimes. These scandals are connected, for example, to illegal party financing and public contracts (Pujas & Rhodes, 1998). The problem in this realm is that, more than in other social spheres, a lot remains in the dark so that even after lengthy inquiries, in many cases there is not much more than speculation and guesswork about the extent and degree of criminal involvement of members of the power elites.[17]

It seems to be a characteristic trait of the treatment of organized crime all over Europe that socially more or less marginalized crime networks receive continuous attention, whereas potentially more harmful crime networks, with greater capacities to manipulate institutional decisions and to profit from lucrative opportunities in the area of business crime, tend to be the subject of scandals that only sporadically occupy the minds of the public and law enforcement. Therefore, the emergence of a clearer picture of organized crime in Europe will not only depend on further police investigations, journalistic inquiries, and scientific research per se; it may also depend on a reorientation of the focus of attention, away from the black-and- white dichotomies that currently influence the perception of organized crime.

NOTES

1. See von Lampe (1999, 2001a) on the historical origins of the organized crime concept.

2. Interestingly, the American debate had repercussions even in Italy where the public found renewed interest in the Sicilian Mafia (Lupo, 2002).

3. It should be noted that a similar reaction had been prompted within the United States. States with no Cosa Nostra family found it difficult to adopt the New York–centered conception of organized crime that emerged from the influential Kefauver and McClellan hearings in the U.S. Senate during the 1950s and early 1960s and from the Presidential Task Force on Organized Crime of 1967 (see von Lampe, 1999, 2001a).

4. The Krays and Richardsons were two pairs of brothers who had each established some dominance in their respective parts of London over illegal and shady businesses. The Krays were publicity hounds and consciously imitated American mobsters. The Richardsons, in contrast, kept in the background but also indulged in uncontrolled violence. The Krays and the Richardsons were convicted and sentenced to long prison terms in separate high-profile trials in the late 1960s (Campbell, 1994; Mack & Kerner, 1975).

5. In 1963, after 9 months of meticulous planning, a team of London underworld figures robbed the Royal Mail night train on its way from Glasgow to Euston and stole £2,500,000 (Campbell, 1994).

6. For an analysis of the situation in the United Kingdom since the 1970s, see Hobbs (1994, 2001).

7. The English translation, quoted in Levi (1998), is as follows:

Organised crime is the planned violation of the law for profit or to acquire power, which offences are each, or together, of a major significance, and are carried out by more than two participants who co-operate within a division of labour for a long or undetermined time span using a.) commercial or commercial-like structures, or b.) violence or other means of intimidation, or c.) influence on politics, media, public administration, justice and the legitimate economy. (p. 335)

The provisional E.U. definition of organized crime used in the context of the annual situation reports is also influenced by the BKA definition:

In order to speak about organised crime at least six of the following characteristics need to be present, four of which must be those numbered 1, 3, 5 and 11: 1. Collaboration of more than 2 people; 2. Each with own appointed tasks; 3. For a prolonged or indefinite period of time (refers to the stability and (potential) durability); 4. Using some form of discipline and control; 5. Suspected of the commission of serious criminal offences; 6. Operating at an international level; 7. Using violence or other means suitable for intimidation; 8. Using commercial or businesslike structures; 9. Engaged in money laundering; 10. Exerting influence on politics, the media, public administration, judicial authorities or the economy; 11. Determined by the pursuit of profit and/or power. (Commission of the European Communities, 2001, Annex)

8. For a more refined typology of legal-illegal interfaces, see Passas (2002); on a typology pertaining specifically to postcommunist countries, see Karklins (2002).

9. According to the German annual organized crime report for 2001, for example, less than 5% of organized crime cases involved corruption (Bundeskriminalamt, 2002a); conversely, the situation report on corruption for the same year lists only 0.4% of the cases with an organized crime context (Bundeskriminalamt, 2002b). Likewise, van Duyne (2002), in an empirical study of criminal financial management in the Netherlands, found little support for a tendency of "organized criminals" to infiltrate legitimate businesses.

10. See von Lampe (2002a) with regard to cases of police corruption in Germany.

11. For an analysis of the effects of the transition process on the police in the case of Hungary, see Kertész and Szikinger (2000).

12. For the development in particular countries, see Foglesong and Solomon (2001) for the Ukraine; Karabec, Diblíková, and Zeman (2002) for the Czech Republic; and Siemaszko (2000) for Poland.

13. On the situation of Western businesses in Russia, see Bagelius (2003) and SINUS München (2000).

14. Differences in the legal framework within the European Union have been detailed, for example, in the area of combating product piracy (Hetzer, 2002) and money laundering (Ambos, 2002). For discussions of the trends and difficulties in European police and judicial integration, see Aden (2001) and Tak (2000).

15. The 2002 E.U. Organised Crime Report contains only a brief reference to six Austrian cases of suspected nuclear smuggling, none of which involved persons who "were able to prove they were indeed in possession of such material suitable to build weapons of mass destruction" (Europol, 2002, p. 39).

16. For a critical view on this assessment see Gerber and Killias (2003).

17. For discussions of the Tangentopoli scandal in Italy, see Giglioli (1996) and Nelken (1996); for a discussion of the Tangentopoli scandal and the Propaganda 2 scandal in the overall context of recent Italian history, see Ginsborg (2001); for an insider's view of the Elf-Aquitaine scandal in France, see LeFloch-Prigent (2001); for an assessment of the party finance scandal involving former German chancellor Kohl, see Dreher (2002); for an analysis of the 1998–1999 European Commission scandal, see MacMullen (1999).

REFERENCES

Adamoli, S., Di Nicola, A., Savona, E. U., & Zoffi, P. (1998). *Organised crime around the world*. Helsinki: European Institute for Crime Prevention and Control, affiliated with the United Nations.

Aden, H. (2001). Convergence of policing policies and transnational policing in Europe. *European Journal of Crime, Criminal Law and Criminal Justice, 9,* 99–112.

Ambos, K. (2002). Internationalisierung des strafrechts: Das beispiel "Geldwäsche" [Internationalization of criminal law: The case of "money laundering"]. *Zeitschrift für die Gesamte Strafrechtswissenschaft, 114,* 236–256.

Anderson, A. G. (1979). *The business of organized crime: A Cosa Nostra family.* Stanford, CA: Hoover Institution Press.

Arlacchi, P. (1993). *Men of dishonor: Inside the Sicilian mafia* (M. Romano, Trans.). New York: William Morrow. (Original work published 1992)

Bagelius, N. (2003). *Svenska företag åter i Österled: Hur svenska företag positionerade sig i Öst och minskade sin exponering för risk och osäkerhet* [Swedish companies returning to Eastern Europe: How Swedish companies captured positions in the East and managed their uncertainty and risk exposures]. Stockholm, Sweden: Stockholms Universitet.

Baloun, V., & Scheinost, M. (2002). Economy and crime in the society in transition: The Czech Republic case. In P. C. van Duyne, K. von Lampe, & N. Passas (Eds.), *Upperworld and underworld in cross-border crime* (pp. 43–59). Nijmegen, Netherlands: Wolf Legal.

Behr, H.-G. (1985). *Organisiertes Verbrechen* [Organized crime]. Düsseldorf, Germany: Econ.

Benninger, P. (1999). Rumänische diebesbanden sind auch in der Schweiz aktiv [Romanian gangs of thieves are also active in Switzerland]. *Kriminalistik, 53,* 625–629.

Besozzi, C. (2001). *Illegal, legal–egal? Zu entstehung, struktur und auswirkungen illegaler märkte* [Illegal, legal—who cares? On the emergence, structure and consequences of illegal markets]. Bern, Switzerland: Haupt.

Black, C., Vander Beken, T., & De Ruyver, B. (2000). *Measuring organised crime in Belgium: A risk-based methodology.* Antwerpen, Belgium: Maklu.

Block, A. A. (1983). *East side, west side.* New Brunswick, NJ: Transaction.

Boer, M. den (2001). The fight against organised crime in Europe: A comparative perspective. *European Journal on Criminal Policy and Research, 9,* 259–272.

Bovenkerk, F. (1998). Organized crime and ethnic minorities: Is there a link? *Transnational Organized Crime, 4,* 109–126.

Brown, P. (1999). Nordic motorcycle gangs. *International Criminal Police Review, 474–475,* 36–39.

Bruinsma, G., & Bernasco, W. (2004). Criminal groups and transnational illegal markets: A more detailed examination on the basis of social network theory. *Crime, Law and Social Change, 41,* 79–94.

Bundeskriminalamt [Federal Criminal Investigation Office]. (2002a). *Lagebericht organisierte kriminalität 2001 Bundesrepublik Deutschland, Kurzfassung* [Situation report organized crime 2001 Federal Republic of Germany, short version]. Wiesbaden, Germany: Author.

Bundeskriminalamt [Federal Criminal Investigation Office]. (2002b). *Lagebild korruption Bundesrepublik Deutschland 2001* [Situation report corruption Federal Republic of Germany 2001]. Wiesbaden, Germany: Author.

Campbell, D. (1994). *The underworld.* London: BBC Books.

Catanzaro, R. (1992). *Men of respect: A social history of the Sicilian mafia* (R. Rosenthal, Trans.). New York: Free Press. (Original work published 1988)

Commission of the European Communities. (2001). *Towards a European strategy to prevent organised crime. Joint report from Commission Services and Europol, 13 March 2001.* Brussels, Belgium: European Commission and Europol.

Dobovšek, B. (Ed.). (2004). *Roundtable on organised crime (collection of reports): Slovenian presidency of the Adriatic-Ionian Initiative.* Ljubljana, Slovenia: Ministry of the Interior, Police.

Dreher, K. (2002). *Kohl und die konten: Eine schwarze finanzgeschichte* [Kohl and the accounts: A black history of finance]. Stuttgart, Germany: Deutsche Verlags-Anstalt.

Duyne, P. C. van. (1996). The phantom and threat of organized crime. *Crime, Law and Social Change, 24*, 341–377.

Duyne, P. C. van. (1997). Organized crime, corruption and power. *Crime, Law and Social Change, 26*, 201–238.

Duyne, P. C. van. (2002). Crime-entrepreneurs and financial management. In P. C. van Duyne, K. von Lampe, & N. Passas (Eds.), *Upperworld and underworld in cross-border crime* (pp. 61–83). Nijmegen, Netherlands: Wolf Legal.

Duyne, P. C. van. (2003). Organizing cigarette smuggling and policy making, ending up in smoke. *Crime, Law and Social Change, 39*, 285–317.

Duyne, P. C. van. (2004). The creation of a threat image: Media, policy making and organized crime. In P. C. van Duyne, M. Jager, K. von Lampe, & J. L. Newell (Eds.), *Threats and phantoms of organised crime, corruption and terrorism* (pp. 21–50). Nijmegen, Netherlands: Wolf Legal.

Duyne, P. C. van, Pheijffer, M., Kuijl, H. G., Van Dijk, A. T. H., & Bakker, G. J. C. M. (2001). *Financial investigation of crime: A tool of the integral law enforcement approach*. The Hague, Netherlands: Koninklijke Vermande.

Egmond, F. (1996). Between town and countryside: Organized crime in the Dutch Republic. In E. A. Johnson & E. H. Monkkonen (Eds.), *The civilization of crime: Violence in town and country since the Middle Ages* (pp. 138–152). Urbana & Chicago: University of Illinois Press.

European Monitoring Centre for Drugs and Drug Addiction. (2002). *2002 annual report on the state of the drugs problem in the European Union and Norway*. Lisbon, Portugal: Author. Retrieved May 11, 2004, from http://ar2002.emcdda.eu.int/en/home-en.html

Europol. (2002). *2002 EU organised crime report: Non-classified version*. The Hague, Netherlands: Author.

Fijnaut, C. (1990). Organized crime: A comparison between the United States of America and Western Europe. *British Journal of Criminology, 30*, 321–340.

Fijnaut, C., Bovenkerk, F., Bruinsma, G., & Van de Bunt, H. (1998). *Organized crime in the Netherlands*. The Hague, Netherlands: Kluwer Law International.

Finckenauer, J. O., & Voronin, Y. A. (2001). *The threat of Russian organized crime*. Washington DC: U.S. Department of Justice.

Finckenauer, J. O., & Waring, E. (1998). *Russian mafia in America: Immigration, culture, and crime*. Boston: Northeastern University Press.

Flormann, W., & Krevert, P. (2001). *In den Fängen der Mafia-Kraken: Organisiertes Verbrechen in Deutschland* [In the tentacles of the Mafia octopuses: Organized crime in Germany]. Hamburg, Germany: Verlag E. S. Mittler & Sohn.

Foglesong, T. S., & Solomon, P. H. (2001). *Crime, criminal justice, and criminology in post-Soviet Ukraine*. Washington DC: U.S. Department of Justice.

Freemantle, B. (1995). *The octopus: Europe in the grip of organised crime*. London: Orion.

Galeotti, M. (1998). The mafiya and the new Russia. *Australian Journal of Politics and History, 44*, 415–429.

Gambetta, D. (1993). *The Sicilian mafia: The business of private protection*. Cambridge, MA: Harvard University Press.

Gerber, J. (2000). On the relationship between organized and white-collar crime: Government, business, and criminal enterprise in post-communist Russia. *European Journal of Crime, Criminal Law and Criminal Justice, 8*, 327–342.

Gerber, J., & Killias, M. (2003). The transnationalization of historically local crime: Auto theft in Western Europe and Russia markets. *European Journal of Crime, Criminal Law and Criminal Justice, 11*, 215–226.

Giglioli, P. P. (1996). Political corruption and the media: The Tangentopoli affair. *International Social Science Journal, 149*, 381–394.

Ginsborg, P. (2001). *Italy and its discontents: Family, civil society, state 1980–2001*. London: Allen Lane.

Glinkina, S. P. (1994). Privatizatsiya and kriminalizatsiya: How organized crime is hijacking privatization. *Demokratizatsiya, 2*, 385–391.

Gropp, W., & Huber, B. (Eds.). (2001). *Rechtliche initiativen gegen organisierte kriminalität* [Legal initiatives against organized crime]. Freiburg, Germany: Edition Iuscrim.

Gruppo Abele. (2003). *Synthetic drugs trafficking in three European cities: Major trends and the involvement of organized crime–final report.* Turin, Italy: Author.

Hajdinjak, M. (2002). *Smuggling in Southeast Europe: The Yugoslav wars and the development of regional criminal networks in the Balkans.* Sofia, Bulgaria: Center for the Study of Democracy.

Haller, M. H. (1992). Bureaucracy and the mafia: An alternative view. *Journal of Contemporary Criminal Justice, 8*(1), 1–10.

Haut, F. (1999). Organized crime on two wheels: Motorcycle gangs. *International Criminal Police Review, 474–475,* 25–35.

Hess, H. (1998). *Mafia and mafiosi: Origin, power and myth.* New York: New York University Press.

Hetzer, W. (2002). Godfathers and pirates: Counterfeiting and organized crime. *European Journal of Crime, Criminal Law and Criminal Justice, 10,* 303–320.

Hobbs, D. (1994). Professional and organised crime in Britain. In M. Maguire, R. Morgan, & R. Reiner (Eds.), *The Oxford handbook of criminology* (pp. 450–456). Oxford, UK: Clarendon Press.

Hobbs, D. (2001). The firm: Organizational logic and criminal culture on a shifting terrain. *British Journal of Criminology, 41,* 549–560.

Hobbs, D., & Dunnighan, C. (1998). Global organised crime: Context and pretext. In V. Ruggiero, N. South, & I. Taylor (Eds.), *The new European criminology: Crime and social order in Europe* (pp. 289–301). London: Routledge.

Hobbs, D., Hadfield, P., Lister, S., & Winlow, S. (2002). "Door lore": The art and economics of intimidation. *British Journal of Criminology, 42,* 352–370.

Holyst, B. (1999). Organized crime in Eastern Europe and its implications for the security of the Western world. In S. Einstein & M. Amir (Eds.), *Organized crime: Uncertainties and dilemmas* (pp. 67–96). Chicago: Office of International Criminal Justice.

Jenkins, P. (2001). *Beyond tolerance: Child pornography on the Internet.* New York: New York University Press.

Johansen, P. O. (1998). Smuggling alcohol: Organized crime the Norwegian style. In *Årsrapport 1998* (pp. 1–11). Oslo, Norway: Institutt For Kriminologi Universitetet I Oslo.

Joossens, L. (1999). *Smuggling and cross-border shopping of tobacco products in the European Union.* Report for the Health Education Authority, London. Retrieved May 12, 2004, www.ash.org.uk/html/smuggling/pdfs/heajoossens.pdf

Joossens, L., & Raw, M. (1998). Cigarette smuggling in Europe: Who really benefits? *Tobacco Control, 7,* 66–71.

Junninen, M., & Aromaa, K. (2000). Crime across the border: Finnish professional criminals taking advantage of Estonian crime opportunities. In P. C. van Duyne, V. Ruggiero, M. Scheinost, & W. Valkenburg (Eds.), *Cross-border crime in a changing Europe* (pp. 107–129). Tilburg, Netherlands, and Prague, Czech Republic: Tilburg University and Institute of Criminology and Social Prevention, Czech Republic.

Karabec, Z., Diblíková, S., & Zeman, P. (2002). *Systémy trestní justice v Evropě a Severní Americe: Česká Republika* [Criminal justice systems in Europe and North America: the Czech Republic]. Prague, Czech Republic: Institut pro kriminologii a sociální prevenci.

Karklins, R. (2002). Typology of post-communist corruption. *Problems of Post-Communism, 49*(4), 22–32.

Kelly, E. (2002). *Journeys of jeopardy: A review of research on trafficking in women and children in Europe.* Geneva, Switzerland: International Organization for Migration. Retrieved May 12, 2004, from www.iom.int/documents/publication/en/mrs%5F11%5F2002.pdf

Kerner, H.-J. (1973). *Professionelles und organisiertes Verbrechen: Versuch einer bestandsaufnahme und bericht über neuere entwicklungstendenzen in der Bundesrepublik Deutschland und in den Niederlanden* [Professional and organized crime: Attempt to assess and report on recent developments in the Federal Republic of Germany and in the Netherlands]. Wiesbaden, Germany: Bundeskriminalamt.

Kertész, I., & Szikinger, I. (2000). Changing patterns of culture and its organisation of the police in a society of transition—Case study: Hungary. *European Journal on Criminal Policy and Research, 8,* 271–300.

Killias, M., & Aebi, M. F. (2000). Crime trends in Europe from 1990 to 1996: How Europe illustrates the limits of the American experience. *European Journal on Criminal Policy and Research, 8,* 43–63.

Kleemans, E. R., & Van de Bunt, H. G. (1999). The social embeddedness of organized crime. *Transnational Organized Crime, 5,* 19–36.

Krevert, P. (1997). *Schutzgelderpressung: Das grosse geschäft mit der Angst* [Protection rackets: The big business with fear]. Lübeck, Germany: Schmidt-Römhild.

Lampe, K. von. (1999). *Organized crime: Begriff und theorie organisierter kriminalität in den USA* [Organized crime: Concept and theory of organized crime in the U.S.A.]. Frankfurt am Main, Germany: Peter Lang.

Lampe, K. von. (2001a). Not a process of enlightenment: The conceptual history of organized crime in Germany and the United States of America. *Forum on Crime and Society, 1,* 99–116.

Lampe, K. von. (2001b). Organisierte Kriminalität unter der Lupe: Netzwerke kriminell nutzbarer kontakte als konzeptueller zugang zur OK-problematik [Organized crime under the magnifying glass: Networks of criminally exploitable ties as a conceptual approach to the OC-problem]. *Kriminalistik, 55,* 465–471.

Lampe, K. von. (2002a, September). Assessing organized crime: The case of Germany. *ECPR Standing Group eNewsletter Organized Crime.* Retrieved May 11, 2004, from http://members.lycos.co.uk/ocnewsletter/SGOC0902/german.html

Lampe, K. von. (2002b). The trafficking in untaxed cigarettes in Germany: A case study of the social embeddedness of illegal markets. In P. C. van Duyne, K. von Lampe, & N. Passas (Eds.), *Upperworld and underworld in cross-border crime* (pp. 141–161). Nijmegen, Netherlands: Wolf Legal.

Lampe, K. von. (2003). Organising the nicotine racket: Patterns of criminal cooperation in the cigarette black market in Germany. In P. C. van Duyne, K. von Lampe, & J. Newell (Eds.), *Criminal finances and organising crime in Europe* (pp. 41–65). Nijmegen, Netherlands: Wolf Legal.

Lampe, K. von, & Johansen, P. O. (2004). Criminal networks and trust: On the importance of expectations of loyal behaviour in criminal relations. In S. Nevala & K. Aromaa (Eds.), *Organised crime, trafficking, drugs: Selected papers presented at the Annual Conference of the European Society of Criminology, Helsinki 2003* (pp. 102–113). Helsinki, Finland: HEUNI.

Lee, R. W. (1998). *Smuggling Armageddon: The nuclear black market in the former Soviet Union and Europe.* New York: St. Martin's.

Lee, R. W. (2003, Spring). Nuclear smuggling: Patterns and responses. *Parameters, 33,* 35–50. Retrieved May 12, 2004, from http://carlisle.www.army.mil/usawc/Parameters/03spring/lee.pdf

LeFloch-Prigent, L. (2001). *Affaire Elf, affaire d'état* [The Elf affair, affair of the state]. Paris: Le Cherche Midi.

Lehti, M., & Aromaa, K. (2004). Trafficking in women and children in Europe. In S. Nevala & K. Aromaa (Eds.), *Organised crime, trafficking, drugs: Selected papers presented at the Annual Conference of the European Society of Criminology, Helsinki 2003* (pp. 114–128). Helsinki, Finland: HEUNI.

Levay, M. (2000). Social changes and rising crime rates: The case of Central and Eastern Europe. *European Journal of Crime, Criminal Law and Criminal Justice, 8,* 35–50.

Levi, M. (1998). Perspectives on "organised crime": An overview. *The Howard Journal, 37,* 335–345.

Lindlau, D. (1987). *Der mob: Recherchen zum organisierten Verbrechen* [The mob: Research on organized crime]. Hamburg, Germany: Hoffmann und Campe.

Lupo, S. (2002). *Die Geschichte der Mafia* [The history of the Mafia] (A. R. Luperti & B. Lindecke, Trans.). Düsseldorf, Germany: Patmos. (Original work published 1996)

Mack, J. A., & Kerner, H.-J. (1975). *The crime industry.* Westmead, UK: Saxon House.

MacMullen, A. (1999). Fraud, mismanagement and nepotism: The Committee of Independent Experts and the fall of the European Commission. *Crime, Law and Social Change, 31,* 1999, 193–208.

Mitsilegas, V. (2001). Defining organised crime in the European Union: The limits of European criminal law in an area of "freedom, security and justice." *European Law Review, 26,* 565–581.

Nelken, D. (1996). The judges and political corruption in Italy. *Journal of Law and Society, 23*(1), 95–112.

Neubacher, F. (2002). Strukturen und strategien der Mafia: Einblicke in die neuere Italienische literatur [Structures and strategies of the Mafia: Insights into the more recent Italian literature]. *Neue Kriminalpolitik, 14,* 44–46.

Nillson, A. (1998). International Atomic Energy Agency Programme against Illicit Trafficking in Nuclear Materials and Radioactive Sources. *Transnational Organized Crime, 4,* 315–320.

Okólski, M. (2000). Illegality of international population movements in Poland. *International Migration, 38*(Suppl. 1), 57–87.

Osyka, I. (2000). Organised economic crime problems in the Ukraine. In P. C. van Duyne, V. Ruggiero, M. Scheinost, & W. Valkenburg (Eds.), *Cross-border crime in a changing Europe* (pp. 130–144). Tilburg, Netherlands, and Prague, Czech Republic: Tilburg University and Institute of Criminology and Social Prevention, Czech Republic.

Paoli, L. (1998). Criminal fraternities or criminal enterprises? *Transnational Organized Crime, 4,* 88–108.

Paoli, L. (1999). The future of Sicilian and Calabrian organized crime. In S. Einstein & M. Amir (Eds.), *Organized crime: Uncertainties and dilemmas* (pp. 155–186). Chicago: Office of International Criminal Justice.

Paoli, L. (2002). The development of an illegal market: Drug consumption and trade in post-Soviet Russia. *British Journal of Criminology, 42,* 21–39.

Paoli, L. (2003). The "invisible hand of the market": The illegal drugs trade in Germany, Italy, and Russia. In P. C. van Duyne, K. von Lampe, & J. Newell (Eds.), *Criminal finances and organising crime in Europe* (pp. 19–40). Nijmegen, Netherlands: Wolf Legal.

Passas, N. (1998). Globalization and transnational crime: Effects of criminogenic asymmetries. *Transnational Organized Crime, 4,* 22–56.

Passas, N. (2002). Cross-border crime and the interface between legal and illegal actors. In P. C. van Duyne, K. von Lampe, & N. Passas (Eds.), *Upperworld and underworld in cross-border crime* (pp. 11–41). Nijmegen, Netherlands: Wolf Legal.

Pearson, G., & Hobbs, D. (2001). *Middle market drug distribution.* London: Home Office.

Peev, E. (2002). Ownership and control structures in transition to "crony" capitalism: The case of Bulgaria. *Eastern European Economics, 40*(5), 73–91.

Pieke, F. N. (2002). *Recent trends in Chinese migration to Europe: Fujianese migration in perspective.* Geneva, Switzerland: International Organization for Migration. Retrieved May 11, 2004, from www.iom.int/documents/publication/en/mrs%5F6%5F2002.pdf

President's Commission on Organized Crime. (1986). *The impact: Organized crime today.* Washington, D.C.: Author.

Pujas, V., & Rhodes, M. (1998). *Party finance and political scandal in Latin Europe.* Florence, Italy: European University Institute.

Ratzel, M. -P., & Lippert, F. (2001). International organisierte kraftfahrzeugkriminalität [Internationally organized motor vehicle crime]. *Kriminalistik, 55,* 705–713.

Rebscher, E., & Vahlenkamp, W. (1988). *Organisierte kriminalität in der Bundesrepublik Deutschland: Bestandsaufnahme, entwicklungstendenzen und bekämpfung aus sicht der polizeipraxis* [Organized crime in the Federal Republic of Germany: Assessment, trends and countermeasures from the perspective of the police practice]. Wiesbaden, Germany: Bundeskriminalamt.

Rebscher, E., & Vahlenkamp, W. (1991). Organized crime in the Federal Republic of Germany. In E. Kube & H. U. Störzer (Eds.), *Police research in the Federal Republic of Germany* (pp. 179–187). Berlin, Germany: Springer.

Rixdorf, W. (1993). *Das steinerne gesicht: Der pate von Danzig Nikodem Skotarczak* [The stone face: The godfather of Gdansk Nikodem Skotarczak]. Berlin, Germany: Karin Kramer.

Roberts, K., Adibekian, A., Nemiria, G., Tarkhnishvili, L., & Tholen, J. (1998). Traders and mafiosi: The young self-employed in

Armenia, Georgia and Ukraine. *Journal of Youth Studies, 1,* 259–278.

Ruggiero, V. (1996). *Organized and corporate crime in Europe: Offers that can't be refused.* Aldershot, UK: Dartmouth.

Salt, J. (2000). Trafficking and human smuggling: A European perspective. *International Migration, 38*(Suppl. 1), 31–54.

Schelling, T. C. (1971). What is the business of organized crime? *Journal of Public Law, 20*(1), 71–84.

Schmidt, U. (1993). Regierungs- und vereinigungskriminalität [Government crime and crime connected with the unification]. *Kriminalistik, 47,* 521–532.

Schneider, F., & Enste, D. (2000). *Shadow economies around the world: Size, causes and consequences* (Working paper WP/00/26). Washington, DC: International Monetary Fund. Retrieved May 11, 2004, from www.uni-koeln.de/wiso-fak/eekhoff/mitarb/schatten/imfwp.pdf

Sehr, P. (1995). *Internationale kraftfahrzeugverschiebung* [International trafficking in motor vehicles]. Lübeck, Germany: Schmidt-Römhild.

Sharpe, J. A. (1996). Crime in England: Long-term trends and the problem of modernization. In E. A. Johnson & E. H. Monkkonen (Eds.), *The civilization of crime: Violence in town and country since the Middle Ages* (pp. 17–34). Urbana and Chicago: University of Illinois Press.

Sieber, U. (1998). Euro-fraud: Organised fraud against the financial interests of the European Union. *Crime, Law and Social Change, 30,* 1–42.

Sieber, U., & Bögel, M. (1993). *Logistik der organisierten kriminalität* [Logistics of organized crime]. Wiesbaden, Germany: Bundeskriminalamt.

Siemaszko, A. (Ed.). (2000). *Crime and law enforcement in Poland on the threshold of the 21st century.* Warsaw, Poland: Oficyna Naukowa.

SINUS München (2000). *Wie sicher lebt und arbeitet man in Moskau? Erfahrungen und urteile von Deutschen 1999* [How safe is living and working in Moscow: Experiences and assessments by Germans 1999]. Moscow: Friedrich-Ebert-Stiftung Moskau.

Skaperdas, S., & Syropoulos, C. (1995). Gangs as primitive states. In G. Fiorentini & S. Peltzman (Eds.), *The economics of organised crime* (pp. 61–82). Cambridge, UK: Cambridge University Press.

Skoblikov, P. A. (1999). *Vzyskaniye dolgov i kriminal* [Debt collection and crime]. Moscow: Yurist.

Sobolev, V. A., Rushchenko, I. P., & Volobuev, A. F. (2002). *Organized criminal groups in Ukraine: traditional and typical (sociological essay).* Kharkov, Ukraine: National University of Internal Affairs.

Sterling, C. (1994). *Thieves' world: The threat of the new global network of organized crime.* New York: Simon & Schuster.

Stille, A. (1995). *Excellent cadavers: The Mafia and the death of the first Italian republic.* New York: Pantheon Books.

Tak, P. J. P. (2000). Bottlenecks in international police and judicial Cooperations in the EU. *European Journal of Crime, Criminal Law and Criminal Justice, 8,* 343–360.

Tarrius, A. (1999). Les fluidités de l'ethnicité: réseaux de l'économie souterraine transfrontalière de produits d'usage licites ou illicites [The fluidities of ethnicity: Webs of the cross-border underworld economy of legal and illegal products]. *Déviance et Société, 23,* 259–274.

Transparency International. (2002). *Transparency International corruption perceptions index 2002.* Berlin, Germany: Author. Retrieved May 11, 2004, from www.transparency.org/cpi/index.html

Varese, F. (2001). *The Russian Mafia: Private protection in a new market economy.* Oxford, UK: Oxford University Press.

Vocks, J., & Nijboer, J. (2000). The promised land: A study of trafficking in women from Central and Eastern Europe to the Netherlands. *European Journal on Criminal Policy and Research, 8,* 379–388.

Volkov, V. (2000a). Between economy and the state: Private security and rule enforcement in Russia. *Politics and Society, 28,* 483–501.

Volkov, V. (2000b). The political economy of protection rackets in the past and the present. *Social Research, 67,* 709–744.

Wamers, P. (1996). *Illegaler technologie-transfer: Eine sonderform der organisierten kriminalität*

[Illegal transfer of technology: A special form of organized crime]. Lübeck, Germany: Schmidt-Römhild.

Weerman, F. M. (2003). Co-offending as social exchange: Explaining characteristics of co-offending. *British Journal of Criminology, 43*, 398–416.

Weschke, E., & Heine-Heiss, K. (1990). *Organisierte kriminalität als netzstrukturkriminalität: Teil 1* [Organized crime as net structured crime: Part 1]. Berlin, Germany: Fachhochschule für Verwaltung und Rechtspflege.

Williams, P. (1999). Getting rich and getting even: Transnational threats in the twenty-first century. In S. Einstein & M. Amir (Eds.), *Organized crime: Uncertainties and dilemmas* (pp. 19–63). Chicago: Office of International Criminal Justice.

Woodiwiss, M. (2001). *Organized crime and American power: A history.* Toronto: University of Toronto Press.

Zaitch, D. (2002). *Trafficking cocaine: Colombian drug entrepreneurs in the Netherlands.* The Hague, Netherlands: Kluwer.

Zimmerli, S. (1999). Die Territorialität der outlaw motorcycle clubs [The territoriality of outlaw motorcycle clubs]. *Montasschrift für Kriminologie und Strafrechtsreform, 82*, 320–339.

21

Organized Crime in Latin America

MAURICIO RUBIO

ROMÁN ORTIZ

The intellectual and legal tradition in Latin America that makes a categorical distinction between politically motivated and common everyday criminality is a long one. This has been one of the obstacles to confronting organized crime in the region in an efficacious manner. This chapter argues that the line that separates criminal organizations from insurgent groups, or terrorists, is increasingly tenuous, confused, and irrelevant for the purposes of internal security. The chapter is divided into four sections. In the first part, the theories from which the recommendation to distinguish the rebel from the criminal is derived are summarized and the limitations of this proposal to the understanding of Latin American reality are demonstrated. In part two, evidence is offered on the progressive participation of Latin American insurgent movements in criminal activities and on the

inevitable politicization of drug-trafficking organizations. In the third section, the impossibility of designing domestic security strategies without moving beyond this dichotomy is discussed. Finally, a brief list of the persistent obstacles to a correct understanding of organized crime in Latin America concludes the chapter.

REBELS AND CRIMINALS: THE THEORY AND ITS LIMITATIONS

The distinction between political and common crime that characterizes Latin American thought has two dimensions. At the positive or explanatory level, it is understood that political criminals differ from their ordinary brethren basically in their intentions and not in their actions. It is thought that the common criminal is inspired to seek personal

Caribbean Sea

Trinidad and Tobago

Guyana

Suriname

French Guiana

Venezuela

State of
Antioquia

• Medellin

• Cali

Colombia

Ecuador

Galapagos
Islands
(Ecuador)

Peru

Brazil

Pacific
Ocean

Bolivia

Paraguay

Atlantic
Ocean

Chile

Argentina

Uruguay

Falkland
Islands
(U.K.)

financial reward, while the political delinquent is socially and altruistically motivated (see Orozco, 1992).[1] Another description of the political lawbreaker is that of the social bandit suggested by Hobsbawm (1991)—an individual who rebels against unjust rule and has wide support among the peasant classes.[2] The third categorization is that of Carl Schmitt, who presents four distinctive features of the *partisan* (his term): He is an irregular combatant, he acts in response to a profound political adherence, he is highly mobile, and, again, he has an "intimate relationship with a specific population and a territory" (quoted in Pizarro, 1996, p. 42).

In a second, normative, dimension, the theory suggests that only ordinary criminals should be penalized and that the rebel must be accorded a privileged treatment: In this case, above all, negotiation should be sought.[3] For different reasons, it is considered that a criminal sanction against rebels is not only unworkable[4] but can even be counterproductive.[5]

The critique of this distinction between political crime and common crime can be summarized in two points. The first is its excessive adherence to 19th-century modes of thought and the failure to incorporate theoretical developments that have occurred in the social sciences, most particularly those related to the rational choice model, organizational theory, and institutional analysis. The second, more pertinent, point is its obvious divergence from the contemporary conditions found in the region's countries, which show serious discrepancies with the ideal-type classification schemes that have been proposed. As shown in the next section, in the Latin American reality, there are numerous symptoms of some profound interdependencies between rebels and criminals. To insist on classifying them independently is a dead-end street. This approach has not only lost its explanatory power but, even

more important, has failed to contribute satisfactorily to the development of sound public policy.

CRIMINALIZED REBELS AND POLITICIZED CRIMINALS

The overlapping of politically motivated violence and organized crime began to become visible at the close of the Cold War era. The process was the product of a transformation of both the politically motivated armed groups and the criminal ones. Among the former, the changes were centered on the search for greater financial independence: They diversified their repertoire of funding activities alongside their political actions. The insurgents used criminal tactics to reach financial autonomy—kidnapping, drug trafficking, extortion, and the like. On the other hand, the growth of the economic dimension of organized crime made its growing political implications inevitable. This tendency was particularly visible in the case of the drug trade. The enormous proceeds from the drug business created the need and at the same time provided the means to influence the state. For that reason, the mafia groups set in motion a gamut of strategies that ranged from financing and participating in electoral politics to corruption and even terrorism. All that was supported by the sectors of the population who benefited from the production and sales of drugs. The inclination of the drug traffickers to compete for power ended up transforming criminal bands into political actors determined to force changes in the direction of governments, to provoke their fall or to promote the candidacies of their allies.

For Latin American insurgent organizations, the process of criminalization began with the changes unleashed with the dissolution of the Soviet Bloc. Throughout the Cold War era, the continent's armed groups relied on financial and military support from abroad to consolidate themselves. With some exceptions—such as the Castro campaign in

Cuba—the armed movements depended on the support of ideologically kindred states or those with strategic interests in common. The principal state promoters of insurgent activities in Latin America were the countries of the Eastern Bloc. Thus, the political and military expansion of the Salvadorian Farabundo Marti Front for National Liberation (FMLN) would have been impossible without the sustained backing of the Cuban and Nicaraguan governments sponsored by the Soviet Union (Moroni & Spencer, 1995). As well, governments that were not Soviet allies chose to support violent political organizations. For example, Venezuela offered critical support to the Nicaraguan Sandinista Front for National Liberation (FSLN) during the guerrilla campaign that culminated in the overthrow of Anastasio Somoza. The U.S. government was also the main supporter of the counterrevolutionary formations that opposed the Sandinista regime.

A number of different factors provoked a slow but steady change toward a model of a financially and militarily independent insurgency. At the beginning, certain guerrilla organizations assumed such radical ideologies that it distanced them from possible backers. This was the case of the Sendero Luminoso [Shining Path] (SL) from its origins in 1980. This group promoted an extreme reading of Maoism that not only divorced them from the orthodox communist states such as Cuba or the Soviet Union but also made them the enemies of the People's Republic of China, which they considered to be a revisionist government without a revolutionary bent. As a consequence, the SL was trapped in a political isolation that forced it to find its own sources of financing. The solution arrived in the mid 1980s when a column installed itself in the Alto Huallaga and began to offer protection to growers and traffickers in exchange for a percentage of the production or the drug shipment (Mason & Campany, 1995). It was the beginning of a close relationship between the drug trade and the SL. As a result, the group was able to survive in the regions where the crops from which drugs are produced are grown, despite the blows to its structure in the big cities and the areas of legal agriculture during the 1990s.

A decade later, with the disintegration of the U.S.S.R. and the Cuban crisis, the sources of state-sponsored support for Latin American guerrilla and terrorist groups dried up. This change put many armed organizations in a difficult position that led them to abandon the armed struggle and begin peace talks. The FMLN in 1992 and the Guatemalan National Revolutionary Union (URNG) in 1996 are cases in point. However, other organizations bet on the expansion of criminal activities to finance their revolutionary agenda. The most visible example of this tendency was the case of the Revolutionary Armed Forces of Colombia (FARC). During the Cold War, this organization maintained limited links with Moscow and Havana. Beginning in the early 1980s, the FARC were not able to remain aloof from the expanding drug trade and followed a similar trajectory to that of the SL, providing armed protection for the illicit crops. Given that historical development, it was natural for the FARC to opt to expand their involvement in the drug trade to consolidate financial independence in the aftermath of the disintegration of the Soviet Bloc (Rangel, 1999). This process implied a slow but steady penetration of the insurgents into the different phases of growing, processing, and marketing the drug. The FARC began by guarding and growing the coca bushes. Later, they built and managed their own drug-processing facilities. And finally, they began to act as suppliers of the drug, or drug traffickers. The discovery that the FARC was supplying drugs to the Brazilian drug lord "Fernandiño" and to the Mexican bands involved in the "Tijuana Cartel" demonstrates the FARC's criminalization.

Drug trafficking has not been the only criminal activity of the guerrilla organizations.

Ideological considerations have pushed some armed groups to distance themselves from drug trafficking as a source of revenue. This has not diverted them from the same process of criminalization; it has, however, led them to engage in different criminal activities to finance themselves. A good example is the Colombian Army of National Liberation (ELN). This group thought that the drug trade was incompatible with the revolutionary ethic, but they saw no problem with systematically kidnapping people to collect funds, which converted them into one of the leaders of the country's kidnapping industry. Certain armed organizations have chosen to finance themselves through activities other than drug trafficking not for ideological reasons but, rather, for economic or geographic convenience. Thus, some sectors of the Colombian paramilitary movement finance themselves by exploiting emerald deposits situated in the country's heartland, where they maintain a strong presence. In any case, Latin American guerrilla and terrorist organizations seem to have incorporated into their repertoire a growing number of criminal activities aimed at ensuring their financial autonomy. Put another way, politically motivated violence has taken on criminal overtones.

In parallel fashion, the development of organized crime in Latin America has given it a size and breadth of interests that necessarily led to its politicization. The most visible case has been that of the groups associated with the drug trade. The first relevant experience of politicizing criminal activity in Latin America was the consolidation of the Medellin Cartel in the middle of the 1980s (Gugliotta & Leen, 1989). With a virtual monopoly over cocaine production and exporting, the group led by Pablo Escobar became immersed in a multidimensional process of politicization. To begin with, the cartel sponsored several social projects in the region of Antioquia, gaining popular support among the lower classes. Meanwhile, the group infiltrated legal politics

by contributing to election campaigns, and Escobar himself actually won a seat in the Congress. Finally, it exerted military pressure with its own paramilitary organizations such as MAS (Death to Kidnappers) or made agreements with guerrilla groups such as the FARC or the M-19 (April 19 Movement) (MacDonald, 1989). The criminal activities of the Medellin Cartel were definitely politicized in the confrontation with the Colombian State over the legislation authorizing the extradition of Colombian citizens to face drug-trafficking charges in the U.S. justice system. To pressure the government and stop extradition, the Medellin Cartel unleashed an intensive terrorist campaign in the country's main cities using the name "The Extraditables" (Labrousse, 1993). In this fashion, Escobar confronted Colombian authorities by making use of an illegal armed strategy—terrorism—with the objective of forcing a change in a legal instrument—extradition. He was behaving exactly as do organizations that are commonly classified as politically motivated criminals.

Despite the fact that the Medellin Cartel's campaign of terror resulted in an all-out confrontation with the Colombian State that ended in Escobar's death and the dismantling of his group, Latin American criminal organizations continue to use political strategies in defense of their interests. The combination of sponsoring social welfare efforts, political corruption, and armed pressure that is chosen to influence state apparatuses has varied according to circumstances. Thus, the Cali Cartel rejected the use of terrorism to pressure Colombian authorities (Buckman, 1994) and, as an alternative, practiced an organized form of corruption and the use of social assistance programs to develop a support network. This two-pronged strategy allowed the cartel to protect their criminal activities with a web of corruption that extended to the highest levels of the public administration.

Since the mid-1990s, the break up of the Cali Mafia has left the control of the Colombian drug market to other smaller organizations. This fragmentation has not changed the mafias' need to intervene in the political sphere to protect their interests; however, it has changed the strategies used to achieve this goal. The use of corrupt practices to penetrate legal political activities has continued, as has the recurrent use of terrorism to defend their interests. At the same time, the cooperation between the Colombian armed organizations and the drug mafias has shifted significantly. Drug traffickers with more limited resources have had to become the junior partners of groups such as the AUC (United Self-Defenses of Colombia) or the FARC. So, the drug lords continue to enjoy political protection but at the cost of a greater dependency on the biggest players in the Colombian armed conflict.

Mexico is another example of the tendency to politicization of organized crime. Mexican drug-trafficking mafias have also set in motion a series of strategies to influence the state and gain political protection for their interests (Sánchez, 1996). Along with the use of patronage to gain the sympathy of the poorer strata in the areas where they operate, the Mexican cartels have also resorted to the practice of corruption, threats, and an association with terrorist groups. The successive dismantling of mafia groups operating along the U.S. border has highlighted the networks of political corruption on which the expansion of drug trafficking in this Aztec nation has relied. In 1996, the arrest of the Gulf Cartel leader was possible due to the imprisonment of an important political figure who apparently had been protecting him. Later, in an especially striking corruption case, the connections between the person responsible for the Mexican war on drugs and the head of the Ciudad Juarez Cartel were laid bare. At the same time, the use of politically motivated violence by Mexican drug traffickers became obvious with the assassination of a presidential candidate in 1994. Since then, Mexican drug traffickers have continued to use corruption and violence

to defend their interests in the border areas through which drugs transit to the United States. Furthermore, the drug mafias have established links with Mexican terrorist groups in a very similar move to the one made by their Colombian counterparts. In fact, since the end of the 1990s, the networks for heroin production in Guerrero state have relied on the support of the Popular Revolutionary Army, EPR, guerrilla movement both for protection for their laboratories as well as for their drug shipments (Wrighte, 2002). This is a case that demonstrates that the connection between drugs and terrorism is not exclusively a Colombian affair—it is a reflection of the tendency of organized crime and politically motivated violence to fuse.

INTERNAL OBSTACLES TO CONFRONTING ORGANIZED CRIME

The overlapping between politically motivated violence and organized crime poses a difficult challenge to public policy in a number of ways. First, the legal and judicial apparatuses of the Latin American states have differentiated the treatment accorded to rebels and to common criminals. In general terms, this distinction has centered on a privileged status for offenders deemed to be politically motivated while an effort is made to fully apply the criminal code to so-called common criminals. This then appears to legitimate the state to negotiate with guerrillas and terrorists. To obtain their demobilization and return to a noncriminal life, they are awarded amnesties and even offered a gamut of economic and political incentives, which can include employment plans or positions in public administration. Although experiences of quasi-political negotiations with criminal groups are not unheard of, these talks are seen as something out of the ordinary and clandestine in nature. On the other hand, talks with insurgent organizations are seen as the ideal fashion to move peace-building efforts forward. It is clear then that when the issue is confronting actors who increasingly combine elements of criminal activity and political influence, this schema is obsolete.

A second problem created by the fusion of politically motivated violence and crime is that it makes the development of a security policy difficult. Moreover, it exceeds the capacity of state apparatuses that were set up to handle the problems of common crime and politically motivated violence separately. Politicization has offered criminal actors the possibility of developing a social base and ways to influence state institutions, something that limits the efficacy of repression. In parallel fashion, criminalization provides armed groups with the means to ensure their financial autonomy and ways to contact international criminal networks, something that makes the processes of political negotiation more fraught. In fact, government authorities can find themselves having to combat drug cartels possessing a similar network of social support to the ones built by insurgent organizations and terrorist groups with the financial capacity of the big crime bosses.

Finally, the overlap between organized criminality and politically motivated violence produces difficulties when it comes to designating the agencies that will be responsible for confronting illegal groups. These groups are difficult to define as political adversaries of the state or bands of common criminals. Normally, in Latin America, the police have been the ones in charge of the struggle against organized crime, and the armed forces have taken charge of counterinsurgency. Increasingly, two factors have combined to confound the separation between military and police tasks. On one hand, with each passing day it is more difficult to make the distinction between criminal groups and insurgent organizations on the ground. On the other hand, the police in Latin America have not been able to deal with threats to domestic security backed by a large amount of money and military force.

In these circumstances, the continent's governments have turned increasingly to the use of the armed forces in the struggle against criminal elements. The armies of some Central American republics have been deployed repeatedly to confront ordinary crime waves. Something similar has occurred when public safety has been seriously jeopardized in the slums of Rio de Janeiro. Broad sectors of public opinion have been skeptical of the role of the military in maintaining public safety.

In summary, the appearance of actors that move between common criminality and terrorism has made the maintenance of the traditional distinction between them an increasingly tenuous proposition. On the contrary, it seems more useful to begin from the basis that a democratic state cannot negotiate its legal framework when it has popular support. With this restriction in mind, the decision to begin talks with illegal groups should not be conditioned on a presumed distinction between political and criminal actors, because they are ever more difficult to separate. The willingness of the state to decree amnesties and make other discretionary concessions to demobilize illegal groups should be guided by an evaluation of the impact of these measures on security more than by the supposed intentions of the groups' members.

In addition, the struggle against corruption, the fight against organized crime, and the antiterrorist strategies must be considered together insofar as getting results in one setting without making progress on the other fronts would be extremely difficult. Likewise, the distinctions between counterinsurgency operations and counternarcotics operations will have to be reviewed to the extent that their targets increasingly are the same.

THE INTERNATIONAL STRUGGLE AGAINST ORGANIZED CRIME

The portrait of a small Latin American country virtually controlled by mafia groups is no mere fictional account. It seems clear that when one speaks of confronting transnational armed groups that have the capacity to corrode or debilitate state apparatuses, it is necessary to coordinate forces at the international level. Alas, the progress that has been made in this direction suffers from the same basic fault that has plagued efforts at the national level: a current diagnosis that does not fully represent the reality of organized crime.

At the end of 2000 in Palermo, Italy, 124 member countries of the United Nations signed the Convention against Transnational Organized Crime (hereafter, the convention) in which they sought to harmonize the criteria for its definition and unify the weapons to combat it.[6]

Several different developments led up to the signing of the convention. First, local criminal organizations, such as the Colombian cartels, moved onto the world stage. Second, new groups began to appear day after day, many times in the form of networks or in association with legitimate businesses. Third, the range of the criminal activities broadened and diversified. Fourth, organized crime began to be recognized as an attack on sovereignty and democracy and as a source of state corruption.

On another front, different developed countries began to devote attention to the problem of illegal immigration in the 1980s. This combination of criminal organizations that surpass the local arena together with greater international mobility of persons is what made it pertinent to reconsider the traditional schema for analyzing organized crime.

Like the contemporary literature on mafia organizations, the convention rejects the notion of defining organized crime by using the specific illegal activities conducted by each group and opts to emphasize the elements common to the majority of the organizations. Although they do not share the same objectives, they do follow a similar pattern. The convention proposes that certain behaviors common to organized crime be classified in

domestic legislation as crimes independently of the specialized criminal practice of each organization. It includes four basic offenses: participation in organized criminal groups, money laundering, corruption, and obstruction of justice.

The definition of organized crime is still subject to debate. As would be expected, each person is most sensitive to the type of organized crime afflicting his or her society.[7] It is in the context of this debate that the importance of the convention should be highlighted because it goes beyond the definition of organized crime that starts from specific activities—activities that change and thus have hindered the characterization of the groups that execute them. To the contrary, the convention suggests that attention be concentrated on a few basic elements, common to a broad range of criminal groups, independently of their origins or stated objectives.

Since the beginning of the 1970s, Thomas Schelling (e.g., Schelling, 1971) has argued that the crucial difference between garden-variety crime and organized crime is that the latter seeks to govern and control the entire underworld economic structure. Only in organized crime is the collection of taxes and the imposition of regulations on businesses, whether illegal or legal, an objective. So the core activities of organized crime are related to the illegal markets not because control is sought over the production and distribution in these markets but, rather, because in the illegal activities there is no possibility of turning to the state to enforce contracts or resolve conflicts. Schelling's conception of organized crime is that of a quasi-government, or protector, of the criminal world that establishes and enforces its own rules of the game. That is essentially the position of Diego Gambetta (1993) as well, who suggests a view of the mafia boss as an individual who oversees exchange and protects agreements.

Using this conception of organized crime as a parallel state that regulates and oversees the activities of the underworld, it is possible to identify a limitation to the convention: It limits the objectives of organized criminal groups to the search for financial profit. This limitation not only contradicts recent literature on mafia groups but also ignores the fact that, as we see in Latin America, the line that separates the economic from the political is even more tenuous in the underworld than in legitimate enterprise.

Throughout the preparatory stages leading up to the convention, the existence of connections between organized crime and terrorism was acknowledged; at the end of the day, however, it was thought better to limit it to offenses producing an economic benefit. Only when the terrorist attacks occurred in the United States did people's concerns about the advisability of recognizing the close connections between terrorism and organized crime take wing, and an effort was made to amend the convention.[8]

It is difficult not to underline the fact that the convention is based on a partial, and idealized, vision of the legal and judicial systems of the societies in which organized crime has attained its most consolidated power. This bias is visible in several dimensions: first, in the emphasis it gives to offenses that are still not in the legislation of numerous countries, which implicitly assumes sophisticated and efficacious criminal investigation systems, to the detriment of more basic criminal behaviors—such as murder, kidnapping, or extortion—that both characterize organized crime and constitute the basis of mafia power in less developed societies. Second, it shows a lack of recognition that in many societies in which mafia groups arise or operate, it does not work very well to discriminate organized crime from activities of the general public. This can be due to the importance of the informal sector in the economy, the lower penetration of the tax system, or the excessive regulation of conducts such as money laundering or bribing public officials. In many cases, it defines what are practically

routine activities associated with any productive activity. Third, the language downplays the existence of corruption or threats to the judicial system, supposing implicitly that the legislative, and executive, branches are free of such influences. We saw earlier that this is not a reasonable assumption for countries highly influenced by organized crime.

Another noteworthy aspect of the convention, and of the contemporary analysis of organized crime in general, relates to the lack of interest in the origin of mafia groups, especially in the mechanisms used to recruit members. Appreciation is growing that the process of joining criminal organizations is more sophisticated and complex than the hazy image of some adult and rational lawbreakers getting together to commit offenses would have it. In particular, two other methods in common use in Latin American societies to broaden the mafia groups' membership are not contemplated: press-ganging, or tricking minors into participating, and the subcontracting and use of services provided by youth gangs. There are many testimonies to the forced recruitment of minors, including children, by guerrilla and paramilitary groups in Colombia (González, 2002). There is also ample data on the stimulating effect that drug trafficking had on the development of juvenile gangs of *sicarios* or paid killers in cities such as Cali or Medellin (Salazar, 1994). In Central America, the available information shows a high association between the presence of the so-called *maras*, or youth gangs, and the influence of organized crime in the area. In Nicaragua and Jamaica, there is evidence that mafia bosses contract juvenile gangs for purely political tasks. Also in Central America it was found that one of the elements that help explain the individual decisions of young people to join a gang is the presence of organized crime in their environs (Rubio, 2003a, 2003b).

In the international context, it is to be expected that the inconsistencies that have already been observed in different countries between the instruments to combat organized crime and the analysis and legal treatment of the juvenile offenders will increase. The situation of minors has still not been recognized, and the problem of the connections that are known to exist between juvenile delinquency and organized crime has not yet been tackled explicitly. In Honduras, for example, it seems clear that the youth gangs not only play an important role in the domestic drug distribution system but also constitute sophisticated mechanisms of recruitment and training for the ranks of organized crime, which leans on them and uses the advantages offered by a more lenient youth code to the utmost (Rubio, 2003a).

Finally, it is worth mentioning some inherent problems in the measurement of the phenomenon, a requisite for its adequate analysis. In most of the developed countries, the basic indicators of the presence, or influence, of organized crime come from intelligence information originating in the security agencies. If, as the literature recognizes, one of the main effects of organized crime is the co-optation, through corruption or threats, of such security agencies or the judicial system, not much can be expected in terms of quality and reliability of data generated therein. Above all, this applies when the information is most needed—that is, when organized crime is flexing its muscles.

It is now a widely recognized and documented fact for Latin America that, for different reasons, not even data on the reporting of offenses to the police are reliable. It is also known that the problem with the figures reported in police statistics is particularly acute in those places where the influence of armed groups is greater (Rubio, 1999). In this context, the problems of information on organized criminal activities, at the most basic level, are far from insignificant.

Where the influence of organized crime is low or moderate, it has been found that a good indicator of the presence of these activities is the homicide rate. The relationship between drug trafficking and violence has been recognized in the literature and tends to be corroborated in the data both for Latin American and for developed countries. However, in those places where organized crime has consolidated itself successfully, this type of measurement can be inadequate because the "parallel state" established by mafia groups can be perfectly consistent with low rates of violence. A good example of this scenario is Surinam, an important staging ground for the trafficking of cocaine to Europe, with a long history of guerrilla presence, and, simultaneously, very low crime rates.

As was found in the analysis of urban crime, it has been increasingly accepted that the best alternative to police crime records is victimization surveys. The solution to the problem of information on organized crime could be the same: direct surveys of households or young people. Exercises along these lines in both Colombia and Central America show that the answers to very simple survey questions can be a valuable source of information on organized crime—and practically the only one available.

Sadly, this type of effort is not undertaken in Latin America for the simple reason that there are no resources, when the amount required is infinitesimally small compared with what the developed world has indicated a willingness to invest in security. How paradoxical that in the era in which organized crime is recognized to be one of the main threats to global security and, simultaneously, that the main groups are born and mature in the countries of the third world, empirical research on crime continues to be limited to what happens in the developed countries and stays on the backburner, when it is not totally abandoned, in the very places where the phenomenon originates.

Without a solid empirical base on what is really happening in Latin America and in general in the countries where mafia groups arise, it is likely that certain very primitive caricatures will persist, such as the notion that only criminals are selfish and should be punished, whereas rebels sincerely seek social justice and societies should make deals with them. That is how anomalous situations are perpetuated such as that of state agencies in certain countries implacably pursuing producers of crops, which, although illegal in the first world, are traditionally grown by peasants—or international agencies and NGOs insisting that kidnappers, or terrorist organizations, be negotiated with at any cost.

NOTES

1. Orozco (1992) makes use of the ideas of Gustav Radbruch, the early 20th-century German criminologist.

2. Hobsbawm (1991) defines three types of social bandits: (1) the Robin Hood, to whom are attributed "all the positive moral values of the people and all their modest aspirations"; (2) the Brazilian Cangaceiro who "expresses above all the capacity of the common folk, humble folk, to terrorize the more powerful: he is avenger and righter of wrongs"; and (3) the Turkish Haidukes who represent "a permanent element of peasant resistance to the lords and the state" (p. 63). See also Hobsbawm (1965).

3. "The dominant forms of urban violence in Colombia are not negotiable, as is the violence produced by confrontations of armed apparatuses struggling for the control of the State or seeking a change of the existing political regime in Colombia" (Comisión de Estudios sobre la Violencia, 1995, p. 71).

4. Along the lines of Radbruch, Orozco (1992) comments, "Neither punishment nor reeducation and not even deterrence through fear are appropriate for a man who feels no guilt and who is not susceptible, therefore, to either remorse or reeducation, and perhaps not even fear" (p. 37).

5. "As concerns the general deterrent function, the German jurist (Radbruch) says that it is deformed in the case of the politically committed offender, to the point that before producing fear, it produces martyrs" (Orozco, 1992, p. 37).

6. See the Convention against Transnational Organized Crime and its Protocols (Document: A/55/383). Available online at www.undcp.org/palermo/theconvention.html.

7. While North Americans emphasize the notion of supply of illicit goods with spontaneous demand—drugs, gaming, prostitution—European concerns include topics such as illegal immigration. Countries affected by terrorism have supported the idea of a definition that would allow the activities of the groups that do not necessarily seek economic advantage to be covered.

8. With the signing of U.N. Security Council Resolution 1373, adopted on September 28, 2001(http://usinfo.state.gov/topical/pol/terror/un.htm).

REFERENCES

Buckman, R. (1994). The Cali Cartel: An undefeated enemy. *Low Intensity Conflict & Law Enforcement, 3*(3), 430–452.

Comisión de estudios sobre la violencia. (1995). *Colombia: Violencia y democracia* [Colombia: Violence and democracy] (4th ed.). Bogotá: National University, Colciencias, Institute of Political Studies and International Relations.

Gambetta, D. (1993). *The Sicilian Mafia: The business of private protection.* Cambridge, MA: Harvard University Press.

González, G. (2002). *Los niños de la guerra.* [Children of the war] Bogotá, Colombia: Planeta.

Gugliotta, G., & Leen, J. (1989). *Kings of cocaine.* New York: Simon & Schuster.

Hobsbawm, E. J. (1991). Historiografía del bandolerismo [A historiography of banditry]. In G. Sánchez & R. Peñaranda (Eds.), *Pasado y presente de la violencia en Colombia* [Past and present of the violence in Colombia] (2nd ed.). Bogotá, Colombia: Instituto de Estudios Políticos y Relaciones Internacionales (IEPRI) y el Centro de Estudios de la Realidad Económica (CEREC).

Hobsbawm, E. J. (1965). *Primitive rebels: Studies in archaic forms of social movement in the 19th and 20th centuries.* New York: Norton Library.

Labrousse, A. (1993). *La droga, el dinero y las armas* [The drug, the money and the arms]. Madrid: Siglo XXI.

MacDonald, S. B. (1989). *Mountain high, white avalanche: Cocaine and power in the Andean States and Panama.* New York: Praeger.

Mason, T. D., & Campany, C. (1995). Guerrillas, drugs and peasants: The rational peasant and the war on drugs in Peru. *Terrorism and Political Violence, 7*(4), 140–170.

Moroni, J. A., & Spencer, D. E. (1995). *Strategy and tactics of the Salavadoran FMLN guerrillas: Last battle of the Cold War, blueprint for future conflicts.* Westport, CT: Praeger.

Orozco, I. (1992). *Combatientes, rebeldes y terroristas: Guerra y derecho en Colombia* [Fighters, rebels and terrorists: War and law in Colombia]. Bogotá, Colombia: Instituto de Estudios Políticos y Relaciones Internacionales (IEPRI), Temis.

Pizarro, E. (1996). *Insurgencia sin revolución* [Insurgency without revolution]. Bogotá, Colombia: Tercer Mundo, Instituto de Estudios Políticos y Relaciones Internacionales (IEPRI).

Rangel, A. (1999). Las FARC-EP: Una mirada actual [The FARC-EP: A present view]. In M. L. Deas & M. Victoria (Eds.), *Reconocer la guerra para construir la paz* [Understanding war to build peace] (pp. 21–51). Bogotá, Colombia: Editorial Norma.

Rubio, M. (1999). *Crimen e impunidad, precisiones sobre la violencia* [Crime and impunity: Some clarifications on violence]. Bogotá, Colombia: Uniandes, Tercer Mundo.

Rubio, M. (2003a). *Infractores, delincuentes juveniles y mareros en Honduras* [Offenders, juvenile delinquents, and gangs in Honduras]. Mimeo. Washington, DC: Inter-American Development Bank.

Rubio, M. (2003b). *Sin educación y con poder: Pandillas juveniles en Managua* [Without education and with power: Young gangs in Managua]. Mimeo. Washington, DC: Inter-American Development Bank.

Salazar, A. (1994). *No nacimos pa semilla* [Not born for seed]. Bogotá, Colombia: Centro de Investigaciones y Educación Popular (CINEP).

Sánchez, J. (1996). *Narcotrafficking in México.* Carlisle, PA: U.S. Army War College, Carlisle Barracks.

Schelling, T. C. (1971). What is the business of organized crime? *Journal of Public Law, 20*(1), 71–84.

Wrighte, M. R. (2002). The real Mexican terrorist: A group profile of popular revolutionary army (EPR). *Studies in Conflict and Terrorism, 25*(4), 207–225.

22

Organized Crime in North America

JAMES O. FINCKENAUER

JAY ALBANESE

*T*he Godfather, The Sopranos, Goodfellas, *Scarface,* and *The Gangs of New York* are a few of the hundreds of films, television shows, and books that depict aspects of organized crime in North America. But virtually no one can separate which of these is fact and which is fiction (in fact, nearly all are fiction). The blurring of fiction and reality makes it difficult to have an accurate understanding of organized crime. Greater accuracy is crucial if public opinion, legislation, and the criminal justice system are to properly respond to the actual threat of organized crime in North America.

North America includes the countries of Canada, the United States, and Mexico. Each is a large country sharing long land borders and massive coastlines that provide access to both the Atlantic and Pacific Oceans. Therefore, the countries of North America are very accessible not only to each other but also from many locations around the world.

Mexico, in particular, is strategically positioned, linking South and Central America to the United States and to Canada as well. The long Mexican land and water borders provide ideal launching points for smuggling people and products to both the United States and Canada, which have large consumer populations that enjoy a high standard of living and income. As a result, North America's geographic location, land and water border access, links to Central and South America, and high standard of living combine to create an attractive environment for organized crime.

HISTORICAL CONTEXT

Organized crime in North America is not a singular phenomenon. It always has been composed of a variety of groups, both large and small, that emerged to exploit particular criminal opportunities. If the terminology had been in use 200 years ago, early European settlers in North America might have been accused of involvement in organized crime activity for avoiding European taxes, engaging in planned thefts from public transport, and bribing government officials to secure favors. Organized crime, indeed, is characterized by planned illegal acts involving multiple offenders who engage in ongoing or recurrent criminal activities.

Traditional crimes associated with organized crime include illegal gambling, prostitution, loan-sharking, drug trafficking, selling stolen property, and extorting money from business owners. But this list is expanding dramatically with changes in the global economy, technology, and communications. For example, arrests in Long Island, New York, revealed a modest home being used to produce 10,000 bootlegged CDs each week and homeowners connected to known organized crime groups who allegedly helped in the illegal distribution of these CD copies (Holloway, 2002). In another case in Australia, it was found that criminal groups in Canada, Malaysia, and Europe had tapped into data cables from department stores to copy credit card information and transmit it overseas, which was then used to produce fake cards that were imported back into Australia (Nicholson, 2003). These examples demonstrate that the types of offenses associated with organized crime change as opportunities and circumstances change. Easy access to the Internet and ease of international air travel are as important to the expansion of human trafficking and fraud as was the invention of the automobile 100 years ago in creating new opportunities for smuggling goods by land and for various types of car registration and ownership frauds.

DESCRIBING ORGANIZED CRIME IN NORTH AMERICA

Organized crime can be described in terms of the activities it engages in or by the groups involved. There are advantages and disadvantages to each approach. The offenses are finite in any given historical period, and they always involve some variation of provision of illicit goods (e.g., stolen property, drugs), provision of illicit services (e.g., prostitution, gambling, loan-sharking), the infiltration of business (e.g., extortion and protection rackets), or some combination of these. What changes by region are the kinds of groups that engage in these activities. The history of criminality in a region, its economic standing, geographic location, national and ethnic customs and beliefs, and political climate are all important factors in shaping the kinds of organized criminal groups that develop in a country or region (Albanese, Das, & Verma, 2003).

Of the myriad forms of organized crime in North America, five major types are selected for examination here. Although other kinds of organized crime can be found in North America, such as outlaw motorcycle gangs, the five types we have chosen are well documented, have been in existence for a relatively long time, and have been subject to study by many researchers and criminal justice practitioners. Thus, the probability of finding valid and reliable information about these types is quite high. As other groups emerge and manage to survive, our knowledge of their structure and operations will grow as well. The five types described here are Cosa Nostra groups, Russian groups, Chinese groups, Mexican groups, and Canadian groups.

Cosa Nostra

La Cosa Nostra or LCN—also known as the Mafia, the mob, the outfit—is a collection of Italian-American organized crime "families" that has been operating in the United States and parts of Canada since the 1920s. Beginning during the time of Prohibition and extending into the 1990s, the LCN was clearly the most prominent criminal organization in the United States. Indeed, it was synonymous with organized crime. In recent years, the LCN has been severely crippled by prosecutions, and over the past two decades, it has been challenged in a number of its criminal markets by other organized crime groups. Nevertheless, LCN remains a viable organization. The LCN still has greater capacity to gain monopoly control over criminal markets, to use or threaten violence to maintain that control, and to corrupt law enforcement and the political system than does any of its competitors. As one scholar has pointed out, "No other criminal organization [in the United States] has controlled labor unions, organized employer cartels, operated as a rationalizing force in major industries, and functioned as a bridge between the upperworld and the underworld" (Jacobs & Gouldin, 1999, p. 128). This capacity distinguishes the LCN from all other criminal organizations in the United States.

Each of the so-called families (whose members usually are not related) that make up the Cosa Nostra has roughly the same organizational structure. There is a boss who exercises general oversight of the family and makes executive decisions. There is an underboss who is second in command. There is a senior adviser or consigliere. And then there are a number of "capos" (capo-regimes) who supervise crews made up of "soldiers," who are "made members" of Cosa Nostra. The capos and those above them receive shares of the proceeds from crimes committed by the soldiers and associates. The illicit operations of the soldiers and associates are not run by the bosses or capos, but the latter are paid a percentage of the profits for "protection" services and for their affiliation with the enterprise.

Made members, sometimes called "good fellows" or "wise guys," are all male and all of Italian descent. The estimated made membership of the LCN is 1,100 nationwide in the United States, with roughly 80% of the members operating in the New York metropolitan area. Five crime families make up the LCN in New York City: the Bonanno, the Colombo, the Genovese, the Gambino, and the Lucchese families. There is also LCN operational activity in Boston, Chicago, Philadelphia, and the Miami/South Florida area, but much less so than in New York. In other previous strongholds such as Cleveland, Detroit, Kansas City, Las Vegas, Los Angeles, New Orleans, and Pittsburgh, the LCN is now weak or nonexistent. In addition to the made members, there are approximately 10,000 associate members who work for the families. Until the recent demise of much of its leadership, a commission of the bosses of New York's five LCN families coordinated control of labor unions, construction, trucking, and garbage hauling companies and resolved disputes between families (Schweizer, Nishimotto, Salzano, & Chamberlin, 2003). In Canada, the influence of Cosa Nostra is felt primarily in the provinces of Ontario and Quebec (Criminal Intelligence Service Canada, 2002). Some of this is "spillover" influence from U.S. families across the border, but Hamilton, Toronto, and Montreal have a history of separate Cosa Nostra groups that have been known to communicate with groups in the United States.

LCN does not enjoy general social acceptance and support. With the exception of a few ethnic Italian neighborhoods where certain of the more brazen exploits and some of the community "good deeds" of bosses are admired, Italian organized crime reinforces a stigma that most Italian-Americans want to eliminate. Along with the stronger effectiveness of law enforcement, the absence of support for the LCN means that recruitment has become difficult. Some families have disappeared, and others are only 10% to 50% of their size 30 years ago. At the same time, however, it is the community's desire for illicit goods and services that continues to help fuel the survival of the Cosa Nostra and all other organized crime groups.

Becoming a made member of LCN requires serving an apprenticeship and then being proposed by a boss. This is followed by gaining approval for membership from all the other families. Once approved, there is a secret, ritualized induction ceremony. Made membership means both honor and increased income. It also, however, entails responsibilities—in particular taking an oath of *omerta*. *Omerta* demands silence to the outside world about the criminal affairs of the family, never betraying anyone in the family, and never revealing to law enforcement anything that might incriminate anyone in organized crime. The penalty for violating this oath is often death. At the same time, the fact that there are over a 100 Cosa Nostra members in the U.S. federal witness protection program (who testified in court against their former colleagues) suggests that omerta is not nearly as effective as it once was.

Violence

Cosa Nostra, over many years, established its reputation for the ruthless use of violence. This violence has occurred mostly in the form of beatings and killings. Personal violence, and to a lesser degree violence against property—bombings, arson, explosions—is the typical pattern of the systematic use of violence as a tool of doing business. Violence, and subsequently just the threat of violence, was the means by which the LCN gained monopoly control over its various criminal enterprises. It discouraged and eliminated competitors, and it reinforced the reputation and credibility of the LCN. Violence was also used for internal discipline. Murder, or conspiracy to commit murder, has often appeared as one of the predicate offenses in RICO (Racketeer-Influenced and Corrupt Organizations) prosecutions.

That violence continues to be an LCN tool is evidenced in two incidents carried out at the behest of the former head of the Gambino crime family in New York, John Gotti. In a 1997 trial, a member of the Gambino family testified about a torture killing that had been ordered by Gotti. The victim apparently fired a shot at Gotti. He was tortured with lighted cigarettes and a knife, shot in the buttocks, carried in the trunk of a car, and ultimately killed with five shots to the head. In the second example, the same John Gotti, from his federal prison cell, contracted with two members of the white supremacist group the Aryan Brotherhood to kill the former consigliere of the Gambino crime family who had threatened to kill him. In 1999, a member of the Lucchese crime family (also based in New York) was charged with conducting a 15-year reign of terror against competitors in the private sanitation business. The charges included setting fire to trucks and buildings of rival carters, damaging businesses that dared to hire carters outside the LCN cartel, and killing a salesman for a rival carting company (Mustain & Capeci, 2002).

The history of violence and the LCN demonstrates the importance of reputation in this respect. Peter Reuter (1982) has made the point that that when there is sufficient credible evidence of the willingness to use violence, *actual* violence is rarely necessary. This is especially true when the targets are not professional criminals. The Cosa Nostra personifies this principle.

Economic Resources

One of the LCN's major assets is its general business acumen. They are best described as being entrepreneurial, opportunistic, and adaptable. They find ways to exploit market vulnerabilities while at the same time maintaining the necessary stability and predictability that business requires to be profitable. One of the ways they do this is by taking over only a piece of a legitimate business—and providing a service in return—rather than taking over the whole business (Jacobs & Gouldin, 1999). The latter would, of course, require a management responsibility that they do not want to handle.

LCN's illegal activities cover a wide range. Gambling and drugs have traditionally been their biggest moneymakers. Loan-sharking is linked to these activities, because the money loaned is often first obtained through gambling and drug transactions. Extortion of businesses for "protection" from damage (by the extortionist) is an example of how the reputation for violence is important in order to instill the necessary fear in victims so they will pay extortion demands. When the fear is high enough, of course, actual violence is not needed (and sometimes can impair the victim's ability to pay).

The specialties of the five New York LCN families include labor racketeering, various kinds of business racketeering, bid rigging, business frauds, and industry cartels. In these areas, the LCN demonstrates its most effective penetration of the legitimate economy. Labor racketeering involves organized crime control of labor unions. With this control, gained by the threat and use of violence, large sums of money are siphoned from union pension funds, businesses are extorted in return for labor peace and an absence of strikes, and bribes are solicited for sweetheart contracts. Another specialty, business racketeering, has occurred in New York City in the construction, music, and garbage industries. The LCN controls unions, bars, strip joints, restaurants, and trucking firms. The five families have also controlled at various times the Fulton Fish Market, the Javits Convention Center, the New York Coliseum, and air cargo operations at JFK International Airport, among other targets. Again the principal tools of control are bribery and extortion (Jacobs, Friel, & Radick, 1999).

One of the best examples of an LCN cartel was their monopoly of the waste-hauling industry in New York City for almost 50 years. LCN used its control of local unions to set up a cartel, which monopolized the industry by threatening business disruption, labor problems, and personal violence (Jacobs & Hortis, 1998). Using this monopoly control, the LCN forced participants and consumers to pay inflated prices for waste hauling—a practice known as a "mob tax." Over the years, this mob tax cost the industry hundreds of millions of dollars.

Partly in reaction to effective law enforcement and prosecutions in recent years, the Cosa Nostra has diversified its activities and extended its penetration in legal markets by switching to white-collar crimes (Raab, 1997). They have carried out multimillion dollar frauds in three areas in particular: health insurance, prepaid telephone cards, and through victimizing small Wall Street brokerage houses. Professional know-how is demonstrated in each of these scams. In an example of their health insurance frauds, mobsters set up Tri-Con Associates, a New Jersey company that arranged medical, dental, and optical care for more than 1 million patients throughout the country. They used nonmob employees of Tri-Con as managers and intimidated health insurance administrators into approving excessive payments to the company. With the prepaid telephone cards, the Gambino family set up a calling card company that stole more than $50 million from callers and phone companies by means of fraudulent sales. In the case of the stock market, LCN members and associates offered loans to stockbrokers who were in debt or needed capital to expand their businesses. The mobsters then forced the brokers to sell them most of the low-priced shares in a company before its stock was available to investors through initial public offerings. They quickly inflated the value of the shares by spreading positive (but false) information about the company and then selling the shares, making huge profits before the overvalued stocks plunged in value (*Organized Crime*, 2000).

LCN's monopoly control over various illegal markets, and its diversification into legal markets, has so far not been matched by any other criminal organization in the United States. This is so despite its having been substantially weakened over the last two decades.

Political Resources

In its heyday, the LCN exercised its political influence mostly at the local level, through its connections with the political "machines" in which bribery was the common method of operation, in U.S. cities such as New York, New Orleans, Chicago, Kansas City, and Philadelphia. With the demise of these machines, came the advent of political reforms stressing open and ethical government and increasingly effective law enforcement. Many of the avenues for corrupt influence were subsequently closed. Today, the LCN exercises political influence only in certain selected areas, where politicians remain open to bribery and kickback schemes.

With respect to police and judicial corruption, there is much more evidence of this in the past than there is today. In recent years, there have been a handful of corruption cases involving law enforcement and one or two involving judges linked to LCN families. In Chicago, for example, a federal investigation of corruption in the courts (and city government more generally) led to 26 individuals—including judges, politicians, police officers, and lawyers—pleading guilty or being convicted at trial (Woodiwiss, 2001, p. 306).

In one of the most notorious cases in recent years, a former FBI supervisor in Boston admitted to accepting $7,000 in payoffs from two FBI mob informants. The two mobsters were major figures in New England organized crime. A second FBI agent was subsequently convicted with alerting the informants to investigations in which they were targets and with protecting them from prosecution (Lehr & O'Neill, 2000).

There has never been any evidence that LCN has had direct representation in the Congress of the United States, nor in the U.S. executive or diplomatic service. Neither is there any evidence that the LCN has ever been allied with armed opposition groups such as terrorists, guerrillas, or death squads. In this respect, the LCN exemplifies one of the traditional defining characteristics of organized crime in that its goal is an economic rather than a political one. Where there has been political involvement, it has been for the purposes of furthering economic objectives.

Responses of Law Enforcement Agencies to LCN

Law enforcement, and particularly U.S. federal law enforcement, has been tremendously successful in combating LCN over the past 20 years. Crime families have been infiltrated by informants and undercover agents, and special investigating grand juries have been employed in state and local jurisdictions. The techniques employed in these cases include electronic surveillance, the use of informants, the witness protection program, and the RICO Act. The RICO statute has clearly been the single most powerful prosecution tool against the LCN (Jacobs, Panarella, & Worthington, 1996). There are now state RICO statutes (to prosecute state crimes) as well as the federal law. RICO enables law enforcement to attack the organizational structure of organized crime and to levy severe criminal and civil penalties, including forfeitures of illegally obtained assets. The threat of these penalties has convinced many made members of the LCN to become informants or to seek immunity from prosecution in return for becoming cooperating witnesses. If their life is in danger, they are placed in the witness protection program and relocated. Civil remedies have included the court-appointment of monitors and trustees to administer businesses and unions that had been taken over by the LCN, to ensure that these enterprises remain cleansed of corrupt influences (Jacobs, Friel, et al., 1999).

Two of the latest weapons against LCN penetration of sectors of the legitimate economy are regulatory initiatives. These are administrative remedies designed to expand a local government's ability to control public services such as waste hauling and school construction. The first instance involves the creation of a regulatory commission. New York City, for example, created the Trade Waste Commission that ended the LCN cartel in the waste-hauling industry in that city through a process of licensing, investigation, competitive bidding, rate setting, and monitoring (Jacobs & Hortis, 1998).

A second example is the creation of a private inspector general. These inspector generals are hired in industries that have historically been controlled by organized crime and, in this case, the LCN. For instance, the school construction industry in New York City had a history of corruption, and a School Construction Authority (SCA) was created. This SCA then used a private inspector general to monitor its contractors, to establish corruption controls, and to report back to them on contractor conduct (Jacobs, Friel, et al., 1999).

Russian Organized Crime in the United States

Consider the case of the Gufield-Kutsenki Brigade in New York. It had just six active members and five or six associates, who engaged in an array of illegal activities, including extortion, abduction, bombings, prostitution enterprises, and white-collar frauds such as Medicaid fraud. Thomas Firestone, the Assistant U.S. Attorney who prosecuted this group, found, "It was very loosely structured, with no formal inductions, no formal rules of conduct, no affiliation with a bigger organization, no soldiers or captains, no single boss" (cited in Berkeley, 2002, p. 1). This Russian organized crime group is fairly typical and demonstrates the differences between the Russians and the Italians.

Russian organized crime (ROC) is an umbrella phrase that captures a variety of crime groups and criminal activities. In some instances, the crimes and the forms of criminal organization in the United States differ from those of ROC in Russia or elsewhere in the world. This may be a result of differing external environments and criminal opportunities. Because of the proliferation of groups, there is not a specific organizational structure that can be delineated as if it described one criminal organization. Even the characterization "Russian" is used generically to refer to a variety of Eurasian crime groups—many of which are not Russian. Among the active criminals in the United States are Armenians, Ukrainians, Lithuanians, and persons from the Caucasus region of the former Soviet Union (Chechens, Dagestanis, and Georgians). The media and law enforcement call these groups various names—Russian mafia, Russian mob, Organizatsya, Bor, or Bratva. Some of the group names refer to geographical locations in Russia—Izmailovskaya, Dagestantsy, Kazanskaya, and Solntsenskaya. The latter are indicative of the local geographically defined roots of some Russian crime groups.

It is estimated that approximately 15 of these loosely categorized criminal groups are operating in the United States and that 8 or 9 of them maintain at least some links to Russia. A report from the Center for Strategic and International Studies estimates that 200 large ROC groups are currently operating in 58 countries worldwide, including the United States (Webster, Borchgrave, & Cilluffo, 2000). An empirical study of ROC in the U.S. concluded that

[the] structure does not look like either what is commonly understood to be the structure of organized crime or a mafia in the conventional sense of those terms. The networks are neither highly centralized nor dominated by a small number of individuals. Those individuals who do have particular influence seem to occupy their positions on the basis of their personal characteristics. . . . This means that the networks lack . . . continuing structures. . . .

On the other hand, it is clear that these structures are not simply small groups of criminals essentially acting independently of one another. . . . Instead, there is broad connectivity among most of the actors. They may not be directly connected to a large number of others, but they are indirectly connected to many. This allows the networks a great deal of flexibility in the organization of their offenses, which means they can be responsive to the opportunities for illegal undertakings that develop. Given such an opportunity, a member of these large networks can access partners who are either generalists or specialists, can raise capital, and can access other needed resources. (Finckenauer & Waring, 1998, p. 164)

The segment of ROC most similar to traditional forms of Italian-American organized crime—in terms of hierarchy, internal codes of conduct, recruitment, and internal conflict resolution—is what is known as the *vory v zakone* or "thieves-in-law" (see Chapter 20, this volume). Other than a belief that certain Russian criminals in the United States have themselves been *vor,* there is little evidence of any organized presence of the *vory v zakone* in North America.

Violence

The threat and use of violence is a defining characteristic of ROC. Violence is used to gain and maintain control of criminal markets, and retributive violence is used within and between criminal groups. The common use of violence is not surprising, because extortion and protection rackets are staples of Russian criminal activity. ROC has engaged extensively in contract murders, kidnapping, and arson against businesses whose owners refuse to pay extortion money.

The Tri-State Joint Soviet-Émigré Organized Crime Project looked specifically at violent crimes in the New York, New Jersey, and Pennsylvania region. Their report indicates that Russian criminals have been implicated in numerous murders, attempted murders, assaults, and extortion. As evidence of their intimidation effect, witnesses to crimes often

cannot be found, or both witnesses and victims refused to cooperate in investigations. Of 70 murders and attempted murders over a 15-year period, all suggest that the victim, the perpetrator, or both were involved in ongoing criminal activity. In some cases, there was evidence to indicate the victim was attacked as a result of a dispute between two individual criminals or gangs or in retaliation for a prior violent act. The homicides in some cases appeared to have been well planned, and assassins or hit men were used.

Those who carried out the attacks often used distractions, decoys, or other tricks to gain advantage over victims. Fifty-three homicides involved the use of guns, including automatic, semi-automatic and silencer-equipped handguns. Victims were often shot either at close range . . . or from a moving vehicle. (New York State Organized Crime Task Force et al., 1996, pp. 19–20)

The report concluded that a great deal of the violence attributable to ROC in the United States was a result of the unregulated competition that exists in their criminal ventures.

Russian Criminal Business

With the principal exceptions of extortion and money laundering, ROC has had relatively little or no involvement in some of the more traditional crimes of organized crime, such as drug trafficking, gambling, and loan-sharking. On the other hand, these varied criminal groups are extensively engaged in a broad array of frauds and scams, including health care fraud, insurance scams, stock frauds, antiquities swindles, forgery, and gasoline tax evasion schemes. Russians have recently become the principal purveyors of credit card fraud in the United States, supplanting the West African scams.

ROC is very adept at changing criminal activities and diversifying into new criminal markets. For example, financial markets and banks have become new targets of criminal opportunity for ROC, as witnessed in two recent prosecutions: *U.S. v. Alexander Lushtak* alleges a multimillion dollar investment fraud scheme and the subsequent laundering of nearly 2 million dollars of proceeds of that scheme by depositing monies involved in the fraud in an account at the Bank of New York; and *U.S. v. Dominick Dionisio* charges two persons alleged to be associated with the LCN and an alleged member of the "Bor" ROC group with operating a multimillion-dollar investment fraud and laundering the proceeds of the scheme.

As criminals from the former Soviet Union become more assimilated into American society, they are moving into legitimate businesses, such as the textile industry and the movie business. But in many cases, these businesses are used for money laundering. Money laundering is also at the heart of one of the best known of the more recent cases of ROC activity in the United States. That case involves the U.S. government indictment of four individuals and two companies in connection with the laundering of more than $7 billion through the Bank of New York (BONY). The case exemplifies a number of economic resource issues. First, the monies laundered represent a mix of income from criminal activity in Russia and money being hidden from the Russian government. ROC uses members of financial institutions such as bank insiders to launder criminal money and also helps Russian businesses and individuals move their own assets out of Russia so as to evade Russian law enforcement and tax officials. Second, the BONY case illustrates the diversification and blend of legal and illegal activities. This blend increases enormously the difficulty faced by law enforcement in dealing with money laundering by ROC in separating the income earned by legal business versus illicit activity. Third, there is clearly a capacity to tap professional know-how in the financial schemes of

ROC. As the bond and stock fraud cases illustrate, some of those associated with ROC work primarily in the legitimate sector of the economy.

Contrary to its pervasive corrupt political influence in Russia and the other republics of the former Soviet Union, ROC has had little or no political influence in North America. Although they have the financial capacity to do so, Russian criminals have not cultivated the political and law enforcement contacts necessary to corrupt them. There have been no reported cases of police or judicial corruption. There is no evidence that ROC has attempted to manipulate either politicians or the political process, that they have managed to get criminals elected or appointed to political office, or that they have influenced media coverage of issues. Similarly, there is no evidence of any connections between ROC and political terrorism in North America.

Combating Russian Organized Crime

The U.S. law enforcement strategy for combating ROC was outlined by the then Assistant Attorney General in charge of the Justice Department's Criminal Division in congressional testimony in 1999. This strategy includes expanding the U.S. presence in other countries and building the new relationships needed to attack transnational crime. That presence includes both law enforcement personnel overseas and attorneys to facilitate requests for mutual legal assistance and extradition, provide substantive legal guidance on international law enforcement and treaty matters, and increase cooperation with foreign police and prosecutors. The U.S. Department of Justice has stationed resident legal advisers, who provide training and technical assistance to foreign prosecutors, judges, and police, in a number of countries, including Russia, Ukraine, Latvia, and Georgia (*Oversight of the Criminal Division*, 1999).

In addition to its headquarters focus, the FBI has created units to combat ROC in its field offices in a number of U.S. cities. Also, major police departments such as New York City and Los Angeles have likewise created specialized units to target Russian crime in their jurisdictions.

As part of their study of ROC in America, Finckenauer and Waring (1998) interviewed émigrés from the former Soviet Union now living in Brighton Beach in Brooklyn, New York—the largest Russian community in the United States. The picture of ROC that emerged from these interviews reflects citizen awareness, cultural acceptance, and the role of the mass media in influencing perceptions. In most cases, the interviewees learned about ROC from the media, not from personal experience. Consequently, they often had only stereotyped or vague images of what ROC is and does. Their views represent the popularized version of ROC in the United States as being a Russian mafia. This is a view promulgated not only by the press and other media, but also by law enforcement, and as such, it tends to be self-reinforcing. The mafia stereotype has not only been misleading in terms of understanding the phenomenon, but it has also been an impediment to developing effective law enforcement strategies.

Although survey respondents believed Russian crime to be widespread, they also believed that the vast majority of Russian émigrés were not involved in this crime. There is less of an acceptance of ROC in the immigrant community than there is a detachment from it and an effort to dissociate oneself from it. There is also resentment expressed by many in the Russian immigrant community that the typical American seems to see them only as organized criminals—as Russian mafiosi. Overcoming this negative stereotype will take time.

Chinese Transnational Organized Crime: The Fuk Ching

The organizational structure of Chinese organized crime in the United States is quite complex. Broadly defined, there are a great variety of Chinese criminal organizations that include gangs, secret societies, triads, tongs, Taiwanese organized crime groups, and strictly U.S.-based tongs and gangs. According to Ko-lin Chin, the foremost academic expert in the United States on Chinese organized crime, there is no empirical support for the belief that there is a well-organized, monolithic, hierarchical criminal cartel called the "Chinese Mafia." Chin (2000) says, "My findings . . . do not support the notion that a chain of command exists among these various crime groups or that they coordinate with one another routinely in international crimes such as heroin trafficking, money laundering, and the smuggling of aliens" (p. 123).

This analysis concentrates on the Fuk Ching gang, which is active in New York City, generally regarded as one of the most powerful, and also transnationally active, Chinese organized crime groups in the United States. Fuk Ching is estimated to have approximately 35 members, with another 20 members currently in prison. Other gangs in New York City include the Ghost Shadows, Flying Dragons, Tung On, and Born-to-Kill. The New York City gangs, like the Fuk Ching, mainly operate extortion and protection rackets in defined neighborhoods in New York's Chinatown. Their victims are mostly businesses in Chinatown. In California, the Chinese organized crime presence and problem is quite different from that in New York. In California, the dominant groups are the Wo Hop To and the Wah Ching.

One of the structural characteristics that makes Chinese organized crime different from other forms is the relationship between some of the street gangs and certain adult organizations, or tongs. The Fuk Ching, for example, is affiliated with the Fukien American Association. The Fukien American Association—as with other tongs and their relationships with gangs—provides the Fuk Ching with a physical place to gather and hang out. They allow the gang to operate on their (the tong's) territory, thus legitimizing them with the community. They also provide criminal opportunities (such as protecting gambling operations), as well as supplying money and guns. The Fuk Ching originally emerged in New York in the mid-1980s, and as with other gangs, their main criminal activity in Chinatown was extortion. They were founded by a collection of young men (youths in their late teens and early 20s) from Fujian province in China—many if not all of whom had criminal records in China. Fuk Ching recruitment today continues to be among Fujianese teenagers (Huston, 2001).

Tong-affiliated gangs, like the Fuk Ching, have an *ah kung* (grandfather) or *shuk foo* (uncle) who is their tong leader. The top gang position is the *dai dai lo* (big big brother). Communication between the tong and the gang occurs principally between these two individuals. Below the *dai dai lo* in descending order are the *dai lo*(s) or big brothers, the *yee lo/saam lo* (clique leaders), and at the bottom the *ma jai* or little horses. A variety of norms and rules govern the gangs. These include respecting the *ah kung,* beating up members of other gangs on your turf, not using drugs, following the orders of the *dai lo,* and not betraying the gang. Rules violators are punished, sometimes severely, through physical assault and killing (Booth, 2001).

Violence

Use of violence within the group and against other organized crime groups is very prevalent. Disputes over territory and criminal markets among the gangs are typically resolved using *kong so,* a process of peaceful negotiation. When this does not occur, however, the resolution is usually a violent one, in which guns are used against rival gang members. Law enforcement authorities believe that an escalation of gang violence has taken place in recent years, due in part to the advent of the Fuk Ching

and to gang involvement in alien smuggling activities. Based on his research, Chin (2000) concludes the following with respect to Chinese gang violence in general:

> The capacity for violence appears to be one of the key defining characteristics of street gang culture. Its employment, however, is shaped and determined by a cluster of constraints related to profit-generating goals. Violence between and among gangs is regulated through an agent or ah kung who attempts to channel aggressive behavior in ways that effectively maintain gang coherence. Gang coherence in turn supports the gang's involvement in extortion activities and in the provision of protection services to organized vice industries in the community. (p. 138)

The Fuk Ching are violent, but their use of violence is not very sophisticated or specialized. It is not the systematic use of violence (including threats) to protect and gain monopoly control of criminal markets associated with mature forms of organized crime. Instead, the Fuk Ching violence is more likely to be random street-level violence, with guns, employed by anyone in the gang. Sometimes this violence is sanctioned by superiors, and sometimes not.

Criminal Activities

Alien smuggling is the illegal movement of migrants across national borders, and human trafficking is migrant smuggling that includes coercion and exploitation. The Fuk Ching is extensively involved in both types of activities. Indeed, these criminal activities, along with kidnapping, are the main transnational crimes of the Fuk Ching. Their dominance is related to Fujian Province being the principal source of Chinese people smuggled and trafficked into North America. On the domestic scene, their main criminal activities in New York City's Chinatown are extortion and gambling. Each

Chinese gang dominates these crimes in their particular Chinatown neighborhoods. This includes the Fuk Ching.

The professionalism and sophistication of the Fuk Ching are quite low, again compared with more traditional forms of organized crime. The same is true of other Chinese criminal gangs operating in the United States. This may be due to their generally being much younger than LCN or ROC figures. Also, their criminal activities are not particularly sophisticated, although the Fuk Ching may be becoming more complex in their organizational structure as they become more heavily engaged in human trafficking, which requires a greater degree of planning and organization.

Chinese gangs are quite active in legitimate businesses in New York City's Chinatown. For example, they own or operate restaurants, retail stores, vegetable stands, car services, ice cream parlors, fish markets, and video stores. On a higher, more professional level, they also own or operate wholesale supply firms, factories, banks, and employment agencies (Chin, 2000). In addition, on the West Coast, Chinese gangs are believed to have penetrated the entertainment industry. Perhaps it is because of their relatively small size, the youth of their members, their lack of business experience and acumen, and the geographical constraints in which they operate that Chinese gangs such as the Fuk Ching do not seem to play significant roles in the broader legitimate economy.

Political Connections

The expert consensus is that the Fuk Ching, like other Chinese gangs, does not have the connections and stature to make them capable of corrupting U.S. police and judges. There have been only one or two cases of police corruption (none in recent years), and no cases of judicial corruption involving Fuk Ching.

As to political influence, there is some ability to manipulate the political system through corruption in China—namely, in Fujian Province and with respect to their human trafficking enterprise. In the United States, however, there is no evidence of corrupting the political process, of getting members elected or appointed to political office, or of being able to manage media coverage of their activities. They are influential only in Chinatown, and their connections to U.S. politicians are nonexistent. Any political influence Chinese gangs have is exerted through the tongs with which they are affiliated. For example, it is reported that the head of the Fukien American Association once gave $6,500 to a New York City Mayor's reelection campaign (Kleinknecht, 1996, p. 168). Tongs and other Chinatown community organizations benefit in some ways from the Chinese gangs' threats of extortion because business owners donate money to the associations in the belief that this will buy them protection (Chin, 2000). There is no evidence that Chinese gangs are involved with political terrorism either abroad or at home and no evidence that they are associated with armed political groups of any kind.

Law Enforcement Response

The New York City Police Department (NYPD), which polices the neighborhood in which the Fuk Ching are active, uses all the standard law enforcement practices commonly used to combat organized crime. These include informants, undercover investigators, and electronic surveillance. In addition, both the police and the FBI support and encourage extortion victims to use telephone hot lines to report their victimization. The NYPD has also created an Asian Gang Intelligence Unit that employs street patrols to monitor street gangs.

Of the 15 Chinese crime groups indicted under the RICO Act between 1985 and 1994, one involved the Fuk Ching. In that case, 20 defendants were charged with, and pled guilty to, murder. The investigation was conducted jointly by the FBI and the NYPD.

On the international level, U.S. law enforcement has undertaken a number of initiatives to improve international cooperation against Chinese organized crime groups. These include the creation of the International Law Enforcement Academy (ILEA) in Bangkok, Thailand, and sponsorship of numerous international meetings on Asian organized crime. Annual meetings of the International Asian Organized Crime Conference attract more than a thousand law enforcement officials from dozens of countries. Both the ILEA and the conferences promote interaction among officials of affected countries and lead to better cooperation and more reliable information.

Many crimes in Chinese-American communities—especially drug trafficking, money laundering, and human trafficking—are linked to China. Chinese gang members flee to China when sought by American law enforcement. Ko-lin Chin (2000) recommends that "deportation, extradition, joint operations, and intelligence sharing among law enforcement authorities from various countries . . . be carried out routinely, . . . extradition treaties . . . be instated . . . [and that] U.S. authorities . . . be more culturally sensitive in dealing with foreign law enforcement agencies" (p. 187).

Public Awareness

There is not general cultural acceptance of Chinese gangs such as the Fuk Ching in Chinatown. Most Chinese business owners comply with gang extortion demands because compliance is easier and less risky than resistance. As previously indicated, the gang affiliation with a tong gives them a degree of acceptability in the neighborhoods associated with that particular tong. The gang must be tolerated in order to gain any benefit that accrues from the tong. It would seem that there is little need in Chinatown for awareness-raising campaigns on organized crime or for sensitizing citizens to the dangers and threats posed by Chinese gangs. The Chinese who live in these neighborhoods are fully aware and fully sensitized. Rather than public information campaigns, Chinese businessmen would prefer a tougher criminal justice system. As Chin (2000) reports, "They [Chinese businessmen] would like to see harsher punishment for offenders, the reinstitution of the death penalty . . . , and the deportation of chronic Chinese criminals" (p. 98). They also want to see many more Chinese police officers in their neighborhoods.

Because of the compartmentalized nature of Chinese organized crime in the United States, the public at large is little aware of and little concerned about what is going on in Chinatowns in U.S. cities. National media pay relatively little attention to these problems. For example, an Internet search of major U.S. newspapers under the topic "Asian organized crime" for the period January 1, 1998, to August 1, 2000, produced only 13 articles.

Chinese involvement in human smuggling, however, may be the exception to this rule. Chinese human smuggling has received considerable attention. A conference in Washington, D.C., on human smuggling pointed to five possible reasons for the high public profile given Chinese smuggling operations: (1) They are expensive, (2) associated human rights abuses are considerable, (3) they are highly efficient, (4) there is an enormous potential pool of migrants, and (5) collecting intelligence and other information from China is extraordinarily difficult (Heckman, Wunderlich, Martin, & McGrath, 2000). Human trafficking activities by Chinese gangs such as the Fuk Ching are contributing to this higher profile.

Mexican Drug Cartels

For years, the border between Mexico and the United States has been crossed by millions of Mexican nationals going north in search of work. Most are hard-working, law-abiding citizens, looking for legitimate opportunities to better socioeconomic circumstances for themselves and their families. But some are criminals. And during the decade of the 1990s especially, those criminals became more organized, more sophisticated, and more violent, as they sought and gained considerable control over the lucrative drug business in North America.

With names like the Juarez cartel, and the Cardenas-Guillen, Valencia-Cornelio, and Caro-Quintero organizations, various organized crime groups have operated in and from Mexico. It is estimated by U.S. law enforcement that there are roughly 100 to 200 members in the main groups, such as those named above. The Carillo Fuentes organization (highlighted below) is estimated to have more than 500 members. These numbers do not include the thousands of operatives in the various affiliated networks operating in the United States and Canada.

The major groups in Mexico itself are said by U.S. law enforcement to be fairly centrally organized. The distribution networks in the United States and Canada, on the other hand, are more fragmented. The core criminal organizations and their extended networks are composed of Mexican nationals living in Mexico, Mexican Americans, and Mexican immigrants living in the United States. The vast majority (estimated at about 85%) is male.

U.S. law enforcement characterizes the Mexican drug-trafficking groups as being mobile and operating with great stealth in the United States. Consequently, they have no established, continuous bases but, rather, operate mainly in ethnic enclaves in major cities. Those cities include Chicago, New York, Los Angeles, and Houston.

The principal criminal activities of these groups clearly revolve around the manufacturing and trafficking of drugs. Heroin, cocaine, marijuana, and methamphetamines are procured, produced, transported, distributed, and sold—often in elaborate partnerships with Colombian and Dominican criminal groups.

They have also collaborated with LCN and other U.S. organized crime groups.

The main drug customers are, not surprisingly, in the United States and, to a lesser extent, in Canada. The transnational nature of Mexican organized crime is not limited to North America in that, for example, their cocaine comes from Colombia, the precursor chemicals for producing methamphetamine come from various countries, and they launder money in the Caribbean and certain Latin American countries.

According to the FBI and other law enforcement officials, the criminal activities in which these Mexican criminal organizations are involved, besides drug trafficking and money laundering, are armed robbery, kidnapping for ransom, extortion, and illegal dealing in firearms. Money laundering of the illegal proceeds from drug trafficking is a dominant criminal activity. For the most part, any other criminal activities in which the Mexicans become engaged are for purposes of furthering their drug business. Their annual average income from all these illicit activities is estimated to be in the billions of dollars.

The main criminal groups make extensive use of violence—more so in Mexico itself than in the United States. This distinction is said to be the result of a desire to avoid attracting undue attention. Violence is employed both internally—for discipline and to quell power struggles—and against other organized crime groups. The violence in Mexico is perpetrated in the form of intimidation, torture, and assassinations. Businesspeople, law enforcement officials, and government officials have been murdered in recent years when they became an impediment to the flow of drugs and money. In the United States, as indicated, there is less use of violence, and it is mostly directed against law enforcement personnel working near the southwest border (*Black-Tar Heroin*, 2000).

With respect to cocaine, the Mexican drug traffickers have business arrangements with the Colombians who grant the Mexicans a portion of the cocaine shipments they transport. This means they both traffic for the Colombians and also deal on their own. With heroin, it is estimated that Mexico is now the second largest source of the heroin used in the United States. The cartels are the predominant foreign source of marijuana in the U.S., and their labs in Mexico and California are estimated to produce about 85% of the methamphetamine distributed in the U.S. (*Black-Tar Heroin*, 2000).

The various Mexican criminal organizations also make extensive use of corruption in Mexico. The targets of this widespread corruption range all the way from poorly paid local police officers to high-ranking elected and appointed officials. The combination of violence and intimidation and the vast sums of money have effectively undermined efforts by Mexican law enforcement to combat these criminals and have also made collaborative efforts between Mexican and U.S. law enforcement very problematic. That does not mean that there have not been some successes, as the following case examples from a study compiled by the U.N. Center for International Crime Prevention demonstrate (see Centre for International Crime Prevention, 2000, pp. 138–140).

Carillo Fuentes Organization

Based in Ciudad Juarez, the Carillo Fuentes criminal organization is a major trafficker of cocaine, heroin, and marijuana. The Rodriquez Orejuela crime group in Cali, Colombia, and the Ochoa brothers in Medellin have been the organization's principal cocaine sources. The Carillo Fuentes organization maintains regional bases in Guadalajara, Hermosillo, and Torreon, Mexico, as storage locations for the drugs to be shipped north. With single operations worth $20 to $30 million, it is estimated the group has generated tens of millions of dollars in profits per week.

The dominant figure in the organization, Amado Carrillo Fuentes, was instrumental in creating the Mexican Federation of Drug Cartels, which developed a number of the joint ventures with Colombian cartels. Amado had extensive links with high-level law enforcement and military officials and became known as the "Lord of the Skies," because of his reputation for transporting large amounts of cocaine by air across the U.S./Mexican border. In a rather bizarre incident, he died in 1997, following surgery carried out to change his appearance. Amado's brother then took over the organization, but a violent internal struggle ensued, and the Mexican Federation of Drug Cartels has subsequently broken up into several cells (Centre for International Crime Prevention, 2000, pp. 138–139).

Arellano-Felix Organization

According to the U.N. study, the Arellano-Felix organization is "one of North America's most violent drug trafficking cartels" (Centre for International Crime Prevention, 2000, p. 139). A "family business," the organization was controlled by the Arellano-Felix family of seven brothers and four sisters. The two dominant brothers were Benjamin and Ramon. For more than a decade, this family controlled the movement of cocaine, heroin, marijuana, and methamphetamine across the San Diego/Tijuana border. Of the seven organizations in Mexico that are said to control the illegal drug market, Arellano-Felix is considered to be the most dominant and dangerous, killing scores of rivals, enemies, and potential witnesses.

The group cooperates with other criminal groups, has extensive political influence in Mexico, and has penetrated the legitimate economy to a considerable degree. It has also been able to continue operations despite the arrests and loss of key leaders. But the Mexican Federal Police killed Ramon Arellano Felix in February 2002, and, also in 2002, his brother Benjamin was arrested. It remains to be seen what the long-term effects of these actions will be.

Canadian Organized Crime

The primary organized crime groups in Canada are of four types: Asian groups, East European groups, Italian groups, and outlaw motorcycle gangs. Like the United States and Mexico, Canada is a large country, so there is tremendous variation within its borders—from a number of very large metropolitan areas to expanses of rural areas that are hundred of miles across.

Asian organized crime groups have been identified in British Columbia, Ontario, and Quebec, the provinces that contain Canada's largest cities: Vancouver, Toronto, and Montreal. Some of the Asian groups are actually street gangs that engage in drug trafficking or perform criminal activities for more sophisticated organized crime groups. Asian groups on Canada's west coast have been found to be involved in trafficking drugs, firearms, and human beings. The primary drugs that are trafficked are heroin, cocaine, and ecstasy. During 2001, all major heroin seizures involved Asian-based crime groups (Criminal Intelligence Service Canada, 2002). Some of these drugs have been found to have been smuggled into the United States by individuals of Chinese descent. Vietnamese-based groups have been found to be extensively involved in large-scale cultivation of marijuana across Canada. In one operation, organized crime members of Chinese descent bought marijuana from Vietnamese-based drug-trafficking gangs to transport in the United States (Organized Crime Agency, 2003).

Since a high-profile case in 1999 involving four ships and 600 illegal Chinese migrants attempting to enter Canada, there have not been any large-scale human-smuggling attempts into Canada by boat. Instead, commercial airplanes are now the transport of choice. In one case, two Chinese-Canadian citizens were caught trying to smuggle four Chinese nationals across the Niagara River into the United States. The Chinese nationals had arrived in Canada through Vancouver airport ("Immigrant Smugglers," 2002).

A recent study interviewed 50 high-level drug traffickers in Canada who were serving prison sentences. These offenders represented a number of different racial and ethnic categories and, surprisingly, 60% had operated small, legal businesses prior to becoming drug dealers (Desroches, 2000). This suggests that market demand and opportunities, as well as entrepreneurial skills, are factors in the expansion and contraction of the illicit drug industry. Drug monies fuel a variety of activities, possibly including terrorism. According to a report by the Royal Canadian Mounted Police, heroin arriving through Montreal and Toronto comes from Pakistan and Afghanistan, and about $20 million each year finds its way back to those source countries, helping to fund terrorism (Moore, 2002).

Significant law enforcement efforts have been made in Canada. One of them is the Anti-Smuggling Initiative that focused on alcohol and tobacco smuggling, and on the profits from it that are used to fund other illegal activities. An evaluation of that program concluded that a substantial reduction was achieved in the contraband tobacco market, but it is unclear whether a simultaneous reduction in Canadian cigarette taxes also played a role in this decline. There was evidence as well that the law enforcement effort had the effect of displacing smuggling groups to use other locations and methods (Schneider, 2000). This experience indicates the need for continued and varied enforcement efforts combined with demand-reduction efforts to offset the adaptability of criminal organizations to changes in risk.

CONCLUSION

Organized crime in North America is shaped by the presence of three geographically large countries that share very long land borders as well as extensive coastlines along the Atlantic and Pacific Oceans. The economic disparities between Canada and the United States on one hand and Mexico on the other, create a lucrative supply-and-demand environment, and the land and water access facilitates trafficking routes for illicit goods, services, and human smuggling.

Organized crime historically has been shaped by the presence of Cosa Nostra groups, composed primarily of Italian-Americans whose influence is concentrated in major U.S. cities and also spills over into cities in Canada and Mexico. An unprecedented prosecution effort during the 1980s and 1990s severely reduced the strength of the Cosa Nostra groups. These prosecution efforts in the United States corresponded with global political changes that included the fall of the Soviet Union, the emergence of the newly independent states of Eastern Europe, and a growing ease of international travel and communication.

What might have been localized organized crime problems just a generation ago have become manifestations of transnational organized crime as criminal groups from Eastern Europe and Asia have found North America to be a desirable market for the provision of illicit goods and services that support organized crime enterprise. Criminal groups within North America also have exploited new opportunities for crime. The growing recognition of the size and importance of organized crime operations that emanate from a variety of foreign countries distinguishes concern about organized crime today from the more local concerns about Cosa Nostra groups and other city-based gangs in years past.

It remains to be seen whether North America can reduce its high demand for illicit products and services (especially drugs), secure its borders from outsiders interested in exploiting the region, and prosecute those individuals and organized crime groups already in either Canada, Mexico, or the United States. The long-term solution to organized crime is a reduction in the demand for the products and services that support it, but in the short-term, greater efforts at detection and prosecution will be necessary to disrupt more effectively both foreign and North American organized crime groups. These efforts will be most effective if pursued collaboratively.

REFERENCES

Albanese, J., Das, D., & Verma, A. (Eds.). (2003). *Organized crime: World perspectives*. Upper Saddle River, NJ: Prentice Hall.

Berkeley, B. (2002, August 19). Code of betrayal, not silence, shines light on Russian mob. *New York Times*, p. A1.

Black-tar heroin, meth, cocaine continue to flood the U.S. from Mexico: Hearing before U.S. House of Representatives, Subcommittee on Criminal Justice, Drug Policy and Human Resources. (2000, June 30). (Testimony of Joseph D. Keefe).

Booth, M. (2001). *The dragon syndicates: The global phenomenon of the triads*. New York: Carroll & Graf.

Centre for International Crime Prevention. (2000). Appendix: Overview of the 40 criminal groups surveyed. *Trends in Organized Crime, 6*(2), 93–140.

Chin, K. (2000). *Chinatown gangs: Extortion, enterprise, ethnicity*. New York: Oxford University Press.

Criminal Intelligence Service Canada. (2002). *Annual report on organized crime in Canada 2001*. Retrieved May 13, 2004, from www.cisc.gc.ca

Desroches, F. J. (2000, Fall). Drug trafficking and organized crime in Canada: A study of high level drug networks. *Nathanson Centre Newsletter*, p. 26.

Finckenauer, J. O., & Waring, E. J. (1998). *Russian mafia in America*. Boston: Northeastern University Press.

Heckman, F., Wunderlich, T., Martin, S. F., & McGrath, K. (2000, June). *Transatlantic workshop on human smuggling*. Conference report. Georgetown University, Washington,

DC. Retrieved May 13, 2004, from www
.uni-bamberg.de/projekte/humsmug/cr_e.pdf

Holloway, L. (2002, December 2). Arrests illustrate
a growing concern over bootlegged recordings.
New York Times, p. C10.

Huston, J. (2001). *Tongs, gangs, and triads:
Chinese crime groups in North America.*
New York: Writer's Club Press.

Immigrant smugglers caught in broad daylight.
(2002, May 6). *Edmonton Journal,* p. 1.

Jacobs, J. B., Friel, C., & Radick, R. (1999).
*Gotham unbound: How New York City was
liberated from the grip of organized crime.*
New York: New York University Press.

Jacobs, J. B., & Gouldin, L. P. (1999). Cosa Nostra:
The final chapter? In M. Tonry & N. Morris
(Eds.), *Crime and justice* (Vol. 25, pp. 129–190).
Chicago: University of Chicago Press.

Jacobs, J. B., & Hortis, A. (1998). New York City
as organized crime fighter. *New York Law
School Law Review,* 42(3 & 4), 1069–1092.

Jacobs, J. B., Panarella, C., & Worthington, J.
(1996). *Busting the mob: United States v. Cosa
Nostra.* New York: New York University Press.

Kleinknecht, W. (1996). *The new ethnic mobs.*
New York: Free Press.

Lehr, D., & O'Neill, G. (2000). *Black mass:
The Irish mob, the FBI, and a devil's deal.*
New York: Public Affairs.

Moore, D. (2002, July 15). Canadian drug trade
aids terrorism. *Ottawa Citizen,* p. A2.

Mustain, G., & Capeci, J. (2002). *Mob star:
The story of John Gotti.* New York: Alpha
Books.

New York State Organized Crime Task Force et al.
(1996). An analysis of Russian émigré crime.
Transnational Organized Crime, 2(2-3), 1–25.

Nicholson, B. (2003, July 20). Cyber gangs
skim millions in Australia. *Sunday Age*
(Melbourne), p. 4.

Organized Crime Agency of British Columbia.
(2003). *Annual Report 2001.* Retrieved May
13, 2004, from www.ocabc.org/publications/
OCA_Annual_Report_2001.pdf

*Organized crime: Hearing before the U.S. House
of Representatives Committee on Finance and
Hazardous Materials.* (2000, September 13).
(Testimony of Thomas V. Fuentes). Retrieved
May 13, 2004, from www.fbi.gov/congress/
congress00/fuentes.htm

*Oversight of the Criminal Division of the
Department of Justice: Hearings before the
Subcommittee on Criminal Justice Oversight
of the U.S. Senate Committee on the Judiciary.*
(1999, July 27). (Testimony of James K.
Robinson).

Raab, S. (1997, February 10). Officials say mob is
shifting crimes to new industries. *New York
Times,* p. A-1.

Reuter, P. (1982). *The value of a bad reputation:
Criminals, cartels, and barriers to entry.* Santa
Monica, CA: RAND.

Schneider, S. (2000, Winter). Organized contraband
smuggling and its enforcement in Canada: An
assessment of the anti-smuggling initiative.
Trends in Organized Crime, 6(2), 3–31.

Schweizer, H. O., Nishimotto, C., Salzano, J., &
Chamberlin, M. T. (2003). Organized crime: A
U.S. perspective. In J. Albanese, D. Das, &
A. Verma (Eds.), *Organized crime: World per-
spectives* (pp. 22–45). Upper Saddle River, NJ:
Prentice Hall.

Webster, W. H., de Borchgrave, A., & Cilluffo, F.
(2000). *Russian organized crime and
corruption: Putin's challenge.* Washington,
DC: Center for Strategic and International
Studies.

Woodiwiss, M. (2001). *Organized crime and
American power: A history.* Buffalo, NY:
University of Toronto Press.

23

Juvenile Justice in the International Arena

JOHN WINTERDYK

Even though official crime rates dropped throughout the early 1990s in some countries, "the pervasiveness of juvenile offending as a problem makes historical and cross-cultural study of juvenile justice relevant."

—Bala & Bromwich, 2002, p. 16

Because young people generally represent a subservient class and are comparatively powerless, concerns about the welfare and discipline of young persons have plagued societies for centuries. For example, if one were to examine the history of child-rearing patterns throughout the ages, one would find that our ideas about how to raise and discipline children have been fraught with ambiguity, inconsistency, and fundamental ignorance concerning the nature of youth. Lloyd deMause (1974) and Philippe Ariès (1962) offer insightful reviews as well as opposing perspectives on the evolution of views of children and youth throughout the ages (see Box 23.1). For example, deMause asserts that "the history of childhood is a nightmare from

which we have just begun to awaken" (p. 1). In spite of their different approaches, deMause and Ariès share a perspective that speaks to the challenges societies have faced in trying to raise children into adults regardless of social class or culture.

Conversely, others have focused their attention on delinquency in the aftermath of the "child saving" movement of the late 1800s, the key proponents of which in North America included Lewis Pease, Samuel Gridley Howe, and Charles Loring Brace. The phrase *child saver*, popularized by Anthony Platt (1977), points out that in North America our concern with youth emerged from a group of middle- and upper-class citizens who imposed their values on delinquent youth. As Platt

457

Box 23.1 The Roots of Child Welfare

One of the first comprehensive attempts to explain delinquency was initiated by social work pioneer Jane Addams, a member of the well-meaning "society" of women in Chicago (i.e., Hull House) who recruited psychiatrist Dr. William A. Healy (1869–1963) in the early 1900s to conduct a longitudinal study of several hundred young offenders. In his 1915 book *The Individual Delinquent: A Textbook of Diagnosis and Prognosis for All Concerned in Understanding Offenders,* Healy focused on a wide range of potential causes of delinquency, from "the influence of bad companions" to "the love of adventure, early sex experiences and mental conflict" (see Krisberg & Austin, 1978, p. 31). As Jones (1999) observes, however, Dr. Healy's efforts and ideas failed to eliminate delinquency or the troublesome behavior of youth.

---

notes, the individuals in this movement began to use such terms as *disease* and *illness,* implying that delinquency is some kind of pathology and that delinquents need to be treated "like irresponsible, sick patients" (p. 45).

DELINQUENCY AS A GROWING INTERNATIONAL ENIGMA

Although the circumstances of the past may be somewhat blurred with respect to how accurately they have been reported and how we choose to interpret them, the fact remains that we have been dealing with the dilemma of youth crime for a very long time. As we begin a new millennium, the mass media and the public continue to focus on youth crime and violence among youth. In Canada, for example, public reaction to several violent crimes committed by adolescent boys and girls in the 1990s was instrumental in the forging of new legislation, in April 2003, for young offenders: the Youth Criminal Justice Act. Yet, while Canada struggles to find a balance between accountability and rehabilitation, other countries (including a number of Latin American nations) continue to resort to less tolerant measures. Some countries, such as Nepal, still allow mentally ill children to be jailed and chained, in clear violation of Article 37 of the U.N. Convention on the Rights of the Child (CRC;

see Box 23.2). And although the legal systems in most countries recognize that young persons (i.e., children and adolescents) are different from adults, there are notable disparities in how various nations respond fiscally, legally, politically, and socially to these differences.

Furthermore, if official and unofficial crime data are any indication, we would be somewhat hard-pressed to deny the fact that, irrespective of formal differences among nations, the issue of juvenile delinquency has grown into a significant contemporary social problem. Even though it is difficult to make simple statistical comparisons among countries because of differences in recording and reporting methods, terminology, and languages, when the majority of reporting countries draw similar conclusions, the nuances of any limitations become moot. Also perplexing are the diverse ways in which nations have evolved control, intervention, prevention, and treatment strategies to handle young offenders—all this in spite of international agreements that have established standards and norms for the handling, processing, and treatment of such offenders.

At the Eighth and Ninth U.N. Congresses on the Prevention of Crime and the Treatment of Offenders, aside from the recognition of conventional and nonconventional crimes as a growing problem, participants also reported

---

Box 23.2 Article 37 of the U.N. Convention on the Rights of the Child

---

Article 37 of the CRC provides the child with the right to be protected from the following kinds of treatment:

- Torture
- Other cruel, inhumane, or degrading treatment or punishment
- Capital punishment
- Life imprisonment without possibility of release
- Unlawful or arbitrary deprivation of liberty

---

that youth crime is increasing around the world—especially in countries experiencing economic and political transition ("Crime Congress," 1995). A U.N. report published in 1995 noted that the average age of onset of delinquent behavior was dropping. These observations, combined with the fact that in the year 2000 more than 50% of the world population was under the age of 15, serve to further "highlight the seriousness of the problem of juvenile delinquency and youth crime" (United Nations, 1995, p. 17). Furthermore, the CRC acknowledges that one of its challenges is the fact that "some States are moving toward increasingly punitive systems of juvenile justice, with children beaten and arbitrarily detained by police and forced to share prisons with adults in inhumane conditions" (see UNICEF, n.d.).

Although not all countries are experiencing the pragmatic concerns about youth crime that seem to accompany certain social, economic, and political changes, it is important that we recognize, examine, and understand the significance and relevance of the diverse ways in which young offenders are treated within their nations' respective justice systems (Bala & Bromwich, 2002; Winterdyk, 2002; see also Table 23.1).[1] Youth crime is not by definition transnational in its scope, but it is an international problem, and it raises cross-national concerns. Furthermore, the issue of how nations should respond formally to youth crime has been addressed by the United

Nations, the Human Rights Convention, and Amnesty International, as well as at national and even continental levels for some time now.

In an effort to complement the focus of this anthology, in this chapter I examine some of the key articles of the U.N. Convention on the Rights of the Child as well as other international documents that have created standards and guidelines by which all nations (or at least member states) have agreed to abide. These points will serve as the basis for some observations concerning how well member states are able to embrace the established standards and norms. The chapter will then move on to a discussion of some promising alternative strategies that might help to encourage greater compliance with the CRC among and between participating nations.

MODELS OF JUVENILE JUSTICE

First, however, a few words are in order concerning the various models of juvenile justice found around the world. Ever since the emergence of the welfare model of juvenile justice in 1899, with the establishment of the first juvenile court in the United States, there have been ongoing concerns and debates about which correctional philosophies (e.g., "just deserts," rehabilitation-treatment, legalistic versus participatory, corporatist versus crime control) offer the most appropriate societal responses to youth crime (see Table 23.1 for

Table 23.1   Summary of the Features of Juvenile Justice Models

Features	Participatory Model	Welfare Model	Corporatist Model	Modified Justice Model	Justice Model	Crime Control Model
General	Informality Minimal formal intervention Resocialization	Informality Generic referrals Individualized sentencing Indeterminate	Administrative decision making Offending Diversion from court/custody programs	Due process Informality Criminal offenses Bifurcation: soft offenders diverted, hard offenders punished	Due process Criminal offenses Least restrictive alternative/ sanctions/ educational concerns	Due process/ discretion Offending/status offenses Punishment/ retribution Determinate sentences
Key personnel	Educators	Child-care experts	Juvenile justice specialists	Lawyers/child-care experts	Lawyers	Lawyers/criminal justice actors
Key agencies	Community agencies/citizens School and community agencies	Social work agencies	Interagency structure	Law/social work agencies	Law	Law
Tasks	Help and education team	Diagnosis	Systems intervention	Diagnosis/punishment	Punishment	Incarceration/ punishment
Understanding of client behavior	People basically good	Pathology/ environmentally determined	Unsocialized	Diminished individual responsibility	Individual responsibility	Responsibility/ accountability
Purpose of intervention	Reeducation	Provision of treatment (*parens patriae*)	Retraining	Sanctioning of behavior/provision of treatment	Sanctioning of behavior	Protection of society/retribution, deterrence
Objectives	Intervention through education	Respond to individual needs/ rehabilitation	Implementation of policy	Respect individual rights/respond to special needs	Respect individual rights Punishment	Order maintenance
Countries	Japan	Austria, The Netherlands, India, South Korea, Italy, Scotland, Belgium	England/Wales, Hong Kong	Canada, South Africa	Germany, Russia, China, Namibia	United States, Hungary

SOURCE: Adapted from Winterdyk (2002). Copyright 2002. Reprinted with permission of Canadian Scholars' Press.

NOTE: As indicated in the text, no country's juvenile justice model is absolute; the designations shown here are intended to reflect general characteristics of the listed countries' juvenile justice systems. For example, in recent years an increasing number of countries have taken steps to embrace the CRC and other international standards that share many of the characteristics of the welfare model of juvenile justice.

a summary of the features of the various models). Although no individual country can be characterized as being truly representative of any one model, the models provide frameworks that are useful for describing and differentiating among nations' treatment of youthful offenders and allow for objective comparative analysis. For example, in Canada, we have what has been described as a *modified justice model* (Corrado, Bala, Linden, & LeBlanc, 1992; Winterdyk, 2002) because while the Youth Criminal Justice Act is a federal piece of legislation, the provinces have some discretion in how they interpret the act (see, for example, Bala 2003; Fetherston, 2000). The province of Quebec, for instance, tends to embrace a welfare approach, whereas some of the western provinces tend to follow a justice model. Yet all Canadian provinces are required to follow the general provisions declared in the act. Similarly, since the 1980s, Australia has moved away from a dichotomized justice and welfare approach to a more welfare-based model, yet Western Australia's Crime (Serious and Repeat Offenders) Sentencing Act of 1992 has been criticized for breaching a number of U.N. conventions (Atkinson, 1997). However, when one considers the juvenile justice system in Australia, it is important to recognize that each of that nation's six states and two territories is responsible for its own juvenile justice system, and, as O'Connor, Daly, and Hinds (2002) point out, "The answer to the question 'Who is a juvenile?' differs between jurisdictions" (p. 225). Even so, South Australia is commonly credited with establishing the world's first children's court and was the first state in Australia to introduce family conferencing on a formal basis.

Hence a close examination of the juvenile justice systems in most countries will reveal that the laws on which these systems are based (that is, in those countries that have dedicated juvenile justice legislation) tend to be subject to interpretation. In some cases, the laws may be interpreted in ways that do not reflect the characteristics generally associated with particular countries' identified juvenile justice models.

It is beyond the scope of this chapter to provide a comprehensive overview of the juvenile justice models in use in various countries, but the information in Table 23.2 serves to illustrate the diversity among nations. This table also indirectly illustrates the challenge that international recommendations and guidelines face within member countries attempting to fulfill their commitment to the CRC and other conventions.

INTERNATIONAL STANDARDS AND GUIDELINES FOR THE TREATMENT OF YOUNG OFFENDERS

Interestingly, neither the United Nations' Declaration of the Rights of the Child in 1924 nor its Declaration of the Rights of the Child in 1959 made any specific reference to juvenile justice. Even the Standard Minimum Rules for the Treatment of Prisoners issued by the United Nations in 1955 made no reference to the handling of juvenile offenders. It was not until the 1980s that the United Nations began to consider juvenile justice as a subject matter. At the Seventh U.N. Congress on the Prevention of Crime and the Treatment of Offenders, held in Beijing, China, in May 1984, the United Nations endorsed the Standard Minimum Rules for the Administration of Juvenile Justice. These standards, commonly referred as the Beijing Rules, are widely viewed as the most important (but not the only) guidelines for improving the quality of juvenile justice globally. Unfortunately, given the diversity in economic, political, and social factors among the world's nations, it is questionable whether such ideas can be universally embraced. However, this does not excuse countries from attempting to follow the essential recommendations. For example, the Centre for Europe's Children and the Oisin program of the

Table 23.2   Juvenile Delinquency: Country Profiles

Country	Minimum[a]– Maximum Age	Conditions/Justice Model[b]
Argentina	16–18	Legal system for juveniles has been described as similar to that of Italy; youth regulated under the Penal Regulations for Youth Law 22.778, 1980; very little research on youth crime (only one study in 1994)/**Justice model**[c]
Australia	10–16/17	Two jurisdictions have minimum age lower than 10/**Welfare model**
Austria	14–19	Juvenile Justice Act 1988, amended 1993; from 1981 to 1991, youth conviction rates dropped (1,799 to 763)/**Modified justice model/welfare model**
Barbados	7–16	Juvenile Offenders Act 1932; although system modeled after British tradition, it includes heavy reliance on police cautioning; little research on the effectiveness of the system/**Corporatist model**
Belgium	16–18	Children ages 6–15 dealt with informally/**Welfare model with penal exceptions**
Bulgaria[d]		Influence of Roman civil and criminal law/**Modified welfare-justice model**
Canada	12–18	**Modified justice model**
Cayman Islands	8–17	Children ages 8–13 classified as young persons; ages 14–17 classified as juveniles/**Welfare model**
China	14–25	Children partially responsible officially until age 18; law requires limited punishment; between 1977 and 1991, steady increase in crime, with proportionate amount of young offenders **Participatory model** with **justice** elements
Cuba	6–16	Progressive **welfare-based model** introduced by Castro regime in 1959 for "children with conduct problems"
Egypt	15–18	Juvenile Law No. 31 (1974); youth are segregated by age (12 and under, 13–14, 15–18); under 15 required to attend school, over 15 must receive vocational skills; judge aided in deliberation by two (appointed) experts, one of whom must be female/**Corporatist model**
England	12–18	**Corporatist–mixed model**
Finland	15–21	Three important age limits—15, 18, and 21; under 15 not liable; penal code recommends lighter sentences for children younger than 18; 17 and younger considered "child," 18 to 21 considered "juvenile"; 1991 proposal to lower minimum age to 14 in response to increase in youth crime/**Justice model**
France	13–18	Problem youth addressed under Ordinance No. 45-174 of February 2, 1945, modified 1958 and 1970; specially trained children's judges/magistrates and social services for educational help; compared with most Western European countries, rate of increase among the lowest (2% from 1992 thru 1993)/**Welfare model** (social defense system)
Germany	14–17	Youth 18–20 may be transferred to juvenile court/**Justice model**
Hong Kong	16–20	Children ages 7–15 classified as juveniles/**Corporatist model**
Hungary	14–18	No separate juvenile legislation/**Crime control model**
India	7–16 for boys; 18 for girls	**Welfare-justice model**
Italy	14–18	**Welfare-justice model**

(Continued)

Table 23.2 (Continued)

Country	Minimum[a]–Maximum Age	Conditions/Justice Model[b]
Israel	13–18	Juvenile Offenders Section (JSO), 1959; ethical code of JSO personnel goes beyond the limits established by the Youth Act stressing protection/**Corporatist model**
Japan	14–20	**Participatory model**
Jamaica	7–14	New legislation was introduced in 2001/The new legislation resembles a **corporatist model**
Namibia	15–18	**Justice model** (although still very much in developmental stage)
The Netherlands	12–18	**Modified justice model**
New Zealand	14–17	Criminal responsibility begins at age 10, but unless *mens rea* can be proven, no conviction possible until age 14; exceptions to rule are murder and manslaughter/**Welfare model**
Norway	15–18	Minimum age raised from 14 to 15 in 1990; 18-year-olds most frequently represented; recidivism rate continues to climb (41% among young offenders)/**Welfare-modified justice model**
Philippines	9–15	Youth offenders ages 15–17 receive suspended sentences; offenders 18–20 are criminally responsible but entitled to leniency/**Welfare-justice model**
Poland	13–17	Responsibility based on mental and moral ability; 16- to 17-year-olds can be held criminally responsible/**Justice model**
Russia	14–18	**Justice model** (but attempting to embrace **welfare** principles)
Scotland	8–16	Upper age limit 18 if already under supervision/**Welfare model with penal exceptions** applied for ages 8–15; **justice model** elements with **welfare exceptions** applied for ages 16–18
Singapore	7–12	Islamic law sets minimum age of criminal responsibility at puberty/**Welfare-justice model**
South Africa	15–18	**Modified justice model**
South Korea		**Justice-welfare model**
Sweden	15–20	Known as "juvenile criminals"; youth ages 15–17 given special consideration/**Justice model**
Switzerland	15–18	Youth ages 7–14 considered children, 15–17 considered adolescent, 18–25 considered young adults (treated less severely than older adults)/**Crime control model**
Tanzania	7–15	Relatively new legislation/elements of **welfare model**
United States	7–15+	Upper limit can range up to age 20 in some states; for most it is 17/**Crime control model**

SOURCE: The information in this table comes primarily from data supplied by foreign embassies and/or relevant juvenile departments. In some cases insufficient information is available to describe the model of justice or any other characteristics.

a. Five countries still practice capital punishment of juvenile offenders: Bangladesh, Barbados, Iran, Pakistan, and the United States.

b. Names of models are provided only for countries in which sufficient information is available to allow a description of their juvenile justice practices.

c. The models (identified by bold type in this table) are the models found in Table 23.1.

d. Some countries do not recognize a minimum age of criminal responsibility, hence no age is given here. In 1804, the Napoleonic Code in France was one of the first laws to prescribe limited responsibility to offenders under the age of 16.

European Commission publish a newsletter, *JUMPletter,* which in June 2002 examined the initiatives from within the European Union to address juvenile crime through social prevention. The Oisin program was established in 1996 by the European Parliament under the field of Justice and Home Affairs. Its objective is to "promote exchange and training of, and co-operation [among], law enforcement authorities" in Europe.

In 1998, UNICEF incorporated the Beijing Rules into the *Implementation Handbook for the Convention on the Rights of the Child.* Other significant U.N. declarations pertaining to juvenile justice include the U.N. Guidelines for the Prevention of Juvenile Delinquency (known as the Riyadh Guidelines) and the U.N. Rules for the Protection of Juveniles Deprived of Their Liberty, both of which were issued in 1990.

The following section examines some of the key standards and explores the extent to which signatories of the standards have been able to actualize them.

HIGHLIGHTS OF THE U.N. CONVENTION ON THE RIGHTS OF THE CHILD

> *Mankind owes to the child the best that it has to give.*
>
> —U.N. Declaration of the Rights of the Child, 1924

In accordance with a welfare model of juvenile justice (see Table 23.1), the Beijing Rules state that the objectives of a nation's juvenile justice legislation should focus on furthering the well-being of the juvenile and her or his family (1.1) and on developing conditions that will ensure a meaningful life in the community for the youth (1.2); in addition, the administration of juvenile justice should represent an integral part of the natural development process of the country. If countries are to meet these

objectives, why is it that the United Nations has fair to excellent information on adult offenders, yet very limited data on young offenders (see Hamilton, 2002)? This lack of central information makes cross-national comparative study of juvenile justice very difficult.

The broad nature of the U.N. principles allows for considerable latitude of interpretation and may account in part for some of the diversity witnessed among those countries that claim they are trying to adhere to the guidelines. For example, juveniles in Sudan, Zimbabwe, and Singapore can still face flogging, amputation, and execution, and juveniles in Kenya are regularly locked up with adults because the country has only one juvenile court. Chinese law includes a provision that allows a 16-year-old to receive a suspended death sentence that can be carried out when the youth turns 18 (Prince, 1997). Several years ago, some Iranian teenagers were sentenced to 10 lashes and a fine of 100,000 rials (approximately $30 U.S.) each for attending a dance party that included both boys and girls. (This mixing of the sexes among unmarried persons is forbidden under Islamic laws; see "Iranian Teens," 1999.) According to the U.S. Department of Justice, even in the United States some 75% of juvenile facilities "lack adequate health care, security, and access to suicide-prevention programs" (cited in Prince, 1997). Meanwhile, in the Caribbean, due to economic factors, many juveniles remain unrepresented by legal counsel at trial (Singh, 1999). The countries in these examples would seem to fall short of U.N. standard 2.3(a), which says that "efforts shall be made to establish in each national jurisdiction . . . provisions . . . to meet the varying needs of juvenile offenders, while protecting their basic rights."

As Table 23.2 illustrates, there is considerable variation among countries concerning the age of criminal responsibility. The Beijing Rules (i.e., 4.1) simply state that the beginning age shall not be fixed at too low an age level. The rules recommend that in determining the lower limit, legislators should keep in mind the factors of emotional, mental, and intellectual maturity. Consequently, we see the age of responsibility ranging from as low as 6 in Mexico and 7 in Thailand and Kenya to as high as 16 in Argentina. Ironically, the rules offer even fewer guidelines for the upper limit of juvenile responsibility. This would appear to reflect a clear lack of social, psychological, and biological understanding of adolescent development. For example, most related studies show that whereas adolescence begins between the ages of 10 to 13 and peaks around age 15, the neurological and social development of individual adolescents can vary depending on a wide array of factors. Therefore, rather than trying to clarify such matters, the Beijing Rules speak to legislative consideration in this case.

South Africa, for example, in 2002 introduced the Child Justice Bill, which for the first time in that country's history established legal provisions to deal with child offenders. Prior to enactment of the bill, children between 7 and 14 years of age were assumed to not possess criminal capacity, but the bill now sets the minimum age of criminal responsibility at 10. In principle, the Child Justice Bill represents South Africa's effort to embrace a number of the standards set out in the U.N. convention. Similarly, in November 2002 Namibia passed the Juvenile Justice Bill, which focuses on several key aspects, such as age of responsibility, criminal capacity, police procedures, and sentencing options. The bill represents a sharp move away from a justice model to a modified welfare model. It includes provisions to reduce the age of criminal responsibility from 14 to 10 and to exclude youth between the ages of 10 to 14 from criminal responsibility. Yet the bill allows the court to overrule these provisos if it can be "proven beyond reasonable doubt that the offender had such capacity" (Schulz, 2002). Furthermore, the bill offers no clear rationale for the establishment of the upper age limit. However, such ambiguity can also be found within many of the more established juvenile justice systems around the world.

The aim of juvenile justice, according to the Beijing Rules (i.e., 5.1), should be that any reaction to juvenile offenders should always be in proportion to the circumstances of both the offender and the offense. However, any action should emphasize, foremost, the well-being of the juvenile. This section of the rules represents conflict between the classical doctrine of criminology and the positive doctrine of criminology. Appreciating that the principle is meant as a guideline, it is both vague and untenable, given that no legislation can equitably apply a fair reaction at an individual level. Rather, for any juvenile justice system to work effectively, it must apply general standards that are consistent in their ideology and grounded in empirical evidence.

Again, when we look at the aims of the countries that are signatories of the CRC standards, we see that the scope for interpretation is excessively broad and appears to be more reflective of political agendas than of any intent to represent the true needs of young persons. In Honduras several years ago, two 16-year-old street children escaped a government-run youth center and were found dead two days later. The police were suspected of committing the killings even though Honduras has ratified the CRC (Prince, 1997). In Canada, the new Youth Criminal Justice Act aims to command the respect of Canadians by holding young offenders responsible for their actions and ensuring meaningful consequences for those who commit certain offenses.

The scope of discretion (section 6) laid out in the Beijing Rules calls for "sufficient accountability at all stages and levels in the exercise of any such discretion." A number of countries have taken notable steps to broaden their scope of discretion when dealing with young offenders. India, even though representative of a welfare model of justice, has taken additional steps to embrace the fundamental principles of its model. In 2000, India's new

Juvenile Justice (Care and Protection of Children) Act introduced provisions that make the juvenile justice system more child-friendly in promoting opportunities for proper care and protection of young persons. The act also makes a clear distinction between juvenile offenders and neglected children. Perhaps most impressive in a country with limited resources, the new act requires that all cases relating to juveniles be completed within a 4-month period (T. Chakraborty, personal communication, November 5, 2002).

Further evidence of the general lack of participation of member states in implementing the U.N. standards and norms is the fact that in 1999 the U.N. Committee on the CRC issued a recommendation calling on member states to give priority attention toward full implementation of Articles 37, 39, and 40 of the convention. The committee also urged the U.N. High Commission for Human Rights to do what it could to encourage and/or assist member countries to implement the standards fully. For example, it seems ironic that the most powerful country in the world, the United States, signed the CRC in 1995 but has yet to ratify its signature. The only other U.N. member state that has not ratified the CRC is the African country of Somalia. Somalia currently has no functioning government, and so is unable to ratify anything. In spite of its intention to ratify, the United States has allowed some 9 years to pass since it signed the convention. Therefore, the United States is not obliged, nor has it made any overt effort, to make this legal commitment to children or to embrace international customary law. The American absence is a significant statement that undermines the goodwill and positive intentions of the rest of the members of the international community as they strive to reach some uniformity in the treatment and handling of young offenders.

One recommendation that has been put forth to assist in the implementation of the CRC and the monitoring of compliance is that member countries should regularly submit statistics on their juvenile justice systems and on juvenile offenders. According to a report prepared by Hamilton (2002), however, at present participation in such data collection is all but absent, with the modest exception of a few countries. Even though such statistics may not provide reliable figures on youth crime, they would provide a basis on which some comparisons could be made and then steps could eventually be taken to streamline recording methods and practices. In the meantime, the rhetoric concerning the rights of the child will continue until the public and governments are prepared to embrace the reality of the plight of children. For example, the United Nations has reported that in 2000 some 300,000 children served as soldiers, and in 1999 about 160 million children were malnourished (see UNICEF, n.d.).

What becomes evident when we evaluate the application of international guidelines and standards to countries that are signatories of the CRC is that, irrespective of any models of juvenile justice, no country is able to implement and/or actualize the guidelines and standards uniformly. Furthermore, many of the states that can be characterized as developing nations simply have not had the resources or the political will to implement juvenile justice systems (or have been inordinately slow in doing so). What becomes evident is that each country's juvenile justice system has evolved since it was first introduced, and, although nations might strive to honor the CRC, pragmatic factors such as social values and norms, economic standards, cultural ideologies, and political and public opinion continue to compromise the establishment of universal standards for juvenile justice.

Hamilton (2002) concludes that the member states of the CRC have "been notoriously slow at implementing Articles 37, 39, and 40" (p. 1). In fact, she further notes that virtually all states have been, or could be, criticized for their "failure to fully implement them" (p. 1). These are daunting accusations, but they are based in reality. As I have already noted, for most countries the failure to follow or to establish a system of juvenile justice that embraces the CRC standards and norms is rooted in an inability to inform and educate citizens properly about the true nature and extent of juvenile offending, the administration of juvenile justice, and the efforts being made in some nations to curb offending or to rehabilitate offenders. Even though juvenile offending and juvenile justice are universal concerns, countries continue to legislate models of justice that are often dictated by political agendas and public opinion even as they attempt to acknowledge the standards of the CRC.

As noted above, and as illustrated in Table 23.2, it is evident that the administration of juvenile justice is more a reflection of the social and political will of the state than of the universal interests of young persons in conflict with the law. When the administration of justice is dictated by political (i.e., human-made) laws instead of scientific/natural laws, we typically end up with a legal system that is consistent with the conflict model. Political laws are based on political power and have no stability, whereas scientific laws are based on common law principles and reflect consensus. Therefore, the more juvenile justice systems move away from scientific laws, the more thinly protected the rights of children and young offenders will be.

IS THERE AN ALTERNATIVE?

Some topics are invested with enormous social importance but blessed with little reliable information.

—Stephen Jay Gould, *The Mismeasure of Man*, 1981

In spite of the seemingly pessimistic nature of the above discussion, it is possible that we can learn from our mistakes by looking at the successes some countries have had in implementing the CRC standards. It would appear that although the CRC offers a solid foundation from which to address and administer juvenile justice, the international efforts of different regions that share some key characteristics might represent a more prudent approach. For example, Oisin has set out to critically analyze and compare best practices throughout the program's European members across a range of areas. This initiative is similar in scope to studies conducted in the United States by the Office of Justice Programs and the National Institute of Justice, such as their Juvenile "Breaking the Cycle" Evaluation, among other projects.

In addition, developing countries need support as they attempt to implement juvenile justice systems or revise their existing systems in accordance with the social and political climate. Hence a staggered implementation approach might be prudent; until the public is willing to support any new approach, legal and political initiatives will only be partially honored.

Finally, if societies are going to address juvenile crime effectively, we must let go of the misguided notion that laws can be used either to exert control over youth or to facilitate social change. As reflected in the CRC and some other international initiatives, we need to humanize youth justice by supporting social prevention programs that are able to provide young people with constructive opportunities. We also need to explore and examine systems that embrace community involvement in ways that promote social cohesion rather than undermine social bonds.

CONCLUSION

Juvenile delinquency is a fascinating problem that appears to have puzzled societies for centuries. This has been reflected not only in the vast diversity of child-rearing and disciplinary practices throughout the ages but in the varying juvenile justice system approaches to addressing youth crime. In addition, the

United Nations and other international bodies have attempted to help define fundamental standards and guidelines for the handling and processing of juveniles offenders.

In spite of all the efforts and resources that have been directed toward the problem of young offenders, successes have been limited, and agreement on "what works" remains entangled within social, economic, and political climates that at the end of the day serve primarily the well-being of the providers and seldom the youth. However, in recent years, various regions of the world have been engaged in initiatives that focus on social prevention and crime prevention through an interdisciplinary and integrated approach. These efforts show promise and are consistent with the scientific/ natural approach to social harmony.

We have seen that crime trends and patterns share many characteristics internationally. They vary only in extent. Therefore, the issue of youth crime is an international matter and should be studied within an integrated and comparative context. Until we can collectively begin to move in this direction, we will live in a world in which our most valuable resource, our youth, remains a visionary objective rather than a reality.

NOTE

1. Throughout this chapter, I use the terms *juvenile delinquency* and *youth crime* interchangeably.

REFERENCES

Ariès, P. (1962). *Centuries of childhood: A social history of family life.* New York: Vintage.

Atkinson, L. (1997). Juvenile justice in Australia. In J. Winterdyk (Ed.), *Juvenile justice systems: International perspectives.* Toronto: Canadian Scholars Press.

Bala, N. (2003). *Youth criminal justice law.* Toronto: Irwin Law.

Bala, N., & Bromwich, R. J. (2002). Introduction: An international perspective on youth justice. In N. Bala, J. P. Hornick, H. N. Snyder, & J. J. Paetsch (Eds.), *Juvenile justice systems: An international comparison of problems and solutions.* Toronto: Thompson Educational Publishing.

Corrado, R. R, Bala, N., Linden, R., & LeBlanc, M. (Eds.). (1992). *Juvenile justice in Canada.* Toronto: Butterworth.

Crime Congress targets terrorist crimes, firearms regulations, and transnational crime. (1995). *CJ International, 11*(4), 4–6.

deMause, L. (1974). The evolution of childhood. In L. deMause (Ed.), *The history of childhood.* New York: Peter Bedrick.

Fetherston, D. W. (2000). The law and young offenders. In J. Winterdyk (Ed.), *Issues and perspective on young offenders in Canada* (2nd ed.). Toronto: Harcourt Brace.

Hamilton, C. (2002). *Juvenile justice: The role of statistics and public perception.* Paper prepared for the Office of the High Commissioner for Human Rights, Geneva.

Iranian teens to be whipped for dance party [Electronic version]. (1999, August 25). *Calgary Herald.* Available at www.calgaryherald.com (subscription required) and www.csmonitor.com (fee access).

Jones, K. (1999). *Taming the troublesome child: American families, child guidance, and the limits of psychiatric authority.* Cambridge, MA: Harvard University Press.

Krisberg, B., & Austin, J. (1978). *The children of Ishmael.* New York: Mayfield.

O'Connor, I., Daly, K., & Hinds, L. (2002). Juvenile crime and justice in Australia. In N. Bala, J. P. Hornick, H. N. Snyder, & J. J. Paetsch (Eds.), *Juvenile justice systems: An international comparison of problems and solutions* (pp. 221–254). Toronto: Thompson Educational Publishing.

Platt, A. M. (1977). *The child savers* (2nd ed.). Chicago: University of Chicago Press.

Prince, C. J. (1997, October 22). Justice lags for world's juveniles [Electronic version]. *Christian Science Monitor International.* Available at www.calgaryherald.com (subscription required) and www.csmonitor.com (fee access).

Schulz, S. (2002). *Juvenile justice in Namibia: Law reform towards reconciliation and restorative justice*. Unpublished manuscript, Polytechnic of Namibia, Department of Legal Studies.

Singh, W. (1999, April). *A regional report: Latin America*. Paper presented at the International Penal Reform Conference, London.

UNICEF. (n.d.). Introduction. In *Convention on the Rights of the Child*. Retrieved December 1, 2002, from http://www.unicef.org/crc/crc.htm

United Nations. (1995). *Ninth United Nations Congress on the Prevention of Crime and the Treatment of Offenders* (A/CONF.167/7). Vienna: U.N. Crime Prevention and Criminal Justice Branch.

Winterdyk, J. (Ed.). (2002). *Juvenile justice systems: International perspectives* (2nd ed.). Toronto: Canadian Scholars Press.

24

Symbolic Law, Isolationism, and the Death Penalty

DAVID KEYS

Murray Edelman (1964) has remarked that the public often bases its attitudes toward government not on empirical facts or interests, but on whether given laws are symbolically reassuring. Edelman concludes, "Political acts or events in the news commonly mean different things to different groups of spectators, dividing men rather than uniting them" (p. 12). The capital punishment laws that exist in 38 U.S. states, as well as in U.S. federal and military jurisdictions, have significant qualities, both symbolic and instrumental. They serve as a moral response to high rates of homicide in the southern United States, where violent crime and executions are most common, and they are also a morally repugnant symbol to the minority of Americans who oppose state-sanctioned killing (Galliher,

1989) as well as to a majority of nations in the world (Radelet, 2003). In some instances, capital punishment is a remnant of colonial domination and institutionalized oppression (Galliher, Koch, Keys, & Guess, 2002). Very few homicide convictions result in actual executions, as the five U.S. states that lead in executions demonstrate,[1] yet the perceived need for the threat of such violence has a currency in the United States that does not exist in other nations of the Western Hemisphere or in other industrialized countries, with the exceptions of Japan and China.

The U.S. position on capital punishment has been the foundation for disputes with other nations; it has created tensions surrounding the executions of foreign nationals who have been tried and sentenced in the United States,

AUTHOR'S NOTE: I owe a debt of gratitude to Robert Weiss, Tony Poveda, and Mike Radelet for their assistance in the writing of this chapter.

contradicted progressive social trends within the European Union, jeopardized the delicate relationship between the United States and Mexico, and thrown obstacles in the way of the humanitarian objectives of the United Nations. Although other issues—concerning international criminal courts, control of weapons of mass destruction, and the use of internationally sanctioned force—have hobbled U.S. diplomatic efforts at the beginning of the 21st century, the use of capital punishment by the majority of U.S. domestic jurisdictions has added emotional fuel to a crisis that threatens to further isolate the United States from the rest of the world. This chapter examines the circumstances surrounding the use and the abolition of capital punishment in the world while also addressing the effects on diplomatic relations of the continuing advocacy and practice of executions in the United States.

AMERICAN EXCEPTIONALISM, SOCIAL PEACE, AND THE DEATH PENALTY

Poveda (2000) builds a compelling case for U.S. "domestic exceptionalism," putting forth the idea that internal political conditions (conservatism), economic conditions (decreasing real wages), and social conditions (incomplete assimilation of African Americans) have tended to set the United States apart from its technically sophisticated Western counterparts on the issue of the death penalty. The blooming of hard-line conservative politics following the 1980 presidential election, the decrease of well-paying manufacturing jobs, and the persistent open wound of race relations in the United States constitute, in Poveda's view, the foundation of support for capital punishment.

Poveda (2000) identifies a trend toward abolition of capital punishment in most Western nations that was sustained throughout the 20th century, but he does not attempt to characterize those nations or those that retain and regularly use capital punishment. Of the 89 nations (Amnesty International,

2001) that continue to use the death penalty, 37 have predominantly Muslim populations or very significant minorities using systems of Islamic justice; 31 are found on the African continent, and another 12 are in and around the Caribbean Basin and were formerly European colonies. Of the remaining nations in the Americas, only Guatemala and the United States still use capital punishment. Excluding the People's Republic of China and Japan, the United States is the only technically sophisticated, industrialized nation in the world to use the death penalty regularly.

Among those nations that have abolished capital punishment since the end of World War II, membership in the European Union has been a significant force in reform, although some have emerged from periods of authoritarian government and sought liberal reforms, including the abolition of executions. Cambodia sought abolition in 1989 after its terrible encounter with the Khmer Rouge, and the Dominican Republic (1966) and Spain (1978) sought to limit the power of government in this manner following the overthrow of long-standing military juntas headed by Generals Trujillo and Francisco Franco, respectively. A similar circumstance accompanied abolition of the death penalty in Haiti in the wake of the infamous dictator François (Papa Doc) Duvalier, who oversaw his country's last legitimate execution in 1972. The Haitian people realized full abolition in 1989 under his son, François (Baby Doc) Duvalier, Jr. Chile abolished capital punishment relatively recently, after a long and bloody experience with right-wing extremism headed by General Augusto Pinochet and the resurgence of the Left, which was nearly wiped out after a 1973 military coup and the assassination of President Salvador Allende. Nicaragua abolished the death sentence in 1979, following the ouster of the infamous Somoza family, which had governed that country since 1932, and Romania did so in 1989 after the grisly Christmas Day execution of former premier

Nicolae Ceausescu and his wife, which was nationally televised.

Probably the most surprising and numerically significant abolition of capital punishment came in South Africa in 1995, a change that was enacted after a long period of state-sponsored and secret executions by the white apartheid governments, which ended their reign in 1991. Within the United States, Alaska and Hawaii both abolished executions as soon as they had appropriated the necessary elements of home rule and universal suffrage, primarily in response to the fact that nearly all of the individuals executed there in the past had been people of color (Galliher et al., 2002). Hawaii in particular was keen to nullify capital punishment laws because the death penalty had fallen exclusively on Asians and Asian Americans during the island's tenure as a feudal kingdom and U.S. territory (Galliher et al., 2002, pp. 148–149).

Among the most far-reaching examples of the abolition of capital punishment, South Africa is exceptional in that its negation of the death penalty, enacted by President Nelson Mandela, immediately preceded the establishment of the Truth Commission, the body empowered to investigate and try members of the former apartheid governments for abuses while in power. It was Mandela's intention to limit the commission's sentencing latitude in an effort to promote restorative justice in a country that stood at the brink of civil war for more than four decades.

The reforms noted above paint a clear image, showing that the abolition of capital punishment is a major step toward the promotion of racial peace and social healing. These reforms also constitute tacit recognition that capital punishment excites retribution and delays the formulation of coolheaded solutions to social problems. Although there are distinct differences between the nations named above and the United States, problems of racial/ethnic tensions and ideological polarization do exist in the United States, and it cannot be denied

that executions have been, and continue to be, a flash point in the debates surrounding those problems. All Americans who desire social peace within the United States and improved relations between the United States and its Western partners must consider the issue of capital punishment in terms of its substantial limitation or eventual abolition.

INTERNATIONAL LAW AND U.S. COMPLIANCE

Over the past half century, international policy and law have consistently moved toward a global moratorium on and/or abolition of capital punishment, with significant steps employed to restrict and narrow the use of the death penalty. As of 2002, more than half the countries in the world had either abolished capital punishment by statute or were in a condition of *virtual abolition,* in which death penalty statutes exist but are never used.

Since 1930, the various states and other jurisdictions of the United States have executed 4,755 people, more than 300 of whom were juveniles at the time they committed their crimes. When the pace of U.S. executions began to increase in the 1990s, the United States came into serious conflicts with other nations over the use of capital punishment (Espy & Smylka, 1994, 2002). In a foreign policy sense, the use of executions by the U.S. federal government and 38 U.S. states poses serious obstacles to the United States' making moral and diplomatic connections with other advanced nations of the world and hinders the United States in securing, in the world's eyes, the role of a cooperative nation governed by legal standards and moral tenets.

Almost immediately following the establishment of the United Nations, a movement began within that body to control and reduce the use of deadly force by member states; this movement has gained in momentum since 1980. As of 2003, more than half of the U.N. member nations had either abolished their capital punishment laws or had stopped using their existing death penalty statutes (Radelet, 2003). The following list briefly describes some of the ways the United Nations and other international organizations have worked in opposition to capital punishment since 1948:

- *1948:* The United Nations adopted, without a dissenting vote, the Universal Declaration of Human Rights, proclaiming the right of every individual to protection from deprivation of life. The declaration states that no person shall be subjected to unusual or degrading punishment and that the death penalty violates both of these fundamental rights.
- *1963:* The Vienna Convention on Consular Relations (April 24) sought to regularize the procedures under which foreign nationals who are detained, indicted, tried, and sentenced in foreign countries can have access to their home countries' consuls.
- *1966:* The United Nations adopted the International Covenant on Civil and Political Rights (ICCPR; see United Nations, 1992), Article 6 of which states that "no one shall be arbitrarily deprived of his life" and that the death penalty shall not be imposed on pregnant women or on any persons who were under the age of 18 at the time their crimes were committed. In addition, Article 7 of the ICCPR states that "no one shall be subjected to torture or to cruel, inhuman or degrading treatment or punishment."
- *1984:* The U.N. Economic and Social Council adopted, and the General Assembly endorsed by consensus, the Safeguards Guaranteeing Protection of the Rights of Those Facing the Death Penalty. These safeguards state that no one under the age of 18 at the time of his or her crime shall be put to death and that anyone sentenced to death has the right to appeal the conviction, to petition for pardon, or to request a commutation of sentence.
- *1989:* The U.N. General Assembly adopted the Second Optional Protocol to the ICCPR. The goal of this protocol is the abolition of the death penalty.
- *1990:* The General Assembly of the Organization of American States adopted the Protocol to the American Convention on Human Rights, which provides for the total abolition of the death penalty, allowing for its use in wartime only.
- *1993:* The International War Crimes Tribunal stated that the death penalty is not an appropriate punishment, even for such offenses as crimes against nature and genocide.
- *1994:* In the U.N. General Assembly, Italy introduced a draft resolution aimed at establishing an international moratorium on executions, making several key points about the philosophical gap that exists on this issue between the United States and the rest of the world. The Italian delegation cited the fact that the war crimes tribunals in the former Yugoslavia and Rwanda dispensed with the death penalty and repeated what has become a familiar refrain, that the "abolition of the death penalty contributes to the enhancement of human dignity and progressive development of human rights" (U.N. Document A/49/234, 1994, cited in Schabas, 1997, pp. 112–126).
- *1995:* The U.N. Convention on the Rights of the Child acquired the force of international law. Article 37(a) of this convention prohibits the use of the death penalty for any person under the age of 18 at the time of his or her crime.
- *1999:* The U.N. Commission on Human Rights (UNCHR) passed a resolution calling on all member states that were continuing to utilize capital punishment to progressively narrow the numbers and types of offenses under which convicted defendants may be sentenced to death.
- *2001:* The UNCHR approved a European Union motion requesting that member nations impose a moratorium on executions.
- *2002:* In February, the Council of Europe's Committee of Ministers adopted Protocol 13 to the European Convention on Human Rights, which in substance is the first legally binding international treaty to abolish capital punishment in all circumstances. In May, 36 countries became signatories to the convention immediately upon its opening (Amnesty International, 2003).

As late as May 2, 2002, the United States, over the signature of President George W. Bush, specifically agreed to assist and ensure European Union policies, among them Section II (Global Challenges), Paragraph 3, of the Joint European Union–United States Action Plan, which reads as follows:

We will:

- identify means of strengthening international judicial assistance and cooperation in the obtaining of evidence and other relevant information;
- cooperate on the judicial seizure and forfeiture of assets;
- identify means to strengthen and improve international mechanisms for extradition, deportation, mutual legal assistance and other cooperative action to ensure that international fugitives have "nowhere to hide";
- cooperate in promoting the work of the Hague Conference on Private International Law and the International Institute for Unification of Private Law (UNIDROIT).

One might assume that entering into such an agreement would require full cooperation with the International Court of Justice (ICJ) and with U.N. authorities that often work in conjunction with the European Union. However, these well-publicized summit meetings have had little effect on the day-to-day treatment of foreign nationals confined and condemned in the United States or on the practice in many U.S. jurisdictions of charging juvenile defendants as adults (European Union Council on Human Rights, 2002).

COMPLICATIONS IN U.S.-MEXICAN RELATIONS

Article 36 of the Vienna Convention on Consular Relations (1963), signed and ratified by the United States in 1969, states:

If he so requests, the competent authorities of the receiving State shall inform the consular post of the sending State if a national of that State is arrested or committed to prison. The said authorities shall inform the person concerned without delay of his rights under this sub-paragraph.

Among a variety of functions aimed at ensuring due process for the accused, this convention guarantees assistance of consul and the defendant's right to an open and fair trial. This includes the foreign defendant's rights to understand the nature of the charges brought (and to have the assistance of an interpreter if necessary) and to be protected against self-incrimination, whether through coerced confession or compulsion to testify against him- or herself. However, despite these protections, more than 50 foreign nationals whose treatment has apparently not been in compliance with the convention are currently awaiting execution in U.S. prisons.

The relationship between the United States and Mexico has suffered considerable setbacks since the late 1990s owing to tensions around the emotional issues of immigration and capital punishment. These two issues are intertwined because the U.S. states that border Mexico have engaged in efforts to make immigration more difficult and to create circumstances that would serve to make the United States less attractive to immigrants, particularly those from Latin America.

In the first major congressional action on immigration in a decade, the U.S. House of Representatives in March 1996 passed, by a vote of 333 to 87, the Immigration and National Interest Act, a bill designed to crack down on illegal immigration. This act's most controversial element is that it allows increased vigilance at popular border crossings, which has had the effect of forcing those seeking illegal entry into the United States to use rural desert routes that have proven deadly, not only because of climatic hazards, but also because of vigilance movements among U.S. nationals whose members murder illegal aliens out of the sight of traditional law enforcement agencies. Subsequent to passage of the act, U.S.-Mexican relations were complicated by a rise in vigilante movements against illegal migrants trying to cross into California, Arizona, New Mexico, and Texas. If this bill led to a perception among Mexicans that the United States places a very low value on the lives of persons who cross the border illegally, the use of the death penalty on Mexican nationals has assured them that this is so.

President Vicente Fox, the Mexican head of state, canceled a trip to Texas and a meeting with George W. Bush in August 2002 as a "repudiation" of the decision of a Texas court to execute Javier Suarez Medina, 33, who was convicted of killing Dallas undercover police officer Lawrence Cadena in 1988. The Mexican newspaper *La Jornada,* which has traditionally been very critical of Fox's policies and those of his conservative National Action Party, commented in an editorial, "The presidential determination to cancel the trip to Texas is consistent with the defense of life, dignity and of the traditional posture of Mexico against the death penalty, and as such it deserves society's full approval and support" ("Fox Visit," 2002). The Medina execution precipitated the imposition by Mexico's highest court, the Suprema Corte de Justicia de la Nación (SCJN), of new restrictions on previous rulings that allowed the extradition of Mexican citizens to the United States. Previously, in an effort to help the United States prosecute drug traffickers, Mexico allowed the extradition of Mexicans to the United States on a variety of criminal charges. In its October 2, 2002, ruling, however, the SCJN curtailed the Mexican government's authority to extradite any Mexican citizen facing any punishment harsher than the equivalent of Mexico's life sentence, which stands at maximum of 60 years in prison. This break in diplomacy immediately threatened

the operation of the justice system in Bexar County, Texas, in that the SCJN has refused to allow the extradition of a high-profile murder suspect, Eric Quesada, on the grounds that he faces the possibility of a death sentence in the United States. Bexar County officials are faced with the choice of dropping capital charges or allowing Quesada to go free in Mexico (Rodriguez, 2002). The problem is even more pronounced in California, where, according to California prosecutors, more than 60 murder suspects have crossed the border into the Mexican state of Baja California (Miller, 2002). Los Angeles County prosecutors recognize that Mexican officials traditionally do not extradite their own citizens back to the United States for trial, but the fact that they have recently become reluctant to return U.S. citizens owing to the possibility of capital punishment or sentences of life without parole (Miller, 2002) is causing concern north of the border ("Refuge in Mexico," 2003).

Mexico has also pressed its case in the International Court of Justice in the case of *Avena and Other Mexican Nationals,* consolidated in *Mexico v. United States of America* (2003). Mexico's petition to the ICJ, filed January 9, 2003, contended that Avena and others had been denied their consular rights under provisions of Article 36 of the Vienna Convention on Consular Relations. An examination of the cases of foreign nationals on U.S. death rows reveals that, in nearly every case, the arresting authorities failed to notify the detained foreign nationals of their rights to communicate with their consular representatives, to make subsequent consular visits, and to have access to attorneys. In that Article 36 ensures that all persons arrested outside of their home countries have the means at their disposal to prepare an adequate defense and to receive the same treatment before the law as domestic citizens, compliance with the law is an essential feature of international relations. In *Mexico v. United States,* Mexico asserted that the United States did not comply with the law, and foreign nationals, confronted by an unfamiliar legal system, were tried and sentenced to death without the support they should have received from the authorities of their native countries. Since 1993, the United States has executed at least 5 foreign nationals, including citizens of the Dominican Republic, Mexico, and Cuba. Currently, 51 Mexicans await execution on U.S. death rows. California (36), Texas (25), and Florida (22) prisons are currently detaining the majority of the foreign nationals slated for capital sentences, with 29 other states and the federal government holding lesser numbers.

On February 5, 2003, the ICJ unanimously ordered in the case of *Mexico v. United States*:

(a) The United States of America shall take all measures necessary to ensure that Mr. Cesar Roberto Fierro Reyna, Mr. Roberto Moreno Ramos, and Mr. Osvaldo Torres Aguilera are not executed pending final judgments in these proceedings;

(b) The Government of the United States of America shall inform the Court of all measures taken in implementation of this order.

Justice system authorities in Harris County, Texas, have not acknowledged receipt of the ICJ order, nor has any sentence of the individual named above, Cesar Reyna, been stayed, commuted, or set aside. In addition, Texas authorities commented in 2003 that the ICJ "had no jurisdiction in Harris County criminal matters and that the [presumably U.S.] Department of Justice has not seen fit to inform the county of the international court's ruling" (Harris County Circuit Court Clerk's Office, personal communication, 2003).

What are the consequences of ignoring an ICJ order, even if it is interpreted as international interference in Texas justice? Miller (2003b) has broached this question in the state's leading professional journal for attorneys, *Texas Lawyer*:

The United States expects Mexico to continue to respect its legal obligations on water rights, tariffs, extradition, and drug trafficking, not to mention the Vienna Convention requirements when US citizens are arrested south of the border. (One would think most Texans gladly would trade a delay in two executions for progress on water rights and extradition.) But a high price may be paid if the United States continues to ignore international law on an issue that Mexico regards as vital. (p. 38)

The idea behind the Vienna Convention is that consuls are uniquely placed to provide essential services to their nationals, including legal advice and assistance, translation, notification of family, the transfer of documentation from the native country, and observation of court hearings. Part of the philosophy of noncompliance that local jurisdictions hold is based in the reality that consular personnel have legally obstructed the attempts of law enforcement authorities to extract confessions from suspects and mitigated the efforts of prosecutors to pressure defendants into pleading guilty. In turn, part of the resentment that foreign governments feel toward noncompliant jurisdictions is founded on the emphasis that the U.S. Department of State places on Article 36—specifically, that it considers notification for American citizens taken into custody beyond U.S. borders to be a serious matter, but has taken no real steps to ensure compliance of U.S. justice agencies with the Vienna Convention or to correct past violations that have resulted in foreign nationals' being condemned to death and executed. At its core, the United States' habit of ignoring the concerns of foreign governments' efforts on the part of their citizenry endangers all Americans who travel abroad.

From the Mexican perspective, immigration crackdowns and systematic refusals to grant internationally guaranteed rights are part of a seamless U.S. policy of exclusion and calculated symbolism designed to threaten

Mexicans in the United States and deter further immigration. Chief among the symbols are the treatment, convictions, and executions of Mexican nationals in the United States for crimes that would not have merited the death sentence in Mexico. In a larger sense, the failure to comply with ICJ rulings is a serious blow to U.S. credibility. As Miller (2003b) puts it:

> With its rejection of virtually every major UN initiative, from the Kyoto Treaty to the International Criminal Court [and now add the war on Iraq and the negation of the Nuclear Non-Proliferation Treaty of 1995], the Bush Administration has given the impression that it lacks a long-term commitment to international law. (p. 38)

The conduct of U.S. state courts in death penalty cases involving foreign nationals creates two troubling realities:

1. It reverses or obstructs a trend in international lawmaking that has sought to institute standards and norms that acknowledge "a nexus between our nation's own judicial traditions and the opinions of mankind" (Levesque, 2001, p. 756).
2. It creates the impression that U.S. courts are not motivated by respect for international law. Rather, as articulated by Justice Blackmun, "at best, the present Supreme Court enforces some principles of international law and some of its obligations some of the time" (Levesque, 2001, p. 757).

Complicating the implementation of international law and the prerogatives of U.S. state and local jurisdictions, the issue of the execution of juveniles has become a serious stumbling block for the United States. Article 6 of the ICCPR states that "sentence of death shall not be imposed for crimes committed by persons below eighteen years of age and shall not be carried out on pregnant women." Although the United States signed and ratified the ICCPR, the U.S. government has not acted to

implement it in local circumstances, as expressed in the U.S. declarations and reservations to the treaty:

3. The United States reserves the right, subject to its Constitutional constraint, to impose capital punishment on any person (other than a pregnant woman) duly convicted under existing or future laws permitting the imposition of capital punishment, including such punishment for crimes committed by persons below eighteen years of age.
4. That because US law generally applies to an offender the penalty in force at the time the offense was committed, the United States does not adhere to third clause of paragraph 1 of article 15.
5. . . . the United States reserves the right, in exceptional circumstances, to treat juveniles in the criminal justice system. (ICCPR Declarations and Reservations; see United Nations, 1992)

COMPLICATIONS IN U.S.-EUROPEAN RELATIONS

The problem of lack of consular access for foreign nationals charged with capital crimes in the United States have not been limited to Mexicans alone. The Federal Republic of Germany has also filed suit against the United States in the International Court of Justice on behalf of two German nationals, brothers Karl and Walter LaGrand, who were charged with murder in Arizona. The ICJ suit alleged very similar circumstances to those alleged in *Mexico v. United States*. The decision of the 15-judge panel (14 votes to 1) reads, in part:

> Finds that, by not informing Karl and Walter LaGrand without delay following their arrest of their rights under Article 36, paragraph 1 (b), of the Convention, and by thereby depriving the Federal Republic of Germany of the possibility, in a timely fashion, to render the assistance provided for by the Convention to the individuals

concerned, the United States of America breached its obligations to the Federal Republic of Germany and to the LaGrand brothers under Article 36, paragraph 1;

IN FAVOUR: President Guillaume; Vice-President Shi; Judges Bedjaoui, Ranjeva, Herczegh, Fleischhauer, Koroma, Veresh-chetin, Higgins, Parra-Aranguren, Kooijmans, Rezek, Al-Khasawneh, Buergenthal (United States);

AGAINST: Judge Oda (Japan). (*Federal Republic of Germany v. United States of America*, 2001)

Unfortunately for the LaGrand brothers, the state of Arizona carried out their executions as scheduled in the spring of 1999, Karl LaGrand dying by lethal injection on February 24 and Walter LaGrand on March 3. Although the ICJ decision came more than 2 years after the LaGrands were executed, Germany also petitioned the ICJ, seeking assurances that the United States would never repeat the errors. The ICJ noted:

(6) Unanimously,

Takes note of the commitment undertaken by the United States of America to ensure implementation of the specific measures adopted in performance of its obligations under Article 36, paragraph 1 (b), of the Convention; and finds that this commitment must be regarded as meeting the Federal Republic of Germany's request for a general assurance of non-repetition. (*Federal Republic of Germany v. United States of America*, 2001)

Despite the ICJ's ruling in this case that the United States must give reasonable assurance that consular access would be a reality for at least German nationals arrested in the United States, more legal difficulties loomed on the horizon for foreign nationals sentenced to death in U.S. courts. As of February 1, 2003, there were 112 foreign nationals sitting on American death rows. California had the

greatest number, with 36. Of the five U.S. states where executions are most frequent, only Missouri had no foreign nationals on death row; among the others, Texas had 25; Florida, 22; Oklahoma, 4; and Virginia, 1. Of the 112 foreign nationals awaiting execution, 56 are citizens of nations that either have abolished capital punishment or have not used it in decades; 51 are from Mexico, 3 are from the United Kingdom, 3 are from Colombia, 3 are from El Salvador, and 1 is from Peru. With the precedents set in the ICJ concerning consular access for foreign nationals in the LaGrand and Avena cases, the outlook is gloomy for the United States and the potential for more embarrassment is real.

Critics of the U.S. position in regard to ICCPR declarations and reservations say that reserving the right to execute persons for crimes they committed when they were juveniles violates the entire spirit of the treaty, and that this amounts to a repudiation of the spirit of the treaty rather than an endorsement of it. Amnesty International (1986) has insisted that the United States, through either legal complication or overt violation, fails to abide by the covenant it has promised to uphold, and that this results in the execution of individuals who are protected by international law. In cases where defendants have attempted to invoke the protection of international treaty, American domestic courts have insisted that "rights under International common law must belong to the sovereigns, not to individuals," meaning that individuals have no standing and no right to invoke international treaty in an effort to guide or restrict sentencing (*United States v. Hensel*, 1983; *United States v. Noriega*, 1990).

This interpretation has come under fire in the U.S. District Court of Northern Illinois. In the case of Gregory Madej, a Polish foreign national, U.S. District Judge David Coar ruled in the summer of 2002 that a decision of the International Court of Justice "conclusively determines that Article 36 of the Vienna

Convention creates individual enforceable rights" (*United States ex rel. Gregory Madej v. James M. Schomig*, 2002). Madej claimed that Chicago police and Cook County prosecutors had violated his right to consular assistance, and Judge Coar noted in his ruling that the defendant's rights under the Vienna Convention "were clearly violated." Madej still sits in an Illinois jail.

GLOBAL TRENDS AND THE CURRENTS OF U.S. CAPITAL PUNISHMENT

Amnesty International–Italy has a tradition of casting golden floodlights on the Coliseum in Rome on the night following a death sentence commutation somewhere in the world. On Saturday, February 3, 2003, this lighting took on a particularly intense meaning, as 167 condemned inmates on death row in Illinois had their sentences commuted to life by Governor George Ryan, who was to leave office the following Monday. Marco Bertotto, spokesman for Amnesty International in Italy, commented that Ryan's move was one of the most important gestures of the preceding 25 years in the history of the death penalty in the United States. Citing the "arbitrary and capricious, and therefore immoral" elements of capital punishment in Illinois, Ryan took phone calls from several world leaders, among them Mexican President Vicente Fox, who expressed his "profound appreciation for the historic decision," as did Walter Schwimmer, secretary-general of the 44-nation Council of Europe, who was quoted as saying, "I sincerely hope that this is a step forward to the abolition of the death penalty in the whole of the United States" ("Opponents of Death Penalty," 2003). Ryan suspended executions in Illinois after journalism students at Northwestern University uncovered facts that exonerated 13 Illinois death row inmates. The discovery of these wrongful convictions led to the establishment of the Illinois State Commission on the

Death Penalty, which subsequently issued a report in which it stated specific concerns and recommended that the state should cease executions.

The United States in the Eyes of Other Western Nations

Political leaders outside the United States have reason to congratulate Governor Ryan, but many also seem impatient, and in some cases distraught, concerning the lack of flexibility the United States has shown on the issue of limiting or abolishing executions. This seems justified when one recognizes that the United States has long been the exception to progressive movements regarding punishment around the world. Over the past two centuries, throughout the world, there has been a significant decrease in the number of offenses that are punishable by death. From 1700 to 1772, Great Britain had five classes (with dozens of offenses in each class) of death-eligible crimes, which led to 1,242 hangings. The United Kingdom abolished executions in 1965 (Linebaugh, 1992). France, which used the guillotine liberally in the 18th and 19th centuries, carried out its last execution in 1977 (Spierenburg, 1998). The British colonies had similar sentencing patterns, and the early United States resembled its Anglophile legal heritage, adding a number of offenses in response to the demands of slavery (known in total as the Black Codes) and the Reconstruction era.

However, the United States has not followed the same progressive pattern of reduction in the number of death-eligible crimes as have European Union nations and most of its Latin American neighbors (Sherman, 1994). Although death sentences for robbery, cattle rustling, and horse theft long ago became relics of the U.S. frontier, executions for rape were eliminated rather late in the United States compared with other nations. This change came in 1977 with the case of *Coker v. Georgia,* and it was accomplished largely on the premise that the death sentence for rape was a remnant of white supremacy; it was only tacitly acknowledged that death constituted disproportionate punishment for the crime of rape.

In the face of the growing movement to abolish executions through international organizations, the United States has hardened its legal structure toward those convicted of homicide. Although support for the death penalty has increased solidly in the United States, from a low of 38% in 1965 to about 67% of those polled in 2001, increasing numbers of U.S. citizens have come to the conclusion that the death penalty does not deter further murders (see Tables 24.1 and 24.2).

Since 1976, all U.S. states that have the death penalty, as well as the federal government, offer lethal injection as a method of execution, whether as one alternative or the only method (U.S. Bureau of Justice Statistics, 2001). Many critics of capital punishment cite this as a broad effort to sanitize state killing and avoid well-publicized errors such as those that have occurred with the use of other methods of execution, such as lethal gas and electrocution (Radelet, 2003). It has not

Table 24.1   Approval/Disapproval of Capital Punishment in the United States, 1965–2001 (in percentages)

Year of Poll	Believe in It	Opposed to It	Not Sure
2001	67	26	7
2000	64	25	11
1999	71	21	8
1997	75	22	3
1983	68	27	5
1976	67	25	8
1973	59	31	10
1970	47	42	11
1969	48	38	14
1965	38	47	15

SOURCE: Data from Harris Poll (2001).

NOTE: Respondents were asked, "Do you believe in capital punishment, that is, the death penalty, or are you opposed to it?"

Table 24.2   U.S. Public Opinion of Executions as Deterrence, 1976–2001 (in percentages)

Year of Poll	Deters Others	Not Much Effect	Not Sure
2001	42	52	7
2000	44	50	7
1999	47	49	4
1997	49	49	2
1983	63	32	5
1976	59	34	7

SOURCE: Data from Harris Poll (2001).

NOTE: Respondents were asked, "Do you feel that executing people who commit murder deters others from committing murder, or do you think such executions don't have much effect?"

gone unnoticed that the United States has progressively revealed other elements of its justice process through the televising of arrest and court processes, but has resisted similar exposure of executions.

The United States has also expanded the number of death-eligible offenses. The Violent Crime Control and Law Enforcement Act of 1994 (known as the Omnibus Crime Bill of 1994) and the Anti-Terrorism and Effective Death Penalty Act of 1996 together added 60 offenses to those now punishable by death. These include terrorist homicide; murder of a federal law enforcement, judicial, or corrections official; drug trafficking associated with a murder; "drive-by" homicide with a handgun; and carjacking that results in death. The bills also provided for capital punishment in cases of significant drug-trafficking offenses even when there are no related homicides.

Probably most troubling to legal progressives throughout the world is the systematic rollback of constitutional provisions taking place in the United States, such as the removal of basic constitutional due process and the placement of strict limitations on habeas corpus appeals in the federal courts. Citing the need for more discernible symbolic artifices, advocates of the death penalty in the United States have argued that execution is ineffective as a deterrent to other crime in part because of the extended interval between conviction and the carrying out of a death sentence. The Omnibus Crime Bill death penalty provisions target habeas corpus as the problem and mandate that convicted defendants be prevented from demanding independent federal court review on claims of wrongful conviction or sentencing. For example, the bill limits a condemned prisoner to a solitary federal appeal, which must be filed within 6 months after the expiration of the state appellate process. In addition, it prohibits federal magistrates from granting appeals without a finding of unreasonable state court action. It is possible for a given

defendant to be executed without realizing one appeal in the federal judiciary. The scope and content of this legislation runs counter to the trend in every other progressive nation. The net effect has been to open a larger cultural, social, and legal gulf between the United States and its Western partners.

THE STATUS OF THE VATICAN IN THE GLOBAL DEATH PENALTY DEBATE

Vatican City and its head, the pope, play a pivotal role in the international debate on capital punishment. Pope John Paul II has had considerable influence in the area of human rights since he assumed the leadership of the Holy See in 1978, both as the religious leader of 62 million American Roman Catholics and 1.2 billion Roman Catholics worldwide and as the head of state of a sovereign nation. This dual role has allowed the Catholic Church to work in opposition to the death penalty on nearly all levels, from community organization efforts and execution vigils to transnational diplomatic initiatives, supplemented by high-profile, religious-based, moral campaigns advocating a right to life, in forms such as national councils of bishops, papal encyclicals, and personal appeals and visits by the pope. At its very heart, the papacy founds its teachings and policies on the Gospels and on the revelations of the saints. In his encyclical letter of 2002, Pope John Paul II stated:

> As Saint Ambrose writes: "Once the crime is admitted at the very inception of this sinful act of parricide, then the divine law of God's mercy should be immediately extended. If punishment is forthwith inflicted on the accused, then men in the exercise of justice would in no way observe patience and moderation, but would straightaway condemn the defendant to punishment. . . . God drove Cain out of his presence and sent him into exile far away from his native land, so that he passed from a life of human kindness to

one that was more akin to the rude existence of a wild beast. God, who preferred the correction rather than the death of a sinner, did not desire that a homicide be punished by the exaction of another act of homicide."

The weight of papal condemnations of capital punishment is clear if one looks carefully at a world map. In almost every country where Roman Catholicism is the primary religious choice of the populace, or even that of a significant minority, execution has been legally or virtually abolished. European and Latin American nations have nearly eradicated the incidence of state-sponsored death, in large part because of consistent, dogged resistance in the form of both pastoral and lay influences on nearly every social level. For his own part, the pope has continued to travel to countries in Latin America and the European Union with an unrelenting pro-life message, which includes denunciation of abortion along with capital punishment. In those areas where the Vatican's influence is felt the least (e.g., the Islamic world, South Asia, and East Asia), nations have stubbornly adhered to policies of capital punishment. However, in Latin America and Europe, the underlying foundation of moral persuasion provided by Vatican efforts has prepared the political ground for Latin American courts and officials of the European Union to carry forth difficult programs of legal reform, moratorium, and abolition. Visits by the pope can be very powerful, putting pressure on previously comfortable politicians to use their powers of commutation, as was seen in the United States in 1999, when John Paul II traveled to St. Louis, Missouri, and pleaded for the life of a man condemned to die for two murders in that state. The Democratic governor, Mel Carnahan, a Protestant and supporter of executions, relented and commuted the death sentence of Darrell Mease to life, despite strong opposition from his own administration, the public, and

police authorities ("Pope Pleads," 1999). It has become abundantly clear that proximity to the pontiff is a powerful force on politicians.

CAPITAL PUNISHMENT ON THE FUTURE GLOBAL LANDSCAPE

Samuel Huntington, in his well-known *The Clash of Civilizations and the Remaking of World Order* (1996), states that the "Western belief in the universality of culture suffers from three problems: it is false; it is immoral; and it is dangerous" (p. 2). Huntington, recognizing the decline of the world of the Cold War, which was divided between liberalism and socialism, cites "culture" and "civilization" as the future divisions across the globe, specifically along "fault lines" roughly defined by ethnic culture and religion. In the process, he draws a gloomy picture, asserting that the remedies for serious stress on international stability will be avoidance of "fault line wars," mediation of conflicts by "core states" in areas of intercivilizational strife, and, most important, efforts by all peoples to find and expand values, institutions, and practices held in common. Huntington argues that "civilizational stability" is the strongest foundation for world peace and that intercivilizational exchange is the most effective policy for achieving it. Although Huntington's view has been criticized as a bunker mentality and much of his book cites the rise of identity politics as negative and irrational (Elliot, 1996), there is positive element in its doomsaying. A stable and peaceful world will be one in which nations can reconcile differences in beliefs and emotions in a forum that is committed to the maintenance of a multipolar—that is, multicivilizational—world and not one of paternalist assumptions pointing to an assumed universality of values and institutions.

The use of capital punishment is one of the issues that separate the United States from other civilized countries, such as France and every other country in the European Union.

Felix Rohatyn (2001), who served as the U.S. ambassador to France from 1997 to 2000, has sketched out what he calls "America's deadly image," saying that while the French are thankful for U.S. aid in the past, they very much view the United States as morally deficient. This idea dovetails with the impression that Robert Kagan (2003) draws in his study of post–World War II Europe and the United States, in which he says that Europe has sought peace and stability through the rule of law and diplomacy, frowning on the use of force and power politics, particularly that brand increasingly popular in the United States following the Vietnam War. It was no surprise to the United States when officials of the European Union, considering a draft agreement between members and the United States on extradition, gave in to French objections to language that would obligate a member state's cooperation in extraditing an individual vulnerable to capital punishment ("EU/US Extradition Agreement," 2003). The results are divergent views on political strategy and corroding cohesion between the United States and its traditional allies. The United States may find that long-term fallout from ignoring a world court is disastrous for security concerns, particularly when the country needs help abroad (Miller, 2003a).

It is apparent that a majority of U.S. citizens perceive capital punishment to be a necessary symbolic, if not instrumental, tool for criminal justice; but, as Edelman (1964) says, "political acts mean different things to different people" (p. 12). The issue of capital punishment considered across international borders creates significant intellectual inertia. Although nearly every national poll conducted in Europe, the Western Hemisphere, and Asia shows that populations of those countries overwhelmingly support the use of executions at home, noteworthy hesitation and opposition emerge when people consider the idea of citizens of their own countries suffering the ultimate penalty applied by another nation-state. In addition, a growing number of governments, many of which share basic cultural, geopolitical, and diplomatic strategies with the United States, oppose the use of capital punishment and view it as an issue that must be put to rest before existing relations can be strengthened and productive diplomacy achieved. As the globe grows ever smaller, reform and reassessment of capital punishment in the United States will be not only advisable but critical, particularly in a world such as the one that Huntington (1996) describes.

NOTE

1. Oklahoma responded with executions in about 0.91% of total homicides in the period from 1976 through 2001, which places it far ahead of the other four states: Virginia, 0.74%; Texas, 0.61%; Missouri, 0.54%; and Florida, 0.22%. I have tabulated these figures based on data gathered from the FBI's *Uniform Crime Reports* (1965, 1969, 1970, 1973, 1976, 1983, 1997, 1999, 2000, 2001) and from the Espy File (Espy & Smylka, 1994, 2002).

REFERENCES

Amnesty International. (1986, 2001, 2003). *Annual report*. New York: Author. (Annual reports are available online at http://web.amnesty.org/report2003/index-eng)

Edelman, M. (1964). *The symbolic uses of politics*. Champaign: University of Illinois Press.

Elliot, M. (1996, December 1). When cultures collide. *Washington Post*, p. C8.

Espy, M. W., & Smylka, J. O. (Comps.). (1994, 2002). *Executions in the United States, 1608–2002: The Espy File* [Computer file]. Ann Arbor: University of Michigan, Inter-University Consortium for Political and Social Research.

European Union Council on Human Rights. (2002, May 2). *Joint European Union–United States Action Plan* (EU/US summit proceedings). Washington, DC: Author.

EU/US extradition agreement suspended over French concerns. (2003, March 1). *European Report*, p. 25.

Federal Bureau of Investigation. (1965, 1969, 1970, 1973, 1976, 1983, 1997, 1999, 2000, 2001). *Uniform crime reports*. Washington, DC: Government Printing Office.

Fox visit to Texas canceled. (2002, August 16). *La Jornada*, pp. 1–2.

Galliher, J. F. (1989). *Criminology: Human rights, criminal law and crime* (Rev. ed.). New York: Simon & Schuster.

Galliher J. F., Koch, L. W., Keys, D. P., & Guess, T. (2002). *America without the death penalty*. Boston: Northeastern University Press.

Harris Poll. (2001, July 20–25). *Surveys on criminal justice*. Rochester, NY: Author.

Huntington, S. P. (1996). *The clash of civilizations and the remaking of world order*. New York: Simon & Schuster.

Pope John Paul II. (2002). *Encyclical letter evangelium vitae*. Rome: Holy See of Rome.

Kagan, R. (2003). *Of paradise and power: America and Europe in the new world order*. New York: Alfred A. Knopf.

Levesque, C. A. (2001). The International Covenant on Civil and Political Rights: A primer for raising a defense against the juvenile death penalty in federal courts. *American University Law Review, 50*, 755–792.

Linebaugh, P. (1992). *The London hanged: Crime and civil society in the eighteenth century*. New York: Cambridge University Press.

Miller, J. M. (2002, November 17). "Tough on Crime" may backfire. *Los Angeles Times*, p. M5.

Miller, J. M. (2003a, February 24). The costs of not respecting a world court are greater than ever. *Legal Times*, p. 6.

Miller, J. M. (2003b, March 3). US should respect World Court's order. *Texas Lawyer, 18*, 38.

Opponents of death penalty hail Illinois governor. (2003, January 13). *Manchester Guardian*, p. 2.

Pope pleads for Mease. (1999, January 28). *St. Louis Post-Dispatch*, p. 1A.

Poveda, T. G. (2000). American exceptionalism and the death penalty. *Social Justice, 27*, 252–267.

Radelet, M. L. (2003). *Post-Furman botched executions*. Retrieved May 19, 2004, from the Death Penalty Information Center Web site: http://www.deathpenaltyinfo.org/article.php?scid=8&did=478

Refuge in Mexico: Murderers find a constitutional safe haven. (2003, February 9). *San Diego Union-Tribune*, p. G2.

Rodriguez, I. (2002, September 16). Mexico protects murder suspect. *San Antonio Express-News*, p. 1A.

Rohatyn, F. G. (2001, February 20). America's deadly image. *Washington Post*, p. A9.

Schabas, W. A. (1997). *The international sourcebook on capital punishment*. Boston: Northeastern University Press.

Sherman, E. (1994). The US death penalty reservation to the International Covenant on Civil and Political Rights: Exposing the limitations of the flexible system governing treaty formation. *Texas International Law Journal, 29*, 69–86.

Spierenburg, P. (1998). The body and the state: Early modern Europe. In N. Morris & D. Rothman (Eds.), *The Oxford history of the prison* (pp. 44–70). New York: Oxford University Press.

United Nations. (1992). *International Covenant on Civil and Political Rights (ICCPR)* (Treaty Series, Vol. 999, UNTS 171). New York: Author.

U.S. Bureau of Justice Statistics. (2001). *Sourcebook of criminal justice statistics*. Washington, DC: U.S. Department of Justice.

Cases Cited

Coker v. Georgia, 433 U.S. 584 (1977).

Federal Republic of Germany v. United States of America, International Court of Justice (LaGrand brothers) (2001).

Mexico v. United States of America, International Court of Justice (Avena and other Mexican nationals) (2003).

United States v. Hensel, 699 F.2d 18 (1st Cir.), cert denied, 461 U.S. 958, 103 S. Ct. 2431, 77 L. Ed. 2d 18 (1983).

United States v. Noriega, 746 F. Supp. 1506 (S.D. Fla. 1990).

United States ex rel. Gregory Madej v. James M. Schomig, No. 98 C 1866 (2002).

Index

485

About the Editor

Philip Reichel is Professor of Criminal Justice at the University of Northern Colorado. His teaching, research, and writing interests include comparative justice systems and the broad area of corrections. He has served as a consultant to the National Institute of Justice. His published articles appear in many professional journals, and he has provided entries for several encyclopedias, has authored and coauthored several book chapters, and is the author of two textbooks—*Comparative Criminal Justice Systems: A Topical Approach* (4th ed., 2005), and *Corrections: Philosophies, Practices, and Procedures* (2001). Dr. Reichel's comparative justice interests have resulted in invitations to speak at the University of Warsaw, the University of Vienna, the University of Innsbruck, and the University of Bremen. In 2003, he was selected by his university as the 2003–2004 Distinguished Scholar, and he was asked to provide a contribution for an anthology of 14 esteemed scholars who have made a significant contribution to the discipline of criminal justice within a comparative/international context (*Lessons From International Criminology/Comparative Criminology/Criminal Justice*, 2004). He earned his Ph.D. in sociology from Kansas State University.

About the Contributors

Jay Albanese is Chief of the International Center at the National Institute of Justice. He is on leave from his position as Professor of Government and Public Policy at Virginia Commonwealth University. He is Past President of the Academy of Criminal Justice Sciences (ACJS) and is currently Executive Director of the International Association for the Study of Organized Crime (www.iasoc.net). He is the author of books that include *Criminal Justice* (3rd ed., 2005) and *Organized Crime in Our Times* (2004) and is coeditor of *Organized Crime: World Perspectives* (2003). He earned his Ph.D. from the School of Criminal Justice at Rutgers University.

Christine Alder is Principal Research Fellow in the Criminology Department at the University of Melbourne, Australia. As a feminist, her previous research and teaching has focused on women and crime. Her publications include *The Police and Young People in Australia* (1994, coedited with R. White); *Child Victims of Homicide* (2001, with K. Polk); and *Critical Chatter: Women Human Rights Activists in South East Asia* (2003, with C. Lambert and S. Pickering). More recently, she has had articles (coauthored with K. Polk) published in international journals in the area of art and crime. She has a Ph.D. in sociology from the University of Oregon.

Claudia Angermaier is currently working as a research assistant at the Criminal Law Department of the University of Vienna and writing her doctoral thesis on the issue of amnesties in international law. Her research focus is international criminal law and transitional justice. She received her B.A. in philosophy and psychology at the University of Witwatersrand in South Africa and completed her Mag. Iur. law degree at the University of Vienna.

Kevin Bitten is a graduate student in the Department of Criminal Justice at Northern Arizona University. When not struggling with the burdens of graduate education, he is also a social justice advocate, private investigator, and avid bicycle racer.

Sandeep Chawla has been Chief of Research at the U.N. Office on Drugs and Crime (UNODC) since 1994, leading the development of UNODC's research and analysis capabilities over this period. The systematic publication of research findings, analytical studies, statistics, and annual estimates of the extent of illicit drug production, trafficking, and abuse, reflected in the *World Drug Report,* the annual *Global Illicit Drug Trends* publications, and the *Studies on Drugs and Crime* series all occurred during this period. He is the editor of the U.N. *Bulletin on Narcotics,* which is one of the oldest journals in the field, having been in continuous publication since 1949. More recently, he led the team that produced an extensive study on *The Opium Economy in Afghanistan* (2003). Prior to joining UNODC, he worked for the United

Nations as a development policy adviser, specializing in social development. He has lectured at universities in several countries and continues to teach international history and political economy at the university level in Vienna. He earned his Ph.D. from the University of Delhi, India.

Harry R. Dammer is Associate Professor of Sociology and Criminal Justice at the University of Scranton in Scranton, Pennsylvania. He is the author of *Religion in Corrections* (1999), coauthor of *Comparative Criminal Justice* (2000, with Erika Fairchild), and coauthor of *The Offender in the Community* (2003, with Todd R. Clear). He has also published or copublished numerous articles, manuals, and professional reports on a variety of criminal justice topics. In 1993–1994, he was awarded a Fulbright Scholarship to teach and conduct research in Germany. He has served as consultant to the National Institute of Justice, the National Institute of Corrections, the American Correctional Association, and the National Conference of Christians and Jews. He received his Ph.D. from Rutgers University.

Mathieu Deflem is Assistant Professor of Sociology at the University of South Carolina. His specialty areas are law, social control, comparative-historical sociology, and theory. He is author of *Policing World Society* (2002) and editor of *Habermas, Modernity, and Law* (Sage, 1996) and *Terrorism and Counter-Terrorism: Criminological Perspectives* (2004). He received a Ph.D. in sociology from the University of Colorado.

Andrea Di Nicola is a researcher in the sociology of deviance at the School of Law at the University of Trento (Italy) and Research Coordinator (Trento office) for Transcrime, Joint Research Centre on Transnational Crime, Università di Trento and the Università Cattolica di Milano. His main research expertise and publications concern migration and crime as well as trafficking in human beings, economic and organized crime prevention, and evaluation of crime reduction policies. He is one of the authors of the volume *Organised Crime Around the World* (HEUNI). He earned his Ph.D. in criminology at the University of Bari-Trento.

David Felsen is Visiting Assistant Professor at Temple University in Philadelphia. His research interests are in the fields of international political economy, international security, and comparative public policy, with a regional focus on Europe. He received his doctorate in politics from the University of Oxford in the United Kingdom.

James O. Finckenauer is a Distinguished Professor II in the Rutgers University School of Criminal Justice. His teaching, research, and writing concern juvenile delinquency and juvenile justice, domestic and transnational organized crime, and a variety of comparative criminal justice issues. His published articles have appeared in many scholarly journals, encyclopedias, and periodicals, and he has authored, coauthored, or edited seven books. He is the current editor of the journal *Trends in Organized Crime* and the President of the Academy of Criminal Justice Sciences. From 1998 to 2002, he was the Director of the International Center for the National Institute of Justice. He earned his Ph.D. in human relations from New York University.

Maria (Maki) Haberfeld is Chair of the Department of Law, Police Science, and Criminal Justice Administration at John Jay College, City University of New York. Prior to coming to John Jay, she served in the Israel National Police and left the force at the rank of lieutenant. She also worked for the U.S. Drug Enforcement Administration, in the New York Field Office, as a special consultant. Her research interests and publications are in the areas of private and public law enforcement—specifically, training, police integrity, and comparative policing. Her most recent involvement in Eastern Europe includes redesigning the basic academy curriculum of the Czech National Police, with the emphasis on integrity-related training. Her book on police training, *Critical Issues in Police Training,* is the first comprehensive text ever published about all the aspects of police training in the United States. She earned her Ph.D. at John Jay College.

Ni (Phil) He is Assistant Professor of criminal justice at Northeastern University. His primary teaching and research interests include comparative criminology and criminal justice, quantitative methodology and policing. He has had significant experience working on several large-scale international and national research projects as a research analyst. His scholarship can be found in variety of refereed professional journals, and he is the author of *Marx, Durkheim and Comparative Criminology* (1998). He received his Ph.D. in criminal justice from the University of Nebraska at Omaha.

Cindy Hill is an analyst in social legislation in the domestic security section of the Congressional Research Service at the Library of Congress. There, she provides nonpartisan assistance in response to requests from members and committees of Congress at all stages of the legislative process for subject areas, including the Justice Department budget, tracking crime trends, and domestic intelligence issues. She earned her Ph.D. in criminal justice from Sam Houston State University.

Frank Höpfel holds a Chair in Criminal Law and Procedure at the University of Vienna. He has published widely on issues of substantive and procedural criminal law, including the system of sanctions in Austria, the European Union, and beyond. He served as Visiting Professor at St. Mary's University, San Antonio, Texas, and Ljubljana University, Slovenia, and as consultant with the U.N. High Commissioner

of Human Rights in China. He received his Dr. Iur. degree from the University of Innsbruck.

Matti Joutsen is Director of International Affairs at the Ministry of Justice of Finland, in which capacity he continues to be very active in the work of the European Union, the Council of Europe, and the United Nations. He has served as Director of the U.N. Regional Crime Prevention Institute for Europe and as the interregional adviser for the U.N. Crime Prevention and Criminal Justice Program. His expertise includes comparative criminal justice systems, victim issues, and transnational organized crime. His published articles appear in many professional journals around the world. He has a J.S.D.(hab.) and an M.S.(Pol.Sc.), both from the University of Helsinki.

Elizabeth Joyce works in the U.N. Office on Drugs and Crime, where she manages U.N. technical assistance to countries that are developing anti–money laundering and counterfinancing of terrorism mechanisms, and she supervises a research program. She previously worked at the international consultancy Oxford Analytica and the Institute for European–Latin American Relations in Madrid. She is an editorial board member of the journal *Global Crime.* She was a Fulbright Senior Scholar at Georgetown University, Washington, D.C., where she published a book about responses to the drug trade in Latin America, *Latin America and the Multinational Drug Trade.* She has a Ph.D. in politics from Oxford University, where, as a Reuters Fellow, she conducted research into international cooperation on illicit drugs and transnational crime.

Akis Kalaitzidis is Assistant Professor of political Science at Central Missouri State University. His research and teaching interests are the European integration process, international security, and comparative political economy. He received his Ph.D. in political science from Temple University.

David Keys is Associate Professor and Chair of the Department of Sociology and Criminal Justice at the State University of New York–Plattsburgh. His teaching, research, and writing expertise include social history of the death penalty, sociological studies of opiate addiction, and correctional cultures. His published articles appear in professional journals, he has provided entries for encyclopedias, and he is coauthor of several books, including *Confronting the Drug Control Establishment* and *Sex and Sociology*. He earned his Ph.D. in sociology from the University of Missouri–Columbia.

Dae-Hoon Kwak is nearing completion of his master's degree in criminal justice at the University of Nebraska at Omaha. He has worked for the Juvenile Justice Institute at UNO as research assistant since March 2003. His major research interests are criminal justice program and policy evaluation, quantitative criminology, computer crime, and spatial analysis using graphic information systems, or GIS. Most recently, one of his articles received the Best Thesis Award (2003) from the 4th National Criminal Justice Thesis Competition sponsored by the Korean Institute of Criminology. He received his bachelor's degree in criminal justice with a specialization in corrections from Kyonngi University in South Korea (2001).

Daniel J. Mabrey is pursuing his Ph.D. in criminal justice at Sam Houston State University. His research interests include terrorism and extremist violence, transnational crime, comparative criminal justice systems, and future issues in criminal justice. He is also the technology editor for *Crime and Justice International,* a bimonthly magazine dedicated to identifying and analyzing issues and trends in international criminal justice.

Chris E. Marshall is Associate Professor of Criminal Justice at the University of Nebraska at Omaha. He teaches statistics and research methods courses at UNO. His research interests are varied and include transnational computer crime, international use of private security, international self-reported criminality, domestic violence, career criminal research, and theory construction. His current methodological focus is on improving ways of visualizing and exploring data, including multivariate data, and exploratory data mining of large data sets. He earned his doctorate in sociology from Iowa State University.

William H. McDonald is chairman of the Criminal Justice Program at Monroe College in the Bronx, New York. McDonald served as a detective with the Washington, D.C., Metropolitan Police and as a Special Agent with the U.S. Treasury Department. He was also a visiting professor at the Police Staff College in Bramshill, England. His research interests and publications focus primarily on policing, criminal investigation, and comparative police issues. A Neiderhoffer Fellow, he earned his Ph.D. in criminal justice from the City University of New York.

Raymond Michalowski is Arizona Regents Professor of criminal justice and Adjunct Professor of Sociology at Northern Arizona University. His scholarly works include *Order, Law, and Crime* (1985); *Radikale Kriminologie* (1989); *Run for the Wall: Remembering Vietnam on a Motorcycle Pilgrimage* (2001); *Crime, Power, and Identity* (2002); and *State-Corporate Crime: Wrongdoing at the Intersection of Business and Government* (in press), as well as over 50 articles and chapters on topics including criminological theory, corporate crime, the political economy of crime and punishment, and crime and justice in Cuba.

Grant Niemann has served as Principal Legal Adviser to the Darwin-based Northern Land Council, as the Assistant Director of Legal services for the Australian Government Solicitor's office, as Commonwealth Deputy Director of Public Prosecutions in Adelaide, and as a prosecuting counsel in the Australian War Crimes Prosecutions. In 1994, he was appointed Senior Trial Attorney of the International Criminal Tribunal for the former Yugoslavia in The Hague, The Netherlands. He had responsibility for the first prosecutions to come before the tribunal, including the prosecution of Tadic. In 2000, he left The Hague and accepted an academic appointment at Flinders University in South Australia. He has an LLB, LLM, Grad. Dip. Pub. Law, FFUE, and Grad. Cert. Ter. Edu. and is currently writing a Ph.D. thesis on international criminal law. He is a graduate of Sydney University Law School.

Román Ortiz is Professor and Researcher at the Economic Development Research Center (CEDE), School of Economics at Los Andes University (Bogotá), where he focuses on the analysis of political violence and terrorism phenomena in Latin America. He has previously taught and researched these topics at Spanish academic institutions such as the General Gutierrez Mellado Institute and the Ortega y Gasset Institute. Included in his most recent publications is the paper "President Alvaro Uribe's Counterinsurgency Strategy: Formula for Victory or Recipe for a Crisis?" published by the Elcano Institute in Madrid. He has a degree in political science.

Thomas Pietschmann has worked since 1993 for the U.N. International Drug Control Programme (now U.N. Office on Drugs and Crime), first as a program officer for Southwest Asia and since 1994 in the research section. He is mainly responsible for trend analysis of illicit drug markets and was involved in a number of UNDCP/UNODC publications, including *A Global Review on Amphetamine-Type Stimulants* (1996); *The Social and Economic Consequences of Drug Abuse* (1997); *World Drug Report,* 1997 and 2000; *Global Illicit Drug Trends* 1999, 2000, 2001, 2002, 2003; and *Afghanistan's Opium Economy: An International Problem* (2003). He earned his Ph.D. at the University of Economics and Business Administration, Vienna.

Kenneth Polk is Professorial Fellow in the Criminology Department at the University of Melbourne. His major research and writing has been in the area of violence and homicide, but his most recent work has dealt with issues relating to art and the problem of the illicit traffic in antiquities. Among his published books are *Schools and Delinquency*; *When Men Kill: Scenarios of Masculine Violence*; and *Child Victims of Homicide* (with Christine Alder). He earned his Ph.D. in sociology from the University of California–Los Angeles.

T. Hank Robinson is the Director of the Juvenile Justice Institute in the Criminal Justice Department at the University of Nebraska at Omaha. He oversees a number of research projects at the federal, state, and local level. The scope of his research ranges from juvenile assessment and diversion to probation practices to gun violence reduction. He earned his doctorate in criminal justice from the University of Nebraska at Omaha.

Mitchel Roth is Associate Professor of Criminal Justice at Sam Houston State University. His teaching, research, and publication interests have focused on a diverse range of issues, including comparative policing, organized crime, history of criminal justice, and violence in American history. He has published numerous articles and seven books, including *Crime and Punishment: A History of the Criminal Justice System* (2004) and *Historical Dictionary of Law Enforcement* (2000). He is currently at work on the *History of the Houston Police Department* for the Houston Police Officers Union and *Prisons and Prison Systems: A Global Encyclopedia*. He earned a Ph.D. in history from the University of California–Santa Barbara.

Mauricio Rubio, an economist and sociologist, is a Ph.D. candidate in economics at Harvard University and currently works at Instituto

Universitario de Investigación en Seguridad Interior at UNED University, Madrid. His main fields of research include organized crime, criminal justice, and youth gangs in Central America. He publishes articles mainly in journals in Latin America and Spain. He is working on a book about kidnapping in Colombia. He has a Diploma de Estudios Avanzados from Universidad Complutense de Madrid in sociology.

Mark Shaw is Crime Prevention and Criminal Justice Officer in the Anti–Organized Crime and Law Enforcement Unit, Human Security Branch, U.N. Office on Drugs and Crime, Vienna. Previously he was Ford Foundation Research Fellow at the South African Institute of International Affairs, Director of the Monitoring and Analysis Unit of the South African Secretariat for Safety and Security, and head of the Crime and Policing Program at the Pretoria-based Institute for Security Studies. He has written widely on crime and policing issues in Southern Africa and is author of *Crime and Policing in Post-Apartheid South Africa* (2002). He holds a Ph.D. from the University of Witwatersrand, Johannesburg.

Klaus von Lampe is a Researcher at Free University Berlin and Chair of Criminology. His articles and reviews appear in political science and criminological journals. He is the author of *Organized Crime: Begriff und Theorie organisierter Kriminalität in den USA* (Concept and Theory of Organized Crime in the U.S.) and coauthor/coeditor of *Upperworld and Underworld in Cross-Border Crime* and *Criminal Finances and Organising Crime in Europe*. He received his doctoral degree in law (criminology) from Goethe University Frankfurt Main, Germany.

Gail Wannenburg is Research Fellow at the South African Institute of International Affairs. She leads the SAIIA's war and organized crime program, which examines the impact of organized crime on current conflicts, postconflict reconstruction, and peace building in Africa. She has conducted research on issues of political conflict and organized social violence, crime and policing, and postconflict reconstruction during her work in the human rights nongovernmental organization sector and at the Truth and Reconciliation Commission, where she had extensive links with civil society partners in Africa. She has recently worked within the European Union development program in South Africa as a justice, good governance, and human rights adviser. She has a BA.LLB from the University of Natal.

Richard H. Ward is Dean and Director of the Criminal Justice Center at Sam Houston State University in Huntsville, Texas. Prior to this, he served as Associate Chancellor (1994–1998) and as Vice Chancellor for Administration (1977–1994) at the University of Illinois at Chicago. He is the author of numerous books and articles in the field and has directed research projects in excess of $8 million. He has lectured extensively in more than 40 countries throughout the world on law enforcement administration and investigative methods and has been a consultant to police departments in the United States and to international organizations. A former New York City detective, he holds a doctorate in criminology from the University of California at Berkeley.

Robert P. Weiss is currently Professor of Sociology and Criminal Justice at State University of New York at Plattsburgh. His research interests include the sociology of punishment; the social history of crime, policing, and prisons; criminal justice privatization, and comparative penology. He has published scholarly articles in several edited books and in a wide array of academic journals, including *The Historical Journal, Social History,* and *Criminology*. He has edited two books: *Social History of Crime, Policing and Punishment* (1999) and *Comparing Prisons Systems: Toward a Comparative and International*

Penology (1998, with Nigel South). He earned his Ph.D. in sociology at Southern Illinois University at Carbondale.

Jonathan R. White was Dean of Social Sciences at Grand Valley State University in Grand Rapids, Michigan. After the tragedies of September 11, 2001, he was seconded to the federal government to direct a counterterrorist training program. He has worked with law enforcement agencies in North America, Europe, and Australia. He is the author of several books, including *Terrorism: An Introduction; Terrorism and Homeland Security* (in press); and *Defending the Homeland: Domestic Intelligence, Law Enforcement, and Security*. His Ph.D. is from Michigan State University in criminal justice.

John Winterdyk teaches in the Department of Justice Studies at Mount Royal College in Calgary, Alberta. His teaching, research, and writing expertise include theory, research methods, and various comparative justice areas. His published articles appear in various professional journals, and he has (co)authored/edited nine textbooks/anthologies, including *Juvenile Justice Systems: International Perspectives* (2nd ed., 2002); *Adult Corrections: International Systems and Perspectives* (2004); and *Lessons From Comparative International Comparative Criminology/Criminal Justice* (2004, with Liqun Cao). He is also the editor of the *International Journal of Comparative Criminology*. He was the first to obtain a Ph.D. in criminology from Simon Fraser University in 1988.